Archaeology in America

Archaeology in America
An Encyclopedia

Volume 1
Northeast and Southeast

Francis P. McManamon, General Editor
Linda S. Cordell, Kent G. Lightfoot,
and George R. Milner, Editorial Board

GREENWOOD PRESS
Westport, Connecticut • London

Library of Congress Cataloging-in-Publication Data

Archaeology in America : an encyclopedia / Francis P. McManamon, general editor ; Linda S. Cordell, Kent G. Lightfoot, and George R. Milner, editorial board.
    v. cm.
  Includes bibliographical references and index.
  Contents: v. 1. Northeast and Southeast — v. 2. Midwest and Great Plains/Rocky Mountains — v. 3. Southwest and Great Basin/Plateau — v. 4. West Coast and Arctic/Subarctic.
    ISBN 978–0–313–33184–8 (set : alk. paper) — ISBN 978–0–313–33185–5 (v. 1 : alk. paper) — ISBN 978–0–313–33186–2 (v. 2 : alk. paper) — ISBN 978–0–313–33187–9 (v. 3 : alk. paper) — ISBN 978–0–313–35021–4 (v. 4 : alk. paper)
  1. United States—Antiquities—Encyclopedias. 2. Excavations (Archaeology)—United States—Encyclopedias. 3. Historic sites—United States—Encyclopedias. 4. Archaeology—United States—Encyclopedias. 5. Canada—Antiquities—Encyclopedias. 6. Excavations (Archaeology)—Canada—Encyclopedias. 7. Historic sites—Canada—Encyclopedias. 8. Archaeology—Canada—Encyclopedias. I. McManamon, Francis P. II. Cordell, Linda S. III. Lightfoot, Kent G., 1953– IV. Milner, George R., 1953–
  E159.5.A68   2009
  973.03—dc22   2008020844

British Library Cataloguing in Publication Data is available.

Library of Congress Catalog Card Number: 2008020844
ISBN: 978–0–313–33184–8 (set)
        978–0–313–33185–5 (vol. 1)
        978–0–313–33186–2 (vol. 2)
        978–0–313–33187–9 (vol. 3)
        978–0–313–35021–4 (vol. 4)

First published in 2009

Greenwood Press, 88 Post Road West, Westport, CT 06881
An imprint of Greenwood Publishing Group, Inc.
www.greenwood.com

Printed in the United States of America

The paper used in this book complies with the
Permanent Paper Standard issued by the National
Information Standards Organization (Z39.48–1984).

10 9 8 7 6 5 4 3 2 1

Cover: Fort Sumter and view of Charleston Harbor, South Carolina. Fort Sumter is an important site of the American Civil War. On April 12, 1861, Confederate artillery fired upon this Federal fort, which surrendered two days later marking the beginning of the Civil War. For related essays, see Steven D. Smith, "Historic Period Military Sites in the Southeast" and Robert S. Neyland, "The CSS *Hunley* Shipwreck: The Recovery and Investigation of a Civil War Submarine."

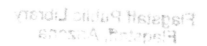

CONTENTS

About the Editorial Board and *About the Contributors* can be found in volume 4.

VOLUME 1: NORTHEAST AND SOUTHEAST

NORTHEAST LIST OF ENTRIES

PREFACE

In 2000, the Harris Interactive polling company carried out a national public opinion poll to discover what adult Americans knew and believed about archaeology. The results of this survey, *Exploring Public Perceptions and Attitudes about Archaeology* by Maria Ramos and David Duganne (Harris Interactive, 2000; <http://www.nps.gov/archeology/pubs/harris/index.htm>), showed that 76% of Americans expressed a high or moderate interest in archaeology and archaeological sites. Nine out of ten respondents said that students should learn about archaeology as part of their education. However, the study also revealed a lack of specific understanding about American archaeology. Few of the respondents could name an American archaeological site, for example.

Until now, there has been no readily accessible text that summarizes information about a large number of important, interesting North American archaeological sites for the general public, teachers, and high school and college students. This encyclopedia describes the basic information about important North American archaeological sites. The essays are written by experts, avoiding jargon and explaining technical terms for a general audience. Each essay includes references to additional information, more detailed articles, books, and reports for readers who want to investigate the sites in more detail. The Harris Interactive study, by the way, indicated that 33% of Americans learn about archaeology through "books and encyclopedias."

Archaeology in America began in May 2001, with a series of emails among Kevin Downing, now Senior Acquisitions Editor for the Greenwood Publishing Group, Dwight Pitcaithley, then Chief Historian of the National Park Service, and me (Frank McManamon). Kevin had approached Dwight about the possibility of creating a reference book focused on the archaeology of the United States. Dwight put Kevin in touch with me; many discussions later, following substantial work on Kevin's part to make suitable arrangements, and the encyclopedia project was launched.

From the beginning, the goal was to assemble an encyclopedia that covered ancient and historic period archaeological sites in North America from northern Mexico to the Arctic Ocean shore. Sites dating from the earliest habitation of North America (as much as 20,000 years ago) through those from the 20th century would be included. We agreed that entries would be written by experts, but for the nonspecialist, and would summarize the investigations and interpretations for the sites covered. Criteria for selection of entries would include the importance of the site(s) to our understanding of the history of human habitation and the variety of cultural adaptations in North America. We also wanted to ensure that each essay would identify useful and more detailed sources of further information for readers who want to pursue the topic further. We wanted each essay to describe whether the sites written about are interpreted in a museum or can be visited as part of a public park with interpretive programs.

We agreed that our intended audience was members of the general public with an interest in American archaeology, high school and college students and instructors, and the public, college, and university libraries that serve these groups. The essays in the encyclopedia would provide clear, concise summaries of archaeological investigations and interpretations of the most important ancient and historic period sites in northern Mexico, the United States, and Canada. We were fortunate that Linda Cordell, Kent Lightfoot, and George Milner agreed to serve as the encyclopedia's editorial board. Each of them assembled lists of sites and topics for essays for the regions they were most familiar with. I worked with each member of the editorial board on the final list of essays for the encyclopedia.

We were fortunate to have Dr. Thalia Grey serve as managing editor in the first years of effort. When Thalia had to leave the project for family reasons, the ever-positive, hypercompetent Shana Jones stepped in to complete the complex organizational task of securing essay texts, proposed illustrations, and administrative documents from over 300 contributors.

I am very grateful to all of our contributors for their efforts in writing essays, submitting illustrations, editing essays, providing recommendations, and the many individual acts of assistance performed by so many to bring this project to a successful conclusion. My special thanks to colleagues in the National Park Service and other public agencies who took their personal time to prepare their essays. It is personally gratifying to me to see among our contributors colleagues from academic institutions, private consulting firms, museums, as well as public agency archaeology programs. This mix of contributing experts shows the variety of individuals and organizations that are part of contemporary archaeology in America. We appreciate the patience of all our contributors with the long process that the production of this encyclopedia has involved. Special thanks to Terry Childs, Barbara Little, and Karen Mudar for their unofficial advice, collegiality, and support during the difficult several last years.

We appreciate the dedication of Lisa Connery and her copy-editing team at Publication Services, Inc., and Liz Kincaid for her work with illustrations. We express also our appreciation to Marc Fairbanks and Steve Hackenberger for working with us on the national and regional maps, in particular to Marc for his careful electronic cartography throughout the map editing process.

My personal and profound thanks for their support of this project go to Kevin Downing and Shana Jones. It is not too much to say that without their support for and work on this project, it would not have happened. Kevin provided much of the vision for this project and made arrangements at the press and in the staffing of the project that enabled me to work on this project outside and independent of my NPS duties. He championed the encyclopedia at Greenwood throughout its development and production. Shana's organizational skill and diligence made it possible to coordinate the efforts of our many contributors. My appreciation to my valued colleague and friend, Dwight Pitcaithley, for his original suggestion that Kevin and I discuss this project, should be apparent to all. The advice and editorial assistance of Linda Cordell, Kent Lightfoot, and George Milner have been essential. Without their assistance the product would not have been possible. In addition, Margaret Lyneis, my colleague and teacher, provided important advice about the Great Basin/ Plateau essay list. My NPS colleague, Ted Birkedal, provided useful and appreciated advice about potential entries and authors for Alaska.

It is impossible to take on such a large project as this encyclopedia without affecting one's personal life. My partner and wife, Carol, has provided essential support, especially during the intensive last year of this project. Addie and Kate, our daughters, have been sources of strength with their cheerful questions about "How's that encyclopedia going?" Flax has provided an important rationale for those necessary relaxing walks. My appreciation and thanks to all who have helped in the many ways they have supported this project. It is my hope that this work will enable more people to learn about, appreciate, and embrace as their own the rich archaeological record of America.

Francis P. McManamon

ARCHAEOLOGY IN AMERICA—IT'S RIGHT UNDER OUR FEET

INTRODUCTION

The archaeology of America is all around us. The artifacts, remains of ancient and historic structures, and cultural features that were created, used, and abandoned by people and cultures of earlier times compose the archaeological record of North America. The geographic area covered by the essays in this encyclopedia extends from the Arctic Ocean to northern Mexico. In addition, the influences of the ancient and historic cultures of central Mexico are discussed in a number of the essays on the ancient and historic Southwestern sites. We have included essays about ancient, as well as historic period sites, and on topics that cover all of the time periods that humans have occupied North America. Although archaeologists have not yet discovered exactly when the first Americans entered and began the human history of the Americas, it is clear that these first colonizers arrived at least 16,000 years ago (see the essay about the earliest inhabitants by Jim Dixon in the Arctic-Subarctic section). European contact with the Americas began with Norse voyages about 1,000 years ago (see the essay about the Norse settlement at L'Anse aux Meadows, Newfoundland, by Brigitta Wallace in the Northeast section). Africans and Asians also have come to this continent, and their histories and heritages are found in the American archaeological record and in essays in these volumes.

Essays have been written to be understood and used by general readers with an interest in archaeology but no special background or training in the subject. Authors have avoided using jargon and technical expressions. Where specialized terminology has been necessary, the editors have provided clarifications in the text. There also is a glossary including specialized terms used throughout the volumes. The essays also will be useful for students in high school and college as introductions to archaeological topics and for information about specific sites. Even professional archaeologists will find these essays to be helpful introductions to sites that they might not be familiar with and general topics in parts of North America that they are not specialists on.

The sites covered in these essays reflect the full range of archaeological site types in North America and the broadest range of archaeological topics. Readers will find essays about sites in rural, even wilderness settings, as well as those in densely urban places. Essays describe sites that include substantial amounts of ancient or historic buildings above ground, as well as sites that are buried deeply by sediment and soil, in caves or rockshelters, or deep under water.

This encyclopedia includes over 350 essays written by experts and describing hundreds of the most important, prominent, and interesting archaeological sites in North America. The authors bring firsthand experience and understanding of the sites and general topics that they write about. Readers will find essays that describe:

- *The oldest sites* in North America (see, for example, the essays about Meadowcroft Rockshelter by Jim Adovasio in the Northeast section, about Paleoindian sites by Bonnie

Pitblado in the Great Plains–Rocky Mountain section, and about "On Your Knees Cave" by Jim Dixon in the Pacific Northwest portion of the West Coast section);

- *The earliest American architecture*, such as the earthen monuments and mound complexes of the Mississippi River valley and the Ohio River valley, the coastal Southeast, and the ancient Southwest (see, for example, the essays about Watson Brake by Joe Saunders in the Southeast section; about ancient architecture by George Milner in the Midwest section; about shell-ring architecture by Mike Russo in the Southeast section; and about Chaco Canyon Great Houses by Steve Lekson and Hohokam platform mounds by Glen Rice, Arleyn Simon, and David Jacobs in the Southwest section);
- *Ancient cities and towns* of North America (see, for example, the essays about villages in the Mohawk valley by Dean Snow in the Northeast section; about Moundville by Margaret Scarry in the Southeast section; about Cahokia, Angel Mounds, and Aztalan by John Kelly, Chris Peebles and Staffan Peterson, and Lynn Goldstein, respectively, in the Midwest section; about Tyounyi and Tsankawi pueblos by Tim Kohler, Wupatki by Chris Downum, Pueblo Grande by Todd Bostwick, and Paquime [Casas Grandes] by Paul Minnis and Michael Whalen in the Southwest section; and, about Cathlapotle by Ken Ames and Virginia Parks in the Pacific Northwest part of the West Coast section);
- *The earliest European sites* in North America (see, for example, essays about L'Anse aux Meadows by Brigitta Wallace, Jamestown by Andrew Veech, and Chesapeake Bay settlements by Barbara Little in the Northeast section; about Santa Elena by Stanley South and Chester DePratter and St. Augustine by Dennis Blanton in the Southeast section; and about Tumacacori, San Antonio area missions, and the El Camino Real trail by Jeremy Moss, Susan Snow, and Ed Staski, respectively, in the Southwest section);
- *Colonial era settlements* (see, for example, essays about the African Burial Ground and other archaeology of lower Manhattan by Andrew Pickman and Rebecca Yamin in the Northeast section; about Fort St. Joseph by Michael Nassaney in the Midwest section; about pueblos and missions in the Salinas and Galisteo Basin areas of New Mexico by Kate Spielmann and Mark Lycett, respectively; about Spanish and Russian colonial sites in California by John Johnson and Glenn Farris, respectively, in the California portion of the West Coast section; and about Russian colonization by Aron Crowell in the Arctic and Subarctic section);
- *Historic period urban and industrial sites* (see, for example, essays about Northeastern cities and industrial sites by Steve Mrozowski and Paul Shackel, respectively; about Midwest urban sites by Paul Mullins; about historical and industrial sites in the Great Basin and Plateau by Don Hardesty; and about the Kennecott Mine in the Pacific Northwest and Southeastern Alaska portion of the West Coast section);
- *Historic period military sites* from the Revolutionary War through World War II (see, for example, essays about Revolutionary War and Civil War sites by David Orr and Steve Smith in the Northeast and Southeast sections, respectively; about the Wilson Creek and Pea Ridge battlefields by Doug Scott in the Midwest section; about the Palo Alto battlefield by Charlie Haecker in the Southwest section; about the Manzanar World War II internment camp by Jeff Burton, Allika Ruby, and Sharon Waeckter in the California portion of the West Coast section; and, about the USS *Arizona* by Larry Murphy and Matt Russell in the Hawaii portion of the West Coast section).

Using the Encyclopedia

Organization of the Entries

This encyclopedia is organized geographically into four volumes with eight sections representing general regions of North America north of Mexico: Northeast, Southeast, Midwest, Great Plains–Rocky Mountains, Southwest, Great Basin–Plateau, West Coast, and Arctic-Subarctic. Because of the large size and diversity, the West Coast section is subdivided into portions focused on California, Hawaii, and the Pacific Northwest and Southeast Alaska. The regions generally conform to large-scale geomorphologic and climatic patterns in North America. They also reflect general culture areas that have been identified by past archaeological and anthropological research. In general, these regions also witnessed different patterns of historical events and developments.

Within each section, the essays are organized with general-topic essays first, arranged in roughly chronological order. Following the general essays are essays describing individual sites, or groups of related sites. These also are organized in general chronological order; that is, essays covering older sites generally come first. However, in some sections, the organization is more geographically oriented because it made more sense to do so. Each section also includes a short introduction to the region, a list of the essays, and a map showing the general locations of sites mentioned in the essays in that section.

Measurements in Space and Time

Archaeological investigations involve a lot of measurements. During excavations, archaeologists typically measure where artifacts are found relative to a three-dimensional matrix that encompasses the site area, or the area being excavated. This kind of spatial control of artifact locations is necessary to describe and analyze the archaeological site after excavation. Spatial relationships among artifacts (as well as other kinds of materials or samples) collected as part of excavation are necessary to infer behavioral, cultural, and temporal similarities or differences among the artifacts and other material. These similarities and differences are the fundamental data used by archaeologists to interpret the human behavior, cultural expressions, and changes or stability over time that the site reflects.

Since measurements are so important to archaeology and archaeological interpretations, the essays in this encyclopedia often refer to measurements of one or another sort. Our essays include the use of both English and metric measurements. Usually if an author has used English measurements, a metric equivalent has been added, and vice versa. The scientific nature of archaeological surveys and excavations lead most investigators to use metric measures as their standard. However, for some kinds of sites, in particular those that relate to the English colonial period or later American eras, English measures directly reflect the measuring system used by the original builders or settlers. In these cases, using English measures for archaeological recording may make both description and interpretation of the archaeological record easier.

As readers might expect, archaeologists are obsessed with time and temporal relationships. They study events or ways of life that date to certain time periods, and so must know that the archaeological materials they examine are from that determined date. Archaeologists study how human behavior or cultural patterns change over time, and so must be sure that they can accurately assign different sets of behaviors or patterns to different time periods. In its earliest days, archaeology relied on linking artifacts to datable inscriptions or artifacts found in the same context with them—for example, ancient Greek or Latin inscriptions, or ancient Egyptian hieroglyphs in a tomb containing artifacts. Coins with dates or that could be dated also have often provided a means of dating other artifacts found with them by association.

Cultural levels or soil layers within archaeological sites can be dated relatively if the sites are stratified. A site is stratified if it has overlapping layers of soil and artifacts, in a "layer cake" pattern. The arrangement of layers, or "strata," within archaeological sites is interpreted according to the principle of "superposition." This principle states that the strata that lie above other strata are younger in time. This permits interpretations of the relative age of artifacts and other cultural remains within a stratified site. In some cases, if the strata are very distinctive and shared among sites, it may be possible to infer the relative chronologically order among a group of sites. Stratigraphic analysis of archaeological sites was developed in the late nineteenth and early twentieth centuries (Harris 1989, 7–22; Renfrew and Bahn 2000, 19–66, 117–128). Unless one or more of the strata can be dated to a particular time or range of times, the chronological relationship among the strata is relative, one being simply older or younger than the other, based on superposition.

Absolute, or chronometric, dating is another general class of chronological methods. It differs from relative dating in that absolute methods result in a specific date or date range for the object, site, or portion of a site being dated (see Renfrew and Bahn 2000, 128–162). Tree rings, lake varves (regular clay deposits), radiocarbon, and other physical or chemical methods are used to obtain absolute dates. Of course, each of these methods has its own requirements, which are often quite specific and highly technical. All methods are never applicable to all artifacts or sites and, for some artifacts and sites, none of these methods is usable. Each method also has its own specialized terminology. For the essays here, authors have used more general references to the ages and dates associated with the sites and topics they are describing. Readers typically will find references to sites dating to 1,000 years ago, or 450 years ago, or about 15,000 years ago. In some essays authors have been more specific or precise with chronological information—for example, when temporal distinctions between sites, or strata within sites, or components of sites are important and close. In these cases, authors have used the type of date that is most sensible in the context of the topic. In general, the essays use the BC/AD time scale; in some cases BP (years before present, which by convention refers to AD 1950, in keeping with the standard for radiocarbon dating) is used. When more specific dating is required, authors or editors have provided more detailed explanations.

Visiting Sites or Museums and Further Reading

Archaeological sites usually also have collections, notes, reports, and data related to them that were collected as part of the investigations of the sites. These collections and records are also considered to be important archaeological resources and typically are cared for by public agencies, museums, and universities (see Sullivan and Childs, 2003, for more about the curation of archaeological collections and records). Many of the archaeological sites described in the essays are interpreted for the public, or have museum exhibits that display collections and information related to them. Each essay includes information about opportunities for visitation where this is possible, as well as lists of more detailed sources—in print or available via the Internet—for readers who seek additional information about the sites or topics.

THE ARCHAEOLOGICAL RECORD OF NORTH AMERICA AND ITS VALUE

America's archaeological sites are sometimes quite obvious, as with the visible remains of ancient earthen mounds, Revolutionary War or Civil War battlefield earthworks, ancient Southwestern cliff dwellings and pueblos, the remains of historic fortifications and industrial complexes, or other above-ground structures. Other kinds of archaeological sites—the vast majority, in fact—are much less visible, most frequently hidden beneath the ground surface or dense vegetation.

Hundreds of the most visible and significant archaeological sites in North America are recognized formally as national parks, historic sites, or other official designations. Hundreds of thousands, or even millions, of less obvious but also important, sites exist throughout the continent. Public lands frequently contain important archaeological sites that are connected to compelling stories about the long history of this land, yet are all but invisible to the naked eye. For example, Cape Cod National Seashore in Massachusetts, created by Congress to preserve public recreational spaces and natural resource values, as well as historical resources on the outer Cape, contains hundreds of archaeological sites.

Some American archaeological sites package stories of thousands of years of ancient American history. A history that is far too unfamiliar to most Americans today. Others contain information that provides details about hundreds of years of historical settlement, development, and cultural change on well-known parts of America. Archaeological sites are found on public lands throughout North America—for example, in the well-known national parks of Yellowstone and Death Valley, in national forests and wildlife refuges, and in the vast public lands of Alaska and northern Canada. Archaeological sites on public lands are an important part of the legacy of Americans, and agencies that manage those lands typically are responsible to the American people for the appropriate use, preservation, and protection of these resources. Of course, there are archaeological sites outside of national parks and other public lands as well, and federal, tribal, state, and local laws exist to ensure that the value and importance of archaeological and other historic resources, such as historic buildings, are taken into account and weighed against the benefits projected from development or other potentially damaging activity.

Archaeology, Commemoration, and Heritage

American archaeological resources are a nonrenewable and irreplaceable national heritage. They are sources of information for forming more complete views of the history—ancient, colonial, and modern—of the cultures and land of North America. Information from archaeological sites, collections, reports, and data is essential for comprehending ancient times and historical events for which there is no written record. Archaeological resources also can be places, objects, or information charged with commemorative value related to culturally or politically important events, individuals, or groups. National Park Service archaeologist Barbara Little states the potential value of archaeology broadly when she writes that it

> offers opportunities for us to become aware of our common humanity and our common struggles. In the face of cynicism and despair, archaeology can offer glimpses into the human story as a source of hope and renewal. We can all hope that respect—at least tolerance but perhaps even celebration—will flow from the present to the past and back again to the present. (Little 2007, 16)

Archaeological sites are places associated with past people, events, and historical patterns. These associations give many archaeological sites personal or community commemorative value. Knowing about these places and having a sense of what happened at each of them provide an important temporal context for modern life. The archaeological investigation of these sites provides us with knowledge about them, the individuals who used them, and the events that transpired at these places. American historian and former director of the National Park Service Roger Kennedy remarked that such places and knowledge about them play an essential role in "sustaining the American heritage and the American community" (Kennedy 1994, 33).

Another noted historian, David Lowenthal, comments on the relationship of archaeological remains, appreciation of the past, and the connections individuals draw between themselves and archaeological and historic places:

> Memory and history both derive and gain emphasis from physical remains. Tangible survivals provide a vivid immediacy that helps to assure us there really was a past. Physical remains have their limitations as informants, to be sure; they are themselves mute, requiring interpretation; their continual but differential erosion and demolition skews the record; and their substantial survival conjures up a past more static than could have been the case. But however depleted by time and use, relics remain essential bridges between then and now. They confirm or deny what we think of it, symbolize or memorialize communal links over time, and provide archaeological metaphors that illumine the processes of history and memory. (Lowenthal 1985, xxiii)

The associations that Lowenthal describes are created by individuals who use the archaeological and historical context provided by places to construct their own identities or to evaluate personal conditions. In some situations, these associations benefit modern communities, in terms of both the cohesion resulting from a shared historical context and the benefits of tourism. The latter benefit, which typically is mixed with costs, is derived from people's desire to enjoy the archaeological or historical sites in or near the community, stimulating the local economy in the process.

That Americans recognize and appreciate the commemorative associations and value of archaeological sites is demonstrated by the large number of archaeological places identified as, or as part of, national, state, regional, and local parks and sites throughout the nation. Some archaeological places are designated for specific events or individuals, such as Franklin Court in Philadelphia, Jamestown National Historical Site (NHS), Little Big Horn NHS, Monticello, and Mt. Vernon. Others commemorate broader historical patterns or periods in American history and prehistory, such as Saugus Ironworks NHS in Massachusetts, Hopewell Culture National Historic Park (NHP) and Serpent Mound State Memorial in Ohio, Etowah Indian Mounds State Historic Site in Georgia, Moundville State Monument in Alabama, Cahokia Mounds State Historic Site in Illinois, Pecos NHP in New Mexico, Canyon of the Ancients National Monument in Colorado and Utah, and Casa Grande Ruins National Monument and Pueblo Grande City Park in Arizona. This brief listing mentions only a very small selection of the rich national assortment of archaeological and historic places that draw tourists intent upon visiting them and other, nearby sites and parks (see Slick 2002 for a discussion about archaeology and tourism).

In addition to the potential economic benefits, archaeology enriches communities by allowing them to devote their energy and resources on objectives associated with their locality. Spinoffs from individual archaeological projects have had a ripple effect through communities, touching public schools, museums, neighborhood activities, and the design of public places. Examples of such community involvement can be found in Baltimore, Maryland; Alexandria, Virginia; Pensacola, Florida; St. Augustine, Florida; and Tucson, Flagstaff, and other parts of Arizona. Pam Cressy, longtime city archaeologist for Alexandria, Virginia, did not exaggerate when she wrote that

> every community in America has an archaeological heritage which, if managed
> properly as a public resource, can help us recognize and celebrate the
> accomplishments of our predecessors. Archaeology brings the American legacy to life.
> (Cressy 1987, 6; see also Cressy's essay about archaeology in Alexandria in the
> Northeast section)

As Brian Fagan, noted archaeologist and author of many popular books about archaeology and archaeological sites, has remarked, all archaeology, like politics, is local. In some instances, archaeological discoveries may have national or international import, but they always have local interest.

> Few archaeologists will ever find a pharaoh's tomb or buried gold . . . most finds are
> of purely local, or perhaps regional, importance, even sometimes, frankly dull. But the
> information that comes from them is of more than passing local significance and
> educational value. This is where archaeologists can work miracles with public
> relations, provided they develop close links with the local media. (Fagan 1991)

In addition to personal considerations and reflections, the commemorative benefit of archaeological places may act on a wider social scale. Writing of the ancient monumental architecture found in the midwestern and southeastern United States, from the upper Mississippi and Ohio valleys to the gulf coast, Roger Kennedy (1994, 1–6) notes that these substantial examples of ancient engineering reflect complex human social organization and skill that ought to give modern Americans an appreciation of the achievements and potential of non-Western cultures and their modern descendants. Following this appreciation, one hopes, will come tolerance and the possibility of cooperation among people of varying ethnic backgrounds.

For Native Americans, the associations with ancient archaeological sites often are more directly cultural. These links hold special commemorative value associated with ancient histories of creation, special events, and epic journeys. Native American associations with archaeological sites provide opportunities for archaeologists to work directly with American Indians to examine the ways in which their different approaches to understanding the past are complementary (see, for example, the essays in Dongoske et al. 2000). Archaeologists Anne Pyburn and Richard Wilk urge archaeologists to act on this challenge and opportunity:

> Archaeology can be used in the service of native people by reconstructing some of the
> heritage that has been lost through conquest and deprivation. Archaeologists can also

offer real support for developing tourism, jobs, crafts industries, self-respect, education, and public awareness. It is absolutely crucial that archaeological reconstructions not be framed as "gifts from the archaeologists," but as the results of scientific research, which is a technique of understanding that is useful and available to anyone. (Pyburn and Wilk 1995, 72)

Cultural associations with historic period sites are also important for other groups of Americans. Places such as Jamestown in Virginia and early European settlement sites in Canada, New England, the Southeast, and the Southwest hold cultural associations for Americans of other backgrounds. African Americans recently experienced a cultural connection with the discovery, investigation, and, after some controversy, commemoration of the African Burial Ground in lower Manhattan (see the essay about this site in the Northeast section). In order for such cooperation to work, however, each side must not only respect the position of the other, but also be able and willing to be effective advocates of their own perspective. Archaeologists must emphasize the benefits of an archaeological approach to investigating and understanding the past.

Archaeology, Anthropology, and History

Archaeological resources are valuable for the information they convey about the cultures and history of the past through scientific investigation. This information helps us to understand larger patterns of cultural and human development throughout the past—for example, the expansion, or contraction, of settlements or land use over a large area, or the development of agriculture and other technological innovations, or the evolution of social organization. The distinguished archaeologist Bill Lipe noted that the ability to provide information about the past is the principal benefit of archaeology:

> The primary social contribution of archaeology . . . [is] the production and
> dissemination of new information about the past based on the systematic study of the
> archaeological record . . . most sites in fact gain their primary social value because
> they have the potential to contribute new information about the past when subjected
> to archaeological study. (Lipe 1996, 23)

A sense of place and cultural context comes from anthropological and historical interpretations derived from archaeological investigations. The importance of scientific investigation of archaeological sites, as opposed to the haphazard, individual collecting of artifacts, has been recognized since the nineteenth century (Willey and Sabloff 1993). The public benefits from the information and artifacts recovered were the primary considerations behind the Antiquities Act of 1906, which established these fundamental aspects of United States law and policy regarding archaeological and historical resources (see the essays in Harmon et al. 2006).

The information from archaeological sites has particular attractions for educators and school children. Educators have discovered that archaeology can provide stimulating subject matter for teaching a wide range of subjects (for example, the essays in Smardz and Smith 2000). Fay Metcalf, an American educator familiar with issues at the local, state, and national levels, recognizes the excitement and intrigue that archaeological approaches and information can bring to formal education. She points out that using material culture, its spatial context, and archaeological methodology promotes complex thinking skills involving the evaluation of data, the construction of inferences, and the flexibility of interpretations (Metcalf 2002). Archaeology has obvious connections with history, geography, and social studies generally. All American school children study United States history, state history, and ancient history at least twice during a normal 12-year elementary and secondary education. Information from archaeological investigations can address pre-European United States history, early contact between Native Americans and European colonists, and later periods of U.S. history. Archaeology is a basic source of information about ancient civilizations and cultures. Many teachers have found that incorporation of archaeological information and discussions of how the investigation of material remains can illuminate aspects of history stimulates student interest. Archaeological examples provide intriguing introductions to topics in biology, chemistry, and physics. For example, radiocarbon dating is a natural entry point to a discussion of general atomic structure, and two- and three-dimensional coordinate geometry can be explored using standard archaeological horizontal and vertical recording of artifacts and features. It is estimated that 90 percent of the American public support the inclusion of archaeology in the school curriculum (Ramos and Duganne 2000).

"Diversity" is a word frequently used these days, yet American cultural diversity is, in fact, deeply embedded in our history, heritage, and identity. Archaeology and the stories it can tell about people in both the ancient and recent past is a portal through which we can access American diversity. The physical archaeological record—artifacts, structural remains, and their locational contexts—are the evidence of past diversity among Americans of different cultures. Some of these differences have persisted, others have been modified, and some are now only historical. Dealing with diversity has been an aspect of much of American history. The encounters and relationships among different cultural groups continue to challenge people today who are struggling with issues that sometimes are mistaken for new. Diversity is not new; cultural conflicts and clashes and accommodation are not new. The challenges of living in a changing environment are not new either. Results from the study of archaeological resources and an archaeological perspective can lend insights into contemporary efforts to work cooperatively and recognize the merit of other points of view.

Public Interest in Archaeology

In 1999 archaeologists in federal agencies and national archaeological organizations joined in a cooperative effort to conduct a national survey to determine Americans' opinions and level of understanding regarding archaeology and archaeological resources. The survey was carried out by Harris Interactive, a national political and social polling research company. Harris contacted a random sample of 1,016 adults across the continental United States (Ramos and Duggane 2000). Questions centered on the public's grasp of, and participation in, archaeology. The poll showed substantial public interest in archaeology and archaeological sites and support for public and educational archaeological programs.

The poll found that most Americans support the goals and practice of archaeology, endorse laws protecting archaeological sites and artifacts, and think archaeology is important to today's society. The results also indicate that Americans are unclear about the primary activities of and topics studied by archaeologists, yet a majority (60 percent) believe in the value to society of archaeological research and education.

A large majority of the public (96 percent) believe that there should be laws to protect public archaeological resources, but are less certain toward laws pertaining to materials found on private land. Many people (80 percent) agree that public funds should be used to protect archaeological sites. Most Americans are aware that archaeologists study ancient civilizations and the human past, with more than one-third (38 percent) mentioning Egyptian sites such as the pyramids and the Valley of the Kings as some of the most important archaeological discoveries. More recent discoveries also received public attention; 83 percent of respondents expressed awareness that archaeologists also study the nineteenth and twentieth centuries, and 77 percent identified archaeologists as shipwreck investigators.

The majority of respondents learned about archaeology through television (56 percent) and books, encyclopedias, and magazines (33 percent), followed by newspapers (24 percent). Learning about archaeology in college was mentioned by 23 percent of respondents. Others noted that they had learned about archaeology in secondary school (20 percent) or at the primary level (10 percent). A large majority (90 percent) believed that students should learn about archaeology as part of the school curriculum from their earliest years. Most of the public (88 percent) have visited a museum exhibiting archaeological material, while more than 1 in 3 people (37 percent) have visited an archaeological site.

Some archaeologists always have regarded public interpretation as an important aspect of their work. For example, during the first decade of the twentieth century, excavations by Smithsonian Institution archaeologist Jesse W. Fewkes at Spruce Tree House and Cliff Palace in the newly created Mesa Verde National Park (established in 1906) were intended primarily to publicize the existence of the cliff dwellings and to stabilize the ancient buildings so that early tourists could more easily and safely visit them. However, it has only been since the 1980s that advocacy for public outreach programs and heightened awareness of the need for public interpretation or a public outreach product as part of archaeological studies has become widespread in the discipline. The survey results suggest fertile ground for effective public education and outreach, but ground that must be cultivated to achieve fruitful results. Important findings include that Americans believe archaeology is important and valuable and that Americans are interested in learning about the past through archaeology. They believe archaeology is important because learning about the past helps us understand the modern world.

PUBLIC ARCHAEOLOGY IN NORTH AMERICA

Thomas Jefferson, often credited with being America's first archaeologist, conducted one of the earliest scientific investigations in the New World when he excavated a Native American burial mound near his property at Monticello, Virginia (see the essay about Jefferson's sites by Jeff Hantman in the Northeast section). Jefferson was one among a number of Enlightenment-influenced American scholars who collected accounts about ancient monuments being found in the interior parts of America. Traders and settlers encountered ancient earthen and stone mounds and mounded earthen complexes as they moved into the Ohio River valley, other midwestern valleys, and the interior Southeast (see the essays by Martin Hawley, George Milner, and others on the ancient architecture, mound sites, and mound complexes in the Midwest section). The first publication of the then-fledgling Smithsonian Institution presented a systematic report, including hundreds of maps and sketches showing these ancient places and some of the artifacts from them: *Ancient Monuments of the Mississippi Valley* (1848), by Ephriam G. Squier and Edwin H. Davis.

In the newly formed United States, explorations of ancient stone and adobe architectural sites in the southwestern part of the country began during the first half of the nineteenth century. Military and scientific recording expeditions in the American Southwest reported finding the remains of structures and settlements through the western landscape. In the late nineteenth century, concern about the looting of these ancient places for building stone and scarce wood led to the passage of the Antiquities Act of 1906. This law was intended to protect such ancient sites for all Americans for their historic, educational, and scientific value. Throughout the twentieth century, important archaeological sites or areas were preserved by presidents who used the authority of the Antiquities Act to create national monuments with special protections on public lands. National park units also were created by congressional action to protect and provide for public interpretation of some of these sites.

Perhaps the earliest example of this type of publicly funded scientific documentation, stabilization, and conservation occurred at Casa Grande Ruin, near the modern town of Coolidge, Arizona, in 1891. This occurred shortly after preservation activists from Massachusetts prevailed upon the United States Congress to protect the site from homesteading and vandalism. In 1892 President Benjamin Harrison issued an executive order designating Casa Grande Ruin and 480 acres around it for permanent preservation because of its archaeological value. Casa Grande includes the Great House, a unique, multi-story classic period Hohokam (AD 1300–1450) structure, and its immediate surrounding compound walls and area (see the essay by James Bayman in the Southwest section). In the case of Casa Grande, these early efforts were followed by protection activities under the management of the National Park Service, including public interpretation, research, and regular maintenance programs.

Throughout the twentieth century, the involvement of public agencies in archaeology and archaeological resources grew. Large-scale archaeological fieldwork was undertaken as part of Franklin D. Roosevelt's New Deal "back to work" programs in the 1930s. Following World War II, archaeological investigations became part of the planning procedures undertaken in advance of large dam and reservoir construction in major North American rivers. Growing out of these public archaeological activities, much of modern public archaeology occurs as part of what has become known as "cultural resource management," or CRM. The term CRM developed within the discipline of archaeology in the United States during the early 1970s. The first use of the term "cultural resources" is attributed to specialists within the National Park Service in 1971 or 1972. Shortly after this the word "management" was linked with cultural resources by the 1974 Cultural Resource Management Conference held in Denver. This conference was attended by many of the individuals working actively on the problems associated with preservation of archaeological sites in the United States (Fowler 1982).

Early proponents and developers of CRM recognized that the concept included not only archaeological sites, but also historic buildings and districts, engineering structures, and other kinds of cultural resources. Despite this early recognition of the broad nature of CRM, the term frequently is used as a synonym for archaeology done in conjunction with public agency actions or projects. Imprecise usage and lack of rigorous adherence to definitions are common to a range of terms related to CRM, such as "historic preservation," "archaeological resource management," and "heritage management." This situation is not too worrisome; all of these terms are relatively new, and in time their definitions and associations will become more precise. However, to avoid misunderstanding, contemporary workers in these various fields must define the terms explicitly as they use them in their own work.

CRM developed from two related archaeological concerns. First, there was a concern about the destruction of archaeological sites due to modern development such as road construction, large-scale agriculture, and housing. Much of this development was sponsored, endorsed, or funded by the federal government. This concern was an extension of earlier ones about large-scale federal construction projects, most notably the river basin reservoir construction program of the Corps of Engineers and the Bureau of Reclamation that developed in the late 1940s and early 1950s. In the United States, archaeology undertaken as part of these construction programs was termed "salvage archaeology" by those who viewed it as second-rate work—or, more positively, "rescue archaeology" or "emergency archaeology" by those who argued that it was necessary and generally effective at saving some of the archaeological data from sites that would otherwise be destroyed. Emergency archaeology focused on saving archaeological data and remains through rapid excavation of sites prior to their destruction from modern construction projects.

The second concern that led to the development of CRM was dissatisfaction with the emergency archaeology approach itself. Although emergency archaeology resulted in the excavation of sites and the preservation of some data and remains, critics justifiably pointed out that frequently the excavations were not followed by adequate data description, analysis, reporting, or synthesis of the investigation. The collections and records from many salvage projects also were poorly cared for after the investigation ended. Perhaps most problematic was the fundamental failure of the emergency archaeology approach to modify development projects so that sites could be conserved and protected rather than destroyed, even though the destruction was preceded by scientific excavation.

One consequence of the heightened concern about environmental issues during the late 1960s and the 1970s was the enactment of laws to protect important aspects of the cultural and natural environment. Prominent among these laws were the National Historic Preservation Act of 1966 (NHPA) and the National Environment Policy Act of 1969 (NEPA). Both of these statutes had important effects on the development of CRM in the United States. Both laws required that federal agencies take historic properties, defined broadly and including archaeological sites, into account as agencies planned, reviewed, or undertook projects or activities. NHPA requires federal agencies to identify, evaluate, and protect historic properties on land over which they have jurisdiction or control. These new requirements and government involvement had two immediate effects on the development of CRM, leading to (1) the employment of professional archaeologists in public agencies and private firms to do the archaeological work required by the new laws and regulations, and (2) increased attention devoted to archaeological resources as part of the planning of public agency operations and projects.

A National Network of Public Agency Archaeologists

During the 1970s the public began to employ professional archaeologists in numbers never before seen and to place them in offices throughout their organizations. This was especially true among federal land managing agencies, such as the Bureau of Land Management and the Forest Service. Prior to this period, the relatively few professional archaeologists employed in federal service were located in the National Park Service and the Smithsonian. Agencies, such as the Federal Highway Administration and the Environmental Protection Agency, that did not manage land but provided funding or licensing for development projects, such as, highways, wastewater treatment facilities, and energy plants, tended not to employ many archaeologists on their staffs. More frequently, these agencies met their CRM responsibilities by requiring their fulfillment by the state agencies or private firms that carried out the development projects. This pattern eventually led to the hiring of professional archaeologists by the state agencies and private firms that found themselves required by federal agencies to carry out necessary cultural resource studies. By the early 1980s, federal and state agencies had developed a network that included hundreds of professional archaeologists filling positions in headquarters, regional, and local offices and undertaking a variety of activities to implement CRM laws, policy regulations, and guidelines. At the state government level, State Historic Preservation Offices established by the NHPA and its implementing regulations required that each state office have a professionally qualified archaeologist on its staff. This in particular helped in the establishment of a national network of professionally qualified archaeologists in the public sector.

A similar growth in the professional employment of archaeologists occurred in private firms. Such firms ranged in size from large national or international consulting firms that needed to comply with NHPA and NEPA requirements for many of the public projects they bid on, to small, newly organized firms set up to undertake specific CRM investigations required by public agencies.

These rapid, substantial changes within the archaeological community in the proportions of professional employment, duties, and responsibilities resulted in discussions, debates, and disagreements regarding the benefits of CRM and the quality of archaeological work done as part of it. Not all of the issues raised in the professional turmoil over CRM have been resolved. However, the general tenor of the debates and disagreements has moderated from vitriolic to collegial. Much of the contemporary archaeological fieldwork done in the United States is tied to CRM. Many, perhaps most, professional archaeologists support a conservation approach to treatment of the archaeological record that has as one major goal the management of resources for long-term preservation. There is general agreement that the archaeological network among public agencies and the statutes, policies, regulations, and guidelines that protect archaeological resources are important to maintain and perhaps strengthen.

Archaeological Resources and Planning

Both the NHPA and NEPA require that federal agencies take account of cultural resources in planning their own programs or projects that they are undertaking with state or local agencies or with private firms. The term "cultural resources" is not used in either statute. NHPA uses the term "historic property" to cover a wide range of cultural resource types, explicitly referring to archaeological resources; NEPA uses the term "human environment," which has been interpreted to include archaeological resources. Both laws are important because they establish a national policy of considering the effect of public actions on the natural and historic environment during the planning stages of public projects. This consideration requires the identification, estimation, and evaluation of impacts on archaeological resources prior to decision-making about proceeding on projects that will result in harm to significant resources. The approach to planning required by NHPA and NEPA has moved archaeologists into the planning process. Although emergency situations requiring that archaeological investigations take place during the construction phase of projects, immediately preceding the bulldozers, still occur, they are much less common than during the days of "salvage archaeology."

Key Activities of Contemporary CRM

There are three general kinds of activities in CRM related to the consideration of archaeological resources: (1) identification and evaluation of resources, (2) treatment and care of the resource, and (3) long-term management of the resource.

Identification and Evaluation

Identification and evaluation of archaeological resources is an essential aspect of CRM and one that is particularly challenging for some kinds of archaeological sites. Discovery of sites that are hidden or unobtrusive and in areas where visibility is poor usually is difficult. For example, many archaeological resources do not contain architectural remains to help signal their existence and location. Frequently archaeological sites are buried below the surface or, if on the surface, are hidden by thick vegetation. Relatively costly and labor-intensive investigations frequently are necessary for the discovery of archaeological resources, much more so than for other kinds of cultural resources, such as historic structures.

The evaluation of archaeological sites involves the determination of the importance or significance of each site or of a group of sites. Most often such significance is based upon what can be learned about the past from the resource being evaluated. However, archaeological resources also may be important because they are associated with important individuals, events, or historical patterns, or because they illustrate important aspects of architecture or design. In most cases, the information needed for archaeological evaluations to be made also requires labor-intensive investigations, in these cases at the site level.

In United States CRM law and regulations, archaeological resources must be determined to be significant enough to be listed on or eligible for listing on the National Register of Historic Places to be considered for preservation in the context of federal undertakings or programs. On federal lands, archaeological resources also are protected from deliberate damage by the provisions of the Archaeological Resources Protection Act (ARPA). This requires that the removal or excavation of archaeological resources be undertaken only as part of a scientifically based investigation, unless these resources have been determined to be no longer "of archaeological interest." Land managers may make a determination that resources have lost their significance under procedures established in the regulations implementing ARPA only after careful consideration of the facts of a case.

Treatment and Care

After archaeological resources have been identified and evaluated as being important enough for some kind of further treatment and care, the exact kind of treatment must be decided upon. There are two general kinds of initial treatments: (1) excavation, data recovery, and documentation prior to site destruction; or (2) in situ preservation of the site. Frequently, of course, a site is not destroyed totally by a construction project, and a portion of the site might be saved in situ while another is excavated prior to destruction. At present, archaeological resources discovered and evaluated as significant that are within the impact area of a public construction project usually are excavated and their data recovered as an agreed-upon means of mitigating the impact of the federal undertaking. There are moves afoot to use site avoidance and preservation more frequently in such situations, but the general pattern at present is to condone data recovery as an acceptable means of impact mitigation. For archaeological resources on public land that are not threatened with destruction by modern construction or agency operations, *in situ* preservation is the more common treatment.

When *in situ* preservation is selected, the agency responsible for management of the resource must also decide if further intervention to stabilize, maintain, or protect the resource is necessary and whether the agency wants to interpret the site actively. If any of these more detailed kinds of treatments is deemed necessary, agency personnel must take further steps to implement them. A site, for example, might be threatened with erosion by fluctuating lake levels and may need shoreline stabilization to protect its deposits. In other situations, an agency office might decide that a site's location near a visitors center or public reception area provides an opportunity for public interpretation of the site. In either case, the agency will undertake additional steps to carry out the treatment decisions that it makes regarding the *in situ* preservation of the resource.

Long-Term Management

The long-term management of archaeological resources is a requirement placed upon each federal agency by the Antiquities Act, ARPA, and Section 110 of the NHPA. For land managing agencies, management focuses on three main duties: (1) carrying out programs to identify and evaluate archaeological resources on the lands they are responsible for, (2) executing the treatments decided on for *in situ* archaeological sites on agency lands, and (3) caring for the archaeological collections, reports, and records related to the sites that were once on agency lands. For public agencies that do not manage land, the first two aspects of long-term management may not apply or may apply only in a few instances. However, the third aspect of long-term responsibilities will apply for these agencies to the extent that their projects and programs have resulted in the excavation of archaeological sites.

PRESERVING ARCHAEOLOGICAL RESOURCES IN NORTH AMERICA

In Canada, the Parks Canada Agency is responsible for archaeological resources of the national parks and preserves, national historic sites, and other public lands administered by Parks Canada. Each province is responsible for archaeological resources within its territory and has established provincial government programs designed for the preservation and protection of these archaeological resources. Except for Ontario and Quebec, archaeological discoveries are the property of the province. Development projects that require formal environmental assessments under national or provincial laws generally require an assessment of the archaeological sites that will be disturbed by the proposed development.

In the United States, there are roughly a dozen major federal land managing agencies, that is, agencies that are responsible for managing from one million acres to hundreds of millions of acres of federal land and the archaeological resources in it. There are about half a dozen federal agencies that either fund or issue permits for substantial development actions and regularly require archaeological investigations as part of these developments. These federal development and regulatory agencies typically have state-level counterparts that are responsible for conducting or contracting for the archaeology required by the federal agencies. There are also state agencies that manage archaeological resources on state land; also, with increasing frequency, municipal, county, and tribal agencies are taking on some archaeological preservation responsibility.

To simplify somewhat, we can say that in the United States the management of archaeological resources is conducted in two ways: (1) by federal agencies on the lands that they administer, and (2) by state, tribal, or local agencies on the lands they administer. On private lands in the United States, there is no public agency responsible for direct archaeological resource management; however, in each state officials, referred to as State Historic Preservation Officers, play a central role in maintaining inventories and information about archaeological sites in each state and advising federal and other state agencies when their activities may impact significant archaeological sites.

Individuals who are interested in participating in archaeological investigations or public agency preservation activities may be able to do so through local agency offices. In the United States the Bureau of Land Management, the National Forest Service, and the National Park Service all have active programs for individuals who wish to become involved in these kinds of activities as volunteers. Local governments and state or tribal governments also sometimes sponsor such volunteer programs. These opportunities give everyone who is interested and willing to contribute some of their time, experience, and skills the ability to contribute to the study, interpretation, and preservation of our American archaeological heritage.

Further Reading: Cressy, Pamela J., "Community Archaeology in Alexandria, Virginia," *Conserve Neighborhoods* 69 (1987): 1–7; Dongoske, Kurt E., Mark Aldenderfer, and Karen Doehner, eds., *Working Together: Native Americans and Archaeologists* (Washington, D.C.: Society for American Archaeology, 2000); Fagan, Brian M., "The Past as News," CRM 14(1) (1991): 17–19; Fowler, Don D., "Cultural Resource Management," in *Advances in Archaeological Method and Theory*, edited by M. B. Schiffer (New York: Academic Press, 1982), 1–50; Harmon, David, Francis P. McManamon, and Dwight T. Pitcaithley, *The Antiquities Act: A Century of American Archaeology, Historic Preservation, and Nature Conservation* (Tucson: University of Arizona Press, 2006); Harris, Edward C., *Principles of Archaeological Stratigraphy* (New York: Academic Press, 1989); Kennedy, Roger G., *Hidden Cities: The Discovery and Loss of Ancient North American Civilization* (New York: The Free Press, 1994); Lipe, William D., "In Defense of Digging: Archeological Preservation as a Means, Not an End," CRM 19(7) (1996): 23–27; Little, Barbara J., *Historical Archaeology: Why the Past Matters* (Walnut Creek, Calif.: Left Coast Press, 2007); Lowenthal, David, *The Past Is a Foreign Country* (Cambridge: Cambridge University Press, 1985); Metcalf, Fay, "Myths, Lies, and Videotapes: Information as an Antidote to Social Studies Classrooms and Pop Culture," in *Public Benefits of Archaeology*, edited by Barbara J. Little (Tallahassee: University of Florida Press, 2002), 167–175; Pyburn, K. Ann, and Richard R. Wilk, "Responsible Archaeology Is Applied Anthropology," in *Ethics in American Archaeology: Challenges for the 1990s*, edited by Mark J. Lynott and Alison Wylie (Washington, D.C.: Society for American Archaeology, 1995) , 71–76; Ramos, Maria, and David Duganne, *Exploring Public Perceptions and Attitudes about Archaeology* (Washington, D.C.: Harris Interactive and the Society for American Archaeology, 2000), www.nps.gov/archeology/pubs/Harris/index.htm (online August 12, 2008); Renfrew, Colin, and Paul Bahn, *Archaeology: Theories, Methods, and Practice* (New York: Thames and Hudson, 2000); Schiffer, Michael B., and George J. Gummerman, eds., *Conservation Archaeology: A Guide for Cultural Resource Management Studies* (New York: Academic Press, 1977); Slick, Katherine, "Archaeology and the Tourism Train," in *Public Benefits of Archaeology*, edited by Barbara J. Little (Tallahassee: University of Florida Press, 2002), 219–227; Smardz, Karolyn, and Shelley J. Smith, *The Archaeology Education Handbook: Sharing the Past with Kids* (Walnut Creek, Calif.: AltaMira Press, 2000); Sullivan, Lynne P. and S. Terry Childs, *Curating Archaeological Collections* (Walnut Creek, CA: AltaMira Press, 2003); Willey, Gordon R., and Jeremy A. Sabloff, *A History of American Archaeology*, 3rd ed. (San Francisco: W. H. Freeman, 1993).

Francis P. McManamon

Northeast Region

KEY FOR NORTHEAST REGIONAL MAP

1. *Monitor* National Marine Sanctuary
2. Albany area: Fort Orange National Historic Landmark, Rensselaerswyck, Beverwyck, Schuyler Flatts/Van Rensselaer's farm
3. Cactus Hill
4. Philadelphia: Independence Square, Franklin Court, Fort Mifflin, Front and Dock Streets, National Constitution Center site, and the President's House site
5. Cape Cod National Seashore: Nauset Archaeological District, High Head sites, the Indian Neck Ossuary, and the Wellfleet Tavern
6. Cocumscussoc
7. Queen's Fort
8. Mount Desert area: Taft's Point shell midden, Fernald Point, Duck Harbor, Fraser Point
9. Robinson House
10. Harper's Ferry National Historical Park
11. Mohawk River valley
12. Saratoga Battlefield
13. Accokeek Creek and Nanjemoy Creek Ossuaries
14. L'Anse aux Meadows National Historic Site
15. Lower Manhattan: Broad Financial Center, Stat Huys, 7 Hanover Square, 64 Pearl Street, 207 and 209 Water Street, the Five Points Neighborhood, and the African Burial Ground National Monument
16. Connecticut River valley sites
17. St. Mary's City
18. Meadowcroft Rockshelter
19. Boston and Charlestown area: Boston Harbor Islands, Boylston Street Fishweir, Massachusett Hill Quarries, the Braintree slate quarry, the Central Artery sites, Charlestown City Square Archaeological District, North End sites, Long Wharf, Town Dock, Boston African American Meeting House and Abiel Smith School sites
20. Long Island, NY area sites
21. Yorktown shipwreck sites
22. Martha's Vineyard and Nantucket
23. Fort Ticonderoga, Lake Champlain
24. Alexandria historic sites
25. Debert
26. Red Bay National Historic Site
27. Monacan ancient and early historic period sites
28. Thomas Jefferson-related sites: Shadwell, Monticello, Poplar Forest sites
29. Annapolis historic sites
30. Lowell historic sites
31. Sylvester Manor
32. Deerfield area sites
33. Minute Man National Historical Park
34. Salem Maritime National Historic Site
35. St. Croix Island International Historic Site
36. RI-1000
37. Bull Brook
38. Powhatan Chiefdom sites
39. Jamestown and other early Colonial sites
40. Fort Pemaquid
41. Pointe-à-Callière, Montréal
42. Lake Champlain area sites
43. Port au Choix National Historic Site
44. Reagen
45. Vail
46. Shoop
47. Shawnee-Minisink
48. Plenge
49. Sheep Rock Shelter
50. Williamson
51. Thunderbird
52. Otter Creek
53. Lamoka Lake
54. Bewerton sites: Oberlander and Robinson
55. Roundtop and Castle Creek
56. Barnes and McNab
57. Tadoussac
58. Mount Vernon
59. Williamsburg
60. Fort William Henry
61. Valley Forge National Historical Park

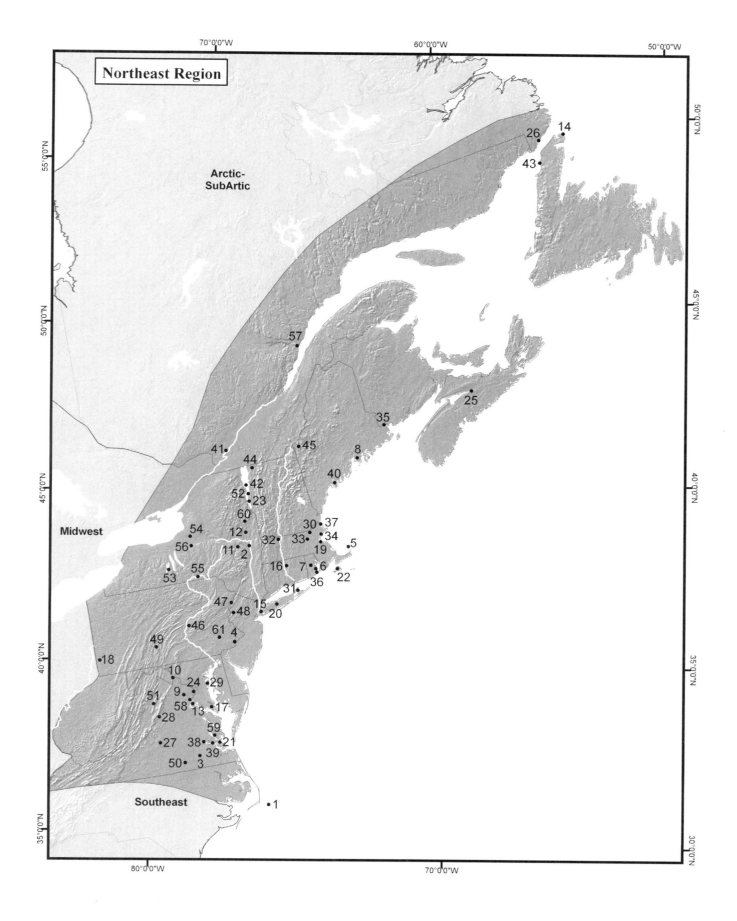

Northeast Region

Arctic-SubArtic

Midwest

Southeast

INTRODUCTION

This section of *Archaeology in America* includes essays about archaeological sites in the Northeast region of North America. This region includes the Maritime Provinces of Canada and the St. Lawrence River valley, the New England states, New York, Pennsylvania, New Jersey, Maryland, Delaware, Virginia, and West Virginia. The regional boundary extends into the Atlantic Ocean to encompass the shipwreck site of the USS *Monitor*.

The region includes the northern Atlantic coastal plain from Virginia to southern New England, and beyond this the rocky coasts of northern New England and the Canadian Maritimes. The Appalachian Mountains run up the middle of the region from western Virginia to the Gaspé Peninsula on the Gulf of St. Lawrence. The region is bordered on the west by the St. Lawrence River valley and the lower Great Lakes. In western Pennsylvania rivers begin to feed the upper Ohio River valley, which runs into and through the Midwest region.

In the Northeast region rivers, lakes, and coasts often have been the focus of human settlement and activities. Archaeological sites related to these settlements and activities are the subject of many of the essays in this section of *Archaeology in America*. The geographical foci of these essays include portions of the Connecticut, Hudson, Susquehanna, and Shenandoah rivers; Lake Champlain; and Chesapeake Bay. These important natural features influenced ancient and historic period human communications and enterprises throughout the region.

Before 15,000 years ago, two-thirds of this region, the area north of an east-west line from the southern coast of New England to mid-Pennsylvania, was covered by the glaciers of the most recent Ice Age. South of that line, however, the region includes some of the earliest ancient sites in North America (Cactus Hill and Meadowcroft Rockshelter). Once the glaciers had retreated north, the region was quickly explored and new resources exploited, and eventually all parts of the region were settled by the earliest Americans.

The northernmost portion of this region, Newfoundland, contains both ancient sites from thousands of years ago and the earliest European site (the Viking settlement at L'Anse aux Meadows). The earliest permanent settlement by the English (Jamestown) and one of the earliest permanent French settlements in North America (Montreal) are located in the region.

European exploration and settlement of the Northeast region are well represented in the archaeological record. Essays in this section describe the archaeological sites related to the interaction between the original Native American inhabitants and European explorers and colonists, the economic and social development of early European colonies, historic agriculture and industrial developments, urbanization, the American Revolution, and the American Civil War.

The archaeological sites described and interpreted in these essays extend in time from the earliest human settlements, sites in the southern portion of the Northeast that were occupied even during the maximum expanse of the glaciers of the last Pleistocene Ice Age, to those that relate to the American Civil War and developments of the nineteenth century.

We have focused these essays on the most important and interesting archaeological sites and topics in the Northeast region. Readers can learn more about these sites, and others as well, by using the sources of information and references in the last section of each essay. Many of the sites can be visited as part of national, state, or local public parks.

The articles in the Northeast section of *Archaeology in America* include eight general essays on topics that cover ancient or historic time periods. The general essays are followed by forty-seven essays on specific archaeological sites or about archaeological sites in a particular region, such as the Mohawk Valley of New York or Cape Cod or Long Island or the Lake Champlain area. These more specific essays are arranged in roughly chronological order.

ENTRIES FOR THE NORTHEAST REGION

OVERVIEW OF THE ARCHAEOLOGY OF THE NORTHEAST

For the Northeast, the ancient archaeological record is as rich as for anywhere else on the continent, but because of the historically early settlement of the region by European colonists it is also unusually rich in archaeological sites from historic times. Of course, the most ancient peoples of the region can be known only through archaeological science, but because the documentary history of European colonization is so incomplete, archaeology is also indispensable for the study of colonial sites.

PALEOINDIANS

The earliest site in the region is Meadowcroft Rockshelter in western Pennsylvania. The earliest human occupation there probably dates to at least 12,800 BP, perhaps earlier. The Paleoindian period, the hallmark of which was the Clovis projectile point, came later, 11,200 to 10,000 years ago. Shoop, West Athens Hill, Reagan, Bull Brook, Sheep Rock, Shawnee-Minisink, Plenge, and Debert are important Paleoindian sites in the northern part of the region. Cactus Hill, Thunderbird, and Williamson are key sites containing Paleoindian and perhaps earlier evidence in the southern part. The Paleoindians who left remains at these sites appear to have spread rapidly across the continent after the close of the Younger Dryas climatic episode, a period of renewed severe cold that followed a generally warming climate and is considered the last gasp of the Pleistocene.

Paleoindians ranged far and traveled light, using the spear thrower (*atl atl*) as their principal weapon. Although their hallmark spear points seem to brand them as hunters, their subsistence base was already broad. Paleoindians hunted, gathered, and foraged for what they could find in an unfamiliar and still unstable range of environments. They did not erect permanent homes, and the exigencies of frequent relocation and exploration did not often allow for the luxury of caching supplies for later use. These were people who could not always be sure that they would come this way again. Yet just like all other human societies, the thin, mobile population of Paleoindians needed networks of human contact for the sake of security, food sharing, and finding mates. Exquisite Clovis points made from high-grade cherts moved through these networks as gifts, the physical evidence of trading partnerships that bound small bands together over vast distances. For example, red jasper points from eastern Pennsylvania lithic sources ended up on sites in New York's Hudson Valley, and points of high-quality Onondaga chert from around Syracuse ended up on the Shoop site in central Pennsylvania.

ARCHAIC ADAPTATIONS

The end of the Pleistocene was marked by the retreat of glacial ice that had covered the Northeast to as far south as Long Island and had formed a sinuous line running across northern New Jersey and Pennsylvania. Warmer conditions beginning around 10,000 BP brought widespread ecological changes to the ancient landscape south of the ice margin. The Holocene was and continues to be a long period of post-Pleistocene climatic cycling. Deciduous tree species expanded out from refuge areas to form the vast hardwood forests of the Eastern Woodlands. Growing human populations used their ingenuity and natural resources to adapt and readapt to the evolving environments of the region, even as the overall climate cycled between warm and cool conditions every 1,500 years or so.

Post-glacial changes were even more dramatic north of the line marking the southernmost advance of the ice sheet. The recently deglaciated landscape of the Northeast was initially barren and cold. New drainage systems cut through the glacial gravels, and new soils had to evolve atop them as grasses and sedges pioneered the return of plant life. Conifers followed, and eventually broadleaf beech, maple, oak, and other deciduous trees spread northward as well. All of this gradual change provided context for the earliest human inhabitants of the region and the archaeological sites they left behind.

The millennia of the Holocene that lie between the passing of the Paleoindians and rise of cultivation and settled life in the Northeast are known as the Archaic time period. This is customarily divided into four periods: the Early, Middle, Late, and Terminal Archaic. The Boylston Street fish weirs illustrate how Native Americans took advantage of stabilizing river channels and sea levels to construct structures to impound fish. Daily tides brought high water and hungry fish into shallow water, and the weirs allowed fishermen an easy harvest. Elsewhere in the Northeast other sites document the development of new tools, materials, and techniques to improve hunting and food gathering. Some of these even led to early cultivation of native plants, almost unintentional tending that encouraged traits that made plants more abundant or more suitable for human consumption. People also learned how to use birch bark to make containers and ultimately canoes for swift travel. They learned how to extract poisonous tannins from acorns in order to grind them into nutritious flour. They learned how to extract creamy vegetable fat from hickory nuts, how to harvest shellfish, and how to tend sunflowers for their seeds and tubers.

Housing remained simple during the Archaic periods, consisting mainly of small peaked or domed structures built of saplings and covered by bark, mats, or hides. Settlement was impermanent, but seasonal movements settled into regular relocations from one traditional site to the next. Winter in a remote hunting camp was probably followed by spring at a favorite set of rapids along the lower reaches of a river, where migrating fish and waterfowl offered relief from deprivation. Summer probably found interior people at sites next to productive marshes or along streams that provided fish and mussels. People living near the ocean favored coastal sites near shellfish beds and tidal marshes full of plant and animal foods. Fall often found people at sites near stands of ripening plants, seeds, berries, and tubers of many kinds. In all of these cases Archaic people were often able to leave specialized equipment behind in caches rather than carrying cumbersome tools, traps, and weapons everywhere through the course of the year. Seasonal returns to traditional sites meant that things even as large as dugout or birch bark canoes could be hidden and retrieved when it came time to return.

As local populations grew and settled into seasonal routines within traditional territories, the need for long-distance social links waned. The long-distance networks of trade in fine projectile points that had characterized Paleoindian society disappeared during the course of the Early and Middle Archaic periods. This is seen in the growing parochialism of local Archaic cultures and their increasing differentiation over time as they all became more adapted to their local conditions.

MARITIME ARCHAIC
An impressive culture arose during the Late Archaic along the northern New England coast and into the Maritimes and Newfoundland. This phenomenon, often referred to as the Maritime Archaic, involved the invention and development of large dugout canoes and their use for marine hunting and fishing. Wood does not hold up for long in the acidic northern soils, so the archaeological evidence for the canoes exists mainly in the form of large woodworking adzes and gouges made from fine-grained stone. The ancient existence of seagoing dugouts is inferred from the existence of such tools, which would have been used to manufacture them, and from the remains of large ocean fish found in

archaeological deposits from this period. Among the species taken by these marine hunters was swordfish, a dangerous prey that could only have been taken at sea. These people buried their dead in graves that were often lined with bright red powdered hematite and provided with offerings of implements of several kinds. These sometimes included decorated swordfish swords or elegant slate bayonets that seem to be impractical stone copies of the swordfish daggers.

Maritime Archaic cemeteries were often sited on natural gravel knolls or other prominent locations that presaged later artificial burial mounds in the Eastern Woodlands. Their red ocher linings led many people to refer to this group as the "Red Paint People" in the early days of Northeastern archaeology, but there is no reason to believe that they were anything but an ancient American Indian culture. There are many Maritime Archaic sites in Maine and New Brunswick, but one of the most spectacular is the site of Port aux Choix on the much more distant northern tip of Newfoundland. Fine-grained Ramah "chert" (actually a quartzite) from nearby Labrador was traded throughout the Maritime Archaic network. The appearance of this material in graves indicates that long-distance trade in superior raw materials, a practice that had died out after the passing of Paleoindians, was revived in the Late Archaic.

The Northeast Archaic periods drew to a close during the first millennium BC. People began making and using bowls of steatite (soapstone) where that material was available in southern New England and the mid-Atlantic area. The steatite vessels presaged the later introduction of pottery from the south. Both stone and pottery bowls would have been maladaptive in earlier, more mobile Archaic cultures, but they were well adapted to the emerging needs of the Terminal Archaic. Associated with this development was the appearance of a range of new projectile point types, often made from rhyolites and other tough stone rather than chert. New burial practices and increasing reliance on the cultivation of regional semi-domesticated plants also accompanied these shifts. These trends can be studied in many of the more specific entries on archaeological sites in this volume.

EARLY WOODLAND
Burial mound building became widespread in the interior Eastern Woodlands during the first millennium BC, but it did not spread deeply into the Northeast. The millennium or so that this culture lasted is sometimes referred to as the Early Woodland period. The earliest mound-building culture was Adena, which was centered in southern Ohio. Adena mound building spread only into the western margins of the Northeast. However, Adena-style burials complete with exotic grave offerings like those found in Ohio have sometimes turned up in New York, New Jersey, and Vermont. These probably mark distant nodes on the Adena trade network where

local people were able to mimic the practices of the centers in southern Ohio.

MIDDLE WOODLAND

Adena was followed by the Hopewell culture, which emerged around 200 BC. This inaugurated the Middle Woodland period, which persisted until around AD 800. The two cultures overlapped in time in and around southern Ohio for about three centuries. Adena waned and Hopewell culture underwent an expansion that built upon the older Adena trade network and stimulated imitation across much of the Eastern Woodlands east of the Mississippi and south of the Great Lakes. Some mounds were constructed in the Northeast, particularly in Pennsylvania, New York, and Ontario, but the practice never took hold elsewhere in the Northeast. What mounds were built in the Northeast were also simple compared with the elaborate mounds and geometric earthworks constructed by Hopewell architects in southern Ohio. This may be because the Northeast was dominated at this time by southward-expanding speakers of Algonquian languages, who arose from a very different tradition. Cultures in the Northeast continued their less spectacular evolution through the heyday of Adena and Hopewell culture. Hopewell lasted until around AD 400, after which the trade network fell apart.

Pottery became a regular craft through Early and Middle Woodland times in the Northeast, and the variable decorative styles have provided archaeologists with important tools for recognizing temporal and cultural differences across the region. The bow and arrow might have been an important factor in the rise of conflict and the demise of long-distance trading in the later centuries of the Middle Woodland period. The new weapon replaced the spear thrower, which had been the hunting tool of choice for millennia. But the bow and arrow was as effective against other humans as it was against game, and it probably contributed to growing strife across the region. It might have been the adaptive edge that enabled the Algonquians to spread into the Northeast, but its effects eventually went far beyond that expansion.

Local food resources continued to be cultivated, and some plants became near domesticates. But the lifestyle of the cultures of the Northeast continued to emphasize seasonal mobility between traditional habitation sites and exploitation of a wide range of hunted and gathered foods.

LATE WOODLAND

The Late Woodland period began around AD 800, but as with other archaeological periods the timing of the transition varies from place to place in the Northeast. The hallmarks of the period are the arrival of maize as a dependable domesticate and the appearance of the more densely populated permanent villages that horticulture made possible. Maize was a topical domesticate that had been in the Southeast for some time, but

the emergence of strains that could mature in shorter growing seasons and the development of farming techniques that used it as a staple crop propelled the growth and dispersal of new robust villages of farmers.

The spread of farming villages was encouraged by the climatic episode known as the Medieval Maximum, a period of global warming that peaked around AD 1000. While farming and village life sometimes spread to former hunter-gatherers, the aggressive expansion of farming communities into areas previously occupied by thinner populations also occurred. The latter process is the best explanation for the appearance of Iroquoian languages in the Northeast. Communities speaking Northern Iroquoian languages spread across the glacial soils of New York and southern Ontario during the warm episode, displacing the thinner population of Algonquian-speaking hunter-gatherers. Modern genetic evidence confirms that this process involved migration and displacement rather than the adoption of maize and language switching by people already living in the region.

Northern Iroquoian villages eventually spread down the St. Lawrence, splitting Eastern Algonquian cultures from those of the Great Lakes region. Still later, Eastern Algonquians living in southern New England and the mid-Atlantic part of the Northeast adopted farming, along with larger and more permanent villages. North of the ecological limits of native farming the Algonquians of the region remained hunter-gatherers, traveling by birch bark canoe whenever possible and maintaining a way of life much like that of earlier Archaic societies. This was the cultural configuration of the region when European colonists began to arrive.

EUROPEAN COLONIZATION

The first Europeans in the region were Norse settlers who arrived by way of Iceland and Greenland during the episode of global warming around AD 1000. The site of L'Anse aux Meadows in northern Newfoundland marks their brief effort to colonize the region. Later attempts by Europeans to colonize the Northeast in the sixteenth century were similarly unsuccessful in most cases. Though many coastal explorations did not leave detectable traces on land, Cartier's exploration of the St. Lawrence and the English Roanoke colony in Virginia were failed attempts that left archaeological evidence behind. Less famous but still significant were various Basque, English, and French fishing stations on the coast of Newfoundland, which also left important archaeological remains.

European colonization began in earnest early in the seventeenth century. Champlain established a French settlement at Tadoussac in 1600; at Port Royal, Nova Scotia, in 1605; and at Quebec in 1608. The first successful permanent English settlement was Jamestown, Virginia, in 1607. The English unsuccessfully attempted another colony at Popham, Maine, the same year. Hudson's exploration of eastern New York was followed by Dutch colonization in 1614. The Dutch later briefly colonized part of Delaware as well.

An epidemic devastated the Indian communities of southeastern New England in 1617, making it easier for the English founders of Plymouth to establish themselves there in 1620. This initial New England colony was followed by a migration of thousands, and during the decades that followed English settlements sprang up all along the New England coast from Maine to Connecticut. Swedish colonists settled along the lower Delaware River in southeastern Pennsylvania and adjacent Delaware.

Archaeological research at all sites of early European settlement has done much more than illustrate history already known from documentary sources. Written sources tend to be few and incomplete; much of what is known about the colonial history of the Northeast has come from historical archaeology.

LATER NATIVE AMERICANS

American Indian communities that were in direct contact with European colonists tended to fare poorly through the course of the seventeenth and eighteenth centuries. The Indian nations of southern New England were reduced by the Pequot War and the King Philips War as well as by diseases. The Powhatan chiefdom, which dominated coastal Virginia until the coming of the Jamestown colonists, broke up into a scattering of tribal communities after sustained contact with the English.

The first smallpox epidemics appeared in the region in 1634. This disease was common in Europe by this time, where it tended to be a childhood disease that conferred lifelong immunity on those who survived it. All American Indians were susceptible to the smallpox, and adults were particularly likely to die from it. Mortality rates around 60 percent were common in Indian communities. Other European infections such as measles, influenza, and scarlet fever spread epidemically as well, putting further downward pressure on Indian populations. European settlement advanced relentlessly at the expense of less permanent Indian settlements, which were also reeling from the effects of the epidemics. The Eastern Algonquians fared worst, and it is surprising that several of them managed to survive. The more northerly Algonquian nations, such as the Penobscots, Passamaquoddys, Abenakis, and Micmacs, benefited from their greater distance from large European settlements.

The Northern Iroquoians in the interior were also devastated by seventeenth-century epidemics, but they survived by being farther from European settlements and by playing French, Dutch, and English political interests off each other. The Northern Iroquoian nations had fallen into conflict with each other before the arrival of Europeans. This led groups of them to form weak defensive confederacies during the sixteenth century. The best known of these was the League of the Iroquois, a confederation of the Mohawk, Oneida, Onondaga, Cayuga, and Seneca nations. The Mohawks were crippled by the 1634 smallpox epidemic,

but they were also in a position to take advantage of Dutch and French firearms and other resources. They and the other Iroquois nations managed epidemics and wars by absorbing large numbers of refugees from less fortunate Algonquian and Iroquoian nations. The League of the Iroquois was largely responsible for the destruction of the other Iroquoian confederacies (Huron, Neutral, and Erie) by the middle of the century. They also all but destroyed some other independent Iroquoian nations, such as the Susquehannocks. The Iroquois themselves took in many refugees that were products of these wars.

The longhouse villages of the Iroquois continue to be a focus of archaeological study. Such villages were only semipermanent because the Iroquois nations practiced upland swidden cultivation that required the constant opening of new fields as old ones became unproductive. A village was built to last a decade or two, after which it was abandoned and a new one built closer to the more recently cleared active fields. As a result, Iroquois sites tend to be large and substantial villages that are relatively easy to explore because they do not reflect the confusion produced by long occupations. They are also numerous because every community produced several per century. One fully excavated seventeenth-century Mohawk village, Caughnawaga, is open to the public near Fonda, New York. Indian Castle, the upper Mohawk village of the eighteenth century, is a national landmark west of Fort Plain.

LATER HISTORICAL ARCHAEOLOGY

The colonial cities of the Northeast persist as modern metropolitan centers. Cities such as Philadelphia, New York, Albany, Hartford, Providence, and Boston have rich records of historical archaeology that often turn up before and during the course of modern construction. Because of the deep modern history of the Northeast, historical archaeology is a larger enterprise than prehistoric archaeology there. Archaeological details clarify ambiguities in documentary sources and provide modern visitors with meaningful access to their past. This is particularly important for the majority of modern people whose ancestors are little documented, let alone celebrated, in the written record.

Battlefields are also important archaeological sites that help modern visitors understand America's past. These are often difficult sites for archaeologists because they tend to be large areas that were occupied only briefly by Colonial, Revolutionary, or Civil War armies. Moreover, some are located in areas where more recent construction or agriculture has damaged or obscured the archaeological record. Nevertheless, battlefields such as Saratoga, Gettysburg, Antietam, Manassas, Richmond, and Fredericksburg-Spotsylvania, all of them units of the National Park system, provide ample opportunities for visitors to learn about key moments in the nation's history. Many other battlefields and nonmilitary historic sites are owned and maintained for public use by the National Park Service and various state and local agencies. Most of them have archaeological resources that inform the larger stories these sites have to tell.

Further Reading: Grummet, Robert S., *Historic Contact: Indian People and Colonists in Today's Northeastern United States in the* *Sixteenth through Eighteenth Centuries* (Norman: University of Oklahoma Press, 1995); Snow, Dean R., *The Archaeology of New England* (New York: Academic Press, 1980); Snow, Dean R., *The Iroquois* (Cambridge, MA: Blackwell, 1994); Trigger, Bruce G., ed., *Northeast*, Vol. 15 of the *Handbook of North American Indians* (Washington, DC: Smithsonian Institution Press, 1978).

Dean R. Snow

EARLIEST INHABITANTS OF THE NORTHEAST

By 14,000 years ago, glaciers had retreated to just north of the present location of the international boundary between Canada and the United States, except for high-elevation areas. Vegetation in northern New England was primarily spruce-park woodland with hardwoods invading from the south during warm periods before and after the Younger Dryas (an especially cold period from about 12,900 to 12,300 years ago). Oaks and temperate pine species are present in New Jersey, Delaware, and southern Pennsylvania. By the time of the later Paleoindian occupation of the Templeton site in Connecticut (about 11,000 years ago) tree species indicating a warmer climate, including red oak and either juniper or white cedar, were present. Soil developed only after areas were re-vegetated as the glaciers retreated northward. Megafauna species that lived in unglaciated parts of the northeast during the glacial ages included mastodon, giant beaver, and stag elk. At Hiscock, a paleontological site in New York, excavations of pond sediments have documented over sixty different animal species, including such megafauna species from the glacial period. These excavations also have recovered human artifacts, such as five fluted points, culturally modified megafauna remains, and other Paleoindian tools from pond sediments. Humans, mastodons, condors, and other animals all used this site, but the temporal context of its use by humans is not clear. The extent to which use of the glacial-period pond at Hiscock by human groups and megafauna species overlapped is difficult to determine.

The arrival of the first human immigrants to the Northeast, about 12,900 years ago, coincided approximately with the beginning of a particularly cold period near the end of the last glacial age known as the Younger Dryas period. At this time glacial ice still covered much of Canada north of the Gulf of Saint Lawrence, but the extinction of the large Ice Age mammals was nearly complete.

Some of the largest Paleoindian period campsites in the Northeast were discovered in the 1950s. Two of these large sites, Shoop in Pennsylvania and Bull Brook in Massachusetts, have yielded hundreds of fluted points and other chipped stone artifacts from an early hunting culture. The earliest widespread human occupation in the southern portion of the Northeast (Pennsylvania and New York State) is recognizable by the presence of Clovis-style fluted points. The Clovis culture is known to have occupied many parts of North America during the Paleoindian period. This early culture is evidenced in part by a very distinctive artifact, the Clovis point. This is a long, narrow, thin, lance-like point with a distinctive central flute running parallel along its length. After Clovis groups initially occupied a region, their descendants adapted to local conditions and resources. Some elements of their basic technology, artifact types, and probably other aspects of culture as well, were modified to account for new conditions and environmental changes. In the northern Northeast, the modified Clovis culture is sometimes referred to as the Bull Brook culture or phase, using the name of a large Paleoindian period site found near Ipswich in northeastern Massachusetts. Chipped stone projectile points and knives made by this culture are comparatively refined, with longer flutes and a deeper basal concavity. Radiocarbon dates from Northeastern Bull Brook phase sites are generally younger than dates for Clovis sites in the Western United States. Points from the Vail and Debert sites, with their very deep basal concavities, can be considered an extreme version of the Bull Brook fluted point type.

Following the Bull Brook phase is a succession of distinctive fluted and nonfluted hafted spear point or knife types. Radiocarbon dates associated with these points at Northeast sites indicate that they are generally younger than similar point types found to the west, for example, in the Great Lakes region. Cumberland-style points are long, narrow, fluted points with distinctively fishtailed bases. They are more common in the southern reaches of the Northeast. The Neponset site in Massachusetts yielded fluted points similar to a different style known as the Barnes type, along with chipping debris, an associated feature that dates to about 12,000 years ago. Another type, known as the Holcombe point type, is smaller and thinner than other Paleoindian period points found in the Northeast. Excavated in advance of construction of a Wal-Mart store,

1 Meadowcroft
2 Shoop
3 Shawnee-Minisink
4 Corditape
5 Potts
6 Kings Road and West Athens Hill
7 Dutchess Quarry Cave
8 Port Mobil
9 Hiscock
10 Lamb
11 Arc and Emanon Pond
12 Turkey Swamp
13 Plenge
14 Reagan
15 Israel River Complex
16 Whipple
17 Templeton
18 Allenís Meadows
19 Sugarloaf/DEDIC
20 Bull Brook
21 Wapanucket
22 Varney Farm and Hedden
23 Magalloway River complex
        including Vail
24 Michaud and Lamoreau
25 Dam, Nicholas and Esker
26 Munsungun Lake complex
        including Windy City
27 Neville and Manchester complex

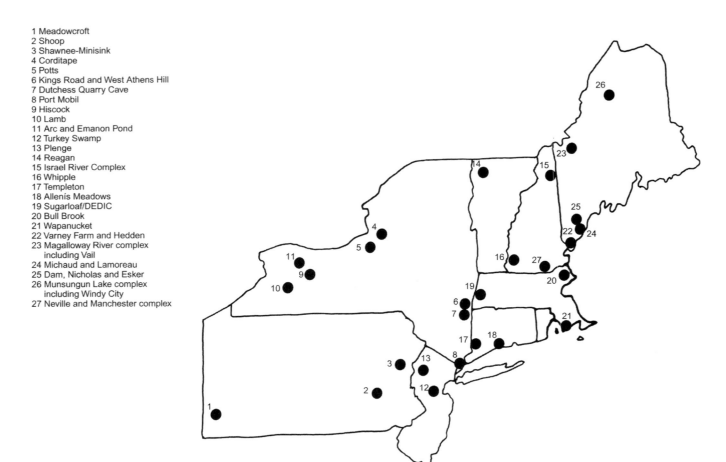

Locations of some of the Paleoindian sites mentioned in this essay.   [Juliet Morrow]

the Nicholas site is a single-component Holcombe site in Maine that yielded several dozen tools made from the distinctive stone type known as Mt. Jasper rhyolite. The Esker site is another late Paleoindian Holcombe site in Maine.

Except for Dutchess Quarry Cave in New York, Paleoindian sites in the Northeast lack remains of megafauna (mastodon, mammoth, horse, etc.) such as those found at Clovis sites in the western United States because the region was probably not inhabited until after the demise of the megafauna, about 12,900 years ago. Fluted-point sites in the Northeast are typically not deeply buried. Over 1,400 fluted points have been identified across the Northeast, most of them found on the surface of the ground after the plowing of agricultural fields. Stratified sequences containing fluted points of different styles are not as common in the Northeast as in other regions. However, at Meadowcroft Rockshelter and at the Shawnee-Minisink site, deep stratified Paleoindian through Woodland period sequences have been excavated. The transition from the Paleoindian to the Early Archaic time period begins earlier in the southern

reaches of the Northeast. The Early Archaic period began about 11,500 years ago. In Delaware, southern Pennsylvania, New Jersey, and southeastern New York at this time, people were making Hardaway-Dalton—style points or knives, which are wider and more triangular than the earlier fluted points and have notches chipped at the lower corners or low on the blade of the point. In Maine people continued to make nonfluted, lanceolate spear points. The Varney Farm site in Maine is a single-component Late Paleoindian site entirely excavated prior to land leveling that produced an assemblage containing parallel-flaked lanceolate points along with end scrapers and side scrapers dating to about this time period.

Until the twentieth century, caribou had been present throughout New England and was one of the prey of the Northeast's earliest inhabitants. Caribou (*Rangifer tarandus*) remains have been identified by Arthur Speiss at the Bull Brook in Massachusetts and Whipple in New Hampshire. Caribou remains and a tooth of an extinct giant beaver (*Castor canadensis*) were identified at Dutchess Quarry

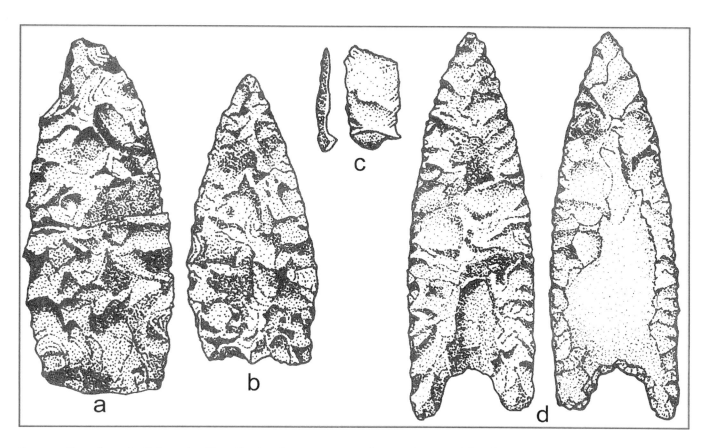

Stone artifacts from the Debert site, Nova Scotia, showing stages in the manufacture of fluted points. Shown are: a roughly shaped bifacial preform intended to be finished as a point (a); a preform with the base shaped and prepared for the removal of a central flute (b); a short flute flake removed from the preform, shown both in section and plan views (c); each side of a fluted point shown with a short central flute removed from the side shown on the left (d). [© National Museums of Canada]

Caves, but the association with Paleoindian artifacts is uncertain. For most of the human occupation of the Northeast region, the animals available were entirely modern species. Humans were active agents in modifying the environment, but the environment also limited what was possible for human societies during the Paleoindian and Early Archaic periods. Some of the detectable changes in technology and settlement appear to be coincident with the transition to a post–Ice Age, essentially modern environment.

The majority of items that survive from the Paleoindian and Archaic periods are tools and ornaments made of stone. Containers, clothing, tool hafts, spear shafts, and other objects certainly were made of organic resources such as wood, leather, and fiber, but these natural materials rarely survive in open-air archaeological sites. In fact, the stone items that hunter-gatherers relied on, and by which modern people know them best, were probably the smallest component of their material culture by volume and probably also by weight. Stone was, however, a much relied upon resource considering the time that was spent procuring it, manufacturing tools from

it, and maintaining these tools. Fluted point–making people had a preference for high-quality, cryptocrystalline (very fine-grained) stone, such as jasper, chert (also called flint), agate, quartzite, silicified sediment, rhyolite, quartz crystal, and other siliceous rocks. The typical Paleoindian chipped-stone tool kit of the Northeast contained a hafted biface (a core of stone flaked on both sides) and flakes tools such as end scrapers, side scrapers, and gravers (sharp-ended tools used for incising or drilling holes). In areas where chert or flint occurred as nodules of at least fist size, production of blades is evident. Shoop is one such site in the Northeast where large blades and the cores from which blades were detached have been recovered. Blades could be modified into other tools such as end scrapers or used unchanged for tasks that required a sharp cutting edge. The large blades and blade cores at the Shoop site and the Clovis point from Shawnee-Minisink in eastern Pennsylvania as well as isolated fluted points from New York State support the presumption of an initial Clovis population in at least the southern portion of the Northeast. A number of chipped-stone Paleoindian tools found at Shoop were made from a source some 250 miles north in New York.

Many of the same tools used during the Paleoindian period continued to be made and used in the Early Archaic period. Innovations in chipped-stone technology during the Early Archaic period, beginning about 9,000 years ago, include the development of heavy-duty woodworking tools (adzes), drills/awls, notching of projectile points and knives, and use of stones (as anvils for cracking nuts and as grinding stones) to process plant foods. The chipped-stone adze was used for felling trees and removing limbs, making dugout canoes from large logs, and shaping logs for dwellings, drying racks, and other structures. Early Archaic period stoneworkers also originated lateral edge serration (sawlike projections) on hafted chipped-stone bifaces as an adaptation for sawing and cutting and alternate beveling (resharpening one edge on opposing faces of a bifacial tool) to conserve blade width. Early Archaic tool kits were comparatively diversified. Rather than one hafted biface that served as both a knife and spear (as was the case for fluted and nonfluted lanceolates during the earlier Paleoindian period), two hafted biface types became the norm—one that served as a knife and the other for use primarily as a spear but also serving as a knife when needed. Notching allows for the use of a wide blade on a relatively narrow haft. This innovation greatly increased the lifespan of the projectile/knife by allowing many more resharpenings than would be possible for a narrow, lanceolate point form like a Bull Brook point. Although hunting terrestrial animals to obtain meat, hides, bones, and sinew was undoubtedly very important during the Paleoindian and Early Archaic periods, fishing and gathering of wild plants also took place. Although fish bones have been found, fishing implements have not.

Taken together, the faunal and archaeobotanical evidence suggests a more generalized, opportunistic foraging strategy during the Paleoindian period in the Northeast. There is evidence of caribou utilization by Paleoindians at Bull Brook, Whipple, and Dutchess Quarry Caves. Fish scales and seeds (acalypha, blackberry, hawthorn plum, buckbean, grape, chenopod, hackberry) were recovered from the archaeological level associated with Clovis-style artifacts at Shawnee-Minisink along with an unidentified berry seed from the Michaud site in Maine. The Hedden site, also in Maine, showed evidence of possible utilization of blackberry, grape, sarsaparilla, and bunchberry. The dearth of Paleoindian period anvil or nutting/grinding stones and other, similar types of stone tools suggests that plant processing did not become a common activity until the Archaic period. But mounting evidence suggests that people in the Paleoindian and certainly the Early Archaic periods probably consumed fleshy fruits such as grapes and berries. Utilization of wild plant seeds, roots, bark, shoots, stalks, berries, and nuts probably increased through trial and error, as Paleoindian groups

became familiar with the natural resources of the Northeast region. Refined archaeological recovery methods like fine wet sieving and flotation applied in future excavations of early sites (deeply buried sites and sites in anaerobic environments that preserve organic remains in particular) will undoubtedly provide additional evidence for a wide variety of plants used for foods, medicines, smoking, beverages, dyes, and raw materials for crafts.

Paleoindian societies are believed to have been based on flexible, kin-based bands that consisted of a dozen to perhaps several dozen individuals. The larger sites in the Northeast such as Vail, Debert, Shoop, and Bull Brook may represent seasonally reoccupied locations where more than one band aggregated, possibly during seasons when food was plentiful, to exchange not only food and other material goods but also ideas and stories, and to find mates. The sparsity of artifacts from excavations of small Paleoindian campsites such as the Avon and Dam sites in Maine, the Whipple site in New Hampshire, and sites of the Israel River Complex in New Hampshire suggest not only that group numbers were small but also that people probably did not live in year-round permanent settlements. The occurrence of chipped-stone tools made of cherts and other fine-grained lithics and deposited at Paleoindian campsites hundreds of miles from their geologic sources is evidence of long-distance migration by individuals or groups to the region and in different parts of the Northeast, and possibly of intergroup trade once groups became more settled in specific regions. Distributions of chipped stone sources (Onondaga, Normanskill, and Munsungun cherts, Mt. Jasper rhyolite, Kineo rhyolite, Cheshire quartzite, etc.) and the artifacts made from them indicate travel distances of hundreds of kilometers to and from stone sources or trade with groups positioned between these sources. Either way, Paleoindian groups appear to have been highly mobile. In the Northeast, Paleoindian sites are recorded in major stream valleys, in rockshelters, and on the margins of former glacial lakes. It is probable that people camped in coastal environments, but submergence, erosion, and wave action make the preservation of potential coastal sites highly unlikely, and access to potential former coastal site locations, now underwater on the coastal shelf, is extremely limited.

Excavated between 1973 and 1978 by a team led by archaeologist James Adovasio, the Meadowcroft site is a rockshelter with the longest sequence of human occupations yet documented in the United States. But the site is most famous for the controversy it sparked as a result of radiocarbon dates for the lowest cultural stratum, IIa. Dates obtained for this stratum range from 19,000 rcybp (radiocarbon years before present) at the bottom to 11,300 ± 700 rcybp at the top. Based on these very early dates and their association with an assemblage of stone tools including a small lanceolate point fragment, other bifacial tools, small blades, and debitage (tool manufacturing debris), Adovasio argues that the lower and middle levels of stratum IIa at Meadowcroft are of pre-Clovis age. From the earliest levels modern fauna occur to the exclusion of Ice Age remains. The absence of evidence for the Pleistocene to Holocene transition at this deeply stratified site is difficult to reconcile with the very old radiocarbon dates. The stratum IIa radiocarbon dates have not replicated elsewhere in the Northeast and so remain controversial (Adovasio et al. 1999). Additional research on the site and in the region could help address the proposition of pre-Clovis antiquity for this important site.

Shawnee-Minisink is located on a terrace of the Delaware River in eastern Pennsylvania. Archaeological deposits at the site extend to a depth of about 10 feet below the surface. Archaeologists from American University excavated about 25 percent of the site over a four-year period in the mid- to late 1970s. Excavations recovered over 55,000 artifacts from an area of about 3,900 square feet. The site contains a stratified sequence of buried living surfaces with the lowest cultural stratum dating to the Paleoindian period. Two high-precision radiocarbon dates recently obtained on carbonized hawthorn plum seeds from a hearth in the Paleoindian level were $10,940 \pm 90$ and $10,900 \pm 40$ rcybp (circa 12,900 to 13,000 years old). The Early Paleoindian (Clovis) archaeological level at the site is completely sealed and separated from a Late Paleoindian component by as much as three feet of sterile river sand. The Clovis artifacts from the site include a complete fluted biface of Onondaga chert (native to upstate New York), bifacial preforms, and dozens of unifacially flaked tools: end and side scrapers, gravers, cores, hammerstones, and many retouched and utilized flakes, as well as an abundance of debitage from making and resharpening chipped-stone tools. Most of the chipped-stone tools were manufactured from a locally available black chert. In the Clovis level, hearths contained carbonized seeds, fish bones, stone tools (mainly black chert end scrapers), and debitage. A large corner-notched projectile represents the diagnostic hafted biface for the Early Archaic component. This was named the Kline type after the discoverer of the Shawnee-Minisink site. Archeologists excavated several examples of this point type along with scrapers, drills, a graver, cores, cobble tools, utilized flakes, and debitage. Compared to the Clovis level, a much wider variety of stone raw materials, particularly jasper, occur in the Early Archaic level.

Located in the mountainous interior of northwestern Maine, the Vail site lies along the eastern shore of a reservoir inundated in 1911 from the damming of the Magalloway River (Gramly 1982). Erosion due to fluctuating reservoir levels exposed a homogeneous tool assemblage interpreted as a single cultural component, with many tools similar to those from the Debert Paleoindian site in Nova Scotia. The site consists of different areas with concentrations of artifacts (inferred to be "kill sites" and an associated habitation) with tool fragments refitted between them, indicating that the activities at the site took place simultaneously. Ongoing research in the vicinity of Vail has resulted in the identification of a concentration of early Paleoindian sites in this region of Maine.

The Templeton site, also known as 6LF21, is 150-square meter single-occupation Paleoindian campsite located 1.5 meters below ground surface on the banks of the Shepaug River in Connecticut. Excavated in 1977, the site was radiocarbon-dated to $10,190 \pm 300$ years. Excavations recovered large quantities of tools used for a wide variety of inferred functions, including hideworking, woodworking, plant processing, hunting, bone working, and tool manufacture. Based on its long flute, recurved haft margins, and flaring ears, the single unfinished fluted point excavated at the site could be related to the Barnes-style point, also found at the Neponset site. Two unifacially flaked miniature fluted points were also recovered from this significant site. Miniature fluted points are common in the Great Lakes area and have been interpreted as toys as well as components of medicine bags.

Further Reading: Adovasio, James, D. Pedler, J. Donahue, and R. Stuckenrath, "No Vestige of a Beginning nor Prospect for an End: Two Decades of Debate on Meadowcroft Rockshelter," in *Ice Age People of North America*, edited by Robson Bonnichsen and Karen Turnmire (Corvallis: Oregon State University Press, 1999), 416–431; Boisvert, Richard A., "Paleoindian Occupation of the White Mountains, New Hampshire," *Geographie Physique et Quarternaire* 53(1) (1999); Byers, Douglas S., "Bull Brook: A Fluted Point Site in Ipswich, Massachusetts," *American Antiquity* 19 (1954): 343–351; Curran, Mary Lou, "New Hampshire Paleo-Indian Research and the Whipple Site," *New Hampshire Archeologist* 33/34 (1998): 29–52; Custer, Jay F., and R. Michael Stewart, "Environment, Analogy, and Early Paleoindian Economies in Northeastern North America," in *Early Paleoindian Economies of Eastern North America*, edited by Kenneth B. Tankersley and Barry L. Isaac, Research in Economic Anthropology, Supplement 5 (Greenwich, CT: JAI Press, 1990), 303–322; Dincauze, Dena F., "Fluted Points in the Eastern Forests," in *From Kostenki to Clovis: Problems in Late Paleolithic Adaptations*, edited by O. Soffer and N. D. Praslov (New York: Plenum Press, 1993), 279–292; Dincauze, Dena F., "The Earliest Americans: The Northeast," *Common Ground* (Spring/Summer 2000): 34–42, www.nps.gov/history/archeology/ Cg/spr_sum_2000/dincauze.htm (accessed November 13, 2007); Ellis, Christopher J., A. C. Goodyear, Dan F. Morse, and K. B. Tankersley, "Archaeology of the Pleistocene-Holocene Transition in Eastern North America, *Quaternary International* 49/50 (1998): 151–166; Gramley, Richard M., "The Vail Site: A Palaeo-Indian Encampment in Maine," *Bulletin of the Buffalo Society of Natural Sciences* 301982 (1982); Haynes, Gary A., *The Early Settlement of North America, the Clovis Era* (Cambridge, UK: Cambridge University Press, 2002); Spiess, Arthur E., Deborah Brush Wilson, and James Bradley, "Paleoindian Occupation in the New England-Maritimes Region: Beyond Cultural Ecology," *Archaeology of Eastern North America* 26 (1998): 201–264.

Juliet E. Morrow

ARCHAIC PERIOD ARCHAEOLOGY
IN THE NORTHEAST

The Northeast region of North America encompasses Virginia, Maryland, Delaware, Pennsylvania, New York, New England, and, in Canada, Quebec and the Maritime Provinces. This region was home to Native American peoples between about 8000 and 1000 BC (about 10,000 to 3,000 years ago); this span of time is referred to by archaeologists as the Archaic era. Archaeologists have divided the era into four periods: the Early Archaic, Middle Archaic, Late Archaic, and Transitional Archaic.

The Archaic era is a long period of human adaptation to post-Pleistocene environmental conditions. In the middle and northernmost Northeast, including parts of Pennsylvania, New York, New England, and the Canadian provinces, the Early Archaic was the time of glacial retreat and expiration. Climatic changes throughout the Archaic era resulted in waning and waxing distributions of various tree species, understory plants, and associated faunal communities. Perhaps the most important result of these climatic shifts was the overall expansion and increased abundance of natural resources, both plants and animals, for human groups to use as food and sources of raw material for manufacturing tools. The Archaic cultural groups were able to move without major obstacles throughout upland settings, onto stabilized terraces, and into coastal marsh edges. The expanded resource opportunities were reflected in the burgeoning array of tool forms created specifically to expedite food procurement from newly accessible environmental niches. The tool forms included both chipped stone and ground stone in addition to a number of specialized bone tools such as fishhooks.

As the Archaic populations in various areas of the middle and upper Northeast expanded their ranges, broader communication networks appear to have been established. By the Late Archaic, cultural traditions originating to the west in the area known as the Laurentian Shield of Canada and to the south in the lower Northeast and Southeast regions were entering New England and eastern Canada. Both the Laurentian and Susquehanna traditions added new tools and tool forms to the region's cultural assemblies and also, presumably, associated processing technologies. Among these tools were steatite (soapstone) bowls, Marcy Creek–style ceramics, broad chipped-stone blades, and the Brewerton-style projectile points. Also present during the Late and Transitional Archaic periods were the so-called Small Stemmed Tradition projectile point types.

Not unexpectedly, most of the Early and Middle Archaic sites located and tested so far have either been surface components, in both upland and lowland settings, or deeply buried occupation zones in lowland riverine settings. Complex upland sites include the Lamoka Lake Site in New York. Deeply buried sites with multiple layers of occupation include the Gould Island, Kent Hally, and Sandts Eddy sites in Pennsylvania; the Neville and Stark sites in New Hampshire; the Wheeler's site near the mouth of the Merrimack River in Massachusetts; and the lower Hudson River shell middens in New York.

The Early Archaic period sites throughout the region are noted for quartz tool assemblages. The reason for this is not clear as the preceding Paleoindians typically produced their projectile points and other chipped-stone tools using high-quality cryptocrystalline (very fine-grained) stone raw materials. The Early Archaic projectile point styles, such as the Kirk, Palmer, and bifurcate-base projectile point styles, were first manufactured in the Southeast and the southern part of the Northeast region. Throughout this area, low-quality quartz, quartzite, and other granular metamorphic rocks were commonly utilized by Early and subsequent Middle Archaic cultural groups.

The subsequent Middle Archaic period is characterized by the widespread adoption of locally developed projectile point and other tool forms and the use of metamorphic and igneous rock to shape tools either by chipping or smoothing them into various shapes. These stone types did not replace quartz; all three types were used, and there was a decided preference for argillaceous shale, chert, jasper, and rhyolite. The Middle Archaic period is marked by the presence of stemmed and triangular projectile point styles. The named projectile points vary in distribution subregionally and include such types as Neville, Stark, and Merrimack point styles in the upper Northeast. The Middle Archaic stone tool assemblages also included *atl atl* (a spear-throwing stick) weights, full-grooved axes, gouges, and ulus (a half-moon-shaped tool probably used for scraping).

The repeated use of particular locations appears to have been common through the Archaic. At the Neville site in New Hampshire and the Sandts Eddy site in Pennsylvania, Paleoindian period, Archaic era, and Woodland era components are all present. At the Gould Island and Jacobs sites in Pennsylvania, Late and Transitional Archaic occupation zones underlay Woodland occupation levels. Similarly, at the Greenwich Cove site on Narragansett Bay in Rhode Island, Wheeler's site in Massachusetts, and the Turner Farm site in coastal Maine, Late and Transitional Archaic levels are vertically and horizontally separable from Woodland occupation areas. The repetitive use of particular locations indicates that similar natural resource exploitation strategies were at play through much of the Archaic and Woodland eras. This does not mean, however, that new approaches were not utilized.

Such new strategies were reflected in the expansion of projectile point, scraper, and container forms during the Late Archaic and Transitional Archaic. At one point in the terminal Late Archaic, small Brewerton series and Small Stemmed Tradition projectile points were used simultaneously with the broad-blade Susquehanna Tradition points. The latter projectile point tradition included such point types as Snook Kill and Susquehanna. Perhaps the most compelling change in the tool kit, however, was the introduction of hard-wall container technology. By the end of the Late Archaic, the steatite (soapstone) bowl had been introduced into New England from the mid-Atlantic region in conjunction with the Susquehanna Broad point.

The use of hard-wall containers is an important step in food preparation technology. While soft-wall hide and basket containers can be used successfully for both boiling and steaming, they are inappropriate for long-term stewing or braising, where direct heat is needed. Based on the number of recovered examples in New England, steatite bowl use was not widespread; nor subsequently, in the terminal Transitional Archaic, was the use of Marcy Creek steatite-tempered ceramics. Their mere presence, however, facilitated the swift acceptance of ceramic technology, although in New England the number of Native American ceramic wares and types never rivaled those developed in the mid-Atlantic and middle Northeast states.

For the most part, the Transitional Archaic, the last phase of this general time period, is delimited based on the occurrence of projectile points like the Orient Fishtail style, which have been found both with and without steatite containers, steatite-tempered ceramics, or the first sand- and grit-tempered ceramics. The latter included such ceramic types as Vinette I in the middle Northeast and Thom's Creek in the mid-Atlantic. The occurrence of these pottery types and others truly heralds the arrival of the Woodland era.

Further Reading: Barber, Russell J., *The Wheeler Site: A Specialized Shellfish Processing Station on the Merrimack River*, Peabody Museum Monograph No. 7 (Cambridge, MA: Harvard University Press, 1982); Bernstein, David J., *Prehistoric Subsistence on the Southern New England Coast: The Record from Narragansett Bay* (New York: Academic Press, 1993); Bourque, Bruce J., *Diversity and Complexity in Prehistoric Maritime Societies: A Gulf of Maine Perspective* (New York: Plenum Press, 1995); Raber, Paul A., Patricia E. Miller, and Sarah M. Neusius, eds., *The Archaic Period in Pennsylvania: Hunter-Gatherers of the Early and Middle Holocene Period*, Recent Research in Pennsylvania Archaeology No. 1 (Harrisburg: Pennsylvania Historical and Museum Commission, 1998); Ritchie, William A., *The Archaeology of New York State*, rev. ed. (Harrison, NY: Harbor Hill Books, 1980); Snow, Dean R., *The Archaeology of New England* (New York: Academic Press, 1980).

Carol S. Weed

ANCIENT VILLAGE LIFE IN THE NORTHEAST

Village life in the Northeast did not arise until the Archaic cultures that characterized human adaptation through most of the Holocene evolved into the more sedentary societies that dominated the southern part of the region in the most recent millennia. Sedentary village life was the consequence of the development of plant cultivation as the primary means of subsistence, and the population growth made possible by farming.

By 1000 BC people of the Adena culture were building burial mounds in southern Ohio. They persisted for over a millennium, overlapping in time with Hopewell culture, which had arisen in roughly the same area by 200 BC. Hopewell culture spread more widely in the Eastern Woodlands, but by AD 400 both Adena and Hopewell cultures had waned. Both cultures were economically based on cultivated food crops developed in the region combined with traditional hunting, fishing, and gathering, and neither culture featured settlements that were sizable or permanent. Their geographic foci were their mounds and earthwork complexes, not their residences. All of this changed with the arrival of maize after AD 500.

Maize is a tropical domesticate that originated in Mexico many centuries earlier. It spread northward into the Eastern Woodlands slowly, an addition to crops of more local origin at first, and perhaps reserved for elite consumption when and where it was initially adopted. By AD 1000 the potential of maize as a staple crop was being realized; it became much more generally and widely used. New, larger communities that depended heavily upon it began to appear in the southern parts of the Eastern Woodlands. No longer just an elite food, maize came to dominate diets in these communities, its productivity and storage capacity turning it into the amazing staple it now is worldwide.

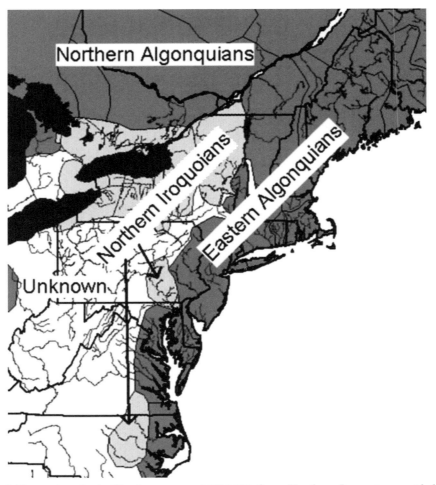

Northern Iroquoians and Algonquians in the Northeast around AD 1600. Some Northern Iroquoians resided in North Carolina and Virginia. The Susquehannocks had moved recently to southern Pennsylvania.   [Dean Snow]

The Northeast remained remote from these evolutionary changes in native horticulture until around AD 1000. At about that time, climatic warming across the Northern Hemisphere combined with the emergence of new maize strains to make horticulture a viable option northward from its range up till then. The new strains of flint maize that could mature in as few as 120 frost-free days allowed the domesticate to spread as far north as the Great Lakes, southern Ontario, and southern New England. The northward spread of maize horticulture did not unfold rapidly, for it entailed profound societal changes. Archaeologists still debate the specifics, searching for ways to separate cases in which maize spread from one society to another from those cases where societies with maize physically expanded or relocated into regions previously the exclusive domains of hunter-gatherers.

A map of American Indian cultures circa AD 1500 reveals two great cultural blocs in the Northeast. In the sixteenth century Northern Iroquoians occupied the Appalachian uplands

of interior Pennsylvania and New York, a domain that extended to southeastern Ontario and the St. Lawrence lowlands of Quebec. The rest of the Northeast was the domain of cultures and societies speaking Algonquian languages. The Algonquians were village-dwelling horticulturalists in the southern part of their range, but their relatives in northern New England, northern New York, and from Lake Huron northward could not, or did not, adopt horticulture and remained hunter-gatherers. All of the Northern Iroquoians were horticulturalists, and they lived in permanent village communities that were large and dense compared to those of their Algonquian neighbors.

During the second half of the twentieth century most archaeologists working in the Northeast assumed that both the Algonquian and the Iroquoian cultures of the region evolved in place from earlier cultures. The in situ model of archaeological interpretation emerged partly as a reaction to earlier speculative migration scenarios, partly to uncouple linguistics and

Detail of a Northern Iroquoian longhouse from "Plan de Fort Frontenac ou Cataracouy," dated to about 1720. [Courtesy of Edward E. Ayer Collection, The Newberry Library, Chicago]

archaeology, and partly to simplify interpretation. But the model has been found unsustainable in the face of archaeological evidence for discontinuity in the centuries prior to AD 1000, and DNA evidence that shows the Iroquoians and Algonquians to be distinct biologically as well as linguistically. The evidence now suggests that the Northern Iroquoians have been in the region for just over a millennium, and that they did not emerge in situ among Algonquian neighbors.

The language families of the long sequence of Archaic cultures that preceded the Iroquoians and Algonquians in the Northeast remain unknown and probably unknowable. Linguists generally doubt the validity of language reconstructions based on analysis of recorded descendant languages if the reconstructions reach back more than two millennia. Linkages between related languages become tenuous and linguistic dating becomes unreliable at greater time depths. Fortunately there is little doubt about the validity of the Algonquian family of languages. Internal linguistic evidence suggests that speakers of Proto-Algonquian originated around the lower Great Lakes and spread southward to modern Pennsylvania and westward to the prairie during the first millennium AD. The adaptive advantage that made this expansion possible was probably the bow and arrow, which had been introduced from the north.

South of the early Algonquians were the Iroquoians of the Appalachians. All of them were maize horticulturalists by

AD 1000. The Southern Iroquoians left only one descendant group, the historic Cherokees. The Northern Iroquoians responded to the opportunities presented by warming climate and access to new strains of maize by expanding into areas they had not previously occupied. Some of them left the Appalachians for new locations in the Carolina Piedmont, where they remained until European colonization prompted them to move north and take refuge with the League of the Iroquois in the eighteenth century. The best-known descendant group of these Carolina Iroquoians are the modern Tuscaroras.

Other Northern Iroquoians gradually shifted northward in an adaptive expansion into present-day New York and southern Ontario. Their adaptive advantage was that they were already maize horticulturalists. Their adaptation allowed them to live in relatively large and dense permanent villages with which the thinner and more mobile population of Algonquian hunter-gatherers could not compete effectively.

The Iroquoian villagers practiced a shifting form of cultivation usually referred to as swidden farming. In the absence of large domesticated animals to provide manure and traction, Iroquoian farming involved the clearing of upland forest by the girdling of large trees and the burning of underbrush. Skeletal trees provided firewood but little shade, so the plots remained sunny and fertile until nutrients were depleted and weeds and pests took over. Over the years older fields were

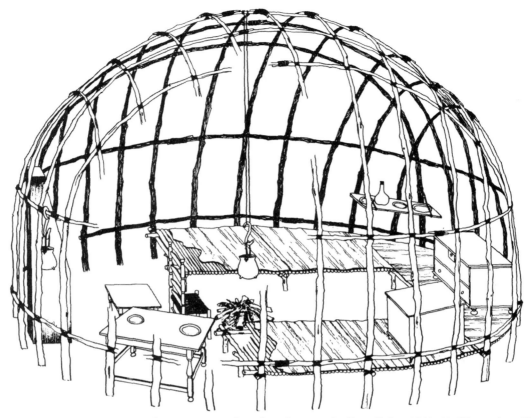

Western Niantic wigwam in cutaway view without coverings, based on drawings by Ezra Stiles, 1760–62. [Reproduced by permission of the Society for American Archeology from *American Antiquity*, Vol. 40, No. 4, p. 439, 1975.]

abandoned and new ones were opened, ever farther from the small compact villages.

Pressures prompting village relocation built up as soil fertility declined and firewood was exhausted. Eventually a village would relocate, often moving only a few kilometers to be closer to active fields and new sources of firewood. If the move was prompted by warfare or some other extraordinary circumstances, the villagers might move a hundred kilometers or more to gain safety and a new start. This pattern of movement, which produced clusters of village sites around the region, was observed by Champlain and reported in his journals as still operating in the seventeenth century.

IROQUOIS CULTURE

The full suite of known traits for the sixteenth-century Northern Iroquoians took centuries to develop. Beans, another tropical crop that spread only slowly northward from Mexico, were not added to the list of staples until after AD 1200. Tropical squash also spread north to augment or replace the native squash already domesticated in the Eastern Woodlands. Together squash, maize, and beans eventually formed the famous "three sisters," the nutritionally complementary staples of later Northeastern farmers. Similarly, the large, dense longhouse

towns of the sixteenth-century Northern Iroquoians emerged through a long evolutionary development. Longhouses were neither as large nor as numerous in the early Northern Iroquoian communities. Finally, collared pottery, small triangular arrow points, and other diagnostic artifacts of the later Northern Iroquoians also emerged slowly over centuries of technological evolution. Nevertheless, the archaeological sites and artifacts of the ancestral Northern Iroquoians of a millennium ago distinguish them from their contemporaneous Algonquian neighbors.

EASTERN ALGONQUIAN DEVELOPMENT

Algonquian populations were either displaced or absorbed by Northern Iroquoians who expanded northeastward through the interior of the Northeast during the height of the climatic episode known as the Medieval Maximum. The Eastern Algonquians from New England south were cut off from easy communication with other Algonquian populations west or north of the Northern Iroquoians. Some of the Eastern Algonquians expanded southward through the rich maritime lowlands of the Atlantic seaboard, establishing themselves as far south as coastal North Carolina. Maize farming was passed on to many of them from the Iroquoians, augmenting

Engraving by De Bry, based on a watercolor painting of a Powhatan village by John White, 1585–86.   [Library of Congress]

the abundant natural resources from southern New England south. However, with so many alternative resources, farming did not become an exclusive activity among the Eastern Algonquians, and it appears even to have been shunned by some of those who lived in particularly rich coastal locations. Where farming was most productively combined with hunting and gathering, population densities rose to a point that

prompted the formation of chiefdoms, as in the case of the sixteenth-century Powhatans of coastal Virginia.

NORTHERN IROQUOIAN VILLAGE LIFE

The permanent compact longhouse villages of the Northern Iroquoians would have been impossible without farming and matrilineal social organization. Staple crops that could be stored for future consumption made such communities sustainable; matrilineal organization made them viable and politically tolerable. Their multifamily longhouses were organized internally by senior women, their sisters, and their daughters. A house consisted of a line of compartments, each with a central fireplace with a pair of nuclear family berths facing each other across the central aisle. Compartments were added to the longhouse as the extended family grew, each marriage requiring half a compartment for the new couple and, eventually, their children.

Iroquois women were careful to space the births of their children to avoid having more than one nursing infant at a time. Family size was maintained at around five, including the parents. Thus, ten was the average number of people living in each longhouse compartment.

Each longhouse was laid out three arm spans (fathoms, the term and measure used at the time) wide, and each compartment had about the same length. That gave each nuclear family a space of about one by three fathoms, about 100 square feet (10 square meters). Occupying perhaps a third of this space was an enclosed sleeping berth, its lower platform about knee high. Elsewhere were small areas for food preparation tool manufacture, sewing, craft production, and so on. There were no inside bathrooms, and messy tasks such as hide tanning were done outdoors. Maize and other crops were sometimes stored in grass-lined storage pits in the earthen floor, but maize was also stored in bark barrels located in storage rooms at the ends of the longhouses.

The village was the domain of Iroquoian women. Senior women kept the peace in the densely packed villages. Fraternal groups of adult men who might otherwise have formed dangerous factions were broken up by the practice of matrilocal residence. The women of every longhouse belonged to a specific named clan, of which there were three to eight no matter how many longhouses were in the village. Young women were not allowed to marry men from their own clans. Young men moved away from fathers and brothers when they married, taking up residence with their new wives in longhouses filled with in-laws. A young man might find a clan brother or two in his new home, but all of the women and unmarried young men in the residence would belong to his wife's clan. The practice allowed villages to grow to as many as 2,000 inhabitants before the number of households got too large to be managed by the informal network of senior matrons and the men they appointed to run village affairs.

The forest beyond the bounds of the village and its agricultural fields was the domain of Iroquoian men. There the fraternal groups that were scattered in the village could come together as bands of hunters, warriors, or diplomats, depending on the circumstances. All Northern Iroquoian people belonged to one of about eight clans, to which membership was inherited from one's mother. Clan affiliation signaled real kinship between the related fathers, sons, brothers, and cousins who made up a band of men abroad in the forest. It also gave them all fictive kinship with men having the same

clan identities in other nations of the Eastern Woodlands, including Algonquians and other non-Iroquoians. This facilitated temporary lodging and trading partnerships, an important lubricant for trade over the network of trails that had been worn into the forest floor for centuries. Back in the home villages clan affiliations served to regulate marriage and politics, but trading, not those more recent supplementary functions, appears to explain the origin of clans.

THE LEAGUE OF THE IROQUOIS

Population growth and regional competition led to increasing conflict between Northern Iroquoian groups as well as between them and non-Iroquoian neighbors by the late fifteenth century. Conflict was facilitated by the Iroquoian belief that almost any death was the result of a deliberate act by an enemy, even if that act was nothing more than presumed sorcery. Further, they believed that wrongful deaths had to be avenged. The result was a growing spiral of conflict as one death led to another. Village matrons usually kept this from rupturing relations within villages, and neighboring villages typically also avoided conflict. But revenge-motivated violence against more distant villages grew out of control. Villages became larger as neighboring communities came together for mutual protection, and the larger villages often relocated to protected hilltops. The spiraling warfare eventually led to the formation of larger confederacies, nonaggression pacts between sets of village clusters.

Confederacies known as the Erie, Huron, Neutral, and Iroquois formed and survived into the seventeenth century. The best known of these, the League of the Iroquois, still survives in attenuated form. This confederacy is known to its members as the Hodenosaunee, the people of the longhouse. It was composed of the Seneca, Cayuga, Onondaga, Oneida, and Mohawk nations, which were distributed across what is now upstate New York. Known early on as the Five Nations, they became the Six Nations in the eighteenth century when the Tuscarora nation moved north to join their Northern Iroquoian relatives. We know the most about the League of the Iroquois because warfare and disease ended all the other Northern Iroquoian confederacies in the seventeenth century, before they could be described by historians and ethnologists.

The League of the Iroquois was structured on clans and traditional funerary ritual. Because warfare was so often prompted by revenge, condolence ritual was invoked frequently as a means to deflect blame away from allies. Men appointed from leading families by clan matrons conducted the business of the League, traveling on diplomatic missions to other nations in the League and beyond. There were fifty League Chiefs or "Sachems," but they were not evenly distributed between the Five Nations. Equal representation was not necessary, for all decisions had to be unanimous. In the absence of unanimity individual nations often acted alone, a characteristic that betrays the weakness of this form of confederacy. However, even when nations acted alone they avoided conflict with other League members. The League came apart in the course of the American Revolution, when the Oneidas sided with the revolutionaries while most members of the other nations sided with the British.

EASTERN ALGONQUIAN VILLAGE LIFE

The Eastern Algonquians of northern New England and the Maritime Provinces of Canada lived beyond the line of 150 frost-free days, too far north to risk dependence upon domesticated crops. They remained hunters and gatherers into the period of first contact with European colonists. They lived for part of each year in villages that were typically situated at the heads of tidal estuaries. These locations allowed them to harvest both the spring and fall runs of migratory fish. From them they could move in small family groups upstream into traditional hunting areas, particularly during the winter. At other times they could move in similarly small groups to coastal locations, where they could exploit marine food resources.

The forests of northern New England and the Maritimes contain birch trees that provide bark suitable for the light swift canoes that were developed by the early Algonquians. They traveled long distances using birch bark canoes. Whereas Iroquoians used long overland trails, pedestrian travel in northern New England was mainly over short portages between navigable streams.

Ironically, although the villages of northern New England were often seasonally vacant, they persisted in the same locations for very long periods because, unlike Iroquoian villages, they did not have to relocate periodically for horticultural reasons. Eastern Algonquian populations from Massachusetts southward were denser, for there horticulture was possible. Farming families dispersed to scattered summer residences near active fields, and at other times they dispersed elsewhere to hunt and fish. Unfortunately, preferred central locations at the heads of estuaries were the same sites favored by later European settlers, and few archaeological traces remain of Eastern Algonquian towns.

Giovanni da Verrazzano's exploration of the southern New England coastline in 1524 revealed many Eastern Algonquian settlements and many fields with associated summer houses. Traces of both have been found by archaeologists, including a field of corn hills preserved by a migrating sand dune.

Population densities were higher farther south along the Atlantic coast. They were dense enough in the Potomac area of Virginia to produce a large number of villages, many of which are known to archaeologists. Contemporary records are very limited for these people compared with the interior Iroquoians, but it is known that a combination of diseases and dislocations drastically altered village life early in the contact period. Villages were numerous enough to allow the emergence of chiefdoms in this part of Eastern Algonquian territory. The best known of these is the Powhatan chiefdom, named after its leader. Polities such as this one were fragile; chiefdoms cycled in and out of existence as men like Powhatan recruited political tributaries and built chiefdoms that would not last long after their deaths. Occasionally a chiefdom arose that was sustained by a succession of chieftains, but none survived the pervasive disruptions of European colonization.

John White's paintings (1585–86) of village life in native Virginia (present-day North Carolina) are our best documentation of the Eastern Algonquians of that part of the Northeast. Harriot's engravings from the same period provide additional detail, especially with regard to the impact of disease, but many engravings were not made from life and err by including details drawn from other parts of the Americas.

Further Reading: Fiedel, Stuart J., "Middle Woodland Algonquian Expansion: A Refined Model," *North American Archaeologist* 11 (1990): 209–230; Hulton, Paul, *America 1585: The Complete Drawings of John White* (Chapel Hill: University of North Carolina Press, 1984); Kerber, Jordan E., *Archaeology of the Iroquois: Selected Readings and Research Sources* (Syracuse, NY: Syracuse University Press, 2007); Potter, Stephen R., *Commoners, Tribute, and Chiefs: The Development of Algonquian Culture in the Potomac Valley* (Charlottesville: University Press of Virginia, 1993); Snow, Dean R., *The Archaeology of New England* (New York: Academic Press, 1980); Snow, Dean R., *The Iroquois* (Cambridge, MA: Blackwell, 1994); Snow, Dean R., "The Architecture of Iroquois Longhouses," *Northeast Anthropology* 53 (1997): 61–84; Tooker, Elisabeth, "Clans and Moieties in North America," *Current Anthropology* 12 (1971): 357–376; Trigger, Bruce G., ed., *Northeast*, Vol. 15 of the *Handbook of North American Indians* (Washington, DC: Smithsonian Institution Press, 1978).

Dean R. Snow

EARLY EUROPEAN SETTLEMENTS IN THE NORTHEAST

The early colonization of the northeastern United States and Canada is largely characterized by initial interactions between aboriginal groups and European explorers. These explorers, arriving mainly between 1500 and 1700, were largely motivated by European attempts to acquire goods for such mercantile corporations as the Dutch West Indian Company and to acquire land for the British and French crowns. Aboriginal groups occupied all of the Northeast at the time of European contact.

Confederacies and tribes included the Five Nations Iroquois, who occupied the Mohawk, Susquehanna, and Seneca river valleys of New York; the Mahicans, who occupied the Hudson valley; the Pequots, who occupied the Connecticut River valley; the Narragansett, Wampanoag, and Massachusetts, who occupied what is now eastern Massachusetts and Rhode Island; a number of smaller tribes occupying what is now northern New England; and the Micmac, who occupied northern New Brunswick, Prince Edward Island, and Nova Scotia.

From the last quarter of the sixteenth century to the middle of the seventeenth century, European efforts to establish colonies in North America were fueled by economic motivations and a need to acquire goods from aboriginal groups. A primary goal of these interactions was to acquire goods for shipment to and sale at European markets. Europeans formed trade alliances with aboriginal groups for highly prized furs and animal pelts. Among the most important commodities were beaver pelts, which were sent back to Europe for use in felt hats and miscellaneous clothing items. In exchange, European explorers brought copper kettles, glass beads, and blankets to trade with Native groups. These items quickly replaced traditional stone, bone, and ceramic objects. Copper projectile points replaced chert and quartz points, copper kettles replaced clay vessels, and glass trade beads replaced shell and wampum beads.

Early European settlements in North American started as small colonies, fishing stations, or trading posts located along coastal areas and major waterways, as evidenced by the early Viking settlement at L'Anse aux Meadows in Newfoundland and the seasonal European fish and whale processing stations in the Gulf of St. Lawrence. Small populations of fishermen, trappers, traders, and mercantile businessmen occupied many of these settlements. During the second half of the seventeenth century, larger settlements and religious missions were constructed further inland to accommodate a growing population who were fleeing religious prosecution in Europe. The Dutch, French, and British were the earliest groups to establish settlements in the Northeast.

Dutch traders occupied New York from approximately 1609 to 1664. General Peter Minuit, who was working for the Dutch West India Company, established the earliest settlements. Minuit, who purchased the island of Manhattan for 60 guilders from Algonquian groups, continued to build settlements along the Hudson River. Included among these settlements were those at New York City (New Amsterdam), Kingston (Wiltwyck), and Albany (Fort Orange). In New York City and Albany the remnants of the original Dutch settlement are mainly below the surface archaeological sites (Bradley 2007; Cantwell and Wall 2001). In Kingston many of the original structures of the fort remain standing today. Remnants of the wooden stockade that surrounded the settlement were discovered during an archaeological excavation in 1971. Additional Dutch settlements on Governor's Island, just off of the tip of Manhattan, remain as evidence of the early Dutch occupation of New York.

The French occupied much of the St. Lawrence valley and Quebec, establishing one of the earliest settlements at Tadoussac in 1599. One of the earliest explorers in the region was Jacques Cartier. Cartier, a French navigator and explorer, interacted with Native groups at the St. Lawrence Iroquois village of Hochelaga, near the current city of Montreal, Quebec, in 1535. The village of Hochelaga was described as an impressive village with more than a thousand occupants. It is not known how long the village was in existence, but it had disappeared by the time Samuel de Champlain visited the St. Lawrence valley in the early seventeenth century.

The French made inroads into the Dutch market in beaver pelts and furs by setting up trade networks in upstate New York in the early seventeenth century. By cutting into the Dutch fur trade, the French were able to form alliances with Iroquois groups and redirect the flow of resources through central and eastern New York (Jameson 1909; Snow et al. 1996). This prompted the Dutch to renegotiate with aboriginal groups over the procurement of furs. In addition, the Dutch looked to capitalize on other potential markets in southern New England.

A primary goal of the French was to convert the local aboriginal populations to Catholicism. The French mission of Saint-Marie-Among-the Hurons was one of the earliest missions established. Located near the city of Midland, Ontario, Saint-Marie-Among-the Hurons was established in 1639 by Jesuit missionaries as a base from which they could convert the local Huron population. The mission contained several buildings, including a cookhouse, a blacksmith shop, and residences. Between 1646 and 1649, the Huron-Iroquois War broke out, killing much of the local aboriginal population. During fighting, eight Jesuit missionaries were killed and are now collectively known as the Canadian Martyrs. In June 1649 the Jesuit priests chose to burn the mission rather than risk having it attacked by local Iroquois groups. Archaeological excavations at the mission site during the late nineteenth century and the first half of the twentieth century located many of the buildings associated with the mission as well as the graves of two of the Jesuit priests buried there (Kidd 1949).

Prior to European contact, the Pequots occupied much of southeastern Connecticut and were reported to have had as many as 8,000 members living within an area measuring several hundred square miles. The Dutch were among the first Europeans to encounter Native groups. One of the first explorers to interact with the Pequots was Adrian Block, who explored the Connecticut River valley. Block and other Dutch traders were anxious to procure beaver pelts from the Pequots for use in the manufacture of felt garments in Europe.

European and aboriginal contacts were not always positive, with European diseases such as smallpox, diphtheria, and influenza often infecting native populations. The Pequots of the Connecticut valley experienced two severe epidemics that wiped out more than half of the tribe. The first of these occurred between 1616 and 1619, and the second occurred between 1633 and 1634. The later epidemic affected much of the Northeast, including groups in the central and eastern Mohawk valley, St. Lawrence valley, and the Canadian Maritimes. These epidemics were especially deadly to younger and older members, making it difficult for many groups to retain their culture. Survivors were often displaced from traditional lands and forced to live with neighboring tribal groups.

Soon, however, increased tensions over the supply of furs, land ownership, and the European incursion into the Connecticut valley by the Massachusetts Bay Colony culminated in the Pequot War. The war, which occurred between 1636 and 1638, had a devastating effect on the Pequots, killing many tribal members. As a result of losing the war, the Pequots were displaced from their homeland and given land at Noank. The Pequots acquired the land in 1651, only to have it taken away in 1666.

In eastern Massachusetts, the Plymouth (1620) and Massachusetts Bay colonies were among the first British settlements established in North America. The latter, established in 1630 in what is now Boston, spread quickly, with additional settlements at Salem, Gloucester, and Charlestown soon constructed. The Massachusetts Bay Colony, unlike some of the other European colonies, was not focused on the accumulation of beaver pelts and the procurement of other trade items. Puritan settlers fleeing religious prosecution in England largely occupied the settlements. Over the next forty years, the Massachusetts Bay Colony would play a significant role in transforming Massachusetts into an important commonwealth and North American colony.

L'ANSE AUX MEADOWS

L'Anse aux Meadows, located at the tip of the island of Newfoundland, Canada, is the earliest authenticated European settlement in North America. Established around AD 1000 by the Vikings, it is not known who or in what context the site was occupied. Many believe that the site is Leif Erikson's "Vinland" while others believe the site may have been occupied as a trading post and supply station for explorers along the St. Lawrence River.

Archaeological excavations of the site in 1960 revealed evidence of at least eight buildings, including a smithy shop and lumberyard that supported shipbuilding. Several houses were also uncovered, including a large structure measuring approximately 15 meters wide. The wooden structure contained several rooms suggesting different living areas within the building. The site was named a World Heritage site by the United Nations Educational, Scientific, and Cultural Organization (UNESCO) and is currently open to tourists.

TADOUSSAC

The French post at Tadoussac (Quebec, Canada) was one of the earliest European occupations in North America. Jacques Cartier first described Tadoussac, and the bay surrounding it, when he explored the St. Lawrence River and Saguenay Fjord in 1535. Established in 1599 by Francis Grave and Pierre Chauvin, Tadoussac was France's first trading post in the New World. Although the site survived through the early seventeenth century as a trading post, attempts to establish a larger settlement there were not successful. During the site's first winter of occupation, many of the settlers died due to the harsh living conditions. Samuel de Champlain visited the trading post in the early 1600s. Champlain is credited with documenting the village's location and geographic setting on historical maps.

Occupation of Tadoussac continued into the late seventeenth century, with the site serving as an important mission. A log chapel built on the site in 1747 by Jesuit missionaries is known as the "Indians Chapel." During the late nineteenth and early twentieth centuries, the local community remained an important lumber and dairy location. Today, the village surrounding Tadoussac is a major tourist destination in southern Quebec.

FORT NASSAU

Fort Nassau (Castleton Island, New York) was established along the east side the Hudson River, south of Albany, in 1615. The fort, which was situated to capitalize on trade with Native Americans who traveled along the river, was occupied for only a few years until 1618, when flooding of the Hudson River forced abandonment of the island. A few years later, the Dutch West India Company would build Fort Orange upriver from Fort Nassau and establish it as the first permanent Dutch settlement in North America.

Historic records indicate that the fort was probably a square building measuring approximately 50 feet square. The fort was probably not occupied by a large group of people but rather by a few settlers whose main purpose was to initiate trade with Native Americans. Recent excavations on Castleton Island by the New York State Museum's Cultural Resource Survey Program have produced evidence of early European ceramic vessel fragments, handmade brick fragments, wrought-iron nails, and other building materials intermixed with incised ceramic vessel shards and chipped-stone tools manufactured by Native groups (Sopko 2007). A standing structure believed to date to the Dutch occupation of the island is also present.

FORT ORANGE

Fort Orange, located along the Hudson River in the present-day city of Albany, New York, was built in 1624–25 by members of the Dutch West India Company; the site replaced Fort Nassau, which was destroyed in 1618 by flooding. The fort, established as an early trading post, provided aboriginal groups with ready access to trade goods. Trade with Mohawk and Mahican groups was important, and the fort was situated along an overland pass uniting the Mohawk and Hudson rivers (Snow et al. 1996). The overland pass allowed Native groups to avoid the treacherous drop in the river at Cohoes Falls. For several years, the occupants of Fort Orange maintained a vast trade network that supplied large quantities of furs for shipment to Europe. During the early 1630s the quantity of supplied furs began to drop off. Suspecting that the primary cause of the decline was the growing French presence in the St. Lawrence valley, the Dutch West India Company decided to send an envoy.

Harman Meyndertsz van den Bogaert, a barber-surgeon stationed at Fort Orange, was dispatched to the Mohawk valley in 1634 to negotiate with the Mohawks regarding the declining number of furs being supplied to the Dutch West India Company. During his journey through the valley, van den Bogaert kept a journal of the villages that he visited and the cultural behaviors of the region's Native groups. His descriptions document the various Mohawk "castles" located along the Mohawk River and document the health conditions, healing rituals, and village life of the Mohawk Iroquois (Snow et al. 1996).

Today, archaeological evidence of Fort Orange remains below the modern city (Bradley 2007). Archaeological excavations conducted by Dr. Paul Huey (Huey 1988) in the 1970s revealed portions of the original Dutch settlement and the buildings contained within the fortification's walls. Archaeological evidence combined with seventeenth-century historical maps indicate that Fort Orange was constructed near the Hudson River possibly to facilitate the loading and unloading of ships. Artifacts recovered from the site include Dutch tiles, ceramics, and architectural remains. The site was likely surrounded by a wooden stockade and other fortification.

POINTE-À-CALLIÈRE

The site of Pointe-à-Callière in Montréal, Quebec, initially was a fourteenth-century Native American hunting and fishing station. Several hundred years later, French explorers looking to set up settlements along the St. Lawrence River once again occupied the site. The earliest European occupation of the site occurred in 1642 with the French settlement of Fort Ville-Marie. The site was occupied throughout the seventeenth century, serving as the home of the governor of Montréal in 1688.

Archaeological evidence of this settlement is found today in the subsurface remains of the first Catholic cemetery in the city. The cemetery was first used in 1643 and continued to be used until approximately 1654. Graves of both Europeans and Native Americans can be found throughout the cemetery. Scientific examination and analysis of the human remains provide information about health and disease in this early community. Evidence of later settlements dating to the British occupation of the city is also present, including an eighteenth-century street, wooden palisade, and guardhouse. The archaeological remains from Pointe-à-Callière are interpreted and preserved as part of Montréal's history museum, a tourist attraction in the old city part of downtown Montréal.

Further Reading: Bradley, James W., *Before Albany: An Archaeology of Native-Dutch Relations in the Capital Region 1600–1664* (Albany, NY: New York State Museum, 2007); Cantwell, Anne-Marie, and Diana diZerega Wall, *Unearthing Gotham: The Archaeology of New York City* (New Haven, CT: Yale University Press, 2001); Huey, Paul R., "Aspects of Continuity and Change in Dutch Material Culture at Fort Orange, 1624–1664," Ph.D. diss. (University of Pennsylvania, College Park, 1988); Jameson, J. F., ed., *Narratives of New Netherland, 1609–1664* (New York: Barnes and Noble. 1909); Kidd, Kenneth E., *The Excavation of Sainte-Marie I* (Toronto: University of Toronto Press, 1949); Mealing, S. R., *The Jesuit Relations and Allied Documents* (Toronto: McClelland and Steward, 1963); Snow, Dean R., Charles T. Gehring, and William A. Starna, *In Mohawk Country: Early Narratives about a Native People* (Syracuse, NY: Syracuse University Press, 1996); Sopko, Joseph, *Cultural Resources Site Examination Report of Castleton Landing, Rensselaer County, New York*, report prepared for the New York State Department of Transportation and the Federal Highway Administration (Albany: New York State Museum, 2007).

Christina B. Rieth

MILITARY SITE ARCHAEOLOGY IN THE NORTHEAST

Military site archaeology has become an important branch of the larger field of historical archaeology. Battlefields, forts, and camps have been the subjects of increasing scrutiny, and important discoveries are being made as new technologies and methods assist archaeologists in their search for these sites. Military site archaeologists combine the historical and documentary record with the archaeological data and produce a holistic account of battle and military activity. Applying this approach to the American Revolution and Civil War can be beneficial to the interpretation and understanding of these hotly debated periods of American history.

Additionally, the imperatives of preservation have stimulated much work in this long-neglected field of American archaeology. Agencies such as the National Park Service need this work to preserve their most significant military sites. Finally, new applications of scientifically based methodologies have been critical in understanding battlefields and military sites and in properly locating them on the landscape.

USA 1777 button found at Valley Forge.   [BRAVO, Dan Sivilich, 2007]

The work of National Park Service archaeologist Douglas Scott in the early 1980s at the site of the Battle of Little Big Horn has been seminal for other archaeologists who have adopted his controlled metal detecting methodology in properly mapping and explaining battlefields. The establishment in 2000 of an international biennial conference of battlefield archaeologists at Glasgow University called Fields of Conflict has also significantly contributed to the growing popularity of battlefield and military site archaeology.

REVOLUTIONARY WAR ARCHAEOLOGICAL SITES

Among the earliest examples of American military site archaeology in the Northeast were the "digging expeditions" of William F. Calver and Reginald Pelham Bolton, two "amateur" archaeologists who associated themselves with the New York Historical Society in 1917. These two men interpreted the artifacts they excavated at British Revolutionary War camps on the Hudson River as "historical documents" and began to rigorously classify and identify these objects. Using British and American regimental buttons, for example, Calver and Bolton were able to flesh out the scanty historical documents and provide valuable data on the organization and location of these forces during the Revolutionary War campaigns on the Hudson highlands. Both of these pioneers

demonstrated that archaeology could be used to show that history was a process and that artifacts led to the real peopling of events.

Revolutionary War forts and camps are prolific in the Northeast and are archaeologically important because, unlike the case for battlefields, the passage of time allows occupational trash to accumulate. The New York sites of Fort Stanwix and Fort Ticonderoga have been the focus of archaeological investigations. Fort Stanwix was completely rebuilt from the archaeological traces uncovered, and its excavation produced a substantial amount of military artifacts as well as important evidence for the life of the soldier from the French and Indian War until the end of the Revolutionary War. Now a National Park Service site, it occupies much of the center of Rome, New York. Its excavated material has shed new light on garrison life during the Revolutionary War. Renamed Fort Schuyler, the fort played an important role in defeating the British in the late summer of 1777 and upsetting the British strategy, which ultimately failed at Saratoga. The American victory at Saratoga, New York, the most critical Revolutionary War battle fought in the Northeast, seriously damaged British hopes to win the conflict. David Starbuck and Dean Snow have conducted tests on the Saratoga battlefield.

One of the best examples of the role military site archaeology can play in properly interpreting a site is the work conducted by

Earthworks near Fort Morton, 1865. [Library of Congress]

David Starbuck at Mount Independence, Vermont. This was a massive, 13,000-man encampment occupying a 300-acre site on the Vermont side of Lake Champlain, directly across from Fort Ticonderoga. In the early fall of 1776 a large garrison won a bloodless victory against the British invading column from Canada. Realizing they were outnumbered and facing the heavily armed fortresses (Fort Ticonderoga and Mount Independence), the British retreated before the advent of winter. During the winter a few thousand colonial soldiers endured severe weather but resolutely held their ground. Mount Independence is the largest military fortification in the Northeast built specifically for the needs of the American Revolution. It is an excellently preserved site and contains collapsed chimneys and hearths from numerous soldiers' huts, blockhouses, shops, and earthen entrenchments. Much information survives to attest to the nature of the soldier's dietary and medical practices. One broken wine bottle, subsequently mended, has "James Hill 1777" written on it.

An important analogue to Mount Independence, Vermont, is the legendary site of Valley Forge, Pennsylvania. Wrapped in national myth, this famous winter encampment site of Washington's Revolutionary army has been examined archaeologically for over five decades. First, it was metal-detected by amateurs in the 1950s and 1960s. Buttons, musket balls, and soldier's accoutrements were unearthed and the non-metal objects (such as animal bone and ceramics) were largely ignored. In the early 1960s the site was excavated as part of one of the first classes in historical archaeology at the University of Pennsylvania taught by John Cotter, a pioneer in the field. Digging at the site of the Pennsylvania Brigade, Cotter found several huts and their associated artifacts. Later Cotter excavated at the Outer Line sites associated with the Virginia brigades and discovered more of the same. The National Park Service acquired the state park in the late 1970s and a survey was undertaken by the University of Pennsylvania. This survey, which was largely geophysical and noninvasive, used the 1777–78 winter camp site as a laboratory to test new developments in geophysical prospecting and remote sensing. This formed the basis for the excavations at the Outer Line and at Conway's Brigade in the 1980s. Several hut sites were excavated, but these endeavors concentrated on nondestructive methodologies. Spurred by a grant from Aurora Foods (maker of Log Cabin Syrup), the National Park Service opened up a larger section of the Revolutionary War camp, again at the site of the Pennsylvania Brigade. A virtual section was plotted from the rear of the brigade to the front using Von Steuben's manual as a guide. This resulted in the uncovering of large sections of the original eighteenth-century surface with associated work areas, hut sites, roads, kitchens, fireplaces, and shaft features. The latter were especially rich, and much contemporary data emerged from this three-year effort (1999–2002). During the spring of 2007 a new archaeological project was undertaken between Temple University's Department of Anthropology and the Washington Memorial Chapel. Using BRAVO (the Battlefield Restoration and Archaeological Volunteer Organization, under the leadership of Dan Sivilich), a controlled metal-detecting survey found clusters of architectural and related artifacts that have produced on a GIS map two striking linear patterns strongly suggesting the presence of a brigade line. The hope is that future excavations will assist in determining exactly who was here in 1777–78.

The Battle of Cooch's Bridge in Delaware, the opening of the 1777–78 Philadelphia Campaign started by General Howe's invading British army, has been studied and a new interpretation developed by Wade Catts. Catts used both the amateur- and professionally recovered archaeological material to re-assess the location of the opposing forces. BRAVO's important work at Monmouth battlefield, the site of the closing battle of the campaign in New Jersey, was begun in 1987 at the Monmouth Battlefield State Park and is ongoing. With the cooperation of Garry Wheeler Stone, the archaeological data has produced an extremely accurate image of the battle that took place on June 28, 1778. The work has identified battle lines, troop movements, locations of landscape features such as orchards, and artillery emplacements. The BRAVO survey even determined the types of weapons used.

Finally, the last battle of the Revolutionary War, the Siege of Yorktown in the late summer and fall of 1781, was examined archaeologically by Norm Barka and the College of William and Mary survey in the mid-1970s. The siege lines, intact mortar bombs, and fortification locations were mapped, and many artifacts and other archaeological materials pertaining to the siege were unearthed and eventually exhibited in the National Park Service Visitors Center of Yorktown. A corresponding underwater survey of the sunken British vessels of 1781 was undertaken in the late 1970s.

CIVIL WAR ARCHAEOLOGICAL SITES

Without a doubt the American Civil War is the most important historical event in the nineteenth century and perhaps since the founding of the Republic in 1776. No other topic has produced so much popular and scholarly material or generated so much discussion. Edmund Wilson praised the participants of the Civil War as articulate and literate. But the archaeological record has until just recently made little impact on the interpretive record. However, since the late 1970s the number of archaeological studies of Civil War sites in the Northeast has greatly increased. The features and artifacts in the ground have been carefully analyzed and the large number and great variety of historical documents and images have been carefully sorted and examined. Military sites that have been studied have refined interpretations regarding ethnicity, social and economic status, race, and gender. Yet, as archaeologist Steven D. Smith says, "The most important way archaeology can contribute information germane to the study of the Civil War is by excavating sites in order to establish basic, but very necessary, archaeological facts." Battlefields have been explored utilizing new techniques, such as controlled metal detecting and geophysical survey. Again, encampments have been very useful in providing significant data for the researcher.

The National Park Service has sought during the past three decades to survey its major battlefield parks. For example, Gettysburg National Military Park had a comprehensive archaeological survey in the 1990s, but this study needs to be updated. Each of the three main days of the July 1–3, 1863, battle has been the subject of an archaeological study. In the late 1970s surveys were done at the McPherson Barn site, the locale of the July 1 action. The house site nearby was tested by park archaeologist Jill Halchin in the 1990s and its foundations uncovered. The Rose Farm and Kitchen were analyzed in the 1980s by the National Park Service and much material dating to the July 2 battle was discovered. Finally, the William Bliss House, destroyed by command of the Union Army just before the July 3 Confederate attack known as Picket's Charge, was left untouched until it too was tested by the National Park Service. The cellar fill was impressive, proving that Bliss had little time to remove his prize possessions and also demonstrating the validity of a claim for remuneration he filed with the government after the battle (he never received any compensation). Some of the items mentioned in his detailed inventory of lost possessions were actually discovered in the small tests conducted in the cellar. The site certainly has the potential to dramatically demonstrate the extent of civilian losses during the Civil War if it is fully excavated in the future.

Nearby Antietam National Battlefield in Maryland also has been investigated archaeologically. Most dramatic is the discovery of the remains of an individual member of the Irish Brigade studied and reported on through the joint efforts of Stephen R. Potter and Doug Owsley. Here an archaeologist and forensic specialist teamed up to present an unrivaled portrait of a soldier who would otherwise have remained anonymous. Other studies at Antietam have used spent bullets to map troop movements and artillery fragments to indicate locations of major attacks and battle episodes.

The three edited works principally done by Clarence Geier are indispensable for the study of Northeast Civil War military site archaeology (see Further Reading). Geier has researched Civil War archaeological sites in the Fredericksburg area. He completed the excavation and discovery of the Spindle House (Battle of Spotsylvania Court House, Virginia), excavated the sites at the sunken road and Marie's Heights at Fredericksburg, Virginia, and has done work surveying the Battle of the Wilderness, Virginia. Much of this is landscape archaeology at its best, combining the rich cartographic and documentary sources with archaeological testing and examination. At Chancellorsville, Virginia, Dan Crozier of Temple University excavated the tavern site in the 1970s, unearthing parts of the foundation and associated artifacts, and also uncovered parts of Catharine Furnace, Virginia, a site associated with the Wilderness and Chancellorsville battles. This latter site has been reexamined in the last several years, with additional information on its ancillary structures and support features documented. Using Bruce Bevan's rich mesh of geophysical techniques followed by archaeological verification, the site of the Widow Tapp Cabin, so important to the Battle of the Wilderness was discovered and interpreted by the National Park Service. Near this site occurred the famous "General Lee to the Rear" episode of the battle.

Further south, the Petersburg Campaign of 1864–65 has been the focus of numerous archaeological tests and surveys by the National Park Service at Petersburg National Battlefield during the 1970s and 1980s. The site of the Crater attack of July 30, 1864, was first explored by archaeologist Edward Rutsch during the mid-1970s. Rutsch exposed the tunnels that Pennsylvania troops from coal mining communities dug to plant the explosive mine. Later the National Park Service tested the Confederate Picket Line, which was impacted by the explosion, and then the Union Picket Line, located in front of the Union earthworks. In 1978–80 geophysics again combined with archaeology to locate the foundation of the Taylor House, which was vital in establishing the Union earthworks across from the Crater site. The foundation was robbed by the Union troops for the construction of Fort Morton, situated to the south of the house. Here the Union attack on the Crater originated; once more a geophysical survey plotted the "anomalies," and the archaeologists tested and verified the location of the fort's principal elements, which are now visibly marked for all to see. Most of the Petersburg earthworks, now largely invisible, can be mapped and tested using this combination of geophysics and conventional archaeology.

The nearby Hare House site had been discovered earlier by archaeologists John Cotter and Brooke Blades, who demonstrated this site's rich potential for further research. Like the Bliss House at Gettysburg, it was destroyed during the Petersburg siege, with the intact furnishings collapsing into the cellar.

The City Point, Virginia, headquarters complex for the Petersburg campaign was acquired from the Eppes family (who had owned it since the seventeenth century) in late 1979. At that time Ulysses S. Grant's original headquarters cabin was still standing in Fairmount Park, Philadelphia, where it had been since August 1865, when it was moved there as a gift by the Commanding General of the Union Army. The cabin was given to the National Park Service, dismantled, and moved to City Point. After the discovery of the cabin's original foundation, it was re-erected on its original

site, completing a removal and return journey experienced by few such ephemeral structures. Archaeology also has revealed some of the buildings used by the army to supply the great investing force before Petersburg in 1864–85. A live, 100-pound Parrot rifle unexploded shell (a very large artillery shell) was found on the City Point bluff and immediately deactivated and preserved.

Cemeteries have also been the subject of scrutiny by Civil War archaeologists. An excellent example is the small African American cemetery found in Delaware City, Delaware, which had been long forgotten, hidden by the encroaching marsh. After a survey conducted by the author in 1984–90, the military headstones of five previously unknown free black soldiers of the United States Colored Troops were discovered. Their war records, "unearthed" in the National Archive, told a hitherto neglected story of sacrifice and heroism.

Today military site archaeology of the American Civil War stands at a threshold. With luck, further research will lead to new discoveries of how these scenes of violent action (battlefields) and long stretches of loneliness and boredom (camps) contribute to the nation's past and present.

Further Reading: Calver, William L., and Reginald P. Bolton, *History Written with Pick and Shovel* (New York: New York Historical Society, 1950); Geier, Clarence R., Jr., and Susan E. Winter, eds., *Look to the Earth: Historical Archaeology and the American Civil War* (Knoxville: University of Tennessee Press, 1994); Geier, Clarence R., Jr., and Stephen R. Potter, eds., *Archaeological Perspectives on the American Civil War* (Knoxville: University of Tennessee Press, 2000); Geier, Clarence R., Jr., David Gerald Orr, and Matthew B. Reeves, eds., *Huts and History: The Historical Archaeology of Military Encampment during the American Civil War* (Gainesville: University Press of Florida, 2006); Hanson, Lee, and Dick Ping Hsu, *Casemates and Cannonballs: Archaeological Investigations at Fort Stanwix National Monument* (Washington, DC: U.S. Department of the Interior, 1975); Parrington, Michael, Helen Schenck, and Jacqueline Thibaut, "The Material World of the Revolutionary War Soldier at Valley Forge," in *The Scope of Historical Archaeology: Essays in Honor of John L. Cotter* edited by David G. Orr and Daniel G. Crozier (Philadelphia: Temple University Laboratory of Anthropology, 1984); Starbuck, David, *The Great Warpath: British Military Sites from Albany to Crown Point* (Hanover, NH: University Press of New England, 1999).

David G. Orr

HISTORIC ARCHAEOLOGY OF NORTHEASTERN CITIES

The archaeological research that has focused on the growth and development of Northeastern cities reflects their positions as the centers of economic and cultural life in the region. Unlike the predominantly rural South, the Northeast, particularly New York and New England, was home to several cities that served

as the commercial hubs of a seaborne trade—including the slave trade—that fueled the growth of a European-centered world economy between the sixteenth and eighteenth centuries. With the coming of industry to the region in the late eighteenth and early nineteenth centuries, the cities of the Northeast experienced yet another period of transformation. In seaport communities such as Boston, Massachusetts, and Providence, Rhode Island, factories were constructed to support new manufacturing enterprises. Others communities, such as Lowell and Lawrence, Massachusetts, and Manchester, New Hampshire, were new cities that had grown from cow pastures into densely populated cities within a generation.

Archaeologists working in the cities of the Northeast have focused on community-wide processes such as the creation of urban space facilitated through a combination of draining low-lying areas along the coast followed by large-scale filling operations. They have approached this dynamic spatial activity by looking at the changes in human life resulting from these spatial modifications that accompanied the changing economies of the region's urban centers. Archaeologists have also focused their efforts on studying the populations of these various communities and the social diversity driven by both economics—the emergence of class differences, for example—and ethnic, religious, and racial divides. The mosaic-like characteristics of the social geography of these cities has been explored by archaeologists through the lens of landscape studies and studies of material culture.

Like most regions of North America, much of the archaeology carried out in the Northeast has been driven by modern development. This is especially true of large-scale projects in cities such as New York, Boston, and Providence, Rhode Island. The Central Artery/Tunnel Project in Boston, for example—more popularly known as the "Big Dig," the largest public works project in American history—uncovered the archaeological remains of sites ranging from a 3,000-year-old Native American habitation on Boston's pre-colonial shoreline, to an array of sites dating to the colonial and industrial periods (Cheek 1998). The African Burial Ground project in New York awakened the interests of a descendant community (La Roche and Blakey 1997). Their involvement in the project created a blueprint for urban projects throughout the United States. The Foley Square project focused on a neighborhood of lower Manhattan that nineteenth-century writers described as Hell's Kitchen. In this instance archaeological data produced a portrait of domestic life that contrasted dramatically with that depicted in the literature of the day (Yamin 1998, 2001). The Providence Place Mall project in Providence, Rhode Island, led to the excavation and analysis of the state's largest nineteenth-century prison (Garman 2005).

The fact that most of the sites investigated in urban centers of the Northeast have come as the result of cultural resource management (CRM) projects has done little to dampen their scholarly appeal. In fact, projects such as the Big Dig, the Providence Place Mall, and Foley Square have resulted in a scale of excavation not feasible outside the context of development-driven investigations. The scope of these projects has, for example, allowed archaeologists the opportunity to examine the production of urban space on a scale that would not have been possible in more traditional, research contexts. The financial and political power needed to support development of this magnitude has been a mixed blessing, however. On the one hand, the resources made available to conduct archaeology in cities such as New York and Boston have produced rich, deeply contextualized investigations. Sadly, these same studies have accompanied projects that resulted in the destruction of a fragile archaeological legacy of immense significance.

Fortunately the archaeologists working in the cities of the Northeast have taken full advantage of the opportunities accorded them to explore a variety of interpretive questions concerning the initial colonization and subsequent urbanization in the region. Finding common threads among these many studies is perhaps best accomplished by focusing on the analytical constructs of materiality and spatiality. The analytical framework of materiality involves studying human relationships through the investigation of material remains, such as artifacts of different styles or functions, as well as other material remains from archaeological sites. A focus on spatiality involves the study of human relationships by investigating spatial differences or similarities in the distribution of artifacts, buildings, or other detectable aspects of human culture (for more detailed discussion of these concepts, see Mrozowski 2006, 5–16; Preucel and Meskall 2004, 11–16; Soja 2000, 6–12). Materiality encompasses all facets of material life, and this includes the related concept of embodiment and the notion of the human body as an aspect of material culture (Meskall and Joyce 2003; Sofaer 2006). Conceiving of the body as part of the broader study of materiality also has allowed urban archaeologists working in the Northeast to connect data concerning health and sanitation to broader issues of class conflict and social inequality in cities such as New York (Cantwell and Wall 2001; Geismar 1993), Newport, Rhode Island, and Lowell, Massachusetts (Mrozowski 1991, 2006), and Providence, Rhode Island (Garman 2005).

Linking the body to materiality is just one example of the manner in which the notion of material culture has been expanded as an analytical construct. In a more traditional sense materiality has been used as a lens for examining the growth and maintenance of group identity (such as belonging to a particular ethnic group or a particular class or type of working group) over both time and space. Investigation into how material remains or certain kinds of artifacts, for example, relate to different group identities has taken several forms. It has been examined through studies of landscape, foodways (how foods are procured, prepared, and consumed), leisure time, and consumption at the site, household, and neighborhood levels. Other factors, such as ethnicity, race, class, and gender, have also been examined in terms of their influence on the formation of identity. Using the dual lens of materiality and spatiality it is possible to traverse the landscape of archaeological research carried out in the cities of the Northeast through the region's initial colonization and its subsequent urbanization.

INITIAL COLONIZATION

Virtually all of the major cities in the Northeast were settled in areas that had formerly been sites of Native American habitation. So it should come as little surprise that large CRM projects carried out in these communities have found ample evidence of this earlier occupation (Cantwell and Wall 2001; Cheek 1998). Archaeologists working in these communities have also unearthed substantial evidence of early filling operations. Although much of the evidence for such activities is linked to the accelerated expansion that took place during the nineteenth century, the draining of wetlands and their filling took place in most coastal communities even during the seventeenth century (Cantwell and Wall 2001; Kelso 1998; Mrozowski 1987). In some instances the impact of these changes on biotic communities has also been examined. Gerald Kelso (1998) has examined these processes in Boston, for example, as have Rothschild and Balkwill (1993) in New York. In both communities, early clearing and filling had a rather pronounced effect on the nature of plant and animal communities. Over time as habitats were altered, or lost altogether, wild plant and animal communities changed. Rothschild (1989; 2003, 86–89) found that faunal species diversity was affected by the steady urbanization of New York and other factors linked to early colonization of the Northeast. In other contexts indigenous landscapes were rapidly replaced by those dominated by introduced plant species (Kelso 1998; Mrozowski 1987; Rothschild 2003, 132–134).

The colonization of the Northeast also resulted in the Creolization (cultural mixing) of foodways practices. This too took several forms. In New Amsterdam, Native American foodways practices were adopted by Dutch colonists (Cantwell and Wall 2001, 177–180; Janowitz 1993, 20–21; Rothschild 2003, 158–160). In other parts of the Northeast foodways traditions came together to form hybrid cultural forms (Cheek 1999). As the populations of the region's urban centers began growing, they created a ready market for goods produced in their surrounding hinterlands. These maturing markets marked one facet of the region's growing urbanization, a process that also resulted in the depletion of local animal and plant communities as noted earlier (Rothschild and Balkwill 1993). Evidence for the growth of these markets has been uncovered in urban contexts throughout the region, including Salem (Bowen 1990), and Boston (Cheek 1999; Landon 1996), Massachusetts, Newport, Rhode Island (Bowen 1990; Mrozowski 2006), and New York (Cantwell and Wall 2001).

URBANIZATION

By the early eighteenth century the cities of the Northeast had become densely populated urban communities that were the commercial centers of the region. The need for a diversified workforce resulted in urban populations that reflected the transformative power of colonization to bring people from across the globe into new relationships. This was especially true in cities such as Boston, New York, and Newport, where Europeans, Native Americans, and enslaved Africans found themselves intertwined in social relations of various kinds. The region's long history of diversity continues into the present, as the politics surrounding the African Burial Ground Project attest (Cantwell and Wall 2001; La Roche and Blakey 1997). The descendents of those buried during the eighteenth and nineteenth centuries came together to insist on having a say regarding the ultimate disposition of their ancestors' remains, and as a result the project featured major public involvement. The resiliency of community is also evident in other investigations of African American sites in New York (Cantwell and Wall 2001) and Boston (Landon 2007).

Archaeological studies that span the eighteenth and nineteenth centuries focused overwhelmingly on the intersection of variables such as race, class, and gender in the construction of individual and community identity. These same studies also looked at the role of consumerism in the expression of identity. In Boston, studies linked to the Big Dig were able to examine the growth of class distinctions in the city during the late seventeenth and early eighteenth centuries as well as the way social inequality was expressed biologically in different patterns of sanitation and disease (Bain 1998; Kelso 1998). Similar studies of sanitation and disease have been carried out in New York (Bonesara and Raymer 2001; Cantwell and Wall 2001; Geismar 1993), Newport, Rhode Island (Mrozowski 2006; Reinhard et al. 1986), and Lowell, Massachusetts (Mrozowski et al. 1996; Mrozowski 2006).

If there is a single topic that has occupied the interests of urban archaeologists working in the Northeast, it is class and the way it intersects with other variables such as race, gender, and ethnicity. In a series of studies Diana Wall examined the manner in which gender, ethnicity, and class converged to find expression in household-level identity (Wall 1991, 1993, 2000). Several studies have called into question the popular characterizations of class in nineteenth-century social commentary and the materiality of the groups described. The work of Rebecca Yamin and her colleagues on the Foley Square project have provided numerous examples of the middle-class sensibilities evident in the assemblages from the notorious Hell's Kitchen area of New York (Yamin 1998, 2001). Similar results were found in Lowell, Massachusetts, where the amount of yard space available for leisure time or gardening was apportioned expressly along class lines. These types of rigid class divisions were also reflected in the living conditions of the various groups of workers. Management-level households were provided with the latest in water and waste management technology while the city's mill operatives continued to use long-outlawed privies (Mrozowski 2006, 97–112). These obvious class differences were not as visible when material culture from housing associated with four different classes of workers from Lowell were compared. In this instance the class differences were much less obvious, marking the apparent blurring of lines between the working-class and middle-class residents of the city (Mrozowski 2006).

The power of factory owners in cities such as Lowell to affect the lives of their workers was embedded in a deeper cultural dialogue concerning class in the nineteenth century. The rhetoric surrounding social issues such as temperance was heavily laden with class connotations, yet archaeology in the cities of the Northeast have unearthed evidence of an obvious disconnect between imagery and reality. This is certainly the case in New York (Fitts 1999; Reckner and Brighton 1999; Yamin 1998, 2001) as well as in Lowell (Mrozowski 2006). Societal commentary also played an important role in notions of crime and punishment, and this in turn influenced the construction and operation of prisons. A prime example of this comes from the work that James Garman (2005) carried out in association with the excavation of the Rhode Island state prison in Providence. Here the roles of religion and ethnicity played out in the amount of space provided for inmates and their overall well-being in a population in which the Catholic Irish of Rhode Island were disproportionately represented. In this important study Garman is able to link the practices of confinement and punishment to social rhetoric of the day concerning deviance. The experience of Irish prisoners in Rhode Island is just one of many such stories that mark the rich and sometimes sordid histories of those who lived in the cities of the Northeast.

Further Reading: Bain, Alison, "A Seventeenth Century Beetle Fauna from Colonial Boston," *Historical Archaeology* 32(3) (1998): 32–48; Bonasera, Michael, and Leslie C. Raymer, "Good for What Ails You: Medicine Use at Five Points," *Historical Archaeology* 35(1) (2001): 49–64; Bowen, Joanne, "Faunal Remains and Urban Household Subsistence," in *The Art and Mystery of Historical Archaeology*, edited by Anne Yentsch and Mary C. Beaudry (Boca Raton, FL: CRC Press, 1990), 267–281; Cantwell, Anne-Marie, and Diana diZerega Wall, *Unearthing Gotham: The Archaeology of New York City* (New Haven, CT: Yale University Press, 2001); Cheek, Charles, ed., "Perspectives on the Archaeology of Colonial Boston: The Archaeology of the Central Artery/Tunnel Project, Boston, Massachusetts," *Historical Archaeology* 32(3) 1998; Cheek, Charles, "An Evaluation of Regional Differences in Colonial English Foodways," in *Old and New Worlds*, edited by Geoff Egan and Ronald L. Michael (Oxford: Oxbow, 1999), 349–357; Fitts, Robert K., "The Archaeology of Middle-Class Domesticity and Gentility in Victorian Brooklyn," *Historical Archaeology* 33(1) (1999): 39–62; Garman, James, *Detention Castles of Stone and Steel: Landscape, Labor and the Urban Penitentiary* (Knoxville: University of Tennessee Press, 2005); Geismar, Joan H., "Where Is Night Soil? Thoughts on an Urban Privy," *Historical Archaeology* 27(2) (1993): 57–70; Janowitz, Meta F., "Indian Corn and Dutch Pots: Seventeenth Century Foodways in New Amsterdam/New York," *Historical Archaeology* 27(2) (1993): 6–24; Kelso, Gerald K., "Pollen Analysis of the Feature 4 Privy at the Cross Street Back Lot Site, Boston, Massachusetts," *Historical Archaeology* 32(3) (1998): 49–62; Kelso, Gerald K., and Mary C. Beaudry, "Pollen Analysis and Urban Land Use: The Environs of Scottow's Dock in 17th, 18th and Early 19th Century Boston," *Historical Archaeology* 29(1) (1990): 61–81; Landon, David B., "Feeding Colonial Boston: A Zooarchaeological Study," *Historical Archaeology* 30 (1996); Landon, David B, ed., *Investigating the Heart of a Community: Archaeological Excavations at the African*

Meeting House, Boston, Massachusetts, Andrew Fiske Memorial Center for Archaeological Research Cultural Resource Management Study No. 22 (Boston: University of Massachusetts, 2007); La Roche, Cheryl J., and Michael L. Blakey, "Seizing Intellectual Power: The Dialogue at the New York African Burial Ground," *Historical Archaeology* 31(3) (1997): 84–106; Meskall, Lynn M., and Rosemary Joyce, *Embodied Lives: Figuring Ancient Maya and Egyptian Experience* (London: Routledge, 2003); Meskall, Lynn M., and Robert W. Preucel, eds., *A Companion to Social Archaeology.* (Oxford: Blackwell, 2004); Mrozowski, Stephen A., "Exploring New England's Evolving Urban Landscape," in *Living in Cities*, edited by Edward Staski (Ann Arbor, MI: Society for Historical Archaeology, 1987), 1–9; Mrozowski, Stephen A., "Landscapes of Inequality," in *The Archaeology of Inequality*, edited by Randell H. McGuire and Robert Paynter (Oxford: Basil Blackwell, 1991), 79–101; Mrozowski, Stephen A., *The Archaeology of Class in Urban America* (Cambridge: Cambridge University Press, 2006); Mrozowski, Stephen A., Edward L. Bell, Mary C. Beaudry, David B. Landon, and Gerald K. Kelso, "Living on the Boott: Health and Well Being in a Boardinghouse Population." *World Archaeology* 21(2) (1989): 298–319; Mrozowski, Stephen A., Grace H. Zeising, and Mary C. Beaudry, *Living on the Boott: Historical Archaeology at the Boott Mills Boardinghouses, Lowell, Massachusetts* (Amherst: University of Massachusetts Press, 1996); Preucel, Robert W., and Lynn M. Meskall, "Knowledges," in *A Companion to Social Archaeology*, edited by Lynn M. Meskall and Robert W. Preucel (Oxford: Blackwell, 2004), 3–22; Reckner, Paul E., and Stephen A. Brighton, "'Free From All Vicious Habits': Archaeological Perspective on Class Conflict and the Rhetoric of Temperance," *Historical Archaeology* 33(1) (1999): 63–86; Reinhard, Karl. J., Stephen A Mrozowski, and Kathleen K. Orloski, "Privies, Pollen, Parasites and Seeds: A Biological Nexus in Historical Archaeology," *MASCA Journal* 4(1) (1986): 31–36; Rothschild, Nan A., "The Effects of Urbanization on Faunal Diversity: A Comparison between New York and St. Augustine, Florida, in the Sixteenth to Eighteenth Centuries," in *Quantifying Diversity in Archaeology*, edited by R. D. Leonard and G. T. Jones (Cambridge: Cambridge University Press, 1989), 92–99; Rothschild, Nan A., *Colonial Encounters in a Native American Landscape: The Spanish and Dutch in North America* (Washington, DC: Smithsonian Books, 2003); Rothschild, Nan A., and Donna Balkwill, "The Meaning of Change in Urban Faunal Deposits," *Historical Archaeology* 27(2) (1993): 71–89; Sofaer, Joanna R., *The Body as Material Culture: A Theoretical Osteoarchaeology* (Cambridge: Cambridge University Press, 2006); Soja, Edward W., *Postmetropolis: Critical Studies of Cities and Regions* (London: Blackwell, 2000); Wall, Diana diZerega, "Sacred Dinners and Secular Teas: Constructing Domesticity in Mid-19th-Century New York," *Historical Archaeology* 25(4) (1991): 69–81; Wall, Diana diZerega, *The Archaeology of Gender: Separating the Spheres in Urban America* (New York: Plenum Press, 1993); Wall, Diana diZerega, "Family Meals and Evening Parties: Constructing Domesticity in Nineteenth-Century, Middle-Class New York," in *Lines That Divide: Historical Archaeologies of Race, Class, and Gender*, edited by James A. Delle, Stephen A. Mrozowski, and Robert Paynter (Knoxville: University of Tennessee, 2000), 109–141; Yamin, Rebecca, "Lurid Tales and Homely Stories on New York's Notorious Five Points," *Historical Archaeology* 32(1) (1998): 74–85; Yamin, Rebecca, "Alternative Narratives: Respectability at New York's Five Points," in *The Archaeology of Urban Landscapes: Explorations in Slumland*, edited by Alan Mayne and Tim Murray (Cambridge: Cambridge University Press, 2001), 154–170.

Stephen A. Mrozowski

HISTORIC INDUSTRIAL ARCHAEOLOGY SITES

INTRODUCTION

The rise of industry in the United States during the nineteenth century impacted landscapes, labor, gender roles, and living conditions. Today what remains of much of America's early industries are rusting factories, abandoned buildings, deserted mines, scarred landscapes, and decaying cities and towns. These are all reminders of an economy that was dominated by industrial capitalism for more than a century. Over the past several decades communities have debated about how to use these abandoned industrial properties. Strategies have included redevelopment, reuse, commemoration, and elimination. These are all policies that affect the way we remember the industrial past. Archaeologists are involved in documenting this past, although there are different approaches on how best to interpret the meaning of these places. The traditional focus of the industrial archaeologist has been to record the engineering and technological feats of past generations. However, those subscribing to the new labor history movement see the job of an industrial archaeologist as using these places to address issues of labor and working-class conditions.

Many ex–factory workers are happy to see their former places of employment destroyed and removed from the landscape. They feel that their time in the factories was a degrading period in their life. Preserving and remembering these places is not a community priority for them. This reaction is telling, because many of the industrial-site museums throughout the United States promote the importance of industrialization at the expense of the story of the worker. However, the preservation, stabilization, and restoration of industrial sites can be useful in interpreting and understanding work conditions that people faced in industries. Telling the story of labor's struggle can make the preservation of industrial complexes acceptable to a greater portion of the working-class community.

LABOR'S HERITAGE

As the United States and Great Britain moved into their post-industrial phases, industrial archaeology developed to allow the recording and preservation of the remains of industries before they disappeared from the landscape. Industrial archaeology includes the documentation of bridges, canals, railways, factories, mills, kilns, and mines. In most cases anthropological questions are not addressed and the study of the machine takes precedence over the people involved in the industry. This tradition is reflected in the flagship journal of U.S. industrial archaeology, *IA: The Journal of the Society for Industrial Archaeology*, and its British counterpart, *Industrial Archaeology Review*. While some of the more recent articles in these journals acknowledge the important role workers once played at these sites, authors tend not explore labor issues in detail. The articles often focus on machines, machine products, physical layout, and power systems. While many historians and anthropologists have made labor an important theme in their studies of industrial society, archaeologists working in industrial contexts often do not make this connection.

The study of labor at industrial sites follows the development of other new radical traditions, such as the civil rights movement, the feminist movement, and the American Indian movement. The new labor history, with its emphasis on workers and their families, allows for a search for agency and resistance. Workers are humanized, and studying them provides a more in-depth understanding of laborers' work habits, their domestic life and interactions within the community, and their leisure activities.

An important project now underway in the National Park Service is the Labor Archaeology National Historic Landmark Theme Study. The document provides a brief overview of work cultures in the United States from the colonial period until recent times. The study examines the experience of workers and addresses issues such as ethnic histories, labor mobility, community studies, worker experiences, women and minority studies, and political behavior. It provides archaeological case studies of sites that are on the National Register of Historic Places and explores issues of labor archaeology at industrial sites. Following are several issues addressed in the study that help to humanize the conditions and situations of industrial life.

Workers' Housing

The examination of workers' housing provides a glimpse of how industry impacted the daily lives of workers and their families. During the early industrial era many companies provided housing for their workers. Industrialists dictated working conditions and processes, and they could control workers' behavior away from the factory by instituting housing regulations. The archaeology at Lowell, Massachusetts, shows that the industrial town contained rows of similar-looking boardinghouses situated in close proximity to the factory. The interiors created an atmosphere of egalitarianism, as all of the rooms were the same size.

However, not all industries operated in this fashion. In the early nineteenth-century government town of Harpers Ferry the Ordnance Department didn't initiate any form of paternalism. This lack of control came to haunt those who tried to manage labor in the gun factory. Workers built their own houses and their families expressed their own personal identities within their individual homes. The domestic landscape of Harpers Ferry appears to have been haphazardly built, unlike the standardized boardinghouses found in the industrial Northeast. The archaeological record shows that armory workers occasionally practiced their craft at home until about 1841, when the military took over control of the facility and made all workers abide by a standard work discipline. After this date armory work was no longer performed in a domestic context.

Resistance

The imposition of rules, regulations, and industrial discipline often met with various forms of resistance. For instance, at Harpers Ferry the armorers responded to the new work discipline with strikes and factory slowdowns. There is also a case of a dissatisfied unemployed worker who murdered his former supervisor. Although the murderer was tried, convicted, and executed, he became a folk hero for the armorers' struggle to retain their craft as they lost control over the means of production. At other industrial places, such as Lowell, Massachusetts, the corporate paternalism that controlled boardinghouse living appears to have been resisted by covert activities, such as drinking alcohol in the backyards and disposing empty containers in the privy.

At the John Russell Cutlery Company on the Green River near Greenfield, Massachusetts, archaeologists discovered a large quantity of inferior or imperfectly manufactured parts related to interchangeable manufacturing near the former cutting room and trip hammer shop. While it would be easy to conclude that these artifacts form a typical industrial waste pile, archaeologists looked at the larger context of nineteenth-century industrial labor relations and they concluded that this assemblage is a reflection of workers' displeasure with the new industrial work system. The higher-than-usual proportion of wasted materials is an indication that workers intentionally damaged goods because of their dissatisfaction with the work process.

Striking is a significant form of resistance and is a focus of the archaeology at the Ludlow Tent Colony Site in Colorado. The Colorado coal strike ignited a year-long cycle of violence and retribution beginning in 1913 and culminating when the militia charged the tent colony and set fire to the tents, killing two women and eleven children. The archaeology examines the formation of temporary communities, protest labor movements, and government and military intervention. With the support of the United Mine Workers of America, archaeology is raising the visibility of this bloody episode in labor relations and is helping to make this incident a part of the broader public memory.

Environment, Health, and Industry

Industrial archaeology can examine the health conditions at industrial sites and towns. For instance, many mining sites endangered the health and lives of workers. Work sites were often unstable, machinery often malfunctioned, pollution and harmful fumes contaminated the air, and workers often put in exhaustive work hours. These are all conditions that led to accidents, chronic illnesses, and deaths. Until about the mid-twentieth century, industrialists paid little attention to the impact that factories had on the surrounding environment until workers, scientists, and environmentalists brought these issues to the forefront of the American conscience.

Archaeologists have demonstrated the effectiveness of using soil samples from the area in and around factories and dwellings to search for toxins and to examine general health conditions. Privy samples at workplaces reveal the presence of parasites and other toxins, indications of poor health. Pollen and macrofloral samples also supply information about the changing landscape and its relationship to shifting ideals related to industrialization. The presence of medicinal and alcohol bottles at workers' houses provide clues about general health conditions. Industrial pollution has had a devastating affect on humans, and it is important that these issues be made part of the story of industrial archaeology.

A study of human osteological remains comparing medieval urban and early industrial sites in England shows the devastating impact of industrialization on children. Children from industrial towns showed a higher rate of mortality, retarded growth, higher levels of stress, and a greater prevalence of metabolic and infectious diseases. Children from an industrial town were also more than an inch shorter than those from a contemporary urban trading town. Although differences between urban and rural populations did exist previously, industrialization had the greatest impact on child health.

MAKING THE STUDY OF INDUSTRY PUBLIC

Industrial archaeology can lead to a better understanding of life and work in an industrial capitalist system. The Historic American Buildings Survey/Historic American Engineering Record (HABS/HAER) is an important federal government program that helps in making a record of industrial sites. The program documents important architectural, engineering, and industrial sites throughout the United States and its territories. HABS was founded in 1933 as a New Deal public employment program for architects, draftsmen, and photographers to record a cross section of American architecture. Founded in 1969 through the cooperation of the National Park Service, the Library of Congress, and the American Society of Civil Engineers, HAER's goal is to document significant engineering and industrial sites in the United States. All HABS/HAER collections are archived at the Library of Congress, where they are made available to the public, and the program is part of the National Park Service (http://www.cr.nps.gov/habshaer). Several notable projects have developed from these programs. For instance, in 1987 America's Industrial Heritage Project, now called the Southwestern Pennsylvania Heritage Preservation Commission, began a long-term project inventorying surviving historic engineering works and industrial resources in the region.

Places to Visit

There are a growing number of industrial archaeology site and museum interpretations that describe the industrial past and emphasize the importance of labor. Industry is an important part of our national history. Since the agricultural revolution, no other process in human history has so changed the way people use the earth's resources, or the way humans work and live. Abandoned mills, factories, and mines are scattered throughout the American landscape. While these landscape signatures beg for the interpretation of the machinery, it is important to remember that the part of the history that is no longer visible on the landscape are the workers and their families. It is essential that any narrative about the industrial revolution include the story of labor as well as capital.

In the American Southwest, many of the company mining towns and large labor encampments from the late nineteenth century followed a grid pattern that reflected order and rationality, while the smaller towns formed in linear strips along roadways. Some of these places still survive as small towns or abandoned places visible from the roadside. Tens of thousands of abandoned mines are scattered throughout the region. In Colorado alone there are 23,000 inactive and abandoned mines and mining communities. The mines are mostly unsafe, containing unstable soil, unsafe roofs and ladders, deadly gases, poisonous snakes, and dangerous explosives. However, throughout the region there are a handful of places that are stabilized and safe and that encourage heritage tourism.

Mining attracted Europeans of many different nationalities, but the Chinese also had a major impact on western mining. The government prohibited Chinese mining, but after 1870 it was allowed to lease mining operations. Several Chinese companies mined the Warren district in Idaho and the workers left an impressive archaeological signature. Archaeologists found the remains of canvas and repair tools, indicating that workers constructed impermanent homes in a distinctive Chinese style. Their assemblage contained imported Asian goods such as kitchen utensils and opium bottles, and the workers built Chinese-style garden terraces. Their mining techniques and tools were also different from those of the European Americans.

Mining occurred in other regions of the United States, and Buxton, Iowa, is a compelling example of a predominantly African American mining town. African Americans were generally disenfranchised from industrial labor after Emancipation. However, when Caucasian workers at Mucakinock, Iowa, struck for higher wages, the Consolidation Coal Company recruited African Americans from Virginia. By 1881 there were over 4,000 African Americans working in the mining town. The operation was abandoned and relocated to Buxton along with the workforce and supporting community. Buxton flourished for several decades and was then abandoned in 1923 when the mining operations ceased. At its peak it had 6,000 residents with 5,500 of them claiming African ancestry.

One newspaper called it "the Negro Athens of the north." Buxton became a ghost town as many of its residents moved to other mining operations in Illinois. The archaeology of Buxton shows that the residents were part of the regional, national, and international trade networks. The spatial layout is a reflection of power and separation. The superintendents' residences stood on an isolated scenic hilltop across a valley overlooking the main part of town.

Copper and iron mine communities once formed a mighty industry in the Great Lakes region. Many of these places are closed, while a few have been stabilized and are interpreted to the public. Keweenaw National Historical Park, located in the Upper Peninsula of Michigan, celebrates and interprets the copper mining industry. The park preserves the heritage of copper mining in a setting where many of the original structures and landscapes of the copper era are still present. The interpretation shows how copper mining generated thriving industries in a remote region of the United States. Copper mining in the Upper Peninsula lured immigrants from distant places, employing people from over thirty different ethnic groups. The architecture and design of the industries is evidence of a corporate-sponsored community of a type often found in early American industry. The archaeological sites in the region are associated with the oldest known mining activity in the Western Hemisphere, dating back some 7,000 years. However, historic copper mining in this region pioneered technological advancements that were later used in mining throughout the world. Other places include Klondike Gold Rush National Historical Park, which interprets the gold rush but is also closely associated with the mining in Alaska. Several reports exist on the archaeology of domestic structures.

In the East the Eckley Miners Village, near Hazleton, Pennsylvania, interprets life associated with nineteenth-century anthracite mining. In 1971 a group of businessmen organized the Anthracite Historical Site Museum, Inc., and purchased the village of Eckley, with 200 residents still living there. They deeded the land over to the state in order to create the country's only mining town museum. Today fewer than two dozen people reside in Eckley. The associated museum displays the hardships of life in a mining community, such as impoverishment, illness, accidents, death, and labor discontent.

In a restored boardinghouse in downtown Lawrence, Massachusetts, is a museum operated by the Lawrence Heritage State Park that interprets one of the largest strikes in the U.S. textile industry, the Bread and Roses Strike of 1912. Immigrant women from thirty different nationalities struck in Lawrence for better wages and improved work conditions. In sympathy, the strike spread throughout the Northeast region, closing many of the textile industries. These industries eventually left the Northeast, and Lawrence is now one of the poorest cities in Massachusetts, suffering from the loss of its major economic base. Today there are mixed reactions to this strike's commemoration in the form of an annual Bread and

Roses festival that strives to interest nontraditional communities in labor's heritage. The Labor Day festival promotes the city as a "special place in American labor history, and as the quintessential 'Immigrant City,' both past and present."

Another exhibition that includes the story of labor is the Museum of Work and Culture in Woonsocket, Rhode Island. The museum interprets the experience of the French Canadian immigrant workers by using oral histories and material culture. Visitors venturing through the exhibits can read about and listen to the workers' stories and learn about how they coped with substandard working and living conditions. This exhibition effectively examines the historical development of labor and class and shows the impact of industrialization on work, domestic lifestyles, and health conditions.

The city of Lowell, Massachusetts, also embraces its industrial past. Statues have been placed around the town to celebrate the efforts of industrial workers. At Lowell National Historical Park many of the exhibits present a history that includes the story of both labor and capital. One exhibit extols the material benefits of industry but also explains labor strife. Visitors are also invited to walk through the mill with earplugs while more than 100 machines operate simultaneously. The experience helps one understand the strain on the mill girls and later immigrants as they labored ten hours per day.

Several exhibitions are featured in Harpers Ferry National Historical Park, which interprets nineteenth-century industry in the town. One exhibition focuses on the early industrial development of Harpers Ferry, describing some of the machinery found in the early armory. This exhibition is occasionally staffed, and interpreters demonstrate the historic wood lathe. Across the room is a display that shows the different types of water power used in nineteenth-century Harpers Ferry. Another exhibit, in Lower Town, illustrates how armory workers may have practiced their craft in a piecework system at home until about 1841, when the military took control of the facility and made all workers abide by a standard work

discipline. Another exhibit interprets daily life in a boardinghouse. The families that inhabited the places had a high disease rate, as indicated by the high concentration of parasites found in the privy, and they also relied heavily on self-medication. A walking trail through an archaeological preserve known as Virginius Island provides an overview of a nineteenth-century mill village. In addition to museums and sites that illustrate examples of American industrialization, there are an increasing number of articles and books from which interested readers can learn more about historic period industrial archaeology and the Americans who were the industrial workers.

Further Reading: Casella, Eleanor C., and James Symonds, eds., *Industrial Archaeology: Future Directions* (New York: Springer, 2005); Gordon, Robert B., and Patrick M. Malone, *The Texture of Industry: An Archaeological View of Industry in North America* (New York: Oxford University Press, 1994); Hardesty, Donald L., *The Archeology of Mining and Mines: A View from the Silver State*, Special Publication Series No. 6 (Rockville, MD: Society for Historical Archaeology, 1988); Historic American Building Survey/ Historic American Engineering Survey, National Park Service Web site, http://www.cr.nps.gov/habshaer; Kemp, Emery L., ed., *Industrial Archaeology: Techniques* (Malabar, FL: Krieger, 1996); Leary, T. E., "Industrial Archaeology and Industrial Ecology," *Radical History Review* 21 (1979): 171–182; Mrozowski, Stephen A., Grace H. Zeising, and Mary C. Beaudry, *Living on the Boott: Historical Archeology at the Boott Mills Boardinghouses, Lowell, Massachusetts* (Amherst: University of Massachusetts Press, 1996); Palus, Matthew, and Paul A. Shackel, *"They Worked Regular": Craft, Labor, Family and the Archaeology of an Industrial Community* (Knoxville: University of Tennessee Press, 2006); Shackel, Paul A., *Culture Change and the New Technology: An Archaeology of the Early American Industrial Era* (New York: Plenum, 1996); Wallace, Anthony F. C., *Rockdale: The Growth of an American Village in the Early Industrial Revolution* (New York: W.W. Norton, 1980).

Paul A. Shackel

ANCIENT SITES IN THE FAR NORTHEAST

New England and the Maritimes

The First Northeasterners

Knowledge of the earliest human inhabitants at or near the far northeastern limit of their distribution in northeastern North America, including New England and the adjacent Maritime Provinces, has been significantly expanded in the past thirty years or so. In this area, designated as the "far

Northeast," evidence of the Paleoindian period is now generally dated from about 11,000 to 9,000 years ago, or about 9000–7000 BC, and perhaps slightly earlier and/or later based on regional evidence. In the far Northeast, the Paleoindian period can be now concretely subdivided into the Early

Paleoindian and the Late Paleoindian periods. The temporal boundary between these periods is roughly correlated with the end of the Ice Age conditions of the Pleistocene epoch and the beginning of the post–Ice Age Holocene epoch at around 10,000 years ago, or 8000 BC. Various subdivisions of the Early Paleoindian and Late Paleoindian periods can also be established, but these are more provisional due to the difficulties of respectively dating them based on available evidence. Subsequent occupation by people referred to as the Maritime Archaic Culture occurred from about 7,500 to 3,200 years ago along the Maine coast and in Newfoundland, particularly in the area of the west coast near Port au Choix.

The Early Paleoindian period was the time of the first arrival of Native American/First Nation pioneering colonists in the region, and their presence is marked by highly distinctive fluted points, among other tool forms. The Early Paleoindian period began in the far Northeast around 11,000 years ago and it lasted until about 10,200–10,000 years ago, when fluted points were abandoned in this region, as elsewhere across the continent. At the time, Late Pleistocene conditions included colder climatic patterns and different weather than today, and the vegetation combined both tundra and forest parkland, among other types, in the far Northeast. Animals that would become extinct by the end of the Pleistocene, such as mammoths and mastodons, and colder-climate species such as barren ground caribou were present in at least some portions of the region. Much of modern-day eastern and central Canada was seemingly not inhabitable during this period due to the presence of glacial and peri-glacial conditions, including a large marine invasion in the St. Lawrence valley and glacial lakes in different areas.

Regional Early Paleoindian groups had a technology much like that of other contemporaneous Paleoindians across all portions of the continent then habitable. Flaked-stone tools, sometimes used in composite constructions—for example, knives, punches, and scrapers in antler, bone, or wood hafts—were characteristic at the time, and few if any ground stone tools are represented. Regional groups in the far Northeast seemingly shared similar hunter-gatherer subsistence and mobility/settlement patterns with those who lived in comparably cold, glaciated settings across the North American continent during the Early Paleoindian period, but these contrasted with those who lived in warmer, non-glaciated portions of the continent. In the glaciated northern areas, there was no advantage in living close to the numerous regional waterways; instead people often chose strategic settings for habitation that afforded them vistas for watching game and access to open, upland travel routes.

The still more enigmatic Late Paleoindian period followed the Early Paleoindian period and lasted about 1,000–1,500 years after about 10,000 years ago, or 8000 BC. The Late Paleoindian period was marked by continuation of many aspects of the preceding flaked lithic technology, but

new styles of projectile points were developed to replace the fluted points. Regional Late Paleoindian projectile point styles were based on elongated lanceolate forms that were often very finely flaked beyond even the mastery of their Early Paleoindian predecessors. These Late Paleoindian forms were broadly similar to other styles in the plains and farther west, but they were rather different from those found to the south beyond the glaciated Northeast.

The Late Paleoindian period was a time when the Ice Age climate and vegetation had largely ameliorated in the far Northeast, although conditions were still different from those of later Holocene times. Forests, sometimes strongly dominated by conifers, became widespread in all the highest elevations, and many large game animals disappeared locally, especially the gregarious barren ground caribou. Consequently, some changes in subsistence can be inferred, and these are more clearly demonstrable in mobility/settlement patterns, as Late Paleoindian groups came to live along waterways for travel reasons and presumably subsistence as well. Late Paleoindian populations expanded into previously uninhabited portions of the far Northeast, including the Gaspé Peninsula of Quebec and New Brunswick, for example. They also expanded northward elsewhere in Quebec and other portions of Canada as glacial and peri-glacial conditions were transformed by the gradual warming, ultimately reaching into what is today considered the far northern subarctic and even the Arctic.

In the far Northeast, we can now recognize six or seven presumed fairly sequential projectile styles for the entire Paleoindian period. Based largely on the recent comparative research of James Bradley and Arthur Spiess, these include (in descending temporal order) the Bull Brook, Debert/Vail, Michaud/Neponset, and Nicholas point styles for the Early Paleoindian period, and the Agate Basin–related, Dalton-related, and Ste. Anne/Varney styles for the Late Paleoindian period. Among the Early Paleoindian styles, all are fluted except for the Nicholas style, which is often nonfluted, whereas none of the Late Paleoindian styles are fluted. These match undated but presumably contemporaneous styles in the Great Lakes region, but more work needs to be done in both areas and elsewhere to refine Paleoindian dating in all cases. This task is complicated by the imprecision inherent in radiocarbon dating in general and dating the Late Pleistocene/Early Holocene in particular. Several of the most important radiocarbon-dated Paleoindian sites in the far Northeast are summarized next.

THE BULL BROOK SITE, EASTERN MASSACHUSETTS

The Bull Brook site in Ipswich, Massachusetts, was identified by a number of avocational archaeologists in the early 1950s during sand and gravel mining. Bull Brook is situated about 12 m above several nearby salt marshes and is only about 5 km from the modern seacoast. Ultimately, these avocational and professional archaeologists, Douglas Byers and Douglas Jordan, excavated the undisturbed portions of the site and in the process discovered that it consisted of a large oval configuration of smaller elliptical loci about 7 m long at most. There are over 42 of these loci at Bull Brook; some are matched by cross mends of broken artifacts, and all seem to represent possible house areas or other activity areas. These are now interpreted as representing contemporaneous occupation in most if not all cases. They were arrayed over an area around 100 m long and as large as 80,000 square meters. No one has produced a comprehensive Bull Brook site report yet, given the nature of its investigation and the large size of the available collections.

A series of six radiocarbon dates was obtained by Byers for Bull Brook; they produced an average date of about 9,000 years ago, or 7000 BC, and several other dates have been obtained more recently, but none of these is clearly reflective of the true age of the site. The tool sample includes many fluted points, but it has yet to be tallied and reported in its entirety. Nonetheless, it may exceed 8,000 or even 10,000 tools, according to John Grimes. Various lithic materials are found within the combined collection, minimally including presumed Munsungan chert from northern Maine, Champlain and Hudson valley cherts, and Pennsylvania jasper from southeastern Pennsylvania, among other materials, including rhyolite from northern New Hampshire. Among several burned faunal samples of mammal remains, caribou bones have been identified by Arthur Spiess from several contexts, along with one beaver bone. Various authors have identified this as an unusually large, pioneering site of the Early Paleoindian period, perhaps a "base camp" or "marshaling area" for further initial human colonization, and representing a high degree of mobility, given the largely non-local, exotic lithic materials. Brian Robinson has recently begun investigation of the site mapping issues and other provenience questions as part of a planned full documentation of Bull Brook.

THE DEBERT SITE, CENTRAL NOVA SCOTIA
The Debert site, as well as others in a local Belmont, Nova Scotia, complex, was discovered after its surface was partially disturbed by military operations. The Debert site is situated 3–4 km from the ocean near the Minas Basin and 400 m from the nearest tributary of the Chiganois River. It was excavated during the mid-1960s by a professional research team, including Douglas Byers and George MacDonald, and ultimately fully documented in a published report by MacDonald. A series of fourteen radiocarbon dates obtained by Byers average around 10,600 years ago, or 8600 BC, which is generally believed to be an accurate date for the site and is now assigned roughly to the middle portion of the Early Paleoindian period, both temporally and stylistically.

A series of artifact concentrations, roughly 55 to 180 square meters in size, demarcate at least eleven activity areas at

Debert, much like but sometimes larger than those at Bull Brook. As at Bull Brook, some other activity areas were likely destroyed. All of these may again represent individual houses, given the typical association of hearths with them. More than 4,400 lithic tools were reported by MacDonald, including about 140 fluted points, many fragmentary, and other biface "knives," drills, wedges, and "scrapers" of different types. Unlike those found at Bull Brook, the lithic raw materials are predominantly local Minas Basin chalcedony and other materials from nearby. No organic artifacts or food remains were recovered, but Debert has been often interpreted as another contemporaneous set of activity areas attributable to a pioneering Early Paleoindian group, as a "macro-band camp," or as a "marshaling area" for local colonization, like Bull Brook (and Vail, described next).

THE VAIL AND ADKINS SITES, NORTHWESTERN MAINE
The Vail and Adkins sites were discovered during the 1970s and 1980s by a combination of avocational and professional investigators along an inundated stretch of the upper Androscoggin River in interior, upland Maine near its border with New Hampshire and Quebec. Richard M. Gramly undertook systematic excavations at the main portion of the Vail site, which includes at least eight loci, or activity areas, and covering at least about 5,600 square meters in total. He worked there several times when water levels permitted during the early 1980s and soon fully reported his initial Vail research. Six radiocarbon dates were obtained from the Vail site, the three most reliable of which average about 10,500 years ago, or 8500–8600 BC, much like the average for Debert.

In 1983 the Vail "kill" site was identified about 250 m away from the larger Vail habitation site and excavated soon thereafter. Remarkably, at least five fluted points could be matched between the main site, or "habitation" area, and the "kill" area. This lends strong support to the "kill" site hypothesis, since the point tips found at the "kill" site could be fit together with fluted point bases found at the habitation area. The small Adkins site, covering only about 50–60 square meters with a small adjoining stone structure, was discovered around the same time in 1984. The stone structure, less than 3–4 meters in overall diameter, was interpreted as a storage chamber, or "cache," for meat. Gramly fully excavated the Adkins site and removed the "cache" structure for display at the Maine State Museum, but he continues to work at Vail and other nearby sites when circumstances permit.

Over 3,800 tools and fragments were cataloged at the time of Gramly's first major publication regarding Vail, including 79 fluted points and other artifacts very much like the Debert specimens in many ways. The Vail tools represent cherts from Munsungan Lake in northern Maine, the Champlain and Hudson valleys, southeastern Pennsylvania, and other areas, suggesting wide-ranging mobility in the standard scenario, much like the case at Bull Brook. Vail too may be a "macro-band camp" or a "marshaling area" for local colonization. In any case, even in the absence of subsistence remains, the local Vail area demonstrates probable evidence of intercept hunting and meat storage.

THE VARNEY FARM SITE, WESTERN MAINE

The Varney Farm site was first identified through a cultural resource management archaeological study conducted in 1993 where an erosion stabilization project was planned on a farm in Turner, Androscoggin County, Maine. Situated between small brooks flowing into the Nezinscot River 100 m distant and about 10 m above the river, the Varney Farm site was extensively excavated by several teams led by the present author in 1994 and 1998. A combined area of about 770 square meters was ultimately salvaged before most of the Varney Farm site was destroyed, representing excavation of about 90–95 percent of the total area. Of nine radiocarbon dates, possibly six can be related to the Late Paleoindian occupation at Varney Farm, including dates of about 9,400 years ago and five others between about 8,700 and 8,400 years ago, with an average of about 8,500 years ago. Thus, Varney Farm may date at about 7400–7500 BC, or around 6500–6600 BC, but the earlier date seems more likely, given other regional evidence.

The Varney Farm site represents a single occupation unequivocally related to the Late Paleoindian period. A total of 326 tools and more than 4,900 flakes were cumulatively excavated from Varney Farm. Virtually all of these lithic specimens are related to the Norway Bluff locale of Munsungan chert from northern Maine, suggesting long-range mobility within Maine in this case. Most representative of the Late Paleoindian period are the 19 individual parallel-flaked points that demonstrate very carefully executed flaking and remarkable thinness. Biface preforms, biface drills, uniface "scrapers," and various modified flake tools are also represented in the Varney Farm sample. The Varney Farm site provides a rare example of a discrete Late Paleoindian occupation in the far Northeast, and more such sites are sorely needed to shed more light on this transitional period between the Early Paleoindian and Archaic periods.

PORT AU CHOIX SITES, WESTERN COASTAL NEWFOUNDLAND

The earliest inhabitants of this area are referred to as belonging to the Maritime Archaic culture. They survived as hunters and gathers, not practicing agriculture and generally utilizing maritime natural resources. During this time period, roughly 7,500–3,500 years ago, people following this way of life, referred to by modern archaeologists as the Maritime Archaic culture, lived in various parts of Atlantic Canada, Maine, and northern Labrador.

Around Port au Choix, archaeological studies conducted since the late 1940s by Elmer Harp, James Tuck, and Priscilla Renouf have investigated ancient burial sites and domestic sites. The sites associated with this culture are known for the use of maritime resources, beautifully crafted polished stone tools and artifacts made from bone, and ceremonial graves in which red ocher was used as a decorative aspect of the burial process.

Further Reading: Bourque, Bruce J., *Diversity and Complexity in Prehistoric Maritime Societies: A Gulf of Maine Perspective* (New York: Springer, 1995); Bourque, Bruce J., *Twelve Thousand Years: America Indians in Maine* (Lincoln: University of Nebraska Press, 2001); Bradley, James W., *Origins and Ancestors: Investigating New England's Paleo Indians* (Andover, MN: Robert S. Peabody Museum of Archaeology, 1998); Curran, Mary Lou, "Paleoindians in the Northeast: The Problem of Dating Fluted Point Sites," *Review of Archaeology* 17(1) (1996): 2–11; Davis, Stephen A., "Debert/Belmont Complex," in *Archaeology of Prehistoric Native North America: An Encyclopedia*, edited by Guy Gibbon (New York: Garland, 1998), 199–200; Dincauze, Dena F., "Pioneering in the Pleistocene: Large Paleoindian Sites in the Northeast," in *Archaeology of Eastern North America: Papers in Honor of Stephen Williams*, edited by James B. Stoltman (Jackson: MS: Department of Archives and History, 1993), 43–60; Gramly, Richard M., *The Vail Site: A Palaeo-Indian Encampment in Maine* (Buffalo, NY: Persimmon Press, 1982); Gramly, Richard M., "Kill Sites, Killing Ground and Fluted Points at the Vail Site," *Archaeology of Eastern North America* 12 (1984): 110–121; Gramly, Richard M., *The Adkins Site: A Palaeo-Indian Habitation and Associated Stone Structure* (Buffalo, NY: Persimmon Press, 1988); Grimes, John R., "A New Look at Bull Brook," *Anthropology* 3(1–2) (1979): 109–130; MacDonald, George F., *Debert: A Paleo-Indian Site in Central Nova Scotia*, Anthropology Papers No. 16 (Ottawa: National Museums of Canada, 1968); Petersen, James B., "Preceramic Archaeological Manifestations in the Far Northeast: A Review of Recent Research," *Archaeology of Eastern North America* 23 (1995): 207–230; Petersen, James B. "Foreword: West Athens Hill, the Paleoindian Period, and Robert E. Funk in Northeastern Perspective," in *An Ice Age Quarry-Workshop: The West Athens Hill Site Revisited*, by Robert E. Funk, New York State Museum Bulletin 504 (Albany: University of New York State Education Department, 2004), xi–xlix; Petersen, James B., Robert N. Bartone, and Belinda J. Cox, "The Varney Farm Site and the Late Paleoindian Period in Northeastern North America," *Archaeology of Eastern North America* 28 (2000): 113–140; Port au Choix National Historic Site of Canada Web site, http//www.pc.gc.ca/lhn-nhs/nl/portauchoix/indes_e.asp; Renouf, Priscilla, and Trevor Bell, "Integrating Sea Level History and Geomorphology in Targeted Archaeological Site Survey: The Gould Site (EeBi-42), Port au Choix, Newfoundland," *Northeastern Anthropology* 59 (1999): 47–64; Spiess, Arthur, Deborah Wilson, and James Bradley, "Paleoindian Occupation in the New England–Maritimes Region: Beyond Cultural Ecology," *Archaeology of Eastern North America* 26 (1998): 201–264; Tuck, James A., "An Archaic Indian Cemetery at Port au Choix, Newfoundland," *American Antiquity* 36 (1970): 343–358; Tuck, James A., *Ancient Peoples of Port au Choix, Newfoundland*, Institute of Social and Economic Research, Social and Economic Studies, No. 17 (St. John's: Memorial University of Newfoundland, 1976).

James B. Petersen

MEADOWCROFT ROCKSHELTER AND NEARBY PALEOINDIAN SITES

Pennsylvania and New Jersey
Paleoindian Sites in the Mid-Atlantic Area

Lying on the southeastern border of the American Northeast, the eastern border of the Midwest, and the northern border of the Southeast, the Commonwealth of Pennsylvania constitutes a unique physiographic, ecological, and prehistoric cultural crossroads. Within or immediately adjacent to its current political boundaries are a series of archaeological sites that collectively span the entire known occupational sequence for eastern North America.

These sites, which include two closed (i.e., cave or rockshelter) and three open-air sites, occur in diverse physiographic and geomorphologic contexts. However, despite these contextual differences, all of the sites served the same basic function: all were seasonally focused campsites whose aboriginal inhabitants visited episodically, apparently for generally short periods. Fortunately, several of the sites produced organic materials that have helped to illuminate the hunting and collecting activities of the native populations who utilized these localities. Additionally, the lithic raw materials represented at each site provide insights into territorial ranges and exchange networks in Paleoindian and Archaic times.

All of the sites discussed here have significantly influenced the history of archaeological research in eastern North American. Collectively, they have helped frame our views of Paleoindian and Archaic adaptations east of the Mississippi while also providing crucial data on more fundamental issues such as dating the arrival and characterizing the behavioral repertoires of the first Americans.

MEADOWCROFT ROCKSHELTER

Meadowcroft Rockshelter is a deeply stratified, multi-component site located about 30 miles southwest of Pittsburgh, Pennsylvania, in the Pittsburgh Low Plateau section of the Appalachian Plateaus physiographic province. The site is situated on the north bank of Cross Creek, a small tributary of the Ohio River that lies 7.6 miles to the west. Declared a National Historic Landmark in 2005, Meadowcroft was owned by the late Albert Miller, whose family settled the area in 1795. The site was brought to the attention of J. M. Adovasio in 1973 and became the focal point of a long-term multi-disciplinary project. Fieldwork began in 1973 and continued thereafter every year until 1978. Additional excavations were conducted in 1983, 1985, 1987, 1993–94, 2003, and, most recently, 2007.

The eleven natural soil strata at Meadowcroft currently represent the longest occupational sequence in the New World. The site has yielded a remarkable corpus of artifactual, floral, and faunal data firmly anchored by some fifty-two stratigraphically consistent radiocarbon dates spanning more than fifteen millennia of autumn-focused, short-term visits. The site's earliest occupants were part of a cultural group referred to by archaeologists as the Miller complex, which appears to represent the pioneer population in the upper Ohio Valley.

The dating of the Miller complex is problematic. A series of thirteen stratigraphically consistent radiocarbon dates are available from the Stratum I-II interface, near the deepest part of the archaeological deposit through middle Stratum IIa at Meadowcroft. Of these, only six dates have clear, undeniable, and extensive artifact associations. Applying a conservative interpretation of the chronometric data, the minimum age for the Miller complex is 10,050–8050 BC. If the six deepest dates unequivocally associated with cultural materials are averaged, then the Miller complex was present at this site and in the contiguous Cross Creek drainage between about 12,605 BC and 12,005 BC. While virtually all authorities concede an age of at least 10,850 BC, for the strata associated with the Miller complex, some have suggested that the earlier dates may be contaminated and are anomalously old. Repeated laboratory examinations, including accelerator mass spectrometry determination, however, have consistently failed to detect any particulate or nonparticulate contaminants (Adovasio et al. 1999).

The environment of Pennsylvania at the time of the initial Miller complex occupation is not known with any certainty. It appears that a mosaic of different peri-glacial habitats coexisted in Pennsylvania, with genuine tundra or steppe-tundra conditions generally occurring at the higher elevations and occasionally rather different conditions at other localities, particularly those at lower elevations. These latter settings apparently included boreal and even limited deciduous vegetation in short-lived combinations that Stephen C. Porter, an authority on North American Late Pleistocene climates, has called "ecologically anomalous" by Holocene standards (Porter 1988, 19). Indeed, at the time of the first human colonization, Pennsylvania, like other parts of the Northeast, was characterized in some areas by vegetational communities with no modern analogues at all.

The same situation apparently also existed regarding diverse Late Pleistocene faunal (animal) communities. These

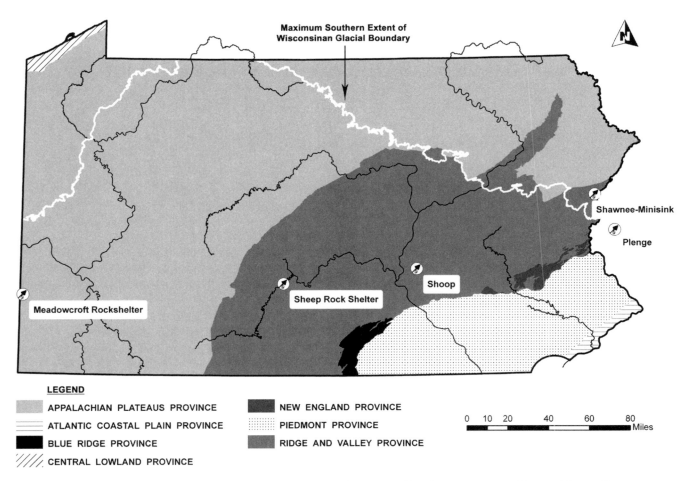

Meadowcroft Rockshelter and other important sites in the Pennsylvania and New Jersey regions.   [James Adovasio]

often included now-extinct species along with modern species still found in North American northern boreal forests or southern woodlands. These late glacial period vegetation and animal communities reflect environmental conditions that neither exist today nor have existed for many millennia. In short, while the "fine strokes" remain to be added, the developing picture of Late Pleistocene environments in Pennsylvania is more diverse and complex than previously suspected. Whatever its exact character, the areas of Pennsylvania and perhaps portions of Ohio that were available to their first human inhabitants appear to have been amply stocked with a variety of resources that these early settlers could exploit for food and raw materials using highly specialized as well as more generalized subsistence strategies.

The inventory of flaked-stone artifacts from lower and middle Stratum IIa at Meadowcroft contains small prismatic blades (long, thin flakes of stone with sharp and generally parallel edges) that were detached by skillful stone tool makers from small prepared stone cores. Although cores themselves were not recovered at Meadowcroft, the artifact assemblage from the nearby and apparently contemporaneous Krajacic

site contains a variety of the distinctive Meadowcroft-style blade implements and several small, cylindrical polyhedral cores. Recovered after the initial study of the Meadowcroft lithic assemblage had been undertaken in 1975, the Krajacic cores precisely parallel the core reduction stone tool manufacturing strategy previously posited for the Meadowcroft blades.

In 1976 a small, lanceolate biface, subsequently called the Miller Lanceolate projectile point, was found in situ on the uppermost living floor of lower Stratum IIa at Meadowcroft. This floor is bracketed above and below by radiocarbon dates from samples of charcoal from fire pits of about 9350 BC and 10,850 BC, respectively. This nonfluted biface is the only Miller Lanceolate point thus far recovered (as of 2007) from a directly dated stratigraphic context—although others have been recovered elsewhere in the Cross Creek drainage—and particular care must be exercised in formulating even a provisional typological definition.

Collectively, this data suggests that the first inhabitants of eastern North America employed a technologically standardized and sophisticated core-and-blade–based industry. In form and style the core and blade artifacts are similar to those found in Eurasiatic regions at roughly the same time period, or slightly earlier. Intriguingly, the Miller complex lithic tool kit has been virtually duplicated (although using different raw materials) at another early site in Virginia, Cactus Hill. Significantly, the dates from Cactus Hill suggest that the Miller-like materials from that locus are essentially the same age as those from Meadowcroft.

Unfortunately, the picture of the subsistence strategies of these earliest inhabitants of the eastern United States is quite unclear. Although 115,166 identifiable bones and bone fragments have been recovered from Meadowcroft Rockshelter, only 11 identifiable bone fragments and less than 11.9 grams (0.42 oz) of plant remains derive from middle and lower Stratum IIa. If all the identified faunal items from these levels represent food remains, which is highly unlikely, then these human populations exploited white-tailed deer and perhaps much smaller game, at least while living at the rockshelter. The meager floral remains suggest possible utilization of hickory, walnut, and hackberry. It is conceivable and likely that these populations may have exploited large and now-extinct Pleistocene big game animals, notably mastodon, but there is no evidence of such predation.

The later strata at Meadowcroft (IIb–XI) span the entire Archaic and Woodland time periods and cultural traditions found in the upper Ohio Valley. Later use of the site conforms to the basic patterns established during the early Paleoindian occupation. Throughout its Archaic tenure, the site served as a fall-centered collection locus for itinerant populations exploiting the Cross Creek valley and contiguous uplands via a very broad spectrum resource collection strategy. Even after the appearance of horticulture in the general study area, this site use pattern continued until the region was depopulated shortly before the onset of the historic period.

In the long view, it appears that the Miller complex populations can be tentatively characterized as generalized hunter-foragers rather than specialized hunters and, furthermore, that despite their geographically circumscribed distribution, they represent the baseline (as of 2007) for all subsequent cultural development in both the upper Ohio Valley and eastern North America.

SHOOP

Shoop is a very large (40 acres) Paleoindian site located in central Pennsylvania within the Appalachian Mountain section of the Ridge and Valley physiographic province. It is situated on a ridge overlooking Armstrong Creek, about 6 miles (9.6 km) east of the Susquehanna River. The Shoop site was discovered by avocational archaeologists in the 1930s and has been heavily collected largely by nonprofessionals ever since. Professional interest in the site was stimulated by John Witthoft, who in 1952 published a major article detailing his technological analysis of artifacts recovered from an extensive surface collection of about 20 acres. This article had a significant effect on shaping Paleoindian research in eastern North America and was the catalyst for many later technical analyses of Shoop lithic material. Interestingly, despite all of the intensive laboratory research and the prominent place Shoop occupies in the Paleoindian literature, no extensive excavations have ever been conducted at the site. As a result, the subsurface stratigraphy is little known and no direct chronometric dates are available from any of the lithic assemblages recovered to date.

All of the artifacts collected or observed at Shoop are limited to the plow zone and appear to be concentrated into at least fifteen distinct clusters. These clusters range about 50 to 300 feet in diameter and often contain high percentages of heat-spalled material, suggesting the nearby presence of as yet undetected and potentially intact subsurface fire features. Within each cluster, the proportion of finished tools to debitage (stone debris from chipped-stone tool manufacturing or maintenance) is very high, and the assemblage of tools is dominated by end unifaces, utilized flakes, side unifaces, terminal-stage bifaces, projectile points, so-called wedges, drills, notched pieces, awls, and acuminate flakes of varying configurations. The suite of approximately 145 whole or fragmentary fluted projectile points from Shoop clearly places the site in the Clovis horizon, which appears to be firmly dated elsewhere to a relatively short 200-year time span in the early tenth millennium BC. Unlike the case for Meadowcroft, there appears to be little or no later intensive utilization of this locality.

Not surprisingly, in the absence of subsurface investigations, the general character of site use at Shoop remains enigmatic. Shoop is located in a very different ecological setting from most other Paleoindian sites in Pennsylvania, and its hilltop location has occasioned considerable speculation about what activities occurred at the site. It has been repeatedly suggested that Shoop may have been located near a major Late Pleistocene caribou migration route and, hence, functioned as a specialized migratory game hunting and processing locality. Direct evidence for such a function, however, is very limited. That the bulk of the raw material utilized for durable tool manufacture at Shoop putatively derives from Onondaga chert outcrops some 250 miles north of the site suggests some degree of long-distance travel, but the role and frequency of that travel by the site's occupants is presently unknown.

Whatever its primary function(s) were, Shoop is one of the largest Clovis era sites in all of North America and suggests that Paleoindian population densities were considerably higher than those postulated on the basis of many Paleoindian sites in the Northeast, which are typically spatially diminutive with small artifact assemblages.

SHAWNEE-MINISINK

The Shawnee-Minisink site (36MR43) is an open locality situated on the second terrace above the confluence of the Delaware River and Brodhead Creek in northeastern Pennsylvania, within the Appalachian Mountain section of the Ridge and Valley physiographic province. Shawnee-Minisink exhibits a southern exposure with higher terrain directly to the north and west. The terrace below the site is an outwash deposit attributable to the last glacial period, as are other geomorphologic and topographic features in the immediate vicinity. The terrace occupied by Shawnee-Minisink is of mixed alluvial and eolian origin and has been incised by an old meander channel of Brodhead Creek.

Shawnee-Minisink was discovered in 1972 by avocational archaeologist Donald Kline, whose three excavated test units revealed that the site was deeply stratified and, like Meadowcroft, contained evidence of all of the periods of aboriginal occupation known in Pennsylvania and eastern North America. One of the test units produced a radiocarbon date attributable to the mid-ninth millennium BC in apparent association with Paleoindian materials.

In 1974 and for three years thereafter, the site was intensively investigated by the Upper Delaware Valley Early Man project. During the course of those investigations, about 25 percent (3,900 square feet) of the estimated total site area was excavated and a very large corpus of artifactual and ecofactual material was recovered under rigid provenience controls. Space limitations preclude all but a summary discussion of the nearly 11,000–radiocarbon year sequence at Shawnee-Minisink, but extended comments are warranted on the Paleoindian and Archaic occupations.

The Paleoindian component at Shawnee-Minisink occurs within a depositional unit composed of loess-derived silty loam. It is completely sealed from overlying components by up to one meter of sterile alluvial sand and may represent—with the singular exception of the Clovis component at Gault in Central Texas—the least disturbed Paleoindian fluted point occupation in North America. Multiple radiocarbon determinations on this component place the earliest Paleoindian utilization of the site at around 11,000 years ago.

As with Shoop, the recovered lithic assemblage is dominated by end unifaces and utilized flakes with other unifaces, flake knives, bifaces, notched pieces, and discoidal and tabular cores represented in relatively low numbers. Projectile points include but a single complete lanceolate fluted specimen. However, unlike Shoop, where subsistence-related activities are far from clear, the early Paleoindian component from Shawnee-Minisink produced a variety of carbonized seeds and fish bone, most of which derived from intact features. The diversity of plant foods and occurrence of fish bone, coupled with the multiplicity of tool types, suggests that, as at Meadowcroft, the inhabitants of Shawnee-Minisink followed a broad-spectrum subsistence strategy with very short-term seasonal occupations at the site. Interestingly, unlike the case for Shoop or, for that matter, Meadowcroft, most of the raw lithic material utilized during the early Paleoindian occupation of Shawnee-Minisink was locally derived black chert.

The later Paleoindian component at Shawnee-Minisink has not been directly dated, but its stratigraphic position suggests an age of about 10,000 years. The lithic assemblage from this occupation is significantly different from the fluted-point component both in terms of tool type and its use of a greater variety of nonlocal raw materials. It is suggested that the basic site function(s) may have changed during this time as reflected by a toolkit directed toward miscellaneous sawing, cutting, and chopping activities.

Stratified above the late Paleoindian component are six Early Archaic living surfaces with lithic artifacts that include both well-known early eastern Archaic point types as well as distinctive local projectile point forms. The Early Archaic occupations are not directly dated by radiocarbon, but based on chronologically well-documented artifact styles, these components are estimated to be 7,000 to 9,500 years in age.

PLENGE

The Plenge site is not located within the Commonwealth of Pennsylvania but, rather, in New Jersey, about 20 miles east of Shawnee-Minisink on a gently sloping terrace of the Musconetcong River within the Reading Prong section of the New England physiographic province. Geomorphologically, Plenge is located between two terminal moraines. The site lies only 646 feet from the Musconetcong River's southern bank about 12 miles north of its confluence with the Delaware River.

Discovered in the late 1960s and the object of limited excavations by Herbert C. Kraft in 1972, Plenge is a large open site encompassing at least 23 acres. Extensive cultivation has turbated the soil profile, and some authorities suggest that no undisturbed stratigraphy remains. Like Meadowcroft and Shawnee-Minisink, Plenge contains evidence of both Archaic and Woodland occupations, but the site is principally known for its Paleoindian component.

Limited excavations and surface collections have yielded some 131 fluted bifaces and at least 1,400 other lithic tools. In addition to fluted points, artifacts found at the site include nonfluted triangular and pentagonal points. Other types of artifacts found include many end and side unifaces as well as utilized flakes. Other forms include notched pieces, denticulated pieces, and various types of perforators. No intact cultural features were encountered, and the site is not directly dated.

The presence of both fluted and presumably later nonfluted points of Paleoindian age suggests that Plenge was revisited over a long period of time and that its initial occupation may have been contemporary with those at Shoop and Shawnee-Minisink. Interestingly, in contrast to Shawnee-Minisink, the lithic assemblage from Plenge evidences the exploitation of a wide range of lithic sources, some of which may derive from the nearby glacial moraines. Other, more distant sources include the Jasper quarries at Macungie, Vera Cruz, and Durham in Lehigh and Bucks counties, Pennsylvania, as well as Onondaga outcrops far to the north. Kraft suggested that, like Shoop, Plenge was intentionally located near a migratory game corridor and may have served as a specialized hunting, collecting, and processing locus. Its close proximity to fresh water may also have facilitated the collection of shellfish.

SHEEP ROCK SHELTER

Sheep Rock Shelter is a large, partially dry, deeply stratified rockshelter located on the north bank of the Raystown Branch of the Juniata River within the Appalachian Mountain section of the Ridge and Valley physiographic province. The site lies some 7 miles upriver from the Raystown Dam and is now completely underwater. Sheep Rock was discovered in 1958 by avocational archaeologist John E. Miller, who investigated the site between 1959 and 1962. The early investigations of Sheep Rock yielded a vast amount of artifacts and environmental material and also demonstrated that the site deposits were at least 20 feet deep. Additional major excavations were conducted at the site in 1966 and 1967 under the supervision of Joseph Michels and Ira Smith, revealing a very complex stratigraphic record with evidence of nine more or less discrete occupational components. Unlike the sites discussed previously, Sheep Rock did not produce Paleoindian materials, although a Paleoindian component may have existed in the deepest but, unfortunately, least explored portion of the site.

The earliest documented occupation at Sheep Rock is attributable to the Early Archaic time period, radiocarbon dated to 6800 BC. Thereafter, the site was intermittently visited throughout the remainder of the prehistoric period and into the protohistoric through the late seventeenth century AD. Recovered evidence indicates that throughout its long occupational history, Sheep Rock served as a locus for broad-based, seasonally focused hunting and collecting activities. A wide array of wild edible plant resources were exploited by the site's inhabitants, including walnuts, chestnuts, hickory nuts, hackberries, cherries, and wild plums. Though most of the fauna recovered from Sheep Rock probably accumulated naturally and represents raptor prey, it is highly probable that some of the assemblage reflects human hunting and subsistence at the site. Faunal species exploited include elk, white-tailed deer, woodchuck, beaver, porcupine, as well as several varieties of duck, goose, trumpeter swan, and a number of fish.

Of the sites discussed here, Sheep Rock is unique for the inventory of perishable artifacts and materials recovered from the largely dry upper layers of the site. These include knotted and unknotted plant fiber–derived cordage, braided and plaited specimens, basketry, and textile materials. The dry layers also yielded worked and unworked leather, wood, grass, and feather materials. Collectively, this perishable artifact inventory provides an unparalleled window into the "soft technology" of Pennsylvania's early aboriginal inhabitants. Given the documented ethnographic and archaeological association of such materials with families, the Sheep Rock perishable artifacts also provide a means for at least faintly illuminating technologies associated with female rather than exclusively male activities.

Further Reading: Adovasio, James, D. Pedler, J. Donahue, and R. Stuckenrath, "No Vestige of a Beginning nor Prospect for an End: Two Decades of Debate on Meadowcroft Rockshelter," in *Ice Age People of North America*, edited by Robson Bonnichsen and Karen Turnmire (College Station: Texas A&M University Press, 1999), 416–431; Carr, Kurt W., "The Shoop Site: Thirty-Five Years After," in *New Approaches to Other Pasts*, edited by W. F. Kinsey and R. W. Moeller (Bethlehem, CT: Archaeological Services, 1989), 5–28; Carr, Kurt W., and J. M. Adovasio, eds., *Ice Age Peoples of Pennsylvania*, Recent Research in Pennsylvania Archaeology No. 2 (Harrisburg: Pennsylvania Historical and Museum Commission, 2002); Cox, Steven L., "A Re-Analysis of the Shoop Site," *Archaeology of Eastern North America* 14 (1986): 101–170; Fogelman, Gary L., *Shoop: Pennsylvania's Famous Paleo Site: A Popular Version* (Turbotville, PA: Fogelman, 1986); Kraft, Herbert C., "The Plenge Site: A Paleo-Indian Occupation Site in New Jersey," *Archaeology of Eastern North America* 1 (1973): 56–117; McNett, Charles W., *Shawnee Minisink: A Stratified Paleoindian Site in the Upper Delaware Valley of Pennsylvania* (New York: Academic Press, 1985); Michels, Joseph W., and Ira F. Smith, *Archaeological Investigations of Sheep Rock Shelter, Huntington County, Pennsylvania*, Vols. 1 and 2 (State College: Pennsylvania State University, Department of Sociology and Anthropology, 1967); Porter, Stephen C., "Landscapes of the Last Ice Age in North America," in *Americans Before Columbus: Ice Age Origins*, edited by Ronald C. Carlisle, Ethnology Monographs No. 12 (Pittsburgh: University of Pittsburgh, Department of Anthropology, 1988), 1–24; Wilmsen, Edward N., *Lithic Analysis and Cultural Inference: A Paleo-Indian Case* (Tucson: University of Arizona Press, 1970).

James Adovasio

PALEOINDIAN AND EARLIER SITES IN VIRGINIA

The Shenandoah Valley and Southeastern Virginia
The Cactus Hill, Williamson, and Thunderbird Sites

Virginia is a geologically diverse state that stretches from the Atlantic Ocean on the east some 600 miles along its southern border well into the Appalachian Mountains at its western tip. However, during the earliest Paleo-American (also referred to as Paleoindian) times, when Canada and the northern parts of the

United States were covered by a large polar ice cap, Virginia's eastern edge was approximately 140 miles further out to sea. In other words, Virginia Beach would have been 140 miles inland and the Chesapeake Bay was a large river valley. The plants and animals also were notably different, with mastodon and other

Three Williamson Clovis artifacts.   [Michael F. Johnson]

large animals living in a spruce-pine forest with possibly mixed grassland, and probably even tundra at higher elevations in the mountains of northern and western Virginia.

It was into this environment that the first Americans arrived. For many years archaeologists thought that they arrived at the end of the last Ice Age, some 13,000 years ago. These early hunter-gatherers made and used tools, in particular long, finely shaped, lance-like stone projectile points with a central flute along the center of the face, parallel with the edges. These distinctive points are called Clovis points, after a town in New Mexico near where positive evidence of a direct association between people and ancient mammoth was first identified in the 1930s.

In the mid-1940s, Dr. Ben C. McCary, a French professor at the College of William and Mary, began a survey of what he called "Folsom points" (another, later, style of fluted projectile point) found in Virginia. His survey involved recording and publishing his findings on these distinctive points in the quarterly bulletin of the newly formed Archeological Society of Virginia. The "McCary Fluted Point Survey," as it was to become known, became the vehicle through which the Williamson site was discovered in 1949. Forty-four years later, the McCary Fluted Point Survey also led to the pre-Clovis discovery at the Cactus Hill site, discussed later.

Technically, Williamson is not a single site but a "complex" of at least six sites centered on an outcrop of Coastal Plain chert, from which most of the Williamson artifacts were made. Because of the association, this stone type is now commonly referred to as "Williamson chert." The chert seems to have been the primary reason that Paleo-American hunter-gatherers chose that location in which to congregate. The vast number of Williamson chert Paleo-American artifacts identified over the last 60 years from the Williamson complex and surrounding counties in southeastern Virginia indicate that the complex was a hub of activity lasting throughout the Paleo-American period in the region.

In the 1960s members of the Archeological Society of Virginia found a new Paleo-American site, located in the Shenandoah Valley near Front Royal, Virginia. They reported the site to Dr. William Gardner of Catholic University. Subsequent testing and archaeological field schools by Catholic University led to the discovery of another major quarry-centered site complex, which they called Thunderbird. This complex was situated on a large jasper stone outcrop and was the site of one of the largest concentrations of Paleo-American activity yet discovered. Unlike Williamson, Thunderbird and related sites were deeply stratified, buried under up to four feet of sediment. The site is so well preserved

A Cactus Hill point held in hand.   [Michael F. Johnson]

that it reveals distinct areas where one can detect the "shadow" of where a person sat while making a stone tool. It is also possible that the site contains the remains of posts from a large structure, possibly built by the Paleo-American inhabitants.

The Williamson and Thunderbird complexes have provided Virginia archaeologists with not one but two opportunities to look at how Paleo-American hunter-gatherers settled on the landscape. Virginia archaeologists now believe that the people who made Virginia's Clovis period artifacts were organized into small groups, called "micro-bands," each of which occupied a distinct territory throughout most of their lives. Groups of these micro-bands maintained wider family relationships with neighboring micro-bands. One of the important ways these social, and perhaps economic, relationships were reinforced was for a related group of micro-bands to periodically meet at a major quarry, such as Williamson or Thunderbird. Archeologists call these larger groups of micro-bands "macro-bands." Archeologists think there were at least two Clovis period macro-bands in Virginia and they were centered on the Williamson and Thunderbird quarries.

Although Williamson and Thunderbird are the most famous Paleo-American site complexes in Virginia, many other contemporary but smaller sites have been found across the state. The McCary Fluted Point Survey has also recorded more than 1,000 Clovis points from these sites and other

isolated contexts. It has always been a problem for Virginia archaeologists to explain how such a well-established Paleo-American culture as Clovis could have suddenly appeared out of nowhere in Virginia and the rest of North America. A possible answer came with the discovery of the Cactus Hill site.

Following up on investigations of Clovis points reported to the McCary Fluted Point Survey, archaeologists in the 1990s discovered evidence of pre-Clovis human activity at the Cactus Hill site in southeastern Virginia. Coupled with evidence from other sites in the Americas, the evidence from Cactus Hill would help reopen the debate about the chronology and nature of the initial peopling of the Americas.

In the mid-1990s two teams of archaeologists, working independently, found distinct stone blades, cores, tools, and points in stratified context below the well-established 13,000 BP (before the present) Clovis levels on the site. These stone artifacts were not only different from the Clovis artifacts found immediately above but even more different from the later Archaic and Woodland artifacts stratigraphically above the Clovis layer. One team, headed by Joseph M. McAvoy, obtained radio carbon dates on both the Clovis and deeper pre-Clovis levels. The Clovis date calibrated to approximately 13,000 BP and the pre-Clovis date to almost 18,000 BP.

The fact that points (probably for spears) identical to the early Cactus Hill points had been recorded on numerous surface sites in southeastern Virginia indicated that the people who used them knew the area and had settled into patterns that reflected

An excellent shot of the detailed excavation at Cactus Hill.   [Michael F. Johnson]

an intimate understanding of the local environment. In other words, these earliest groups of regional inhabitants were successfully adapted. This assumption fits well with what had already been learned from the Williamson and Thunderbird site complexes with regard to the Clovis settlement patterns.

With most of the rest of Cactus Hill having been destroyed by artifact hunters, archaeologists in the region have turned to searching for other sites like it. Only through the diligent and careful methods used by professional archaeologists can we hope to tease out the sensitive scientific data that will tell us who the pre-Clovis people were and where they came from.

Further Reading: Gardner, William M., ed., *The Flint Run Paleo-Indian Complex: A Preliminary Report 1971–73 Seasons*, Occasional Publication No. 1 (Washington, DC: Catholic University of America, Department of Anthropology, Archeology Laboratory, 1974); Johnson, Michael F., "Paleoindians Near the Edge: A Virginia Perspective," in *The Paleoindian and Early Archaic Southeast*, edited by David G. Anderson and Kenneth E. Sassaman (Tuscaloosa: University of Alabama, 1996); McAvoy, Joseph M., *Nottoway River Survey—Part I: Clovis Settlement Patterns*, Research Report No. 1 (Sandston, VA: Nottoway River Publications, 1992); McAvoy, Joseph M., and Lynn D. McAvoy, *Archeological Investigations of Site 44SX202, Cactus Hill, Sussex County, Virginia*, Research Report Series No. 8 (Richmond: Virginia Department of Historic Resources, 1996); McCary, Ben C., *Survey of Virginia Fluted Points*, Special Publication No. 12 (Richmond: Archeological Society of Virginia, 1991); Wittkofski, J. Mark, and Theodore R. Reinhart, eds., *Paleoindian Research in Virginia: A Synthesis*, Special Publication No. 19 (Richmond: Archeological Society of Virginia, 1989).

Michael F. Johnson

LAKE CHAMPLAIN AREA ANCIENT SITES

Vermont and New York
Ancient Sites Around the Lake

The Lake Champlain basin provides an important north-south travel corridor between the Atlantic coast and the St. Lawrence valley in conjunction with the Hudson valley, with possible connections to the east and west as well. The Green Mountains and the Adirondack Mountains bound the Lake Champlain drainage basin to the east and west, respectively. The Champlain basin has been variably occupied throughout the span of Native American/First Nations occupation in the glaciated portion of northeastern North America, that is, over the past 11,000 years or so, since the time of a local marine invasion during the Late Pleistocene epoch in the Northeast. However, many Native activities were seemingly concentrated on or near the lake proper, because of its ecological richness. The pre-European Native occupational record can be outlined based on long-term avocational collecting and professional excavations, primarily consulting archaeology work before development. This record can be divided into three periods locally: the Paleoindian period, 9000–7000 BC; the Archaic period, 7000–1000 BC; and the Woodland period, 1000 BC–AD 1600.

The earliest occupation of the Champlain basin is marked by occasional discovery of Early Paleoindian fluted projectile points, like those found in most other areas of North America. Of local Early Paleoindian evidence, the Reagen and Davis sites are probably the two best known, but other Early Paleoindian sites have been recently discovered. Late Paleoindian occupation, after the abandonment of fluted points for the use of parallel-flaked ones, also is represented in the basin, at the Reagan site and other new discoveries that date to around the time of the transition from the Late Pleistocene Ice Age to the post–Ice Age period, the Holocene epoch. During the subsequent Archaic period, human populations in the basin began to grow rapidly as environmental conditions moderated and new technologies were developed to harvest and process key resources. Local Native populations seemingly reached their peak densities by about 6,000 to 5,000 years ago and thereafter during the Late Archaic period, with varying connections to other areas of eastern North America during the Archaic period. The local record for the Early Archaic period is best marked by the recently discovered John's Bridge site, while the Late Archaic period is best known at the KI and Otter Creek No. 2 sites, along with a few others.

By about 3,000 years ago at the onset of the Woodland period, local Native populations in the Champlain basin were well connected to other groups in eastern North America through intensive trade networks, and they added pottery to their technological repertoire. They also shared in dramatic mortuary practices during the end of the Archaic period and Early Woodland times, as locally represented by the Isle La Motte and Boucher sites, among others. Trade continued into the Middle Woodland period between about 2,000 and 1,000 years ago, but seemingly diminished to a large degree when the Late Woodland began, around AD 1000, at the time that farming became locally common in warmer basin settings. The Winooski, Donahue, and Headquarters sites document this transition from hunting and gathering to simple farming in the basin, and the Bohannon site documents the local emergence of proto-Iroquoian peoples after AD 1300. The arrival of Samuel de Champlain in 1609, a Frenchman who gave his name to the lake, marks the end of the prehistoric era, by which time most Native groups had been forced out of the basin by intertribal competition and open hostilities. Only the Paleoindian and Archaic period sites noted above are discussed here due to space constraints.

THE REAGEN SITE, HIGHGATE, VERMONT

The Reagen site in northwestern Vermont was one of the very first Paleoindian sites discovered in the Northeast during the late 1920s or early 1930s by several avocational artifact collectors. Situated on a Late Pleistocene landform about 100 m above the Missisquoi River and back about 13 km from modern Lake Champlain, the Reagen site covers about 8,000 square meters of an eroding sandy ridge top, with a commanding view of the river about 1.3 km away. Once the significance of fluted points had been demonstrated by finds in the American Plains and Southwest, the Reagen site was conclusively related to these discoveries by the New York State Archaeologist, William A. Ritchie. In 1953 Ritchie initially summarized 179 Reagen tools and ornaments in five major categories, plus additional flake specimens, and about ten or eleven different raw materials. Fluted points and nonfluted points were both present, as were other bifaces, but uniface scrapers and other, similar tools predominated. In 1957 Ritchie published photographs of most of these specimens. Ritchie clearly recognized that this was an Early Paleoindian site, and he correctly suspected that it dates toward the end of this period. He further surmised that subsequent Late Paleoindian evidence is also represented at Reagen. Recent re-analysis of surviving portions of the Reagen collection by the present author demonstrates the general accuracy of Ritchie's early report, especially in terms of the multiple occupations, although he did not necessarily recognize the different stages of lithic reduction represented. Local Champlain valley chert and quartzite is represented in the recently studied collection, along with nonlocal cherts from New York State and rhyolites from Maine and New Hampshire, among other exotic sources.

THE DAVIS SITE, CROWN POINT, NEW YORK

Like Reagen, the Davis site was discovered by an avocational archaeologist and analyzed and reported by William Ritchie in the 1960s, but in this case the site is situated only about 37 m above the current level of Lake Champlain near the lake shore in New York State. The Davis site is known from a small collection of ten lithic specimens recovered over an area of about 1,300–1,400 square meters. It produced five fluted points, which seem to be earlier than the Reagen examples, but not of the earliest regional form, such as those at the Bull Brook site in eastern Massachusetts. Five uniface tools are also represented at Davis. Possibly local and nonlocal cherts and jaspers are represented in the Davis collection.

THE JOHN'S BRIDGE SITE, SWANTON, VERMONT

The John's Bridge site was discovered in 1979; one part of the site was investigated as part of a cultural resource management study in advance of new bridge construction across the Missisquoi River in northwestern Vermont. Situated close to the river on a bedrock knoll, John's Bridge is a small campsite attributable to the Early Archaic period and is radiocarbon dated to about 8,100 years ago, or 6100–6200 BC. An excavation area of about 33 square meters produced eleven newly recognized "Swanton corner-notched" projectile points, biface point preforms, tabular "choppers," uniface scrapers, and other tools, as well as over 23,000 flakes. Small amounts of mammal (possible deer) and catfish bones were also recovered. Notably, unlike the overwhelming majority of Paleoindian finds, virtually all of the lithics at John's Bridge seem to have been manufactured from local Champlain basin lithic sources, suggesting a much more locally focused mobility for the Archaic hunter-gatherers here relative to their Paleoindian predecessors.

THE KI SITE, RUTLAND COUNTY, VERMONT

The KI, or Ketcham's Island, site is situated on a low bedrock knoll island adjacent to the Otter Creek in the south-central portion of the Champlain basin. Extensively excavated by several avocational archaeologists in the late 1950s and early 1960s, this site was later tested and briefly reported by William Ritchie. It is a classic representation of the earliest portion of the Late Archaic period, or the Vergennes phase of the Laurentian tradition, but there are

no reliable radiocarbon dates for KI. One circular structure, about 4.6 m in diameter and marked by post molds and a low earth mound, may represent a small house at KI. A single, poorly preserved human skeleton with red ocher was associated with this structure. Deer and bear bones were also recovered. Along with many flakes, about 218 lithic tools and a single native copper tool were recovered, of which most are hunting and processing tools. The "Otter Creek side-notched" points, slate points and ulu knives, stone abrading rods, and spear thrower weights are most distinctive, clearly reflecting the Laurentian tradition. The copper specimen is a gorge (presumably used for fishing). With the exception of the copper, virtually all of the tools represent locally available Champlain basin lithic materials, and as with John's Bridge, one can infer a locally focused hunter-gatherer population.

THE OTTER CREEK NO. 2 SITE, RUTLAND COUNTY, VERMONT

Like KI, the Otter Creek No. 2 site is situated on a low bedrock knoll island near the Otter Creek, and it produced a remarkably similar set of artifacts, again attributable to the Vergennes phase of the Laurentian tradition. The Otter Creek No. 2 site was excavated by another set of avocational archaeologists and Ritchie during the 1970s; they identified a small Vergennes phase locus about 135 square meters in size within the context of larger multiple occupation deposits spanning the Late Paleoindian to Woodland periods. A single radiocarbon date of about 5,100 years ago, or 3100–3200 BC, seems to accurately date the Vergennes phase occupation at the Otter Creek No. 2 site.

Otter Creek No. 2 also produced a Vergennes-related sample of over 200 tool specimens, including five or six native copper gorges, 13 bone and antler tools, and 186 lithic tools and other remains, along with many flakes. Of the Vergennes phase lithic tools at Otter Creek No. 2, "Otter Creek side-notched" points, slate points and ulus, and stone rod abraders are the most distinctive. Six human burials, including four children and two adults, may be related but could not be dated. None included obvious mortuary goods, except one that had an associated dog burial. Vergennes-related food remains at Otter Creek No. 2 apparently include deer, bear, beaver, muskrat, possible dog, turkey, other birds, and turtles. This site seemingly represents the typical economy within the context of the Champlain basin all through the Archaic and Woodland periods before the local advent of substantial farming during the Late Woodland period, although non-subsistence aspects of the economy clearly changed well before subsistence did.

Further Reading: Haviland, William A., and Majory W. Power, *The Original Vermonters: Native Inhabitants, Past and Present*, rev. ed. (Hanover, NH: University Press of New England, 1994);

Petersen, James B., "Preceramic Archaeological Manifestations in the Far Northeast: A Review of Recent Research," *Archaeology of Eastern North America* 23 (1995): 207–230; Petersen, James B., "Foreword: West Athens Hill, the Paleoindian Period, and Robert E. Funk in Northeastern Perspective," in *An Ice Age Quarry-Workshop: The West Athens Hill Site Revisited*, by Robert E. Funk, New York State Museum Bulletin 504 (Albany: University of New York State Education Department, 2004), xi–xlix; Ritchie, William A., "A Probable Paleo-Indian Site in Vermont," *American Antiquity* 18(3) (1953): 249–258; Ritchie, William A., *Traces of Early Man in the Northeast*, New York State Museum and Science Service Bulletin 358 (Albany: University of the State of New York, 1957); Ritchie,

William A., *The Archaeology of New York State*, rev. ed. (Garden City, NY: Natural History Press, 1969); Ritchie, William A., "The Otter Creek No. 2 Site in Rutland County, Vermont," *Bulletin and Journal of the Archaeology of New York State* 76 (1979): 1–21; Thomas, Peter A., "The Early and Middle Archaic Periods as Represented in Western Vermont," in *Early Holocene Occupation in Northern New England*, edited by Brian S. Robinson, James B. Petersen, and Ann K. Robinson (Augusta: Maine Historic Preservation and Maine Archaeological Society, 1992), 187–203; Thomas, Peter A. "Vermont Archaeology Comes of Age: A Perspective on Vermont's Prehistoric Past," *Journal of Vermont Archaeology* 1 (1994): 38–91.

James B. Petersen

LAMOKA LAKE AND NATIVE AMERICAN ARCHAEOLOGY OF NEW YORK

Central New York State

Ancient and Early Historic Period Native American Sites

INTRODUCTION

Central New York includes major rivers that meander across low-lying land bordering Lake Ontario, one of the Great Lakes of North America. South from this plain is a significant rise in elevation leading up to the Allegheny Plateau. On the plateau are the narrow Finger Lakes, remnants of melted glacial ice. From these lakes flow the creeks that merge into south-flowing rivers, such as the Susquehanna, which attracted generations of early peoples, whose histories are buried within these valleys.

People walked the lands of central New York as early as 12,000 years ago, (10,000 BC), stalking elephant-like mammoth and mastodon, as well as small animals and migratory waterfowl. Forays into this region continued long after the large mammals became extinct (ca. 8000 BC). However, it was not until a period known as the Late Archaic (ca. 4000–1500 BC) that the migratory hunter-gatherers began to call this region home. The sites created by these peoples take us on a journey through time starting with their nomadic beginnings, and culminating in the formation of the powerful *Haudenosaunee* (Iroquois) Confederacy of Nations.

LAMOKA LAKE, SCHUYLER COUNTY, NEW YORK

Nestled between two of the "minor Finger Lakes" (Waneta and Lamoka) on the Allegheny Plateau, the archaeological site at Lamoka Lake defines an important part of the Late

Archaic period (4000–1500 BC). What archaeologists call the Lamoka culture refers to groups who used narrow-stemmed stone projectile points as tips for spears or javelins, and worked wood with a stone tool called a beveled adze. The people of the Lamoka culture moved their camps seasonally but also established large camps at the shallow ends of the Finger Lakes. The discovery of the Lamoka Lake site spurred new interpretations about year-round settlements during an era when hunter-gatherer groups were assumed to have moved frequently.

In 1925 Dr. William A. Ritchie, State Archaeologist of New York, began a series of excavations at Lamoka Lake. These excavations identified an unusually large site, covering 2.5 acres maximum, many times larger than the typical sites of this era. Ritchie and his associates made several astounding discoveries. The site contained an extensive "midden," an accumulation of decomposed organic refuse that contained thousands of stone artifacts, animal bones, and nutshells. Archaeologists uncovered a multitude of small round stains from decayed wooden posts forming several rectangular patterns. These characteristics suggest that the site was occupied on a year-round basis, or at least semi-permanently. Ritchie interpreted these patterns as houses, and estimated that the site could have housed as many as 150 to 200 people.

Researchers also found over 8,000 "netsinkers" (notched stones used to anchor fishing nets), bone hooks, and numerous fish bones. The midden and cooking hearths contained the bones of many large and small mammals. Also, there were large quantities of charred acorns, indicating that the Lamoka people relied heavily on nuts to support their resident population. A series of carbon-14 dates derived from charred wood and nuts indicated that people lived at the site from 2800 to 2200 BC.

Human burials on the site showed that most of the people were slender with elongated heads. Some of the people died violent deaths; one skull fracture was fatal, and another person had several wounds from projectile points. The inference from these is that some form of warfare, possibly raids by other groups, threatened the inhabitants of the site.

The Lamoka Lake site is privately owned and protected; it is not open for public visitation. A visual interpretation of the site is presented at the New York State Museum in Albany.

BREWERTON: OBERLANDER AND ROBINSON SITES, ONONDAGA COUNTY

A decade after the excavations at Lamoka Lake, Ritchie visited the lakeside community of Brewerton. In the shadow of eighteenth-century Fort Brewerton, the Oneida River rises from the foot of Oneida Lake and meanders across the Ontario lakeplain. Ritchie explored several areas along both banks of the river; two of these areas were the Oberlander and Robinson sites. Expecting to see Lamoka traits, Ritchie was surprised to find different kinds of artifacts. He interpreted these as belonging to a different ancient culture that he called Brewerton. As with Lamoka, Brewerton characterized a hunter-gatherer lifestyle that involved seasonal movements of small groups of people among a regular series of sites. The outlet of Oneida Lake proved to be an advantageous location for larger, and longer-term, settlements.

Brewerton is distinct from Lamoka in many ways. The people were more robust than the slender individuals who lived at Lamoka Lake. The artifact assemblage contained broad-bladed projectile points that were usually notched at the base. These points greatly outnumbered other tool types, resulting in interpretations of Brewerton as specialized hunters in contrast to Lamoka fishers. Brewerton sites also yielded an unusual variety of woodworking tools: adzes, celts, gouges, and drills. In combination with tools made of native copper from the western Great Lakes, these traits suggested a people who traveled extensively in canoes along the east-west series of Great Lakes.

Brewerton sites also produced a group of different tools related to fishing: stone plummets, bone harpoons, and sharp bone needles, referred to as gorges. People of the Brewerton culture focused their fishing efforts on seasonal fish runs into Oneida Lake by funneling them into stone structures (weirs),

where they were speared or caught on lines of bone gorges anchored by stone plummets.

The two sites at Brewerton were large (3 and 2 acres, respectively), with thick refuse middens. It is likely that these sites housed substantial numbers of people. A small group may have remained throughout the year to protect the rich hunting and fishing grounds. Smaller sites with Brewerton points are found throughout central New York in many contexts (small streams, lakes, uplands, and marshes). However, none of these smaller sites contains the wealth and diversity of artifacts found at Brewerton.

From the vantage point of eighteenth-century Fort Brewerton, a restored historical site, the landscape that once housed the ancient Brewerton sites can be viewed. The Fort Brewerton Historical Society (Route 11, Brewerton) houses collections from this "prehistoric capital" of New York.

THE OWASCO HEARTLAND: ROUNDTOP AND CASTLE CREEK, BROOME COUNTY

Around AD 900, sites in central New York show early evidence of agriculture and village life. A series of sites near the confluence of the Susquehanna and Chenango rivers illustrates these ancestral Iroquoian occupations, often referred to as the Owasco culture.

The Roundtop site in Endicott, New York, provided the first evidence of Owasco village life found by archaeologists. Recorded by Arthur C. Parker, State Archeologist of New York, in the 1920s, the site was frequented by amateur archaeologists until the 1960s, when the New York State Museum and the State University of New York at Binghamton conducted extensive excavations. Researchers found at least two overlapping longhouses, hundreds of storage pits and hearths, and thousands of decorated pottery shards and stone artifacts. Roundtop captured nation-wide attention when analysts found maize, beans, and squash, the "Three Sisters" of Iroquois mythology. They dated charred wood from pits to AD 1070, yielding the earliest evidence of agriculture in the Northeast. During the 1990s a re-analysis of individual specimens using a more direct dating method (AMS) found early dates for charred maize found at the site, but much later dates (post–AD 1300) for beans. However, Roundtop still stands as an early Owasco village site, with examples of the first longhouses occupied in central New York.

West of Roundtop on the Chenango River is the Castle Creek site, a village situated on a prominent knoll. Of particular note was the discovery of a "palisade," or ring of posts surrounding the rim of the knoll. Palisades typically denote a need for protection, but they might alternatively, or simultaneously, have symbolic meaning.

The site was discovered during commercial gravel mining operations in the 1920s, and Foster Disinger, the

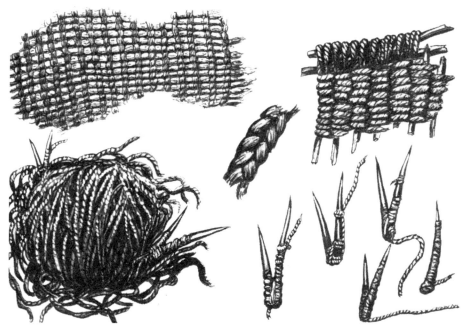

Castle Creek site cordage. Original is curated by the Broome County Historical Society, Roberson Museum, Binghamton, NY. [Courtesy of the Broome County Historical Society]

director of the Roberson Museum in Binghamton, funded an early excavation. William Ritchie followed with more intensive excavations in 1933. The site produced hundreds of post molds, interpreted as longhouse dwellings. Radiocarbon dates suggest that people lived at Castle Creek during AD 1200–1300.

Excavations revealed incredible preservation of cordage and bone. There were examples of twined and woven baskets made of basswood bast and hemp fiber. There also was a rare example of preserved fiber fish lines with attached fish hooks made from hawthorn spines. Bone and antler artifacts included picks, possibly used for planting; numerous needles made from bird bones; and awls. Many of these artifacts are curated at the Roberson Museum in Binghamton, and several are on display.

THE IROQUOIS HEARTLAND: BARNES AND McNAB, ONONDAGA COUNTY

By the fifteenth century AD, the archaeological evidence shows that people began to move to larger villages in the northern part of central New York. The sequential history of settlement in the Iroquois Heartland documents a gradual movement through time to the current homeland of each Haudenosaunee Nation. In central New York, the sequence describes the formation of the Onondaga Nation. Pivotal sites in that sequence are Barnes and McNab, the last villages before contact by European groups. These sites are also part of a "paired" sequence with similar sites in

nearby valleys that shared unique aspects of their material culture.

The McNab site is located on Chittenango Creek at the outlet of Cazenovia Lake. No published manuscripts exist on the site, but amateur archaeologists have shared their results with writers of regional books on the Onondaga. Much more is known about the Barnes site, which is located on Limestone Creek, about 2 miles west of Cazenovia. Both sites cover large areas, as much as 8 acres, with the potential to accommodate a substantial number of people. By this time, village locations had shifted to elevated plateaus bordered by ravines, but much less attention was paid to constructing protective palisades than in previous time periods. This suggests an era of decreased warfare, possibly related to the peace pact among the Iroquois Nations. Both sites also contained more ornaments and ritual objects than nearby sites, as well as demonstrating more embellishment of everyday items. For instance, the Barnes site produced a rare, well-preserved collection of polished bone artifacts, including fish hooks, weaving needles, harpoons, and awls. Adorning clay pipes and pottery at both sites were striking human face effigies, a rare occurrence for this time period. Finally, there were several polished pendants, slate disks with center holes, and beads. The material culture is a visual display of the rich cultural, ritual, and artistic traditions that formed the basis for the Onondaga peoples encountered by French, English, and Dutch visitors to the region in the seventeenth century.

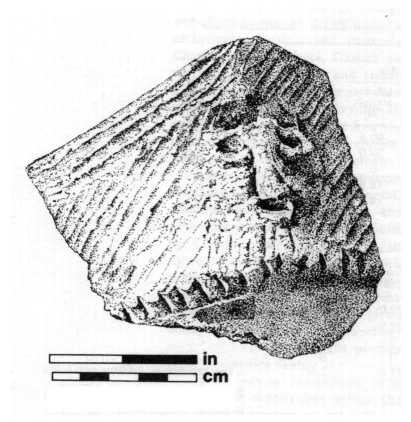

Barnes Site pottery shard with a face effigy. [Reprinted from *Evolution of the Onondaga Iroquois: Accommodating Change: 1500–1655* by James W. Bradley by permission of the University of Nebraska Press. © 1987 by James W. Bradley.]

Further Reading: Bradley, James, *Evolution of the Onondaga Iroquois* (Syracuse, NY: Syracuse University Press, 1987); Funk, Robert E., *Archaeological Investigations in the Upper Susquehanna Valley, New York State*, Vol. 1 (Buffalo, NY: Persimmon Press Monographs in Archaeology, 1993); Funk, Robert E., *Archaeological Investigations in the Upper Susquehanna Valley, New York State*, Vol. 2 (Buffalo, NY: Persimmon Press Monographs in Archaeology, 1998); Hart, John P., and Hetty Jo Brumbach, The Death of Owasco. *American Antiquity* 68(4):737-752; Ritchie, William A., *The Archaeology of New York State*, rev. ed. (Garden City, NY: Natural History Press, 1969); Ritchie, William A., and Robert E. Funk, *Aboriginal Settlement Patterns in the Northeast*, Memoir 20 (Albany: New York State Science Service, State Education Department, 1973); Tuck, James A., *Onondaga Iroquois Prehistory* (Syracuse, NY: Syracuse University Press, 1971); Versaggi, Nina M., *Hunter to Farmer: 10,000 Years of Susquehanna Valley Prehistory* (Binghamton, NY: Roberson Museum and Science Center, 1986).

Nina M. Versaggi

NATIVE AMERICAN SITES ON LONG ISLAND

Eastern Long Island, New York
Ancient to Historic Sites in Coastal New York

Archaeologists believe that Native Americans arrived in the Long Island Sound region sometime prior to 10,000 years ago and that for many thousands of years the island's harbors and coves were home to large populations of Native groups. Throughout at least the last five millennia of the prehistoric era, Native Long Islanders lived in permanently established coastal communities and seldom ventured far from their homes for any of life's basic necessities. Settlements on the region's protected shores provided easy access to food, industrial resources, and transportation

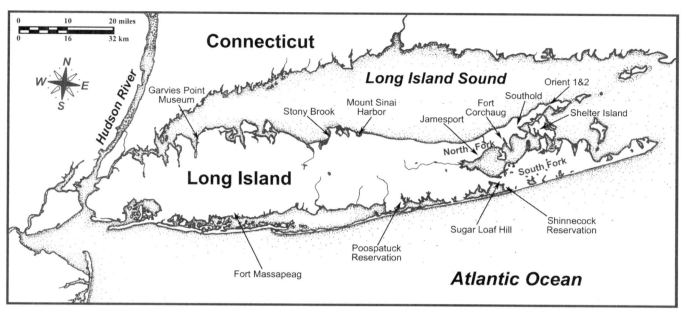

Important Native American sites on Long Island. [David J. Bernstein]

routes. Occasionally, they traded or traveled in order to obtain foreign products such as stone bowls or high-grade rocks for making chipped-stone tools, but their prime focus was always on the efficient utilization of resources found close at hand. Archaeological evidence suggests that an economy based on gathering, hunting, and fishing provided a resource base more than sufficient to support stable, enduring communities that were occupied more or less continuously throughout the year.

Researchers typically employ a system of three periods to divide the timespan between the first settlement of the region by Native peoples and the arrival of the European explorers and colonists in the sixteenth century (see Table 1). The earliest inhabitants of Long Island are usually termed Paleoindians. Although the date of their initial arrival is not certain, it is likely that they settled in the area not long after the retreat of the glacial ice that covered Long Island during the later stages of the Pleistocene glacial

epoch. The environment of Long Island was much different when it was first settled than it is today. Most important, Long Island was not an island at this time. Due to the lower level of the sea (sea level subsequently rose gradually due to melting of glacial ice), the shoreline of the Atlantic Ocean was hundreds of miles south of its present location. Further reflecting conditions of an early post–Ice Age landscape, the vegetation was relatively treeless and probably resembled the tundra of modern Alaska and northern Canada. Although little is known of Paleoindian lifeways, it is assumed (based on comparisons with modern hunting groups and archaeological information from better-known areas of the Northeast and North America) that group sizes were fairly small and that settlements were moved during the course of a typical year.

The Archaic period is characterized by the gradual development of modern environmental conditions. Humans adapted to the abundant resources provided by interior woodlands, ponds, and rivers as well as the coastal estuaries by exploiting a broad range of food (e.g., nuts, large and small game, seed-bearing plants, fish) and industrial products (stone for making tools and weapons, plants for baskets and textiles, bark for house construction, etc.). By 3000 BC Long Island was substantially populated, with inhabitants probably numbering in the thousands for the island as a whole. Archaeological evidence of this apparent population explosion is found in the tremendous number of archaeological sites dating to this period and by the size of the individual settlements, some of which exceed 10 acres.

The so-called Terminal Archaic period (1000–700 BC) is renowned for its elaborate funerary rituals (discussed later).

Table 1   Prehistoric Chronology for Long Island

Period	Approximate Dates
Late Woodland	AD 1000–1500
Middle Woodland	AD 0–1000
Early Woodland	700 BC–AD 0
Terminal Archaic	1000–700 BC
Late Archaic	4000–1000 BC
Middle Archaic	6000–4000 BC
Early Archaic	8000–6000 BC
Paleoindian	10,500–8000 BC

On Long Island, cemetery complexes containing cremated human and animal remains, stone bowls made from imported (from Rhode Island, Connecticut, or Pennsylvania) steatite (also known as soapstone), fishtail-shaped projectile points, red ocher, and other symbolically important materials date to this time. Locally, pottery makes its first appearance during the Terminal Archaic.

Archaeologically, little behavioral change is observable during the Woodland period. Some artifact forms (e.g., projectile point shape) are altered and pottery seems to become increasingly important over time, but the long-established economic pattern of the exploitation of a broad range of natural resources continues. During the Late Woodland (about AD 1000–1500), agriculture (especially corn and beans) became very important in the economies of native groups living along the Hudson River and in what is now upstate New York. The importance of agriculture on Long Island is still not well known and is a topic much debated by archaeologists. Regardless of the importance of foods such as corn, beans, and squash in the diet, it is clear that Native peoples on Long Island continued to hunt, gather, and collect the abundant products of the natural environment.

Native cultures were greatly changed with the European arrival in the fifteenth and sixteenth centuries. Infectious diseases took a heavy toll, and Indians were increasingly marginalized economically. However, even though Native communities were ravaged by diseases and social disruption, they were able to maintain many of their traditional lifeways. There was continuity in belief systems and the structure of social relations despite the horrendous impact of infectious diseases introduced by Europeans. These traditions continued well after European contact, and Native peoples still actively maintain their ancestral communities and cultures. They live today on state-recognized reservations (Shinnecock and Poospatuck) and in enclaves throughout Long Island.

ORIENT BURIALS
Archaeologically, Long Island is best known for a series of Native American mortuary sites called the Orient Burials that date to approximately 1000–700 BC. Named for the easternmost point on the North Fork of the island, the Orient Burials were first excavated in the 1930s by a group of avocational archaeologists led by a local farmer, Roy Latham. The Latham group excavated at four hilltop sites: Orient 1 and Orient 2 on the eastern end of the North Fork, Jamesport on the North Fork just east of the head of Peconic Bay, and Sugar Loaf Hill in the Shinnecock Hills on the South Fork. The avocationalists did not keep detailed records (even by early twentieth-century standards) of their excavations and the materials that they recovered; hence, most of the information on this ceremonial complex comes from the subsequent work of William Ritchie (1903–95), the longtime New York State Archaeologist. In the 1950s Ritchie re-excavated two of the sites (Jamesport and Sugar Loaf Hill) and published his

findings (including the first radiocarbon dates for the burial complex) along with the results from contemporary Native American domestic sites in the landmark book *The Stony Brook Site and Its Relation to Archaic and Transitional Cultures on Long Island.* Ritchie was able to determine that the Long Island burials were highly varied; some tombs housed the remains of single individuals, whereas others apparently contained the cremated remains from several deceased persons. The offerings from the Orient burial sites, especially the imported steatite bowls, the large deposits of powdered red ochre, and the fire-making kits comprised of iron pyrites and quartz strikers, are extraordinary but still await full interpretation.

Many of the materials excavated by Latham can be seen at the Southold Indian Museum on Bayview Road in Southold, New York. The museum is open to the public on Sundays from 1:30 to 4:30 pm, and by appointment.

SHELTER ISLAND AND MOUNT SINAI HARBOR
Most of the recent scientific research has taken place on Shelter Island and at Mount Sinai Harbor, and has been conducted by former and present archaeologists (especially Kent G. Lightfoot and David J. Bernstein) at the State University of New York at Stony Brook. Investigations in these locales have demonstrated the existence of fairly sedentary coastal communities of hunter-gatherer-fishers prior to the European arrival. As was the case in many of the mainland areas surrounding Long Island Sound, most essential activities were centered around tidal creeks and marshes. These were optimal locations for exploiting a diverse array of resources (coastal and terrestrial) and were chosen as the settings for residential bases.

The Garvies Point Museum and Preserve in Glen Cove, New York, has an excellent collection of Native American artifacts from the north shore of Long Island and elsewhere in the region. These materials are very typical of those routinely found by local archaeologists and are virtually identical to those recovered on Shelter Island and at Mount Sinai Harbor. The museum offers educational programs for school groups and the general public and is open Tuesday to Sunday from 10:00 am to 4:00 pm.

NATIVE AMERICAN FORTS
Among the more important of the seventeenth-century archaeological sites are the forts constructed by Native Americans along the coast of Long Island during the early years of European exploration and settlement. Current thinking holds that these were secure positions for the large-scale production and trade of wampum. These shell beads were mass-produced and used as currency by the European traders and colonists, and were the medium of exchange for the trading of furs with inland groups. In addition to serving as wampum manufacturing and trading centers, it is likely that the fortifications also served as refuges and strongholds

during times of conflict between Native groups. The best known of the forts is Fort Corchaug, located on Downs Creek on the North Fork of the island in the town of Southold. Initially documented in the 1930s and 1940s by the famed archaeologist Ralph Solecki, Fort Corchaug was more thoroughly excavated in the 1960s by Lorraine Williams as part of her doctoral research at New York University. It is estimated that the roughly 34,000-square-foot wooden fort and the immediate surrounding area were utilized by the Corchaug Indians from the 1630s to the 1660s.

Fort Corchaug is a National Historic Landmark and, along with the contemporary Fort Massapeag Archaeological Site in Oyster Bay, is one of only two Native American archaeological sites on Long Island listed in the National Register of Historic Places. Administered by the Peconic Land Trust, the Fort Corchaug and Downs Farm Preserve is open daily and features a small visitor center and marked walking trails.

Further Reading: Bernstein, David J., "Long-Term Continuity in the Archaeological Record from the Coast of New York and Southern New England, USA," *Journal of Island and Coastal Archaeology* 1 (2006): 271–284; Ritchie, William A., *The Stony Brook Site and Its Relation to Archaic and Transitional Cultures on Long Island,* Bulletin 372 (Albany: New York State Museum and Science Service, 1959); Strong, John A., *The Algonquian Peoples of Long Island from Earliest Times to 1700* (Interlaken, NY: Empire State Books, 1997).

David J. Bernstein

ANCIENT ARCHAEOLOGY OF THE LOWER CONNECTICUT RIVER VALLEY

Along the Connecticut River in Connecticut
Ancient Life Along the Lower Connecticut River

The Connecticut River is the dominant watercourse in New England. Along its 655-kilometer (407-mile) passage from north to south, it demarcates the border between Vermont and New Hampshire, passes through western Massachusetts, bisects the state of Connecticut, and then flows into Long Island Sound in the town of Old Saybrook. Its original name and transliteration, *Quinnehtukqut*, meaning "beside the long tidal river," was bestowed by the aboriginal residents of its lower reaches, and the river has long been a defining resource for the people living within its valley and along its many tributaries. The *Quinnehtukqut* supplied an abundance of food for human consumption, especially in the form of freshwater fish and shellfish. It dominates the local landscape through its meandering and yearly flooding, providing fertile soil suitable for agriculture and serving as a major artery for trade and transportation. Human beings have long been aware of the productivity of the river, establishing their camps, villages, forts, and cities within its broad valley.

Excavations by the Public Archaeology Survey Team (PAST) from the University of Connecticut and by John Pfeiffer (1986) during the 1980s at the Dill Farm Site in East Haddam provide a glimpse into aboriginal settlement of the Connecticut River Valley, especially during the Early Archaic period, about 8,000 years ago. The Dill family found and collected over a dozen bifurcate-based projectile points on their farm, artifacts diagnostic of the Early Archaic period. Additionally, three bifurcate-based points along with secondary retouch flakes were recovered in subsequent excavations by PAST and Pfeiffer. One of four features excavators identified at the site, a basin-shaped hearth, contained hazelnut and walnut fragments, suggesting a fall occupation or possible storage beyond the seasonal availability of these nut foods (Pfeiffer, personal communication 1986). A radiocarbon sample obtained from this feature yielded a date of 8560 ± 270 years BP. Pfeiffer believes that the quartz quarry blocks and large flakes recovered from another site feature represent a cache and this "indicates that the site was important enough to be scheduled into the seasonal round and periodically revisited" (Pfeiffer 1986, 31). Whether this represents the emergence of regular seasonal movements to exploit natural food resources occurring in different parts of the territory settled by the human cultures that occupied the river valley is still being studied.

Further north in the Connecticut valley, stone projectile points and other artifacts recovered from the WMECO site located within the Riverside Archaeological District near the Connecticut River in Gill, Massachusetts, (Thomas 1980) indicate a nearly continuous sequence of occupations from the Middle Archaic through Middle Woodland periods (about 7,000 to about 1,500 years ago). Stone tools, including scrapers, drills, oval-shaped blades, flake knives, large hammerstones, and choppers, from the lowest excavation levels suggest that a variety of activities occurred during the early occupation of the site. Rapids and falls at this stretch of the Connecticut River obstructed the progress of large numbers of salmon and shad that ascended the river during the spring and summer, enough that they could be caught with spears and seines. Fish elements found in the faunal assemblage at WMECO provide clear evidence of the importance of this resource in the diet of the groups that lived at this site. In addition, the surrounding wetlands and uplands provided a variety of resources that must have been important considerations in the selection of this site by Native American groups. Thomas (1980) suggested that these resources may have been sufficient for seasonal gatherings of "small" bands (about 25 people). Growth rings on fish vertebrae, believed to be those of anadromous shad, and reptilian elements (snake and turtle) recovered through careful excavation of archaeological deposits suggest that this site was occupied during the spring through summer over the earliest portion of its use, in the Middle Archaic period.

Located in South Windsor, Connecticut, on the east bank of the Connecticut River, Woodchuck Knoll was a Late Archaic occupation of the river floodplain (McBride 1984). Its excavation was directed by then State Archaeologist Douglas F. Jordan of the University of Connecticut. The location appears to have been occupied twice, as there are two stratigraphically distinct occupation layers. The older layer has produced radiocarbon dates that indicate a short-lived occupation a little more than 3,500 years ago. Artifacts recovered through excavation include a corner-notched Brewerton projectile point, a style typical for the site's Late Archaic period of occupation. The far more extensive upper layer at the site dates to about 3,220 years ago. The upper layer is thicker and is rich and dark in organic waste, including charcoal, floral remains, and bits of bone. The density and extent of the layer suggest a far larger and longer occupation, representing what appears to have been a semi-permanent base camp that likely was part of a broad settlement pattern that included hunting camps and food gathering stations located away from the home base (McBride 1984).

The site's excavators recovered an abundance of small-stemmed quartz spear points in the occupation of 3,220 years ago. Also recovered were caches of split quartz cobbles, a product of the primary step in the production of stone tools. Excavators also found a large number of quartz waste flakes, which together with the split cobbles indicate that stone tool manufacturing and maintenance were important activities at the site.

Food remains recovered by archaeologist Kevin McBride (1984) in his analysis of the soil from the many storage and cooking features excavated at Woodchuck Knoll indicate the use of a broad range of natural foods in the subsistence of the site's inhabitants. McBride found the remains of hickory nuts and walnuts, as well as the seeds of goosefoot (*Chenopodium*) and American lotus. These foods would have been available

in the late summer through fall, and this suggests that the site was occupied at least during these seasons. Of course, the ability to store food can extend a village's occupation beyond the seasons during which the foods can be harvested. Of interest in this regard is the fact that McBride found the remains of granary weevils (*Situphilus* sp.) in some of the features. As these insects currently are found in stored grain, their presence at Woodchuck Knoll is an indicator that the site's inhabitants were storing seeds for future use.

Excavations by the Albert Morgan Chapter of the Archaeological Society of Connecticut and testing by the Public Archaeology Survey Team during the mid-1970s through the early 1980s at Salmon Cove in East Haddam yielded Susquehanna Tradition projectile points and related artifacts, typically dated to about 3,000 years ago. Whether the appearance of this style of "broad blade" in the lower Connecticut River valley reflects the migration of new groups into the area, a technological development by groups already in the area, or the result of trade has yet to be resolved (Snow 1980). If new groups did enter southern New England with distinctive new projectile point styles, their occupations seem to coincide with the presence of indigenous groups using narrow-stem projectile points because both types of projectile points appear at many sites. The settlement systems of human groups during this time period appear to have focused on riverine settings, specifically terrace edges, with floodplains and uplands being used for task-specific activities and temporary camps (McBride 1984). PAST reported that the Salmon River Cove I site was a village settlement encompassing approximately 10,000 square meters. In addition to the projectile points, flakes, various stone tools, and ceramics were recovered at the site.

The Loomis II site is located on the west bank of the Connecticut just south of its confluence with the Farmington River in the town of Windsor, Connecticut (Feder 1981). Dating to 1,950 years ago, Loomis II is an Early Woodland occupation of the Connecticut valley. Researchers from the Farmington River Archaeological Project recovered an array of stone tools at the site, including Jack's Reef corner-notched projectile points and large quantities of lithic debitage (the waste products from chipped-stone tool manufacturing). Ceramics at the site included stamped and cord-marked shards. Faunal and botanical remains recovered from cooking locales include the bones of whitetail deer and an assortment of nuts, including acorns, hickory nuts, and chestnuts.

Loomis II's location at the confluence of a navigable north-south watercourse, the Connecticut, and a significant and similarly navigable tributary, the Farmington, likely enabled the site's inhabitants to take advantage of the extensive trade networks that were becoming established in the Woodland period. The geographic diversity of the sources of raw materials used by Loomis II's inhabitants to produce tools is evident in the lithic assemblage. Whereas the overwhelming majority of lithics, both tools and debitage, at Late Archaic sites such as Woodchuck Knoll were of locally available quartz, large percentages of the stone tools and waste flakes recovered at Loomis II were flint and jasper, materials not available in the Connecticut and Farmington River valleys. These "exotic" raw materials found at Loomis II, and that appear in increasing frequency during the course of the Woodland, are superior to most locally available rock in the Connecticut valley in that they are easier to flake and can more readily produce a sharp cutting edge. The most likely source for the flint recovered at Loomis II is the Hudson valley of New York State, and the jasper may have originated in the Delaware River, separating Pennsylvania from New York State.

To the south, in Lyme, Connecticut, archaeologists from the Public Archaeology Survey Team have excavated the Selden Island site. Radiocarbon-dated to approximately 1,000 years ago, Selden Island was home to a Middle Woodland sedentary village. Researchers estimate that they have excavated only about 2 percent of the site and have found more than 2,000 lithic artifacts and 1,000 ceramic shards derived from more than 50 pottery vessels.

A broad subsistence base is indicated by the wealth of faunal and botanical remains recovered from the numerous storage and refuse pits found at Selden Island. The bones of whitetail deer, turtle, squirrel, woodchuck, and assorted birds and fish reflect the significance of hunting in the residents' diet. Remains of acorn and hickory as well as blackberry and bayberry reflect the exploitation of plant resources.

The overall appearance of Selden Island is that of a sedentary village. The rich and clearly demarcated living surface, the density of storage features, and the presence of what appears to be a ceramics manufacturing area support this construct. Following the pattern seen at Loomis II, Selden Island lithics include a broad array of raw materials, including a sizable percentage of nonlocal stone.

European colonists recognized the fertility of the soils in the Connecticut valley as well as the value of the river as an avenue for trade and commerce. The 1633 Dutch settlement in the area of present-day Hartford and the English settlements in Windsor and Wethersfield in the 1633 and 1635, respectively, reflect this recognition. Clearly, the Connecticut valley has a long history of human settlement. The archaeology of the Connecticut valley is illuminating that lengthy history.

Further Reading: Feder, Kenneth L., "Waste Not, Want Not: Differential Lithic Utilization and Efficiency of Use," *North American Archaeologist* 2(3) (1981): 193–205; McBride, Kevin A., "Prehistory of the Lower Connecticut River Valley," Ph.D. diss. (University of Connecticut, Storrs, 1984); Pfeiffer, John E., "Dill Farm Locus I: Early and Middle Archaic Components in Southern Connecticut," *Bulletin of the Archaeological Society of Connecticut* 49 (1986): 19–35; Snow, Dean, *The Archaeology of New England* (New York: Academic Press, 1980); Thomas, Peter A., "The Riverside District, the WMECO Site, and Suggestions for Archaeological Modeling," in *Early and Middle Archaic Cultures in the Northeast*, edited by David R. Starbuck and Charles E. Bolian, Occasional Publications in Northeastern Anthropology (Rindge, NH: Franklin Pierce College, 1980), 73–96.

Kenneth L. Feder and Marc L. Banks

BOSTON HARBOR ISLANDS AND OTHER ANCIENT SITES

Boston, Massachusetts, and Nearby

Ancient Sites Around and Under the Modern City

BOSTON HARBOR ISLANDS, BOSTON HARBOR, MASSACHUSETTS

The Boston Harbor Islands are listed in the National Register of Historic Places, as an archaeological district comprising twenty-one of the thirty-four islands located within Boston Harbor. The district includes pre-contact Native American sites on islands located in six cities or towns (Boston, Hingham, Hull, Quincy, Weymouth, and Winthrop) across three counties (Suffolk, Norfolk, and Plymouth). The islands are all owned by the Commonwealth or its municipalities, except for Thompson Island, which is privately held.

Long recognized by archaeologists for its important prehistoric archaeological resources, the Boston Harbor Islands District contains a wide variety of archaeological sites dating to the Early Archaic through Late Woodland periods (about 9,000–500 years ago). In addition, there are historic-period Native American sites dating to the sixteenth and seventeenth centuries.

Native American use of the harbor islands differed from island to island through time and from season to season. In the earliest period of human occupation (9,000–5,000 years ago), the islands were actually small hills situated on a broad coastal plain traversed by river and wetlands. As the sea level rose, estuaries and tidal mudflats formed. This habitat was rich not only in marine and anadromous fish (fish that migrate upriver to spawn, typically in large numbers during certain seasons) but also in shellfish; coastal, sea, and migratory fowl; and other coastal resources. Eventually (about 3,000–2,500 years ago), as the rise of sea level slowed, the outer hills of this coastal plain became harbor islands, and the inner hills became part of a system of intertidal mudflats and coves that were a primary source of soft-shell clams. The Boston Harbor Islands are the only intact remnants of this ecologically diverse native landscape in the Boston area. Most of the Native American sites on the mainland have been destroyed or are deeply covered by modern development.

Archaeological evidence of the ancient Native American utilization of this changing environment illustrates the flexibility of human adaptation to climatic changes and sea level rise. Preliminary analysis of the distribution of the islands' archaeological sites indicates that the islands located closer to the present mainland were used seasonally from the earliest times through the Late Woodland and historic periods, and the outer islands were not used until the most recent precontact times (Middle and Late Woodland periods, about 2,000–500 years ago), and then only seasonally.

The main type of prehistoric archaeological site found on the islands is called a shell midden. Shell middens are, literally, trash dumps composed mainly of shells and other food refuse. Because of the high lime content of shells, the preservation of organic remains in shell middens is exceptional. Careful excavation of shell middens enables archaeologists to recover artifacts made from organic materials, such as bone tools, as well as tiny, delicate bones and other organic remains that are not commonly preserved in the normally acidic soils of Massachusetts.

Archaeologist Barbara Luedtke found evidence that the harbor islands were shared by the mainland tribes living to the north and the south of the Charles River, and that the territorial boundary cut across the middle of the harbor, along the modern shipping route called the Nantasket Roads. Most interestingly, she found that only one island was shared by the two tribes— Thompson Island; the territorial line cut across the middle of the island. At that boundary, she found evidence of gatherings by both tribes for trade and possibly social and political purposes.

During King Philip's War (1675–1676), the islands played a tragic role in the conflict. Friendly Native Americans from what were called "praying towns" were incarcerated on Deer Island and later on Long Island. Without shelter or provisions, many died during the harsh winter and were buried on those islands. There is a memorial on Deer Island and an exhibit in the historic Deer Island pump station that can be visited.

The Boston Harbor Islands are a unit of the National Park Service and are accessible to the public. For information on schedules, public ferries, and private boat docking information, go to www.bostonislands.org, www.nps.gov/boha/, or www.mass.gov/dcr/metroboston/harbor.htm. The visitor's center on Spectacle Island has an exhibit on the Native American and historic-period occupation of the island.

BOYLSTON STREET FISHWEIR, CHARLES RIVER, BACK BAY, BOSTON, MASSACHUSETTS

The Boylston Street Fishweir was discovered in the first half of the twentieth century during various construction activities under Boylston Street and at nearby building sites in the Back Bay section of downtown Boston (Johnson 1942, 1949). The Back Bay is a modern landform, built in the late nineteenth century after a massive effort to fill in a shallow tidal lagoon in the Charles River. Wooden stakes associated with the fishweir site have been found beneath this deep historic-period fill, stuck in the underlying natural blue clay deposits, at depths of more than 30–40 feet below the modern streets. Radiocarbon dates for the stakes range from about 3,000 to 5,000 years ago (Late Archaic period). Initially archaeologists believed that the stakes made up one large fishweir that would have required a large aggregation of people to construct during the Late Archaic period, when Native Americans lived in relatively small, mobile groups of hunter and gatherers.

Archaeologists Dena Dincauze and Elena Décima excavated fishweir features recently at a construction site on Boylston Street near Clarendon Street, opposite the historic Trinity Church. They found many small stakes and twigs, also dating to the Late Archaic period. They believe that Native people would stand in shallow water and push vertical stakes into the soft mud and clay and interweave twigs and limbs in a horizontal brushwork. The size and scale of the fishweirs indicate that small families would have been very capable of constructing them, with no need for a large workforce. The fishweir would be submerged during high tide, and any unlucky fish trapped behind the wooden weir during low tide could be easily captured in baskets or nets. The fishweirs were used for thousands of years, when ecological conditions in this former lagoon of the Charles River were optimal for catching fish by this method.

The Boylston Street Fishweir is now interpreted as a complex of numerous wooden fishweirs located throughout the Back Bay. The fishweir complex is listed in the National Register of Historic Places as part of the Back Bay Historic District. Although you cannot see the fishweirs because they are deep underground, there is an annual public event on the Boston Common where local Native Americans build a replica of the fishweir and where one can learn more about Native culture in eastern Massachusetts (www.fishweir.org/).

MASSACHUSETT HILL QUARRIES, MILTON AND QUINCY, MASSACHUSETTS

The Massachusett Hill Quarries are located in the Blue Hills Reservation, a state park south of Boston. The Algonquian word "Massachusett" means "at a great hill." It is believed that this was the Native people's name for the Blue Hills. Native people who lived in the Boston area south of the Charles River were known historically as the Massachusett, presumably because their territory included the Blue Hills. The tallest range near Boston, the Blue Hills can be seen from many vantage points, including any of the islands in Boston Harbor.

A volcanic geological feature, the Blue Hills are made mostly of granite, which was quarried historically, most notably to build the Bunker Hill Monument in Charlestown. More highly prized to Native Americans, however, were a slate called Braintree slate and a fine-grained volcanic material known as hornfels.

The Braintree slate quarry site was most heavily used during the Late Archaic period (about 3,000–5,000 years ago) to fashion adzes and gouges used to make dugout canoes and other wooden artifacts. The slate was also used during the Middle Archaic period (about 8,000–5,000 years ago) to make semi-lunar knives (commonly called ulus, from the Eskimo term).

Hornfels was used primarily during the Middle and Late Woodland periods (about 2,000–500 years ago) to make arrowheads, knives, and scrapers. When initially chipped into a blade-like tool, hornfels is characterized by an extremely sharp edge, far superior to many other local stone materials such as quartz or felsite.

The Massachusett Hill Quarries are listed in the National Register of Historic Places within the Blue Hills Multiple Resource Area. The Blue Hills Reservation is open to the public. A number of hiking trails are located near the quarry sites (www.mass.gov/dcr/parks/metroboston/blue.htm).

Further Reading: Dincauze, Dena F., and Elena Décima, "Small Is Beautiful: Tidal Weirs in a Low-Energy Estuary," in *A Lasting Impression: Coastal, Lithic, and Ceramic Research in New England*, edited by Jordan E. Kerber (Westport, CT: Praeger, 2002), 71–85; Johnson, Frederick, ed., *The Boylston Street Fishweir: A Study on the Archaeology, Biology, and Geology of a Site on Boylston Street in the Back Bay District of Boston, Massachusetts*, Papers of the R. S. Peabody Foundation for Archaeology, No. 2 (Andover, MA: Phillips Academy, 1942); Johnson, Frederick, ed., *The Boylston Street Fishweir II: A Study on the Archaeology, Biology, and Geology of a Site on Boylston Street in the Back Bay District of Boston, Massachusetts*. Papers of the R. S. Peabody Foundation for Archaeology 4(1) (Andover, MA: Phillips Academy, 1949); Luedtke, Barbara E., "Archaeology on the Boston Harbor Islands after 25 Years," *Bulletin of the Massachusetts Archaeological Society* 61(1) (2000): 2–11; Ritchie, Duncan, and Richard A. Gould, "Back to the Source: A Preliminary Account of the Massachusett Hill Quarry Complex," in *Stone Tool Analysis: Essays in Honor of Don E. Crabtree*, edited by M. G. Plew, C. Woods, and M. G. Pavesic (Albuquerque: University of New Mexico Press, 1985), 35–53; Simon, Brona G., "Boston Harbor: The Shapes of Things Past and Present," *Bulletin of the Massachusetts Archaeological Society* 63(1–2) (2002): 2–10.

Brona G. Simon

MOUNT DESERT AREA SITES

Coastal Maine

The Archaeology of Ancient Acadia

At one time, Native people lived all along the coast of the state of Maine. The highly crenellated and rocky coastline, stretching 3,000 miles (5,000 km), provided many opportunities for hunters and gatherers enjoying the rich marine and terrestrial ecosystems. Except in the extreme southwest of Maine, agriculture and palisaded villages did not exist in pre-European times. A high tidal range, extending to more than 20 feet (6 m) in eastern Maine, provided a bounty of shellfish—especially mussels and clams—plucked from the exposed rocks and mudflats. The tides also created a highly productive marine system by mixing nutrients from the bottom to the surface, where the sun produced huge plankton blooms, the basic building block of the marine ecosystem. Native people left extensive spreads of mollusk shells together with fish and animal bones, broken tools, and dwellings. These sites are situated in protected coves, usually behind a shellfish mudflat and normally facing south or southeast. Many sites have been lost to coastal erosion, collector predation, and development, but well over 1,000 have been documented to varying degrees of thoroughness. One area where remains of these shell heaps, or middens, can be seen is in the Acadia National Park region, as depicted in exhibits at the Abbe Museum in Bar Harbor on Mount Desert Island.

Although Native Americans had been living in Maine since perhaps 9000 BC (the Paleoindian period), evidence for coastal habitation is restricted to the past 5,000 years because of a rising sea level that inundated earlier sites. Sites dating to between 4000 and 1000 BC belong to the Late Archaic period. The earliest sites feature a strong marine adaptation that includes intertidal species of shellfish, small fish that could be caught in intertidal brush weirs, and offshore

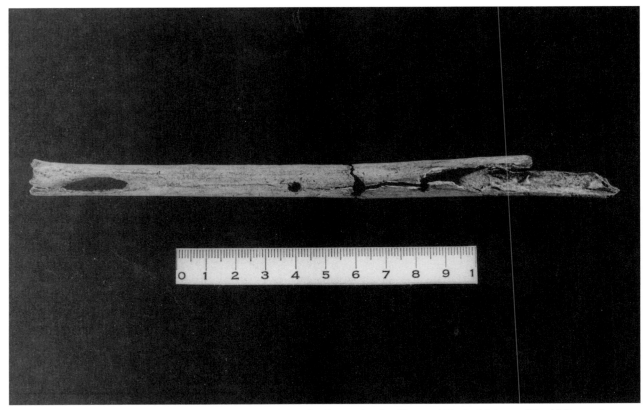

A carved-bone bird flute from the Frasier Point site on Schoodic Point, Acadia National Park, Maine.   [David Sanger]

species, the most prominent of which is the swordfish. The latter, weighing over 100 pounds (45 kg), were taken by a harpoons thrust as the fish basked on the surface. An Abbe Museum exhibit illustrates a 1930s excavation and recoveries, including swordfish objects, from the Late Archaic period Taft's Point shell midden in nearby Frenchman Bay. By 1500 BC swordfish were no longer being captured, probably because surface water temperatures cooled and the swordfish went further offshore. However, the combination of marine and terrestrial remains continues in the shell midden sites right up to the arrival of Europeans in the early seventeenth century.

Within the confines of Acadia National Park archaeological research has revealed additional Late Archaic sites plus those of the following Ceramic or Woodland period, which began around 1000 BC in this area. Numerous artifacts and Abbe Museum exhibits relating to shell midden excavations in Frenchman Bay illustrate aspects of this period. Much of this research occurred at a time when less attention was being paid to internal site organization and recovery of food bones. However, in the 1970s, as part of an overall evaluation of eroding sites in Acadia National Park, the important Fernald Point shell midden was tested by considerable excavation.

Fernald Point is located at the mouth of Somes Sound, which is the only true fiord in Maine. It afforded the residents an ideal fishing location, as documented by the many thousands of fish bones recovered from the site and the deep piles of shellfish, mostly soft-shell clams, dug up from the intertidal mud in front of the site. Seals, attracted to the ebb and flow of tides and fish, were also taken. Remains of terrestrial mammals included whitetail deer and beavers. People were living at Fernald Point prior to 1500 BC—as established by some Late Archaic period artifacts—and left deep, Ceramic period shell midden deposits. University of Maine archaeologists recovered arrowheads, knives, scrapers, and various other stone tools, pottery shards, bone tools, and beaver teeth modified to make cutting and carving tools. Also found were the incomplete remains of at least one oval depression, approximately 10 feet (3 m) on the short axis, which served as a snug foundation for a conical wigwam, likely for winter occupancy. A surprise find was a small cluster of human burials, since repatriated to Maine's Native peoples.

At Duck Harbor, on the Isle au Haut portion of the national park, archaeologists came across a number of sites around the edge of this small embayment. In addition to a small shell midden, the field crew located great numbers of stone chips, the result of extensive stone tool manufacture. Nearby the archaeologists discovered an outcrop of dark rhyolite, a fine-grained volcanic rock, which showed evidence of having been mined for stone implements. This prehistoric quarry, complete with discarded stone blanks and broken hammer stones left from the process of acquiring the rock, is one of a very few known from the coast of Maine. Some flaked stone from several shoreline sites derived from the quarry; others were mined from boulders and ledge outcrops right in the harbor.

In yet another part of Acadia National Park, archaeologists located shell and non-shell sites on Schoodic Peninsula. At the Fraser Point picnic ground, a shell midden produced the usual mixture of terrestrial and marine species, including a very rare bird bone whistle, probably made from a goose leg bone, very similar to one found years earlier, also in Frenchman Bay and now on exhibit at the Abbe Museum. Measurements of these specimens are similar to those of bone whistles found in New York State, which along with a few stone tools made of nonlocal rocks serves as a reminder that people did not live in isolation from other groups.

There are no useful written descriptions of Native people making a living on the shorelines of Maine, so nearly all aspects of their lifestyle have to be constructed from the archaeological evidence and a few oral traditions. Studies of animal and shell remains indicate that small settlements were occupied seasonally, but coastal people occupied the littoral region year round, probably moving around in response to food availability and shelter requirements. For example, more exposed island sites tend to show warm-weather occupation, whereas larger mainland sites selected for winter settlement feature less exposure to cold winds. The small size of house depressions, usually less than 12 feet (about 4 m) on the long axis, suggests nuclear families, which

were probably organized into loose confederations that claimed the right to hunt, fish, and gather in a territory with loosely defined boundaries. Little evidence exists for religious observance, but it seems likely that the people recognized the presence of a spirit world presided over by Gluskabi, a transformer and culture hero who created the land, the animals and plants, and the people.

For many years, the value of the pre-European archaeology of the Acadia National Park area has been appreciated. Unfortunately, the sea level continues to rise and each storm brings more erosion to each site. Many sites have simply disappeared in the past few decades. Development and collector activities have also taken their toll. It is clear, however, that from at least 2500 BC to the coming of the Europeans in the seventeenth century, Acadia National Park and Frenchman Bay constituted an important location for Native peoples. Fortunately, both the Abbe Museum and the national park have sponsored research to help recover some of the evidence. Members of the Passamaquoddy tribe, who currently have two reservations in Washington County, Maine, have ancestors who regularly hunted and fished in the Acadia National Park area and left us the impressive sites along these rocky shorelines.

Further Reading: Abbe Museum Web site, www.abbemuseum.org; Bourque, Bruce J., *Diversity and Complexity in Prehistoric Maritime Societies: A Gulf of Maine Perspective* (New York: Plenum Press, 1995); Bourque, Bruce J., with Steven L. Cox and Ruth H. Whitehead, *Twelve Thousand Years: American Indians in Maine* (Lincoln: University of Nebraska Press, 2001); Sanger, David, "Testing the Models: Hunter-Gatherer Use of Space in the Gulf of Maine, USA," *World Archaeology* 27(3) (1996): 512–526.

David Sanger

CAPE COD NATIONAL SEASHORE

Eastham to Provincetown, Massachusetts
Ancient and Historic Archaeology on the Outer Cape

People have lived on the outer part of the hook of land that forms Cape Cod for thousands of years. Cape Cod and the islands of Martha's Vineyard and Nantucket were formed as massive terminal moraines at the end of the last glacial period in North America, about 15,000 years ago. Ancient artifacts, such as Paleoindian projectile points found at several locations on Cape Cod, indicate that humans have occupied this land, or at least traversed it, for the last 10,000 years. Thousands of archaeological sites exist throughout the cape. A number of these sites have been scientifically studied and

some can be visited. The interpretation of ancient and historic activities at these sites provides a view of human uses of the Cape Cod coastline from earliest times.

The archaeology of Cape Cod has been of interest to inhabitants and visitors for hundreds of years. In his travel narrative about the region, *Cape Cod*, Henry David Thoreau observed that Cape Cod was once "thickly settled" by Indians and that traces of their occupation, in the form of "arrow-heads" and piles of shell, ashes, and deer bones, could be seen around the marsh edges and inlets throughout the cape. More systematic

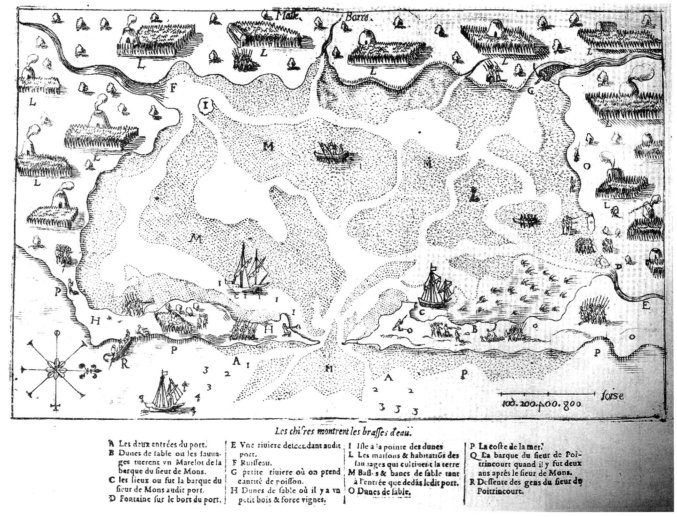

Les chi'res montrent les braſſes d'eau.

A Les deux entrées du port.
B Dunes de ſable ou les ſauuages tuerent vn Marelot de la
   barque du ſieur de Mons.
C les lieux ou fut la barque du
   ſieur de Mons audit port.
D Fontaine ſur le bort du port.

E Vne riuiere deſcendant audit
   port.
F Ruiſſeau.
G petite riuiere où on prend
   cantité de poiſſon.
H Dunes de ſable où il y a vn
   petit bois & force vignes.

I Iſle a la pointe des dunes.
L Les maiſons & habitatiõs des
   ſauuages qui cultiuent la terre
   à l'entrée que dedãs ledit port.
M Baſſis & bancs de ſable tant
O Dunes de ſable.

P La coſte de la mer.
Q La barque du ſieur de Poi-
   trincourt quand il y fut deux
   ans après le ſieur de Mons.
R Deſſente des gens du ſieur de
   Poitrincourt.

Map of Nauset Harbor from the works of Samuel de Champlain, the French explorer who visited outer Cape Cod in 1605 and 1606. The map records incidents during the brief French exploration, including a skirmish with native inhabitants. The map shows a landscape with evidence of a sedentary human way of life, including enclosed corn fields and a fish weir.   [Library of Congress]

and concerted archaeological studies on the outer cape by National Park Service archeologists in the 1980s showed concentrations of ancient villages and activities around Nauset Harbor and Wellfleet Harbor, as well as in the High Head area. Other researchers have found concentrations of sites in Truro near the mouth of the Pamet River and in many locations in the western portion of the cape.

By 5,000 years ago, the human presence on Cape Cod was quite extensive. Artifacts, projectile points in particular, dating from this period are found throughout the cape; however, sites are rare. During this early period of settlement, human groups may have moved seasonally from one part of the cape to another without establishing permanent settlements. It may also be that the remains of such settlements are buried deeply and are rarely found and investigated by archeologists. By 3,000 years ago, people had left dense deposits of ancient

trash, including discarded stone tools, stone flakes used as tools or from tool sharpening, shell from intensive gathering of shellfish for food, fish and animal bone, and ash and stone from fires for cooking and heat. These are found at sites in the Nauset area and probably exist in other areas where settlement was concentrated. Permanent settlement was probably the norm by this time, with parties of men and women traveling out from the villages to hunt or gather food and raw material for making tools, clothing, and shelter.

THE NAUSET ARCHAEOLOGICAL DISTRICT, EASTHAM, MASSACHUSETTS

The Nauset Archaeological District within the southern portion of Cape Cod National Seashore was one focus of substantial ancient settlement since at least 4000 BC. Indians at Nauset Harbor practiced farming and fishing. Farming was simple, using stone hoes and fire-hardened wood tools to work the soil, but rewarding. French explorers and the early English settlers report crop surpluses. In fact, the early Pilgrim settlers purchased corn and other crop foods from the Nauset Indians during the early years of their settlement at Plymouth, just across Cape Cod Bay. One of the means of fishing can be seen in the upper right corner of the map of Nauset by Champlain, which shows a conical weir constructed of saplings and grass rope, designed to capture fish swimming from the marsh into a pond. Radiocarbon dating and information indicating the season in which different species were collected or hunted, based on studies of the shellfish and other faunal remains from ancient shell middens, indicate that people lived here year-round.

The first written account of the area was by Samuel de Champlain, who sailed in on July 21, 1605, and saw a bay with dwellings and cultivated fields bordering it on all sides. He went ashore with some of the crew, and "before reaching [the Indians'] wigwams, [we] entered a field planted with Indian corn . . . [which] was in flower, and some five and a half feet in height. . . . We saw Brazilian beans, many edible squashes . . . tobacco, and roots which they cultivate." He also described the round dwellings, covered by a thatch made of reeds, and the people's clothing, woven from grasses, hemp, and animal skins. As the expedition cartographer, Champlain has left us an informative map of the Nauset Harbor area. Unfortunately, his visit to Nauset ended after four days with a fight between the French and the Indians in which one Frenchman was killed.

When he returned the next year, Champlain recorded in his journal that about 150 people were living around Nauset Harbor and about 500 to 600 were living around Stage Harbor to the south in the area of present-day Chatham. After 1620, English colonists from the settlement at Plymouth visited Nauset many times to buy food and trade. Unfortunately, along with the trade goods, European diseases for which the Indians had no immunity were spread by such contacts. Many of the Nauset Indians died and the population declined drastically. In 1639 about half the English from Plymouth relocated to the Nauset area, settling the town that is now Eastham.

The area can be visited via the Fort Hill unit of the National Seashore, where a trail winds from the top of the hill to the marsh. Visitors can view interpretive displays of the area at the Salt Pond Visitor Center in the park. Additional trails from the visitor center to Coast Guard Beach pass by other ancient archaeological sites. The sites around Nauset Marsh, like most archaeological sites in the eastern part of the country, are hidden from view by soil and vegetation. This protects the sites, but it also makes it difficult for visitors to envision ancient settlements. At Nauset, the Champlain map suggests how houses and cultivated fields must have filled the margins of land around the marsh in pre-European times. The view from the top of Fort Hill overlooking the modern marsh

takes in all of Nauset Harbor, with its steep shorelines and extensive marsh divided by natural channels. Beyond the harbor are the breakers of the Atlantic Ocean. Nauset Beach, a barrier beach with a narrow entrance, protects the tidal lagoon.

PILGRIM HEIGHTS AND HIGH HEAD SITES, NORTH TRURO, MASSACHUSETTS

Another concentration of ancient sites is located at High Head in Truro. There are many archaeological sites in this area; however, most of them lack the dense deposits of trash that archaeologists associate with permanent settlements. Ancient inhabitants were using the High Head area regularly from at least 5,000 years ago, but the activities seem to have been relatively short-term, perhaps specialized hunting or gathering of material or food that grew naturally in the area. Camps probably were set up to carry out these specialized activities and were briefly occupied for short periods of a few days or weeks. The ancient archaeological sites in this area are relatively small and covered by soil and vegetation. Archaeological deposits consist mainly of discarded stone tools, stone fragments broken off when tools were resharpened or maintained in other ways, and stone used for heating in cooking or campfires. The area can be visited via the Smalls Swamp and Pilgrim Spring trails beginning at the Pilgrim Spring parking area of the National Seashore.

THE INDIAN NECK OSSUARY SITE, WELLFLEET, MASSACHUSETTS

Another concentration of ancient activity and settlement was the area around Wellfleet Harbor on the bay side of the cape. One of the most interesting sites in this area is the Indian Neck Ossuary, a burial dating to about AD 1100. "Ossuary" refers to a secondary burial that contains the remains of many individuals. The burials are referred to as secondary because the remains gathered in an ossuary typically were buried or exposed elsewhere first. Since the original, temporary burials the flesh and soft parts of the bodies have decomposed, so by the time the individual remains are collected for the ossuary, only the bones remain. In North America the ossuary form of burial is well known from the periods just before European colonization in the Chesapeake region and northwestern New York and adjacent Ontario. The Indian Neck ossuary is the best known and most completely reported such site in New England.

The site was discovered accidentally in 1979 when a backhoe digging a trench for a home improvement project on private land uncovered human bones. After ascertaining that the human remains were not related to a homicide or other recent event, archaeologists from the National Park Service conducted an archaeological salvage excavation to recover the remains and any information about them before they were destroyed by the modern development. The ossuary burial is quite concentrated, with all the human bone packed together tightly, and covers a roughly oval area with maximum dimensions of approximately 1.5 by 3 meters. The portion of the site that was excavated consisted of the half of the ossuary that was not destroyed by the backhoe digging, and it contained the remains of at least fifty-six individuals. Most age groups and both sexes were represented in proportion to their expected occurrence in a typical human population, except for the absence of very young infants. Judging from the condition of the bone, the community represented by this burial population was relatively healthy. There was little evidence of any dental decay, infectious disease, or malnutrition. The absence of tooth decay suggests that the diet did not at this time include substantial amounts of ground maize, so intensive horticulture probably was not practiced at this time in the area. The ossuary suggests a centralized and communal burial practice, which in turn indicates a sedentary settlement pattern. This site, plus other evidence from sites in the Nauset area, support the existence of settled village life by inhabitants of Cape Cod by as of least 1,000 years ago.

THE WELLFLEET TAVERN SITE, GREAT ISLAND, WELLFLEET, MASSACHUSETTS

Historic-period archaeological sites, mainly small farmsteads widely spaced and linearly arranged along small, east-west running valleys, exist throughout the outer cape. The initial European settlement of the outer cape occurred around 1644, when colonists from Plymouth relocated in Eastham. Historical research tells us that fishing, whaling, trading, and farming all were important for these new inhabitants of the outer cape. One unique site that can be visited is the Wellfleet Tavern site (also known as the Samuel Smith Tavern Site and the Great Island Tavern site) on Great Island, part of the headland that now forms an outer boundary of Wellfleet

Harbor. The site was excavated in 1969 and 1970 by archaeologists Erik Ekholm and James Deetz. Analysis of the artifacts collected by Ekholm and Deetz indicate activity at the site between 1690 and 1740. The artifact types found at the site relate to its designation as a tavern, including high percentages of drinking vessels, pipe stems, and other kinds of glassware.

A park trail around Great Island passes by the Wellfleet Tavern site. Interpretive displays describing and illustrating ancient and historic inhabitants and ways of life on Cape Cod can be found at the National Park Service Salt Pond Visitor's Center just off Route 6 in Eastham.

Further Reading: Bigger, H. P., ed., *The Works of Samuel de Champlain, Volume I (1599–1607)* (Toronto: Champlain Society, 1922) (the map is Plate LXXV, following p. 358); Bragdon, Kathleen J., *Native People of Southern New England: 1500–1650* (Norman: University of Oklahoma Press, 1996); Cape Cod National Seashore, National Park Service, *The Archaeology of Outer Cape Cod*, http://www. nps.gov/caco/ historyculture/the-archaeology-of-outer-cape-cod.htm (accessed March 2008); Cronon, William, *Changes in the Land: Indians, Colonists, and the Ecology of New England* (New York: Hill and Wang, 1983); Ekholm, Erik, and James Deetz, "The Wellfleet Tavern," *Natural History* 80 (1971): 49–56; McManamon, Francis P., "Prehistoric Land Use on Outer Cape Cod," *Journal of Field Archaeology* 9 (1982): 1–20; McManamon, Francis P., and James W. Bradley, "The Indian Neck Ossuary," *Scientific American* 256(5) (1988): 98–104; Moffett, Ross, "A Review of Cape Cod Archaeology," *Bulletin of the Massachusetts Archaeological Society* 19 (1957); Yentsch, Anne E., "Farming, Fishing, Whaling, Trading: Land and Sea as Resource on Eighteenth-Century Cape Cod," in *Documentary Archaeology in the New World*, edited by Mary C. Beaudry (Cambridge: Cambridge University Press, 1988), 138–160.

Francis P. McManamon

MARTHA'S VINEYARD AND NANTUCKET ARCHAEOLOGY

Coastal Massachusetts

Ancient and Historic Native American Sites on the Islands

Martha's Vineyard and Nantucket are the two largest islands off the coast of Massachusetts. This article outlines the long cultural history of these islands using the lens of archaeology.

MARTHA'S VINEYARD

The island of Martha's Vineyard is home to the Wampanoag Tribe of Gay Head/Aquinnah, a federally recognized Indian tribe whose oral traditions tell them that their ancestors lived on *Noepe*, the island's Algonquian name, for at least the past

10,000 years. The Aquinnah have been recorded in historical documents as continuous residents of the land from the first European contact to the present day. The brightly colored clay cliffs that are a landmark of Gay Head document the island's rich geologic history, but also mark the home of Moshup, a giant in Algonquin oral history who lived there when the first Native people arrived.

Located seven miles off the southwestern tip of Cape Cod, Martha's Vineyard covers 120 square miles and is the largest

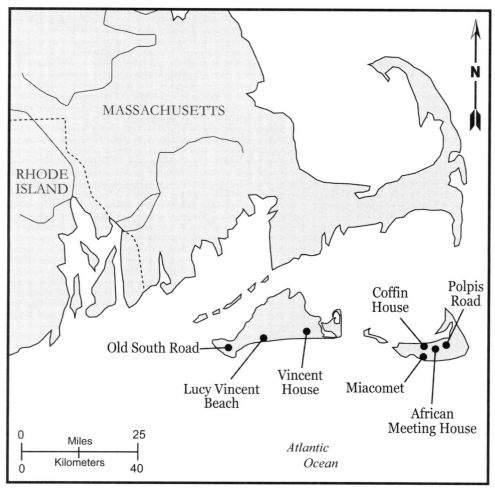

Important sites on Martha's Vineyard and Nantucket.   [Elizabeth S. Chilton]

island in southern New England. The physical isolation of Martha's Vineyard and the unique patterns of settlement on the island have contributed to the preservation of the town of Aquinnah (formerly known as Gay Head) as a primarily Native American community that has been well documented through oral traditions and non-Native historical studies.

Beginning at the turn of the twentieth century, some of the region's prominent archaeologists were drawn to the island, in part because of its remote and relatively undisturbed setting. Harvard's Samuel Guernsey and E. A. Hooten, Douglas Byers and Frederick Johnson of the R. S. Peabody Foundation at Andover, and perhaps most notably New York State Archaeologist William Ritchie excavated complex habitation and ceremonial sites. Their research served as the archaeological framework for the interpretation of Native American settlement and subsistence in southern New England for much of the twentieth century. The full range of Native American occupation on the Vineyard was only partially identified by these early professional and amateur archaeologists; for the most part, these researchers focused on large shell midden

sites, located close to the shoreline and around coastal ponds, that contained dense artifact deposits and were often also used for burial. More recently, cultural resource management (CRM) professionals and academic archaeologists have identified a wider range of site types in virtually all sections of the island and have collected information on the earliest periods of human activity on Martha's Vineyard through the modern period.

As the last glaciers retreated northward from the Vineyard around 14,000 years before the present (BP), the massive release of meltwater caused sea levels to rise slowly over the next few thousand years. Seawater flooded the deeper parts of the Vineyard Sound around 7500 BP, and at about 6000 BP marine waters flooded Nantucket Sound and separated the islands from Cape Cod (Oldale 1992, 100). The present-day coastline of Martha's Vineyard was not established until approximately 3000 to 2000 BP, so it is likely that many of the oldest archaeological sites on the island are now underwater. Nevertheless, Paleoindian spear points in artifact collections indicate that people were living on the island as far back as

12,000 BP. Professional archaeologists have recently documented 9,500-year-old Early Archaic bifurcate-based points in the towns of Chilmark and Aquinnah on the western end of the island, including several sites that were used repeatedly during later periods.

The Late Archaic through Late Woodland periods (7000–450 BP) have been well documented on Martha's Vineyard, with sites identified across the island at shoreline and interior locations. Many of the known sites appear to have been revisited many times, with thick layers of stone tools and waste flakes, shells and animal and fish bone, pottery, and other materials documenting thousands of years of seasonal and semi-permanent habitation. These sites indicate that the environment remained relatively stable over time, providing enough plant and animal resources to sustain populations over many generations.

European accounts of Martha's Vineyard and its inhabitants date to 1602, when Bartholomew Gosnold named the island after his daughter. Gosnold's crew described the Native people as having iron and copper implements, and one individual was said to be dressed in a European fashion (Levermore 1912, 43–54). The description suggests that the Vineyard's Native population was interacting with European explorers or fishing and whaling crews prior to Gosnold's arrival.

The first permanent Euro-American settlement on the island occurred in 1641 when Boston merchant Thomas Mayhew purchased Martha's Vineyard, Nantucket, and the nearby Elizabeth islands. Mayhew sent his son, Thomas Jr., to settle the Vineyard in 1642 with a group of several other families, who formed the town of Great Harbor (today Edgartown) on the eastern end of the island. The younger Mayhew soon began a missionary effort aimed at converting the Native inhabitants to Christianity.

One of the earliest Euro-American sites on Martha's Vineyard has been documented at the circa 1670 Vincent House site in Edgartown. The original structure was built by proprietor William Vincent on the shores of the Great Pond. The property was used as a farm for nearly 300 years before the house was moved to Edgartown center, where it is in use as a museum. Archaeological investigations conducted in 1977 prior to the relocation identified structural elements and features dating to the eighteenth century. More recent archaeological studies in the surrounding area identified the site of a second structure that appears to predate the 1670 house. The site includes a small depression with the remains of a brick center chimney that likely represents a full or partial cellar for the structure that stood above. Other artifacts collected from the site include handwrought nails and brick, fragments of diamond window glass panes, European gunflints, clay smoking pipe fragments, a brass shoe buckle, a pewter or lead button, and bone utensil and comb fragments.

Over much of the eighteenth century, Euro-American settlement spread across the island and the Native American community became more concentrated on the Aquinnah peninsula. Nineteenth-century settlement patterns were focused along two primary east-west roadways that existed in Aquinnah by at least 1852, including the Old South Road. The Aquinnah inhabitants sold grains and other foodstuffs along with fish and feathers to the English, and many men traveled across the world while engaged as skilled mariners in the whaling industry. Archaeological studies and oral histories completed within the Aquinnah homelands have documented more than twenty-five nineteenth-century Native American home- and farmsteads within the Old South Road Community, a residential area that was largely abandoned by the first decades of the twentieth century in favor of locations along the new South or State Road. These sites are rich in architectural detail, domestic goods, and building materials and reflect differences in occupation and land use. Several of the identified farmsteads are quite complex, with the identified remains of large dwellings, barns, outbuildings, animal pens, agricultural fields, and orchards. Other areas contain only a small dwelling or animal pen. The material culture identified at the Old South Road sites is predominantly of Euro-American origin, including tableware service items such as plates, bowls, and cups; personal items such as clay pipes, glass beads, iron buckles, and button backs; and construction materials including bricks, mortar, window glass, chimney glass, and handwrought and machine-cut nails. Despite the presence of these materials, the sites are uniquely Native American, incorporating more traditional materials and elements such as chipped- and ground-stone tools, hearth features, and structural styles that maximized solar exposure and protection from prevailing winds.

The Lucy Vincent Beach Site

The Lucy Vincent Beach site is a palimpsest (a series of overlaying layers, one atop the other) of the Vineyard's deep Native history. The site is located in the town of Chilmark on a 40-foot knoll overlooking Lucy Vincent Beach and the ocean. The site was originally identified when a human burial was discovered in the eroding cliff face in 1995 and another in 1996. After consultations among professional archaeologists, the Massachusetts Historical Commission, the Town of Chilmark, and the Aquinnah, all parties agreed that a full archaeological excavation was warranted. The site was the focus of the Harvard Archaeological Field School in the summers of 1998 and 1999 (see Chilton and Doucette 2002a, 2002b; Largy et al. 2002).

The goals of the excavation were to determine the site boundaries and the temporal/cultural affiliation of occupational episodes, and to identify and excavate features closest to the cliff face because of the threat from erosion. In 1998 and 1999 a total of 80 square meters were excavated, representing 12.8 percent of the estimated site area. A total of 168 features were identified by the excavators, including 130 possible post molds, 31 pit features, one fire hearth, and two human burials.

Most of the interpretations of site chronology are based on the presence of diagnostic artifacts, most of which were found in the plow zone. One possible Late Paleoindian (Dalton-like) quartzite projectile point was discovered in the plow zone, and likely dates to about 10,000–9000 BP. The next oldest artifact recovered was a small Neville projectile point, which likely dates to the Middle Archaic period, about 8000 BP. A variety of Late Archaic (5000–3000 BP) spear points were also recovered, including Brewerton points, Squibnocket Triangles, and Small-Stemmed points. This indicates more frequent use of the site beginning in the Late Archaic period, as is the case elsewhere on Martha's Vineyard (see Ritchie 1969, 230; Richardson 1985). This coincides with the separation of Martha's Vineyard from the mainland at about 6000 BP (Oldale 1992, 100).

The predominant pre-contact use of the Lucy Vincent Beach site took place during the Late Woodland period (AD 1000–1600). This interpretation is based on the presence of Late Woodland ceramics, projectile points, and pit features, and the radiocarbon dating of features. The site was also heavily used during the contact period (AD 1600–1700). Artifacts dating to this period include white clay smoking pipes, gunflint fragments, cut brass, and a carved wooden pipe. Very few nineteenth- or twentieth-century materials were recovered from the site, and those that were found were quite small and likely associated with plowing and manuring of the site (e.g., glass, brick, pottery, and metal fragments).

One of the two definite human burial remnants identified was located under a large hearth and consisted of a partial human cranium. The person was likely male and older than 50 years old at the time of death. This was the only intact fire hearth identified at the site. The hearth contained stone tools, Native ceramic shards, numerous animal and fish bones, and charred plant materials (including maize). Shell species included quahog, soft-shell clam, bay scallop, and whelk; breakage patterns on the latter suggested use for consumption (Shaw 2001). The large amount of food remains in this fire hearth and the association with a secondary burial suggest that this hearth feature is the result of ceremonial feasting. Three wood charcoal dates from this burial indicate that it dates to AD 1000–1500.

The other human burial was discovered at the bottom of a pit feature. Burial 4 was a primary burial and was nearly complete. The individual, nearly complete, was placed at the bottom of a pit in a tightly flexed position. This person was also likely male and about 20 years old at the time of death. The pit feature above the burial contained faunal remains (including shell), chipping debris, Native American pottery shards, and charcoal. Radiocarbon dates from the pit feature above this burial suggest a date of AD 1400–1600.

Although it is likely that most of the site was lost to erosion before it came to the attention of archaeologists, some tentative interpretations can be made on the basis of the data recovered. It is clear that the site has been important to Native Americans for thousands of years, and it continues to be important to the Aquinnah Wampanoag today. The site obviously served a variety of functions and was most intensively utilized during the Late Woodland and contact periods (AD 1000–1700). There is evidence for seasonal settlement: a wide range of plant and animal foods were exploited and consumed at this site, and a number of post molds indicate small seasonal encampments. The presence of freshwater nearby (Chilmark Pond) and the proximity of marine resources within the last several hundred years made this an attractive location, most likely during the warmer months of the year. Preliminary faunal and floral analysis suggest a diverse subsistence base for Native use of the site during the Late Woodland and early contact periods, similar to what Bernstein (2002) reports for Long Island.

NANTUCKET

The distribution of known sites on Nantucket reflects a long history of avocational archaeology and artifact collecting that dates to the nineteenth century. In 1980 Dr. Elizabeth Little of the Nantucket Historical Association (NHA) completed an inventory of Nantucket's pre-contact archaeological sites, and the data gathered as part of this project was used to develop a predictive model for site distribution within various environmental zones across the island (Pretola and Little 1988). This document remains the single comprehensive study of Nantucket's Native American history and has been used as a foundation for subsequent archaeological investigations.

Although no sites dating to the Paleoindian or Early Archaic periods (prior to 7500 BP) have been systematically excavated on what is today Nantucket Island; evidence for the peopling of this area in the distant past includes a number of fluted Clovis- and Dalton-style points in artifact collections, which are known, based on research at other sites, to date to between 12,000 and 10,000 years ago. Middle Archaic deposits dating to 7500–5000 BP appear to mark the earliest occupations at several large multi-component sites on Nantucket and reflect a pattern of site reuse also seen on Martha's Vineyard. Pollen data indicate that after about 5500 BP, the vegetation on Nantucket consisted of a mixed hardwood forest with oak as the dominant species and a slightly less diverse forest makeup than that present on the mainland (Dunwiddie 1990).

Nearly half of the more than 600 projectile points identified in the 1978 NHA survey were Levanna points, considered diagnostic of the Late Woodland period and dating to approximately 1000–450 BP (Pretola and Little 1988). The NHA researchers estimated that local populations were steadily increasing in numbers and reached a peak by the Late Woodland period, when settlement was concentrated in the coastal zone.

Polpis Road Sites

More recently, archaeological investigations completed by the Public Archaeology Laboratory (PAL) as part of the 8-mile Polpis Road Bicycle Path project documented six significant Native American sites, four of which could not be avoided and preserved in place. The Polpis Road project was the first archaeological data recovery program completed on Nantucket Island and resulted in the collection of almost 70,000 artifacts spanning the Late Archaic to Late Woodland and contact periods (Rainey 2004). Post mold stains marking the locations of oval wigwam or *wetu* structures measuring 8 to 9 meters in length were identified at two of the sites in association with storage and trash pits, hearths, and lithic workshop areas. The excavations documented the processing of whitetail deer, rabbit, raccoon, turkey, turtle, muskrat, otter, domestic dog, and domestic cow in addition to spiny dogfish, tautog, Atlantic cod, sturgeon, sea bass, striped bass, gray seal, dusky shark, and a wide range of fresh- and saltwater shellfish species. Maize fragments collected from two of the sites were radiocarbon-dated to the Late Woodland/contact period (AD 1440–1630 and AD 1495–1670). The recovery of several thousand grass, reed, and sedge fragments provides archaeological documentation of the baskets, mat, coverings, and even clothing that were described by early European visitors to Nantucket. The incredibly diverse cultural deposits identified during the Polpis Road Bicycle Path archaeological project generated a wide range of interdisciplinary data that has and will continue to inform our understanding of Native American land use on Nantucket over the past 5,000 years.

The initial English travel to the island of Nantucket can be traced to the late fifteenth-century voyages of John and Sebastian Cabot. Although Nantucket's Native population had sporadic contact with traders and fishing fleets during this period, a permanent Euro-American settlement was not established on the island until 1659, nearly two decades after Thomas Mayhew Sr. had purchased rights to Nantucket, Martha's Vineyard, and the Elizabeth Islands. Mayhew sold Nantucket to a group of ten investors, himself included, and in the next year a group including members of the Coffin, Starbuck, and Mayhew families arrived to lay out house lots and common grazing lands.

Jethro Coffin House

The Jethro Coffin House, constructed in 1686, is the only surviving example of the seventeenth-century colonial settlement on Nantucket. Jethro, a blacksmith, was the grandson of Tristram Coffin, one of the island's original proprietors, and lived in the house with his wife, Mary Gardner, until his death in 1727. The house passed through numerous owners before it was acquired by the Nantucket Historical Association in 1923 and partially restored. The documentation of this significant historic site has included chain of title (deed), genealogical, and archival research, historic architectural analyses,

oral and family histories, soil resistivity studies, and archaeological excavation.

Archaeological investigations completed at the site in the 1970s and 1980s around the house and in the surrounding yard areas identified Native and Euro-American artifacts and features associated with the historic home (Johnson et al. 1985). The artifact deposits included ceramics, clay pipes, bottle and window glass, and structural hardware. A large amount of mammal and fish bone, shellfish remains, and seeds was collected and the analysis of these materials provided important information about diet over time. Evidence of historic-period gardens, cobblestone pavements, and builder's trenches help to reconstruct changes to the property over time and through successive owners. Much of the recovered archaeological data has not been thoroughly analyzed and presents an opportunity for the future study of this important colonial-era site.

Miacomet Village

Native Americans continued to live on Nantucket after the arrival of the fist Euro-American settlers, and one of their eighteenth-century settlements was located near the head of Miacomet Pond. This community, sometimes referred to as a "praying town" because of its association with Christian missionaries such as Matthew Mayhew, included residences, grazing and farm lands, a meeting house, and a cemetery. While Euro-American descriptions of Miacomet Village are present in eighteenth-century texts, small areas investigated by archaeologists prior to house and road construction have revealed additional information about Native lifeways during this period. The Miacomet Indian Burial Ground was located when construction workers exposed human remains in 1987. Reviews of historical maps and deeds, noninvasive soil resistivity testing, and archaeological sampling were used to help identify the boundaries of the burial ground, which may contain the graves of more than 200 Native Americans (Carlson et al. 1992). Historical research indicates that many of the individuals buried at Miacomet may have died during an epidemic in 1762–63 that killed several hundred of the island's Native residents. In 1993 the burial ground was dedicated at a ceremony attended by Native American representatives and town and state officials.

Nearshore or "alongshore" whaling by the colonists began off the south shores of Nantucket after 1690. The Nantucket Indians' involvement in the development of the industry has been well documented: "given the supply of right whales close to shore, and a labor pool of Indians with a maritime aptitude as well as an interest in drift whales, we can readily understand the successful European introduction of alongshore whaling to southeastern New England and eastern Long Island" (Little and Andrews 1982, 29). By the early 1700s, Nantucket had taken the lead in the system of boat whaling from the shore, which involved the construction of lookout stations (called spars) at prominent points along the coast, from which sightings were reported. It was soon recognized that the deep-water sperm whales produced oil of a much finer quality than that of the right whales, which were pursued alongshore. Between 1800 and 1840, Nantucket was known as the "whaling capital of the world," with more than eighty ships spread across the world's whaling grounds. As whale oil was replaced by other fuel sources, the industry dwindled and Nantucket returned to its agricultural subsistence base until tourism revitalized the economy.

Nantucket, like Martha's Vineyard, supported a thriving African American community in the eighteenth and nineteenth centuries. Archaeological investigations at the African Meeting House site (also known as the African Baptist Society Meeting House) on Nantucket have helped to document this connection. The restored post-and-beam building was constructed by African American residents in 1827 and served as a meeting house, school, and church for Nantucket's African American and Native American residents. The structure was maintained as a community space through much of the twentieth century until its acquisition by the Museum of African American History. Archaeological studies completed in the 1990s as part of the site's rehabilitation helped to provide important details about the construction of the building, the layout of the physical landscape in the yard areas, and the types of activities that helped to maintain a unique African American identity on Nantucket through several generations (Berkland 1999).

In sum, Martha's Vineyard and Nantucket have deep and rich histories. Both islands demonstrate continuity in Native history going back at least 10,000 years, before either of these places were islands. They also demonstrate great continuity in Native societies, even in the face of the great changes brought about by Euro-American colonization. Shoreline erosion and development threaten the archaeological evidence for these histories, but landowners, Native American tribes, professional and avocational archaeologists, historical commissions, and the public are among the key stakeholders that have come together in increasing numbers to steward these fragile and non-renewable resources.

Further Reading: Baker, Anne W., "The Vincent House: Architecture and Restoration," *Dukes County Intelligencer* 20(1) (August 1978); Banks, Charles E., *The History of Martha's Vineyard* (Edgartown, MA: Dukes County Historical Society, 1911); Berkland, Ellen, *The Centering of an African-American Community: An Archaeological Study of the African Baptist Society Meeting House, Nantucket, Massachusetts* (Boston: Museum of African American History, 1999); Bernstein, David J., "Late Woodland Use of Coastal Resources at Mount Sinai Harbor, Long Island, New York," in *A Lasting Impression: Coastal, Lithic, and Ceramic Research in New England Archaeology*, edited by Jordan Kerber (Westport, CT: Praeger, 2002), 27–40; Byers, Douglas S., and Frederick Johnson, *Two Sites on Martha's Vineyard*, Papers of the Robert S. Peabody Foundation for Archaeology No. 1 (Andover, MA: Phillips Academy, 1940); Carlson, Catherine, Elizabeth A. Little, D. Richard Gumaer, Leonard Loparto,

and Brenda Baker, *Archaeological Survey and Historical Background Research for the Miacomet Indian Village and Burial Ground, Nantucket, Massachusetts*, report on file (Boston: Massachusetts Historical Commission, 1992); Chilton, Elizabeth S., and Dianna L. Doucette, "The Archaeology of Coastal New England: The View from Martha's Vineyard," *Northeast Anthropology* 64 (2002a): 55–66; Chilton, Elizabeth S., and Dianna L. Doucette, "Archaeological Investigations at the Lucy Vincent Beach Site (19-DK-148): Preliminary Results and Interpretations," in *A Lasting Impression: Coastal, Lithic, and Ceramic Research in New England Archaeology*, edited by Jordan Kerber (Westport, CT: Praeger, 2002b), 41–70; Dunwiddie, Peter W., "Postglacial Vegetation History of Coastal Islands in Southeastern New England," *National Geographic Research* 6(2) (1990): 178–195; Glover, Suzanne, and Kevin A. McBride, *Old Ways and New Ways, 7,000 Years Along the Old South Road: An Archaeological Study* (Gay Head, Martha's Vineyard, MA. Wampanoag Tribe of Gay Head/Aquinnah, 1994); Guernsey, Samuel J., "Notes on Explorations of Martha's Vineyard," *American Anthropologist* 18(1) (1916): 81–97; Johnson, Selin, Marlo Jacobson, J. Clinton Andrews, Louise Hussey, and Elizabeth Little, *Inventory of Artifact Finds from the 1975–1976 Archaeological Excavation at the Jethro Coffin House* (Nantucket, MA: Nantucket Historical Association, Archaeology Department, 1985); Largy, Tonya B., Peter Burns, Elizabeth S. Chilton, and Dianna L. Doucette, "Lucy Vincent Beach: Another look at the Prehistoric Exploitation of Piscine Resources off the Coast of Massachusetts, U.S.A," *Northeast Anthropology* 64 (2002): 67–73; Levermore, C. H., ed., *Forerunners and Competitors of the Pilgrims and Puritans or Narratives of the Voyages Made by Persons Other Than the Pilgrims and Puritans of the Bay Colony to the Shores of New England During the First Quarter of the Seventeenth Century, 1601–1625 With Especial Reference to the Labors of Captain John Smith in Behalf of the Settlement of New England*, 2 vols. (Brooklyn, NY: New England Society of Brooklyn, 1912); Little, Elizabeth A., "A Brief Historical Sketch of Archaeology on Nantucket," in *Widening Horizons: Studies Presented to Dr. Maurice Robbins*, edited by Curtiss Hoffman (Attleboro, MA: Massachusetts Archaeological Society, 1980), 75–79; Little, Elizabeth A., *Initial Predictive Map for Prehistoric Sites on Nantucket*, Nantucket Archaeology Studies No. 1 (Nantucket, MA: Nantucket Historical Association, Archaeology Department, 1983); Little, Elizabeth A., and J. Clinton Andrews, "Drift Whales at Nantucket: The Kindness of Moshup," *Man in the Northeast* 23 (1982): 17–38; Oldale, Robert N., *Cape Cod and the Islands: The Geologic Story* (East Orleans, MA: Parnassus Imprints, 1992); Pretola, John, and Elizabeth A. Little, "Nantucket: An Archaeological Record from the Far Island," *Bulletin of the Archaeological Society of Connecticut* 51 (1988): 47–68; Rainey, Mary Lynne, "The Archaeology of the Polpis Road Bicycle Path: A Landmark in the Study of Native American Lifeways on Nantucket," *Historic Nantucket* 53(3) (Summer 2004): 8–13; Richardson, James B., III, "Prehistoric Man on Martha's Vineyard," *Oceanus* 28(1) (1985): 35–42; Ritchie, William A., *The Archaeology of Martha's Vineyard* (Garden City, NY: Natural History Press, 1969); Shaw, Leslie, "Shell Analysis for the Lucy Vincent Site, Martha's Vineyard, Massachusetts," ms. in possession of the author, 2001; Stachiw, Myron, *Archaeology and Historic Preservation: The Vincent House*, report submitted to Martha's Vineyard Historical Preservation Society (Edgartown, MA, 1978).

Elizabeth S. Chilton and Holly Herbster

ARCHAEOLOGY IN AND AROUND WASHINGTON, D.C.

District of Columbia, Maryland, and Virginia
Ancient and Historic Period Sites

The Potomac is often called "the nation's river." It flows through the capital city, and many prominent men and women of the country's founding generations once called its shores home. In the nineteenth century the tragedy of the Civil War ebbed and flowed across its banks. The blood of over 22,000 casualties washed into Antietam Creek, a tributary of the Potomac, on a single day in 1862. The Potomac has come to be a place firmly established in the historical conscience of this nation.

As a natural feature, the Potomac River casts a significant shadow on the regional landscape. It is one of three major tributaries that feed the great Chesapeake Bay. As it flows eastward from the Appalachian highlands to the bay, its channel traverses a number of distinct provinces. Washington, D.C., is situated near the fall zone of the river (the area where the elevation of the land increases and waterfalls occur in the river channel). From the capital city east to the Chesapeake Bay the Potomac is estuarine, flooded by the sea level rise brought about by the continental glacier's release of trapped water near the end of the Pleistocene some 10,000 years ago. Well above Washington, D.C., the river originates in mountainous highlands and courses through the Appalachian front, meanders down through the ridge and valley and the Blue Ridge Mountains, and then flows across the piedmont's fertile floodplains.

An important feature about the 385-mile journey to the Chesapeake Bay is the distinctive natural corridor the river creates. Almost every conceivable form of travel finds the path of least resistance along this riparian avenue. Native Americans canoed its waters and walked the trails along its shores. Later peoples who would call the region home followed suit and moved westward up the first colonial roads, then by canals and railroads, and eventually on interstate highways. Today fiber-optic cables carrying products of the information age follow that same route. Thus the corridor has always been and remains a conduit of great strategic value. One can follow the Potomac River from its mouth westward to just a few miles short of the Ohio River drainage and mid-continental North America.

FIRST PEOPLE
Native Americans have called the Potomac home for at least 11,500 years. Archaeologists typically divide those millennia into three periods: Paleoindian, around 11,500 to 10,000 years ago; the Archaic period, about 10,000 to 3,000 years ago; and the Woodland period, from about 3,000 years ago until European contact, in the sixteenth and seventeenth centuries.

These subdivisions are of unequal magnitude, but reflect major changes in ecology, and the corresponding human adaptations, after the end of the Pleistocene. Although the last glacial advance of the Pleistocene ground to a halt well north of the region, it affected conditions here. After the end of the Pleistocene it took several thousand years for today's temperate ecology to become reestablished.

The Paleoindian period represents the first unequivocal entrance of humans into the region. Those pioneers, in very small numbers, settled in dense coniferous forests of spruce, fir, and pine. Their tool kit consisted of the ubiquitous fluted point and a small number of other very generalized implements. The fluted projectile was a pan-continental implement of the era, and often all of the implements in the tool kit were flaked from high-quality siliceous rock (very fine-grained stone) that could be easily re-sharpened. Paleoindians were rather mobile, occupying a number of small sites across an expansive settlement area. They moved at regular intervals to situate themselves near seasonally available resources or necessary raw materials.

By 10,000 years ago, the climate had started to ameliorate, and the temperate deciduous forest of today began to establish itself. Such an ecosystem has a higher carrying capacity, which allowed Native populations to expand. With the development of a shrubby understory, the gathering of plant resources became more important. Major game resources included deer, elk, bear, and turkey along with a host of other small mammals, reptiles, and aquatic creatures. The lower reaches of the Potomac began to flood as a result of rising sea level, creating the estuary (a mix of salt- and freshwater) still present today. Certain species established themselves within that estuary in enormous numbers. The Archaic period human groups responded to all of these changes. Populations were still fully dependent on wild resources, but people now had to move less distance to find them. Tool kits became more specialized and varied, an adaptation to the presence of a large variety of new resources.

The following Woodland time period brought even greater changes. The climate had reached modern conditions, the temperate forest was fully established, and sea level rise was beginning to slow. The lower estuarine portion of the Potomac was teeming with aquatic resources. Local populations responded to this richness by becoming more and more sedentary. Occupation sites correspondingly became larger and somewhat more permanent. By AD 1000, domesticated plants, first cultivated in tropical areas of North America, found their

Photograph of William Henry Holmes (circa late nineteenth century) replicating a stone tool in Rock Creek Park, Washington, D.C. Handwritten notation below image (apparently added by Holmes) states, "Holmes in an ocean of the 'paleoliths' of Abbott, Putnam, Wilson, and the rest of the early enthusiasts of American antiquities. All are merely refuse of Indian implement making." [Courtesy of Smithsonian Institution Libraries, Washington, D.C.]

way into the Potomac region and began to be incorporated into subsistence practices. Paramount among the new sources of nutrition were maize, beans, and squash. Soon permanent villages appeared, first in the Potomac piedmont above the city and later farther east along the lower Potomac. The manufacture of ceramic vessels was another hallmark of this era. The earliest agriculturalists probably spoke a dialect of the Iroquois language, but Algonquian dominated downstream. Descendants of these peoples would be the tribes that the first Europeans met and named. At the time of contact, the river more or less formed a border between the Powhatan further south and the Piscataway to the north. There were, however, a number of smaller, nonaligned groups in the area.

BOAT PEOPLE

The flag of the first European ship to enter the Potomac is not known. In 1588 Spanish mariners left an account of their entry into what appears to have been the Potomac River. They referred to it as the San Pedro. The river's most famous early explorer was Captain John Smith, of Jamestown fame, whose visits began in 1607. After 1634 Europeans and those under their control increasingly settled the banks of the Potomac. Two colonial ports—Alexandria, Virginia, and Georgetown, Maryland—would establish themselves by the eighteenth century and became incorporated in the new capital after its

charter in 1790. Alexandria and the surrounding area was retroceded to Virginia in 1847.

The remainder of this article will briefly describe a few of the area's more important archaeological sites.

CATOCTIN CREEK

Catoctin Creek is a Paleoindian site located about 48 miles west of the city near Point of Rocks, Maryland. There, roughly 11,500 years ago, a small band of hunters and gatherers camped above the river. A major attraction for them was a nearby jasper quarry. Jasper is a siliceous rock that can be formed into high-quality, reliable stone tools. At this site Paleoindians once paused to replenish their tool kits. The resulting site consists of discarded, worn-out tools, including several broken fluted points, along with the chippage resulting from the production of replacements. All of that debris lies scattered across a farmer's field bordering the river.

PINEY BRANCH QUARRY

By 4,000 years ago, during the Archaic period, people began to exploit quartzite cobbles that were deposited in great numbers along the hillsides of what is today Rock Creek Park in Washington, D.C. Piney Branch was one stop on the larger seasonal round for the purpose of procuring raw material for tool kits. Rather than carry off the entire rock, individuals

Dog skeleton dating to circa AD 1350 from the Winslow site. This canine, one of five known from the site, was intentionally interred outside one of the small oblong wigwams once occupied within the village.   [Richard J. Dent]

reduced the cobbles to what might be called preforms. Those blanks were then transported and turned into finished tools elsewhere. The ground at Piney Branch is littered with cobbles, flakes, and preform rejects. Archaeologists have found caches of intact preforms at contemporaneous habitation sites waiting to be completed as finished tools.

Piney Branch is famous for the research undertaken there in the late nineteenth century by William Henry Holmes. Holmes was curious about the age of the site. A contemporary, Charles C. Abbott of Trenton, New Jersey, claimed that similar objects he had recovered near Trenton, New Jersey, were of extreme antiquity, dating to long before the end of the Pleistocene. Holmes suggested that the seeming crudeness of the objects was not evidence of great age, but that both sets of artifacts represented an initial step in the lithic reduction process from raw material to finished tool. Holmes was correct, and his study became a landmark in early archaeology.

POPES CREEK

The Popes Creek site is about 60 miles below the city and appears to date to about 2,000 years ago, to the Middle Woodland time period. A highly visible feature of the site at one time were two enormous shell heaps—one to the north covering up to 4 acres and up to 20 feet thick, and another to the south of the creek spreading over 20 acres and averaging 5 feet in depth. These middens of oyster bivalves, some larger than a human hand, are the result of intensive shellfish harvesting of reefs near the confluence of the creek and the river. In the early 1900s, William Henry Holmes reported evidence of circular prehistoric houses on the midden surface, and the site is no doubt the product of many years of harvesting rich shellfish resources of the estuarine portion of the river and repeated human habitation. Both middens have since been intensively mined for the lime contained in the shell, but one can still see part of the midden exposed on the high north cliff. Two authentic Potomac River seafood houses are built on pilings at the mouth of Popes Creek, and one can still enjoy oysters here along with a view of what remains of the ancient midden.

WINSLOW

The Winslow village site is located about 26 miles above Washington, D.C., on the broad and productive floodplain of the Potomac River. Major occupation of the site occurred

Removing lower section of east lift-lock gate from within Lock One of the Patowmack Canal, Great Falls Park.   [Richard J. Dent]

about AD 1350, and village occupants represented some of the earliest agriculturalists in this area. Most archaeologists believe that these peoples migrated into the Potomac valley from the north and probably spoke a dialect of the Iroquoian language. On what is today Maryland's McKee Beshers Wildlife Management Area, these immigrants built a small circular village. The center of that village was an open plaza, probably used for ritual and as a workspace. Subterranean storage and trash pits ringed by small circular wigwams surrounded that common. The deceased of the small community were interred in and around those structures. In addition to human burials, a significant number of dog burials have been excavated in this area. Direct evidence has been found of maize, bean, and squash agriculture. A number of other, similar villages are known along the middle and upper Potomac, and these early planters represented a new era in area lifeways.

PATOWMACK CANAL, LOCK ONE

There are a great number of seventeenth- and eighteenth-century sites along the Potomac associated with historic European settlement. Sites of enslaved Africans and African Americans have also recently been investigated. However, this most recent era in settlement is best exemplified by the archaeological remains of an early historic effort to link Washington, D.C., with the western interior late in the eighteenth century. About 12 miles west of the city, in Great Falls Park, one encounters the ruins of the Patowmack Canal. This was an early attempt to improve transportation using a series of bypass canals around major obstacles. When not in one of these bypass canals, canal boats used the natural river channel. The Patowmack Canal pre-dates the better-known Chesapeake and Ohio Canal, also preserved by the National Park Service on the opposite shore. Lock One was probably the first lift-lock built in America (1797–98). The spectacular five-lock complex of which it is a part overcomes a 77-foot drop in the Potomac River. One can easily visit the lock complex in the park, and the lock gate remains that have been excavated are on display in the visitor center.

Further Reading: Curry, Dennis, *Feast of the Dead: Aboriginal Ossuaries in Maryland* (Crownsville: Maryland Historical Trust Press, 1999); Dent, Richard J., *Chesapeake Prehistory: Old Traditions, New Directions* (New York: Plenum Press, 1995); Hranicky, W. Jack, *Lithic Technology in the Middle Potomac Valley of Maryland and Virginia* (New York: Kluwer Academic, 2002); Metcalf, Paul, *Waters of Patowmack* (Charlottesville: University Press of Virginia, 2002); Potter, Stephen R., *Commoners, Tribute, and Chiefs: The Development of Algonquian Culture in the Potomac Valley* (Charlottesville: University Press of Virginia, 1993).

Richard J. Dent

L'ANSE AUX MEADOWS NATIONAL HISTORIC SITE

Eastern Newfoundland, Canada

Only Known Viking Settlement in the New World

L'Anse aux Meadows is a Viking age West Norse site occupied briefly around AD 1000. Located on the northern tip of Newfoundland's Northern Peninsula, it was a sizable winter base for further exploration. It corresponds to Straumfjord (Fjord of Currents) of the Vinland sagas.

The occupants of L'Anse aux Meadows came from Greenland, where a small group of Icelanders led by Erik the Red had established a colony around AD 985. Iceland and Greenland were chiefdoms, their economies based on livestock farming. Settlement consisted of individual farms; there were no towns or villages. Both countries were dependent on imports such as flour, weapons, glass, and bronze, and luxuries such as spices, wine, fine textiles, artworks, gold, silver, and precious stones. Greenland also lacked timber and iron.

The Viking age covers the period AD 800–1050. The term "Norse" refers to all Scandinavians of the Viking age and early medieval period. "West Norse" includes Icelanders and Greenlanders, who, to some extent, shared language and culture with western Norway.

The voyages of Erik the Red's son, Leif, and other members of his family to regions west and southwest of Greenland around the year AD 1000 are described in the Vinland sagas, a collection of medieval Icelandic manuscripts. The southernmost of these regions was Vinland, Land of Wine. Archaeological work at L'Anse aux Meadows indicates that Vinland comprised the coastal regions surrounding the Gulf of St. Lawrence. L'Anse aux Meadows was the base for the exploration of Vinland and the exploitation of its resources in northeastern New Brunswick.

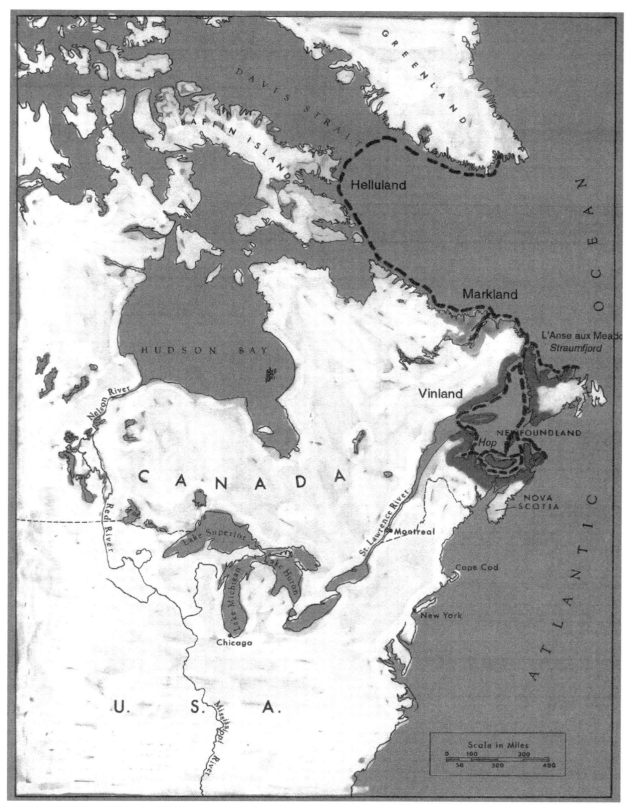

A map showing the route the early Viking explorers took, establishing the settlement of L'Anse aux Meadows.   [Birgitta Wallace]

The ruins of L'Anse aux Meadows from a distance.   [Birgitta Wallace]

THE SITE

The ruins of eight Norse buildings are situated on a narrow terrace encircling a bog 300 feet from the sea. Black Duck Brook, which runs from Black Duck Pond, about half a mile inland, cuts through the terrace and the bog. The present village of L'Anse aux Meadows is situated about half a mile from the site. To the south, the site is framed by a low sandstone ridge. Off the coast are three small islands, one of which, Great Sacred Island, forms a distinct landmark.

The site was occupied by a succession of Native peoples between 4000 BC and AD 1500, but no Natives were present during the time of the Norse.

The Norse buildings were organized into three dwelling complexes and a compound for the manufacture of iron. The dwelling complexes were distributed in a line along the seaside edge of the terrace. Each complex comprised a large hall and a hut, and the southernmost complex also included a small house. The iron-smelting installation, closer to the shore, consisted of an open-ended hut with a stone furnace. Nearby was a charcoal kiln in which fuel was produced for the furnace.

L'Anse aux Meadows was first identified as the likely site of Leif's landing by William F. Munn in 1914. The site was excavated from 1961 to 1968 by Anne-Stine Ingstad, a Norwegian archaeologist, after her husband, Helge Ingstad, was shown the ruins by George Decker, a local fisherman. The site was designated a National Historic Site of Canada in 1969.

Excavations continued under the management of Parks Canada from 1973 to 1976, directed first by Bengt Schonback and later by Birgitta Wallace.

THE BUILDINGS

All the buildings are in the manner of late tenth- and eleventh-century Icelandic architecture, found also in Greenland. Building materials were sod over a timber frame.

The Halls

The two largest halls, at the south and north ends of the terrace, were large, multi-roomed structures. The southern hall had an exterior length of 95 feet and a floor surface of 1,100 square feet, with four rooms in a row. One small and two large rooms served as living quarters, with wooden platforms along the walls and a simple hearth either in the center of the floor or off to one side. The small room provided private quarters for the lord of the manor. The fourth room was a smithy.

The northern hall, with a floor space of 1,720 square feet, was the largest and most complex building on the site. It had six rooms plus a lean-to shed. Two large communal rooms and one small private room formed a row through the center of the house. Another row on the western side of the house contained a kitchen with a stone oven, and two large storage rooms. A shed attached to the eastern side was used for boat repairs. One of the communal rooms had a "longfire" in the center of the floor, consisting of a stone hearth, a cooking pit, and a pit for keeping embers overnight. The central longfires in the other living/sleeping rooms were simpler, and all the rooms had sitting/sleeping platforms along the side walls.

The middle hall was smaller than the other two, with a floor space of only 668 square feet. It lacked the private quarters of the other two halls and had only one communal living/sleeping room. Its longfire was slightly off-center, with a square, slate-lined ember box at one end. There was also a large storage room and a small carpentry shop.

The Small House

Next to the southern hall was a small rectangular house with a fireplace against one wall, backed by a large slab of slate. The house was probably a dwelling and workshop where bog ore was prepared for the making of iron.

The Huts

Two of the huts were square buildings dug into the ground, known as pit buildings. A third hut was irregularly rounded and aboveground. All three were dwellings, the former two possibly also workshops. Pit buildings are a tradition in Scandinavian prehistory from at least the fifth century on. They were especially common in the Viking age, usually built side by side with halls. The round hut had a narrow entrance protected by walls projecting toward the southern hall. A fireplace by the wall indicates that it, too, was a dwelling. The roof had been corbeled. Only outbuildings and low-status dwellings were built this way in Iceland.

The Furnace Hut

The furnace hut was set into the edge of the terrace, its front open to the brook. In the middle of the floor was a small furnace for the manufacture of iron, consisting of a stone shaft made airtight with a thick layer of clay and set over a shallow pit. The nearby charcoal kiln was a simple pit packed with wood, which was set alight, covered with sod, and left to smolder for at least 24 hours. Iron bog ore was collected along the brook bank, where it forms naturally. The furnace was filled with layers of prepared bog ore and heated to a temperature above 1,850°F (1,000°C) with the help of bellows inserted into the front of the shaft. During the firing, non-iron inclusions became liquid and ran down into the pit, forming slag. The iron in the ore dripped down on top of the slag, forming a bun-shaped bloom, which was partially cut and hammered to drive out impurities while still red-hot. As it cooled, it was removed from the furnace hut and taken to the smithy, where it was forged into boat nails.

ARTIFACTS

Most of the artifacts consist of waste from iron manufacture, carpentry, and boat repair. A few small personal items were also recovered.

Iron Waste

Ironworking on the site included both smelting and smithing and the waste from these activities consisted primarily of slag. The iron manufacture had been a single episode, producing only 6.5 to 11 pounds of iron. The workers had been unskilled, so that much of the iron remained in the slag. Iron production was required for nails, used in boat repair; the iron produced would have been sufficient for 100 to 200 nails. The work of forging the iron into nails had taken place in a smithy in the southern hall, where smithing slag was found.

Carpentry Waste

Wood waste from framing the buildings and other activities was thrown into the peat bog. Thanks to the preservative quality of the bog, the debris has survived in excellent condition. The waste, consisting of post and plank ends, shavings, chips, birch bark rolls, and fragments of rope made from twisted spruce roots, was concentrated outside the middle hall complex. Within the waste were broken and discarded objects: a barrel lid, the floor plank for a small boat, an auger bow, a birch bark cup, treenails, and a few objects whose function has not been determined. The waste chips were local wood, but some of the discarded objects were of Scotch pine, a European species introduced into North America only around AD 1500.

Boat Repair

All iron objects found on the site were nails, including eighty-one cut and discarded nails, and one whole unused nail. When iron nails occur in large quantities on a West Norse site, they signal boat repair, as nails were primarily used in Viking ships and boats, not in building construction; the nails rusted with time, and had to be replaced. About 66 percent of the nail fragments were found in the northern complex, especially in the shed, where the repair took place. The boat was small, no longer than about 26 feet, the size of auxiliary boats carried on Viking ships and used as landing and scouting craft. The unused nail differed from the discarded fragments: its iron had a much higher phosphorus content and it was probably made on the site. It was found within the carpentry waste, away from the other nails.

Small Personal Items

A bronze pin had fallen into a forge pit in the smithy; it was a simple "Hiberno-Norse" type of clothing fastener customary throughout the West Norse area. A glass bead had been dropped outside the middle hall, and a gilded piece of a bronze ring (finger ring or suspension loop) was found in the living room of the same hall.

Three objects are associated with women's work: a spindle whorl and a small whetstone found in the boat shed, and a bone needle found in the middle hall. The spindle whorl, the flywheel of a handheld spindle used to make yarn or thread for weaving and knitting, is of soapstone and had been made from a piece of an old soapstone cooking pot or oil lamp. The whetstone is of a typical Viking age form often kept in sewing boxes and used for sharpening small objects such as needles and sewing scissors. The bone needle is of a type used for single-needle knitting, a technique used to make hats, socks, and mitts.

DATE OF THE SETTLEMENT

Dating of the site is based on its architecture, artifacts, and radiocarbon dates. The architecture of the halls is of the style that evolved in Iceland toward the end of the tenth century and remained in vogue into the thirteenth century. Pit buildings were out of style by the eleventh century.

The spindle whorl, the whetstone, the bone needle, and the glass bead were common throughout the Viking period and even later. Only the bronze pin provides a more precise date. It is of a kind in use about AD 920–1050 and was especially common around 950.

Radiocarbon analysis furnishes the tightest date spans. There are a total of 148 radiocarbon dates for the site, about 50 of which pertain to the Norse occupation, ranging from AD 640 to 1150. However, the archaeological evidence is unequivocal that the Norse occupation was brief and limited to one settlement episode. The wide range of dates are on peat, whalebone, and wood, including charcoal, have all been calibrated to take account of differences in the amount of carbon isotope that was naturally in the atmosphere at different times. However, this wide range of dates results from the effect of sample size, marine reservoir effect, and wood age. The most accurate dates are those obtained on a series of young branches and twigs, ranging between AD 990 and 1050, with a mean date of about 1014. There is little doubt that these dates are the ones that come closest to the actual date of occupation.

SIZE OF THE SETTLEMENT AND ITS SOCIAL ORGANIZATION

The settlement was large and the buildings show clear evidence of social stratification. The L'Anse aux Meadows buildings could accommodate between sixty-five and ninety people, most of them in the three halls. The two largest halls were the type of dwelling enjoyed by the elite, chieftains or their near equals. Both were imposing buildings. The southern hall is more than double the size of Erik the Red's last home in Iceland. The northern hall is comparable to the large hall at Sandnes, the chief estate in the West Settlement in Greenland. The middle hall, with its one communal living/sleeping room, was the type used by the well-to-do but not of chieftain status— in this case perhaps a skipper and his crew. The small house is the type of multifunctional dwelling used by day-labor tenant farmers. Finally, the small round hut, as well as the two pit buildings, were dwellings of the kind to which those lowest on the social scale, perhaps slaves, were confined.

The artifacts are less explicit with regard to the status of their owners. Glass beads and bronze adornments were relatively common. Only the gilded brass fragment suggests that its owner possessed a certain amount of wealth. The spindle whorl, the whetstone for needles, and the bone pin indicate the presence of women. All other activities, such as carpentry, iron manufacture, and smithing, were within the male realm. Throughout, there is no evidence of normal household activities, in the form of broken soapstone vessels and dairy pantries, small household knives, and looms. The conclusion one gains from the building and artifact types is that the occupants represented the social spectrum of West Norse society but were predominantly male.

Nine fire strikers of red jasper, worn out and discarded around the halls, give an indication of the national origin of the occupants. Four of the nine pieces were of jasper from western Greenland, and the other five from western and southwestern Iceland. All the Greenland pieces came from the northern complex. Of the five Icelandic pieces, two came from the southern complex and two from the middle, with one found in the northern complex. This could be seen as a corroboration of the Vinland sagas, which suggest that up to two-thirds of the Vinland exploration parties may have been hired Icelanders on at least some voyages, but that leadership and control rested with the Greenland contingent. There is no doubt that the northern complex was *the* most important complex on the site. One may conclude that the northern hall was in fact the hall built by Leif Eriksson.

LENGTH OF OCCUPATION AND ABANDONMENT OF THE SETTLEMENT

The archaeological indicators show that the Norse occupation was short, probably a matter of years rather than decades. The cultural deposits are insignificant and the middens are minute. The iron waste is so limited that it indicates a one-time event. Abandonment of the site was voluntary and orderly, with all household inventory, tools, and substantial belongings removed.

THE FUNCTION OF THE SETTLEMENT

The lack of structures for domestic animals shows that L'Anse aux Meadows was not a normal colonizing settlement. The presence of three large halls so close together and the considerable space devoted to accommodations and storage are also unusual. The exposed location of the settlement directly on the sea indicates that seafaring was the most important aspect of the settlement, not farming.

A piece of butternut wood and three butternuts found in the carpentry waste are proof that the occupants had visited areas farther south. Butternut, also called white walnut, *Juglans cinerea*, is a southern species of wood, not indigenous to Newfoundland. Its northern limit is in northeastern New Brunswick and deep into the St. Lawrence River valley, close to latitude 47° north. The find is significant because wild grapes grow in the same area, proving that the Norse did in fact visit areas where grapes grew wild. In the wild, grapes usually grow among hardwood trees, the vines winding up to the tops of the trees. These trees, felled and shipped back to Greenland, were the *vínvíð*, or "grape trees," of the sagas. Wine was an expensive commodity, cherished by chieftains whose power and political and religious authority were tied to their ostentatious display of wealth and lavish feasts. This significant resource gave its name to the entire region—Vinland, Land of Wine—and L'Anse aux Meadows was its main settlement.

L'ANSE AUX MEADOWS AND VINLAND

L'Anse aux Meadows was a base for exploration and a trans-shipment station for resources collected farther afield. All social levels were represented, from one or more chieftains to slaves. Although its architecture and material culture are typical of early eleventh-century Greenland sites, there is no physical counterpart to L'Anse aux Meadows in the entire West Norse area. Its only parallel is Straumfjord, the northern base described in the Vinland sagas. L'Anse aux Meadows matches Straumfjord in all aspects: type of structures and concentration of people, social organization, and function. In the Vinland sagas, the Norse spent summers in a distant location south of Straumfjord, at Hóp, where they gathered grapes and cut lumber. Hóp means lagoon, salt at flood, fresh at ebb, and sheltered from the sea by extensive sandbars. No doubt this is the place from where the butternuts were transported to L'Anse aux Meadows. A close match to Hóp can be found in the coastal lagoons and rivers of northeastern New Brunswick.

L'Anse aux Meadows is in all likelihood Leif Eriksson's exploration base in Vinland, Straumsfjord or Leifsbúðir (Leif's Camp; Leifsbúðir is simply a literary contraction of Straumfjord and Hóp). Simple calculations of the work hours and materials required to build the settlement along with its number of inhabitants prove that L'Anse aux Meadows cannot be an anonymous settlement unmentioned in the sagas. Greenland, in its early years, with a total population of about 500, was too small a settlement to support more than one such venture. Nor could L'Anse aux Meadows survive as a permanent settlement. The distance from Greenland, about the same as to Norway, was too great to be practical, and the most desirable resources, grapes and hardwood, were even farther away. The same resources and many others could be obtained via Norway, and voyages to Europe were a necessity. It would have strained the small Greenland colony beyond its capacity to maintain traffic in both directions. In addition, the Norse were outnumbered by thousands of people already in Vinland, people with whom they got into conflict almost immediately.

Under these circumstances it is not difficult to understand why Vinland was never colonized, or why L'Anse aux Meadows/Straumfjord was soon abandoned.

VISITORS TO L'ANSE AUX MEADOWS NATIONAL HISTORIC SITE

The site is managed by Parks Canada and is officially open to the public June 1 to October 14, but arrangements can be made to see the site beyond these dates, except during the winter months. There is a visitor center with an exhibit showcasing the most interesting artifacts and a short film detailing the discovery of the site. A boardwalk leads to the site, where the footprints of the buildings can still be seen. Nearby are full-size reconstructions of the southernmost complex. Guides and animators are present on the site during the opening season.

Further Reading: Fitzhugh, William W., and Elisabeth I. Ward, eds., *Vikings: The North Atlantic Saga* (Washington, DC: Smithsonian Institution Press in association with the National Museum of Natural History, 2000); Ingstad, Anne Stine, and Helge Ingstad, *The Norse Discovery of America*, Vol. I: *Excavations at L'Anse aux Meadows, Newfoundland 1961–1968*, and Vol. II: *The Historical Background and the Evidence of the Norse Settlement Discovered in Newfoundland* (Oslo: University of Oslo Press, 1986); Jones, Gwyn, *The Norse Atlantic Saga. Being the Norse Voyages of Discovery and Settlement to Iceland, Greenland, and North America*, new, enlarged ed. (New York: Oxford University Press, 1986); *L'Anse aux Meadows National Historic Site of Canada*, Parks Canada Web site, http://www.pc.gc.ca/lhn-nhs/nl/meadows/index_e.asp (online February 2004); *The Sagas of the Icelanders: A Selection*, preface by Jane Smiley, introduction by Robert Kellogg (New York: Viking Penguin, 2000); Wallace, Birgitta, "The Norse in Newfoundland: L'Anse aux Meadows and Vinland," *Newfoundland Studies* 19(1) (2005): 5–43; Wallace, Birgitta Linderoth, *Westward Vikings: The Saga of L'Anse aux Meadows* (St. John's, NL: Parks Canada and Historic Sites Association of Newfoundland and Labrador, 2006).

Birgitta Wallace

MOHAWK RIVER VALLEY ARCHAEOLOGY

Eastern New York State

Native American Village Sites Along the Mohawk River

The Mohawk valley was the core area of the Native American nation known by the same name. Sites there that date after AD 1000 are relevant to the long developmental history of the Mohawk Nation. Earlier villages in the Mohawk valley were small, and the number of contemporaneous communities multiplied as the overall population grew. After 1450 increasing conflict with nearby nations caused the scattered small communities to consolidate into a smaller number of larger communities, and required village leaders to pick defensible hilltops as new village sites. This lasted until late in the

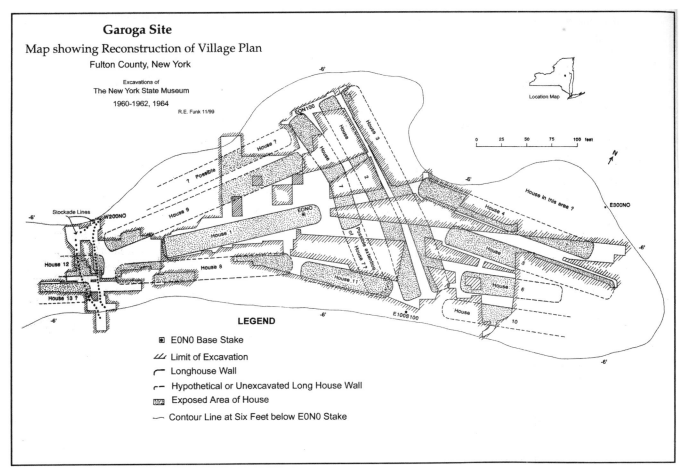

Garoga Site

Map showing Reconstruction of Village Plan

Fulton County, New York

Excavations of
The New York State Museum
1960-1962, 1964

R.E. Funk 11/99

Location Map

LEGEND

- EON0 Base Stake
- Limit of Excavation
- Longhouse Wall
- Hypothetical or Unexcavated Long House Wall
- Exposed Area of House
- Contour Line at Six Feet below E0N0 Stake

Plan of the Garoga site.   [Bulletin #503, printed with permission of the New York State Museum, Albany NY 12230]

sixteenth century, when the League of the Iroquois was formed. Later sites were located nearer the river and major trails. Palisaded Mohawk villages disappeared early in the eighteenth century, replaced by more dispersed faming settlements. Except where noted below, these sites are on private land and not open to the public.

ELWOOD SITE

The Elwood site is a small village site that dates to 1446–76, before small villages consolidated into larger communities on hilltops. It lies on private property in the town of Minden. One complete longhouse was excavated in 1982. This structure probably housed about 40 people. The total population of the village was probably about 100.

GETMAN SITE

The Getman site is located north of the Mohawk River in an area known as Stone Arabia. Like the Elwood site it documents Mohawk small villages prior to their nucleation on defensive hilltops. The village was probably occupied for about a decade in the first half of the fifteenth century. The only excavated longhouse had about 70 residents. There were probably at least 240 people in the village, but no more than 400.

OTSTUNGO SITE

Otstungo lies on private land southwest of the Mohawk River in the town of Minden. It is perched atop a sheer cliff of black shale where Otstungo Creek has cut deeply into the soft bedrock. Otstungo is the earliest and one of the best studied of the large fortified villages built by the Mohawks.

The single excavated longhouse here is probably understood in greater detail than any other Iroquois longhouse. The site is located in a particularly scenic spot, and it was chosen as one of four 1491 villages to be highlighted by *National Geographic* magazine in October 1991.

A huge pine tree once stood near the village entrance. The giant tree was still intact in 1877, but it was gone by 1902. Otstungo was occupied between 1450 and 1525. The maximum population at Otstungo was probably around 630.

GAROGA SITE

The Garoga site is located on a high defensible hilltop in the town of Ephratah, Fulton County, about 11 km from the Mohawk River. The village site was probably occupied during 1525–45 by people who moved there from the Otstungo site.

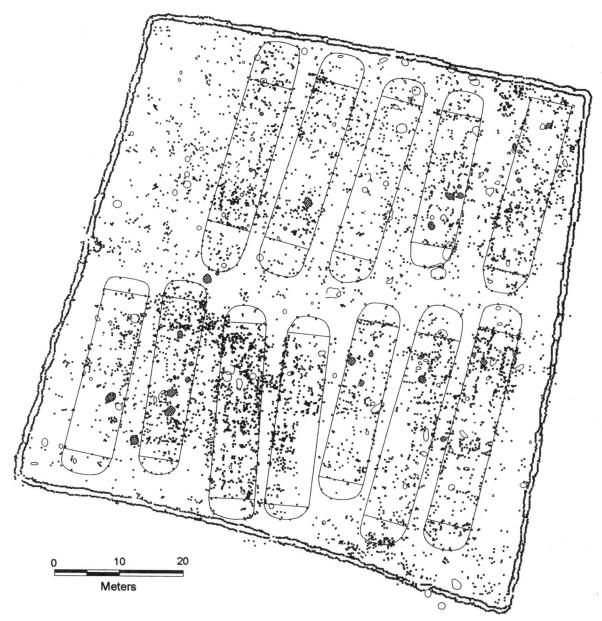

0   10   20

Meters

Post mold patterns, house outline, and palisade at Caughnawaga.   [Dean R. Snow]

Like Otstungo, it was palisaded for defense only across this narrow access.

Major excavations revealed the remains of nine large longhouses and a double palisade across the neck of the site's peninsular hilltop. Later research revealed that there were thirteen longhouses and possible traces of two more. The narrow southwest access to the site is only 27 m wide, and this short stretch was the only area that the residents of Garoga felt compelled to fortify. They built a double palisade of very large posts, apparently after most of the longhouses had been built.

The artifacts from Garoga include a few scraps of metal of European origin, indicating that the site dates to some time

within the 1525–80 period. Garoga was probably occupied around 1525–45. Its population was probably at least 820 people, but estimates of 1,400 or more are not unreasonable.

KLOCK SITE

The Klock site is one of two most extensively studied sites of the period, along with nearby Garoga. It represents the decades during which the beneficial effects of the League of the Iroquois were beginning to be felt by the Mohawks, and military defenses began to relax.

The site lies on a tongue of land that extends eastward from higher ground to the west. Eight houses have been identified at the site, one of which was explored in detail.

Anglican church at Indian Castle.   [Dean R. Snow]

Excavations turned up at least twenty-five pieces of metal. Some of these could be early European trade goods, including a piece of copper and a length of chain found in a post mold. The Klock site might have been occupied later than Garoga, but it is likely that the villages were occupied simultaneously by two separate communities. An occupation in the range of 1525–45 is likely. There were fewer people living at this site than at Garoga, and the two communities might have consolidated subsequently at the very large Smith-Pagerie site.

SMITH-PAGERIE SITE

The Smith-Pagerie site is located on a broad defensible hill about a kilometer northeast of the Garoga site. The site probably dates to 1560–80, and its inhabitants probably moved to it from the Klock and Garoga sites. The Smith-Pagerie site represents the end of a period in which small amounts of European goods were making their way into the Mohawk

valley. It was also a time when captives and refugees from elsewhere in Northern Iroquoia were being absorbed by Mohawk villages. This infusion is reflected in the growing diversity of ceramic styles.

The site had at least sixteen longhouses and perhaps as many as twenty. Possibly the most striking artifact known for the Smith-Pagerie site is a bone comb that was excavated by John Jackowski around or just before the time that the State Museum was also investigating the site. The comb was purchased by the Rock Foundation for curation at the Rochester Museum, and it remains there.

The village probably had a population of at least 1,100 and perhaps twice that many. The number of longhouses at this site is large enough to have accommodated households moving here from both Garoga and Klock. Captives and refugees contributed to the growth and accounted for the new exotic ceramic styles that show up in the archaeological assemblage.

CAUGHNAWAGA SITE

The Veeder site is now known more commonly as Caughnawaga. The site was completely exposed by avocational excavators in the 1950s. Metal stakes were selectively inserted into the molds left by longhouse and palisade posts, and the site is now open to the public. Visitors can walk around the village site and acquire a good sense of the layout of a late seventeenth-century Mohawk community.

The site was purchased by the Franciscan Order Minor Conventuals and excavated under their direction based on their belief that it was the home village of Kateri Tekakwitha. She was an early Catholic convert who in the 1670s moved with Jesuit missionaries and other converted Mohawks to a mission site outside Montreal that is now known as Kanawake. More recent research suggests that Kateri probably lived on the nearby Fox Farm village site, and that Caughnawaga was probably occupied during 1679–93 by around 300 non-Catholic Mohawks.

Caughnawaga had a dozen longhouses of uniform size, arranged in two rows within a square palisade. Standard lengths were typical of the period of demographic upheaval that followed the epidemics of the middle seventeenth century. The square palisade with bastions followed a European pattern that worked better than earlier designs after the introduction of firearms.

FORT HUNTER SITE

The Mohawks shifted from palisaded villages of longhouses to dispersed communities of individual cabins early in the eighteenth century. One such community congregated around the English fortification at Fort Hunter. The fort, Anglican parsonage, and traces of Native structures are preserved in a New York State Historic Site, along with Erie Canal ditches and an aqueduct. The site is open to the public.

INDIAN CASTLE

The second principal community of Mohawks in the eighteenth century was initially in the vicinity of modern Fort Plain. The dispersed community later shifted farther west, and the English built a fort there, naming it Fort Hendrick in honor of a local Mohawk chief. Still later the focus of the community shifted farther west to the mouth of Nowadaga Creek, where it is known today as Indian Castle.

The site is now a National Landmark. Standing structures include the Anglican church, built in 1769 on land donated by the Mohawk chief Joseph Brant. A Dutch barn that might have belonged to Brant also stands on the site, near the ruins of his home. Most of the site is privately owned, but Indian Castle church is often open to visitors.

Further Reading: Funk, Robert E., and Robert D. Kuhn, *Three Sixteenth-Century Mohawk Iroquois Village Sites*, Bulletin 503 (Albany: New York State Museum, 2003); Grumet, Robert S., *Historic Contact: Indian People and Colonists in Today's Northeastern United States in the Sixteenth through Eighteenth Centuries* (Norman: University of Oklahoma Press, 1995); *Native Peoples of New York*, New York State Museum Exhibitions Web site, http://www.nysm.nysed.gov/exhibits/np.html (online April 2005); Snow, Dean R., *The Iroquois* (Cambridge: Blackwell, 1994); Snow, Dean R., *Mohawk Valley Archaeology: The Sites*, Occasional Papers in Anthropology No. 23 (University Park: Penn State University, 1995); Trigger, Bruce G., ed., *Northeast*, Vol. 15 of *Handbook of North American Indians* (Washington, DC: Smithsonian Institution Press, 1978).

Dean R. Snow

RED BAY NATIONAL HISTORIC SITE AND EARLY HISTORIC ST. LAWRENCE SITES

Labrador, Newfoundland, and Quebec, Canada

Basque Whaling and Fishing Sites from the 1500s

In 1992 when much of the western world turned its attention to celebrating the discovery of the Americas by Christopher Columbus, credit spread to the English, the French, and the Portuguese, who also made contributions to the exploration and settlement of the New World. Notably absent from this group were the original European discoverers: the Norse, or Vikings, as they are still popularly known, who about AD 1000 established a settlement on the northern tip of Newfoundland for a few years before returning to Greenland, where they maintained a colony that lasted more than 400 years. Another group even less known for New World exploration are the Basques, a seafaring people with special ethnicity, traditions, and language who lived along the shores of the Bay of Biscay in northern Spain and southwestern France (Barkham 1978; Proulx 1993; Kurlansky 1999; Douglass and Bilbao 2005). They sailed to Newfoundland, Labrador, and Quebec, where they hunted whales, fished, and traded with native groups from the 1520s into the 1600s and later. However, the Basque voyages have been largely missing from the annals of history for the past 300 years. Like the Norse, early Basque voyagers did not establish long-term settlements, come in large groups, or leave a residual population, so their ventures did not produce a large or easily detected legacy that survived into modern times. In fact, knowledge of their contributions to early America discovery has disappeared almost entirely, eclipsed by the growing dominance of other European nation-states that cannibalized their expertise and appropriated their contributions into their own histories of conquest, exploitation, and settlement. With the ascendancy of succeeding European powers, the Basques, who sent more ships across the Atlantic than any other European nation in the sixteenth century, vanished almost without a trace from compendia of early America discovery.

In fact, a record existed in the archaeological sites left behind by the shore-based whale-processing activities of the Basques, but these sites were not readily apparent to modern observers. Another buried record was found in the archives in Spain and France. In the 1970s Selma Huxley Barkham, while researching the voluminous but poorly catalogued sixteenth-century Spanish Basque archives, discovered reports of Basque whaling voyages to southern Labrador and Newfoundland beginning early in the 1500s. One of the documents from mid-century concerned the loss of a whaling vessel named the *San Juan*, which sank in a 1565 storm in the mouth of Red Bay, one of the largest Basque whaling centers on the Labrador coast of the Strait of Belle Isle. The wife of one of the sailors who was lost had sued the ship owners for compensation, and depositions described the circumstances; among other records was the last will and testament of a crew member who died on one of the expeditions. As documents and references to a major whale fishery accumulated, a surprising story, unknown except in vague terms to historians, unfolded. Basque whalers had begun sailing to Newfoundland and Labrador waters to hunt whales at least as early as the 1520s, and by mid-century dozens of vessels were engaged annually in a lucrative fishery that stretched from the western Gulf of St. Lawrence to Chateau in southern Labrador and along the entire west and south coasts of Newfoundland. The fishery declined after the 1580s following the decimation of local whale populations and the loss of many Basque whalers that had been commandeered for the Spanish Armada of 1588 and other military endeavors against England. After 1600, Basque vessels returned sporadically, primarily to fish and trade (Turgeon 1990, 1994), but by this time the Newfoundland fishery was less lucrative and the most experienced skippers and whalers had been hired away by the Dutch for their Arctic and northwest Atlantic whaling ventures.

This history of extensive Basque involvement in early North American discovery is not widely known in Europe or the Americas, and like the intriguing reports that Columbus obtained clues about the existence of an American mainland during a voyage he made west of Iceland in 1480s, the details of the Basque enterprise have not been thoroughly studied, published, or assimilated (Bélanger 1971; Barkham 1977, 1978, 1980, 1984; Huxley 1987; Douglass and Bilkbao 2005, 51–57). At present, information comes from two sources: the Spanish and French Basque archives preserved in municipal centers, and archaeological work in Newfoundland, southern Labrador, and the Gulf of St. Lawrence. From these sources it is possible to piece together the outline of a new and largely unwritten Basque chapter in the history of the Americas.

One reason Basque history has remained obscure is that its geographic focus lies outside the sphere of later colonial settlement and was a commercial enterprise that did not enjoy high-level national sponsorship or the involvement of prominent "adventurers" or patrons whose writings and influence (as in the case of Lord Baltimore's establishment of the short-lived colony of Ferryland, or Martin Frobisher's vainglorious search for a northwest passage to the Orient and attempt to mine gold in southern Baffinland) led these ventures into the pages of history. Yet from forty years of archival studies in Spanish and French Basque archives and a similar period of archaeological work at Basque sites in Newfoundland, Labrador, and Quebec, it is now possible to provide a general outline of Basque history in the Americas as well as specific knowledge of how the Basques' operations were conducted in the field.

Although it is possible that Basque ships were visiting the northwest Atlantic or even Newfoundland waters in the late fifteenth century, it was in the aftermath of John Cabot's voyage of 1498 to Newfoundland and Labrador that Spanish and French Basque whalers and fishermen began sailing regularly to Newfoundland and the Strait of Belle Isle. Their general procedure was to leave the Bay of Biscay in April and May and arrive in the Newfoundland region in June, after the pack ice had dispersed. The ships operated singly or in small groups, depending on their financing and ownership, and they tended to utilize specific harbors and regions rather than range at large on the seas, as was the Dutch pattern in the seventeenth century. Utilizing whaling techniques and a ship-building tradition that had developed in Biscay between the tenth and fifteenth centuries, they harpooned whales with large, double-bladed barbed iron harpoons fixed to wooden shafts, with a line that could be secured to the stem of a light plank whaleboat, known as a chaloupe, manned by several oarsmen. Once captured and lanced, the whale was towed into the harbor where the mother ship was anchored, and the blubber was stripped and the oil rendered in large cast iron kettles over tryworks on shore. In addition to chains of hearths constructed of blubber-stained rock, earth, and discarded clay roof tiles, shore facilities included a cooperage where barrels prefabricated at home were assembled, filled with oil, and sealed. Since the whalers and sailors lived aboard ship, Basque whaling stations consisted only of industrial facilities, and these were roughly assembled and generally consisted of furnaces surrounded by a wood floor or stone slab pavement and a tile-covered roof supported by an open-sided timber framework The season usually ended in late October or November, when the Labrador bays began to freeze and access to harbors became uncertain. Occasionally an early winter storm would freeze the harbors before the ships could depart, and in such cases the crews became stranded and endured a harsh winter, for which they were unprepared and from which some did not survive. However, a successful voyage produced great profit for the owners, and what trickled down to the sailors, supplemented by the private stock of fish and resources garnered during their free time, supported their families at home for a year. Should disaster befall a ship or a sailor, legal recourse was available, and it was from such actions as well as municipal tax records, licenses, insurance documents, and financial records that the business of Basque whaling in the Americas became known historically.

The geography of sixteenth- century Basque whaling, pieced together from documents, maps, and archaeological finds, centered on the Strait of Belle Isle and the Gulf of St. Lawrence, where more than twenty stations were established along the western and southern coasts of Newfoundland, St. Pierre and Miquelon islands, and the north shore of the gulf from the straits nearly to Quebec City. Less activity seems to have taken place along the southern shore of the gulf, where large whales were less common. The archaeological sites left from these activities are mostly small, consisting a few stone oven bases and deposits of blubber-stained rocks and tiles, and occasionally whalebones, which tended to be disposed of alongshore rather than on land.

Major whaling centers like those along the Labrador coast of the Strait of Belle Isle left more substantial archaeological remains. Many of these sites contain several sets of ovens, often owned by different companies or concerns. Because outbound ships were laden with light loads, they had to be ballasted, usually with tiles that upon arrival were used to refurbish winter-damaged tile roofs and served as paving and construction material. However, stone ballast, usually consisting of limestone or other rock local to the ship's home port (but not generally flint nodules, which tended to be a northern European ballast material), was also used and dumped when the ship reached its destination. Ballast for the return voyage was provided by casks of oil, fish, timber, or whatever other materials had been harvested.

Archaeologists working in the straits region prior to the 1970s did not report the presence of tiles—or, if they noticed them, made little of their significance. The early history of this region is complex, and the local population is a mix of French- and English-speaking settlers and fishermen whose origins post-date 1700 and who have no local tradition or knowledge of the region's early history. It was not until Barkham's archival discoveries prompted Jim Tuck of Memorial University and Walter Kenyon, a prominent Canadian historical archaeologist, to explore Red Bay and

other locations that the presence of a century of Basque occupation was identified. Subsequent fieldwork by Tuck and by Robert Grenier of Parks Canada at Red Bay (Tuck and Grenier 1981, 1989), by a Basque archaeological team in Chateau, and by other archaeologists in Newfoundland and Quebec (Lalande 1989) revealed the geographic extent of Basque activities, most of which dated to the sixteenth century and involved whaling.

Although many Basque sites have been found, few besides Red Bay have been investigated thoroughly. Many are known only from the presence of their distinctive tiles, from a note in the historical record, or by the obtrusive ovens. Many sites have been destroyed or covered beneath later settlement, while others, such as those on Île Nue in the Mingan Islands (Drouin 1988), are pristine and have not yet been investigated. The archaeological visibility of tiles and ovens has made the Basque occupation a prominent yet still largely unexplored feature of the gulf's complex 500-year-old historical landscape.

It is from the extensive research at Red Bay that we have some understanding of the operation of a Basque whaling station. Although perhaps not typical because it was larger and occupied more consistently than many other stations, Red Bay has become the "type site" for the sixteenth-century whaling phase of Basque America. However, Red Bay is important for more than its archival studies and land archaeology.

Among the records uncovered by Barkham was information about the loss of the whaling galleon San Juan at Red Bay, known as Butus to the Basques, in 1565 (Barkham and Grenier 1978/79; Grenier 1985). Ready to leave for her home port and loaded with 800 to 1,000 barrels of oil, the San Juan was caught unprepared for one of the fierce fall gales that can strike this region without warning, and it sank in 30 feet of water, only a few feet from one of the large Basque shore stations on the northern side of Saddle Island. Armed with specific archival information, Parks Canada archaeologists directed by Robert Grenier located what is almost certainly the San Juan nearly perfectly preserved in the cold, still waters of the harbor and excavated it, plank by plank between 1978 and 1985 (Grenier 1988, 1989). In addition to recovering detailed information about Basque nautical architecture, the excavation produced a treasure trove of ceramic, wood, and other artifacts that were more intact and better preserved than the artifacts recovered from the nearby land site. Detailed analysis of the ship and its contents, and results of an excavated trench connecting the wreck to the shore, have provided a wealth of data on Basque shipbuilding and the material culture of a mid-fifteenth-century Spanish Basque whaling operation (Light 1992; Ringer 1985; Ross 1985).

The object of Basque interest—the whales and their resources—has also been studied from archaeological recovery of whalebones found in the land site, underwater, and from a whale "graveyard" across Red Bay, where whale remains were dumped after the butchering. It is estimated that as many as 20,000 whales were killed, primarily by Basques, during the sixteenth century. Osteological studies indicate that Basque whalers were catching right whales and bowheads in approximately equal numbers (Cumbaa 1986). North Atlantic right whales are now an endangered species, following their precipitous decline in the sixteenth century, and their population hovers at about 300 animals today. This has led to the belief that Basque whaling may have been a key component in the right whale's decline. However, recent studies using DNA techniques dispute this interpretation. Researchers have discovered that the early osteological identifications over-represented right whales among other whale kills and that their genetic diversity is greater than originally thought (Rastogi et al. 2004). The Basque sixteenth-century hunt, like those of Dutch and later whalers, certainly impacted right whale populations greatly, but other, unknown factors such as disease may also have contributed to their decline.

Another subject of growing interest has been the effect of Basque activities and contacts on the Native peoples of the region. Here the historical accounts have provided relatively little information and give the impression that Basques generally avoided such contacts. Nevertheless contacts did occur and included a variety of types of interactions (Barkham 1980; Douglass and Bilbao 2005, 55). Hostile actions as well as amicable trade transactions are reported, and Inuit are known to have repeatedly raided and burned seasonally abandoned Basque stations to obtain wood planks, boats, iron nails, tools, and other materials. Basque iron, ceramics, and even roof tiles used as surrogates for Inuit soapstone lamps have been recovered at sixteenth- and seventeenth-century Labrador Inuit sites on Eskimo Island in Hamilton Inlet (Kaplan 1985, 56), hundreds of miles north of the Basque whaling stations. Inuit soapstone lamp and pot fragments have also been found in a late sixteenth-century Basque site at Petit Mécatina on the Quebec Lower North Shore (see below) in a context suggesting that an Inuit woman or her family may have been working in a service capacity at a Basque station. Finally, there is growing interest in studies suggesting contact and cultural transfer between Basque whales and cod fishermen with the Miqmaq Indians of northern Nova Scotia and southwestern Newfoundland. These studies explore influences and exchanges in such areas as ethnology, linguistics, folklore, and oral history (Roslyn Frank, personal communication).

To date, most information on Basque history in the Americas has come from their sixteenth-century whaling activities. Following 1600 Basque whaling in the western Atlantic declined as Basques' economic and political power slipped away. Nevertheless, a few Basque ships continued to visit Newfoundland and the gulf, where the crews hunted seals, fished for cod, traded with natives, and conducted opportunistic whaling (Turgeon 1994). These voyages were risky due to competition and attacks from well-armed French, English, and Dutch vessels. However, the voyages remained profitable on a small scale, and Basques continued to venture to the eastern gulf region into the late seventeenth and early

eighteenth centuries. Little is known about the details of these voyages, which have not been researched to the same degree as the sixteenth-century sources. Most of these vessels sailed from the French Basque region.

Even less is known about this late phase of Basque voyaging to America from archaeological sources. However, one site currently being researched on the Quebec Lower North Shore dates to this period. Located 200 kilometers west of the Strait of Belle Isle, the Hare Harbor site on Petit Mécatina Island, near the town of Harrington Harbor, closely follows the pattern known for earlier Basque stations (Fitzhugh 2006). The site, located in a secluded harbor with a high cliff rockshelter, is strewn with red roof tiles identical to those found on earlier Basque sites and has a cookhouse and a blacksmith shop constructed with slab pavements and tile roofs, along with tile-paved pathways. In the cove adjacent to the site are eight linear piles of ship ballast composed of limestone rocks originating from the northern Bay of Biscay, positioned perpendicular to the shore below individual mooring berths. Beneath these berths, underwater excavations have revealed stratified deposits beginning with wood detritus from timber squaring and site construction, followed by phases of whaling and then mass processing of codfish. Within these deposits have been found a variety of Spanish faience tableware and Bergundian storage vessels, together with barrel parts, clay pipes, flint and gunflints, glass, tiles, and even the remains of clothing and shoes.

Identical but more fragmentary remains have been recovered from the Hare Harbor land site, which also contained clay pipes and glass beads dating to about 1680–1720 (Fitzhugh 2006; Herzog and Moreau 2004). Notably absent are the large tryworks of sixteenth-century Basque sites; by this time Basques must have been processing blubber aboard ship and using land facilities primarily for maintenance, cooking, smithy and woodcrafts, production of charcoal, and other activities. Charcoal and artifacts in micro-stratigraphic levels in a boggy area of the site indicate a minimum of eight to ten occupation surfaces, suggesting a decade or more of annual re-occupations. Charred wood floors below the upper slab pavement floors suggest that the site was burned and rebuilt at least once prior to abandonment. An interesting feature of the artifacts recovered from the Basque floors are fragments of soapstone lamps and cooking vessels of Eskimo (Inuit) manufacture, and charred stains of seal oil lamps are also present on the paving stones. Although mutual avoidance seems to have marked the relations between Basques and the Inuit in the sixteenth century (Barkham 1980), the Mécatina site may have utilized an Inuit family as service providers in support of the station's economic and maintenance work.

Hare Harbor conforms to expectations of a late Basque station located in what was probably an increasingly dangerous and competitive frontier region in the complicated political milieu of the late seventeenth century. Its material culture reflects a wider procurement zone in Europe extending well beyond the Basque national area into Spain and western

Europe even while maintaining a basic "Basque" pattern in terms of economic activities, settlement types, and voyage origin. Although Basques seem not to have been able to continue their 300-year tradition of voyaging to Newfoundland and the gulf much beyond 1820, they demonstrated persistence in extracting resources from a region that remained a political and economic frontier throughout this period.

Basque history in the Americas did not end with their withdrawal from the northern fisheries. Back in 'Basque country," once boat building and their marine economy had become eclipsed by other nations, Basque people and culture soon turned to another mode of interaction with America, immigrating as sheepherders to high mountain zones in the western Americas (Kurlansky 1999; Douglass and Bilbao 2005; Totoricaguena 2005). Basques had been settling in Latin America during the early Spanish colonization era, but a massive second wave of emigration beginning in the early nineteenth century brought Basques from their homelands to the northern plains and Rocky Mountains of the United States, as well as to Canada, Mexico, and the Andes. There they established cultural enclaves whose members turned out to be remarkably successful and persistent, not only as pastoralists, but later as restauranteurs, artists, and tradespeople. In the pursuit of these activities Basque identity was retained and strengthened, and in recent times has been encouraged by the creation of Basque study centers in universities; dedication of museums promoting Basque language, history, and culture; and founding of local and regional Basque organizations and publications. Basques continue to make unique contributions to the history of the Americas. Clearly, increased knowledge of their once-obscure sixteenth- to eighteenth-century fisheries and archaeological sites provides this unique ethnic group a strong foundation for claiming European and American legacies.

Further Reading: Barkham, Selma, "The Identification of Labrador Ports in Spanish 16th Century Documents," *Canadian Cartographer* 14(1) (1977): 1–9; Barkham, Selma, "The Basques: Filling a Gap in Our History between Jacques Cartier and Champlain," *Canadian Geographical Journal* 96(1) (1978): 8–19; Barkham, Selma, "A Note on the Strait of Belle-Isle During the Period of Basque Contact with Indians and Inuit," *Études/Inuit/Studies* 4(1–2) (1980): 51–58; Barkham, Selma, "The Basque Whaling Establishments in Labrador 1536–1632—a Summary," *Arctic* 37(4) (1984): 515–519; Barkham, Selma, and Robert Grenier, "Divers Find Sunken Basque Galleon in Labrador," *Canadian Geographical Journal* 97(3) (1978/79): 60–63; Bélanger, R., *Les Basques dans l'estuaire du Saint-Laurent (1535–1635)* (Montreal: University of Quebec Press, 1971); Cumbaa, S. L., "Archaeological Evidence of the 16th Century Basque Right Whale Fishery in Labrador," *Report of the International Whaling Commission*, Special Issue 10 (1986): 187–190; Douglass, William A., and Jon Bilbao, *Amerikanuak: Basques in the New World* (Reno: University of Nevada Press, 2005); Drouin, Pierre, "Les baleiniers basques à l'Île Nue de Mingan," *Archeological Journal of Canada* 12 (1988): 1–15; Fitzhugh, William W., "Cultures, Borders, and Basques: Archaeological Surveys on Quebec's Lower North Shore," in *From the Arctic to Avalon: Papers in Honour of James A. Tuck Jr.*, edited by Lisa Rankin and Peter Ramsden, British Archaeological Reports International Series No. 1507 (2006), 53–70; Grenier, Robert, "Excavating a 400 Year-Old Basque Galleon," *National Geographic* 168(1) (1985): 58–68; Grenier, Robert, "Basque Whalers in the New World: The Red Bay Wrecks," in *Ships and Shipwrecks of the Americas*, edited by G. Bass (London: 1988), 69–84; Grenier, Robert, "Basque Whalers of Labrador," in *Atlantic Visions*, edited by J. de Courcy and D. Sherry (Dublin: Boole Press, 1989), 109–123; Grenier, Robert, Brad Loewen, and J.-P. Proulx, "Basque Shipbuilding Technology c. 1560–1580: The Red Bay Project," in *Crossroads in Ancient Shipbuilding, Proceedings of the Sixth International Symposium on Boat and Ship Archaeology, Roskilde, 1991*, edited by C. Westerdahl, Oxbow Monograph 40 (Oxford: 1994), 137–141; Herzog, Anja, and Jean-François Moreau, "Petit Mécatina 3: A Basque Whaling Station of the Early 17th Century?" in *The Gateways Project 2004: Surveys and Excavations from Chevery to Jacques Cartier Bay*, edited by W. Fitzhugh, Y. Chrétien, and H. Sharp (Washington, DC: Smithsonian Institution, Arctic Studies Center, 2004), 76–87; Huxley, Selma, ed., *Los Vascos en el Marco Atlántico Norte. Siglos XVI y XVII [The Basques in the North Atlantic in the 16th and 17th Centuries]* (San Sebastián: Etor, 1987); Kaplan, Susan, "European Goods and Socioeconomic Change in Early Labrador Inuit Society," in *Cultures in Contact: The European Impact on Native Cultural Institutions in Eastern North America, A.D. 1000–1800*, edited by William W. Fitzhugh (Washington, DC: Smithsonian Institution Press, 1985), 45–70; Kurlansky, Mark, *The Basque History of the World* (New York: Penguin Books, 1999); Lalande, D., "Archaeological Excavations at Bon-Désir: Basque Presence in the St. Lawrence Estuary," *Northeastern Historical Archaeology* 18 (1989): 10–28; Light, J. D., "16th Century Basque Ironworking: Anchors and Nails," *Materials Characterization* 29 (1992): 249–258; Proulx, Jean-Pierre, *Basque Fisheries and Whaling in Labrador in the 16th Century* (Ottawa: Ministry of the Environment, Parks Canada, 1993); Rastogi, Toolika, Moira W. Brown, Brenna A. McLeod, Timothy R. Frasier, Robert Grenier, Stephen L. Cumbaa, Jeya Nadarajah, and Bradley N. White, "Genetic Analysis of 16th-Century Whale Bones Prompts a Revision of the Impact of Basque Whaling on Right and Bowhead Whales in the Western North Atlantic," *Canadian Journal of Zoology* 82 (2004): 1647–1654; Ringer, J. R., "A Summary of Marine Archaeological Research Conducted at Red Bay, Labrador: The 1984 Field Season," in *Archaeology in Newfoundland and Labrador*, vol. 5, edited by Jane Thomson (St. Johns, NL: Government of Newfoundland and Labrador, 1985), 190–223; Ross, S. L., "16th-Century Spanish Basque Coopering," *Historical Archaeology* 19(1) (1985): 1–31; Totoricaguena, Gloria, *Basque Migration and Diaspora: Migration and Transnational Identity* (Reno: University of Nevada Press, 2005); Tuck, James A., and Robert Grenier, "A 16th-Century Basque Whaling Station in Labrador," *Scientific American* 245(5) (1981): 180–188; Tuck, James A., and Robert Grenier, *Red Bay, Labrador: World Whaling Capital A.D. 1550–1600* (St. John's, NL: Atlantic Archaeology Ltd., 1989); Turgeon, Laurier, "Basque-American Trade in the Saint Lawrence during the Sixteenth Century: New Documents, New Perspectives," *Man in the Northeast* 40 (1990): 81–87; Turgeon, Laurier, "Vers une Chronologie des Occupations Basques du Saint-Laurent du XVIe-XVIIe Siècle: un Retour à l'Histoire," *Recherches Amérindiènnes au Québec* 24(3) (1994): 3–15.

William W. Fitzhugh

ST. CROIX ISLAND INTERNATIONAL HISTORIC SITE

Near Calais, Maine

The 1604–05 Winter Encampment of Champlain and du Monts

St. Croix Island is a 3-hectare site of international historic significance located on Maine's northeast coast. It has been confirmed by archaeologists as the location of a 1604–05 settlement led by the Huguenot Pierre Dugua, also known by the title of Sieur de Monts, that immediately preceded permanent French colonization in North America. The settlement history is described and illustrated in detail by Samuel Champlain, who served as Dugua's cartographer and assistant. St. Croix Island served as the expedition's initial base camp while Champlain explored and charted the American coastline as far south as Cape Cod. The island settlement was abandoned after nearly half of the crew of seventy-nine men who wintered there died of scurvy. St. Croix Island is also significant as the first site in North America where the methods of historical archaeology were used to solve a historical problem. By verifying the location of the 1604–05 Dugua settlement through fieldwork in 1796 and 1797, boundary commission members Robert Pagan and Thomas Wright helped to establish the international boundary between Canada and the United States in 1797.

By the early seventeenth century French interests in North America had shifted from seeking the Northwest Passage to China to settlement and economic exploitation. In 1603 Henry IV of France granted exclusive rights to Pierre Dugua for trading and colonization of Acadia, an enormous area located between today's Pennsylvania and Cape Breton Island. Dugua assembled a diverse group for his expedition consisting of 120 men, including Catholics and Huguenots, gentry and commoners. The noted explorer and cartographer Samuel Champlain accompanied the group, which set out in two vessels. After reaching the coast of Nova Scotia in May 1604, they explored the Bay of Fundy. Midway up a river in Passamaquoddy Bay, Champlain discovered an island with excellent prospects for defense as well as for trading with Native Americans. After the island was fortified and cleared of timber, a settlement was laid out on the northern end of the island including nineteen buildings and their gardens surrounding an open square. Both a general view of the island and a detailed view of the settlement or habitation were used to illustrate the 1613 edition of Champlain's book *Les Voyages du Sieur de Champlain*.

As building continued on the island, Champlain left to explore the New England coast with a small group including a Native American guide. He noted and named the Isle du Mont-Desert, known by the same name today as Mount Desert Island, and the Isle au Haut, both locations of today's Acadia National Park units. His barque (a small coastal sailing vessel) reached as far south as Penobscot Bay and the site of present-day Bangor, Maine, before returning to St. Croix Island for the winter. There the expedition members were housed according to their status, with Pierre Dugua lodged in his own house while gentlemen such as Sieur d'Orville and Champlain shared row houses and the soldiers had separate quarters. A chapel was built "in the Indian style" near the southern tip of the island near the cemetery, and another chapel may have been attached to the priest's house. A warehouse and covered workhouse were located within the fortified area.

A group of seventy-nine elected to winter over, and the two ships were sent back to France. This proved to be disastrous for those who remained. Snow began to fall in October and soon the river was filled with ice flows, impeding access to the mainland. Either thirty-five or thirty-six company members died of scurvy during the winter. When a relief party arrived the following summer, the majority of buildings were dismantled and moved to the new settlement of Port Royal in Nova Scotia. The site was briefly re-occupied in 1611 by a Captain Platrier and four others, but any remaining buildings were entirely destroyed by an English expedition in 1613.

HISTORY OF ARCHAEOLOGY

The origins of North American historical archaeology may be traced to St. Croix Island. The 1784 Treaty of Paris set the northeastern international boundary of the United States at the river where the Dugua settlement was located, but the island itself had since been renamed and lost to historical memory. A boundary commission was established in 1794 to decide the issue, and for this purpose, finding physical evidence for the 1604–05 settlement was critical. In 1797 commission member Robert Pagan paid a visit to a local island named Bone Island that Native Americans claimed had been visited by the French in earlier times. Here Pagan found piles of rocks that corresponded with structures shown in Champlain's plan. He exposed walls composed of stone set in clay mortar and found charcoal, bricks, and a stoneware pitcher. Additional evidence convinced the other commission members that they had located St. Croix Island, allowing the international boundary to be set.

In 1949 Congress authorized that St. Croix Island be designated a National Monument. National Park Service

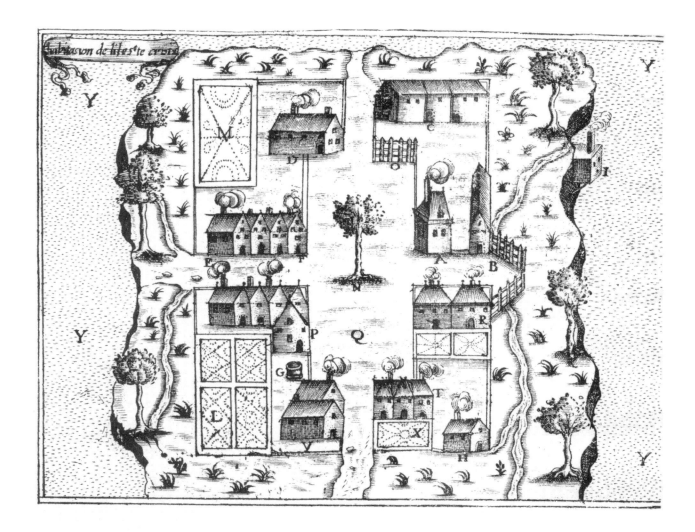

A Logis du fieur de Mons.
B Maifon publique ou l'on paffoit le temps durant la pluie.
C Le magafin.
D Logement des fuiffes.
E La forge.
F Logement des charpentiers
G Le puis.
H Le four ou l'on faifoit le pain.

I La cuifine.
L Iardinages.
M Autres Iardins.
N La place où au milieu y a vn arbre.
O Palliffade.
P Logis des fieurs d'Oruille, Champlain & Chandore.
Q Logis du fieur Boulay, & autres artifans.

R Logis ou logeoiét les fieurs de Geneftou, Sourin & autres artifans.
T Logis des fieurs de Beaumont, la Motte Bourioli & Fougeray.
V Logement de noftre curé.
X Autres iardinages.
Y La riuiere qui entoure l'ifle.

Isle de Sainte Croix, from *Voyages du sieur de Champlain* (1613), page 34.   [Library of Congress]

regional archaeologist J. C. Harrington developed an intense interest in relocating the French settlement. He hired a local archaeologist named Wendell S. Hadlock to locate buildings and to "secure other information pertinent to the historic background of St. Croix Island." By trenching, Hadlock confirmed the locations of both the habitation area and cemetery depicted in Champlain's plans. But nearly twenty years passed until the National Park Service could acquire the entire island and conduct more extensive excavations. In 1968 John Cotter hired Jacob Gruber of Temple

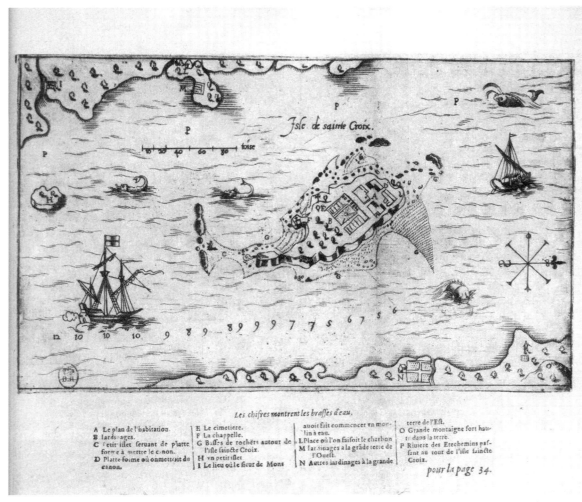

Habitation of Isle de Sainte Croix, from *Voyages du sieur de Champlain* (1613), page 38.   [Library of Congress]

University to reveal more of the French period settlement. This led to extensive stripping of both habitation and cemetery areas, revealing poorly preserved architectural remains and a relatively well-preserved cemetery containing twenty-three graves.

More recent work has included geophysical surveys and a re-analysis of the skeletal remains by a forensic team directed by Dr. Thomas Crist of Utica College. Artifacts from both Hadlock's and Gruber's excavations have been re-analyzed to determine function and regional French origin.

ARCHAEOLOGY OF FRENCH COLONIZATION

Archaeology at St. Croix Island has informed us about the earliest stages of French colonization. Planting an initial colonial settlement on an island was an approach also used by both the Spanish and English in the New World. However, the ease of defending St. Croix Island was outweighed by the problems of provisioning it with food and freshwater. Later French settlements, including Port Royal and Quebec, were situated on the mainland. Ceramics found at St. Croix Island

revealed a diet emphasizing preserved meats containing little or no vitamin C. At later sites there was progressive emphasis on fresh meat and vegetables. The earliest French settlements in Brazil, Florida, and Maine were led by Huguenots and were characterized by religious tolerance. These expeditions were provisioned from Huguenot-dominated ports in Normandy and Brittany, a pattern reflected by the origins of artifacts found at St. Croix Island. However, after the establishment of the One Hundred Associates in 1628, Huguenot involvement in colonizing and provisioning New France diminished.

The St. Croix Island cemetery dating to 1605 is the oldest documented European cemetery in North America. Forensic studies, including DNA analysis, are ongoing, but preliminary data indicates the presence of twenty-five relatively young males ranging in age from 18 to 40. Several individuals reveal skeletal pathologies associated with scurvy, and one individual had been autopsied, the first specifically documented example in North America. With the failure to understand why expedition members were dying over the winter, Champlain wrote in *Les Voyages*, "a post-mortem examination was made of several to investigate the cause of their malady."

Further Reading: Biggar, H. P., ed., *The Works of Samuel de Champlain*, Vol. 1: 1599–1607 (Toronto: Champlain Society, 1971); Cotter, John, "Premier etablissement francais en Acadie—Sainte-Croix," *Dossiers de l'archeologie* 27 (1978): 60–71; Ganong, William Francis, *Ste. Croix (Dochet) Island*, Monographic Series No. 3 (St. John: New Brunswick Museum, 1945); St. Croix Island International Historic Site, National Park Service Web site, http://www.nps.gov.sacr (online April 2005).

Steven R. Pendery

THE ARCHAEOLOGY OF THE EARLY AMERICA

The Virginia and Maryland Chesapeake

Jamestown, the James River Settlements, and St. Mary's City

INTRODUCTION

The Chesapeake Bay of Virginia and Maryland is the largest estuary in the continental United States and ranks among the most dynamic, productive aquatic ecosystems on the entire planet. With its fish-filled waters and agriculturally fertile shorelines, the Chesapeake region has attracted humans to its banks and wooded hinterlands for thousands of years. The Chesapeake's rich archaeological record testifies to the region's complex human story, and many important archaeological sites in the region are both well interpreted and accessible to the visiting public.

Paleoindians were the first to arrive in the Chesapeake, initially traveling there some 12,000 to 15,000 years ago in pursuit of large, migratory game herds. Subsequent Native American generations tied themselves even more permanently to the region by building villages along the bay's freshwater tributaries; planting crops in its alluvial floodplains and clayey uplands, harvesting its oysters and other shellfish, and netting its migratory fish species. Then, in 1607, English colonists arrived in the Chesapeake, determined to mine the region's natural resources and establish new settlements. Conflicts soon arose between these land-hungry English newcomers and local Native Americans, leading ultimately to either the decimation or westward displacement of most Natives.

The Englishmen's insatiable desire for more Chesapeake land was mainly fueled by tobacco, which became their chief source of wealth from the region after 1619. Tobacco yielded these colonists high profits for much of the seventeenth century but demanded constant infusions of new farmland and field labor. Although new farmlands became relatively abundant after Native American displacement, labor shortages remained a chronic problem. Early in the seventeenth century, most Chesapeake laborers were English servants, who worked on tobacco plantations for seven years and then were given their freedom. Servant labor diminished as the seventeenth century progressed, however, while dependence on African-born slaves increased. By 1700 most Chesapeake laborers were African-born slaves, doomed to work on tobacco plantations for the duration of their lives. Despite the tremendous social and economic constraints imposed upon them, these slaves and their descendants succeeded in creating and sustaining a viable culture of their own, distinct from that of their white masters.

Tangible evidence of many early Chesapeake residents—Native American, English, and African—has come to light in recent decades through the aid of archaeology. Archaeological sites discovered in both Virginia and Maryland shed light on how seventeenth- and eighteenth-century Chesapeake residents lived, how they interacted, and how they adapted to their regional environment. Several of the most important colonial Chesapeake sites are open to the public and are described below.

MARTIN'S HUNDRED

Martin's Hundred in James City County, Virginia—like the city of Pompeii near Naples, Italy—is one of those rare archaeological sites that seems to have captured a specific moment in time. In Pompeii's case, the historical clock stopped on August 26, AD 79—the day Mount Vesuvius erupted. At Martin's Hundred (also known as Wolstenholme Towne), time stands frozen on March 22, 1622, the date when Virginia's Powhatan Indians almost wholly destroyed that small English settlement in a devastating surprise attack. Seventy-eight of the settlement's 140 inhabitants were killed by the Powhatans on that fateful March day, and the remaining 62 either were captured or else fled to the safety of the Virginia colony's capital on Jamestown Island. Because of its rapid, unexpected destruction and abandonment, and because it remained undisturbed until its archaeological rediscovery in the 1970s, Martin's Hundred enables visitors to glimpse an isolated English outpost as it existed (and died) in 1620s Virginia.

Martin's Hundred in James City County, Virginia.   [Courtesy of The Colonial Williamsburg Foundation]

In an Elizabethan English context, the term "hundred" connoted a demographic-geographic division that was larger than an Anglican Church parish but smaller than a county. Additionally, the term originally referred to an area of land capable of supporting and mustering 100 militiamen, although the English population of early-seventeenth-century Virginia was too small for that to have been possible. Consequently, the frequent application of "hundred" to outlying Virginia settlements (e.g., Martin's Hundred, Flowerdew Hundred, Bermuda Hundred, Shirley Hundred, Smith's Hundred) likely was a matter of early-seventeenth-century advertising. Stockholders in England called the settlements they underwrote "hundreds" to attract would-be settlers.

Ivor Noël Hume, former Director of Archaeology for Colonial Williamsburg, first stumbled across Martin's Hundred in 1970 and 1971 as he was searching for outbuildings associated with Carter's Grove—the grand, eighteenth-century plantation of the Burwell family. During that initial archaeological fieldwork, Noël Hume's crew exposed a series of graves and refuse pits dating to the early seventeenth century, rather than to the mid-eighteenth century, clueing Noël Hume to the fact that they had discovered something entirely unexpected: a small, early English colonial outpost pre-dating Carter's Grove, which had been lost for some 350 years. After a several-year hiatus, Noël Hume embarked upon a full-scale excavation of Martin's Hundred that ran from 1976 to 1981. That multi-year excavation ultimately exposed a number of spatially discrete archaeological sites (designated Sites A through H) that collectively comprised the heart of the short-lived Martin's Hundred community—the fortified village of Wolstenholme Towne.

Site A represents one of the most complete, best-documented early-seventeenth-century plantation layouts yet uncovered in

The palisaded fort of Wolstenholme Towne at its peak.   [Courtesy of The Colonial Williamsburg Foundation]

the Chesapeake region. It is composed of a dwelling house 40 × 18 feet, two structures 20 × 18 feet, an unusual semi-subterranean structure (possibly a storehouse) measuring 18 × 17 feet, plus numerous fencelines and rubbish pits. Quite likely, Site A was the domestic compound of William Harwood, "governor," or settlement leader of Martin's Hundred.

Site B consists of two structures: a dwelling house 44 × 22 feet and a work shed 30 × 10 feet. The dwelling house ranks as the largest domestic structure yet found at Martin's Hundred (larger even than that of William Harwood), and the shed—entirely open-sided along its 30-foot northern façade—is suspected to be the workshop of colonial Virginia potter Thomas Ward. Also noteworthy about Site B is the fact that it was never plowed after its seventeenth-century abandonment—a rare and fortuitous circumstance in the Chesapeake region. Because of this, Noël Hume was able to conduct rigorous soil chemistry studies and artifact distribution studies at Site B—studies that have provided valuable insights about human and animal traffic, the kinds

of work that occurred, and how the work was organized spatially within a seventeenth-century colonial house yard.

Site C, arguably the most impressive and intriguing site at Martin's Hundred, is the palisaded fort of Wolstenholme Towne itself—built around 1620 and almost certainly the rallying point of colonial defenders during the March 1622 attack. This trapezoidal fort measured roughly 122 × 86 feet, with a square bastion extending from its eastern corner and another from its southern corner. Slot trenches, interpreted as the remains of musketeers' firing platforms, line the interiors of four palisade walls. Three buildings, a well, and several large trash pits were found within the fort's interior. The largest fort building—a hall-and-parlor plan dwelling house measuring roughly 35 × 13 feet—quite likely was settlement leader William Harwood's first home, before the completion of his more elaborate, better-built dwelling house at Site A.

Few places in the Chesapeake region capture the excitement and educational value of archaeology as well as Martin's Hundred—a 2-acre archaeological site with

Excavating the palisaded fort of Wolstenholme Towne.   [Andrew Veech]

adjoining museum situated on the James River 8 miles east of Williamsburg, within the majestic grounds of Carter's Grove Plantation—a Colonial Williamsburg Foundation property. Unfortunately, the site is presently (2007) closed to public visitation. Budgetary shortfalls forced Colonial Williamsburg to close Carter's Grove in January 2003, and the plantation has yet to reopen. It is hoped that the necessary funds will be procured soon to re-open both Carter's Grove and Martin's Hundred to public visitation.

FLOWERDEW HUNDRED

Flowerdew Hundred is located on the south bank of the James River in rural Prince George County, Virginia, approximately 45 miles southeast of Richmond and 12 miles east of Hopewell.

Founded in 1619 by George Yeardley, Virginia's first royal governor, Flowerdew ranks as one of the earliest English settlements established in the Virginia colony after

Jamestown. Newly arriving Englishmen of various social classes and occupations opted to move beyond the comparatively safe and established confines of Jamestown and set up farmsteads within the raw settlement of Flowerdew, along with their wives, children, and indentured servants. Also accompanying them were fifteen of the first twenty Africans who also arrived in Virginia in 1619—the first unfortunate players in what would become America's 250-year-long saga of African slavery. Thus, Flowerdew's relevance to African American history is at least equal to its relevance to seventeenth-century English colonization. Unlike Martin's Hundred, Flowerdew Hundred survived the Powhatan Indian uprising of 1622 with a loss of only six lives. Consequently, Flowerdew served as an important military staging area for the harsh English reprisals that followed the Powhatan uprising.

From an archaeological standpoint, Flowerdew Hundred is notable for the length and continuity of its on-site research

A representation of Flowerdew's English settlement as well as some archaeological details.   [Source: National Geographic Society, *Clues to America's Past*, Washington, D.C.: National Geographic Society, 1976. Credit: Louis S. Glanzman/National Geographic Image Collection]

program. Archaeological investigations, either in the form of active field excavations or subsequent artifact analysis, have been on going at Flowerdew since the early 1970s. From 1971 through 1978 excavations at Flowerdew were carried out by the College of William and Mary, under the direction of Dr. Norman Barka. Then, in 1980, Dr. James Deetz of the University of California, Berkeley, (and later of the University of Virginia) initiated a second, more comprehensive series of excavations at Flowerdew that continued into the early 1990s. Since that time, active archaeological fieldwork at Flowerdew has essentially ceased, with all energies instead focusing on the laboratory analysis and curation of existing artifact collections.

Cumulatively, eighteen distinct archaeological sites have thus far been identified across Flowerdew Hundred, spanning the gamut of Virginia history from initial English settlement through the American Civil War. Eleven of those sites have been excavated, in part or completely, and have generated in excess of 200,000 artifacts. The most remarkable of those artifacts are now on display at Flowerdew's museum—housed in a restored, circa-1850 schoolhouse on the property. Exhibits there present visitors with both an encapsulation of Flowerdew's rich, complex history and a summary of the

archaeological work that uncovered that history. All of the seventeenth-century residents of Flowerdew and its environs—European, African, and Native American—are discussed in the exhibits.

Seven of Flowerdew's eighteen archaeological sites are of particular interest to students of the early historic Chesapeake, since they shed light on the very earliest years of Flowerdew's English settlement—roughly 1620 to 1650. These sites were explored and documented by James Deetz and his students in the 1980s and 1990s, and they bear interesting similarities to and differences from English sites from the same period located at nearby Jamestown Island and Martin's Hundred.

Closest to the James River, Deetz and his archaeological crew uncovered an enclosed compound consisting of a well and two earthfast buildings (buildings with walls supported by pairs of hewn wooden posts set into deep, regularly spaced holes dug into the ground; once set in the ground and backfilled, these posts were either pegged or nailed together with cross beams to form the sides and gables of the house). These were surrounded by a bastioned and ditched palisade fence 240 × 110 feet. One of the earthfast buildings within the palisade likely was a simple dwelling

Excavations from Structure 112 in the New Towne section of Jamestown Island.   [National Park Service, Colonial National Histor-ical Park]

house, but the second quite possibly was a warehouse—one of the two cited in Flowerdew's muster roll of 1625. A second enclosed compound, palisaded and ditched like the first, was discovered 800 feet farther southwest. While no structures were identified within this smaller (60 × 40 feet) compound, the artifacts recovered from it suggest that, like the first, it was intended in part for commercial purposes and in part for defense.

Between these two enclosed compounds Deetz located a line of dwelling houses, most of small dimension and ephemeral, earthfast design. The majority of these small dwelling houses were discernible only from the scattered domestic artifacts left behind. However, one of these dwelling houses left traces that are considerably more substantial and it thus warrants further description. That dwelling house—detected archaeologically by its highly unusual, expensive, and sturdy siltstone foundations—was a massive (41 × 24 feet) hall-and-parlor-plan, a two-story structure with an attached stair tower measuring 8 × 10 feet and an interior, H-shaped hearth. Numerous clay tiles found in and around the dwelling house indicate that it originally had supported an expensive tile roof. The discovery of such a grand dwelling house on the edge of Virginia's early-seventeenth-century frontier was highly unexpected and speaks to the tremendous discrepancies in wealth and status among Virginia colonists. Very few seventeenth-century Virginians possessed either the necessary wealth or stature to

commission such a dwelling house, so obviously this home belonged to someone highly important within the Flowerdew community, quite likely Abraham Peirsey, the prosperous English merchant who purchased the settlement from Governor Yeardley in 1624.

The Flowerdew Foundation offers an array of organized educational programs for students between the ages of 3 and 14. Younger students (ages 3 to 7) may participate in nature programs that emphasize the agricultural use of the property as well as the extensive wildlife population. Older students have the opportunity to work directly with artifacts and primary documents. Additional program components include mapping, orienteering, adaptive use of historic structures, and windmill technology.

JAMESTOWN ISLAND

Jamestown Island is the Chesapeake archaeological site most closely associated by most people with America's English colonial beginnings. This association is understandable and justified, for two good reasons. First, Jamestown is the site of America's first permanent English settlement, established in May 1607. Second, Jamestown is the birthplace of modern historical archaeology—the place where America's fledgling archaeological professionals first employed their evolving excavation techniques on a site pertinent to the country's early-colonial (rather than pre-Columbian) past.

Visitors to Jamestown Island (now known as Historic Jamestowne) will walk away from their experience with a better understanding of this earliest English New World settlement and the ways in which archaeologists are continually gleaning new information about it. New exhibits and displays that expanded and updated archaeological interpretations were created in 2007 for the 400th anniversary of the initial settlement of Jamestown. Jamestown Island continues to be an exciting place for archaeological enthusiasts.

Two organizations jointly own and manage the 1,500-acre island: the National Park Service (NPS) and the Association for the Preservation of Virginia Antiquities (APVA). The National Park Service possesses the vast majority of this land—more than 1,400 acres—which it acquired in 1930. This Park Service land contains at least sixty individual archaeological sites (many in almost pristine condition), spanning the gamut of the region's human history from Paleoindian times to the early twentieth century. Chief among these archaeological sites is the 40-acre village of James Cittie or New Towne, which served as Virginia's colonial capital from around 1620 to 1699. New Towne was the focus of the Park Service's pioneering archaeological excavations of the 1930s and 1950s, conducted under the auspices of Drs. J. C. Harrington (1936–41) and John Cotter (1954–57). Harrington's and Cotter's combined excavations uncovered a total of some 141 structures and 24 wells—a wealth of early Anglo-colonial material culture the likes of which had never before (or since) been seen. The hundreds of thousands of artifacts unearthed during those initial NPS digs (many of which are unique and far older than objects recovered from other, more recent English New World sites) shed light on the experimental beginnings of English colonization in the Chesapeake, prior to the establishment of a regional economy wedded solely to tobacco production and the strict importation of British finished goods.

After the 1950s, Jamestown Island saw almost no new archaeological activity until the 1990s, with the APVA's hiring of Dr. William Kelso and his initiation of the Jamestown Rediscovery project. Kelso felt that the original 1607 James Fort—long speculated to have washed out into the James River—in fact still existed, buried beneath the archaeologically unexplored grounds of the APVA's 22½-acre property, comprising the extreme southwestern corner of Jamestown Island. By 1996 Kelso and his team had uncovered a moat, curved wall trench, and posthole alignments, which collectively formed the eastern bulwark of a triangular, palisaded fort. The many late-sixteenth-century European artifacts recovered from this fort trench made Kelso's discovery undeniable: he had, in fact, found the Jamestown colony's 1607 fort. Kelso's extensive excavations since 1996 have aimed at tracing out the full perimeter of that fort and its interior architectural configuration. The fort is now known to have measured 304 × 304 × 425 feet and to have enclosed some 1.1 acres. At least four early-seventeenth-century structures have been found within the fort to date, situated

parallel to and exactly 10 feet in from the palisade walls. Each of these structures is just one room in width but multiple rooms in length, and each contains an end-room cellar. The precise functions of these early fort structures is a matter of debate: they may have been barracks; one or more may have served as a storehouse. But all of these structures appear to have been built in the "mud and stud" building tradition—a construction technique commonly used in the Lincolnshire region of England during the sixteenth century. In addition to the explorations of James Fort, Kelso also has excavated more than seventy human burials located within a cemetery dating to the infamous 1609–10 "Starving Time." With luck, ongoing analyses of these burials will shed life on the health, nutrition, and causes of death of Jamestown's earliest colonists.

Jamestown Island lies on the north bank of the James River, a short 5 miles from downtown Williamsburg, Virginia. Once on the island, visitors can enter a brand new National Park Service Visitor Center, built in preparation for the 2007 anniversary of the Jamestown Colony. Archaeological digs at James Fort and elsewhere can sometimes be viewed by the public, and numerous excavated artifacts are on display at both the NPS Visitor Center and the APVA archaeology museum. Professional archaeologists may also be interested in arranging a visit to the new Historic Jamestowne Research Center, where the majority of both the NPS and APVA archaeological collections are stored.

Jamestown Settlement, a state-run, living-history museum located immediately off Jamestown Island, is also a worthwhile tourist destination, especially for families with small children. At Jamestown Settlement, visitors can stroll through reconstructed versions of Pasbahey—a James River Powhatan Indian village—and James Fort. Costumed interpreters at both the village and fort describe and demonstrate the day-to-day activities of seventeenth-century living. At Jamestown Settlement one can also see and tour magnificent, almost full-scale reconstructions of the *Godspeed*, *Susan Constant*, and *Discovery*—the three English ships that landed at Jamestown Island in 1607.

ST. MARY'S CITY

St. Mary's City was the Maryland colony's equivalent of Jamestown—the colony's founding settlement and its seventeenth-century capital. Established in March 1634 along an estuary of the Potomac River, St. Mary's City soon grew into the governmental and economic hub of a thriving tobacco colony, just like Jamestown had in Virginia. Yet Maryland's St. Mary's City differed from Virginia's Jamestown in important ways, and these differences make a journey to both colonial capitals worthwhile for comparison's sake.

Maryland, unlike Virginia, was created first and foremost as a religious colony. English Catholics were a persecuted minority in early-seventeenth-century England, so Sir George Calvert—the Lord Baltimore and a prominent Catholic himself—pled for and received a royal charter to establish a Catholic haven in the English New World. This fundamentally religious impetus behind Maryland's creation aligns Maryland conceptually more closely with the Plymouth colony of Massachusetts than with the Virginia colony, despite the fact that Maryland's Chesapeake setting and tobacco economy so closely resemble conditions in Virginia. In truth, many more English Protestants than Catholics actually immigrated to Maryland, so Calvert's intrinsically Catholic motivation behind the colony's founding is often overlooked. But Catholic aristocrats such as the Calverts, Arundells, and Howards continued to rank among Maryland's wealthiest and most powerful throughout the colonial era.

St. Mary's City was largely abandoned by the end of the seventeenth century, due to Maryland legislators' 1695 transfer of their capital from St. Mary's City to Annapolis. The location of the original capital was never completely forgotten, however, and in 1966 the state of Maryland created the St. Mary's City Commission to protect, study, and interpret the now-buried town site. Today, Historic St. Mary's City is a state museum of history, archaeology, and natural history, dedicated to interpreting the first century of English settlement in the Chesapeake region.

The archaeology program at Historic St. Mary's City has been ongoing since 1971, when systematic archaeological investigations began under the direction of Dr. Gary Wheeler Stone. Since that time, St. Mary's City archaeologists have identified and recorded more than 300 sites within the limits of the 1,000-acre National Landmark, spanning the entire history of human life in the Chesapeake region.

Many of the seventeenth-century sites found at St. Mary's City broadly resemble those found in Virginia, illustrating how general cultural continuities spanned the colonial Chesapeake. But certain important St. Mary's sites differ markedly from those found in Virginia, most notably St. Mary's 1667 Brick Chapel, which was fully exposed in 1989–90. This immense masonry church, constructed in the shape of a Latin cross, was one of the largest brick structures ever built at St. Mary's City, and, together with the 1676 Statehouse, it anchored the town's purposefully designed symmetrical layout. The Brick Chapel measured 54 feet long by 57 feet wide across its transepts, and its massive 3-feet-thick, 5-feet-deep foundations suggest a building height of around 23 feet. Archaeological remnants of an imported stone floor, mullion brick window frames, and leaded glass window panes indicate that the chapel was lavishly furnished and likely was constructed by highly skilled artisans.

Over 190 colonial-era grave shafts were discovered in and around the Brick Chapel, the three most noteworthy of which lay within the chapel's north transept. Excavation of these three shafts revealed the well-preserved lead coffins of an adult male, adult female, and infant female, all of whom belonged to early Maryland's ruling Catholic aristocracy. Both adults were positively identified following several years of multidisciplinary analysis, with the man determined to be Philip Calvert, Lord Chancellor of Maryland (d. 1682), and the woman to be his first wife, Anne Wolsey Calvert (d. ca. 1680). The child most likely was Philip's daughter by his second wife, Jane Sewell. The skeletal evidence of dietary deficiency and disease found for these three individuals demonstrates how even wealthy, high-status Marylanders suffered on the seventeenth-century Chesapeake frontier.

Historic St. Mary's City (the official name of this living-history museum/archaeological preserve) is located off of Route 5 in rural southern Maryland, several miles upstream from the mouth of the Potomac River at Point Lookout. By automobile, St. Mary's City is less than two hours from either Washington, D.C., or Annapolis and less than three hours from either Richmond or Baltimore.

Once at St. Mary's, visitors will encounter costumed interpreters stationed at various locations around the original town site. The town's reconstructed buildings—all built with painstaking accuracy and close attention to detail—provide perhaps the most realistic sense of seventeenth-century Chesapeake life to be found anywhere. The reconstructions include the State House of 1676, Smith's Ordinary, and the Godiah Spray Plantation—a working tobacco farm. Docked in the harbor is a replica of the *Dove*, one of the two English ships that first sailed to St. Mary's in 1634. The Brick Chapel is now being reconstructed atop its original foundation and ought to be completed within the next few years.

Further Reading: Cotter, John L., *Archeological Excavations at Jamestown, Virginia* (Washington, DC: National Park Service, 1958); Deetz, James, *Flowerdew Hundred: The Archaeology of a Virginia Plantation, 1619–1864* (Charlottesville: University Press of Virginia, 1993); Gibb, James G., ed., *A Layperson's Guide to Historical Archaeology in Maryland: Examples from the Lost Towns of Anne Arundel Project* (Annapolis, MD: Lost Towns of Anne Arundel Project, 1998); Kelso, William M., and Beverly Straube, *Jamestown Rediscovery, 1994–2004* (Richmond: Association for the Preservation of Virginia Antiquities, 2004); Little, Barbara J., and Richard J. Dent, eds., *New Perspectives on Maryland Historical Archaeology*, Vol. 26, Nos. 1–2 of *Maryland Archeology* (Annapolis: 1990); National Park Service, *Jamestown Archeological Assessment* (Washington, DC: National Park Service, 2003); Neiman, Fraiser D., *The "Manner House" before Stratford (Discovering the Clifts Plantation)* (Stratford, VA: Stratford Hall, 1980); Noël Hume, Ivor, *Martin's Hundred* (New York: Alfred A. Knopf, 1979); Pogue, Dennis J., *King's Reach and 17th-Century Plantation Life*, Studies in Archaeology No. 1 (Annapolis, MD: Jefferson Patterson Park & Museum, 1990); Reinhart, Theodore R., and Dennis J. Pogue, eds., *The Archaeology of 17th-Century Virginia*, Archeological Society of Virginia Special Publication No. 30 (Richmond: Dietz Press, 1993); Shackel, Paul A., and Barbara J. Little, eds., *Historical Archaeology of the Chesapeake* (Washington, DC: Smithsonian Institution Press, 1994).

Andrew Veech

THE ARCHAEOLOGY OF THE POWHATAN CHIEFDOM

James and York Rivers Area, Virginia

Werowocomoco and Other Ancient and Historic Period Sites

Based on archaeological excavations just to the south at the Cactus Hill site, human settlement on the James and York rivers likely dates back to at least 15,000 years ago. Archaeologists in Virginia have divided this long time span into three periods: the Paleoindian period, which ended around 8000 BC; the Archaic period, from 8000 BC to 1200 BC; and the Woodland period, from 1200 BC to AD 1600.

Paleoindian sites along the James and York rivers are extremely rare, undoubtedly due to the very low population densities at that time, with most sites being destroyed over the millennia since then due to natural factors, such as erosion, and human factors associated with modern development. Facing a much colder climate then than today, small Paleoindian bands seasonally moved across the landscape exploiting the availability of animals and wild plants.

Gradually during the Archaic period, with a warming of the climate, populations increased, with a continued reliance on gathering wild plants and hunting animals. It was only during the Woodland period that such cultivated crops as maize, beans, and squash were introduced, allowing for a rapid population increase and a semi-sedentary life, with part or all of the year spent settled in villages where fertile soils were found along the James and York rivers.

By 1607, when the English arrived at Jamestown, the Powhatan chiefdom dominated most of coastal Virginia. This chiefdom, under the rule of Powhatan, contained over thirty districts and a total population of approximately 15,000 persons. Much of this area had been conquered by Powhatan during his lifetime, with the core portion of the chiefdom originating along the James and York rivers. Powhatan inherited his position as paramount chief (a leading or senior chief) and served as both a secular and religious leader. From the perspective of economic institutions, sociopolitical organization, and religious practices, the Powhatan chiefdom was one of the most complex societies existing in eastern North America in 1607.

THE GREAT NECK SITE, VIRGINIA BEACH, VIRGINIA

Situated on the south bank of Broad Bay in Virginia Beach, the Great Neck site once contained nearly continuous archaeological deposits over an area 2 miles long and one-quarter mile wide. It is best known for its well-preserved remains dating to the Middle and Late Woodland periods (about 500 BC to AD 1600), documenting a semi-sedentary lifestyle focusing on the rich estuarine environment of the Chesapeake Bay.

Because of rapid site destruction due to the construction of houses, avocational archaeologists and the Virginia Department of Historic Resources conducted a number of emergency excavations in the 1970s and 1980s in the core portion of the site. Although they were able to sample only limited areas, well-preserved deposits were found virtually everywhere tested. Of particular note, portions of a palisaded village dating to the Late Woodland period were identified, with longhouses found within the palisade.

During the winter of 1585–86, an English party from the just established settlement at Roanoke Island in North Carolina explored to the north in the Chesapeake Bay and noted an Indian settlement named Chesapeake. English maps associated with this exploration place Chesapeake in the vicinity of Broad Bay. Many archaeologists believe that the Great Neck site was the village of Chesapeake, given its location, the dates it was occupied, and its great size. Later, the English wrote that around 1607 the paramount chief Powhatan, upon the advice of his priests, attacked the Chesapeakes and relocated the settlement farther to the west, near modern-day Norfolk. Today, the Great Neck site has been largely destroyed, with only very small portions surviving intact in the yards of modern homes.

THE DUMPLING ISLAND SITE, SUFFOLK, VIRGINIA

Dumpling Island is a remarkably well-preserved village site associated with the Nansemond Indians. Located on the Nansemond River, the 14-acre island is a shell midden with occupation here dating principally to the Late Woodland period (ca. AD 900–1600). Captain John Smith on his 1612 map of Virginia identifies it as a "white Chaukie Iland," undoubtedly because of the white color of the dense shell deposits here.

In 1609 the English at Jamestown set up an expedition under the joint command of George Percy and John Martin to establish an outpost on the Nansemond River. Choosing Dumpling Island, they attacked the Nansemonds there and after defeating them, they burned their houses and ransacked the temples located on the island, desecrating the remains of the deceased chiefs found within the temples. The Nansemonds quickly counterattacked, regained control of the island, and killed many of the English still there.

Test excavations in 1986 and 1995 by the Virginia Department of Historic Resources found the site to be in a remarkably pristine state with excellent preservation of the archaeological

Late Woodland ditches at Werowocomoco.   [Courtesy of Werowocomoco Research Group]

deposits. Dumpling Island was listed on the National Register of Historic Places in 1997. Privately owned and not open to the public, Dumpling Island and the vast marshes surrounding it can be seen from the Nansemond River.

THE TREE HILL FARM SITE, HENRICO COUNTY, VIRGINIA

Situated in the corner of a high terrace overlooking the James River and city of Richmond to the northwest, the Tree Hill Farm site is thought by many archaeologists to be the settlement of Powhatan on Captain John Smith's 1612 map of Virginia. It was also known to the Jamestown settlers as Powhatan's Tower due to its elevated position. According to a 1612 account by William Strachey, the paramount chief Powhatan was born near or at this settlement. Captain John Smith describes it as being palisaded, a rare occurrence in eastern Virginia but not unexpected given its proximity to the hostile Monacans just to the west beyond the fall line at modern-day Richmond.

An intensive archaeological survey in 1988 by the Virginia Department of Historic Resources documented a cluster of Late Woodland/protohistoric Native American artifacts over an area of 180 × 130 meters and including small triangular projectile points and a variety of ceramics. Most typical were shell-tempered pottery shards with both simple stamped and plain surface treatments, with lesser amounts of sand-tempered shards having similar surface treatments. Of particular interest are the sand-tempered simple stamped shards, suggesting interaction with such Iroquoian groups as the Nottoways and Meherrins to the south in Virginia. Being at the virtual southwestern edge of the Powhatan chiefdom, the settlement of Powhatan undoubtedly had established trade networks with neighboring groups, as apparently reflected in the ceramics here.

Being on a privately owned farm, the Tree Hill Farm site or site of Powhatan is not open to the public. However, one can view its setting from Route 10 and looking to the northwest toward the city of Richmond.

THE WEROWOCOMOCO SITE, GLOUCESTER COUNTY, VIRGINIA

At the founding of Jamestown in 1607, Werowocomoco was capital of the Powhatan chiefdom, being the principal residence of the paramount chief Powhatan. Also known as Wahunsenacawh, he ruled over most of eastern Virginia. While a captive, Captain John Smith first met Powhatan at Werowocomoco in December 1607. It was also here at that time that Smith claims his life was saved by Pocahontas. Powhatan abandoned Werowocomoco in January 1609, moving farther west to Orapaks on the Chickahominy River to put additional distance between him and the English as a result of increasing hostilities. At this time, Werowocomoco disappears from English accounts, never to be mentioned again.

Archaeological excavations sponsored by the College of William and Mary and the Virginia Department of Historic Resources were conducted at Werowocomoco from 2003 through 2007. Unique to the site are two parallel ditches predating 1607 by several centuries that divide the 45-acre site into a western component nearest Purtan Bay and an eastern component farther from the water. Archaeologists believe these Late Woodland features may represent a boundary between a secular portion of the settlement nearest the water and a more restricted sacred area inland, denoting both the secular and sacred powers held by Powhatan chiefs. The site was listed on the National Register of Historic Places in 2006. Werowocomoco is privately owned and not open to the public; however, there is a well-illustrated Web site that documents archaeological research that has been conducted there (http://powhatan.wm.edu).

THE PAMUNKEY INDIAN RESERVATION, KING WILLIAM COUNTY, VIRGINIA

When the English arrived at Jamestown in 1607, the dominant group within the Powhatan chiefdom were the Pamunkeys. Today, descendants of these Native inhabitants reside in the center of the territory where their ancestors lived four centuries earlier. Situated on a marsh-rimmed peninsula of 1,000 acres bordering the Pamunkey River in King William County, the Pamunkey Indian Reservation is recognized as a reservation in colonial documents going back to the seventeenth century.

A number of archaeological sites have been identified on the reservation dating back to as early as about 5000 BC and continuing into the modern era. This continuity of occupation leading literally to the present day at the reservation is extremely rare, resulting in high research potential for the sites located here. Only limited archaeological testing has been conducted at the reservation, with all known sites being protected. Listed on the National Register of Historic Places in 1982, the Pamunkey Indian Reservation is open to the public and has a museum with exhibits on local archaeology and the tribe's history.

Further Reading: Gallivan, Martin D., David A. Brown, Thane Harpole, Danielle Moretti-Langholtz, and E. Randolph Turner III, *The Werowocomoco (44GL32) Research Project: Background and 2003 Archaeological Field Season Results*, Virginia Department of Historic Resources Research Report Series No. 17 (2006); Hodges, Mary Ellen Norrisey, *Native American Settlement at Great Neck*, Virginia Department of Historic Resources Research Report Series No. 9 (1998); Reinhart, Theodore R., and Mary Ellen Hodges, eds., *Middle and Late Woodland Research in Virginia: A Synthesis*, Archeological Society of Virginia Special Publication No. 29 (1992); Reinhart, Theodore R, and Dennis J. Pogue, eds., *The Archaeology of 17th-Century Virginia*, Archeological Society of Virginia Special Publication No. 30 (1993); Rountree, Helen C., *The Powhatan Indians of Virginia: Their Traditional Culture* (Norman: University of Oklahoma Press, 1989); Rountree, Helen C., and E. Randolph Turner III, *Before and After Jamestown: Virginia's Powhatans and Their Predecessors* (Gainesville: University of Florida Press, 2002); Rountree, Helen C., Wayne E. Clark, and Kent Mountford, *John Smith's Chesapeake Voyages, 1607–1609* (Charlottesville: University of Virginia Press, 2007); Werowocomoco Research Project Web site, powhatan.wm.edu.

E. Randolph Turner, III

ACCOKEEK CREEK AND NANJEMOY CREEK OSSUARIES

Lower Potomac River Area, Maryland
Native American Burial Sites

These sites are well known for their ossuary burial areas, associated with evidence of nearby habitation. Ossuary burial represents the communal interment of multiple individuals. The practice is well known archeologically in the mid-Atlantic area of the United States and Eastern Canada. In these regions, large ossuary deposits included individuals whose bodies initially (immediately after death) had been deposited elsewhere. Subsequently, the decomposed or skeletal remains of these individuals were gathered together and buried communally in a large, sometimes complexly arranged group burial.

ACCOKEEK CREEK SITE

The Accokeek Creek Site (18PR8) refers to a complex of sites located in the area where Accokeek Creek and the Piscataway Estuary join the Potomac River in Maryland. Archeological research was initiated at this complex in about 1935 by Alice L. L. Ferguson after her 1923 purchase of the "Hard Bargain Farm" on which the complex is located. Evidence of human occupation in the area dates back to much of the Archaic period, but the major features are from the Woodland period and include the historic Susquehannock Fort. Early work at this site was conducted by landowner Ferguson and her geologist husband Henry Ferguson, with some specialized assistance provided by Aleš Hrdlička and T. Dale Stewart of the Smithsonian Institution. Robert L. Stephenson studied the cultural material recovered in his Ph.D. dissertation at the University of Michigan.

The Accokeek Creek Complex includes four distinct major sites: (1) a late prehistoric fortified village site; (2) a smaller stockaded village thought to date between AD 800 and 1000; (3) a site at Mockley Point at the junction of Piscataway Creek and the Potomac River, thought to date from the late Archaic (4,000 to 5,000 years ago) to Woodland times; and (4) the historic Susquehannock Fort located at Clagett's Cove on the Piscataway Estuary.

The late prehistoric fortified village site represents a large occupation site lacking artifacts of European manufacture and likely abandoned around AD 1550. Dominant archeological features include multiple stockade lines and three ossuary burials. At the time of excavation, part of this site had eroded into the river. The original construction likely featured circular stockades surrounding the village with gates to the north and east. Evidence was detected of an earthen rampart, likely constructed for defense purposes. Analysis of archeological materials recovered suggested that agriculture and deer were important in subsistence, but also present were remains of clams, crabs, duck, squirrel, sturgeon, terrapins, and turkey.

Three ossuaries were found within the fortified area. One ossuary was located near the central portion of the site. It measured approximately 10 feet by 16 feet with a depth between 3.8 feet and 4.2 feet. The bone deposit was about 1-foot thick and contained cremated cranial fragments, articulated remains (bones in normal anatomical position), and arrangements of bones suggestive of bundle deposits. At least 288 individuals were represented by skulls.

A second ossuary was found near the most centrally located palisade but was not completely excavated. This deposit measured about 10 feet by 24 feet and was about 3 feet deep. No apparent bundle deposits were detected. It was estimated that about 250 individuals likely were present.

The third ossuary was the smallest, measuring about 8 feet by 17.8 feet. The skull count was 248 with an additional four individuals present in a deposit of cremated bone.

A fourth ossuary was also detected outside the stockade area. It was located about 750 feet southeast of the larger village area. It was the largest and deepest ossuary of the group, measuring 21 feet by 32 feet. The skull count was 618 with evidence of cremated bone as well.

The historic Susquehannock Fort was constructed in 1674 when that group moved into the area. The following year, the fort was attacked and burned by the English community in Maryland and Virginia with Maryland Indian allies. The Susquehannock occupants fled, and the incident contributed to Bacon's Rebellion in Virginia. Excavation revealed an ossuary within the interior of the fort area. This small ossuary was thought to contain less than fifty individuals with some suggestion of articulated remains.

Records also suggest that a small ossuary containing about eleven skulls and historic period artifacts was found in the Mockley Point area, but the exact location is not clear.

THE NANJEMOY CREEK SITE

The Nanjemoy Creek Site (18CH89), also referred to as the Julhe site after the landowner, is located in Charles County, Maryland, about 50 miles south of the present District of Columbia on the north bank of Nanjemoy Creek, a tributary of the Potomac River. Three ossuaries have been located associated with a small habitation area on a 110-foot bluff overlooking Nanjemoy Creek. All three ossuaries lack artifacts of European manufacture and likely date from the Late Woodland period.

The first ossuary was excavated between 1953 and 1955 by T. D. Stewart of the Smithsonian Institution and colleagues. The ossuary was located near the contemporary residence on the property and had been discovered during excavation for the connection of a water pipe to the house. Although most of the skeletal remains were nonarticulated, some evidence for articulation, as well as bundles of remains were detected. Ninety-four skulls were noted at the time of excavation, although later analysis suggested the presence of 131 individuals (sixty-nine adults and sixty-two subadults).

A second ossuary at this site was discovered in 1971 during fence construction on the farm. Excavation of this ossuary was conducted in 1971 and 1972 by T. D. Stewart and Douglas H. Ubelaker of the Smithsonian Institution. The ossuary pit measured about 7.3 feet by 16.5 feet and was located about 96 feet northwest of the first ossuary. Depth of the pit varied from about 1.8 feet to 2.9 feet. The bone concentration itself varied in thickness from about 3 inches to 1.8 feet. The human remains presented a mix of disarticulated bones, distinct bundles, and articulated remains, including three completely articulated individuals. At least 188 individuals were present, including 89 immature individuals. Some bones with evidence of having been burned were present as well.

Demographic analysis suggested a life expectancy at birth of about twenty-one years for the first ossuary sample and twenty-three years for the second one. The extent of articulated remains compared to those not articulated suggested that the second ossuary deposit likely represented an accumulation of about three years. This interval, coupled with the demographic information, suggested a living population size of about 1,441 individuals who constituted the community whose deceased members were buried in the ossuary. Since the habitation area immediately associated with the ossuary appeared to be relatively small, the data suggest that the ossuaries represent interments from settlements in addition to the one at that location.

A third ossuary was detected and excavated at this site in 1980. Detailed analysis is not yet available, but it was located between the previous two ossuaries and associated with evidence of a nearby series of post molds.

Further Reading: Clark, Wayne E., "The Susquehannock Fort: A Historical Overview," in *The Accokeek Creek Complex and the Emerging Maryland Colony* (Accokeek, MD: Alice Ferguson Foundation, 1984), 61–82; Curry, Dennis C., *Feast of the Dead: Aboriginal Ossuaries in Maryland* (Myersville, MD: The Archeological Society of

Maryland, Inc.; Crownsville, MD: The Maryland Historical Trust, 1999); Dent, Richard J., "Archeological Research at the Accokeek Creek Site," in *The Accokeek Creek Complex and the Emerging Maryland Colony* (Accokeek, MD: Alice Ferguson Foundation, 1984), 7–21; Potter, Stephen R., "A New Look at the Accokeek Creek Complex," in *The Prehistoric People of Accokeek Creek*, edited by Robert L. Stephenson (Accokeek, MD: Alice Ferguson Foundation, 1984), 36–40; Potter, Stephen R., *Commoners, Tribute, and Chiefs: The Development of Algonquian Culture in the Potomac Valley* (Charlottesville, VA: University Press of Virginia, 1993); Stephenson, Robert L., and Alice L. L. Ferguson, *The Accokeek Creek Site: A Middle Atlantic Seaboard Culture Sequence*, Anthropological Papers, Museum of Anthropology, University of Michigan, No. 20 (Ann Arbor, MI: University of Michigan, 1963); Stewart, T. Dale, *Archeological Exploration of Patawomeke: The Indian Town Site (44St2) Ancestral to the One (44St1) Visited in 1608 by Captain John Smith*, Smithsonian Contributions to Anthropology, No. 36 (Washington, DC: Smithsonian Institution Press, 1992); Ubelaker, Douglas H., *Reconstruction of Demographic Profiles from Ossuary Skeletal Samples: A Case Study from the Tidewater Potomac*, Smithsonian Contributions to Anthropology, No. 18 (Washington, DC: Smithsonian Institution Press, 1974); Ubelaker, Douglas H., "A Discussion of Mid-Atlantic Ossuaries," in *The Accokeek Creek Complex and the Emerging Maryland Colony* (Accokeek, MD: Alice Ferguson Foundation, 1984), 33–60.

Douglas H. Ubelaker

THE HISTORIC PERIOD ARCHAEOLOGY OF THE CHESAPEAKE BAY AREA

Chesapeake Bay, Delaware, Maryland, and Virginia
Early European Settlements to Colonial Times

Archaeologically, the Chesapeake region is thought of as the parts of Virginia, Maryland, Delaware, and the District of Columbia within the Chesapeake Bay's coastal plain watershed. Both Spain and England attempted very early settlements in the region. In 1607 England succeeded in establishing Jamestown, which is well known as the first permanent English settlement in the Americas. Jamestown did not end other nations' attempts at colonization. The Dutch, for example, attempted a settlement in Delaware in the 1630s, which is commemorated at the Zwaanendael Museum in Lewes.

After initial failures and high mortality rates, colonists capitalized on the high price of tobacco in Europe, clearing and planting extensively. As a result, the tobacco economy encouraged a pattern of settlement that was dispersed

across the landscape. During the seventeenth and eighteenth centuries towns were rare and small because plantations were the centers of the economy. Jamestown and St. Mary's City, founded in 1634, served as colonial capitals through the seventeenth century, but both Virginia and Maryland moved their capitals in the 1690s to Williamsburg and Annapolis, respectively. By that time, European settlement in the region had shifted from an essentially frontier model to become centered on more settled communities. In 1780 the capital of Virginia moved to Richmond and, although Annapolis retained its state government functions, the economic center of Maryland shifted to Baltimore.

Historical archaeologists investigate many kinds of sites, including domestic sites, such as houses and domestic trash deposits; military sites, such as camps and battlefields; craft sites, such as blacksmith shops and printing houses; industrial sites, for example, factories or pottery kilns; commercial sites, such as stores, trading posts, and hotels; institutional sites, including schools, churches, and trade union halls; landscapes, such as formal gardens; transportation features, including canals, locks and lockhouses, turnpike taverns, and pony express trails; and shipwreck sites. Archaeologists often focus on sites where people lived, and these sometimes are associated closely with other types of sites. Military sites, for example, include domestic components, as do many industrial sites, particularly those of early or small-scale manufacturing such as an artisan's household. Shipwreck sites usually contain artifacts that inform us about life aboard a ship.

Many archaeological themes and topics have been investigated at historic period sites in the Chesapeake Bay area. There are some topics that receive more attention depending on the time period being investigated. For example, researchers investigating early colonial settlement (seventeenth century) in the Chesapeake often are interested in cultural contact between Native peoples, Europeans, and Africans and the influences that each group had on the other (Blanton and King 2004; Gallivan 2003, 2004; Potter 1993). Another frequent topic is the colonists' relative self-sufficiency, the extent of reliance on the mother country, and adaptation to both new ecological and social environments on the frontier (Edwards 2004; Galke 2004; Gibb and King 1991; Luckenbach 1995; Miller 1983; Neiman 1986). Some early manufacturing attempts can shed light on self-sufficiency. There were several early attempts at establishing glass factories, for instance. Colonists' early attempts at an iron industry challenged relations with England, which discouraged such industrial development, intending instead for the colonies to provide a market for goods manufactured in England. Archaeological interest in how colonists adapted to their frontier environment has been explored through the analysis of impermanent architecture. Such buildings are marked by earth-fast construction, that is, buildings with wooden rather than masonry foundations that were not built to last for more than a generation. Many archaeologists have interpreted such intentional impermanence an indication of early colonists' intentions of making their fortunes and then returning home (Carson et al. 1981; cf. Horning 2000).

Archaeologists studying the eighteenth-century Chesapeake focus on the ways that people lived after the initial frontier period of colonization, for example, how people fed and clothed themselves and how they made a living. Relatively recently archaeologists have begun to seriously study gender. The careful analysis of artifacts, informed by historical and anthropological understandings of women's and men's idealized roles, sheds light on how such roles changed through time. Many archaeologists are interested in how enslaved Africans resisted slavery and maintained or adapted African cultural traditions. For eighteenth-century studies, cities become an important topic for archaeology in the Chesapeake region because urban places, while still small, by then became more important in colonial political, economic, social, and cultural life.

Plantations were vital parts of the economic and social landscape of the Chesapeake from the earliest settlement through the nineteenth century. Many plantations, which varied greatly in size and structure, have been studied archaeologically, including Custis (Luccetti et al. 1999), Kings Reach (Pogue 1990), Kingsmill (Kelso 1984), Monticello (Crader 1984, 1990; Kelso 1986a, b), and Poplar Forest (Heath 1999). Tobacco was the original basis of wealth, although later economies were based on mixed grain. Historical archaeology of plantations provides opportunities to study not only the economy of the Chesapeake but also the influences of African American heritage and culture and the institutionalization of racism (in addition to plantation studies, see Samford 1996).

However, the archaeology of African Americans is not confined to the study of enslaved life on plantations but includes enslaved people in urban areas and free people in both urban and rural settings from the earliest settlement. One example of finds that indicate the persistence of African traditions is the discovery of several caches of crystals and related materials, perhaps with magical or religious significance, that have been found in urban contexts in pre-emancipation Annapolis (Leone and Fry 1999). Another type of artifact that may tell us more about African life is colonoware, a type of low-fired, hand-built earthenware pottery. Archaeologists disagree about the source of colonoware ceramics and whether they were made and used by African Americans or Native Americans in the region. The Chesapeake provides excellent data for the comparative study of plantation slavery with the southeastern United States, which also has extensive colonoware that is made of native clays but is clearly different from Native American antecedents (Davidson 2004; Emerson 1999; Ferguson 1992; Henry 1992; Mouer et al. 1999; Veech 1997).

During the nineteenth century, earlier small-scale manufacturing turned into full-blown industrial development. There was increasing commerce, industry, agriculture, and regionalism with the pitting of Chesapeake states against each other during the Civil War. In Washington, D.C., archaeologists investigate urban neighborhoods and alley dwellings from the nineteenth and twentieth centuries (Cheek and Friedlander 1990; Little and Kassner 2002; Seifert and Balicki 2005). They study issues that include gender relations, prostitution, ethnicity, class, and neighborhood boundaries.

The Chesapeake region was among the first in the United States to receive serious attention by historical archaeologists. Beginning in 1897 the Association for the Preservation of Virginia Antiquities, which owns parts of James Island, uncovered foundations at Jamestown. Extensive excavation of colonial era remains began in the 1930s at St. Mary's City, Williamsburg, and Mount Vernon. Both private and public entities were involved in this early archaeology. The Rockefeller Foundation created Colonial Williamsburg; the Mount Vernon Ladies Association sponsored work at George Washington's home; and the National Park Service initiated its own excavations at Jamestown in 1934. Large-scale excavations of the 1930s and earlier were concerned with gathering data for architectural reconstructions and served to strengthen an Anglo-American history concerned with the social and political elite. Historical archaeology has continued in the Chesapeake with new projects constantly providing new information and with new research interests sparking a broad range of different types of studies.

In the Chesapeake region, there are numerous opportunities to visit archeological sites in parks and outdoor museums and to view artifacts in traditional museum settings (a list of parks and museums and their Web sites can be found at the end of this chapter). The public has had the opportunity to visit archaeology and its results for several generations. Visitors have been traveling to Jamestown and Colonial Williamsburg since the 1930s. There are also some relatively new public places that provide more opportunities for the interested public. The Delaware Archaeology Museum in Dover, for example, contains displays of archaeological material from thousands of years of human occupation in the state. At the Zwaanendael Museum in Lewes, Delaware, artifacts from the wreck of the HMS DeBraak reveal details of naval life aboard a brig during the heyday of the Royal Navy.

Jamestown, well known as the first permanent English settlement in the Americas, served as the capital of Virginia from 1607 until 1699. A portion of Jamestown Island is now part of Colonial National Historical Park, administered by the National Park Service. Another part of the island is administered by the Association for the Preservation of Virginia Antiquities (APVA). Both organizations work together to provide visitors to the island an interesting and educational experience as they explore the founding and development of the city through the seventeenth century (Kelso 2006).

Williamsburg was the capital of Virginia from 1699 until 1780. Today it is best known as the living museum of Colonial Williamsburg, founded in 1926 by John D. Rockefeller. Archaeology has been an integral part of the restoration efforts since the founding. Visitors today see the results of ongoing research, not only in the architectural reconstructions but also in the artifacts and the information uncovered about living conditions of all segments of society, including enslaved African Americans, artisans, merchants, and the ruling class. Until recently, Colonial Williamsburg

included Carters Grove Plantation, in addition to the main visitor area of the town itself, and interpreted archaeological findings there to visitors. Archaeologists excavated at Wolstenholme Towne within Martin's Hundred, an early seventeenth century settlement, in the late 1970s and revealed earth-fast timber dwellings surrounded by slot fences (Noel Hume 1979). Based on archaeology of a later period, the Colonial Williamsburg Foundation reconstructed slave quarters at Carters Grove Plantation on their original locations, using eighteenth-century building techniques.

Archaeological and historic properties can be visited in unlikely places as well. Kingsmill Plantation, the home of Colonel Lewis Burwell, was built in 1736. Buildings and sites are incorporated into golf courses at the Kingsmill Resort in Williamsburg. The Kingsmill Woods course includes several archaeological site markers, and the Plantation Golf Course includes historic structures and sites (Kelso 1984).

Several plantations on the James River have provided archaeologists with well-preserved resources. Shirley Plantation, founded in 1613 and located in Charles City, offers archaeological and educational programs. Flowerdew Hundred is a Virginia Historic Landmark in Hopewell, located on the James River between Williamsburg and Richmond in Virginia (Deetz 1993). Exhibits, educational programs, and special events are available to visitors seasonally. Three decades of archeology have rewritten what we know historically about relationships among Native Americans, African Americans, and European Americans. Archaeologists also have investigated Curles Plantation, the home of Nathaniel Bacon of Bacon's Rebellion. Bacon's Castle, built in 1665, is a National Historic Landmark and has been open to the public since 1983. Stratford Hall Plantation, home of the Lee family of Virginia, conducts archaeology as well and is located in Stratford, in the vicinity of Fredericksburg.

Americans are familiar with Mount Vernon as the Virginia home of George and Martha Washington and their household. The Mount Vernon Ladies Association, which has owned the site since 1860, has sponsored ongoing archaeological excavations since the 1980s. As in many historic house museums, archaeology contributes to accurate reconstructions and to museum displays. Archaeology at Mount Vernon also influences education programs and interpretive programs, providing information on the lives of enslaved African Americans on the plantation (Bograd and Singleton 1997). Other properties associated with the first U.S. president also have archaeological programs. The National Park Service manages George Washington birthplace near Pope's Creek along the Potomac River near Fredericksburg. Ferry Farm, on the Rappahannock River near Fredericksburg, is a National Historic Landmark because it is Washington's boyhood home.

On the western edge of the Virginia piedmont is Monticello, designed by Thomas Jefferson. Excavations in the 1980s uncovered a strip of slave houses and plantation workshops known as Mulberry Row. Archaeologists have traced changes in both diet and housing of Jefferson's enslaved laborers (Crader 1984, 1990; Kelso 1986 a, b). Other properties belonging to Jefferson also have active archaeological programs. Investigations at Poplar Forest, Jefferson's retreat outside Lynchburg, Virginia, have provided a wealth of data about slave life (Heath 1999).

St. Mary's City was founded in 1634 and was the capital of Maryland until 1694. After the capital moved to Annapolis, the town slowly disappeared from the visible landscape. St. Mary's City is a National Historic Landmark that is significant for its extensive and well-preserved archeological remains. Excavations and analyses since 1971 have identified numerous archaeological sites and provided information for the reconstruction of the core of the town (Miller 1983). A living museum operates now, including living history, as well as museum displays of archaeologically recovered artifacts. Also reconstructed is the ship, the *Dove*, which was one of the vessels that brought Catholic English to the colony in search of religious freedom. Archaeology at two plantations has found direct evidence of early Catholic presence in the colony. St. Inigoes Plantation was established on what is now the Webster Field Annex of the Naval Air Station on the Pautuxent River. Archaeologists have identified a Jesuit Manor house occupied from 1637 to 1660 as well as a residence for Jesuit priests dating from 1700 to 1750.

Jefferson Patterson Park and Museum is located along the Pautuxent River in Calvert County, Maryland, on land donated to the state for the purpose of creating an archaeological preserve and an ecological studies center. The inventory of archaeological sites begins with early Native American occupation. Well-preserved historic period sites range through several centuries, from the seventeenth-century Kings Reach to the nineteenth- to twentieth-century Sukeek's Cabin site. Richard Smith lived at Kings Reach from 1690 to 1715. The Quarter site is believed to have been the home of some of his servants or slaves. Sukeek's Cabin was identified by descendents as the home of a freed, formerly enslaved woman until the 1920s (Pogue 1990; Uunila 2005).

Colonists settled Annapolis in 1649, and the town grew rapidly after the colonial capital was moved there in 1694. The town plan was laid out according to baroque principles of design, with the statehouse and the Anglican church centered in two hilltop circles surrounded by radiating streets. The Archaeology in Annapolis project has been excavating sites in the city since the early 1980s and has contributed to the widespread recognition in American historical archaeology that public education and outreach is an essential part of the discipline's purpose (Leone 2005; Mullins 1999; Shackel et al. 1998; Yentsch 1994). Visitors to Annapolis experience the original town plan, numerous eighteenth-century buildings, and several gardens. The Paca Garden, behind the home of one of the Maryland signers of the Declaration of Independence, was reconstructed based on archaeological evidence. Many of the lots in town contain intact archaeological deposits and have contributed to an archaeological understanding of the city's development.

Archaeologists have worked at many sites in Baltimore, and archaeology is included in the curriculum in Baltimore County's Public Schools. At Brewer's Park, near the harbor and the Betsy Ross House, visitors can see the remains of a Revolution-era brewery as well as artifact displays in the Center for Urban Archaeology.

Although the Chesapeake Bay is notoriously murky for divers, there is a place where divers can investigate an unusual wreck site. The Maryland Historical Trust and the U.S. Navy established a Dive Preserve where visitors can see a German U-boat. This rubber-sheathed U-1105, also known as the "Black Panther" was an early German attempt at stealth technology. The vessel was turned over to the United States at the end of World War II.

Historical archaeology in the Chesapeake Tidewater is both vibrant and productive. This brief description provides an overview and a small sample of the extensive archaeological work in the region.

Further Reading: Alexandria Archaeology Web site, http://www.alexandriaarchaeology.org; Archaeology in Annapolis Web site, http://www.bsos.umd.edu/anth/aia; Association for the Preservation of Virginia Antiquities Web site, http://www.apva.org; The Atlas of Virginia Archaeology Web site, http://state.vipnet.org/dhr/atlas/atlas.htm; Baltimore County Public Schools Web site, http://www.oregonridge.org/archae.php; Blanton, Dennis B., and Julia A. King, editors *Contact in Context: The Mid-Atlantic Region* (Gainesville: University Press of Florida, 2004); Bograd, Mark D., and Theresa A. Singleton, *The Interpretation of Slavery: Mount Vernon, Monticello, and Colonial Williamsburg*, in Presenting Archaeology to the Public, edited by John H. Jameson (Walnut Creek, CA: Alta Mira Press, 1997); Carson, Cary, Norman F. Barka, William M. Kelso, Gary Wheeler Stone, and Dell Upton, "Impermanent Architecture in the Southern American Colonies," *Winterthur Portfolio* 16(1981): 135–196; Cheek, Charles D., and Amy Friedlander, "Pottery and Pig's Feet: Space, Ethnicity, and Neighborhood in Washington, D.C., 1880–1940," *Historical Archaeology* 24(1) (1990): 34–60; Colonial Williamsburg Web site http://www.history.org; Crader, Diana C., "The Zooarchaeology of the Storehouse and the Dry Well at Monticello," *American Antiquity* 49(3) (1984): 542–557; Crader, Diana C., "Slave Diet at Monticello," *American Antiquity* 55(4) (1990): 690–717; DAACS, Digital Archaeological Archive of Comparative Slavery Web site, http://www.daacs.org; Davidson, Thomas E., "The Colonoware Question and the Indian Bowl Trade in Colonial Somerset County, Maryland," in *Contact in Context: The Mid-Atlantic Region*, edited by Dennis B. Blanton and

Julia A. King (Gainesville: University Press of Florida, 2004), 244–264; Deetz, James, *Flowerdew Hundred: The Archaeology of a Virginia Plantation, 1619–1864* (Charlottesville: University of Virginia Press, 1993); Edwards, Andrew C., *Archaeology of Seventeenth Century Homelot at Martin's Hundred, Virginia*, (Williamsburg, VA: Colonial Williamsburg Foundation, 2004); Emerson, Matthew C., "African Inspirations in a New World Art and Artifact: Decorated Pipes from the Chesapeake," in *"I, Too, Am America": Archaeological Studies of African-American Life*, edited by Theresa A. Singleton (Charlottesville: University Press of Virginia, 1999); Ferguson, Leland, *Uncommon Ground: Archaeology and Early African America, 1650–1800* (Washington, DC: Smithsonian Institution, 1992); Flowerdew Hundred Plantation Web site, http://www.flowerdew.org; Galke, Laura J., "Perspectives on the Use of European Material Culture at Two Mid-to-Late 17th Century Native American Sites in the Chesapeake," *North American Archaeologist* 25(1) (2004): 91–113; Gallivan, Martin D., "Reconnecting the Contact Period and Late Prehistory: Household and Community Dynamics in the James River Basin," in *Contact in Context: The Mid-Atlantic Region*, edited by Dennis B. Blanton and Julia A. King (Gainesville: University Press of Florida, 2004), 22–46; Gallivan, Martin D., *James River Chiefdoms: The Rise of Social Inequality in the Chesapeake*, (Lincoln: University of Nebraska Press, 2003); Heath, Barbara J., *Hidden Lives: The Archaeology of Slave Life at Thomas Jefferson's Poplar Forest* (Charlottesville: University of Virginia Press, 1999); Henry, Susan, *Physical, Spatial, and Temporal Dimensions of Colono Ware in the Chesapeake, 1600–1800*, Volumes in Historical Archaeology XXIII, South Carolina Institute of Archaeology and Anthropology (Columbia: University of South Carolina, 1992); Horning, Audrey J., "Urbanism in the Colonial South: The Development of Seventeenth-Century Jamestown," in *Archaeology of Southern Urban Landscapes*, edited by Amy L. Young (Tuscaloosa: University of Alabama Press, 2000); George Washington Birthplace National Monument Web site, http://www.nps.gov/gewa; George Washington's Ferry Farm Web site, http://www.kenmore.org; Gibb, James, and Julia A. King, "Gender, Activity Areas, and Homelots in the 17th Century Chesapeake Region," *Historical Archaeology* 25(4) (1991): 109–131; Jamestown Web site, http://www.nps.gov/colo; Jefferson Patterson Park and Museum Web site, http://www.jefpat.org; Kelso, William M., *Kingsmill Plantations, 1619–1800: Archaeology of Country Life in Colonial Virginia* (Orlando, FL: Academic Press, 1984); Kelso, William M., "The Archaeology of Slave Life at Thomas Jefferson's Monticello: 'A Wolf by the Ears,' " *Journal of New World Archaeology* 6(4) (1986a): 5–20; Kelso, William M., "Mulberry Row: Slave Life at Thomas Jefferson's Monticello," *Archaeology* 39(5) (1986b): 28–35; Kelso, William M., *Jamestown: The Buried Truth* (Williamsburg: University of Virginia Press, 2006); Leone, Mark P., *The Archaeology of Liberty in an American Capital: Excavations in Annapolis* (Berkeley: University of California Press, 2006); Leone, Mark P., and Gladys-Marie Fry, "Conjuring in the Big House Kitchen: An Interpretation of African American Belief Systems, Based on the Uses of Archaeology and Folklore Sources," *Journal of American Folklore* 112(445) (Summer 1999): 372–403; Little, Barbara J., and Nancy J. Kassner, "Archaeology in the Alleys of Washington, DC (with Nancy J. Kassner)," in *The Archaeology of Urban Landscapes: Explorations in Slumland*, edited by Alan Mayne and Tim Murray (Cambridge: Cambridge University Press, 2002); London Town Lost Towns Project Web site, http://www. historiclondontown.com/archaeology.html; Luccketti, Nicholas M., with contributions by Edward A. Chappell and Beverly A. Straube, "Archaeology at Arlington: Excavations at the Ancestral Custis Plantation, Northampton County, Virginia" (Virginia Company Foundation and the Association for the Preservation of Virginia Antiquities, 1999); Luckenbach, Al, *Providence: The History and Archaeology of Anne Arundel County's First European Settlement* (Crownsville: Maryland State Archives and the Maryland Historical Trust, 1995); Maryland Historical Trust Web site, http://www.marylandhistoricaltrust.net; Miller, Henry M., *A Search for the "Citty of Saint Maries,"* St. Mary's City Archaeology Series No. 1 (Saint Mary's City, MD, 1983); Mouer, L. Daniel, Mary Ellen N. Hodges, Stephen R. Potter, Susan L. Henry Renaud, Ivor Noel Hume, Dennis J. Pogue, Martha W. McCartney, and Thomas E. Davidson, "Colonoware Pottery, Chesapeake Pipes, and 'Uncritical Assumptions,'" in *"I, Too, Am America": Archaeological Studies of African-American Life*, edited by Theresa A. Singleton (Charlottesville: University Press of Virginia, 1999), 83–115; Mount Vernon Web site, http://www.mountvernon.org; Mullins, P. R., *Race and Affluence: An Archaeology of African America and Consumer Culture* (New York: Kluwer Academic/Plenum Publishers, 1999); National Park Service Archeology Program, Visit Archeology or the Colonial Chesapeake Tidewater Web site, http://www.cr.nps.gov/archeology/visit/chesarch.htm; Neiman, Fraser D., "Domestic Architecture at the Clifts Plantation: The Social Context of Early Virginia Building," in *Common Places: Readings in American Vernacular Architecture*, edited by Dell Upton and John Vlach (Athens: University of Georgia Press, 1986); Noel Hume, Ivor, *Martin's Hundred: The Discovery of a Lost Colonial Virginia Settlement* (New York: Alfred A. Knopf, 1979); Pogue, Dennis J., *King's Reach and 17th-Century Plantation Life*, Jefferson Patterson Park and Museum Studies in Archaeology No. 1 (Annapolis: Maryland Historical and Cultural Publications, 1990); Potter, Stephen R., *Commoners, Tribute, and Chiefs: The Development of Algonquian Culture in the Potomac Valley* (Charlottesville: University Press of Virginia, 1993); Samford, Patricia, "The Archaeology of African-American Slavery and Material Culture," *William and Mary Quarterly* 3rd Series, Vol. LIII, No. 1 (1996); Seifert, Donna J., and Joseph Balicki, "Mary Ann Hall's House," *Historical Archaeology* 39(1) (2005), in thematic issue, "Sin City," edited by Donna J. Seifert; Shackel, Paul A., and Barbara J. Little, editors, *Historical Archaeology of the Chesapeake* (Washington, DC: Smithsonian Institution Press, 1994); Shackel, Paul A., Paul R. Mullins, and M. S. Warner, editors, *Annapolis Pasts: Historical Archaeology in Annapolis, Maryland* (Knoxville: University of Tennessee Press, 1998); Shirley Plantation Web site, http://www.shirleyplantation.com; St. Mary's City Web site, http://www.stmaryscity.org; Stratford Hall Plantation Web site, http://www.stratfordhall.org; Uunila, Kirsti, "Using the Past in Calvert County, Maryland: Archaeology as a Tool for Building Community," *Society for American Archaeology Archaeological Record* 5(2) (2005): 38–40; Veech, Andrew S., "Considering Colonoware for the Barnes Plantation: A Proposed Colonoware Typology for Northern Virginia Colonial Sites," *Northeast Historical Archaeology* 26 (1997): 73–86; Washington, D.C., Web site, http://www.heritage.umd.edu/DCArchaeologyTour.htm; Yentsch, Anne Elizabeth, *A Chesapeake Family and Their Slaves: A Study in Historical Archaeology* (Cambridge: Cambridge University Press, 1994).

Barbara J. Little

ANCIENT AND HISTORIC ARCHAEOLOGY
OF THE MONACAN INDIANS

The Virginia Piedmont Region
Thomas Jefferson's Archaeology and Later Studies

As documented on Jamestown colonist John Smith's 1612 Map of Virginia, the Monacans occupied the Virginia Piedmont at the time of European contact. Archaeological evidence confirms that the Monacans were living there as well as in the Blue Ridge Mountains and in the Ridge and Valley province west of the Blue Ridge in the centuries before contact. Part of the Eastern Siouan language group, the Monacans were neighbors to the Algonquian Powhatans of the Virginia coastal plain and the Iroquoian-speaking groups to the north and southwest. After 1607 they were also neighbors to the English colony at Jamestown. Archaeological research depicts a society that practiced agriculture since ca. AD 1000, built large and permanent burial mounds, and were a numerous people organized as a polity, which, at times, united the Virginia Piedmont.

The archaeology of the Monacans is as old as American archaeology itself. The mound site at which Thomas Jefferson pioneered American scientific archaeology was a Piedmont Monacan burial mound. Jefferson also observed that there were several others like it in a wide area on both sides of the Blue Ridge Mountains and in the Shenandoah and James River valleys. By the mid-twentieth century, thirteen such mounds had been recorded, and they define the approximate boundaries of the Monacan people between AD 1000 and about AD 1700. Archaeologists refer to this cluster of mounds either as the Lewis Creek Mound complex or, more recently, the Monacan Mounds.

The late twentieth century saw a renewed interest in studying the mounds as a result of the Native American Graves Protection and Repatriation Act and the effort to repatriate human remains to the Monacan Indian Nation, still extant in Amherst County, Virginia. Hayes Creek Mound is one such Monacan mound. In the 1990s, bioarchaeologist Debra Gold analyzed the human remains from the Hayes Creek Mound and the Rapidan Mound. Gold's analysis allows a rich understanding of Monacan health, status, and diet in the prehistoric period.

Chiefly towns were associated with the Monacan mounds. One such place is Monasukapanough, the town site believed to be associated with the Jefferson Mound. Both the residential and the mortuary areas of this site are particularly significant in that they are two of the latest sites known to be occupied by Monacans in the James River drainage, and they were contemporary with the Jamestown colony.

THE JEFFERSON MOUND SITE

Jefferson's 1783 study of the mound site was prompted by correspondence with the French government, which inquired, amidst many other wide-ranging questions, whether the aboriginal people of Virginia built "monuments." To evaluate the "monumentality" of the Virginia mounds, Jefferson used archaeological methods to investigate how and why at least one of the earthen mounds he knew of in central Virginia was constructed. He considered as alternatives whether the mounds were cemeteries for dead warriors buried on the battlefield, or whether they were, instead, the common sepulcher of a community that interred their dead over long spans of time. Jefferson's observations of stratigraphic periodic construction in the accumulation of the mound, the presence of women and children, and the absence of traumatic wounds, led him to conclude that the latter hypothesis was correct. He published his excavation results and interpretations in his 1787 book, *Notes of the State of Virginia*.

The Jefferson Mound and the other Virginia Piedmont mounds are distinct from Mississippian platform and burial mounds, which can be found in southwest Virginia, western North Carolina, and eastern Tennessee. The Piedmont mounds are accretional, having been built up by periodic human burials and associated mortuary ritual activity over centuries. They contain predominantly secondary burials, human interments in which the bones of individuals who had been buried initially elsewhere were periodically gathered up and placed within the mound as single burial features, each containing between twenty and thirty-two individuals. At the Jefferson Mound and the Rapidan Mound, as many as 1,000–2,000 individuals (respectively) were interred, an unusually high figure for any burial site in the eastern United States. The mounds generally have few artifacts associated with them.

Despite several attempts in the early to mid-twentieth century, the Jefferson Mound site has never been relocated, although a fairly precise location is given in his report. New methods of noninvasive testing should help relocate this historic and sacred site.

THE HAYES CREEK MOUND SITE

The Hayes Creek Mound site is one of the thirteen known Monacan mounds, located in Rockbridge County, part of the Ridge and Valley province. Hayes Creek has particular significance among the Monacan mounds because of the early date (1901) of the scientific investigation and publication of the site by Edward P. Valentine. At this time, the mound was oval-shaped, roughly 60 by 64 feet, nearly circular, and its height was 4.5 feet. Valentine reported that within the lifetimes of local inhabitants the mound had been twice that height, and one can then imagine that at the time of its last use in the late prehistoric period it would have been substantially taller than that.

Interments in the Hayes Creek Mound occurred in at least three levels. Burials were of both a flexed individual type and secondary burial features consisting of between two and twenty individuals. A feature unique of the Hayes Creek Mound is a layer of ash at the base of the mound with burnt human bone and a cluster of large stones covering approximately fifty individual skeletons. Slightly more than half of these individuals were buried with grave goods (shells and pendants), although in general artifacts were rare in the mound. Eight fully articulated dog skeletons were interred in the mound and adjacent to human remains. Dog burials are known from other sites in eastern Virginia and across the eastern United States, but are otherwise not commonly seen in the Virginia interior.

Bioarchaeological analysis conducted by Debra Gold of the Hayes Creek population revealed that those interred there had a diet that consisted of approximately 50–75 percent maize (a high percentage), mixed with wild plants and freshwater fish. Interestingly, although Jefferson specifically noted the absence of traumatic wounds at the mound he studied, the Hayes Creek Mound had at least three individuals (6 percent) who suffered, but survived, the impact of a blunt weapon to the head. These populations were in relatively good health, although some illnesses due to infectious diseases, and one case of tuberculosis, were noted.

MONASUKAPANOUGH: A PIEDMONT MONACAN TOWN

The town associated with the Rivanna River burial mound excavated by Jefferson is called Monasukapanough. The name is derived from John Smith's Map of 1612. Monasukapanough in current archaeological writing refers specifically to that area of residential use adjacent to the mound location. In *Notes on the State of Virginia*, Jefferson refers to the mound as located on the low grounds of the Rivanna and across the river from an Indian town. Since Jefferson nowhere else refers to the common occurrence of potsherds or stone tools as occurs throughout Piedmont Virginia floodplains as an "Indian town," this suggests that either the actual remnants of Monacan structures or a local historical memory of the town

was still extant in the 1780s. John Smith identified Monasukapanough with an icon denoting the presence of a "King's Howse," meaning a chief's house. This is the same symbol that marked the town of the chiefly villages (villages in which recognized chiefs resided or were periodically in residence) of the Powhatan, including Werowocomoco, where the Algonquian paramount Chief Powhatan lived. Although the Rivanna River appears to separate the town from the mound, contemporary indigenous Monacan perspectives offer a corrective that the river was the heart of one sacred place, with a domestic area and a burial mound connected by the water, rather than separated by it.

David Bushnell, of the Smithsonian Institution, conducted excavations at Monasukapanough in the early twentieth century. Bushnell was drawn to the place in search of the Jefferson Mound. He did not find evidence of the mound but did uncover a range of artifacts indicating a long-term occupation of the site. Since 2001, the University of Virginia has conducted test excavations in the residential area of Monasukapanough. Still preliminary results indicate that the town site had been occupied sporadically for several centuries due to shifting agricultural strategies. Radiocarbon dates provide evidence of occupation from ca. AD 800 to 1700. Some distinctive seventeenth-century artifact types further confirm that Monasukapanough was occupied during the years of the Jamestown colony. However, as of this date, no European artifacts have been found at Monasukapanough. This could be the result of the small sample excavated, or it could be evidence that at least at this place, as early historic period texts suggest, the Monacans sought no contact or trade with the English colonists. By the late seventeenth century, however, other indigenous Piedmont towns were participating in trade with the English.

Further Reading: Bushnell, David L., Jr., *The Five Monacan Towns in Virginia, 1607*, Smithsonian Miscellaneous Collections, Vol. 82, No. 12 (Washington, DC: Smithsonian Institution Press, 1930); Dunham, Gary H., Debra L. Gold, and Jeffrey L. Hantman, "Collective Burial in Late Prehistoric Interior Virginia: Excavation and Analysis of the Rapidan Mound," *American Antiquity* 68 (2003): 109–128; Gold, Debra L., *The Bioarchaeology of the Virginia Burial Mounds* (Tuscaloosa: University of Alabama Press, 2004); Hantman, Jeffrey L., "Monacan Archaeology of the Virginia Interior, in *Societies in Eclipse: Archaeology of the Eastern Woodland Indians, 1400–1700*, edited by David Brose, C. Wesley Cowan, and Robert Mainfort (Washington, DC: Smithsonian Institution Press, 2001), 107–124; Hantman, Jeffrey L., and Gary Dunham, "The Enlightened Archaeologist," *Archaeology* 46(3) (1993): 44–49; Hantman, Jeffrey L., Karenne Wood, and Diane Shields, "Writing Collaborative History," *Archaeology* 53(5) (2000): 56–59; Monacan Indian Nation Web site, http://www.monacannation.com; Pellerin, Cheryl, "Righting History," *American Archaeology* 5(1) (2001): 29–33; Jefferson, Thomas, *Notes on the State of Virginia*, ed. by William Peden (Chapel Hill: University of North Carolina Press, 1996 [1784]).

Jeffrey L. Hantman

EARLY HISTORIC ARCHAEOLOGY IN ALBANY

Albany, New York

Early Dutch Settlements and Sites

New York State and its capital city of Albany are both named after an English duke, but the initial European settlement here was the creation of a young Dutch republic in the early seventeenth century. The Netherlands was experiencing a golden age of global exploration, commercial success, scientific discovery, and achievement in the arts after its successful liberation from Spain. The diversity and tolerance of the Dutch, along with their emphasis on commerce that required cooperation with natives, provided a unique cultural foundation for their settlement. The English took the Dutch colony of New Netherland in 1664 and administered it until the American Revolution. Archaeological sites in Albany include the Dutch trading company's Fort Orange and town of Beverwyck, the surrounding colony of Rensselaerswyck, and the later English city of Albany. Archaeologists found these sites through investigations of places where modern construction was proposed.

FORT ORANGE NATIONAL HISTORIC LANDMARK

The first permanent settlement at Albany was the Dutch West India Company's Fort Orange, built in 1624. This was a square, earth, and wooden fort about 150 feet on each side with four bastions. It was located at the northern limit of Hudson River navigation and an established overland route west to the Mohawk River.

In 1970 plans to construct an interstate highway along Albany's riverfront threatened the site of Fort Orange. Archaeologist Paul R. Huey excavated beneath the streets and found that 346 years of development did not destroy all traces of the fort. Archaeologists worked under temporary shelters during the winter and identified four buildings within the fort, the east entrance, the stone-lined south moat, and the north inner wall of the defensive work built on the south side of the moat.

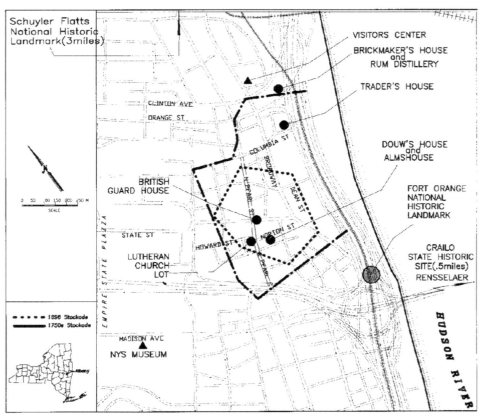

Map of Albany with the location of archaeological sites mentioned in the text.   [Charles L. Fisher]

Examples of finished wampum, approximately 0.25 inches in length.   [Charles L. Fisher]

Three of the buildings were houses, and the other was the brick foundation of either the guardhouse or the brewery. The houses had nonpermanent, wood-lined cellars that contrasted to the evidence of their substantial above-ground appearance that included fireproof red earthenware tile roofs, chimneys of yellow brick, floor tiles, decorative wall and fireplace tiles, and decorated glass windows.

The physical remains at this site differed from popular ideas about life at this trading post. The numerous artifacts related to the fur trade were expected, but the discovery that construction followed designs of similar European structures was new information. The houses were built like houses in the Netherlands and furnished with similar goods obtained from around the world. Many of the artifacts from Fort Orange resembled ones depicted in still-life paintings of Dutch artists. The residents of the fort were not impoverished and suffering in hastily built, inadequate shelters.

RENSSELAERSWYCK
Killian van Rensselaer purchased a large tract of land around Fort Orange from the Mahican Indians in 1630. The settlers of Rensselaerswyck engaged in the lucrative fur trade despite prohibitions. Traders positioned themselves to the north and west of Fort Orange and intercepted the furs before they reached their legal destination.

The lower portion of a wood-lined cellar from one of these illegal trader's huts contained artifacts from both Dutch and Native Americans, who were smoking, drinking, gambling,

Photograph of archaeologists excavating a burial beneath Pearl Street under shelter by artificial light.   [Charles L. Fisher]

and trading at this site. Another house from the 1640s was occupied by a brick maker and had a wooden floor resting directly on the ground. The roof was constructed of red earthenware tiles, and the house had glass windows, delft tiles, and iron hardware. Tobacco smoking pipes, glass trade beads, and wampum were recovered from this site, indicating that trade was an important activity even in this industrial setting. Soil from the surface around this house contained parasite eggs from human waste that was thrown on the ground rather than contained in latrine pits, or carried away in a sewer.

In 1643 Arent van Curler built a Dutch-style house and barn, combined in a single building 120 feet long and 28 feet wide at van Rensselaer's farm, about 5 miles north of Fort Orange. This house had leaded window glass, a brick fireplace, red tile roof, blue painted delft tiles, and iron shutter bolts. A wood-lined cellar beneath this building was found that was 29 feet long, 19 feet wide, and almost 6 feet deep. This Dutch agricultural settlement contained numerous artifacts that emphasize the importance of the fur trade.

BEVERWYCK/ALBANY
In 1652 Peter Stuyvesant established the West India Company town of Beverwyck by removing the houses that were close to the fort and creating a new settlement at least

a cannon shot away. The street plan of that town remains visible today.

The house of Volkert Jansen Douw, a fur trader and member of the Lutheran minority in Beverwyck, was excavated on a lot granted to Douw in 1652. It became the Dutch Reformed Church's almshouse after his death in 1685. The historic remains at this location were preserved beneath a hotel built with a shallow basement.

Archaeologists recorded the wooden cellar, the bricks from the chimney, and the later floor associated with the almshouse. Douw's cellar floor was made of wooden boards about 14 inches wide that were supported by wooden beams placed directly upon the soil. Artifacts associated with Douw's role in the fur trade included lead bars, glass trade beads, wampum, an iron axe, knives, and mouth harps. In addition to the trade items, numerous small seeds of squash or pumpkin, nutshells, and a shoe were recovered from beneath the floorboards.

Artifacts from the almshouse included English ceramics and a large quantity of clamshell. The recovery of shell fragments, unfinished and broken beads, and the tools for making shell beads indicate that the residents worked at manufacturing wampum, shell beads used as money.

The Dutch tolerated minorities, but they restricted public worship in Beverwyck to the Dutch Reformed Protestants. After the English took over the colony, the Lutherans were granted a deed and built a church by 1680. Skeletal remains

Photograph of colonial rum distillery excavation prior to covering it for the parking garage construction.   [Charles L. Fisher]

of five individuals were discovered on this lot, and the analysis of them demonstrated life experiences that included chronic infections during childhood and adulthood, nutritional diseases, and poor dental health. A cast of the female's skull was used as the basis for a facial reconstruction that is currently on display at the New York State Museum.

A large, eighteenth-century rum distillery was discovered and excavated under shelters during the winter of 2000. Rum was made from a by-product of refining sugar, and distilleries developed along with the worldwide trade in sugar, slaves, agricultural products, and manufactured goods. The foundation was 60 × 36 feet in size and contained the remains of twenty-one large wooden vats, a system of wooden pipes beneath the vats, and the stone bases of two stills and the chimney. The largest vats were 8 feet in diameter and could hold 1,900 gallons of fermented liquid.

Members of two Albany Dutch families constructed the distillery outside of the north wall of the city during the French and Indian War. This location allowed them to ignore the city ordinance that prohibited selling alcohol to soldiers or residents. The Dutch preferred drinking beer, wine, or brandy, and the construction of the rum distillery resulted from increased English influence by the middle of the eighteenth century.

Additional changes brought by the English were found at the British guardhouse, where artifacts from the French and Indian War were recovered along with items related to its subsequent use. The guardhouse was constructed by the British

to protect the Dutch population. A variety of artifacts show the soldiers' participation in the local economy, including the production of wampum. The continued military occupation after the war reflects the increased tensions that led to the American Revolution.

VISITING ALBANY ARCHAEOLOGY

There are numerous opportunities for visiting locations of archaeological sites and exhibits in Albany. Archaeological remains beneath the historic streets include churches, houses, markets, and military structures.

A commemorative sign marks the location of Fort Orange National Historic Landmark. Artifacts from the excavation are permanently on display at Crailo State Historic Site about a half mile from Albany in Rensselaer. Brochures for an archaeology walking tour of the city and a film on the archaeology of Fort Orange are available at the Albany County Visitors Center.

Trade artifacts and the facial reconstruction from the Lutheran church lot are on display in the New York State Museum, and an exhibition on the distillery is in process. Artifacts are presently displayed in lobbies of several new office buildings downtown.

Schuyler Flatts, the site of Van Rensselaer's farm, is a town park about 3 miles north of Albany. There is a walking tour with interpretive signs related to the archaeology and history of this National Historic Landmark.

Further Reading: Bradley, James W., *Before Albany: An Archaeology of Native-Dutch Relations in the Capital Region 1600–1664* (Albany: New York State Museum, 2007); Huey, Paul R., "Aspects of Continuity and Change in Colonial Dutch Material Culture at Fort Orange, 1624–1664." Ph.D. diss. (University of Pennsylvania, 1988); Huey, Paul R., "Thirty Years of Historical Archaeology in the City of Albany," in *People, Places, and Material Things: Historical Archaeology of Albany, New York*, edited by Charles L. Fisher (Albany: New York State Education Department, 2003), 11–21; Moody, Kevin,

"Traders or Traitors: Illicit Trade at Fort Orange in the Seventeenth Century," in *People, Places, and Material Things: Historical Archaeology of Albany, New York*, edited by Charles L. Fisher (Albany: New York State Education Department, 2003), 25–38; Peña, Elizabeth S., "Wampum Production in New Netherland and Colonial New York: The Historical and Archaeological Context." Ph.D. diss. (Boston University, 1990); Watervliet City School District, Schuyler Flatts Home Page, http://instruct.neric.org/schuyler (2000).

Charles L. Fisher

DEERFIELD VILLAGE AND NEARBY SITES

Connecticut River Valley, Massachusetts

Ancient and Historic Archaeology in the Connecticut River Valley

Today Deerfield, Massachusetts, is a town of about 30 square miles in western Massachusetts. For thousands of years this place, known by a variety of names, has been an important location for Native peoples as well as people of European and African descent. As a result, the archaeology of this town provides a distinctive window into human life in interior New England over the last 12 millennia.

The town of Deerfield is located at the intersection of a major north-south and east-west transportation corridor (the Connecticut River valley and Deerfield-Miller's River valleys, respectively). Because interior New England is composed of rugged uplands, Deerfield has attracted human settlement for millennia. It has long been a major by-way between Long Island Sound to the south to today's U.S.-Canadian border and the nearby St. Lawrence Valley on the north, as well as between the Hudson Valley to the west and the central uplands of Massachusetts, southern New Hampshire, and beyond to the New England coast to the east. In addition, the floodplain of the Deerfield River offers rich bottomland and a productive environment that is warmer than the surrounding uplands. As a productive habitat for a wide variety of plants and animals, it has attracted first hunter-gatherers and then farmers of all sorts for thousands of years. Nearby falls on the Connecticut River (e.g., Turners Falls) are sources of seasonally abundant anadromous fish (fish that swim upstream in large numbers to spawn), as well as water power for industry. The Deerfield Valley has long been a good place to meet, to rest when traveling, and to settle in the interior of New England. The enduring significance of this place has been captured in the efforts of two historical museums, Pocumtuck Valley Memorial Association (PVMA) and Historic Deerfield, Inc. The preservation of significant aspects of the village-scape from the late eighteenth and early nineteenth century makes visiting the village a

chance to experience and learn about the deep and more recent past of interior New England.

The first people came to the area of Deerfield at least 12,000 years ago, sometime after a large glacial lake had drained about 13,500 years ago (Hart et al. 2008). After the last maximum extent of glaciers about 18,000 years ago, as the glaciers melted and retreated to the north, a glacial lake (extending at its maximum from south of present-day Hartford, Connecticut, to modern White River Junction, Vermont) covered the Deerfield area. After this and associated lakes drained about 13,500 years ago, the environment slowly bounced back as vegetation began to take hold in bare ground left after deglaciation. The environment changed from open spruce woodland, to a mixed coniferous-deciduous forest, to an oak-hemlock forest, to today's oak-chestnut forest (Dincauze and Mulholland 1977). Each of these environmental settings provided homelands for communities of people who left remnants of their ways of life throughout the town. Human pioneers, about 12,000 years ago, established a large settlement (known today as the DEDIC site) near the Connecticut River in the southern portion of the town (Chilton et al. 2005). There are many examples of artifacts dating to the Archaic Period, about 3,000–11,000 years ago, found throughout the area.

The colonizing English encountered people they mistakenly referred to as the Pocumtuck (a word that translates to "swift, shallow, and sandy stream"), a name that has stuck in the English literature ever since. The Pocumtuck lived in the world of oak-chestnut forests and rapid-flowing rivers, along with bear, whitetail deer, shad, turkey, passenger pigeons, various plants with their useful stalks, oils, and delicious berries, and an abundance of trees with acorns and hickory nuts, bark, and sap. The trees and reeds provided materials for shelter, and useful objects were crafted from wood, stone, bone, hides, and clays.

Many of the raw materials for these objects came from the local area, but some were traded over long distances. During the Late Woodland period, about 400–1,000 years ago, the Pocumtuck grew maize, beans, squash, and tobacco, yet they were "mobile farmers" and shifted their encampments seasonally within well-defined homelands (Chilton et al. 2000). They placed their dead on rises of higher ground throughout their homeland. They had thoroughly settled and deeply understood this world, just as had the nearby Nonotuck community to the south in what today is known as Northampton and the Sokoki community not too far to the north. Today we know the names of some of the members of this community from signatures on deeds, such as Mashalisk, a Pocumtuck sunsqa (woman sachem) who signed deeds for what became the English settlement of Pocumtuck and then Deerfield (Bruchac 2005). Records kept by Europeans in the seventeenth century provide further identification, such as Wattawaluncksin, Mashalisk's son, who had accounts with the English trader, John Pynchon. We also know about them from today's Native peoples, descendants of Pocumtucks who were forced off their homeland to live in more northerly villages, such as Odanak (Foster and Cowan 1998, 263–277; PVMA 2004). Finally, the things they left in the ground, now part of archaeological sites, offer additional clues to the lives lead by the members of these communities.

The Pocumtuck, one of several Algonquian-speaking groups in New England, were a major community within the networks of Native social relations. The arrival of Europeans on the edges of these Native networks added new forces to those already driving North American history. Following a number of incidents and conflicts caused by English settlement in southern New England, in 1664 a group of Kanienkehaka (Mohawk) warriors led an attack on a Pocumtuck settlement or fort. This attack is often used in historical writings to mark the disappearance of Native peoples in the Deerfield Valley. However, it is clear from many sources that there was great continuity before and after this attack (Bruchac 2005; Hart and Chilton 2007). Nevertheless, this initial stage of Pocumtuck diaspora created an opening into which European settlers stepped. Europeans became interested in the Deerfield area as the fur and food trade extended up the valley from settlements at Hartford and Springfield in the first half of the seventeenth century, but settlement was out of the question given the significant and strong presence of the Pocumtuck. The 1664 attack coincided with an almost simultaneous land dispute between an English town and a Praying Indian town in eastern Massachusetts. The latter dispute was resolved by permission from the General Court of the English colony of Massachusetts to found a town on 8,000 acres. John Pynchon of Springfield, the "lord" of the valley, obtained deeds from Native people for territory that encompasses today's town of Deerfield. What a desirable tract of land it must have been, with the bottomland cleared for agricultural production and transportation paths and Native homesite locations obvious on the landscape. On a series of rises above the Deerfield River floodplain, in an area intensively used by the Pocumtuck people, the

English surveyed a mile-long street with house lots between 2 and 7 acres in size and rights to property in a variety of fields and woodlots, establishing an anachronistic variation on the English open-field agricultural village plan. This village within the much larger town was settled by the English no later than 1671 (Bruchac 2005; Melvoin 1989; Sweeney 1985; Thomas 1984).

For the next century the English village at Deerfield was variously one of the northernmost outposts of the English world in interior North America, an invasion of a crucial part of the ancient and persistent Pocumtuck homeland, and a symbolic threat of English intentions on New France to the north (what today is part of Canada). The village was substantially abandoned by the English twice in the first thirty years of this period, first in 1675 after a battle between an English supply train and Native forces during King Philip's (or Metacom's) War (1675–1676), and second following a raid on the village during Queen Anne's War (or the War of the Spanish Succession) in 1704. This second raid has reverberated through the centuries with stories about the attack, the taking of captives, and the subsequent insistence by the daughter of a protestant minister to not return to the English from her life with Abenaki and Mohawks. Periods of hostilities between English and Algonquian and Iroquoian peoples and the French were interspersed with periods of trade and peaceful relations. With this back-and-forth movement between the English and various Native and French people, and with the work done by people of African descent held as captives by English elites, the eighteenth-century English colony of Deerfield was interestingly multicultural. A decisive moment was the British conquest of New France in 1763. The English were no longer threatened by the French, and the Algonquians lost a formidable ally. Often presented as the abandonment of southern New England by its Native inhabitants, this European political shift instead led the indigenous peoples of the northeast to use their homelands in new ways, working within the interstices of English settlements, visiting their ancient homelands, and trading with the English and other European immigrants and the descendants of African captives up to today (Burchac 2005; Demos 1994; Haefeli and Sweeney 2003; Melvoin 1989; PVMA 2004; Sheldon 1972).

The English farmers in Deerfield, beginning as early as the 1720s, saw an increase in their material well-being as the region shifted from producing forest surpluses managed by a small number of elites in the Springfield region to the production of agricultural as well as forest products for sale in the sugar islands of the Caribbean. A regional network of elite families of merchants, political office holders, and ministers, became known as the "River Gods" because of the powers they seemed to control. Some of these individuals and families were based in Deerfield; they managed society and profited from this trade. They marked their position with their material world, building distinctive styles of houses and consuming regionally produced household items along with the imported ceramics, textiles, and other goods of the expanding European consumer revolution. This way of life changed after the American Revolution, and the change accelerated with the disruption of U.S. trade with the British Caribbean in the early 1800s, as agricultural production increasingly was oriented toward markets serving the growing populations of the urbanizing and industrializing northeast. Although agriculture was a mainstay of the village in the first part of the nineteenth century, the shift of the locus of commerce out of the village to the southern part of the town left Deerfield Village as a bit of a backwater town. As a result, the village's eighteenth- and early-nineteenth-century houses remained relatively untouched by industrialization and Victorian architectural tastes.

Deerfield Village also became increasingly self-conscious of its own history during the nineteenth century, with one of the earliest attempts of architectural preservation in the United States occurring in the 1848 effort to preserve a house that withstood the 1704 raid. The Pocumtuck Valley Memorial Association was formed in 1870 with a mission to collect materials of the early English settlers and the supposedly vanished Pocumtucks. The village participated industriously in the turn-of-the-century arts and crafts movement. With the growth of the prestigious Deerfield Academy during the first half of the twentieth century and the development of a museum of architecture and decorative arts (now known as Historic Deerfield, Inc.), in the 1940s the village thrived as a place of education and historical preservation (Flynt 2002; Garrison 1991; McGowan and Miller 1996; Paynter 2002).

Deerfield Village and its surroundings have been the focus of archaeological investigations into the Native and more recent European-period histories. Archaeological investigations of the sort considered inappropriate today were conducted in the nineteenth century by Euro-Americans, who sought out, or stumbled across, the settlements and graves of the Native peoples of the Pocumtuck Valley. Some of these early investigators were steeped in perspectives of racism and White supremacy (Bruchac 2007). Although these investigations do not meet today's standards of establishing and observing aspects of archaeological context, they are considered the source on sacred objects by some of the descendent communities. Native American human remains that were excavated or otherwise removed from archaeological sites in the vicinity of Deerfield and are in the collections of the area's colleges and universities may be subject to repatriation by Native communities. Educational institutions are consulting with Native communities on this issue.

Professional archaeology as we now practice it began with investigations of English homelots in the 1970s sponsored by Historic Deerfield, Inc. Beginning in the early 1980s Historic Deerfield and the University of Massachusetts–Amherst Department of Anthropology established a cooperative relationship that has resulted in over two decades of work on sites relating to the European and Native histories of the area around the village. This includes archaeological investigations at ten sites primarily concerned with the post-1670 period and additional work at seven sites informative about Native history of the area. Some of the better known of these are described in the sections that follow.

PINE HILL

The Pine Hill site is located on a knoll in the middle of the Deerfield floodplain in the northern Deerfield Valley, just north of the village's main street. The site was utilized by Native peoples for thousands of years, beginning at least 7,000 years ago. Excavations by faculty and students from the University of Massachusetts–Amherst between 1989 and 1997 centered on a Late Woodland time period component (AD 1000–1600) based on radiocarbon dates. Archaeological evidence revealed that during this time Native peoples returned to the site on an annual basis, primarily during the late summer and fall (Chilton et al. 2000). Post-mold patterns indicated an overlapping pattern of small house structures and a series of seasonal encampments. Subsistence remains included butternut, acorn, hazelnut, chenopodium, maize, small mammals, and moose. There was archaeological evidence for twenty-one subterranean storage or food-processing pits. There was no archaeological evidence for year-round site use, and there were no apparent midden or substantial structures. Artifacts included numerous lithic tools and debitage (small stone fragments from chipped stone tool manufacture or maintenance). Hundreds of ceramic shards were also recovered from the site, which consisted of a minimum of fifty-six vessels (Chilton 1999). Ceramic evidence from this site provided strong support for the model of Pocumtuck peoples as "mobile farmers" within a well-defined homeland. These findings play an important role in our understanding that, unlike their counterparts in Iroquoia (central New York State), some or all of the peoples of the Algonquian northeast lived lives as mobile farmers, productively making their livings without resorting to life in central nucleated villages.

POCUMTUCK "FORT"

In 1995, 2004, and 2006 the University of Massachusetts Archaeological Field School focused on confirming the location of the Pocumtuck "Fort," which is recorded in historic records as having been attacked by the Mohawk in 1664. In 2006 evidence was discovered for a large seventeenth-century Native American site in eastern Deerfield, thought to be the location of the historic "fort" (Chilton and Hart 2008). Thus far, no archaeological or geophysical evidence of fortification has been found, nor have researchers found evidence of violent conflict. This may be because investigations are still in their early stages; it may be because the evidence has been lost due to the looting of the site by enthusiasts and dealers in antiquities; or it may be because the "fort" does not fit archaeological or popular expectations of what a fort should look like. Nevertheless, we have identified scattered post molds and pit features similar to those identified at the Pine Hill site. Artifacts recovered included glass trade beads, cut copper and/or brass, and Native American ceramics. Although the ceramics are very similar to those recovered at Pine Hill, no stone tools or debitage were found at the fort site. Analysis is still ongoing, but thus far remains have been identified of freshwater mussel, a variety of nutshells, and the bones of fish, small mammals, and turtles. A major feature of the work at this site is the collaborative nature of the relationships with a wide variety of stakeholders, including professional, amateurs, local residents, the landowner, and the Massachusetts Commission on Indian Affairs.

NIMS HOUSE

The third Nims House today sits at the junction of the main Village Street and Memorial Street, but in 1704 its predecessor was a ten-year-old house situated just inside the south wall of the village palisade. The house was burned in the raid of 1704, with members of the Nims family killed or taken captive. Sons of Godfrey and Mehitable Nims returned from captivity and in the 1740's built the present house, an interesting example of vernacular New England architecture that rarely survives. Archaeological survey used geophysical methods of magnetometry and resistivity to identify a well-laid stone cellar with a stone floor. The landscape surrounding the cellar has early to mid-eighteenth-century artifacts; the floor itself has small bits of charcoal all supporting the interpretation that this is the cellar for the second Nims house, burned in the 1704 raid. Only the northeast corner of the cellar was investigated, reserving the rest for future excavation. But from this northeast corner an important clue about the seventeenth-century English village emerged. Today the buildings on the street are set with their walls parallel to the street. However, the cellar of the second Nims house is distinctively not parallel to the street, deviating by nearly 40 degrees from the bearing of the street and the rest of the present-day village's buildings. This discovery led to a search of photographic and archaeological data. To date at least four other buildings or features have been identified with orientations not parallel to the street—evidence suggesting that the earliest English village had a more jumbled appearance, with houses probably sited to take advantage of ecological features, such as sunlight by maximizing a southern exposure. The village oriented to the social life of the street that the visitor sees today is an eighteenth-century development, reflecting the modern era's sense of orderliness and symmetry in the landscape and in architecture. The Nims House is a residence owned by Deerfield Academy and is not open to the public, but its southerly lot where the second house stood can be viewed from the street and is visited in archaeology tours organized by Historic Deerfield, Inc.

E. H. AND ANNA WILLIAMS HOUSE

Around 1750, Ebenezer and Abigail Hinsdale, along with a captive African named Meshick, built and resided at what is today known as the E. H. and Anna Williams House, open to the public through Historic Deerfield. Hinsdale built a two-story, central-chimney house that looks very much like the present Sheldon-Hawks House (another Historic Deerfield property) that is directly across the street. Hinsdale was the son of a captive of the 1704 attack. He was also one of the founders of Hinsdale, New Hampshire, and he and Meshick alternately tended Hinsdale's two stores in Hinsdale and Deerfield. The property passed through a number of hands until in 1816, a distant relative, Ebenezer Hinsdale Williams and his wife Anna, bought the homelot. E. H. and Anna Williams were among the wealthiest

families in the region and built an abode to announce their status, transforming the house to the central hallway style, with an "L-shaped" extension for the kitchen and accommodations for hired help, a sophisticated stall-fed oxen barn, and a refined landscape. Visitors to the house have the opportunity to see what stylish rural domestic life was like in the 1820s and 1830s. The restoration is based on probate information, detailed architectural study, and clues from archaeological investigations.

Geophysical archaeological survey was conducted over most of the home lot around the house, in particular on the area between the house and the barn. Williams's stall-fed oxen barn has long been replaced by New England hay barns, but its footings became evident in the geophysical surveys and subsurface archaeological tests. Two cobble floors were probably used by the progressive farmer Williams, as dung floors were also part of his agricultural enterprise. Evidence of a buried land surface all around the house tells of the Williams's desire to landscape (with south-facing terraces) the relatively uneven terrain of the earlier home lot, presenting their remodeled mansion on a suitable viewing platform. They even put in a red-stone walk on the south lawn directing visitors around the house. A privy pit was part of this earlier landscape, used by the previous occupants but filled in by the Williamses with trash, including ceramics and glassware deposited during their move into the remodeled house. The ceramics and glassware provided stylistic information to aid the curators' interpretation of the cryptic entries on E. H. Williams's probate inventory as they installed the exhibit. Below all of this landscaping by the Williamses was the earliest recovered archaeological feature, the trench for a fence. Not in itself remarkable on an agricultural landscape, the trench shares a characteristic with the Nims house cellar; it is oriented nearly 40 degrees from the present street orientation to today's magnetic north. Repeated attempts to better define this fence trench and locate any associated features so far have proven futile. It is a reminder that while much is known about the truly interesting world of the eighteenth and nineteenth centuries in Deerfield, more remains to be discovered about the ways of life when the English, the Pocumtuck, and people from Africa were building the colonial landscape of interior New England.

Further Reading: Bruchac, Margaret M., "Earthshapers and Placemakers: Reflections on Algonkian Indian Stories of the Landscape," in *Indigenous Peoples and Archaeology: The Politics of Practice*, edited by H. M. Wobst and C. Smith (New York: Routledge, 2005); Bruchac, Margaret M., "Historical Erasure and Cultural Recovery: Indigenous People in the Connecticut River Valley," Ph.D. diss. (Department of Anthropology, University of Massachusetts–Amherst, 2007); Chilton, Elizabeth S., "Mobile Farmers of Pre-Contact Southern New England: The Archaeological and Ethnohistoric Evidence," in *Current Northeast Paleoethnobotany*, edited by J. P. Hart, New York State Museum Bulletin, Vol. 494 (Albany: New York State Museum, 1999), 157–176; Chilton, Elizabeth S., and Siobhan M. Hart, "In Search of the Pocumtuck 'Fort': An Artifact of Colonial History," *Historic Deerfield Magazine* (in press, 2008); Chilton, Elizabeth S., Tom Ulrich, and Niels Rinehart, "A Reexamination of the DEDIC Paleo-Indian Site,

Deerfield, Massachusetts," *Massachusetts Archaeological Society Bulletin* 66(2) (2005): 58–66; Chilton, Elizabeth S., Tonya Baroody Largy, and Kathryn Curran, "Evidence for Prehistoric Maize Horticulture at the Pine Hill Site, Deerfield, Massachusetts," *Northeast Anthropology* (59) (2000): 23–46; Demos, John, *The Unredeemed Captive: A Family Story from Early America* (New York: Knopf, 1994); Dincauze, Dena F., and Mitchell T. Mulholland, "Early and Middle Archaic Site Distributions and Habitats in Southern New England," in *Amerinds and Their Paleoenvironments in Northeastern North America*, edited by W. S. Newman and B. Salwen, Annals of the New York Academy of Sciences, Vol. 288 (New York: New York Academy of Sciences, 1977), 439–456; Flynt,, Suzanne L., *The Allen Sisters: Pictorial Photographers 1885–1920* (Deerfield, MA: Pocumtuck Valley Memorial Association, 2002); Foster, Michael K., and William Cowan, eds., *In Search of New England's Native Past: Selected Essays by Gordon M. Day* (Amherst: University of Massachusetts Press, 1998); Garrison, J. Ritchie, *Landscape and Material Life in Franklin County, Massachusetts, 1770–1860* (Knoxville: University of Tennessee Press, 1991); Haefeli, Evan, and Kevin Sweeney, *Captors and Captives: The 1704 French and Indian Raid on Deerfield* (Amherst: University of Massachusetts Press, 2003); Hart, Siobhan M., Elizabeth S. Chilton, and Christopher Donta, "Before Hadley: Archaeology and Native History, 10,000 BC to 1700 AD," in *Changing Winds: Essays in the History of Hadley, Massachusetts*, edited by Marla Miller (Amherst: University of Massachusetts Press, in press); Hart, Siobhan, and Elizabeth S. Chilton, "Community Archaeology and the Pocumtuck 'Fort,'"

Massachusetts Center for Renaissance Studies Newsletter (Autumn 2007); McGowan, Susan, and Amelia F. Miller, *Family and Landscape: Deerfield Homelots from 1671* (Deerfield, MA: Pocumtuck Valley Memorial Association, 1996); Melvoin, R., *New England Outpost: War and Society in Colonial Deerfield* (New York: W. W. Norton and Co., 1989); Paynter, Robert, "Time in the Valley: Narratives Told about Rural New England," *Current Anthropology* 43(Supplement) (2002): 85–101; PVMA (Pocumtuck Valley Memorial Association), *Raid on Deerfield: The Many Stories of 1704*, Vol. 2007 (Deerfield, MA: Pocumtuck Valley Memorial Association, 2004); Sheldon, George, *A History of Deerfield, Massachusetts: The Times When and the People by Whom It Was Settled, Unsettled and Resettled: With a Special Study of the Indian Wars in the Connecticut Valley*, Vols. 1 and 2 (Somersworth, NH: New Hampshire Publishing Co., 1972); Sweeney, Kevin M., "Mansion People: Kinship, Class, and Architecture in Western Massachusetts in the Mid Eighteenth Century," *Winterthur Portfolio* 19(1984): 231–256; Sweeney, Kevin M., "From Wilderness to Arcadian Vale: Material Life in the Connecticut River Valley, 1635–1760," in *The Great River, Art and Society of the Connecticut Valley, 1635-1820*, edited by G. W. R. Ward and W. N. Hosley (Hartford, CT: Wadsworth Atheneum, 1985), 17–27; Thomas, Peter A., "Bridging the Cultural Gap: Indian/White Relations," in *Early Settlement in the Connecticut Valley*, edited by J. W. Ifkovic and M. Kaufman (Westfield, MA: Historic Deerfield, Inc., and Institute for Massachusetts Studies, Westfield State College, 1984), 5–21.

Robert Paynter and Elizabeth S. Chilton

EARLY DUTCH, ENGLISH, AND AMERICAN HISTORIC SITES IN NEW YORK

Lower Manhattan, New York City
The Archaeology of Early Historic New York

The Dutch first settled Lower Manhattan in the 1620s. Beginning at the southern tip of Manhattan Island the city grew northward, reaching the limits of what is now called Lower Manhattan in the early decades of the nineteenth century. Since the late 1970s archaeologists have excavated a number of sites in Lower Manhattan in conjunction with the construction of large office buildings. The excavations have enabled archaeologists to reconstruct aspects of life in New York City during the seventeenth, eighteenth, and nineteenth centuries. The archaeologists have examined the alteration of the original shoreline and the growth of the city as a major seaport during this period.

THE EASTSIDE SITES
From the earliest settlement of the city in the seventeenth century, seaborne commerce was a major focus of the city's economic life, and waterfront property was highly valued. Beginning in the latter portion of that century, new waterfront

property was created by the process of landfilling outward from the city's original shoreline into the East River. As a result, lower Manhattan's East River shoreline is more than three blocks east of its original seventeenth-century location along the route of what is now known as Pearl Street.

Two of the earliest archaeological excavations occurred along the original shoreline on the west side of Pearl Street. At the Broad Financial Center site archaeologists uncovered a portion of a warehouse belonging to the Dutch West India Company and artifacts associated with homes that stood there in the mid-seventeenth century. At the Stat Huys site, archaeologists uncovered the walls and charred wooden basement floor of a tavern built by the English governor, Francis Lovelace, in 1670. At these sites, as well as the others mentioned in this essay, deposits of household artifacts dating to the eighteenth and nineteenth centuries enabled archaeologists to chronicle changes in domestic life during this period.

The first expansion of the city eastward on landfill occurred in the 1680s and 1690s. At the 7 Hanover Square site archaeologists uncovered the foundations of a row of houses built at the time of landfilling. The walls of these houses were built on the beach and in intertidal areas near the shoreline, with landfill being deposited around the walls. This was the earliest solution to the problem of how to keep the landfill from washing away while it was being deposited. At Hanover Square, and at excavations conducted in the basement of a nearby building at 64 Pearl Street, large samples of this early landfill were recovered. It contained many artifacts, including ceramics imported from Holland and England as well as clothing items and food remains, representing refuse discarded by early New Yorkers.

During the eighteenth century, additional landfilling expanded the shoreline eastward, first to Water Street and later to Front Street, one and two blocks, respectively, east of the original Pearl Street shoreline. The deeper waters in this location did not permit the use of building foundations to retain landfill, so other solutions had to be found. One solution was to build wharves. These massive structures served to hold the landfill during filling, and afterwards accommodated ships carrying goods into and out of the port.

The unloading of ships also required the construction of piers that extended into the water perpendicular to the shoreline. Eighteenth- and early-nineteenth-century piers were often built by what is known as the block and bridge method. Square or rectangular "blocks" were constructed of logs and then filled with large rocks or earth to sink them in place in a line extending into the river. Large planks were then used to bridge the gap between the blocks, creating the pier. When the landfilling was later extended into the area adjacent to these piers, horizontal boards were attached to the sides of the blocks in order to keep the landfill from washing away during filling. Portions of these wharves and piers were uncovered at the Assay Office and Telco sites in the 1980s.

Evidence of perhaps the most dramatic solution to the problem of retaining the landfill in deep water was first uncovered in the 1970s during excavations beneath two buildings (207 and 209 Water Street sites) at the South Street Seaport Museum. The archaeologists excavating here uncovered a portion of a wooden ship, the purpose of which became clear several years later, when excavations at the 175 Water Street site uncovered a major portion of an eighteenth-century vessel. Such ships were sunk parallel to the old shoreline to support material deposited during the landfilling process. The ship was partially beneath the Front Street pavement and was apparently sunk during the episode of filling that expanded the city to this location in the second half of the eighteenth century. Thousands of New Yorkers stood in line to see the ship on a cold winter's day in 1982.

The final episode of landfilling on the east side of Lower Manhattan took place during the first decade of the nineteenth century, expanding the shoreline to its present location at South Street. During the following decades, build-ings were constructed on the fill to serve as offices and warehouses for merchants trading in the goods carried in ships that docked at the port facilities. Goods handled by such merchants were recovered from the basements of late-eighteenth- and early-nineteenth-century buildings during archaeological excavations at the 7 Hanover Square, Assay Office, Barclays Bank, and Telco sites. In 1835 a great fire laid waste to a large portion of Lower Manhattan. At the Assay Office site, archaeologists encountered the burnt remains of goods that had been located within the basement of one of these merchants, Anthony Winans. They recovered crates and barrels full of wine bottles and the remains of foodstuffs such as grapes and peppercorns. At the Telco site, an earlier fire in 1816 had consumed the building occupied by a coffee merchant, and excavators recovered thousands of coffee beans from the burned remains of the basement floor.

THE FIVE POINTS NEIGHBORHOOD SITES

In addition to creating new space with landfill, the city spread northward in the nineteenth century. An increased need for workers' housing and the desire to separate home and workplace led to the transformation of former industrial districts into residential neighborhoods. The infamous Five Points neighborhood developed in one of these districts. Dominated by a large freshwater pond called the Collect, the district was first inhabited by artisans who lived and worked on their properties and later by the waves of immigrants who came to New York in search of new lives. The Collect Pond had been filled by 1819, and multistory tenements were built, first to receive Irish immigrants fleeing the potato famines of the 1840s and later for the Italians and Chinese who came in the last decades of the century. The construction of a new federal courthouse just east of Foley Square in the early 1990s provided the opportunity to excavate a large portion of a block that was once part of the Five Points neighborhood, traditionally portrayed as New York City's most notorious slum.

The Pearl Street side of the excavated block housed artisans (e.g., tanners, bakers, carpenters) in the early nineteenth century and mostly Irish laborers at mid-century. The artifacts recovered from the many filled privies and cisterns associated with this sequence of residents revealed contrasting lifestyles. At least one artisan family early in the century maintained an Old World lifestyle, eating from fancy porcelain dishes and sipping wine from delicately etched glasses in an atmosphere that must have been filled with noxious fumes from nearby industries. Food remains, two sets of everyday dishes (for milk and meat, perhaps), and pewter seals marked with Hebrew letters belonged to an orthodox Jewish family that kept a kosher kitchen on Pearl Street in the 1830s. The mid-century Irish residents sought respectability in spite of limited incomes and overcrowded, unsanitary living conditions. The archaeologists identified sets of imported tea and tablewares and clay pipes that showed a disdain for patriotic imagery. Food remains indicated an Irish preference for pork over the fish that was readily available and less expensive.

The Baxter Street side of the block was New York's first garment district. Eastern European Jewish tailors and secondhand clothing dealers lived and worked in single-family houses that had been converted for multiple tenants. They chose different ceramics than the Irish, preferred lamb and fish to pork, and were apparently comfortable with the patriotic imagery that was associated with the anti-Irish Nativist political party. Ethnic identity was clearly maintained at Five Points, although the archaeological evidence does not suggest the kind of violent conflict nor degraded populace that nineteenth-century yellow journalists, and even Charles Dickens, characterized.

In addition to tenements for workers, new housing was also being built for the middle class in nineteenth-century New York. The expansion of New York University's library on Sullivan Street in Greenwich Village provided the opportunity to excavate six lots on the southern edge of Washington Square. Just as on the Five Points site, the artifacts came mainly from trash-filled privies in the former backyards of the house lots. The remains indicate that the mid-nineteenth-century residents were fashion conscious. They had fancy tea sets for entertaining and matching sets of tea and tablewares for family meals that favored the Gothic style. Archaeologist Diana Wall has associated this style with the "cult of domesticity," a code of behavior that emphasized proper manners and Christian morality. Highlighted is the attention paid to children and their upbringing, which was facilitated by gender-specific toys and didactic possessions such as cups with sayings printed on them, or decorated with a child's name or the alphabet. These things were found at Sullivan Street, but they were also found at Five Points, suggesting that the difference between middle-class and working-class values may not have been as extreme in the nineteenth century as often assumed.

Modern buildings have taken the place of most of the archaeological sites discussed here. Visitors interested in what the sites look like today can take the self-guided walking tour (listed in Further Reading) published by Diana diZerega Wall and Anne-Marie Cantwell. The walls of the Lovelace Tavern can be viewed in a sidewalk exhibit on Pearl Street in front of the building numbered 85 Broad Street. A few of the buildings from the nineteenth-century seaport still stand and have been incorporated into the South Street Seaport Museum. An exhibit of artifacts recovered from some of the excavated archaeological sites is displayed at the South Street Seaport Museum's New York Unearthed facility. This display can be visited by appointment. Unfortunately all but 18 of the 850,000 artifacts found on the Five Points site were lost when No. 6 World Trade Center, where they were analyzed and stored, was destroyed on September 11, 2001. The remaining 18 artifacts will eventually be on permanent display in the federal courthouse, known as the Daniel P. Moynihan Courthouse, that now stands on the site. The Sullivan Street artifacts, along with those from many of the other Lower Manhattan archaeological sites, will be permanently curated at the New York State Museum in Albany. Artifacts from early New York City are also on display at the Museum of the City of New York.

Further Reading: Cantwell, Anne-Marie, and Diana diZerega Wall, *Unearthing Gotham: The Archaeology of New York City* (New Haven, CT: Yale University Press, 2001); Wall, Diana diZerega, and Anne-Marie Cantwell, *Touring Gotham's Archaeological Past: 8 Self-Guided Walking Tours Through New York City* (New Haven, CT: Yale University Press, 2001); Yamin, Rebecca, "New York's Mythic Slum, Digging Lower Manhattan's Infamous Five Points," *Archaeology Magazine*, 50(2) (1997); Yamin, Rebecca, Paul Reckner, and Damian Blanck, *The Five Points Site*, General Services Administration Web site, http://r2.gsa.gov/fivept.

Arnold Pickman and Rebecca Yamin

RI-1000, A SEVENTEENTH-CENTURY NARRAGANSETT CEMETERY SITE

Narragansett Bay Area

A Native American Site from the Beginning of European Contact

RI-1000 is a seventeenth-century Narragansett Indian cemetery in North Kingstown, Rhode Island. In the third quarter of the seventeenth century, fifty-six people—women, men, and children—were buried there. In 1982 the unmarked burial site was disturbed accidentally by excavators preparing the area for commercial development.

Because the cemetery was on private land and was without legal protection, the Narragansett Tribe reluctantly agreed to have archaeologists excavate and study the cemetery provided that reburial would occur when the study was completed. Excavations were carried out during the summer of 1983.

The site is important in archaeology for what it tells us about some of the physical, social, and spiritual aspects of the daily lives of people in a Narragansett village during the first few decades of sustained contact with Europeans. The project itself is important as an early example of archeologists and Indian people working together on the excavation and study of a cemetery site and deciding together that the skeletal remains of the dead and their artifacts would be reburied instead of stored or displayed.

The people buried in RI-1000 are part of a tribe that has lived around Narragansett Bay for thousands of years. Tribal oral history, traditions, and archaeological excavations indicate a continuous occupation of the lands around the coastal estuaries and salt ponds and on the islands of Narragansett Bay and Block Island Sound since at least 3,200 years ago. A large year-round settlement on Block Island was established by 2,200 years ago. The residents' diet included locally available fish and shellfish, nuts, and seal; maize cultivation began between 700 and 900 years ago as demonstrated by the presence of maize kernels in many storage and refuse pits found through archaeological studies of village settlement sites at Point Judith and Quononchontaug Ponds along Rhode Island's south coast. The first European descriptions of Narragansett Bay and its people come from the 1524 visit of the Italian navigator, Giovanni da Verrazzano. Near what is now Newport, Rhode Island, he described a coastal village with many circular wigwams, gardens of corn and beans, and a healthy, prosperous, and generous people who showed him great hospitality.

European settlement began in 1636 when Roger Williams, a Puritan minister banished from Boston for his heretical views, established Providence at the head of Narragansett Bay. Relations between the Narragansett and Williams started well, as Chief Sachem Canonicus allowed Williams to establish a trading post near what is now Wickford, Rhode Island, at one of the Narragansett's major settlement areas. Relations soon soured, however, as Narragansett leaders complained to colonial officials that the English could not be trusted and that Narragansett people were suffering from the effects of new diseases, land encroachment, threats of violence, and frequent rumors of war. Open and declared war began in December 1675 when Puritan armies from Massachusetts and Connecticut invaded and brought what is now called King Philip's War to the Narragansett country.

The fifty-six people interred at RI-1000 lived and died during the forty-year period of social and political disruption and upheaval that preceded the King Philip's War. The study of their skeletal remains reveal much about the physical conditions of their lives—the diseases people had, their ages of death, and some general indications of their overall well-being. The biological analysis indicated that the people were under stress. One indication of this is that a disproportionate number of the burials were young people, between the ages of ten and thirty, usually years of good health and physical strength. Evidence from the West Ferry site in Jamestown, Rhode Island, an earlier Narragansett cemetery that was used prior to sustained European contact, suggests a much less stressful time because the largest proportion of people buried there died after reaching the age of fifty. By the 1650s, however, when English settlements were well established throughout southern New England, an alarmingly high proportion of teenage individuals and young adults were dying, threatening the very survival of the community.

The Narragansett were spared the major epidemic diseases that struck Indian villages along the New England coast to the east and north of Narragansett Bay between 1616 and 1622. They were, however, subjected to the steady, relentless effects of chronic diseases such as dental caries (cavities) and tuberculosis. Severe, and in some cases disabling, dental disease was present in many individuals as a result of new foods introduced by Europeans—flour, molasses, and sugar—and poor dental hygiene. Many apparently suffered from tuberculosis, based on the tubercular skeletal lesions exhibited by seventeen of the fifty-six people buried. Because skeletal lesions develop with time, and not all individuals with tuberculosis develop them, it is likely that other people had the disease as well and that it was much more widespread than in pre-contact times. Tuberculosis is often associated with poverty and malnutrition, and the high incidence of the disease at RI-1000 is one indication of how living conditions had deteriorated.

That malnutrition may have been a problem for some of the people is also suggested by the pattern of Harris, or "growth-arrest," lines. These lines are thin dense lenses of bone in the femur (the thighbone) and other long bones. They are detectable with X-rays and are generally considered to represent exposure to episodes of stress such as malnutrition or illness. When Harris line counts are compared to the distribution of wampum among individuals in the cemetery, the pattern suggests that individuals buried with wampum suffered fewer exposures of malnutrition or illness and that people with wampum were healthier, better nourished, and better cared for than others. Wampum is the name given to the small white and purple shell beads that were used to buy food and other items and that ritually symbolized social well-being. The relationship between wampum and growth arrest lines among people at RI-1000 is noteworthy given Roger Williams's observation in the 1630s that Narragansett communities had no beggars and that food was freely and generously shared. By 1648, there were reports that some Narragansett were compelled to buy corn from the colonists, when only a generation earlier Indian people had enabled the English to survive at Plymouth by providing them with corn and sustenance. RI-1000 provides visible, tangible evidence of the breakdown of a people's health and well-being from chronic and debilitating disease and from the stress and malnourishment experienced by those who could not care for themselves.

While the Narragansetts' physical and social well-being worsened, their relationship with the spirit world remained strong, as shown by the way they used the body to symbolize ideas about life and death. Great care was taken in the burial of all the people. All were buried in a flexed or fetal position. This birth posture represents the idea that death is not an end point but simply a change in the state of one's continuing existence as one returns to the womb of mother earth. Similarly, all the people were buried with the tops of their heads pointing to the southwest, toward the home of Cauntantowitt, the creator; and nearly all of the people had their eyes looking to the east, toward the rising sun and a new beginning.

RI-1000 was one of the first Native American cemetery projects in the United States that began with the assumption that most, and perhaps all, of what was taken from the earth would be reburied. At that time there was widespread resistance against reburial among archaeologists because many were concerned that it amounted to an irretrievable loss of scientific data. In Rhode Island, however, there was a precedent for reburial: in 1972 William S. Simmons had arranged for the reburial of skeletal remains from the West Ferry site that he had excavated in the 1960s without tribal participation. So to many Rhode Islanders it was not at all extraordinary when the Rhode Island Historical Preservation and Heritage Commission agreed with the Narragansett Indian Tribe that reburial would be a condition of the project. When the Native American Graves Protection and Repatriation Act

(NAGPRA) became law in 1990, the routine practice of archaeology in Rhode Island was in most respects unaffected, because the debate between archaeologists and Indian people over the control the excavation of burial sites had been settled.

The RI-1000 reburial site is very near the site's original location and may be visited: four large stones mark the outside of the circular area reserved for reburial, which is immediately south of the shopping complex at the southwest corner of the intersection of Routes 102 and 2 in North Kingstown, Rhode Island. The former cemetery site, several hundred feet to the north, is covered by a large asphalt parking area.

Further Reading: Brown, John B. III, and Paul A. Robinson, "'The 368 Years' War': The Conditions of Discourse in Narragansett Country," in *Cross-Cultural Collaboration: Native Peoples and Archaeology in the Northeastern United States*, edited by Jordan E. Kerber (Lincoln: University of Nebraska Press, 2006), 59–75; Narragansett Indian Tribe Web site, http://www.narragansett-tribe.org (online June 2007); Robinson, Paul A., Marc A. Kelley and Patricia E. Rubertone, "Preliminary Biocultural Interpretations from a Seventeenth-Century Narragansett Cemetery in Rhode Island," in *Cultures in Contact: The European Impact on Native Cultural Institutions in Eastern North America, A.D. 1000–1800*, edited by William W. Fitzhugh (Washington, DC: Smithsonian Press, 1985), 107–130; Rubertone, Patricia E., *Grave Undertakings: An Archaeology of Roger Williams and the Narragansett Indians* (Washington, DC: Smithsonian Institution Press, 2001).

Paul A. Robinson

COCUMSCUSSOC, NORTH KINGSTOWN, RHODE ISLAND

Narragansett Bay Area

An Ancient and Historic Indian and Euro-American Site

Cocumscussoc is the Narragansett name for the part of their ancestral homeland in North Kingstown, Rhode Island, bordering Wickford Harbor, one of many small coves around Narragansett Bay. Variously translated as "marshy meadows" and "where there are small sharpening stones," Cocumscussoc commonly refers to the locale that became the site of seventeenth-century European trading posts, an eighteenth-century slave-holding plantation, and nineteenth- and twentieth-century dairy farms. Today, the name is attached to an archaeological site preserved beneath the lawn of a larger historic property that is also the location of Smith's Castle, a two-and-one-half-story wooden structure, built in the late 1670s and recently restored to its eighteenth-century style.

Archaeological evidence suggests a Native presence at Cocumscussoc that dates back long before the arrival of Europeans in the seventeenth century. Some stone points found at locations around Wickford Harbor are more than 8,000 years old. Others dating several thousand years later imply that the area's freshwater streams, such as Cocumscussoc Brook, were important for fishing. Discarded stone tools, stone flakes from tool sharpening, burnt rocks from heating and cooking, and charred hickory nuts found in nearby archaeological deposits from about 2,000 years ago indicate that Wickford Harbor and nearby coves and estuaries were attractive locations of permanent, year-round residents. At the site of Cocumscussoc, archaeologists found stone points and

Aerial view of Cocumscussoc.   [Photograph by Richard A. Gould]

pottery, along with a deposit of stone flakes with traces of charcoal, that provide evidence for Native occupation prior to European traders in the seventeenth century.

Questions about who set up the first trading post at Cocumscussoc, when it was established, and where exactly it was located have been debated for hundreds of years. Some historians say that Roger Williams, popularly known as the founder of Rhode Island, built a trading post at Cocumscussoc as early as 1637. Others point to Richard Smith, who, with John Wilcox, his business partner, conducted trade with the Narragansett for more than a decade before buying Williams's trading house, fields and fences, canons, and rights to use a small island for goats in 1651. Archaeological evidence may not provide the precision to answer these questions unambiguously since material remains used in dating typically cannot pinpoint a site to a particular decade, let alone to within a few years. However, artifacts found in archaeological investigations at the site of Cocmuscussoc by archaeologists from the University of Rhode Island in the 1970s and Brown University in the 1990s, such as a lead seal broken off from a bolt of imported cloth, glass beads, and inner spirals of whelk shells for making wampum (Native beads sometimes used as money), suggest that Indians and Europeans traded there during the seventeenth century. A Native grave excavated at an undisclosed location at Cocumscussoc in 1879 and 1880 that held a human skeleton buried with a brass kettle, white-glazed ceramic cups, a silver-plated spoon, a glass bottle, and other offerings provides additional examples of goods that the Narragansett community living near the trading post might have bartered or bought from Europeans, and then used or gave away to family and friends.

Written accounts suggest that Richard Smith built a more substantial house or enlarged an existing one at Cocumscussoc after the middle of the seventeenth century. During the conflict known as King Philip's War (1675–76), the site was a staging area for New England troops who launched the attack on Narragansetts sheltered in the Great Swamp of South Kingstown, Rhode Island. Archaeology has yet to offer clues to the property damage reported to have been caused by the troops or any evidence to support claims that the Narragansetts burned Smith's strong house (or "castle") in 1676. The only testaments to King Philip's War now visible on the grounds are two boulder memorials with inscribed bronze plaques. One marks the grave of forty soldiers who died at Great Swamp or during the march back to Cocumscussoc. Archaeological and geophysical testing in its vicinity has not revealed any hint of a mass grave or human remains. Therefore, the soldiers may not have been

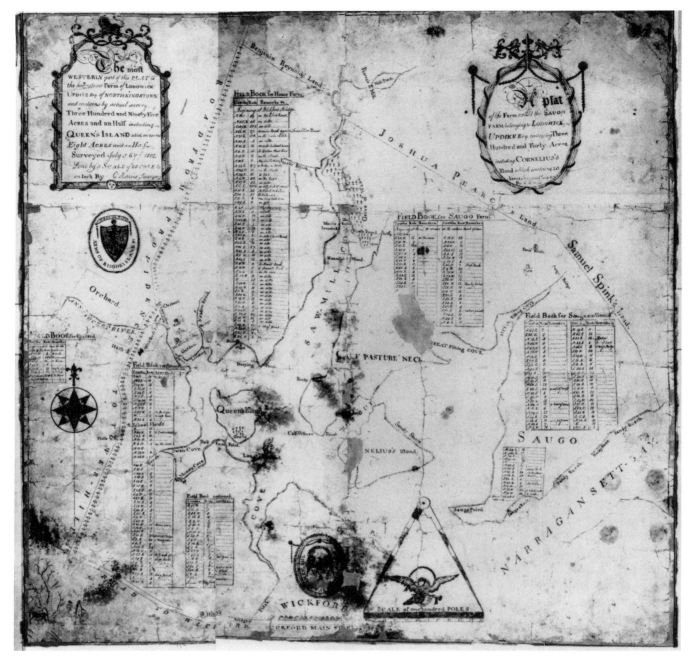

A map of the Updike Plantation (Harris 1802).   [Rhi X5 308. Harris, Caleb, Surveyor. A plat of the Farm called Saugo Farm belonging to Lodowick Updike. Scale [1:20 poles]. North Kingstown, RI. 1802. Ink and gold leaf on paper backed with silk. CARTOGRAPHY. Graphics collection: Map #1172. Courtesy the Rhode Island Historical Society.]

interred at the spot identified by the monument, since a grave containing multiple individuals should leave some archaeological traces.

The abundance of artifacts excavated as part of archaeological investigations and dating between the late seventeenth and the eighteenth centuries tells us about the increasing wealth and social aspirations of Cocumscussoc's owners following King Philip's War. Beginning with Lodowick Updike, who inherited the property from Richard Smith, Jr., in 1692, and continuing

through the eighteenth century, the Updike family ran Cocumscussoc as a plantation and owned slaves, much like planters in the South. Their fields, orchards, and pastures, which at their peak extended over 3,000 acres, produced crop surpluses sold for profit. They made a rich, creamy cheese from the milk of their cows that was a highly regarded export commodity. Today, Smith's Castle looks much like it did during the Updike period, when it was remodeled using a style of building design called Georgian architecture. Excavations on an earthen terrace in the front yard turned up remnants of brick paths from an ornamental garden and discarded tea sets, wine bottles, punch bowls, furniture hardware, and fancy buckles indicative of the Updike's lavish lifestyle. Archaeologists have not located separate slave living quarters or artifacts. However, beyond the house and archaeological site, close to the entrance of property from Post Road, there are stone walls and the foundation of an ice house, used for storing ice harvested from Cocumscussoc Brook, that serve as examples of work probably done by slaves on the Updike plantation.

The plantation era ended in 1812 when Wilkins Updike sold Cocumscussoc. Over the next 125 years, Cocumscussoc had a series of different owners, although less is known about their lives and activities than those of earlier occupants. Drawings and photographs show that they altered the exterior of Smith's Castle and added dairy barns and other outbuildings that are no longer standing. Brown University archaeologists uncovered an extensive drainage system constructed of brick and stone that probably dates to the nineteenth century. In general, artifacts from the site dating to the nineteenth and twentieth centuries are not as elaborate or plentiful as those from the previous era. There are examples of mass-produced dishes and glass ware, including fragments of milk bottles from the modern dairy farm operated at Cocumscussoc during the 1920s and 1930s.

By the late 1930s, the Cocumscussoc dairy farm ceased to exist. Following the sale of the property in 1940, the house and grounds were neglected, vandalized, and almost destroyed. In 1949 a group of concerned local people organized the Cocumscussoc Association, a nonprofit corporation, to preserve Smith's Castle and 2 acres of land surrounding it as a historic site. Since buying the property, the association has acquired more land, restored and maintained the house and grounds, and interpreted them for the public. Visitors can take guided tours of Smith's Castle and explore for themselves the area between the house and the cove that contains the archaeological site.

Further Reading: Fitts, Robert K., "The Landscapes of Northern Bondage," *Historical Archaeology* 30 (1996): 54–73; Rubertone, Patricia E., *Grave Undertakings: An Archaeology of Roger Williams and the Narragansett Indians* (Washington: Smithsonian Institution Press, 2001); Smith's Castle Web site, http://www.smithscastle.org (online June 2005); *Smith's Castle at Cocumscussoc: Four Centuries of Rhode Island History*, an Exhibition [Catalog] Celebrating the 325th Anniversary of the Construction of Smith's Castle in 1678 (Wickford, RI: Cocumscussoc Association at Smith's Castle, 2003); Woodward, Carl R., *Plantation in Yankeeland: The Story of Cocumscussoc, Mirror of Colonial Rhode Island* (Chester, CT: Pequot Press, 1971).

Patricia E. Rubertone

QUEEN'S FORT, NORTH KINGSTOWN, RHODE ISLAND

Narragansett Bay Area

Historic Seventeenth-Century Narragansett Indian Fort Site

Queen's Fort is a seventeenth-century Narragansett Indian stone fortification located on a hilltop about 3.5 miles northwest of Cocumscussoc in North Kingstown. It is named for Quiaipen, a Narragansett sachem or leader, sometimes called Matantuck, Magnus, or the Old Queen, who lived in the Exeter–North Kingstown area. She was killed during King Philip's War by Connecticut forces in a northern Rhode Island swamp in the summer of 1676, just six months after surviving the attack on Great Swamp. During those months, she and other Narragansett survivors evaded capture by occupying Queen's Fort and other places in their ancestral homeland unknown to Europeans. The fort's historical associations with King Philip's War and its stone construction have been topics of much speculation, as well as careful study, for almost 200 years.

The fort consists of dry-laid stone walls built between piles of boulders deposited naturally by glaciers. In some spots, these boulders form part of the fort's walls. Drawings from the nineteenth and early part of the twentieth century suggest that the fort was roughly circular in plan and had as many as four semicircular bastions or tower-like projections. An archaeological site map from the late 1970s shows a similar layout, but only a single bastion and an angular feature identified as a flanker jutting out from its walls. These different interpretations of the fort's design might be related to the difficulties of seeing its outline among all the rocks or to artistic liberties taken by early observers with romanticized visions of hilltop fortifications. It is also possible that time and vandalism have taken their toll and contributed to the fort's deterioration.

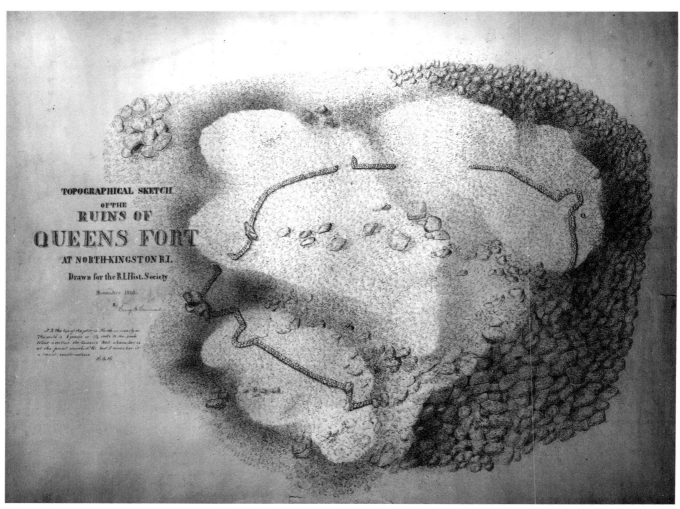

Sketch of Queen's Fort, 1865.   [Rhi X32 60. Henry B. Hammond. Ruins of Queens Fort. North Kingston, RI. 1855. Ink on paper. CARTOGRAPHY. Graphics. Courtesy the Rhode Island Historical Society.]

Some writers suggest that a Narragansett Indian, who Europeans called Stonewall John because of his talents as a stonemason, built the fort. The archaeologist Patrick Malone, an expert on military technology in seventeenth-century New England, says its sophisticated design points to Stonewall John's qualifications and possibly to his familiarity with defensive structures Europeans built to enclose their settlements. However, regardless of whether he or another Narragansett constructed Queen's Fort, stone forts are uncommon. Native peoples in southern New England used stockades, made of logs or wooden poles set in earth, and stone-filled ditches, rather than stone walls, as protection from enemies.

Outside the fort's walls, there is a large clump of boulders that conceals a natural cavern known as the Queen's Chamber (or Bedroom). In the nineteenth century a local historian wrote that "arrows etc." were found inside the chamber. Archaeological excavations in the 1970s did not uncover any artifacts nearby. Of all the locations excavated

within and outside of the fort's walls, archaeologists only found a fragment of a pipe bowl dating from the seventeenth century. The pipe resembles ones recovered from Cocumscussoc and RI-1000.

Because of its unusual construction and the scarcity of artifacts, skeptics say Queen's Fort is merely a geological feature and not an archaeological site. A recent proposal calls it a sacred place rather than a fortification, since its hilltop setting and rocky terrain were unsuitable for habitation and perhaps even hard to defend. However, seventeenth-century Native forts in southern New England are located on hilltops as well as in swamps. A stone fort on a boulder-covered summit may have provided a well-camouflaged hiding place and, unlike Great Swamp, one that colonial troops failed to discover during King Philip's War.

Queen's Fort is on land that is owned by the Rhode Island Historical Society on the south side of Stoney Lane west of Route 2. A roadside marker erected in 1931 to indicate its location is missing, but visitors can find the site by

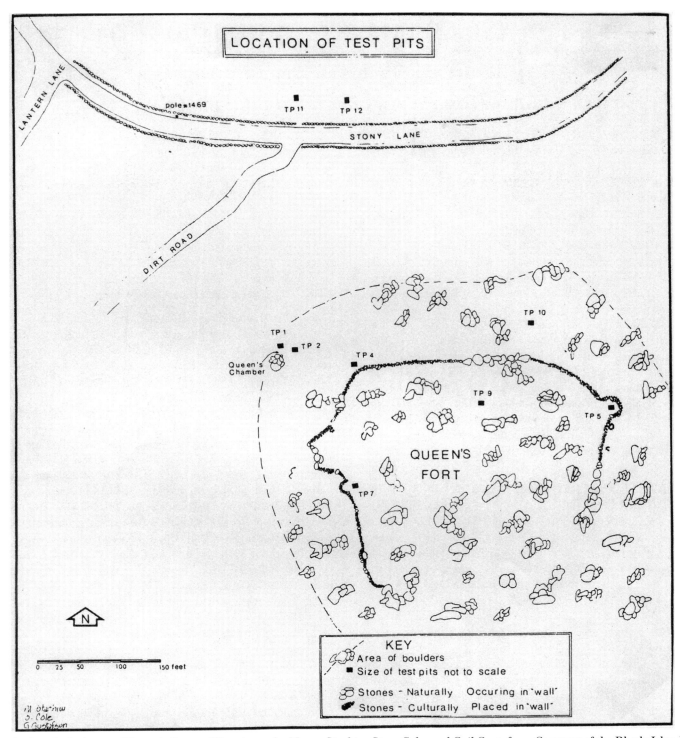

LOCATION OF TEST PITS

KEY
Area of boulders
■ Size of test pits not to scale
Stones - Naturally Occuring in "wall"
Stones - Culturally Placed in "wall"

Archaeological map of Queen's Fort. [Map drawn by Myron Stachiw, Steve Cole, and Gail Gustafson. Courtesy of the Rhode Island Historical Preservation and Heritage Commission.]

following a trail about 200 yards to the west of a stone wall and barn.

Further Reading: Chapin, Howard M., "Queen's Fort," *Rhode Island Historical Society Collections* 24 (1931): 141–156; Malone, Patrick M., *The Skulking Way of War: Technology and Tactics Among the New England Indians* (Baltimore, MD: Johns Hopkins University Press, 1991); Mavor, James W., Jr., and Byron E. Dix, *Manitou: The Sacred Landscape of New England's Native Civilization* (Rochester, VT: Inner Traditions International, 1989).

Patricia E. Rubertone

BOSTON AND CHARLESTOWN HISTORIC SITES

Boston, Massachusetts, and Nearby
Early Historic Sites in and around the City

Europeans had begun visiting the New England coast by the sixteenth century, but they left little documentation or physical evidence. At that time Boston was a small peninsula surrounded by the waters of the Charles River and the harbor and connected to the mainland by a narrow neck. In 1630 William Wood described the peninsula, called Shawmut by the Native Americans, as having a "safe and pleasant Harbor within, having but one common and safe entrance." Since the early 1800s multiple land building campaigns have increased the original landform. Today, one-sixth of Boston is built on manmade land.

Hundreds of historic-period archaeological sites have been located in Boston, dating from the earliest settlement in 1630 to the more recent twentieth-century immigration episodes. The majority of sites are belowground features that have survived extensive urban development. The historical archaeological record of Boston includes both terrestrial and underwater sites and encompasses a variety of types, including military, industrial, commercial, social, recreational, institutional, religious, agricultural, and domestic.

CENTRAL ARTERY/THIRD HARBOR TUNNEL PROJECT

During the 1970s the Central Artery/Third Harbor Tunnel Project, also known as the "Big Dig," initiated the largest highway/tunnel project in the United States. Before construction began the project corridor was archaeologically assessed and tested, and two Boston neighborhoods were found to contain significant, intact sites.

City Square Archaeological District Sites, Charlestown

The planned settlement of the Boston area began in Charlestown, located on the north side of the Charles River across from Boston, in 1629. Settlement commenced with the arrival of an advance party for the Massachusetts Bay Company. Company engineer Thomas Graves selected the City Square site as the heart of a nucleated town, between a fortified hill and the Charles River. In 1630 Governor Winthrop arrived from England with eleven ships of colonists and settled into City Square.

Archaeologists uncovered the remains of Governor Winthrop's "Great House," the colony's political and religious center, and three early household sites, including a tavern. Excavations evaluated pottery, distillery, and wharf sites,

most notably North America's oldest dry dock, contributing important information on the development of the early waterfront district.

The City Square Historic and Archaeological Site is a Boston landmark. The site is interpreted in a public park along Boston's Freedom Trail. Foundation stones from the excavated structures are incorporated into the landscape and mark the original building footprints. This parcel represents thousands of years of human occupation, as determined by a Native American site also uncovered in the area.

The North End Sites, Boston

The North End was the earliest settled and most densely populated neighborhood of Boston, which served as both a residential and commercial district. Three sites were excavated in this neighborhood: the Mill Pond site, Paddy's Alley site, and the Cross Street Backlot site.

The excavations of the Mill Pond site revealed how early Bostonians modified the landscape and captured tidal energy from the harbor to power grist mills located along the edge of an estuary of the Charles River. Building a dam across this shallow "pond" and digging a creek from the "pond" into the harbor allowed the water to drain into the harbor after powering the mills. The area became a prime location for dumping everyday trash. Over a period of twelve years beginning in the early 1800s, the Mill Pond was filled and became Boston's first large-scale land building episode. Archaeologically recovered material reflects the land use history of the parcel and early engineering methods.

The land known as the Paddy's Alley site was purchased in the early 1700s by a metalsmith named John Carnes. Carnes's stone dwelling occupied the center of the property, and his warehouse and workshop were adjacent to his home. The artifacts from the site include both artisan metal hardware and domestic items associated with the daily life of a merchant's family and servants. One indicative item found in the Carnes trash midden was a glass wine bottle seal, which would have attached to the side of the bottle. Most wine seals exhibit only the owner's initials, but here John Carnes's full name appears. Fragments of a colonoware pot, a ceramic type with West Indian origins attributed to African-American makers, were found at this site, providing information on the lives of early black New Englanders.

Katherine Nanny Naylor was listed as the owner of the Cross Street Backlot parcel in the mid-1600s. A privy (outhouse) vault associated with the Naylor household was excavated, dating from the 1660s to early 1700. The dense, well-preserved deposit of a wealthy merchant's family with trade connections around the world was reflected in the many exotic materials recovered. Additional documentary evidence provided a rich, detailed account of the life of a seventeenth-century woman, and contextual studies (pollen, parasite, and insect remains analyses) contributed to a reconstruction of the environment of the area and the health conditions of the residents.

TOWN DOCK AREA AND FANEUIL HALL SITE

The Town Dock site is located in the earliest settled area on the Shawmut Peninsula known as Town Cove. Situated in a small inlet of Boston Harbor, Town Cove was the center of all shipping activities. By 1641 the need for improved waterfront facilities led to the building of wharves and the filling in of adjacent marshlands, which were divided and developed into private parcels. Major thoroughfares were laid out at this time and are evident in the present street plan.

Faneuil Hall was erected in 1742 as a public market and meeting place. Also known as the "Cradle of Liberty" because it was the venue for important pre-Revolutionary meetings, it is a National Historic Landmark operated by the National Park Service. Archaeological investigations revealed evidence that Faneuil Hall was built on part of the former Town Dock that was filled in 1728. The artifact assemblage from the historic landfill deposits contributed significant information on colonial trade, crafts, and lifeways. Ceramic and glass artifacts came from household and tavern sites that were adjacent to the Town Dock and incorporated into the fill material. One uncommon ceramic style found, however, was locally made sugarloaf molds and syrup jars, used in the process of refining sugar. These almost complete vessels provide evidence of activities associated with Boston's role in the Triangle Trade.

Faneuil Hall is open to the public and continues to serve as a venue for public gatherings. A small exhibit of artifacts from the site can be viewed on the second-floor rotunda of Quincy Market, just east of Faneuil Hall. The original shoreline of Town Cove and the footprints of early streets and structures are etched in granite pavers near the Samuel Adams statue on the west entrance to Faneuil Hall.

The nearby Blackstone Block, between North and Hanover streets, features extant early-nineteenth-century street patterns and structures. Many archaeological sites have been excavated within this block. An artifact exhibit in the lobby of the Bostonian Hotel displays a sample of local material culture.

LONG WHARF SITE

By the beginning of the eighteenth century Boston was the busiest port in America, and the need to accommodate large vessels and store goods resulted in the building of Long Wharf. Extending a quarter mile into the harbor, the construction of the wharf made Town Dock obsolete. Archaeological investigations at Long Wharf revealed significant information on wharf building technology, colonial maritime trade, and early Boston foodways.

Today, a significant portion of Long Wharf is buried beneath built land. Standing at the eastern terminus of State Street, which runs on top of Long Wharf, one is offered a linear view to the Old State House similar to the eighteenth-century vista witnessed by new arrivals disembarking from a trans-Atlantic voyage.

FORT INDEPENDENCE, CASTLE ISLAND, SOUTH BOSTON

The earliest fortifications in the Boston area were placed in strategic locations along the harbor's edge. These forts usually consisted of small earthworks armed with cannons. In 1634 a fort was built on Castle Island, just south of the deep water channel entrance into the port of Boston. Archaeological investigations revealed seven subsequent building campaigns at this site and addressed technological and architectural innovations for both the British and the American militia.

Fort Independence, designed by French military engineer Jean Foncin, was completed in 1833 and remains standing on Castle Island today. Archaeological evidence from a privy dating to the mid-nineteenth century reveals information on the leisure time activities of enlisted soldiers and the domestic lives of commissioned officers and their families.

Today Castle Island is connected to the mainland by a causeway built in 1932 and is accessible via public transportation. The site is managed by the Department of Conservation and Recreation. Castle Island also offers wonderful views of Boston, the Inner Harbor, and the Harbor Islands.

AFRICAN MEETING HOUSE

During the late eighteenth century, the neighborhood on the north slope of Beacon Hill was created and built by a free-black community. Facing systematic racism in New England, the community established the African Meeting House, the oldest standing black church building in the United States (ca. 1806), which became an all-purpose community center. This building was used for religious, political, and social activities for the benefit of a community committed to establishing social change and community identity. Archaeological excavations over the last thirty years have uncovered numerous deposits associated with the building of and use of the structure and its rear yard by the occupants.

The site is located at the intersection of Joy Street and Smith Court, and it is open Monday through Saturday, 10 am to 4 pm. The National Park Service conducts tours of the site and the Black Heritage Trail.

The Abiel Smith School, the first school for blacks in Boston, was constructed in 1834–35 adjacent to the Meeting House. After 1855, when legislation was passed ending segregation in Massachusetts schools, it continued to operate as an integrated school until 1881. Archaeological investigations of the school courtyard indicate that the landscape was modified and that creative approaches successfully solved drainage and sanitation problems. The excavation of six privies contributed significant information about the history of the School House, the Boston Public Schools System, and Boston's African American community, including children and Civil War veterans of the historic 54th Massachusetts Volunteer Infantry Regiment.

Further Reading: Beaudry, Mary C., *The Archaeology of Boston* (New Haven, CT: Yale University Press, forthcoming); Cheek, Charles, ed., "Perspectives on the Archaeology of Colonial Boston: The Archaeology of the Central Artery/Tunnel Project, Boston, Massachusetts," *Historical Archaeology* 32 (1998); Langford, Norma Jane, "Colonial Boston Unearthed," *Archaeology* (September 26, 1997), http://www.archaeology.org/online/features/boston/index.html; Lewis, Ann-Eliza, ed., *Highway to the Past: The Archaeology of Boston's Big Dig* (Boston: Secretary of the Commonwealth of Massachusetts, 2001); Museum of African American History, Boston and Nantucket, http://www.afroammuseum.org/; Wood, William, *New England's Prospect* (London: 1634; reprint Amherst: University of Massachusetts Press, 1977), 60.

Ellen P. Berkland

COLONIAL PEMAQUID STATE HISTORIC SITE

Coastal Maine

Seventeenth-Century English Settlement on the Maine Coast

The village of Pemaquid Beach, situated on Maine's south central coast, is the site of one of North America's earliest English settlements. Beginning in the late 1620s, a year-round settlement took root on the Pemaquid peninsula and its offshore islands. Over the next six decades Pemaquid gained prominence as one of northern New England's leading fishing and trading centers. In 1676 and 1689, Wabanaki Indian war parties attacked and destroyed the English settlement. The coastal community that reemerged in the early eighteenth century developed into a modest fishing, farming, and trading settlement.

Today extensive archaeological evidence of this English settlement can be found at the Colonial Pemaquid State Historic Site, a 19-acre property at the mouth of the Pemaquid River. The site provides an in-depth look at life on colonial New England's northeastern frontier. In 1994 the Department of the Interior designated Colonial Pemaquid a National Historic Landmark. Recent archaeological investigations on the upper reaches of the Pemaquid River and the offshore island of Damariscove have uncovered additional remnants of seventeenth- and eighteenth-century Pemaquid.

The roots of the English settlement of Pemaquid date to the first decade of the 1600s. Between 1605 and 1614, English explorers and colonizers such as George Weymouth and John Smith visited the Pemaquid peninsula and its offshore islands. They returned to England with news of a land endowed with valuable natural resources, particularly fish, fur-bearing animals, and timber. They also spoke of an Indian population interested in trade and a climate and resource base capable of supporting year-round settlement. By 1610 English fishermen had established seasonal fishing stations on Monhegan and Damariscove, coastal islands located southwest and southeast, respectively, of the Pemaquid peninsula. They continued to man these seasonal operations until the early 1620s.

Around 1626, two prominent Bristol, England, merchants, Robert Aldworth and Gyles Elbridge, founded a year-round plantation on the Pemaquid peninsula and its offshore islands. The owners and inhabitants of the plantation took advantage of the region's bounty of fish, fur-bearing animals, and timber and their proximity to French Acadia and the Wabanaki Indians. Fishermen from Pemaquid and Massachusetts Bay frequented coastal waters, whereas Indian, French, Massachusetts, and New York traders came to do business. Pemaquid, however, paid for its location on New England's northeastern frontier. In 1676 and 1689, Wabanaki Indian war parties attacked and destroyed the English settlement. The English briefly reestablished a presence with the construction of Fort William Henry in 1692. However, Wabanaki and French forces destroyed the fort four years later. The English did not reoccupy the Pemaquid peninsula for thirty-three years.

In 1729 Englishman Colonel David Dunbar sailed to New England with ambitious plans. Over the next three years, Dunbar oversaw the resettlement of the Pemaquid peninsula and construction of a new fort, Fort Frederick, on the ruins of its late seventeenth-century predecessor, as part of a larger plan to establish a colony between the Kennebec and St. Croix Rivers with Scots-Irish immigrants. His plans, however, were cut short in 1733 with his forced departure to England.

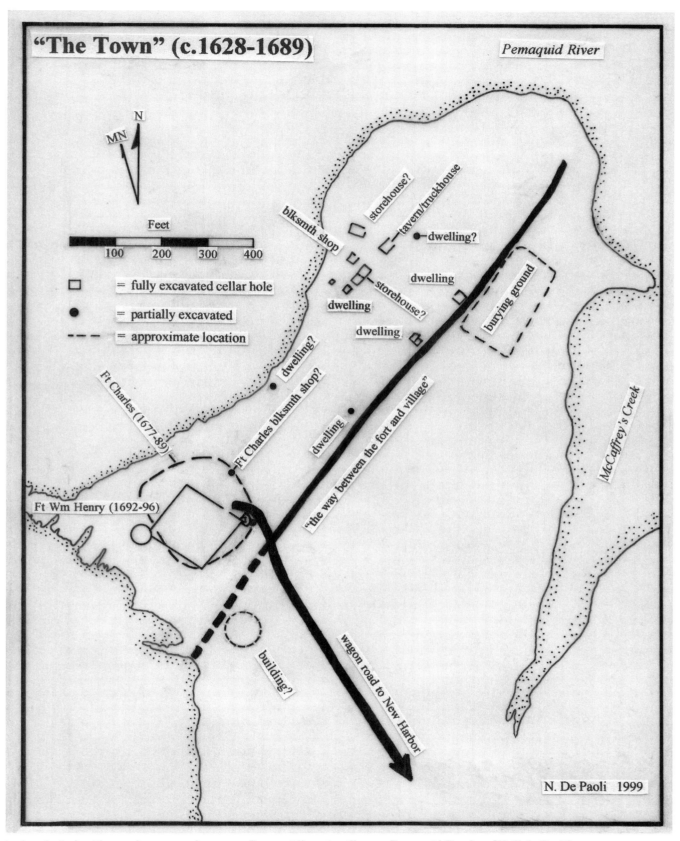

"The Town" (c. 1628-1689)

Pemaquid River

N

MN

Feet

| 100 | 200 | 300 | 400 |

☐ = fully excavated cellar hole

● = partially excavated

- - - = approximate location

blksmth shop

storehouse?

tavern/truckhouse

● dwelling?

dwelling

storehouse?

dwelling

dwelling

burying ground

dwelling?

Ft Charles blksmth shop?

Ft Charles (1677-89)

dwelling

"the way between the fort and village"

Ft Wm Henry (1692-96)

building?

wagon road to New Harbor

McCaffrey's Creek

N. De Paoli 1999

Archaeological evidence of seventeenth-century Pemaquid's main village at Pemaquid Beach.   [Neill de Paoli]

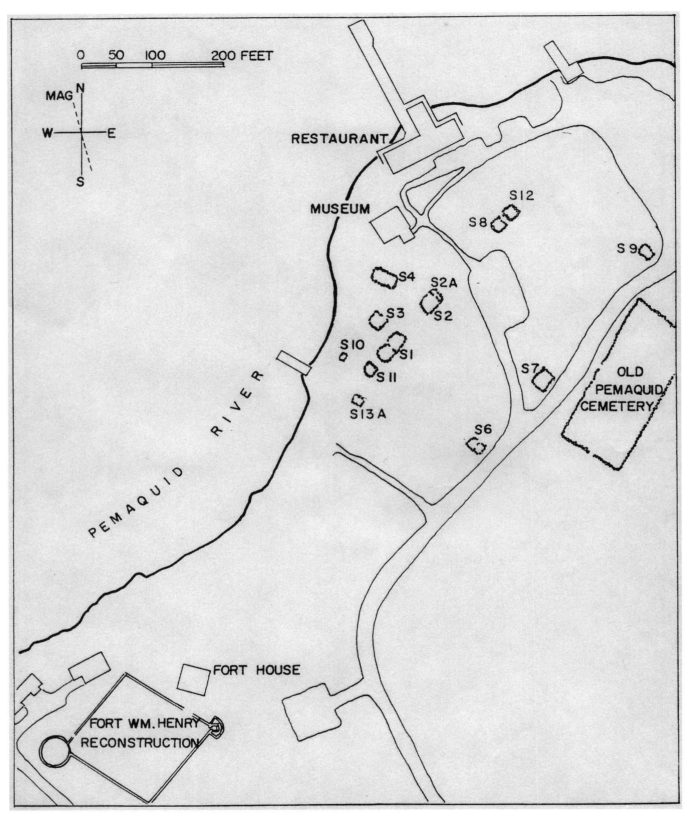

MAG N
W E
S

0 50 100 200 FEET

RESTAURANT

MUSEUM

PEMAQUID RIVER

S12
S8
S9
S4
S2A
S3
S2
S10
S1
S11
S7
S13A
S6

OLD
PEMAQUID
CEMETERY

FORT HOUSE

FORT WM. HENRY
RECONSTRUCTION

Archaeological evidence of the main village during the seventeenth and eighteenth centuries. [Neill de Paoli]

Nevertheless, Pemaquid continued to attract, in the decades that followed, settlers from Massachusetts, New Hampshire, Maine, and Ireland as it reemerged as a modest fishing, farming, and trading settlement.

The historic antiquity of Pemaquid has long attracted the interest of antiquarians, historians, and archaeologists. As early as 1795, Maine historian James Sullivan spoke of the "ruins" of Pemaquid that included a "paved street" and the cellars of thirty to forty homes. Between the early 1890s and 1920, antiquarian John Cartland documented and collected archaeological evidence of Pemaquid's early history. In 1923 the Maine Historical Society hired archaeologist Warren Moorehead to resolve the long-held claim by some that Vikings once occupied Pemaquid. Moorehead's excavations at Colonial Pemaquid and further upriver turned up no evidence of a Norse presence. He did, however, uncover five stone-lined cellar holes and portions of the paved "street" that were part of colonial-era Pemaquid. Moorehead's investigations of the ruins of Fort William Henry exposed the stone foundations to the fort's enlisted men's quarters. In 1964 archaeologist Helen Camp launched the first comprehensive look at this English fishing and trading settlement. During her tenure, Camp's crews unearthed fourteen seventeenth- and eighteenth-century dwellings, storage buildings, a tavern/trading post, a forge, and portions of Forts William Henry and Frederick. More recent archaeological investigations by the late Robert Bradley, Charles Rand, and the author have uncovered additional evidence of the colonial-era settlement and fortifications.

The picture that has emerged from the more than a century and a half of archaeological and historical study of early Pemaquid both contradicts and supports traditional images of early Maine as a regional backwater. Today's Colonial Pemaquid State Historic Site contains the heart of the seventeenth- and eighteenth-century English fishing and trading settlement and the three forts that defended it. The earliest archaeological evidence of the village was a stone-lined cellar, measuring 6 × 8 feet, to a modest single-story dwelling. The home lacked a foundation, sat directly on the ground (earthfast), and had a timber superstructure. The walls were wattle and daub, an old-world wall infill technique consisting of a matrix of wooden saplings or dowels covered with a mixture of straw and clay. The structure was probably built in the 1640s and would have typified Pemaquid homes up through the mid-seventeenth century. It was destroyed in the 1676 or 1689 Indian attacks.

Two additional dwellings represented improvements made in the village at Pemaquid Beach as the seventeenth century wore on. The first timber-framed and timber-clad building, of unknown dimensions, had a large stone-walled cellar measuring 17 × 19 feet. The builders integrated a stone- and barrel-lined well into one of the corners of the cellar's walls for immediate year-round access to fresh water. Archaeologists unearthed a series of trimmed wooden saplings sitting on the cellar's clay floor. The dwelling's occupants probably intended these as "sleepers," raising the floor boards above water seeping into the

cellar. The second dwelling was composed of two segments: one that was earthfast and a second that sat over a stone-walled cellar 18 × 18 feet. Occupants could enter or exit the cellar via a stone-walled bulkhead. Extensive evidence of burning indicated that both of these dwellings were also destroyed during the 1676 or 1689 Indian attacks.

Archaeologists also uncovered the remains of one, and possibly a second, seventeenth-century trading post that was tied to Pemaquid's Indian trade. The first structure consisted of a stone foundation measuring roughly 41 × 25 feet, where archaeologists uncovered a cache of 108 cannon balls. Pemaquid's first manager, Abraham Shurt, may have had this structure erected in ca. 1630 to serve as a fortified communal residence, storehouse, and trading post. The wood-framed and wood-clad storehouse may have been surrounded by a wooden palisade and defended by several cannons and musketeers. The second building was similar in size (35 × 20 feet) and appearance. This building was a trading post and tavern, as evidenced by an array of liquor bottles, wine glasses, glass beads, cloth seals, mouth harps, lead shot, and gun flints recovered from its cellar. Archaeologists unearthed similar evidence of Anglo-Indian trade while excavating the officer's quarters of Forts William Henry and Frederick.

Antiquarians and archaeologists have also uncovered segments of a central cobblestone street and several paved cross streets that extended from the settlement's cemetery over to Fort William Henry and the western shore of the Pemaquid River. The archaeological evidence indicates the paving dates to the seventeenth century; possibly part of New York Governor Edmund Andros's efforts during the mid-1670s to upgrade the key settlements within the Duke of York's holdings in New England and New York. One observer reported at the time of the 1689 Wabanaki attack on Pemaquid that the main street was lined with ten to twelve homes.

The archaeological and historical record has also shown a settlement that, despite its location on New England's northeastern frontier, had diverse commercial links extending north to Nova Scotia, south to Barbados, and across the Atlantic to England, the Netherlands, and the Mediterranean. Archaeological finds have included clay smoking pipes from England's West Country and the Netherlands; ceramic wares from England, France, Spain, Portugal, Italy, and Germany; and coins from Massachusetts, England, and Ireland. Excavators have also found a glass trade bead from Venice, a West African elephant ivory divination tapper, and pieces of coral and coquina ballast probably from the Caribbean.

Visitors to this historic site can explore a museum operated by Maine's Bureau of Parks and Lands that is open to the public from the middle of May until early October. A series of exhibits depicting life in the colonial-era village and the three fortifications are visible in the museum and the restored tower of Fort William Henry. History buffs can also visit the ruins of seventeenth- and eighteenth-century dwellings, storehouses, a forge, fortifications, and a cemetery. The vast majority of the over 100,000 prehistoric and historic archaeological artifacts are stored in an on-site archaeological laboratory.

Further Reading: Bourque, Bruce J., *Twelve Thousand Years. American Indians in Maine* (Lincoln: University of Nebraska Press, 2001); Bradley, Robert, and Helen C. Camp, *The Forts of Pemaquid, Maine: An Archaeological and Historical Study*, Occasional Publications in Maine Archaeology, No. 10 (Augusta: Maine Historic Preservation Commission, 1994); Camp, Helen C., *Archaeological Excavations at Pemaquid, Maine, 1965–1974* (Augusta: Maine State Museum, 1975); Colonial Pemaquid State Historic Site, Friends of Colonial Pemaquid Web site, http://www.friendsofcolonialpemaquid.org; De Paoli, Neill, "Life on the Edge: Community and Trade on the Anglo-American Periphery, Pemaquid, Maine, 1610–1689," doctoral dissertation (University of New Hampshire, 2001); Johnston, John, *The History of Bristol and Bremen, Including the Pemaquid Settlement* (Albany, NY: Joel Munsell, 1873); Judd, Richard W., Edwin A. Churchill, and Joel W. Eastman, eds., *The Pine Tree State from Prehistory to the Present* (Orono: University of Maine Press, 1995).

Neill De Paoli

POINTE-À-CALLIÈRE, MONTRÉAL MUSEUM OF ARCHAEOLOGY AND HISTORY

Montréal, Quebec, Canada
Earliest European Settlement at Montréal

On May 17, 1642, on a point of land at the confluence of the St. Lawrence and another smaller river, Jesuit Father Vimont held a mass celebrating the founding of Montréal, attended by Sieur de Maisonneuve, Jeanne Mance, and their companions. On May 17, 1992, Pointe-à-Callière, the Montréal Museum of Archaeology and History, opened its doors on the very same site. It reveals authentic archaeological remains along an intriguing underground tour route. Pointe-à-Callière is a unique part of Montréal, a cultural and museum complex measuring more than 13,000 square meters.

Until the Museum opened, only historians knew about the "Pointe à Callière," so named because it was here that Chevalier Louis Hector de Callière, third governor of Montréal, had a home built in the 1690s. Today the point has actually become part of the shoreline of the Island of Montréal, but its name lives on and is better known than ever, thanks to the museum.

The museum was founded as part of celebrations to mark Montréal's 350th birthday, and owes its existence largely to the significant archaeological discoveries made on the site during the 1980s. In fact, the museum and its sites are inextricably linked. Rising above evidence of more than 1,000 years of human activity, it houses remarkable architectural remains, displayed in situ with absolute respect for their integrity. Pointe-à-Callière is the only sizeable archaeology museum in Canada.

Set in the midst of a fertile plain, at the confluence of several major navigable waterways, Montréal was long a site where Native groups tied up and camped. Later, in the early days of the colonial era, the town was the final outpost for travelers headed for the interior of the continent. Montréal witnessed many key political and economic events as a jumping-off point for explorers, fur traders, soldiers, and missionaries, as well as a rallying point for diplomatic meetings and trade with the First Nations from the St. Lawrence Valley, the Great Lakes, and the Ottawa River. The Great Peace of Montréal, a 1701 treaty between thirty-eight First Nations and the French, was signed on the very site where Pointe-à-Callière stands today. Following that event, French and Canadian explorers, such as the LeMoyne family and Antoine Laumet de Lamothe Cadillac, all set off from Montréal and founded a number of large American cities, such as Detroit.

MUSEUM BUILDINGS AND ARCHAEOLOGICAL REMAINS UNDERGROUND

The museum is located in Old Montréal, near the Old Port, atop remains of the city's birthplace. The hundreds of artifacts it houses are grouped into seven main sections: the Éperon, a modern building that has won many architectural awards; the archaeological crypt on the lower level and below the Place Royale; the renovated Ancienne-Douane building (Montréal's first Custom House); the large collector sewer, a unique cut-stone structure related to the development of urban sanitation during the early nineteenth century; the Youville Pumping Station, once connected to the collector; the Archaeological Field School; and the former Mariners House. The museum of a site, a history, and a city, Pointe-à-Callière delves into the past to foster a debate on urban issues both local and global and to encourage visitors to reflect on the future. Like an archaeological dig, the route visitors take when exploring

A beautiful panorama of downtown Montréal, Canada.   [Musée d'archéologie et d'histoire de Montréal / Jacques Nadeau]

Pointe-à-Callière is both vertical and horizontal, lined with traces of past centuries.

Marking the entrance to the museum, the Éperon building is an inspiring piece of architecture, rising from the foundations of its predecessor—the Royal Insurance Company building. Like that earlier edifice, the Éperon is triangular in shape and boasts a tower that looks out over the Old Port of Montréal. It houses the reception desk, a multimedia theater, a temporary exhibition hall, and, in the basement, part of the Where Montréal Was Born permanent exhibition.

Just below the main building of the museum, one of the most fascinating archaeological remains is Montréal's first Catholic cemetery. Between 1643 and 1654, thirty-eight burials were recorded in the Notre-Dame parish register. According to the documents, twelve Natives (probably baptized before their death) and twenty-six French people were buried there. The archaeologists uncovered seven graves, one containing the skeleton of a Frenchman. Occupancy levels from the eighteenth and nineteenth centuries were also found.

Archaeological digs and historical research have been going on since 1979 in Place Royale, near the birthplace of Montréal, at the confluence of the St. Lawrence and Little St. Pierre rivers. The fascinating finds there tell us a great deal about the daily lives of Natives and the first Montrealers, many centuries ago. It sits above the remains of fortifications and buildings from the seventeenth, eighteenth, and nineteenth centuries.

The archaeological crypt lies beneath Place Royale and links the Éperon and Ancienne-Douane buildings underground. The archaeological remains and artifacts in the crypt are part of the Where Montréal Was Born permanent exhibition. Among other remains, visitors can see the impressive foundations of the city's fortifications, near the Place du Marché (Marketplace). The fortifications, designed by military engineer Gaspard-Joseph Chaussegros de Léry, were erected between 1717 and 1738, making Montréal the first fortified French town in North America.

The Ancienne-Douane building dates back to 1836–1837 and originally housed Montréal's first Custom House (its name means "the Old Custom House"). It was expanded in 1881. This neoclassical building was the first major project by architect, engineer, and surveyor John Ostell as well as one of the first architectural signs of the British presence in Montréal.

The Youville Pumping Station, erected on the Place D'Youville (just across the street from the Éperon building), was Montréal's first electrically operated wastewater pumping station. The building, now converted into an interpretation center, dates from 1915 and showcases some ingenious artifacts that are nearly a century old. Carefully preserved motors, pumps, valves, and electrical equipment are now used to explain the role, components, and operation of the station. It takes history to a whole new "level"!

FORT VILLE-MARIE REEMERGES

Pointe-à-Callière and the Anthropology Department of the Université de Montréal signed a partnership agreement in May 2002 to create an archaeological field school near the museum's main building in Old Montréal. This location was thought to be the site of the first French settlement in Montreal, Fort Ville-Marie.

Right from the first archaeological digs in 2002, the researchers found confirmation of well-preserved archaeological remains in the levels prior to 1695, the date when Louis-Hector de Callière's residence was built on the former site of Fort Ville-Marie (ca. 1642–1680). These remains were hidden beneath 2.5 meters of archaeological deposits from more recent periods, however, and it took time for an overall vision of the site to emerge as the digs progressed.

In 2004 excavations finally led to the discovery of a well associated with a notarized document from 1658, which officially mentioned the digging of a well in the fort. New discoveries made since then have allowed the archaeologists to conclude that they had found traces of Fort Ville-Marie and to suggest that the dig site was located in the northeast part of the fort. The students and archaeologists turned up many artifacts (animal bones, earthenware, faience and stoneware items, trade beads, etc.) and unearthed a large masonry wall associated with occupations of the Fort Ville-Marie.

Pointe-à-Callière's Archaeological Field School on the site of Fort Ville-Marie and Callière's residence won the Award for Outstanding Achievement from the Canadian Museums Association, in the "research" category, in 2002. The museum also won the prestigious Conservation and Heritage Management Award from the Archaeological Institute of America (United States) in 2006, for its overall conservation efforts.

TEMPORARY EXHIBITIONS AND CULTURAL ACTIVITIES

Along with its permanent exhibitions, since it opened the museum has presented many temporary exhibitions on themes relating to local and international archaeology, history and heritage, culture and artistic creativity, and multiculturalism. Complementing this exhibition program are education and outreach programs and cultural activities that introduce school groups and the general public to other aspects of archaeology and history. Pointe-à-Callière also holds a number of popular cultural activities for the public, ranging from musical performances to theater and demonstrations, including lectures, debates, and participation in Montréal, Quebec, cross-Canada and international events. Its Public Market is one of the highlights of the summer, attracting some thousands of visitors to Old Montréal into eighteenth-century Montreal for one glorious weekend. Many other exciting educational programs and original urban events are presented to the public: from the Port Symphonies, coaxing music from ships' horns in the port in mid-winter, to the Cultural Rendezvous, celebrating the city's cultural diversity.

Further Reading: Boisvert, Nicole, *Pointe-à-Callière, Experience the Past!* (Montréal: Pointe-à-Callière, Montréal Museum of Archaeology and History, 1992); Desjardins, Pauline, and Geneviève Duguay, *Pointe-à-Callière: From Ville-Marie to Montreal* (Montréal: Old Port of Montréal; Sillery: Septentrion, 1992); Lauzon, Gilles, and Madeleine Forget, eds., *Old Montreal. History through Heritage* (Québec City: Les Publications du Québec, 2004); Pointe-à-Callière, Montréal Museum of Archaeology and History Web site, http://www.pacmuseum.qc.ca.

Louise Pothier

THE ARCHAEOLOGY OF SEVENTEENTH- AND EIGHTEENTH-CENTURY NORTHERN PLANTATIONS

Eastern Long Island, New York
The Sylvester Manor Site

Most people living today in the United States equate plantation slavery with the American South, yet during the seventeenth and eighteenth centuries there were many plantations in the Northern colonies that relied heavily upon enslaved Africans and Native Americans as laborers and skilled workers (Berlin 1980, 1998, 2003; McManus 1966; Strong 1996, 1997). Recently, archaeologists working in northeastern North America have begun to examine the lives of those living on plantations, and much of this research has understandably focused on the lives of enslaved Africans (Fitts 1998, 1996; Garman 1998; Bankoff et al. 2001; Sawyer and Perry 2003). Much less attention has been given to the Native American laborers who also toiled on these plantations. Some of them were enslaved, but many appear to have been free to engage in work and economic exchange with the burgeoning Euro-American populations of colonial America.

Sylvester Manor was one of these northern plantations. Established in 1652, it originally encompassed all of Shelter Island, an 8,000 acre island located between the North and South Forks of eastern Long Island, New York. Today the property consists of about 250 acres, including what had been the core of the plantation since it was first established. This includes a manor house dating to about 1735; Quaker and African burial grounds; a large (2 acres) enclosed garden, several cottages, and farm out-buildings. Before the arrival of Europeans the island—known by local Native groups as Manhansack-Ahaquatuwamock, "an island sheltered by islands" (Tooker 1911, 92)—was home to the Manhanset or Manhansacks, a group politically and culturally affiliated with the Montauk of eastern Long Island (Strong 1994; Ales 1993).

During the early colonial period (1630–75) the Native groups of coastal New York and southern New England saw their own political and economic rivalries intertwined with that of the Dutch and English, the major colonial powers in the region (Ales 1993; Priddy 2002; Strong 1996). Competition over both land and political influence kindled clashes that eventually led to the loss of Dutch New Amsterdam to the English and its subsequent recapture in 1674. For the Native populations of eastern Long Island and their leaders, these battles for colonial supremacy may have initially been viewed as a subtext to their own political rivalries, but through shifting alliances and commercial exchange, they sought to turn them to their favor. For the Montauk sachem Wyandanch and his older brother Youghco, leader of the Manhansett, connections to the English were seen as a way of protecting their own interests against those of other Native groups in the region, while for the English it was a way of establishing their claims to lands they sought (Priddy 2002, 26; Strong 1997).

It was against this backdrop that Shelter Island was purchased by Nathaniel Sylvester, his brother Constant Sylvester, Thomas Middletown, and Thomas Rouse in 1651. Constant Sylvester operated two large sugar plantations on Barbados (Constant and Carmichael plantations), where he, Middleton, and Rouse were part of a group of elite planters who dominated the sugar industry on the island. Like so many of the plantations in the Caribbean, Constant and Carmichael plantations relied on foodstuffs and raw materials from off-island to support their operations. Throughout the North American colonies provisioning plantations such as Sylvester Manor were established to meet the needs of the sugar industry in the Caribbean. Documentary sources, although limited in what they reveal about the day-to-day operation of the Long Island plantation, do confirm the fact that livestock, foodstuff, and raw materials such as wooden barrel staves were mainstays of this colonial trade. Documents have also confirmed the fact that Nathaniel Sylvester and his wife Grissell owned at least twenty African slaves. Little is known about the role of these enslaved Africans in the operation of the plantation during the seventeenth century. When they were noted in Nathaniel's 1680 will, they were always discussed as small family units of not more than three members, normally a man, woman, and child. These small groups were given to the individual children of the Sylvesters, suggesting that they probably served as domestics in the household (Mrozowski and Hayes 2007).

If the documentary sources were the only means of developing a portrait of life on this early plantation, then African Americans may well have been considered as the chief source of labor. The archaeology of Sylvester Manor has revealed a very different picture, one in which Native Americans appear to have played a major role in the establishment and operation of the plantation during its first forty years. Archaeological excavations carried out between 1998 and 2007 unearthed remains of several phases of buildings associated with the earliest phases of the plantation. Survey work carried out on other portions of the property confirmed that the 250-acre parcel still owned by the original family contains the core of the original seventeenth-century plantation. Excavations in the plantation core revealed the remains of several buildings that appear to have been demolished at the same time the 1735 manor house was being constructed. The evidence also points to several phases of building linked to the initial establishment of the plantation and its rapid evolution over the next forty years (Hayes 2007).

The initial goal of the investigations at Sylvester Manor was to explore the interaction of the European and African inhabitants of the plantation. Nathaniel and Constant Sylvester were English, but their father's commercial activities resulted in his raising his family in Amsterdam. The preponderance of yellow brick and red ceramic roofing tiles, consistent with Dutch architectural styles of the seventeenth century, suggest that the landscape of the early plantation may have been influenced by Nathaniel's formative years in Amsterdam. It can also be assumed that the Africans who found themselves on Long Island reflected a rich cultural heritage that could have been shaped by time in Africa, the Caribbean, and/or other colonies. The intensity of land use revealed by the archaeology at the manor indicates that work and living space may well have been intertwined, as both Fitts (1996, 1998) and Garman (1998) have suggested. With strong evidence of a Native American presence, the pluralistic space explored through the archaeology at Sylvester Manor contained material culture, faunal, and floral remains as well as architectural debris that all point to a dynamic environment that served as the crucible for cultural mixing.

The results of the investigations at Sylvester Manor to date indicate that during the first eighty years of the plantation's existence it evolved from a provisioning plantation into a tenant-run commercial farm after Nathaniel Sylvester's death in 1680, and then reconfigured into a Georgian-inspired, country estate (Mrozowski et al. 2007). The evidence also suggests that the early plantation may have gone through several smaller transitions. Landscape features such as an ornamental paving believed to date to the 1660s may well have been constructed when the plantation was given manorial status by the English crown in 1666. Although the site produced a wealth of evidence concerning the changing landscape of the plantation, the bulk of the cultural material recovered from the site is linked to provisioning activities, building construction and demolition, and household production and consumption. The most direct evidence of provisioning activities came in the form of slaughter remains found in a large bone pit that appears to date to approximately 1660–1670. The deposit, investigated archaeologically, was dominated by pig and cow remains. Close to two-thirds of the deposit consisted of the remains of thirteen large pigs that it is estimated represented close to 1300 pounds of meat (Sportman et al. 2007). Based on documented estimates that enslaved populations were provided approximately 1 pound of meat per week, the 1,300 pounds represents three months' rations for a force of 100 (Sportman et al. 2007).

In addition to the large slaughtering pit found on the site, structural remains of an early structure were uncovered that may have served as a work house for Native laborers (Hayes 2007; Mrozowski et al. 2007). The dimensions of the building are not clear, but based upon the combination of residue from wampum production, fish bone, and fish scales, it appears to have been the locus of Native American laborers during the earliest phases of the plantation's operation. The interaction of Native American, African, and European cultural practices is also evident in botanical and faunal remains that suggest a creolized (culturally mixed) diet (Sportman et al. 2007; Trigg and Leasure 2007). Similar evidence of creolization and hybrid cultural forms is visible in groups and individual artifacts that exhibit a combination of cultural traits. These include European coins that have been etched with what appear to be small Native American symbols. One such symbol, that of Thunderbird, appears on both a coin and well-worn stone that contains other etchings (Gary 2007). Other evidence includes European bottle glass and flint that appears to have been worked in a manner consistent with Native lithic (stone tool) manufacturing traditions. Finally, the remains of a large Native pot were found that included a European-style handle (Gary 2007).

Taken as a whole the archaeological evidence from Sylvester Manor suggests that Native laborers, enslaved Africans, and Europeans all lived together in a space that was an arena for a series of simultaneous cultural entanglements similar to that theorized by Edward Soja as a space of "interwoven complexity of the social, historical, and spatial dimensions of our lives, their inseparability and often problematic interdependence" (2000, 6–12; see also Harvey 2000, 14–16). This image of a dynamic environment in which cultural traditions were being brought together at places such as Sylvester Manor is also consistent with the growing appreciation archaeologists have for the complexities of most colonial encounters. The archaeological record at Sylvester Manor reflects the global connections of the actors who shaped its history. Compared with evidence from similar archaeological contexts (e.g., Bankoff et al. 2001; Rothschild 2003), a generalized picture emerges that amplifies the creolized and hybrid character of early colonial society and its dynamic quality.

Further Reading: Ales, Marion Fisher, "History of the Indians on Montauk, Long Island" (Master's thesis, New York University), reprinted in *The History and Archaeology of the Montauk*, edited by Gaynell Stone, Vol. 3 of *Readings in Long Island Archaeology and Ethnohistory*, 2nd ed. (Stony Brook, NY: Suffolk County Archaeological Association, 1993), 4–66; Bankoff, Arthur, Christopher Ricciardi, and Alyssa Loorya, "Remembering Africa under the Eaves," *Archaeology* 54(3) (2001): 36–40; Berlin, Ira, "Time, Space, and the Evolution of Afro-American Society in British Mainland North America," *American Historical Review* 85(1) (1980): 44–78; Berlin, Ira, *Many Thousands Gone: The First Two Centuries of Slavery in North America* (Cambridge: Belknap Press of Harvard University Press, 1998); Berlin, Ira *Generations of Captivity: A History of African-American Slaves* (Cambridge: Belknap Press of Harvard University Press, 2003); Fitts, Robert K., "The Landscapes of Northern Bondage," *Historical Archaeology* 30(2) (1996): 54–73; Fitts, Robert K., *Inventing New England's Slave Paradise: Master/Slave Relations in Eighteenth Century Narragansett, Rhode Island* (New York: Garland, 1998); Garman, James C., "Rethinking 'Resistant Accommodation': Toward an Archaeology of African-American Lives in Southern New England, 1638–1800," *International Journal of Historical Archaeology* 2(2) (1998): 133–160; Gary, Jack, "Material Culture and Multi-Cultural Interactions at Sylvester Manor," in "The Archaeology of Sylvester Manor," edited by Katherine Howlett Hayes and Stephen A. Mrozowski, special issue, *Northeast Historical Archaeology*, Vol. 36 (2007); Harvey, David, *Spaces of Hope* (Berkeley: University of California Press, 2000); Hayes, Katherine Howlett, "Field Excavations at Sylvester Manor," in "The Archaeology of Sylvester Manor," edited by Katherine Howlett Hayes and Stephen A. Mrozowski, special issue, *Northeast Historical Archaeology*, Vol. 36 (2007); McManus, Edgar J., *A History of Negro Slavery in New York* (Syracuse, NY: Syracuse University Press, 1966); Mrozowski, Stephen A., and Katherine Howlett Hayes, "The Archaeology of Sylvester Manor," in "The Archaeology of Sylvester Manor," edited by Katherine Howlett Hayes and Stephen A. Mrozowski, special issue, *Northeast Historical Archaeology*, Vol. 36 (2007); Mrozowski, Stephen A., Katherine Howlett Hayes, Heather Trigg, Jack Gary, David Landon, and Dennis Piechota, "Conclusion: Meditations on the Archaeology of Northern Plantations," in "The Archaeology of Sylvester Manor," edited by Katherine Howlett Hayes and Stephen A. Mrozowski, special issue, *Northeast Historical Archaeology*, Vol. 36 (2007); Priddy, Katherine Lee, "On the Mend: Cultural Interaction of Native Americans, Africans, and Europeans on Shelter Island, New York, (master's thesis, University of Massachusetts–Boston, 2002); Rothschild, Nan A., *Colonial Encounters in a Native American Landscape: The Spanish and Dutch in North America* (Washington, DC: Smithsonian Books, 2003); Soja, Edward W., *Postmetropolis: Critical Studies of Cities and Regions* (London: Blackwell, 2000); Sportman, Sarah, Craig Cippola, and David Landon, "Zooarchaeological Evidence for Animal Husbandry and Foodways at Sylvester Manor," in "The Archaeology of Sylvester Manor," edited by Katherine Howlett Hayes and Stephen A. Mrozowski, special issue, *Northeast Historical Archaeology*, Vol. 36 (2007); Strong, John A., "Wyandanch: Sachem of the Montauks," in *Northeastern Indian Lives, 1632–1816*, edited by R. S. Grumet (Amherst: University of Massachusetts Press, 1996), 48–73; Strong, John A., *The Algonquian Peoples of Long Island from Earliest Times to 1700* (New York: Empire State Books, Interlaken, 1997); Tooker, William Wallace, *The Indian Place-Names on Long Island and Islands Adjacent with Their Probable Significations* (New York: G. P. Putnam & Sons, 1911); Trigg, Heather, and Ashley Leasure, "Cider, Wheat, Maize, and Firewood: Paleoethnobotany at Sylvester Manor," in "The Archaeology of Sylvester Manor, edited by Katherine Howlett Hayes and Stephen A. Mrozowski, special issue, *Northeast Historical Archaeology*, Vol. 36 (2007).

Stephen A. Mrozowski

CHRISTIAN INDIAN COMMUNITIES IN NEW ENGLAND AFTER KING PHILIP'S WAR

Eastern Massachusetts

The Archaeology of Eighteenth-Century Christian Indian Settlements

Religion played an important role in the European colonization of the New World. In New England, missionary work among the Native American populations of the region was limited because early Puritans did not see their conversion as a priority (Cogley 1999, 9–22). Eventually a modest program of missionary work was undertaken by John Eliot of the Massachusetts Bay Colony. Eliot sought to prepare those Natives who were interested in Christian conversion by first getting them to adopt English civil and economic practices. The goal was to become more integrated into the economic system and, in this manner, limit their continuing interaction with more hostile Natives in the region (Brenner 1980; Cogley 1999; Salisbury 1974). During the second half of the seventeenth century, fourteen "Praying Indian" communities were established in eastern Massachusetts and northeastern Connecticut. The first of these was called Nonantum Hill, in part of what was then Cambridge, Massachusetts. It was established in 1646 but was later moved to Natick in 1651. Natick was the largest and most stable of the communities (O'Brien 1998). The second town to be established was Hassanamesit, in what is today Grafton, Massachusetts. In most instances, these Christian communities were located in areas that were inhabited by Native groups who sought some alliance with the English for their own protection as much as any desire to partake of God (Brenner 1980, 1984; Salisbury 1974).

Eliot's overall plan was to convert the Native populations of the region to Christianity by first instructing them in the ways of the English. This approach reflected Eliot's religious views that the religious conversion of the Native populations of New England was to be preceded by the conversion of Catholics and Jews in Europe and the Middle East. Events in Europe and England, especially the overthrow of Charles Stuart, lead Eliot to believe that the Natives of Massachusetts Bay could in fact be prepared for conversion as part of the establishment of a "New Kingdom" (Cogley 1999, 90–93). From Eliot's perspective the fact that some Natives already living near the English exhibited interest in the teaching of God was just one facet of what he considered to be conditions ripe for the eventual conversion of large numbers of Natives living in the region. To this end he advocated that the new settlements be based on English town plans with streets, English-style houses, and a meeting house. The meeting house was to serve as the center of these communities, with each being served by a Native teacher. Eliot would visit the villages periodically and was chiefly responsi-

ble for their support. Collecting funds from English benefactors, Eliot made large purchases of English goods that he would then supply to the various communities. Many of these items were to play an important role in the training of Native peoples in the production of goods such as baskets or clothing that they could then sell to the English. In doing so, Eliot sought to Anglicize the Native peoples as a first step in their conversion (Brenner 1988; Cogley 1999; O'Brien 1998).

Natick and Hassanamesit were the two largest Christian communities, each about 3,000 acres, and they were able to weather the effects of Metacom's Rebellion or what the English called the King Philip's War (1675–76). This devastating conflict resulted in a series of Native victories, including the burning of scores of English towns (Lepore 1999). During the conflict some residents of the "Praying Towns" joined Metacom's forces while others were sent to live on Deer Island in Boston Harbor. Many died in captivity and few of those who survived returned to their previous villages.

The archaeology of these Christianized Native American communities has a long history of futility. The remains of these seventeenth-century villages have eluded archaeologists searching for their location. Although cemeteries associated with the "Praying Indian" communities of Natick, Ponkapoag, (Canton, Massachusetts), and Okommakamesit (Marlboro, Massachusetts) have been discovered and examined (Kelley 1999), several attempts to locate the actual villages have proven fruitless (Brenner 1986; Carlson 1986). This futility has led some archaeologists to question whether the descriptions of the towns written by Massachusetts Bay Supervisor of Indian Towns Daniel Gookin during the seventeenth century were accurate (Brenner 1986; Carlson 1986). Some have suggested that while a central meeting house, or what Cogley (1998, 31) calls a "fair house" might have existed in Natick, the populations of these communities continued to be somewhat nomadic and return to the town sites only on a seasonal basis. Cogley disagrees with this interpretation, but only in the sense that Brenner argues that the Native towns were not continuously occupied, residential communities (Cogley 1998, 31–33).

The questions that emerge from this discussion of Natick, the largest of the "Praying Indian" communities underscores a large debate concerning the veracity of Daniel Gookin's 1674 (1970) description of the seven Native communities that had been established before the outbreak of King Philip's War. In most instances Gookin provides a rather upbeat assessment of the communities, noting streets, houses built in the English style, and meeting houses. Despite efforts to identify the remains of several of these communities (e.g., Brenner 1986; Carlson 1986), no remains were uncovered until the late 1990s when a site thought to be associated with the last of the initial seven villages to be established, Magunkgoag, was found as part of the cultural resource management survey in Ashland, Massachusetts. The site was subsequently excavated in 1997 and 1998, with the remains of what is believed to be the community's meeting house the primary focus (Mrozowski et al. 2005). More recently, excavations carried out in Grafton, Massachusetts, have uncovered the remains of a Nipmuc household associated with the eighteenth-century remnants of Hassanamesit (Mrozowski, Pezzarossi, and Law 2006).

The devastating impact of King Philip's War left many of the Christian Native settlements in turmoil. Yet the archaeology at Magunkaquog and Hassanamesit provide detailed evidence of cultural persistence after the war. The same is true of the mortuary data from the Natick, Punkapoag, and Okommakamesit cemeteries. Taken as a whole, the data from these various sites points to the continuation of Native cultural and religious practices throughout the eighteenth century and well into the nineteenth century. The information also adds to a portrait of these communities as being inhabited by Native peoples who practiced a form of cultural mimicry that served to camouflage their continuing adherence to cultural and spiritual practices of long-standing.

NATICK, PUNKAPOAG, AND OKOMMAKAMESIT

The discovery and excavation of Native cemeteries in Natick, Punkapoag, and Okommakamesit were conducted under very different conditions. All three cemeteries were discovered by accident as part of construction activities (Kelley 1999, 67). Natick, being the oldest and largest of the "Praying Indian" towns, is also only one of two such communities to have been continuously occupied, the other being parts of Hassanamesit. The Natick cemetery was first encountered when workmen laying water pipes disturbed several burials in 1877. The poorly documented excavation that resulted in the removal of several graves included little in the way of contextual information, making it impossible to reconstruct associations between individuals and their burial's contents (Kelley 1999, 68–72). The same was true of another collection of artifacts recovered from graves disturbed during the construction of a church foundation in the 1830s. Here again, no contextual information was recorded, making it impossible to link individuals to artifacts recovered from the graves (Kelley 1999, 70–74).

The graves at Okammakamesit were also encountered by accident during construction. In 1951 archaeologists from the Robert S. Peabody Foundation for Archaeology in Andover, Massachusetts, were asked to remove the remains of four individuals encountered during construction for a sewer line.

With limited time, the archaeologists excavated the four burials and returned the physical remains and what few artifacts there were to the Peabody Foundation, where they were rediscovered in 1986 by Catherine Carlson (Kelley 1999, 109). They were later repatriated. Although the collection is limited, the data relating the excavation of the burials was sufficient to determine that the lack of burial goods was not a product of the manner in which the burials were encountered or excavated.

The Punkapoag cemetery was also encountered during a construction project; however, unlike the Natick and Okammakamesit cemeteries, the Punkapoag burials were found in 1988, when Massachusetts law did not permit the destruction of such graves. In consultation with the Massachusetts Office of Indian Affairs, State Archaeologist Brona Simon supervised the removal of those burials that had been disturbed. After the artifacts were recorded and analyzed, they were repatriated in accordance with Native American Grave Protection and Repatriation Act (NAGPRA) regulations (Kelley 1999).

Because of Native American sensitivities surrounding the discussion of burials or of grave offerings, this essay will not discuss in detail the materials recovered from the three Native cemeteries. Some general observations can be offered, however, concerning burial practices and the presence or absence of grave goods, since both pertain directly to the issue of whether practices consistent with Christian teachings were being followed by Native groups in Massachusetts. In this instance the evidence points to a mix of adherence to Puritan religious practices in contrast to those documented from Late Woodland burial contexts. Little can be said concerning the Natick burials beyond that they do appear to have been accompanied by grave offerings. The same was true of the Punkapoag cemetery, where most of the burials contained grave offerings. Although only four burials were excavated in Okammakamesit, only one contained grave goods, and these may have been associated with the coffin used in the burial itself.

Evidence of coffins was found at both Ponkapoag and Okammakamesit. This would have been consistent with Christian practices. This was true of all thirty-two burials found at Ponkapoag (Kelley 1999), yet more than half were also oriented on a northeast-southwest axis, which is more in keeping with traditional Native American practices. The overwhelming evidence of items being purposely placed within the graves is also consistent with Native practices. Many of the artifacts recovered from the cemeteries were of European manufacture. Kelley's comparison of the materials from both the Ponkapoag and Natick cemeteries found almost identical assemblages of grave offerings. The presence of English Midland slipware mugs, for example, as well as English copper pots and thimbles seems to have been the result of a single source, that being John Eliot himself (Cogley 1998, 31–32). The fact that so many of the artifacts were of English manufacture raises questions concerning why they were appearing in burials in such large numbers. Crosby (1988) has argued that Native belief in the spiritual strength of material things, their "manit" made English goods attractive in part because of their assumed connection to the powerful English god. It would make sense then that they would be placed in graves; however, archaeological evidence from both Magunkaquog and Hassanamesit suggest an even deeper explanation.

One item from a Ponkapoag burial worthy of note in this regard is an English copper pot that held the remains of a snake. The presence of a snake in a burial is consistent with Native spiritual practices (Simmons 1986); however, its association with an English manufactured pot represents the kind of hybrid cultural form discussed by postcolonial theorists (Ashcroft 2001, 219; Bhabba 1994, 208; Parry 2004, 56). This example of a hybrid cultural form being created as a result of Native-English interaction is but one instance of this kind of cultural mimicry and creativity that often results from colonial encounters. The archaeology of Magunkaquog and Hassanamesit contains additional evidence of the manner in which English materiality was reinterpreted in Native American society.

MAGUNKAQUOG

The site at Magunkaquog was first discovered by the Public Archaeology Laboratory of Pawtucket (PAL), Rhode Island (Herbster and Garman 1996). Further excavation was conducted by the author through what is now the Andrew Fiske Memorial Center for Archaeological Research at the University of Massachusetts at Boston. Although much of the material from the site has been examined and analyzed by graduate students and staff from the University of Massachusetts at Boston (Mrozowski et al. 2005), some work still is being carried out on the collection.

The 1997 and 1998 excavations determined that the concentration of artifacts originally discovered was part of a large deposit associated with the remains of a dry-laid, field stone and boulder foundation. Excavations over two seasons revealed the full extent of the foundation and a large collection of material culture and faunal material. Additional excavations failed to find any significant concentrations of cultural material and suggested that the foundation was the only concentration of archaeological remains on the site. The only other feature uncovered was an exterior hearth that was at least partially used to heat quartz cobbles, apparently to facilitate the extraction of crystals (Mrozowski et al. 2005). Some quartz crystals were recovered from site; the fact that they were found inside the foundation, near three corners, suggests that this was purposeful. This would not be surprising since the ritual significance of quartz crystals for close to 4,000 years has been documented by archaeologists working in New England.

In addition to the quartz crystals there are also several examples of gunflints made of quartz (Mrozowski et al. 2005).

The late Barbara Luedtke analyzed the gunflints and concluded that the lithic technology they exhibited was consistent with that of Native peoples in the region. In particular, she noted the evidence of use and retouch on all four sides of each gunflint as well as their small size. She interpreted the latter as an example of the Native practice of continuous tool reworking and reuse.

The remainder of the artifact assemblage is dominated by English manufactured goods with some examples identical to those found in graves in Natick and Ponkapoag (Mrozowski et al. 2006). English ceramics and pipes from the site suggest a period of occupation well past that suggested by the sale of the property to Harvard College in 1721. In fact, the material culture suggests that the site remained occupied at least until the mid-eighteenth century (Mrozowski et al. 2005). The assemblage contains horse furniture, bed curtain rings, double drawer pulls and escutcheon plates that seem to indicate a single piece of furniture, upholstery tacks, iron kettle fragments from a single large vessel, iron knives and tools, architectural hardware, thimbles, and a small collection of bottle glass. One of the most indelible characteristics of the assemblage is that it seems to represent what one might expect from a single household. The total ceramic vessel count for the site is small, thirty vessels, but like the house furniture, iron kettle, curtain rings, and furniture hardware, there is a sense that the fragmented pieces represent individual artifacts of each type.

One of the other defining characteristics of the collection from Magunkaquog is that it exhibits Native cultural practices despite the overwhelming number of items of English manufacture. Evidence of these practices include the heating of quartz for crystal extraction, gunflint manufacture and maintenance, the exterior heating evident on red-paste earthenwares that are not used for cooking by the English, and perhaps most importantly the lack of exterior hearth associated with the foundation. Taken as a whole the collection suggests that the foundation may well have been that of what Eliot referred to at Natick as a "fair house" (cited in Cogley 1998, 31). In his description Eliot says there was a loft area for him when he visited and that the building was also where the town's residents kept their valuables (Cogley 1998, 31). This description accords well with the artifact assemblage recovered from inside and immediately around the foundation at Magunkaquog. The use of the term "valuables" is intriguing because it would suggest that according to Eliot these would have been the items of English manufacture he had acquired for each of the villages. It is also possible that the building served as a sort of work house for the native community. This is one way to interpret the thimbles from the site, for example, for use in making or repairing cloths. The presence of horse furniture suggests that the building may have also served as the dwelling of the Native "teacher" in each community, given that horses were often the property of high-status individuals. If so, then the presence of quartz crystals strongly suggests that even the most devoted Christian converts probably layered this set of beliefs over a spiritual topography that remained persistently Native.

When the material from Magunkaquog is compared with the burial information, there are several points worthy of attention. First, and perhaps most obvious, is the large percentage of English material culture found around the Magunkaquog structure and in the graves from Ponkapoag and Natick. Certainly their *availability* for inclusion in the graves is no mystery—the documented purchase by Eliot of items strikingly similar to those recovered seems to explain their presence. The more important question is why they were in the graves, and here it may be that the Native peoples were actively engaged in a form of cultural mimicry that camouflaged their ambiguities concerning the power of the English god and their own future.

The evidence from Magunkaquog may at least partially support Brenner's (1980, 1986) suggestion that the "Praying Indian" towns were relatively autonomous and not residential communities in the sense of year-round occupation. The lack of an interior hearth at the Magunkaquog structure might be interpreted as support for Brenner's argument; however, the longevity of the occupation of the communities also tends to counter the same idea. A middle ground seems the most plausible, where year-round occupation was probably the norm, but movement over the land and between other communities was part of a seasonal pattern of movement. Such an interpretation would also accord with the sum total of the data from Magunkaquog and the cemeteries at Natick and Ponkapoag—that of Native communities experimenting with Christian doctrine and English economic practices while they continued to practice ways they had known for generations.

HASSANAMESIT WOODS

Archaeological evidence from the Sarah Boston farmstead in Hassanamesit Woods in Grafton, Massachusetts, presents a picture different from that of the other four "Praying Indian" communities discussed thus far. It is, for example, a later site linked to the dispersal of former Native lands after King Philip's War. The property identified in a 1728 land allotment as the 100-acre parcel of Peter Muckamoag was most likely part of the original seventeenth-century Hassanamesit community. Muckamoag was married to Sarah Robbins, who is believed to be a descendent of the Nipmuc Sachem Petavit, also known as "Robin." The archaeological investigations of a 206-acre parcel purchased by the Town of Grafton in 2005 discovered the remains of a dwelling site that contains material culture tightly dated to the period 1750–1840. The period of occupation suggested by the material assemblage corresponds to a time when the property was owned by Sarah Phillips's granddaughter, Sarah Burnee, and her great-granddaughter Sarah Boston.

In the period following King Philip's War, all Native lands in Massachusetts were placed under the control of small boards of overseers. All land sales and many commercial transactions involving the members of Native communities such as Hassanamesit were handled by the overseers, including the actual purchase of items such as ceramics, clothes, or building materials (Mrozowski, Pezzarossi, and Law 2006). In one example, Sarah Burnee asks to sell a parcel of land in order to have work done on her dwelling. This transaction took place in 1795, and among other things noted was the purchase of hardware from a local blacksmith named Amos Ellis. This purchase is noteworthy because among a large assemblage of cultural material discovered during three seasons of field work (2004–07), there was a metal tag with the initials "A. Ellis" impressed into it. Tags such as this were often used by artisans and, in particular, blacksmiths to mark their products. In this instance it is especially significant because it confirms that the dwelling remains uncovered in Hassanamesit Woods are most assuredly that improved by Sarah Burnee in 1795 and lived in by her daughter Sarah Boston until the latter's death in 1837.

Sarah Boston was a larger-than-life figure who was the subject of the rich local folklore that has been recorded by local history groups (see Mrozowski, Pezzarossi, and Law 2006). In most respects the portrait of Sarah Boston was less than flattering noting her large size, strange clothing, and predilection for drink. These same characterizations describe her dwelling as derelict and dark. The archaeological evidence points instead to a well-appointed household with ceramics and glassware consistent with the middle-class sensibilities of the period (Mrozowski 2006). It is possible that what Bhabba refers to as mimicry—the appropriation of the cultural trappings of one's oppressors as a form of defiance—represents a form of civil disobedience (Bhabba 1985, 163; see also Ashcroft 2001, 50–55; Parry 2004, 55–72). This interpretation is supported by strong evidence of continuing Native cultural practices during the opening decades of the nineteenth century. Evidence comes in the form of the continuing use of Native stone-working traditions in the quarrying of local stone for the foundation of the building. Despite English legal tradition that noted the original owner of the property in Hassanamesit Woods as Peter Muckamoag, it was his wife, the Nipmuc Sarah Robbins, who continued Native cultural practices by passing the land on to her daughter Sarah Muckamoag who, in turn, deeded it to her daughter Sarah Burnee. Further evidence of persisting Native cultural practices comes in the form of several examples of bottle and tumbler glass being reworked into tools as well as the existence of exterior hearth similar to that found at Magunkaquog.

Taken as a whole, the archaeological evidence of five different Christianized Native communities raises questions about the extent of cultural transformation these groups were experiencing during the late seventeenth and early eighteenth centuries. Continuing Native identity in the use of domestic space, spiritual practices, and technology is evident well into the nineteenth century. From the perspective of the now-repudiated notion of acculturation, it would be easy to interpret the preponderance of English and American manufactured goods as evidence of the rapid adoption of Anglo-American culture. There is, however, enough evidence, albeit subtle, to support a different interpretation—one of cultural continuity and persistence well into the twentieth century.

Further Reading: Ashcroft, Bill, *Post-Colonial Transformation* (New York: Routledge, 2001); Bhabba, Homi K., "Signs Taken for Wonders: Questions of Ambivalence and Authority under a Tree outside Delhi, May 1817," *Critical Inquiry* 12(1) (1985): 144–165; Bhabba, Homi K., *The Location of Culture* (London: Routledge, 1994); Brenner, Elise M., "To Pray or to Prey: That Is the Question, Strategies for Cultural Autonomy of Massachusetts Praying Town Indians," *Ethnohistory* 27(2) (1980): 135–152; Brenner, Elise M., "Archaeological Investigations at a Massachusetts Praying Indian Town," *Bulletin of the Massachusetts Archaeological Society* 47(2) (1986): 69–78; Carlson, Catherine C., "Archival and Archaeological Research Report on the Configuration of the Seven Original 17th Century Praying Indian Towns of Massachusetts Bay Colony," University of Massachusetts Archaeological Services (Amherst: University of Massachusetts, 1986); Cogley, Richard W., "Was Natick a Residential Praying Town in the Period before King Philip's War?" *Bulletin of the Massachusetts Archaeological Society* 59(1) (1998): 31–35; Cogley, Richard W., *John Eliot's Mission to the Indians Before King Philip's War* (Cambridge, MA: Harvard University Press, 1999); Crosby, Constance A., "From Myth to History, or Why King Philip's Ghost Walks Abroad," in *The Recovery of Meaning, Historical Archaeology in the Eastern United States*, edited by Mark P. Leone and Parker B. Potter (Washington, DC: Smithsonian Institution Press, 1988), 193–209; Gookin, Daniel, *Historical Collections of the Indians in New England* (Boston: Towtaid Press, 1970 [1674]); Kelley, John W., "Burial Practices of the Praying Indians of Natick, Panokapoag, and Marlboro," unpublished master's thesis (Department of Anthropology, University of Massachusetts–Boston, 1999); Lepore, Jill, *Name of War: King Philip's War and the Origins of American Identity* (New York: Vantage Books, 1999); Mrozowski, Stephen A., *The Archaeology of Class in Urban America* (Cambridge: Cambridge University Press, 2006); Mrozowski, Stephen A., Holly Herbster, David Brown, and Katherine L. Priddy, "Magunkaquog: Native American Conversion and Cultural Persistence," in *Eighteenth Century Native Communities of Southern New England in the Colonial Context*," edited by Jack Campsi, Occasional Paper No. 1 (Mashantucket, CT: Mashantucket Museum and Research Center, 2005); Mrozowski, Stephen A., Guido Pezzarossi, and Heather Law, "Archaeological Intensive Excavations: Hassanamesit Woods Property, the Sarah Boston Farmstead, Grafton, Massachusetts," Andrew Fiske Memorial Center for Archaeological Research, Cultural Resource Management Study No. 17 (Boston: University of Massachusetts, 2006); O'Brien, Jean M., *Dispossession by Degrees: Indian Land and Identity in Natick, Massachusetts, 1650–1790* (Cambridge: Cambridge University Press, 1998); Parry, Benita, *Postcolonial Studies: A Materialist Critique*. (New York: Routledge, 2004); Salisbury, Neal, "Red Puritans: The 'Praying Indians' of Massachusetts Bay and John Eliot," *William and Mary Quarterly* 31 (1974): 27–54.

Stephen A. Mrozowski

THE AFRICAN BURIAL GROUND NATIONAL MONUMENT

Lower Manhattan, New York City
The Archaeology of Northern Enslavement

Amid the hectic commerce and civic business of lower Manhattan is the final resting place of approximately 15,000 African Americans. They were buried, mainly during the eighteenth century, in the country's oldest known urban African cemetery. On February 27, 2006, using the authority of the Antiquities Act of 1906, President George W. Bush proclaimed a portion of this site a National Monument. The area of the cemetery is estimated to be 7 acres, and the entire site was designated as a National Historic Landmark in 1993. The president's proclamation set aside the National Monument in order to "promote understanding . . . , encourage continuing research, and present interpretive opportunities and programs for visitors to better understand and honor the culture and vital contributions of generations of Africans and Americans of African descent to our Nation" (Bush 2006).

Free and enslaved Africans and African Americans buried their dead in the African Burial Ground, located outside the border of the original colonial town. Burials may have begun as early as the mid-seventeenth century, but mainly the area was used as a cemetery from 1700 onward, by which time many of New York's churches prohibited the interment of free or enslaved Africans in the cemeteries of white congregations (Perry et al. 2006, 40–44). The African Burial Ground con-

Location of the African Burial Ground archaeological site in Lower Manhattan, New York City. Based on Figure 1.1, Archaeological Report of the Excavations of the African Burial Ground, Howard University and the General Services Administration. Electronic report available at www.africanburialground.gov/ABG_FinalReports.htm, accessed December 7, 2007.

tinued in use until about 1795, when the demands of a developing, expanding city and growing population encroached upon and then swept over the cemetery, most of which was in a low-lying area to the east of a north-south ridge upon which Broadway Avenue was constructed. By 1812 many of the graves had been covered with up to 25 feet of historic fill and soil. Not long afterward buildings and streets were constructed atop the newly filled surface, and markings on a few historic maps became the only clues of the existence of the many burials far below the surface.

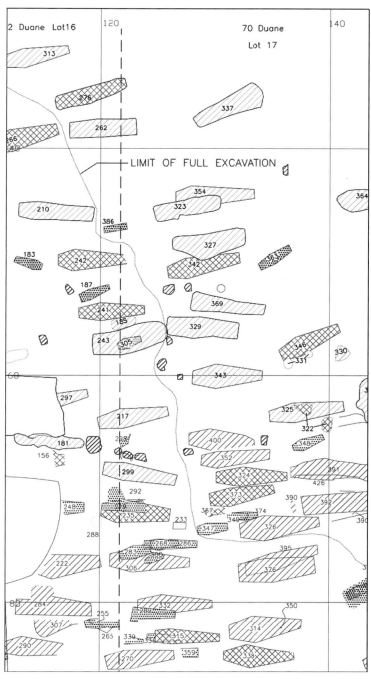

Detail of the site plan showing row-like alignments of graves spanning the site from north to south. The alignments might reflect the original natural contours of the hillside. Based on Figure 5.12, Archaeological Report of the Excavations of the African Burial Ground, Howard University and the General Services Administration. Electronic report available at www.africanburialground.gov/ABG_FinalReports.htm, accessed December 7, 2007.

HISTORICAL BACKGROUND

The first enslaved Africans arrived in New Amsterdam, the Dutch colony located at the southern tip of Manhattan Island, in 1625. African slaves worked as farmers, as builders, and in the fur trade activities of the Dutch West India Company, which controlled the colony. In 1644 the company freed the enslaved on the condition that they pay annually for their freedom in farm produce; however, children of the formerly enslaved remained the property of the company, and the import of enslaved Africans continued. Conditional freedom for some of the enslaved did not eliminate slavery in the colony.

In 1665 the Dutch surrendered New Amsterdam to the English, who continued to use slavery as part of their economic system and practiced it with a harder edge than the Dutch. In Dutch times free blacks, but also enslaved Africans, had some legal and social rights. These rules were changed by the English, who also created the Royal African Company to import slaves directly from Africa to the colony. The British "threatened the position that black people had secured during the first forty years of European and African settlement. The black men and women who came of age under British rule—and who probably compose the majority of those interred in the African Burial Ground—worked harder and died earlier than their . . . forbears" (Berlin and Harris 2005b, 10).

The English renamed the colony, and by the early 1700s there were about 800 African men, women, and children in New York, about 15 percent of the total population. The early documents from which these counts are made do not distinguish how many of the Africans at that time were enslaved and how many free. Africans, whether enslaved or free, provided valuable labor for the commercial and domestic enterprises of the colony. The British enacted a number of laws, referred to as "slave codes," that dictated how Africans could be employed and how enslaved Africans could be freed. The legal restrictions on Africans are interpreted as a major cause of a slave revolt in 1712 in which nine whites were killed. The revolt was unsuccessful; twenty-one enslaved Africans were executed and probably buried in the African Burial Ground. In response to the revolt, even more laws were passed further limiting the rights of Africans and controlling their activities.

In the early and mid-eighteenth century, Europeans in New York outnumbered Africans and people of African descent 5 to 1. However, New York contained the largest number of enslaved Africans of any American colonial settlement other than Charleston, South Carolina. Enslaved and free Africans and African Americans engaged in many kinds of work. Slavery in the urban context of the colonial city involved African women cooking, cleaning, and caring for the children of upper- and some middle-class white households. Enslaved men "worked outside the house, laboring on the docks and warehouses, loading and unloading ships and drays. . . .As the urban slave population grew, slave men also moved into skilled occupations as carpenters, coopers, and the like" (Berlin and Harris 2005b, 11). During these times, 40 percent of New York's households included at least one enslaved African, the largest percentage of any northern colonial settlement (Berlin 1998; Berlin and Harris 2005a; Finkelman 1989; Lepore 2005; McManus 1970; White 1991).

THE UNEXPECTED DISCOVERY OF A DOCUMENTED ARCHAEOLOGICAL SITE
In 1987 the General Services Administration (GSA), the federal agency that provides buildings and office space for

U.S. government agencies, began planning to provide additional courtrooms and office space in the Civic Center–Foley Square area of lower Manhattan. The planning process led to a proposal for a new thirty-four-story office building to be built on a property along Broadway, between Duane and Reade streets. During the planning, environmental and historical research was done to determine what impacts the construction and new building might have on cultural and natural resources. Historical research revealed that the new building's footprint would be within the general area where the African Burial Ground had been located. It was assumed, however, that historic and modern subsurface construction in the area had disturbed most of the area and had likely destroyed most burials. The possibility of small areas of undisturbed archaeological remains from the eighteenth century was recognized, however, and small areas within the project impact area were designated for archaeological field testing (Perry et al. 2006, 1–3).

Limited archaeological testing began in June 1991, and human burials were discovered beneath the modern surface and layers of historic debris and fill that had accumulated over the eighteenth century ground surface. Rather than finding these burials in limited parts of the planned construction footprint, the archaeologists conducting the investigations found many burials throughout the area where the building foundation was to be built. By October, a full-scale archaeological excavation was under way as more and more human burials were discovered. Archaeological investigation continued through the fall, winter, and spring. Excavation areas were covered with temporary structures so that fieldwork could continue during cold and inclement weather. Lighting was strung throughout the structures to enable the archaeologists to work extra hours on the project. The archaeological fieldwork was driven by the need to remove burials from areas where the foundation of the new office building had to be laid. Contrary to the initial assumption that the eighteenth-century African Burial Ground had been destroyed by the subsequent development of the area, many of the burials in the area proposed for construction were intact. The careful uncovering, recording, and removal of these human interments necessarily was very time-consuming.

The fast-paced archaeology continued until July 1992. Community concerns about the treatment of the burials and the earthly remains of New York's earliest Africans and African Americans, which had been growing, boiled over. Local political leaders, the mayor, and congressional representatives demanded that GSA change its plans for the new office building. The archaeological excavations, building construction, and progress on GSA's ultimate plan for the new building were halted. The story of community and political involvement regarding the African Burial Ground is fascinating. Readers who would like more details and perspectives on this matter should consult several of the publications in the "Further Information" section of this essay (e.g., the African Burial Ground Web site; Blakey and Rankin-Hill 2004, 2–37, 98–115; Harrington 1993; LaRoche and Blakey 1997). The political intervention in the project led to GSA revising its construction plans for the new office building to reduce the building footprint, allowing in situ burials to remain in place. The building lobby and adjacent undeveloped space also were designated to include memorials to and information about the African Burial Ground and about African and African American contributions to New York and the United States. Another outcome was the designation of Howard University as the most appropriate institution to carry out the analysis and reporting on the archaeology of the African Burial Ground and the human remains recovered by the excavations, and of Dr. Michael L. Blakey, a distinguished American physical anthropologist who also is African American, as the director of the research project.

RESULTS OF THE ARCHAEOLOGICAL RESEARCH

In addition to its national commemorative and symbolic value, the African Burial Ground is a truly astonishing archaeological site. Its contents and archaeological contexts encompass a rich reservoir of historic and scientific data about the early American past. The archaeological and physical anthropological research on the portion of the site that was excavated for the GSA office building project offer a picture of colonial America that was not widely recognized before this project, and the publicity and controversy that swirled around it, brought it into focus. The existence of slavery in the northern American colonies and early United States and the economic contributions of enslaved Africans and African Americans in this part of the country were highlighted by the existence of this large cemetery in the heart of one of the most prominent American cities.

The total number of graves identified in the excavated portion of the cemetery was 424. These burials contained the skeletal remains of 419 individuals. It is estimated that the excavation area sampled about 4 percent of the total extent of the African American Burial Ground (about 9,500 ft² of a total area estimated at 305,000 ft²). A remarkable homogeneity among the burials and the treatment of the dead can be inferred from the recovered remains (Perry et al. 2006, 447–453). Over 90 percent of the burials were in wooden coffins; all were in an extended supine position, and nearly all were oriented with the head to the west (97.8 percent). Only two coffins included more than one individual, and most graves had individual grave shafts; that is, each interment involved a separate burial. It also appears that the dead were shrouded or wrapped in sheets or fabric of some sort before being placed in the coffin. Small, copper-alloy

straight pins were found with half the burials. These pins would have held in place fabric that covered the deceased. There also was little evidence of regular clothing, for example, buttons or other common fasteners, suggesting that burial customs included covering or wrapping the deceased with a sheet or pieces of fabric, rather than burying them in street clothing.

When the eighteenth-century ground surface was detected and observed before the burial excavation, surface treatments of the grave were observed. For example, Burials 18 and 47 had slabs of stone placed upright above the graves and at the head of the interred individual. In addition, Burial 47 was outlined partially on the surface by stone cobbles. A number of other burials also showed cobble outlines atop the grave shafts (see Perry et al. 2006, 147, figs. 5.7–5.9). Unfortunately, the rapid pace of excavation in 1991 and 1992 may have destroyed remnant eighteenth-century surfaces in parts of the excavated area, preventing the observation of such surface treatments throughout the area.

The dating of individual graves was challenging because few artifacts with definite chronological characteristics were found in the burials. However, researchers used information about coffin shapes, stratigraphic relationships among the burials, the spatial location of burials relative to other eighteenth-century features (mainly pottery kiln waste deposits and fence lines from that period), and artifact dating to infer the relative dates of burials. Four groups of burials divided according to general relative dates were identified by the analysis. The Early Group, which includes 51 burials, seems to pre-date 1730. Most burials were placed in a Middle Group (199) or a Late-Middle Group (60) based upon stratigraphic relationships or, occasionally, datable artifacts. A Late Group (114 burials) was defined based on the placement of burials in the area north of a line where a fence had existed prior to the British occupation of the city during the Revolutionary War; before the removal of the fence, it is assumed that burials in this area would not have been possible. In addition to some chronological order to the burials, the spatial placement of the burials is generally regular. In some portions of the excavated area, burials seem to cluster in groups; in other areas, they seem aligned along a north-south axis (see Perry et al. 2006, fig. 1.7). In one area in the middle of the excavated portion, the general north-south alignment suggests a tracking of the original contour of the eighteenth-century surface (Perry et al. 2006, 149, fig. 5.12).

Extensive historical and physical anthropological research also was conducted as part of the African Burial Ground project, and detailed reports are available (Blakey and Rankin-Hill 2004; Medford 2004). Of the 419 individuals identified by skeletal remains in the archaeological excavations, 301 sets of skeletal remains were sufficiently well preserved for physical anthropological study. For the adult skeletal remains of 171 individuals (56.8 percent of the sample, 102 males and 69 females) ages could be determined. There were 130 subadult (as used in this analysis, age 15 and younger) skeletons (43.2 percent of the sample) for which ages could be determined. Overall mortality (age at death) within the sample of 301 skeletal remains studied was highest for individuals under the age of 2 years and for adults in the third and fourth decades of life (Blakey and Rankin-Hill 2006, 271–281).

Physical examination and recording of bone pathologies, bone element and teeth conditions and markers, and chemical and isotopic investigations of the skeletal remains were performed. A number of general conclusions developed from these studies, although the researchers note that additional studies, in particular more comparative studies with other burial populations, would be valuable. Most "genetic . . . ethnohistorical and chemical evidence indicates that most of the . . . individuals who died as adults were African-born. . . . Conversely, those who died before the first eight years of life were very likely to have been born in New York" (Blakey and Rankin-Hill 2006, 542).

The physical anthropology also reveals through examination of the skeletal remains the hard life endured by the Africans and African Americans buried in the cemetery. "Those who died as children . . . are frequently characterized by delayed growth and development due to a combination of nutritional, disease, and probable work-related stresses. . . . Infants, especially newborns and weaning age children, had especially high levels of new infections, anemia and other indicators of poor nutrition such as growth retardation and stunting" (Blakey and Rankin-Hill 2006, 544).

The skeletal remains of adults also show evidence of lives of hard labor and difficult circumstances for the colonial African and African Americans in New York. "Both African men and women experienced elevated work stresses, with some distribution of load bearing toward the upper spine in women and lower spine in men. . . . It is clear that most men and women were exposed to arduous work for extended periods of time. . . . The physical effects of slavery in New York resemble those of southern plantations and were not in any sense benign" (Blakey and Rankin-Hill 2006, 546).

CONCLUSION

The lives and contributions to America of the men, women, and children at rest in the African Burial Ground National Monument are now commemorated by the new National Monument at the site. Thousands of people have participated in traditional African ceremonies or American-style memorials at the site. In October 2003, following a week of ceremonies and celebrations to honor the importance of historic and modern African and African American contributions to the

United States, the excavated remains were re-interred in an accessible section of the cemetery near the protected, unexcavated graves of their companions. Currently, planning is under way by the National Park Service to interpret the site so that the people and their contributions to the nation will not be forgotten again.

Further Reading: African Burial Ground Web site, www.africanburialground.gov/ABG_History.htm (accessed December 7, 2007); Berlin, Ira, *Many Thousands Gone: The First Two Centuries of Slavery in North America* (Cambridge, MA: Belknap Press of Harvard University Press, 1998); Berlin, Ira, and Leslie M. Harris, eds., *Slavery in New York* (New York: New York Historical Society and the New Press, 2005a); Berlin, Ira, and Leslie M. Harris, "Uncovering, Discovering, and Recovering: Digging in New York's Slave Past beyond the African Burial Ground," in *Slavery in New York*, edited by Ira Berlin and Leslie M. Harris (New York: New York Historical Society and the New Press, 2005b), 1–27; Blakey, Michael L., "Bioarchaeology of the African Diaspora in the Americas: Its Origins and Scope," *Annual Review of Anthropology* 30 (2001): 387–422; Blakey, Michael L., and Leslie M. Rankin-Hill, eds., *The New York African Burial Ground Skeletal Biology Final Report*. vols. 1–2, Report for the United States General Services Administration (Washington, DC: Howard University, 2004); Bush, George W., *Establishment of the African Burial Ground National Monument: A Proclamation of the President of the United States* (Washington, DC: White House, 2006), www.whitehouse.gov/news/releases/2006/02/print/20060227-6.html (accessed December 26, 2007); Cantwell, Anne-Marie, and Diana diZerega Wall, *Unearthing Gotham: The Archaeology of New York City* (New Haven, CT: Yale University Press, 2001); Finkelman, Paul, ed., *Slavery in the North and West*, Vol. 5: *Articles on American Slavery* (New York: Garland Press, 1989); Harrington, Spencer P. M., "Bones and Bureaucrats: New York's Great Cemetery Imbroglio," *Archaeology* (March/April 1993): 28–38, www.archaeology.org/online/features/afrburial/index.html (accessed December 7, 2007); La Roche, Cheryl J., and Michael L. Blakey, "Seizing Intellectual Power: The Dialogue at the New York African Burial Ground," *Historical Archaeology* 31(3) (1997): 114–131; Lepore, Jill, *New York Burning: Liberty, Slavery, and Conspiracy in Eighteenth-Century Manhattan.* (New York: Random House, 2005); McManus, Edgar, *A History of Negro Slavery in New York.* (Syracuse, NY: Syracuse University Press, 1970); Medford, Edna Greene, ed., *The New York African Burial Ground History Final Report*, Report for the United States General Services Administration (Washington, DC: Howard University, 2004); Perry, Warren R., and Michael L. Blakey, "Archaeology as Community Service: The African Burial Ground Project in New York City, " in *Lessons from the Past: An Introductory Reader in Archaeology* (Mountain View, CA: Mayfield, 1999), 45–51; Perry, Warren R., Jean Howson, and Barbara A. Bianco, eds., *New York African Burial Ground, Archaeology Final Report*, 4 vol., Report for the United States General Services Administration (Washington, DC: Howard University, 2006); White, Shane, *Somewhat More Independent: The End of Slavery in New York City 1770–1819* (Athens: University of Georgia Press, 1991).

Francis P. McManamon

ANNAPOLIS HISTORIC PERIOD ARCHAEOLOGY

Annapolis, Maryland

The Colonial Archaeology of Maryland's Capital

Maryland was established as the fourth permanent English colony in North America in 1634, with its capital city chartered in 1667 at St. Mary's City in southern Maryland, the first English settlement. Following the Protestant revolution in England, a new royal governor was appointed for the colony, Francis Nicholson. During the winter of 1694–95 the provincial government was relocated from St. Mary's City to a new capital city for the colony, which was called Annapolis. This locale had initially been settled in 1649 and was then called Anne Arundel Town. Annapolis was given its charter in 1708 and became a center of commercial power, largely enabled by its situation as a mercantile port and through the importation of enslaved Africans, and later on the basis of wealth produced from enslaved labor. It was a cultural center as well, enjoying a golden age during the middle decades of the eighteenth century, until it began to be overshadowed economically by the city of Baltimore to the north in the early nineteenth century. Although slavery provided the basis for great wealth among Maryland's landed elites, Annapolis also had a substantial population of free African Americans in the years before Emancipation. Free blacks forged themselves into communities, sometimes characterized as church congregations, and sometimes as "enclaves" settled into marginal spaces of the city or its outskirts. The nineteenth century brought European immigrants as well, and the United States Naval Academy at Annapolis, established in 1845 and always an important institutional employer within the city, increased that diversity by bringing people from the Philippines after the Spanish-American War. New spaces opened up as the colonial town site was ringed with settlements after the American Civil War, places such as Eastport, Camp Parole, and West Annapolis. The U.S. Naval Academy was also redesigned and enlarged during the early twentieth century, bounding the city's growth to the north. During the early 1950s Annapolis annexed neighboring communities, establishing its present-day boundaries and setting the stage for urban renewal and historic preservation during the 1970s and 1980s. Archaeology in the city is imbedded in these later two moments.

Archaeology in Annapolis (AiA) is the long-term research project created to explore this heritage, a rare combination of a major historic preservation effort supported by local government and scholarship from the department of anthropology at a major research institution, the University of Maryland at College Park. The city of Annapolis has been the subject of systematic excavations of historic materials since 1981, when the Historic Annapolis Foundation and the University of Maryland at College Park began the exploration of sites in the oldest parts of the city for purposes of saving the material, publishing discoveries as scientific knowledge, and incorporating the new knowledge into public programs. The mayor and city council of Annapolis collectively became the third member of this partnership beginning in 1983.

Few American cities have a richer and more intact archaeological record than Annapolis. Major archaeological discoveries have been made within the city, in mostly intact contexts, but these include few prehistoric or seventeenth-century sites. Dr. Al Luchenback, founder of the Lost Towns Project, discovered and excavated Providence, the Puritan settlement allowed by Lord Baltimore in 1649 that marks the actual origin of Annapolis, which sits elsewhere in Anne Arundel County. Over forty archaeological sites have been excavated under the sponsorship of AiA within the city. Significant research within the city of Annapolis includes work on colonial landscapes and gardens, the African and African American history of Annapolis, and a significant focus on public education and interpretation.

ARCHAEOLOGY OF ANNAPOLIS LANDSCAPES

Baroque landscapes and gardens dating from 1695 to the 1770s characterize the planned urban landscapes of the city and have been one of the major contributions to knowledge made through historical archaeology. Baroque design uses landscape to manipulate lines of sight and orient persons visually and spatially to other persons, architecture, and monuments. Baroque design applied to town planning highlighted monarchical authority by putting symbols such as government buildings at the end of long vistas created by the corridor of buildings facing on a street. These designs captured and manipulated perception in a very deliberate way, whether applied to public or private spaces. When Annapolis was established as the new colonial capital in 1694, Governor Francis Nicholson superimposed a new baroque city plan for Annapolis onto a small existing community that had been settled by Protestants in 1649, called Anne Arundel Town. As Annapolis grew, the "Nicholson plan" for the city was carried out, using monumentality and landscape to underscore state authority by aggrandizing the symbols of colonial power and by controlling or directing what people saw. The survival of the historic fabric of Annapolis's colonial period is remarkable, and Nicholson's 1696 planned landscape can still be easily experienced. The modern historic

The 1718 Stoddert survey of Annapolis.   [Matthew Palus]

district, included on the National Register of Historic Places since 1966, relates closely to the earliest known map of Annapolis, the 1718 Stoddert survey.

The most studied feature of the Nicholson plan in Annapolis is the circle that was designed to display the state house. The planned landscape that holds the Maryland Statehouse was systematically excavated in 1990. When the city's plan is viewed in two dimensions, as on a map, there is prominent asymmetry in the way streets enter and leave State Circle, taken by some as a failure in

Nicholson's competence. In contrast, excavations showed that that State Circle was designed as a true geometric egg shape that created the appearance of a harmonious landscape around the state house, and that the landscape had been maintained and rebuilt continually over the eighteenth and nineteenth centuries with its orientation shifting a number of times. These excavations resulted in an understanding that baroque town plans and gardens operated using principals of perspective so as to create optical illusions; for example, the rules of perspective dictate that a circle should be laid out on the ground as an egg if it is to appear as a circle to a person approaching, in this instance, the Maryland Statehouse. Therefore, baroque towns, like baroque gardens, are not to be seen as maps; they are volumes through which people move with vistas as the object of the design and movement.

These principles were embraced by Annapolis elites in the years leading up to the American War of Independence, and were reinterpreted as landscapes that tied together house and garden according to principles of order found in nature. Fourteen baroque gardens were constructed in Annapolis between 1763 and 1774, but importantly these landscapes had a different philosophical premise that conformed to Revolutionary ideologies. Placing neoclassical architecture on the highest terrain, these gardens "fell" away from the house in terraces, concluding either at a curvilinear area designated as a wilderness or at the waterfront. Maps and excavations of at least four of the falling, or descent, gardens in the city demonstrate the use of optical illusions in their design, which was faithfully executed using standard garden encyclopedias and dictionaries from the seventeenth and eighteenth centuries.

ANNAPOLIS AS PART OF THE AFRICAN DIASPORA

A third of Annapolis has always been from Africa or of African descent. Historical archaeology was among the first scholarly disciplines to work with the African descendent community of the city to systematically publicize their history as an object of knowledge and understanding. Ten archaeological sites associated with people of African descent have been excavated. African diasporic history in Annapolis became a major part of AiA's research design after leaders within the descendent community asked for more investigation into the spiritual lives of Africans and African Americans in the past, as well as the history of freedom before and after emancipation.

The investigation into spiritualism led to some of AiA's best-known research questions dealing with practices showing the material culture associated with hoodoo or conjure, terms that are often avoided now in favor of the term "African spirit practices." These practices involve the use of hands, tobys, mojos, or fixings, and many of the concrete manifestations of them can be found archaeologically and

are referred to generically as caches. Current intellectual work on religions derived from Africa tends to see African spirit practices in North America as either creole or hybrid. Modern scholarship that uses hybridity theory sees a creative and new invention in the Afro-Christian church, wherein African traditions are mixed with Christian theology to bring about a whole new and African-derived version of Christianity. Some of the maladies addressed by hands or tobys are rheumatism, headaches, cramps, teething, toothaches, and heart pains. In addition to these medical problems, ritual items warded off harsh events or turned them against those who invoked harmful spirits on others. For example, at the Charles Carroll House site, a cache was found in a basement workroom known to be used during the eighteenth and nineteenth centuries. This cache was made up of twelve crystals, flakes of quartz, a faceted glass bead, and a polished black stone, all covered by an overturned pearlware bowl with an asterisked decoration on its base, and found buried in the northeast corner of the room. According to African spirit practices, crystals could be used to capture and hold spirits, who were in turn used to protect, cure, or take action against a person or situation.

Another important facet of AiA's work has been its research into free life before and after emancipation, showing the means by which middle-class life as well as African diasporic traditions were established and maintained. This is exemplified by Paul Mullins's scholarship concerning excavations done at the Maynard-Burgess House, a house owned by two interrelated African American families from the 1850s to the 1980s. His analysis identified consumer strategies that Black consumers used in their struggle for racial equality from the time of the Civil War through to the civil rights movement. Choices made in the marketplace, for example, the purchase of precanned rather than bulk items to protect themselves from the cheating of racist storeowners, show this negotiation.

Because Annapolis was a node in the plantation economy and all of the city's great homeowners and famous patriotic politicians drew their wealth from farms well beyond the city, including the eastern shore, AiA has excavated extensively at Wye Hall Plantation, built in 1793 by William Paca. Excavations are also ongoing at Wye House Plantation, home of the Lloyd family, made famous by Frederick Douglass, who lived there as a boy early in the nineteenth century, in vivid recollections found in all three of his autobiographies.

ARCHAEOLOGY IN PUBLIC

Archaeology in Public was created in 1981 along with its parent project, Archaeology in Annapolis. An aggressive educational program was defined so that an archaeological environment could be used to change the perception that the past is discovered by archaeologists as opposed to interpreted by them during their work. This educational program was designed with two main goals: (1) to help reenfranchise people by giving them control over their own consumption of history and (2) to illuminate portions of everyday life that are taken for granted but, when given history, can be questioned or challenged. These goals were achieved by a variety of means, which consisted of public tours of in-progress excavations, a guidebook-based walking tour of the historic district, and a slide show/film. Initially, Archaeology in Public met substantial resistance from the profession because it defined education, and specifically public archaeology, as being as important as excavation.

By the late 1990s, AiA was focusing on a new avenue of public education: museum education and programming. The Banneker-Douglass Museum, the state of Maryland's official repository of African American material culture located in Annapolis, became an outlet for archaeological knowledge through a museum-based summer camp that educated young African American students in African history and culture using archaeology as one of the main teaching methods. AiA collaborated on this camp for five summers and is now partners with the Banneker-Douglass Museum, using the museum as the foundation for a majority of AiA's public work.

AiA does not focus its educational efforts only through Archaeology in Public. Three hundred fifty undergraduates have been trained in the University of Maryland's archaeological field school, run by AiA. Many graduate students have received training in Annapolis archaeology; a dozen dissertations have been or are being written, which have led to over six books on the archaeology of the city. Guidebooks, Internet-based information, a geographical information system to the historic district of the city, and streaming video have all been created to introduce findings to constituencies and stakeholders.

Further Reading: Cochran, Matthew, *Archaeology in Annapolis*, Department of Anthropology, University of Maryland, College Park Archaeology in Annapolis Web site, http://www.bsos.umd.edu/anth/aia/index.htm (online January 2007); Hyatt, Harry Middleton, *Hoodoo-Conjuration-Witchcraft-Root-Work: Beliefs Accepted by Many Negroes and White Persons, These Being Orally Recorded among Blacks and Whites* (Hannibal, MO: Western Publishing, 1970–1978 [1935]); Leone, Mark, The *Archaeology of Liberty in an American Capital: Excavations in Annapolis* (Berkeley: University of California Press, 2005); Shackel, Paul A., Paul R. Mullins, and Mark S. Warner, eds., *Annapolis Pasts: Historical Archaeology in Annapolis, Maryland* (Knoxville: University of Tennessee Press, 1998).

Mark P. Leone, Amelia Chisholm, Jennifer J. Babiarz, Matthew Palus, and Lisa Kraus

MINUTE MAN NATIONAL HISTORICAL PARK

Lexington, Concord, Lincoln, Massachusetts
Sites of the Early American Revolutionary War

On April 19, 1775, in the Massachusetts towns of Lexington, Lincoln, and Concord, violence broke out between British Army regulars and colonial militia that marked the beginning of the American Revolution. British troops had ventured west of Boston to seize hidden munitions in Concord, but it soon appeared to residents that the entire town might be destroyed in the process. Turned back at the North Bridge, British soldiers returned to Boston engaged in a running battle with colonial militia companies. News of this event mobilized other New England town militia and led to the Siege of Boston (1775–76). Minute Man National Historical Park (NHP) was established in 1959 to commemorate the events of April 19 and to preserve and interpret its historical, architectural, and archeological legacy. The park consists of three individual units totaling 971 acres and contains twenty-five identified archaeological sites associated with events of April 19, 1775. Archaeology has improved the accuracy of information presented to the public and has shed new light on the lives of Native Americans, American colonists, and some of Concord's most famous early nineteenth-century authors.

NORTH BRIDGE AREA
The North Bridge area features a variety of sites and landscapes focusing on the reconstructed bridge over the Concord River marking the location where the first major skirmish between British Army regulars and colonial militia companies took place. Prone to flooding in the spring, the river contributed to a rich ecological system that supported abundant plant and animal resources of interest to human beings over thousands of years. Here could be found the camp sites of Native Americans between 5,000 and 7,000 years ago. It is likely that they had also cleared areas along the river for agriculture in the decades before European colonists settled Concord in 1635.

The North Bridge area attracted settlement early in Concord's colonial history due to its easy access by land and by water as well as its fertile river terraces. Archaeology has laid bare sections of colonial roads, which provide the basis for some of today's visitors' paths. To the northwest and near present-day Liberty Street are the exposed foundations of the David Brown House, possibly built before 1644. The

North Bridge reconstruction.   [National Park Service]

foundations may represent a four-room house that was supplemented by a second house in the immediate area built between 1752 and 1768. Both of these houses and their respective outbuildings were standing in 1775. The corners of one barn foundation are marked with stone. During the colonial period rural populations tended to occupy dispersed family farmsteads rather than nucleated town centers. Several generations of the same family continued to occupy a single farmstead, augmenting it as necessary. Eventually, successive generations were required to seek land elsewhere or to take up trades. As the fertile Midwest opened for farming in the nineteenth century, New England farmers often sold their rocky farms to recent immigrants and moved on.

Understanding the evolution of the landscape of Minute Man NHP in detail is a complex process involving several different disciplines. Historians have consulted tax lists, land deeds, and genealogical and probate records to establish a chain of ownership dating back to the seventeenth century for individual land parcels. Architectural study helps to determine which houses

were standing in 1775. Archaeology informs us about Concord's agrarian economy and about now-vanished landscape features in the North Bridge area. For example, a late eighteenth-century engraving executed by Amos Doolittle depicts the battle at the North Bridge, showing stonewalls, cleared fields, and buildings in upland areas. These were certainly structures built by members of the Buttrick family, but even the detailed Doolittle engraving does not show exactly where they stood. Two cellars discovered by archaeologists in front of the North Bridge Visitor Center in the 1960s may represent the remains of either the Ephraim or Willard Buttrick houses. The remains of other colonial period structures built by several generations of Buttrick family members are probably preserved elsewhere in this area.

MERIAM'S CORNER

Meriam's Corner is historically significant as the location where British Army regulars clashed with several companies of colonial militia, as the British began their march along the "Battle Road" back to Boston. Here, sandy lowlands on the edge of

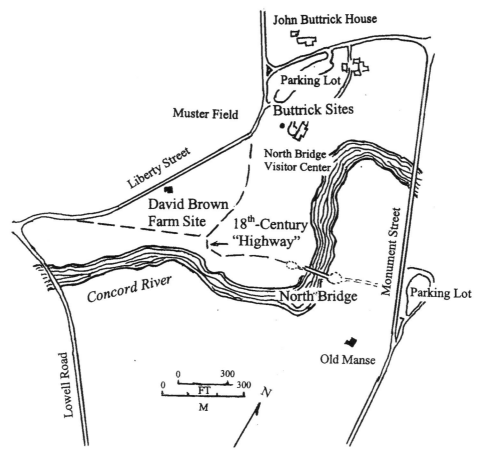

Plan of North Bridge Unit.   [National Park Service]

glacial Lake Concord are dominated by Revolutionary Ridge, a glacial esker landform. This area was attractive to Native Americans during the Late Archaic period in part because of the presence of wetlands, now largely drained. Archaeology has revealed how four generations of the Meriam family adapted to this part of east Concord since settling there in the mid-seventeenth century. The earliest house, built around 1663 by John Meriam, stood midway along the visitor path in front of the Joseph Meriam House (ca. 1705) that is visible today. The earlier structure had two cellars and probably a central chimney. Closer to the intersection of Old Bedford Road and Lincoln Road stood its post-supported outbuildings. In 1775 the older house was owned by Josiah Meriam, and the 1705 house was occupied by Nathan Meriam. On April 19, the column of British regulars passed in front of this cluster of buildings and then regrouped in order to cross the wetlands to the east. In this vulnerable position they were attacked by several colonial militia companies approaching from Old Bedford Road and sheltered behind the Meriam buildings. Archaeology has corrected some of the misconceptions about the Meriam's Corner landscape of 1775, locating Josiah's house and barns and using geological analysis to locate the stream bed of that period. By the early nineteenth century some of the older Meriam houses and

outbuildings were in disrepair and were torn down in order to expand the amount of arable land.

VIRGINIA ROAD AREA

Heading east along Lexington Road, the visitor passes through land owned by members of the Brooks family in 1775, where more fighting occurred on April 19. The Virginia Road area is found just to the north after crossing into the town of Lincoln at Elm Brook. Intense fighting took place along this stretch of narrow, angular road. Much of the surrounding land had been cleared by 1775, and so colonial militia members had to take shelter behind buildings and stone walls to attack British soldiers. Archaeology has helped to verify the location and original surface of the road itself in addition to locating eighteenth-century structures such as the Mason House site, outbuildings and orchard of the Hartwell Tavern, and the immediate landscape of the Samuel Hartwell House site, which was destroyed by fire in the 1960s.

NELSON ROAD AREA

After returning to the North Great Road, or present-day Route 2A, the visitor soon encounters the Minute Man Visitor Center, where exhibits and an orientation film can be viewed.

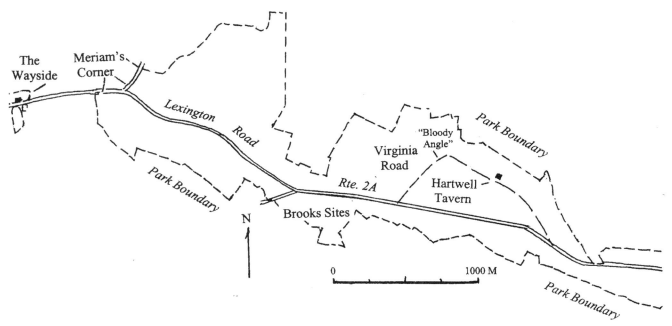

Plan of Meriam's Corner and Virginia Road areas.   [National Park Service]

The Nelson Road area itself can be easily explored by foot. It contains another segment of the eighteenth-century Bay Road with colonial period house sites studied by archaeologists since the 1960s. The roadbed itself was 18 to 22 feet (6 to 7 m) wide, possibly lined with a ditch and grassy shoulder edged by stone walls marking the edges of adjacent fields. On the north side of Nelson Road in 1775 could be found the houses of Daniel Brown and of the brothers Josiah Nelson and Thomas Nelson, Jr., and of their sister Tabitha. The Thomas Nelson, Jr., house was probably built between the 1730s and 1750s and was certainly present in 1775. Tabitha's house was apparently joined to it sometime before both houses were demolished in the 1890s. Such a complicated building history is not unusual for houses at Minute Man NHP, requiring the combined research skills of archeologists, architectural historians, and historians to unravel. Building and landscape complexity creates additional challenges for interpreting these sites to the public because many of the post-1775 modifications may be significant for other reasons and cannot be removed. Minute Man NHP's mission also includes preserving and interpreting evidence of agricultural life regardless of the time period. For example, a post-1775 hop house is visible at the intersection of Nelson Road and Route 2A. This was a facility for drying hops, a flower used for brewing beer. A slow-burning fire was set at the bottom of the kiln of this building, now filled with sand for safety reasons.

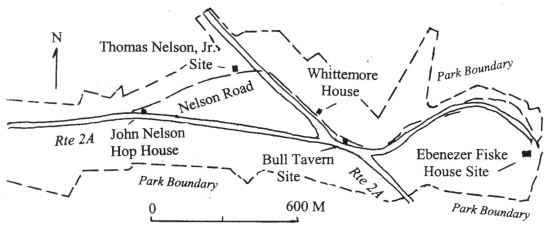

Plan of Nelson Road and Fiske Hill areas.   [National Park Service]

FISKE HILL AREA

The Fiske Hill area contains a variety of sites including Pre-contact period flake scatters dating back between 5,000 and 7,500 years ago. During the later colonial period, one would have encountered a cluster of buildings along a segment of the Bay Road, beginning with Jacob Whittemore's house and continuing a short distance east to the intersection of today's Route 2A and Old Massachusetts Avenue. Only Jacob Whittemore's house remains today, but documentation indicates that his farm buildings included a corn house and cider mill and barn (not in the location of the later barn visible today). There is archeological evidence that a post-1775 blacksmith shop and tavern existed just east of the Whittemore farmstead, but there are questions about their use in 1775. However, the visitor may walk along several segments of the original Bay Road to reach the Ebenezer Fiske site at the far eastern side of the park unit. In 1775 one would have encountered a house, farm buildings, and fences, none of which survive today. At or near the exposed foundation stones stood the house of Ebenezer Fiske, also occupied by his son Benjamin and daughter-in-law Rebecca in 1775 (their two-story central chimney house was probably replaced by another in 1852, whose foundations are visible). Oral history suggests that several British casualties may be buried on the Fiske property.

THE WAYSIDE

The Wayside was the first literary site to be acquired by the National Park Service (NPS), and it consists of a late seventeenth-century residence with later additions and a barn. During the middle of the eighteenth century it was occupied by a variety of farmers and artisans, and in 1775 it was the home of Samuel Whitney, muster master of the Concord Minutemen. Between 1845 and 1852 it was the home of the educator and philosopher A. Bronson Alcott and his wife, Abby, along with their daughters Louisa May Alcott, Anna, Elizabeth, and May. In 1852 it was purchased by author Nathaniel Hawthorne, renamed "the Wayside," and occupied by his family, including his wife Sophia and their three children (a decade earlier Hawthorne and his new wife had occupied the Manse, located close to the North Bridge). The Wayside was designated a National Historic Landmark first in 1963 and later again in 1985. Archaeology has played a role in investigating the shifting configuration of barns and outbuildings and has a high potential to inform us about landscape treatments, interior furnishings, and consumer behavior of some of the house's famous occupants. Due west of the Wayside may be found the exposed foundations of the Eliphelet Fox House, dating to 1666. Henry David Thoreau describes the Fox House as having once belonged to Casey, an African slave owned by Samuel Whitney, but this has not been verified by other sources.

Further Reading: Donahue, Brian, *The Great Meadow: Farmers and Land in Colonial Concord* (New Haven, CT: Yale University Press, 2004); Fischer, David Hackett, *Paul Revere's Ride* (Oxford: Oxford University Press, 1995); Malcolm, Joyce Lee, *The Scene of the Battle, 1775: Historic Grounds Report: Minute Man National Historical Park* (Boston: Division of Cultural Resources, National Park Service, 1985); Minute Man National Historical Park, National Park Service Web site, http://www.nps.gov/mima (online August 2007); Synenki, Alan T., Steven Pendery, and Lou Sideris, *Traces of the Past* (Fort Washington, PA: Eastern National Park and Monument Association, 2002).

Steven R. Pendery

FORT TICONDEROGA AND OTHER LAKE CHAMPLAIN HISTORIC SITES

Vermont and New York

Early Historic Forts and Shipwrecks

Human occupation along the shores of Lake Champlain and Lake George began roughly 12,000 years ago. For millennia native cultures flourished; however, with the 1609 arrival of French explorer Samuel de Champlain, the whole complexion of human history in the region changed. For the next 150 years military conflict between France and Britain dominated Lakes Champlain and George. It was their geographic position in those nations' contested colonial hinterlands that led to their intensive military use, with forts erected along their shorelines and warships sailing their waters. The end of hostilities came with the British victory in the Seven Years War in 1763. Peace, however, was short lived with the American Revolution soon engulfing the region. The early years of the struggle for independence saw considerable conflict on Lake Champlain culminating in the October 1776 fleet engagement at the Battle of Valcour Island. With

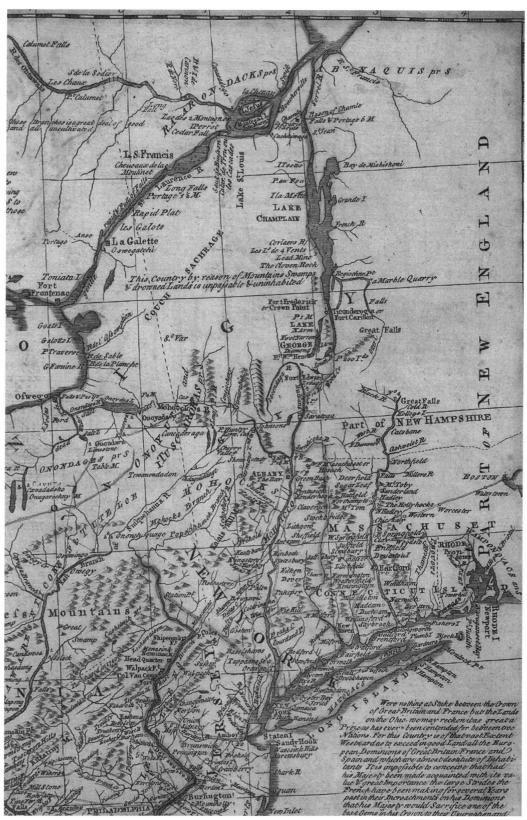

1771 map of the northeastern colonies showing the important geographical position of Lakes Champlain and George. [Library of Congress]

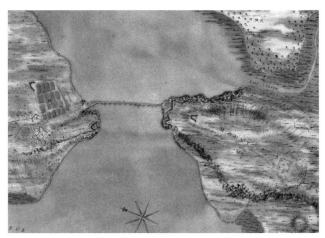

1777 map showing the fortifications of Fort Ticonderoga and Mount Independence.   [Fort Ticonderoga Museum]

the 1783 Peace of Paris, settlement of the region began in earnest. Lake Champlain's final military episode occurred during the War of 1812 with a fleet action between the Royal Navy and the U.S. Navy at the Battle of Plattsburgh Bay. The American victory helped bring an honorable end to the war. During the nineteenth century, the development of steamboats and construction of canals transformed Lake Champlain into a dynamic commercial superhighway. Lake George was not connected to other waterways via canals, thus waterborne commerce was less significant there during the nineteenth century.

During all of these complex and interwoven years of conflict and commerce, archaeological sites both on land and underwater were created. Fortifications built and fought over by French, British, and American forces provide tangible connections to those military periods and lives of their participants. Many of these terrestrial sites have been preserved and protected by the states of Vermont and New York. In recent years, a vast collection of intact submerged wooden watercraft and other underwater cultural remains lying on the bottoms of these lakes have been located and studied. Each state has also established an Underwater Historic Preserve program that provides access to selected submerged sites to divers. The Lake Champlain Maritime Museum provides information about these submerged sites to nondivers and divers alike.

FORT WILLIAM HENRY, LAKE GEORGE
Located at the southern end of Lake George, Fort William Henry was erected by the British in 1755 during their efforts to drive the French out of the Champlain Valley. The fort is best remembered for the French siege directed by the Marquis de Montcalm in the summer of 1757 that resulted in its surrender by the British. The defeated army was attacked in an episode made familiar by the book *Last of the Mohicans* by James Fennimore Cooper. After this massacre the fort was never formally re-occupied.

The site of Fort William Henry was left to return to the elements until the 1950s, when archaeological excavations were begun there. Today a reconstruction of the fort stands on its original site.

FORT TICONDEROGA, LAKE CHAMPLAIN
Fort Ticonderoga is situated on a cape that extends into Lake Champlain and controls the northern end of Lake George. This strategic location led it to be fortified by the French in 1755. In 1758, Fort Carillon, as it was known, was the site of one of the bloodiest battles of the French and Indian War, when the British army attempted a frontal assault on the French lines. More than 2,000 British troops were killed and wounded, and the British invasion force was repulsed.

In May 1775, during the opening months of the American Revolution, the British-controlled Fort Ticonderoga was taken by colonial revolutionaries led by Ethan Allen and Benedict Arnold. The following year Fort Ticonderoga served as an American stronghold while a fleet of warships was built to repel an impending British invasion. The American fleet under Arnold's command engaged a superior Royal Navy fleet on October 11, 1776, in the American defeat at the Battle of Valcour Island. Control of the lake shifted to the British, with the Americans retreating behind the guns of Fort Ticonderoga. In 1777 General John Burgoyne led a British force that took Fort Ticonderoga and Mount Independence, a fortification built the previous winter on the opposite Vermont shore. Just two months later, Burgoyne and his army were defeated at the Battles of Saratoga, thereby changing the prospects for American success.

After the war, Fort Ticonderoga was left to deteriorate. Eventually the property came into the hands of the Pell family, and in 1909 at the 300th anniversary of Champlain's arrival, the Pell family established Fort Ticonderoga as a privately owned but publicly accessible historic site. Today, the Fort Ticonderoga Museum contains an important collection of eighteenth-century military objects, and its Thompson-Pell Research Center and Library provides scholarly access to a significant collection of books, manuscripts, and objects relating to the French and Indian War and the American Revolution. Archaeological studies have been used in the restoration of parts of the fort, and information from these studies enhances the interpretation of the site and its collections.

SHIPWRECKS AS UNDERWATER CULTURAL HERITAGE
Lakes Champlain and George contain a large collection of intact wooden shipwrecks and other underwater cultural heritage. Lake George's shipwrecks relate primarily to the colonial era and most notably include the 1758 British radeau (a historic flatboat carrying cannon) *Land Tortoise* and the sunken fleet of 1758, consisting of seven British bateau (flat-bottomed riverboats). Lake Champlain's shipwreck collection includes the remains of French, British, and American warships from the colonial and early federal era, as well as

The replica canal schooner *Lois McClure* under sail in 2004. [Photograph by Eric Bessette, Lake Champlain Maritime Museum Collection]

nineteenth-century steamboats, sloops, schooners, canal boats, and a horse ferry. There are over 300 known shipwrecks in Lake Champlain.

The shipwrecks resting in Lakes Champlain and George are largely intact because of the relatively stable environment created by their cold freshwater conditions. In 1991 zebra mussels, a nonnative aquatic nuisance species, were found in Lake Champlain. This species, which obscures and degrades shipwrecks, now infests many of Lake Champlain's shipwrecks, although they have not been found in large numbers in Lake George.

THE UNDERWATER HISTORIC PRESERVE SYSTEM

On Lake Champlain and Lake George, public shipwreck access programs for divers have been developed. The approach has been to provide reasonable access to appropriate sites. On Lake George there are currently four sites, including the remarkably intact British radeau *Land Tortoise* (sunk in 1758). On Lake Champlain there are currently eight sites, seven in Vermont waters and one, the steamboat *Champlain II* (1867), in New York waters. The Vermont sites include the hull of the steamboat *Phoenix I* (1815), which burned in a violent fire with the loss of six persons; the *Horse Ferry* (ca. 1825), the *Water Witch* (1832), built as a steamboat and converted to a schooner; and the *General Butler* and the *O.J. Walker*, two canal schooners that sank in Burlington Harbor.

The Lake Champlain Underwater Historic Preserves and the Lake George Submerged Heritage Preserves provide seasonal moorings for each site, permitting divers to easily locate the shipwreck without the need to anchor.

THE LAKE CHAMPLAIN MARITIME MUSEUM

Located at Basin Harbor, Vermont, the Lake Champlain Maritime Museum (LCMM) has been at the forefront of current research of Lake Champlain's historical and archaeological resources. Over the years the LCMM's significant nautical archaeology studies have contributed to the public's renewed interest in Lake Champlain and stimulated a rapid expansion of the museum site. The LCMM campus consists of a dozen buildings, including a Nautical Archaeology Center and a Conservation Laboratory. A wide variety of exhibitions, educational opportunities, and courses and workshops both on campus and off have been developed and implemented. The public is connected to Lake Champlain's extraordinary historic and archaeological legacy through the production of films, the publication of books, and the development of youth and family boat-building experiences. In 2004 the LCMM launched the canal schooner *Lois McClure*, a replica based on the archaeological study of two nineteenth-century canal schooner wrecks in Lake Champlain.

Further Reading: Bass, George F., ed., *Beneath the Seven Seas: Adventures with the Institute of Nautical Archaeology* (London: Thames and Hudson, 2005); Bellico, Russel P., *Chronicles of Lake Champlain: Journeys in War and Peace* (Fleischmanns, NY: Purple Mountain Press, 1995); Bellico, Russel P., *Chronicles of Lake George: Journeys in War and Peace.* (Fleischmanns, NY: Purple Mountain Press, 1999); Bellico, Russel P., *Sails and Steam in the Mountains: A Maritime and Military History of Lake George and Lake Champlain* (revised edition) (Fleischmanns, NY: Purple Mountain Press, 2001); Cohn, Arthur B., *Lake Champlain's Sailing Canal Boats: An Illustrated Journey for Burlington Boat to the Hudson River* (Basin Harbor, VT: Lake Champlain Maritime Museum, 2003); Crisman, Kevin J., and Arthur B. Cohn. *When Horses Walked on Water: Horse-Powered Ferries in Nineteenth Century America* (Washington and London: Smithsonian Institution Press, 1998); Hill, Ralph N., *Lake Champlain: Key to Liberty* (Twentieth Anniversary Edition) (Woodstock, VT: Countryman Press, 1995).

Arthur B. Cohn

SARATOGA BATTLEFIELD

Saratoga, New York

American Revolutionary War Battle Site

New York was a major theater of the American Revolution. The first hostile action in New York occurred on May 10, 1775, when Vermonters led by Ethan Allen and Benedict Arnold took Fort Ticonderoga in a surprise attack. Arnold led another attack against Quebec in September of that year, suffering a bullet wound in the leg during that failed engagement. The crucial turning point of the war was fought at Saratoga, north of Albany, in autumn 1777.

Both Euro-American settlers and native Six Nations Iroquois communities were important participants on both sides in the conflict. Early in the war the easternmost Iroquois nation, the Mohawks, took refuge with their British allies at

Fort Niagara and in Quebec. The Clinton-Sullivan Campaign of 1779 was intended to disperse and punish the western Iroquois nations, the Senecas, Cayugas, Onondagas, and Tuscaroras, who had also sided with the British. The American army marched across central and western New York, burning the villages of those Iroquois nations.

The Oneidas sided with the American colonists around Fort Stanwix in modern Utica. Fort Ticonderoga, Fort Stanwix, and several other Revolutionary War sites, such as Fort Oswego, West Point, and Crown Point, remain preserved and in some cases reconstructed for students, scholars, and the general public.

THE SARATOGA BATTLEFIELD

The Saratoga Battlefield, now a National Historical Park, lies south of Schuylerville, New York, on the west side of the Hudson River. The area of interest to archaeologists and historians of the two battles fought there in 1777 is large, about 3 miles (5 km) in both dimensions. Today it is the only eighteenth-century battlefield in either North America or Europe that is preserved for public benefit entirely within park boundaries.

Archaeological investigation of the Saratoga is a daunting problem. Archaeologists, mindful that their work is both expensive and partially destructive, tend to focus on sites where long occupations are concentrated in small areas. The Saratoga Battlefield is a huge area comparable in size to the pre-Hispanic city of Teotihuacan, Mexico, yet its period of archaeological interest was less than a month. Combinations of low-level aerial photography, magnetometer survey, soil sampler transects, test excavation, historic documentation, and fine-resolution mapping have allowed archaeologists to overcome these problems.

The British intended to take Albany in 1777 by means of a three-pronged attack. One column was supposed to advance northward up the Hudson, but it never materialized. Another was supposed to descend the Mohawk River by way of Fort Stanwix, but it was stopped by American and Oneida units at the battle of Oriskany. The third and largest prong was led by General Burgoyne, southward from Quebec by way of Lake Champlain and the upper Hudson River. Burgoyne's large cumbersome force was harassed and delayed by American forces as it advanced southward along the west side of the Hudson, and by autumn it had still not reached Albany. American resistance stiffened as the British column approached, and the engineer Thaddeus Kosciuszko selected high ground anchored on a bluff called Bemis Heights as a place for the American militia to make a stand.

The Americans dug in on Bemis Heights and below on the Hudson floodplain, straddling the road along which the British had to advance. Kosciuszko anticipated a flanking attack by extending the defensive line for nearly a mile (1.5 km) northwestward to the Neilson Farm, where the line angled sharply back to the southwest for about half that distance to protect the army's western flank. These lines are visible in the park today where entrenchments were dug, and

painted posts mark the location of lines between the more visible archaeological remains.

FIRST BATTLE OF SARATOGA

The British army never made it as far as the American fortification lines. On September 19, 1777, the advancing British army of regulars and volunteers encountered American resistance about 2 miles (3 km) to the north. The British split into three columns, one moving 1 mile, another 2 miles, westward away from the river before striking southward through woods and farmland. American regiments moved forward to engage the British, and heavy fighting ensued. Several regiments on both sides took significant losses before dusk brought an end to the fighting, and the Americans fell back to their fortifications. The British troops dug in, forming a long fortification line that mirrored the one already occupied by the Americans to the south of them across a broad no-man's land.

The western angle of the British line came to be known as the Balcarres Redoubt. North of it, protecting the British western flank was another fortification known as the Breymann Redoubt. Regiments of British regulars took up emplacements between the Balcarres Redoubt and the Hudson River, but the space between the two western redoubts was occupied by only a few Canadian volunteers.

Both armies refined their fortifications and constructed most of what is archaeologically visible today over the subsequent eighteen days. During that time, fresh American volunteers swelled the army blocking the British advance, the weather cooled as the forest turned red, and the British army suffered both camp fever and malnutrition from poor food at the end of its long supply line. Burgoyne knew that he had to reach Albany before winter, and by October it was clear that there was no help on the way from either the west or the south.

SECOND BATTLE OF SARATOGA

On October 7, 1700, British troops under the command of General Simon Fraser advanced with artillery support in a flanking movement southward to the Barber Wheatfield, located in the western part of the no-man's land separating the two armies. The Americans accepted the offer of battle and attacked with over a dozen regular regiments and militia units from Albany and Connecticut, a total of around 8,000 men. Accurate firing by Daniel Morgan's riflemen from the woods to the west of the field mortally wounded General Fraser, and the numerically superior American forces soon drove the British back toward their redoubts.

The mercurial and arrogant Major General Benedict Arnold was present, but he had been relieved of his command by General Gates for having been too aggressive in the earlier fighting on September 19. Although he was without an official command, Arnold played an important role in the battle of October 7. A disorganized American attack on the Balcarres Redoubt failed, with many casualties, once the British troops that had advanced previously fell back into it and reinforced its garrison. Arnold noticed a weakness in the British line between the two redoubts, which was held only by a small number of Canadian volunteers. Collecting fragments of dispersed American units, Arnold used his personal charisma to organize an assault northward across the Canadian position and into the rear of the Breymann Redoubt. With their guns pointed the wrong way British resistance there collapsed quickly, and the day ended with the Americans in possession of the western flank of the British line. Arnold suffered another wound to the leg. Although his bravery and success on the battlefield were later acknowledged by Congress, he was already embittered. He eventually betrayed the Revolution at West Point. A monument to his wounded leg now stands in woods behind the Breymann Redoubt. The monument depicts Arnold's boot but pointedly omits his traitorous name. Its inscription reads in part "The 'most brilliant soldier' of the Continental Army Who was desperately wounded On this spot, the sally port of BURGOYNES GREAT (WESTERN) REDOUBT 7th October 1777. Winning for his countrymen The Decisive Battle of the American Revolution And for himself the rank of Major General."

The British pulled back to their positions on the bluffs overlooking the Hudson. During the night many died of their wounds, including Simon Fraser. The next day Burgoyne and his troops retreated to Schuylerville, where they dug in once again. The dwindling British army was surrounded there by still-growing American forces, and Burgoyne was compelled to surrender on October 17, 1777. British and American entrenchments are still visible around Schuylerville, and a large commemorative obelisk dominates the modern village.

SARATOGA ARCHAEOLOGY
Test excavations carried out as part of a larger archaeological project in 1972 uncovered the remains of two individuals in very shallow graves. One was found in one of the trenches of the Balcarres Redoubt. This individual, who was elderly and probably female, died of a gunshot wound to the head. She might have been the wife of a noncommissioned British officer, some of whom were accompanied by wives and families. Another individual was found in the Breymann Redoubt. His jacket buttons suggested that he was not regular army but rather a volunteer, whose loyalties remain undetermined.

Archaeological investigations by the State University of New York and the University at Albany from 1972 to 1975 led to a correction of previous misunderstandings about the placement of the Breymann Redoubt and revealed previously unknown details about the Balcarres Redoubt.

The probable location of Simon Fraser's grave was investigated, as were sample sections of both the British and the American fortification lines. Regimental buttons and other artifacts allowed investigators to rectify period maps to modern ones, which in turn clarified the deployment of units of both armies in the fall of 1777. Aerial photography and systematic ground truthing also facilitated the locations of key historic roads. Today the Saratoga Battlefield is an exemplary historical park where visitors can acquire an unusually complete understanding of eighteenth-century warfare and a singular event in the history of the United States.

Further Reading: Furneaux, Rupert, *The Battle of Saratoga* (New York: Stein and Day, 1971); Ketchum, Richard M., *Saratoga: Turning Point of America's Revolutionary War* (New York: Henry Holt and Company, 1997); Morrissey, Brendan, *Saratoga 1777: Turning Point of a Revolution* (New York, Osprey Publishing, 2000); National Park Service, Saratoga National Historical Park, History of the Park Web site, http://www.nps.gov/sara/s-prkhst.htm; National Park Service, Saratoga National Historical Park, Maps of the park and battle Web site, http://data2.itc.nps.gov/hafe/hfc/carto-detail.cfm?Alpha=SARA#; Thurheimer, David C., *Landmarks of the Revolution in New York State: A Guide to the Historic Sites Open to the Public* (Albany: New York State American Revolution Bicentennial Commission, 1976).

Dean R. Snow

FRANKLIN COURT, THE PRESIDENT'S HOUSE, AND OTHER SITES

Philadelphia, Pennsylvania

The Archaeology of the Revolution and Early American Republic

Philadelphia, sometimes known as a city of firsts, has led the nation in many areas—the first public school in America, the first university, the first hospital, and the first zoo. Less well known is Philadelphia's claim to a special place in the development of archaeology in the Americas. Beginning in 1743 with the founding of the American Philosophical Society, the city was home to major research institutions that played key roles in American archaeology. In the nineteenth century the Academy of Natural Science and the University of Pennsylvania Museum of Archaeology and Anthropology joined the

Excavations at Franklin Court (seen here in 1960) established the location of Benjamin Franklin's house and left a tangible record for park visitors to see.   [Courtesy of Independence National Historical Park]

Philosophical Society in pushing forward the study of American antiquities. In 1956, with the creation of Independence National Historical Park, a new partner was added, and the interest in American archaeology took a new turn as the city began to look inward toward the study of its own archaeological past. Considering the fruits of this new introspective turn, Philadelphia can fairly be called the place where urban archaeology came of age.

Philadelphia's long and varied history offers rich rewards to the teams of archaeologists who sift its soil for clues about the past. Prior to the arrival of Europeans on the banks of the Delaware River, people inhabited the area for thousands of years. Little is directly know about the earliest inhabitants of what is now Philadelphia. Evidence from elsewhere in the region suggests that migratory bands hunted the length of the Delaware Valley by at least 10,000 years ago. At the time Europeans first explored the length of the Delaware River, they found villages and camp sites along the shores of the river.

By 1681, when William Penn received his charter from King Charles II to the land that was to become Pennsylvania, the original inhabitants of the Philadelphia area had largely been displaced by encroaching Europeans, and their land appropri-

ated by Swedish and Dutch settlers. At the time Penn launched his Quaker experiment on the strip of land between the Delaware and Schuylkill Rivers some fifty farmers worked the land within the present-day boundaries of the city. Settlement spread westward from a nucleus of settlement at the port on the bank of the Delaware River as waves of new settlers built houses and workshops in Penn's newly established town. The new town was never limited solely to English members of the Society of Friends and quickly became home to a large and diverse population. Despite its relatively late founding date, Philadelphia grew rapidly to become one of the largest and most cosmopolitan cities in the English-speaking world. By the time of the American Revolution, the city was a thriving port and a center for learning, science, and the arts. The workshops of the early settlers provided the seed on which grew a mighty industrial engine that, by the middle of the nineteenth century, led the city to boast that it was the "workshop of the world."

For more than fifty years archaeologists have explored the physical remains of Philadelphia's past. Anchored by research conducted in Independence National Historical Park, this work has helped to shed light on the institutions that defined the city and on the people—both humble and

Archaeologists uncovered an entire eighteenth-century neighborhood on the site of the National Construction Center during excavations in 2000. The site offers a unique view of "We the People."   [Courtesy of Independence National Historical Park]

renowned—who shaped its development. This sustained effort has revealed little about those who lived here before the arrival of Europeans. Centuries of urban growth and development have largely destroyed, or at least obscured, these early traces. By contrast, a wide range of historic period sites have been excavated throughout Philadelphia and in the suburbs and hinterlands surrounding the city.

ARCHAEOLOGICAL BEGINNINGS: INDEPENDENCE SQUARE

The authorization of Independence National Historical Park by an act of Congress in 1948 served as the spark that launched sustained interest in the study of Philadelphia's

archaeological past. The genesis of the park grew, starting in the 1920s, from a local interest in preserving sites and buildings associated with the founding of the nation. During World War II fears grew over the perceived threat to Independence Hall and other historic buildings from a fire-bombing attack. Ultimately these wartime fears proved the catalyst that led to the establishment of the park.

An archaeologist was among the team of National Park Service experts assigned to help plan and guide the development of the park. Most of the early archaeological work was conducted in support of this design and development effort. Archaeologists were pressed into service to answer specific questions concerning the location of buildings and features and to uncover the physical layout of historic sites within the park.

Typical of this early work was a series of excavations conducted in Independence Square behind Independence Hall. Although noteworthy in its own right, the square is today best known through its association with Independence Hall. In 1736 the Commonwealth of Pennsylvania designated the area as a public green to compliment Independence Hall (then known as the State House), which was under construction at the north end of the square.

Today Independence Hall is venerated as the site at which the American nation was born. It was within this building, one of the most imposing structures in colonial America, that the Declaration of Independence was adopted. Here, too, the Constitution of the United States was debated and signed. Independence Square was more than just the backdrop to these events. The first public reading of the Declaration of Independence took place within this public square.

Beginning in 1953 Paul J. F. Schumacher became the first archaeologist employed to work in the park. As part of these early efforts he launched an extensive program of excavations within the square that were completed by his successor, B. Bruce Powell, in 1957. A primary goal of this research program was to uncover evidence that would shed light on the appearance of the square from 1785 to 1800. Of particular interest were any remains of the first landscape plan devised by Samuel Vaughan, a close friend of Benjamin Franklin. Vaughan completed the landscaping of the square in 1787 and immediately went on to develop a landscape plan for George Washington's estate at Mount Vernon.

Schumacher and Powell also hoped to establish the location of an observatory that was erected in the square by the American Philosophical Society in 1769. From this observatory successful observations of the 1769 transit of Venus were conducted. The location of the observatory was chiefly sought because it was often cited as the place from which John Nixon first read the Declaration of Independence to a public gathering on July 8, 1776. Recent research has suggested that a temporary stage, rather than the observatory, was used for the reading. At the time that Schumacher and Powell worked, and for many years after, the observatory was believed to be the site of this important event, and its location had long been sought.

Schumacher and Powell employed a standard technique used by archaeologists at the time and crisscrossed the grassy areas of the square with narrow exploratory trenches. Their search for the observatory ended in disappointment when no trace of the structure came to light. These multi-year excavations did, however, reveal much about the history of the square and its evolution from a residential enclave on the edge of the growing town to a venerated public square.

The archaeologists uncovered the home sites of three early residents, the oldest of these tiny houses dated to the closing years of the seventeenth century. Also uncovered was a rubble-filled trench indicating the location of the first wall, built in 1740, that marked what was at the time the south end of the square. Particularly exciting were deposits of red gravel in various locations. These marked surviving traces of Vaughan's original serpentine walks that snaked through the square.

The evidence that Schumacher and Powell amassed helped to paint a picture of the square as a dynamic public space. Traces of its use as a Revolutionary War encampment came to life, including the remains of a chicken dinner on which the solders dined. The locations of buildings, now vanished, were revealed, and an unusual octagonal brick privy (outhouse) pit behind Independence Hall was excavated.

In the end, however, these early archaeological excavations did not contribute directly to what visitors to Independence Square experience. Rather than restoring the Vaughan plan, park planners decided instead to leave in place the landscape plan that the American Institute of Architects designed for the square in 1915.

EXPANDING HORIZONS: INDEPENDENCE NATIONAL HISTORICAL PARK AND BEYOND

The excavations conducted in Independence Square between 1953 and 1957 demonstrated the value of archaeology in locating and documenting vanished landscape features. So too, in a spectacular manner, did excavations at Franklin Court. In 1953 archaeologists began looking for evidence of the Franklin home. Construction on the house began in 1763 and was completed largely under his wife, Deborah's, watchful eye while he was in Europe on diplomatic missions. The house had been demolished in the early nineteenth century, and their first goal was to precisely locate the house, its outbuildings, and details of the surrounding landscape. And this, in due course, they did; first excavating in the street and under the sidewalk, and then exploring the adjacent house lots after the demolition of overlaying nineteenth-century structures. It took three distinct phases of work conducted over three decades to complete the task. Schumacher launched the work in the 1950s, and the search continued under the direction of various archaeologists in the 1960s and the 1970s. Over that time scores of archaeologists, aided by volunteers and laborers, systematically sifted the soil for clues to the site's history.

The picture that emerged tells us much about a great man and his times. The excavations reveal a detailed picture of the home Franklin designed and in which he spent his declining years. Foundation remains and paved cellar floors indicate the layout of the house. Stone foundations and fragments of bricks and plaster tell us that the house was an imposing, substantial structure with carefully plastered and painted walls. Franklin's original and inventive mind is suggested by a unique feature uncovered by the archaeologists. A privy pit adjacent to the house included a brick chute that originally connected to the building; suggesting that Franklin installed a flush toilet within his house. This was an innovative household convenience at a time when other Philadelphia residents relied on outdoor toilets.

A surprising find from a surprising source casts additional light on Franklin's intellect and his place as an eighteenth-century man of science. In 1959 an electrician working in the basement of a building at Franklin Court found a curious object. Close examination revealed it to be a fossil mastodon tooth. In the late eighteenth century, mastodon fossils were the subject of intense interest by those, like Franklin, who studied what was then termed "natural philosophy." The 1959 find is almost certainly a relic from Franklin's collection of such curiosities.

Today, visitors to Franklin Court (located mid-block on Chestnut Street between Third and Fourth Streets) can study some of the fruits of archaeologists' three decades of labor. The site features an innovative and award-winning design completed by noted architect Robert Venturi in 1974. Venturi followed a suggestion offered by archaeologists working on the project and incorporated into his design life-sized steel frame outlines of the Franklin house and the smaller print shop used by his grandson. Underneath the frame of the house, visitors are invited to view the preserved archaeological remains of the house. Looking into these portals, visitors gaze into the past to see what archaeologists saw when they first uncovered these tangible links to Franklin's life.

The elegant ghost-like structures compliment an underground museum that contains exhibits that illustrate Franklin's life and times. A row of restored buildings on Market Street that were once owned by Franklin contain additional exhibits, including a Fragments of Franklin exhibit that features artifacts unearthed from excavations at the site.

The excavations at Franklin Court marked a milestone for archaeologists working in Philadelphia. The success of the project can be measured not just by the accomplishment of its primary goal—the establishment of the exact location of the Franklin house—but also by its success in incorporating the physical remains from Franklin's life into the site plan that the National Park Service implemented. In the ensuing years millions of visitors have had an opportunity to learn from the work of these archaeological pioneers.

Another significant development emerged alongside the unfolding work at Franklin Court. In 1957 John Cotter arrived in Philadelphia to serve as a regional archaeologist with the National Park Service. Soon after his arrival, he initiated excavations at a wide variety of sites across the city. Cotter enlisted both local high school and university students in these projects, including students from the University of Pennsylvania, where he taught the first course in historical archaeology. Cotter broadened the horizons of archaeology in Philadelphia by studying sites beyond Independence Park's boundaries, including sites that represented a broad range of people and institutions from both eighteenth- and nineteenth-century Philadelphia.

The focus was no longer limited to sites of famous events or persons; the goal was no longer primarily to address the needs of historic reconstruction and the preservation of noted buildings. Cotter and his students pressed trowel, pick, and shovel into service at revolutionary-era Fort Mifflin, at the site of the late colonial Bonnin and Morris Porcelain Factory, and at the Walnut Street Prison, the unhappy home of many of the city's debtors and common criminals from 1775 to until 1835. They examined numerous other sites, both residential and otherwise, in the city and in the surrounding region.

Congress's passage of the National Historic Preservation Act in 1966 extended and reinforced the expanded view of archaeology that John Cotter first introduced to Philadelphia. This act mandates that projects with federal funding or involvement must complete a process of review to determine whether significant historical or archaeological resources are present within the project area. If an archaeological site is identified, excavation may be required. Passage of the act contributed to increased attention to archaeological resources across the country, including in Philadelphia.

Excavation of a site at Front and Dock Streets is one example of the kind of projects the act makes possible. In 1984 archaeologists from the firm of John Milner and Associates were retained to conduct archaeological investigations at the site in conjunction with a federally funded urban renewal project. Structural remains and artifact deposits in the cellars and privy pits excavated at the site reveal the evolution of the area from the late seventeenth century into the nineteenth century. Over that period the homes of early settlers gave way to increasingly commercial usage of the site. Domestic trash pits filled with household tableware, including locally made dishes and imported porcelain, are accompanied in later deposits by the discarded stock from warehouses and the shops of merchants. The lobby of the Sheraton Society Hill Hotel, which occupies the site today, features a display of some of the artifacts recovered from the site.

ARCHAEOLOGY OF "WE THE PEOPLE"

The pioneering work of John Cotter and the requirements of the National Historic Preservation Act continued to shape the work of archaeologists in the city from the 1970s into the early years of the twenty-first century. Archaeologists continued to cast a wide net in their effort to shed new light on the lives of the city's residents, both celebrated and humble.

Beginning in 1999 some of the most extensive excavations in the city's history were completed in Independence National Historical Park as part of the ambitious redevelopment of Independence Mall. At Sixth and Market Streets, where a new park and regional visitors center was to be built, archaeologists explored the homes and shops of those who worked and lived in what was a relatively upscale neighborhood in the late-eighteenth through the mid-nineteenth centuries.

William Simmons lived on the site in the 1790s. He served as a government clerk and accountant during the administrations of both George Washington and John Adams at a time when the seat of government was in Philadelphia, prior to its move to Washington, D.C. The abundance of liquor bottles, carafes, decanters, and drinking glasses recovered from a deposit associated with his tenure on the block testifies to Simmons's bachelor status and to the high level of alcohol consumption during the early years of the republic.

In the second quarter of the nineteenth century, members of the Everly family were proprietors of a comb manufactory and a fancy dry-goods store located on the site. A child's miniature tea set and doll parts recovered from their house lot illuminates the youthful pastimes of the Everly children. The middle-class aspirations of the family are evident in the quantities of fine ceramics (including a monogrammed Chinese porcelain tea set) recovered from the site. Archaeologically recovered food remains tell us that the meals served in the Everly household were fitting compliments to this refined tableware and included significant quantities of wild game.

The Independence Visitor Center, which now stands on this spot, houses a permanent display of some of these archaeological remains. These objects provide visitors today with a glimpse into the lives of these long-forgotten Philadelphians.

The analysis of artifacts recovered from the site where the National Constitution Center now stands are providing additional insights into the lives of the diverse inhabitants of late colonial and early federal Philadelphia. Located one block north of the Independence Visitor Center at Arch and Sixth Streets, large-scale excavations at this site produced more than a million artifacts.

The results of this excavation are shedding light on an entire neighborhood and its residents in the years around the birth of the nation. Within the narrow confines of the block in 1795, doctors and wealthy merchants lived side by side with whitewashers, bricklayers, shoemakers, and laborers. Among the house lots archaeologists excavated were the homes of Caleb Cresson, the wealthy merchant who owned and developed much of the block, and Benjamin Cathrall, a Quaker schoolmaster. Also excavated were lots on which Israel Bergo, a free African American of modest means, lived and the home of James Oronoko Dexter. Dexter, also a free African American, hosted founding meetings in this house for the African Episcopal Church of St. Thomas, which was one of the first free black churches in the United States.

The National Constitution Center features artifacts recovered from the site as part of an exhibit that introduces visitors to Philadelphia during the years when the Constitution was being written, debated, and adopted. Nearly 100 objects are on display. Outside the center, an interpretive plaque near the location where James Dexter's house stood provides information on Dexter and other residents of the block.

In the summer of 2005 the National Park Service, in partnership with the National Constitution Center, opened a public archaeology laboratory in the Independence Living History Center located on Chestnut and Third Streets. Artifacts from the National Constitution Center site and from other sites in the park are processed and analyzed in this facility. Visitors to the laboratory can watch the process of analysis unfold on a daily basis and listen as the staff provide an explanation of the ongoing work.

THE PRESIDENT'S HOUSE: CONFRONTING SLAVERY AND FREEDOM THROUGH ARCHAEOLOGY

On March 21, 2007, an extraordinary groundbreaking ceremony took place in the heart of Independence National Historical Park. Several hundred city residents, high school students, and community activists listened as Philadelphia Mayor John F. Street addressed the crowd: "We don't know what we're going to find. But we certainly know we have an obligation to look." Those words prefaced a four-month excavation on the site, now a busy downtown street corner, where in the 1790s presidents George Washington and John Adams lived and worked in a large house with a complex of outbuildings during the period when Philadelphia was the temporary capital of the United States.

In 2002 a local independent scholar, Edward Lawler Jr., published the results of extensive research he had completed on the history of the President's House. His findings sparked wide public interest—and controversy. During the years that President Washington occupied the President's House, he brought nine enslaved Africans to Philadelphia. It was the jarring and deeply disturbing image of Washington, the larger-than-life symbol of the American struggle for freedom, juxtaposed against the largely anonymous enslaved men and women who toiled in obscurity in the shadow of the great man, that sparked a controversy ultimately leading to the 2007 archaeological dig.

Historians, local community activists, the Philadelphia media, and many individual citizens urged that the complete story of the President's House be told, including the stories of Austin, Christopher Sheels, Giles, Hercules, Joe Richardson, Moll, Oney Judge, Paris, and Richmond, the nine slaves the president brought to Philadelphia from his plantation at Mt. Vernon.

In 2007, with federal and city funding for a commemoration secured, and as the planning and design for the proposed commemoration moved forward, the National Park Service joined in partnership with the City of Philadelphia to launch an archaeological excavation on the site. The house was gutted in 1832 and replaced by a row of four stores, each with a deep basement. Consequently, the archaeological team was not optimistic that the site would yield significant evidence of the President's House. But over the four months following the groundbreaking, archaeologists made a series of unexpected finds. Park visitors watched from a viewing platform as remains of the famous house's foundation were revealed.

First, segments of the foundation of the rear wall of the main house came to light. Other discoveries followed in quick succession. Evidence was found of a bow window that President Washington ordered added to the main house. This grand curving window prefigured both the oval rooms in the White House and today's Oval Office. The foundations of the large kitchen building that stood behind the main house were also discovered. This was the kitchen where Hercules, Washington's enslaved chef prior to his escape to freedom in 1797, worked. Two foundation walls marked the location of a previously unknown underground hallway or passage that linked the kitchen to the main house. The passage would have been used almost exclusively by servants and enslaved workers as they went about their daily routines.

The surprising finds garnered wide media interest, and the crowds of visitors grew as the excavation progressed. During the four months of active work more than a quarter of a million people gazed down on the excavation from the viewing platform. Washington's bow window stood a scant 6 feet from the kitchen where Hercules toiled. That small distance, plainly visible to visitors, perfectly encapsulates a central contradiction—the inextricably intertwined themes of slavery and freedom—that runs through American history. The excavations at the President's House demonstrated the power of archaeology to connect contemporary Americans with an important and deeply troubling part of their country's history.

Further Reading: Cotter, John L., Daniel G. Roberts, and Michael Parrington, *The Buried Past: An Archaeological History of Philadelphia* (Philadelphia: University of Pennsylvania Press, 1992); Fowler, Don D., and David R. Wilcox, eds., *Philadelphia and the Development of Americanist Archaeology* (Tuscaloosa: University of Alabama Press, 2003); Independence National Historical Park, National Park Service Web site, http://www.nps.gov/inde/ (online July 2005); Lawler, Edward, Jr., "The President's House in Philadelphia: The Rediscovery of a Lost Landmark," *Pennsylvania Magazine of History and Biography* 126(1) (2002): 5–95; Lawler, Edward, Jr., "The President's House Revisited," *Pennsylvania Magazine of History and Biography* 129(4) (2005): 371–410; Oliver Evens Chapter of the Society for Industrial Archeology, *Workshop of the World: A Selective Guide to the Industrial Archeology of Philadelphia* (Wallingford, PA: Oliver Evens Press, 1990).

Jed Levin

THE ARCHAEOLOGY OF THOMAS JEFFERSON

Monticello, Poplar Forest, and Shadwell, Virginia
Jefferson as Plantation Owner and Architect

Thomas Jefferson, author of the Declaration of Independence and third president of the United States, directed an archaeological excavation of a Native American burial mound near his home in Charlottesville, Virginia, in 1784. Employing stratigraphic method and publishing his results, Jefferson is lauded as America's first scientific archaeologist. It is fitting, then, that two centuries later, archaeological study of Thomas Jefferson's three homes plays a significant role in the modern understanding of Jefferson's life and the lives of the African Americans he enslaved within Virginia plantation society of the late eighteenth and early nineteenth centuries.

Archaeological studies were conducted at Jefferson's birthplace home of Shadwell in the 1950s and again in the early 1990s. At Monticello and at Poplar Forest, archaeological research has been ongoing since 1979 and 1993, respectively. The excavations at Shadwell were concerned with assessing the social and economic standing of Jefferson's father, Peter Jefferson, a pioneer settler in the Virginia Piedmont. Archaeological excavations have shown the household to be similar in material culture to that of the contemporary Tidewater Virginia elites, although smaller and different in design. Thomas Jefferson moved to Monticello in 1770 and lived there until his death in 1826. Archaeological survey and excavation there has focused on the famous house designed by Jefferson but also on the less well-documented associated buildings and landscape. These studies have made significant contributions to understanding the daily lives of enslaved African American workers on the plantation and how the institution of slavery itself changed during Jefferson's lifetime. Archaeological research based at Monticello has also provided insights into plantation-based industrial sites and landscape construction and change over time. Some 90 miles southwest of Monticello, Jefferson built Poplar Forest, often called his retreat and retirement home, but that was also a working plantation with a large enslaved labor force. Archaeology at Poplar Forest has aided in the reconstruction of the house and its man-made landscape as well as a fuller understanding of African American life on that plantation.

SHADWELL

Shadwell is a house and plantation site located on the Rivanna River in Shadwell, near Charlottesville. Peter Jefferson was one of the first Virginians to move from the Tidewater society into the Piedmont foothills of the Blue Ridge Mountains. Shadwell was occupied by Peter and Jane Jefferson and family from around 1739 to 1746 and again from 1753 to 1770. Archaeological research was first conducted there in 1943 to shed light on the poorly understood economic and social foundation of the Jefferson family in the frontier region. Comparatively little documentary evidence speaks to Jefferson's early family history and social standing. The Thomas Jefferson Memorial Foundation, owner of Monticello and Shadwell, sponsored archaeological research at the site in the early 1990s.

Archaeological studies of the house itself show it to be neither a Georgian mansion, such as could be found in the Tidewater, nor a log cabin. It was a well-constructed brick home with four large rooms and a substantial basement—the home of a family of the elite gentry class. Shadwell was part of a new Piedmont plantation society that grew and prospered quickly, dependent on enslaved labor. The material culture recovered from the main house include personal items, such as pieces of Peter Jefferson's survey equipment, and the tea sets and silver typical of the elites throughout the Virginia colony. The challenge of the three- to five-day journey separating Piedmont from Tidewater planters did not affect the participation of the Jefferson family in the British Atlantic trade. Slave quarters at some distance from the main house were excavated, and artifacts were found relating to food acquisition, preparation, and consumption, including fishhooks, as well as items of craft production and spiritual or medicinal ritual practice.

The site is preserved by the Thomas Jefferson Memorial Foundation but is not presently open to the public.

MONTICELLO

Monticello archaeology has played a leading role in the development of historical archaeological methods and in the study of plantations and the lives of enslaved African Americans in the South.

The estate of Monticello was established on approximately 5,000 acres of land that Thomas Jefferson inherited from his father. The first structure on Monticello mountain was built in 1770, and Jefferson is said to have been living in Monticello by 1794 and (with long periods away) until his death in 1826. The plantation included the main house, attached dependencies, adjacent slave quarters, field slave quarters, and extensive gardens. Jefferson responded to the fluctuating tobacco market by substituting a mixed farming regime with wheat as the main crop of the plantation in the 1790s. Jefferson's Monticello diversified in other ways as well, including craft shops and an industrial nailery.

All aspects of the plantation have been studied from an archaeological perspective. An early emphasis employed archaeology to reconstruct the landscape of the plantation. Extensive gardens, a garden pavilion, fence lines, retaining walls, road systems, ditches, and domestic yard trash from the main house were mapped, and some of these features reconstructed. The archaeological study of the lives of the enslaved workers focused on a 1,000-foot street of wooden buildings with stone foundations, wooden chimneys, and earth floors called Mulberry Row. Mulberry Row was located just 300 feet south of the main house. Here were the quarters for the slaves who worked in and around the house, or in the adjacent industrial sites.

Study of Mulberry Row cabins reflects significant change over time in the plantation economy and slave life. The earliest cabins, built around 1770, were approximately 215–260 square feet. In a second phase of construction, the cabins were greatly reduced in size, to roughly 140 square feet. Two structures built in the early nineteenth century then show a return to the size of the first cabins on average. The earliest slave cabins are two-cell structures with one entry; the post-1790 structures are one room with one entry. The change in room size may reflect a shift to kin-based housing emerging in the more diversified plantation economy with task specialization for the enslaved labor force. Archaeological studies at Monticello suggest differences in status between enslaved workers along Mulberry Row, and between those slaves living in Mulberry Row houses and field quarters. Analysis of animal remains shows an increase over time in the frequency of small wild game, suggesting an increase in hunting to enhance upon provisioned foods.

Mulberry Row slave cabins built before 1800 typically contained subfloor pits. These features contained a range of distinctive artifact types, including buttons, pierced coins, cowry shells, and food. Archaeologists have observed that the presence, number, and size of such subfloor pits and their contents are important archaeological measures of continuity and change in slave life, but their specific function is debated. Data from Monticello has been central to that ongoing discussion. At Monticello, there is a decline over time in the number and size of these pits, until the latest quarters have no pits at all. Some have suggested that the pits served as a means of hiding West African–derived ancestral religious and ritual objects in resistance to slave owners and overseers. Others suggest they were root cellars, although perhaps also used to secret away food that was obtained by pilfering or other undercover means. An alternative interpretation sees the pits as a kind of storage place, not to hide objects, but to make access to them more difficult while keeping them in a space that was visible and protected by those who occupied the cabins.

Monticello is a National Historic Landmark and is open to the public. Tours of the main house and Mulberry Row are available year-round. A large museum displays objects from the archaeological studies and interpretation of the lives lived at Monticello.

POPLAR FOREST

Thomas Jefferson inherited the land that would later include the plantation called Poplar Forest from his father-in-law in 1773. Although occasionally using the property as a retreat from Monticello, over the next fifty years the plantation was occupied and worked primarily by slave labor brought to Poplar Forest from plantations across the region. The Poplar Forest economy under Jefferson's direction was diverse, with tobacco, wheat, and hemp all grown and processed there. Construction of Jefferson's design for his octagonal-shaped Poplar Forest home began in 1806.

Archaeology at Poplar Forest began in 1993. Much of the initial work focused on the reconstruction of landscape features. Three slave cabins were found and excavated, yielding over 20,000 artifacts and features including subfloor pits. Along with cooking and serving vessels were found food remains (domestic and wild), pipes, items of personal adornment (e.g., buckles, buttons, and jewelry), and the tools of the crafts worked for the plantation and within the household. The presence of these work-related tools, as well as weapons, ammunition, and locks and keys, lead to debate concerning the right to ownership of some property as well as the negotiation of some rights of privacy for the enslaved. Understanding that any such rights would be severely limited within the institution of slavery, the archaeological evidence at Poplar Forest offers new insight into the day-to-day lives of those who were enslaved there.

Poplar Forest is open to the public and offers tours from April through November. Visitors can observe excavations when in progress as well as the archaeology laboratory.

Further Reading: Archaeology at Poplar Forest Web site, http://www.poplarforest.org/arch.html; Heath, Barbara J., *Hidden Lives: The Archaeology of Slave Life at Thomas Jefferson's Poplar Forest* (Charlottesville: University Press of Virginia, 1999); Heath, Barbara J., "Buttons, Beads, and Buckles: Contextualizing Adornment Within the Bounds of Slavery," in *Historical Archaeology, Identity Formation, and the Interpretation of Ethnicity*, edited by Maria Franklin and Garrett Fesler, Colonial Williamsburg Research Publications (Richmond: Dietz Press, 1999), 47–70; Kelso, William M., *Archaeology at Monticello*, Monticello Monograph Series (Charlottesville: Thomas Jefferson Memorial Foundation, 1997); Kern, Susan, "The Material World of the Jeffersons at Shadwell," *William and Mary Quarterly* 62(2) (2005): 213–242; Monticello Archaeology Web site, http://www.monticello.org/archaeology/index.html; Neiman, Fraser D., "Changing Landscapes: Slave Housing at Monticello," *Scientific American Frontiers*, http://www.pbs.org/saf/a301/features/archaeology.htm.

Jeffrey L. Hantman

THE YORKTOWN SHIPWRECKS

Near the Mouth of Chesapeake Bay, Central Virginia
Revolutionary War Shipwrecks from the Battle of Yorktown

The Yorktown Wrecks National Register site consists of at least nine shipwrecks sunk during the battle of Yorktown (Virginia) in 1781. The Yorktown Wrecks were added to the National Register of Historic Places in 1973, one of the first underwater sites to be placed on the register and the first multiple-shipwreck site to be so recognized. The National Register designation was based primarily on historical documentation, along with limited information about artifacts recovered from shipwreck remains near Yorktown during the 1930s. Not until the 1970s was the area documented by archaeologists.

The Yorktown Wrecks are British vessels sunk during the successful American siege of Yorktown, Virginia, in October 1781. This battle proved to be the last major conflict of the American Revolution, leading to the creation of the United States of America. During the Yorktown Shipwreck Archaeological Project, 1978–1990, nine shipwrecks were located and mapped in the York River near Yorktown. One wreck, the British collier brig *Betsy*, was completely excavated from within a steel enclosure called a cofferdam. The Yorktown Victory Center, a local museum, contains a major exhibition on the Yorktown Wrecks, with a focus on the *Betsy*. The National Park Service's Yorktown National Battlefield Visitor Center also presents information on the naval aspects of the battle of Yorktown.

NAVAL ASPECTS OF THE BATTLE OF YORKTOWN, 1781

After years of conflict in North America and Europe, the American War of Independence had become a frustrating undertaking for the British. By 1781 an unsuccessful campaign in the Carolinas caused the British to revise their war strategy. Sir Henry Clinton, commander of all British forces in North America, ordered Major General Charles Earl Cornwallis to move his southern British Army to the Chesapeake Bay. Once there, Cornwallis was to establish a post that could be easily fortified and would provide an ice-free port for the British naval fleet for the winter of 1780–1781. Cornwallis's position would then be reinforced from New York, with the aim of launching a major offensive against the Chesapeake region the following spring. In late summer, Cornwallis's army occupied and fortified Yorktown, Virginia, on the York River. Cornwallis transported and supplied his army utilizing a fleet consisting of five small warships and approximately fifty transports, armed merchantmen, and other small craft.

Meanwhile, American and French forces, under the command of General George Washington, were anxious for a major victory against the British in order to garner continued war support at home and abroad. When Washington learned of Cornwallis's move to Yorktown, he developed a plan for entrapping and defeating the British there. First, Washington appealed to his French allies to send warships to the Chesapeake. He then moved his army south to Yorktown. In September, when a fleet of British warships attempted to enter the Chesapeake Bay to reinforce Cornwallis in Yorktown, it encountered a French fleet—the support previously requested by Washington. On September 5, the two fleets fought the battle of the Chesapeake Capes. There was no clear victor, but Admiral Thomas Graves, commanding the British fleet, elected to return to New York to refurbish and replenish his ships, leaving the Chesapeake Bay under French control. On October 9, combined American and French forces opened a siege on Cornwallis's position, burning and sinking several British ships including the forty-four–gun HMS *Charon*. Cornwallis soon realized that he was outnumbered and that an escape by sea was no longer possible. He scuttled many of his remaining ships and waited for British reinforcements. On October 19, with no relief in sight, the southern British Army surrendered, thus ending the last major conflict of the American Revolution. Although no detailed records of the ships' disposition have been found, twenty-six British vessels are unaccounted for and are presumed to remain on the bottom of the York River.

RESEARCH AND PROTECTION

A preliminary underwater archaeological survey at Yorktown in 1975 identified the remains of a large wooden shipwreck from which artifacts were being removed by recreational divers. News of this looting resulted in emergency passage of protective legislation by the Virginia General Assembly. A 1976 field school conducted by the Virginia Historic Landmarks Commission (now the Virginia Department of Historic Resources) and the Institute of Nautical Archaeology further documented the wreck discovered the previous year, concluding that it was a large merchant vessel carrying British war materials. Instead of continuing the excavation of the merchant vessel, the commission elected to survey the entire National Register area as a cultural landscape, based on the abundance of historical data suggesting that the area should contain widely dispersed cultural material. In 1978

the Landmarks Commission received a grant from the National Endowment for the Humanities to conduct a comprehensive survey of the entire site. The strategy proved successful. An archaeology team under the direction of John D. Broadwater discovered nine wrecks and concluded that all were British vessels sunk in 1781 during the battle of Yorktown. Cornwallis's largest warship, the HMS *Charon*, was located near Gloucester Point, along with another vessel from which an iron cannon was recovered. Seven wrecks lie near the Yorktown shoreline, six of them parallel to shore as if they were part of the "sinking line" depicted in contemporary maps. In addition, the remains of an eighteenth-century pier were discovered, along with other scattered remnants from the 1781 battle.

Following this successful survey, funds were obtained from public and private sources for the complete excavation of the best-preserved of the wrecks, known only by its site designation, 44YO88. In order to overcome the adverse diving conditions in the York River (poor visibility, strong currents, and stinging jellyfish), the project constructed a cofferdam—a steel enclosure that isolated the wreck site from the surrounding river—allowing the enclosed water to be filtered and clarified. Completed in 1982, the cofferdam proved to be an excellent means for improving research effectiveness on shallow sites, making this the first underwater excavation to take place within a cofferdam. Additionally, a pier connected the cofferdam to the nearby shore, making this one of the first underwater archaeological sites to be accessible to the public.

Shipwreck 44YO88 proved to be a relatively small wooden ship, approximately 23 meters in length at the waterline, with a distinctly box-like shape, typical of eighteenth-century British colliers (coal-carriers). Colliers were frequently leased as military transports because of their hull strength and excellent cargo capacity. The hull, approximately 50 percent intact, contained an interesting variety of naval and military items as well as furniture, furnishings, and personal possessions. Research eventually identified the vessel as the collier brig *Betsy*, built in Whitehaven, England, in 1772. Before being leased as a transport, *Betsy* had been hauling coal from Whitehaven to Dublin every few weeks. The painstaking documentation of the *Betsy* and its contents has shed new light on eighteenth-century merchant ship construction and interior furnishings. In addition, a careful analysis of the hull contents provided insight into the function the vessel served while under contract as a military transport.

Analysis of results from the Yorktown Project was cut short in 1990 by the abolishment of Virginia's underwater archaeology program during a state budget crisis. In spite of this setback, a report was developed privately by the former archaeological director and more than a dozen contributing researchers, with assistance from a grant from the National Endowment for the Humanities. The project revealed new information on eighteenth-century British merchant vessels; developed a detailed description and reconstruction of the *Betsy*, including hull lines and a sail plan; and demonstrated the significant relationships between Yorktown's physical setting and the archaeological evidence from the battle of Yorktown.

Further Reading: Broadwater, John D., "Shipwreck in a Swimming Pool: An Assessment of the Methodology and Technology Utilized on the Yorktown Shipwreck Archaeological Project," *Historical Archaeology* 26(4) (1992): 36–46; Broadwater, John D., "In the Shadow of Wooden Walls: Naval Transports During the American War of Independence," in *The Archaeology of Ships of War*, vol. 1 of *International Maritime Archaeology*, edited by Mensun Bound, Oxford University (Oswestry, Shropshire, England: Anthony Nelson Press, 1995), 58–63; Broadwater, John D., "From Collier to Troop Transport: The *Betsy*, Yorktown, Virginia," in *Beneath the Seven Seas*, edited by George F. Bass (London: Thames and Hudson), 206–210; Greene, Jerome A., *The Guns of Independence: The Siege of Yorktown, 1781* (New York: Savas Beatie, 2005); Sands, John O., *Yorktown's Captive Fleet* (Charlottesville: Published for the Mariners' Museum by the University Press of Virginia, 1983); Sands, John O., "Gunboats and Warships of the American Revolution," in *Ships and Shipwrecks of the Americas: A History Based on Underwater Archaeology*, edited by George F. Bass (London: Thames and Hudson, 1988), 143–168; Yorktown National Battlefield, National Park Service Web site, http://www.nps.gov/colo; Yorktown Victory Center Web site, http://www.historyisfun.org/Yorktown-Victory-Center.htm.

John D. Broadwater

THE ARCHAEOLOGY OF ALEXANDRIA

Alexandria, Virginia

Historic Period Archaeology of Urban Settlement and Trade

Alexandria was established as a port town on the Potomac River in 1749 and has been inextricably linked with major themes of American history since that time. The city founders selected a crescent bay as a safe haven for their wharves and ships. They superimposed a street grid over the landscape while building their homes on a bluff overlooking the bay. Tobacco and later wheat and other grains were produced by Africans and African Americans on large plantations and brought to Alexandria for export. The town became the major port in the region and grew by annexing land, as well as by filling in the bay through a process referred to as "banking out." Ship construction and repair, rope making, baking, and other businesses supported maritime commerce as the town bustled with life in taverns, potteries, breweries, and along the major retail artery, King Street.

Merchants, artisans, maritime workers, agricultural and commercial laborers, planters, and manufacturers interacted in a highly diverse urban community composed of immigrant and native-born peoples with multiple cultural traditions associated with England, Scotland, Ireland, Wales, and west Africa. In the first fifty years, Quakers, Episcopalians, Catholics, and Presbyterians built churches and started cemeteries, as Baptist and Methodist faiths attracted both black and white people in the early nineteenth century. German, Irish, and Jewish immigrants increased the diversity in mid-century. Alexandrians changed their spatial associations over the decades as elite homes and businesses shifted from proximity to the river and the market square in the first fifty years to King Street and Washington Street in the nineteenth century. Enslaved blacks lived within white households, while many free blacks lived independently in their own family homes, most of which formed neighborhoods fostered by white Baptists and Quakers.

The juxtaposition of privilege, commerce, enslavement, and resistance in Alexandria created a dynamic social environment in which freedom was a central issue. Planters such as George Washington and George Mason discussed the rights of the colonies and individuals before the American Revolution, while some enslaved blacks took action to gain liberty by running away from servitude, purchasing their own freedom and suing for manumission. Newly freed blacks established vibrant neighborhoods and churches while most blacks remained legally enslaved. Blacks continued to live with restrictive laws in Virginia, the state whose citizens spawned the earliest code of individual rights in the colonial period.

Originally honored to be included in the new District of Columbia after the Revolution, Alexandrians chafed under the lack of independence while tolerating large slave-trading businesses that robbed others of freedom. Alexandria broke free of Washington, D.C., by building the Alexandria Canal and retroceding to Virginia in the 1840s. Residents lost rights while suffering a four-year occupation by U.S. troops during the Civil War, yet more than 8,000 freedmen gained their liberty by seeking refuge from slavery in Alexandria. Thousands of freedom-seekers died from disease, malnutrition, and lack of shelter while tens of thousands of Union troops lived, recuperated, and died in forts, hospitals, and other Union installations. After the war, black Alexandrians built more neighborhoods and churches, lived under Jim Crow segregation, and staged early civil rights protests. Large factories and processing plants occupied the old town, while new twentieth-century streetcar suburbs formed as railroads eclipsed water transportation.

Alexandria's history and archaeology provide an ongoing case study of urban American transformation. The city of Alexandria has been engaged in archaeology since 1961 due to citizen interest in preservation and knowledge. City government, residents, developers, volunteers, and students have worked in partnership to study, preserve, and interpret the archaeological resources of the city that extend back nearly 10,000 years. The Smithsonian Institution conducted rescue archaeology from 1965 to 1973 on King Street urban renewal blocks, and the city began its own archaeology program in 1975. The Alexandria Archaeology Protection Code, enacted in 1989, requires developers to conduct archaeological investigations when significant resources are threatened by new construction. The code has led to the expansion of the city's history associated with American Indian, plantation, urban residential, cemetery, Civil War, maritime, black, and industrial sites.

The Alexandria Archaeology Museum (105 North Union Street) in the Torpedo Factory Art Center can be visited six days a week to view exhibits, do hands-on activities, talk to the city archaeologists and volunteers, and see artifacts processed in the public laboratory. An annual calendar of events includes walking tours, open houses at site excavations, lectures, and other public programs. Archaeology Adventure Lessons are available to groups (http://www.AlexandriaArchaeology.org).

The city archaeologists study places and artifacts as parts of a wider Alexandria city-site composed of layers of time, each with intertwined activities and cultures. The public can experience this city-site by walking or biking the 23-mile Alexandria Heritage Trail that joins 110 archaeological and historic places and is a segment of the Potomac Heritage National Scenic Trail. A trail brochure is available, as well as a guidebook. Many trail places are open to the public; some have interpretive signs.

CARLYLE-DALTON WHARF SITE
Two of the town's founders, John Carlyle and John Dalton, built one of the earliest wharves in 1759. The city archaeologists discovered the timber crib structure that extended from the base of the bluffs in the center of the crescent bay through muddy flats to deeper water. The cribbing was handmade from huge, yellow pine trees and filled with rocks and earth, probably obtained from grading the bluffs along the streets to give better access to the town. The merchants'

homes on the bluff overlooked the wharf, where they carried on prosperous trade with England, Portugal, and the Caribbean. In the 1780s, this wharf was encapsulated into a new city block; the entire crescent bay was filled by the early 1790s. The wharf is protected today under Cameron Street. The Carlyle House (212 North Fairfax Street) is open to the public and provides a look at mid-eighteenth-century Alexandria elite and enslaved black life.

KEITH'S WHARF SITE
In the 1780s, three merchants joined to build a large wharf at the south end of the expanded town. They also created Franklin Street, the widest road in town, to attract export businesses. Archaeologists found a rich heritage buried beneath an old Ford building and asphalt. A cofferdam allowed the study of the wharf, the hulls of nine vessels, and the Alexandria Marine Railway, a 400-foot-long shipway where a 1,500-ton four-mast schooner was launched in 1883. The resources still exist under the present development, built upon pilings. Several interpretive signs are on the waterfront.

ALEXANDRIA CANAL TIDE LOCK SITE AND PARK
In the 1840s, local merchants raised funds to build a canal from the terminus of the Chesapeake and Ohio Canal in Georgetown to north Alexandria. They intended to restore the town's prosperity after thirty years of declining trade. Completed in 1846, this lock was one of four that lowered and raised canal boats 38 feet from Washington Street to sea level on the Potomac River. The Alexandria Canal revived the town and operated until 1886, with the exception of the Civil War period. Archaeologists excavated and drained the lock, allowing recordation of the stone walls, wooden gates, and metal strap hinges. Since it was not practical to conserve the wooden gates and flooring with continual exposure to the elements, the tide lock was filled with gravel, allowing river water to continue maintaining a stable environment. The tide lock is protected under a shallow reconstruction, the center of a waterfront park with interpretive sign.

500 KING STREET, COURTHOUSE SITE
Before construction of the new city courthouse, excavations yielded more than 2,000,000 artifacts from brick-lined shafts that were used as wells, privies, and trash dumps. The ceramics show the changing tastes of the American middle class and increased mass production, and the use of local business names on bottles and stoneware document the rise of competitive retail sales. A large, brick shaft lined with plaster shows Quaker Robert H. Miller's concern in the 1830s for clean water, given knowledge that waterborne diseases frequently shortened lives. The Miller cistern included a filtration box with twenty-six layers of

materials with decreasing sizes, of gravel, sand, and eventually charcoal. All eleven of the Miller children survived when infant mortality rates were very high. The Lyceum, Alexandria's History Museum (201 South Washington Street) and Barrett Library (717 Queen Street) have information about the town's Quaker community. The library is also the site of the Quaker Burial Ground and extensive archaeological preservation efforts. Artifacts from several King Street sites are at the Alexandria Archaeology Museum. Additional Quaker interpretation is at another archaeological site, the Stabler Leadbeater Apothecary Museum (105–107 South Fairfax Street).

ARELL'S, McKNIGHT'S, AND GADSBY'S TAVERN SITES

Taverns were places for travelers to stay as well as local gathering places hosting itinerant entertainers, political conversations, and balls. Studies of changing designs on drinking vessels from archaeological deposits show shifting loyalties from King George's monogram to the American eagle. Archaeological investigations also show that taverns catered to different clientele. Arell's was a place of good times, where people drank beer, ale, and hard cider from common redware tankards and passed around two-handled posset pots to share a hot drink of spiced milk curdled with wine. They also enjoyed eggs, salad, and fruit. English and Chinese teapots, coffee cups, and teacups document that Alexandrians met at McKnight's to discuss business and politics as in a European coffee house. Gadsby's fine wares confirm its impressive reputation as a tavern that entertained presidents. Gadsby's Tavern Museum (134 North Royal Street) is open to the public. At the corner of North Royal and Cameron streets, visitors can see inside a large ice well that kept foodstuffs cold for use at Gadsby's.

HENRY PIERCY, TILDEN EASTON, AND WILKES STREET POTTERY SITES

Alexandria's potters made utilitarian wares for almost ninety years. Their wares are known from excavations at the potteries, a waster pile, and a retail shop. Piercy, a redware potter from a German tradition settled in town as a disabled veteran of the Revolutionary War. His distinctive wares with slip trailing were made from 1792 to 1809 with local clays, which have a different chemical composition than similar Philadelphia pottery. Excavation of Tildon Easton's kiln (1841–1843) provided the only clues to this previously unknown potter. Three successive individuals operated the major stoneware pottery business on Wilkes Street (1813–1877); they left their names (Milburn, Smith, and Miller) on their wares, which are also identifiable by distinctive forms and blue cobalt designs. Free blacks worked at the Wilkes Street site; at least one was an accomplished potter. Visit the Alexandria Archaeology Museum to see wares from all these sites.

JAMIESON BAKERY SITE

Although a photograph survives of Jamieson's nineteenth-century bakery, it has generally been forgotten how many baking businesses once made sea biscuits or ship's bread for sailors. Sixty-three bakeries advertised in the newspaper over a forty-year period. Archaeology at the Lee Street site discovered four ovens, the firebox, and a brick cistern and filter that probably served as a source of water for the crackers, or may have been used for the steam engine installed by 1850. An iron pipe ran on the floor of the bakery basement between the firebox and steam engine. This modernization maintained Jamieson's competitive edge as the fifth largest business in town. Exhibit and publication are available at the Alexandria Archaeology Museum.

MOORE-McLEAN SUGAR HOUSE SITE

Alexandria was one of the largest producers of refined sugar in America during the first two decades of the nineteenth century. William Moore and, later, Daniel McLean operated the sugar house on North Alfred Street from 1803 until 1828 with the labor of seven African Americans—five men and two boys. Excavation of this site and associated historical research yielded knowledge about Alexandria's role as a producer and exporter of sugar. Study of the archaeological remains revealed much about the nineteenth-century sugar-refining process. Muscavado sugar imported from Cuba was boiled with added ingredients and poured into redware sugar cone molds that were then placed into jars. As the cones dried, the brown impurities drained through the hole in the cone's tip into the jar, leaving a white, hard sugar that was then unmolded and wrapped in paper for sales and shipment. Artifacts are in the Alexandria Archaeology Museum, and a marker is at the site. The African American aspects of the site can be seen at the Alexandria Black History Museum (902 Wythe Street).

ENGLEHARDT BREWERY AND VIRGINIA GLASS COMPANY SITES

Just outside the boundary of eighteenth-century Alexandria, the West family created the first suburb, which was called West End. Situated on a major turnpike, West End attracted businesses that depended upon road transportation and processed products: cattle butchers, coach makers, tanners, saddlers, slave traders, a brewer, and a hotel and beer parlor. By the turn of the twentieth century, a glass factory and wholesale floral business operated in West End. Many of the residents were German, including Henry Englehardt. Excavation at the Englehardt Brewery (1858–1893) resulted in a surprise discovery—a 60-foot-long brick vault that was under the turnpike, now called Duke Street, where the lager beer was kept cold. Also found at the site was the foundation of the German beer parlor, with many beer steins, plates, and stoneware bottles. The pedestrian concourse from the King Street Metro Station under Duke Street to the federal courthouse echoes the beer vault, still preserved just a few feet away. Just a block to the east, the Virginia Glass Company (1894–1916) underground ruins have survived for ninety years. Investigations documented an industrial complex developed by seven German glassmakers, with buildings, furnaces, oven, chimney, airshafts, and thousands of glass artifacts produced for the Robert Portner Brewing Company. Alexandria became a regional center of bottle making with hundreds of men, women, and children working in four factories around the clock before World War I. Factory fires and prohibition brought the end of the town's glass production. The new John Carlyle Park protects and interprets the glass site.

BLACK ALEXANDRIA HISTORIC SITES OF ENSLAVEMENT

Until the Civil War, most of the town's black population was enslaved. Yet a large free black population started as early as 1790. A vast amount of documentary and archaeological information exists on African Americans in Alexandria; however, it is far more difficult to identify sites of enslavement. Only occasionally did blacks without freedom live as heads of their own households, instead of the more common pattern of living within the house or business of the legal owner. Three sites have been excavated. Franklin and Armfield Slave Pen at 1315 Duke Street was the setting from 1828 until 1861 of the shipment of blacks from the surrounding countryside to New Orleans and Natchez. The building still stands and includes a museum. Shuter's Hill Plantation stands on a hill overlooking historic Alexandria. Excavations at the laundry have uncovered the base of the structure, fireplace, paved work area, and thousands of artifacts associated with work and domestic life. One of the residents may have been Esther, later sold to a merchant who fathered her four children. An exhibit can be viewed at the George Washington Masonic Memorial (101 Callahan Drive). The Harriet Williams site provides the only glimpse into a separate household of an enslaved Alexandrian. The artifacts reveal her dependence upon her owner, who lived only two doors away. The Williams household had many large serving pieces—pitchers, bowls, and platters—yet, few if any kitchen wares. Harriet Williams may have cooked the food for both households in the Lindsay kitchen and carried some on the serving pieces to her home. Ink bottles and a child's plate and cup with slogans encouraging hard work show an effort to move beyond the limits of slavery to independence.

FREE BLACK SITES

Esther, enslaved at Shuter's Hill (described earlier) came to live in the neighborhood of Hayti when her sister, Harriet Jackson, purchased and manumitted her and the children. Free blacks moved into Hayti by 1810, when a Quaker started renting to several families. Excavations at two households found house and stable remains, as well as thousands of artifacts of everyday life—fragments of teapots and cups, plates and bowls, stoneware kitchen wares, and tools. A large number of buttons are probably testimony to the women's work doing laundry. The artifacts are indicative of these families' independence—they represent all facets of living. Although free blacks used similar kitchen and dining wares as whites, the dishes did not come from matching sets and were older, perhaps used longer or obtained as previously owned. Rather than spending money on optional items, free blacks invested their capital in buying their own and others' freedom, building homes, and establishing churches. Some of the Hayti homes can still be seen on the 400 block of South Royal Street. The public can visit the Alexandria Black History Museum and Alexandria African American Heritage Park (Holland Lane), the scene of an excavation to protect the Silver Leaf Society's Black Baptist Cemetery.

ALEXANDRIA FREEDMEN'S CEMETERY

During the Civil War, more than 8,000 African Americans fled slavery by entering into Union-occupied Alexandria. These freedmen faced harsh living conditions with little shelter, food, and medical treatment. Many died, and in 1864 the federal government established a burying place at South Washington and Church streets. By the time the government stopped burying destitute blacks in 1869, about 1,800 people—more than half children—were interred here. Archaeological work has identified rows of graves that are still extant, even though two buildings, grading, and a highway cut into the abandoned cemetery. Additional archaeological investigation will locate and protect the remaining graves while the city of Alexandria constructs a memorial park to honor the freedmen.

CIVIL WAR ALEXANDRIA: FORT WARD SITE AND MUSEUM

First constructed by Union troops after the Battle of Bull Run as one of 161 forts defending Washington, D.C., the fort was expanded in 1864. Almost 100 years later, the city sponsored the first archaeological excavation in Alexandria here. More than 90 percent of the site was saved from destruction, and a park was created. The city reconstructed the northwest bastion based upon the investigation, which showed additional features not mentioned in the historical documents. Visit the museum and site at 4301 Braddock Road.

Further Reading: Alexandria Archaeology Web site, http://www. AlexandriaArchaeology.org; Alexandria Archaeology Museum, *A Community Digs Its Past: The Lee Street Site*, (City of Alexandria, VA: 1999); Alexandria Convention and Visitors Association, *A Remarkable and Courageous Journey. A Guide to Alexandria's African American History* (2003); Bromberg, Francine W., and Steven J. Shephard, "The Quaker Burying Ground in Alexandria, Virginia:

A Study of Burial Practices of the Religious Society of Friends," *Historical Archaeology* 40(1) (2006): 57–88; Cressey, Pamela J., *To Witness the Past: African American Archaeology in Alexandria* (City of Alexandria, VA: 1993); Cressey, Pamela J., *Walk and Bike the Alexandria Heritage Trail* (Sterling, VA: Capital Books, 2002); Cressey, Pamela J., Ruth Reeder, and Jared Bryson, "Held in Trust: Community Archaeology in Alexandria, Virginia," in *Archaeologists and Local Communities: Partners in Exploring the Past*, edited by

Linda Derry and Maureen Malloy (Washington, DC: Society for American Archaeology, 2003), 1–18; Hahn, Thomas S., and Emory L Kemp, *The Alexandria Canal: Its History & Preservation* (Morgantown: West Virginia University Press, 1992); Magid, Barbara H., and Bernard K. Means, "In the Philadelphia Style: The Pottery of Henry Piercy," in *Ceramics in America 2003*, edited by Robert Hunter (Milwaukee, WI: Chipstone Foundation, 2003), 47–86.

Pamela J. Cressey

LOWELL NATIONAL HISTORICAL PARK

Lowell, Massachusetts

The Archaeology of Nineteenth-Century Industry and Workers

When the Industrial Revolution came to New England in the late eighteenth century, it started modestly in small villages established along the tributaries of the Blackstone River in Rhode Island and Massachusetts. These small mill villages were the "American" answer to the urban industrial centers of Britain that were looked upon with such moral disdain because of the specters of child labor and worker exploitation. Despite the strong agricultural lobby in Washington and the national preoccupation with "agrarian values," large-scale urban industry did eventually come in the form of the planned industrial cities such as Lowell, Massachusetts. Established at the confluence of the Merrimack and Concord Rivers in northern Massachusetts, Lowell was viewed as one of the wonders of the age. In response to those who viewed urban industry as a drain on the agrarian labor force, and in particular young men, Lowell's founders devised the ingenious idea of using female workers. Combined with a philosophy of corporate paternalism, Lowell's reliance on female labor would prove to be a winning combination that contributed to the growth of a city of more than 40,000.

Over the past twenty years archaeologists have worked to reveal the daily life of Lowell's many classes of workers. Much of this work has focused on the workers who represented the majority of the mill labor force, but attention has also been given to distinct classes of workers including skill laborers and their families, overseers, and company agents. Archaeologists have also concentrated their efforts on unearthing evidence of the technological changes that accompanied Lowell's growth as a center of innovation in both industry and business (Gordon and Malone 1994; Mrozowski 2000). Starting with the work of Robert Schulyer, who concentrated on the housing blocks of the Merrimack Company (1974, 1976), and continuing with the large-scale investigations of the Boott Cotton Mills (Beaudry and Mrozowski 1987a, 1989, 2001;

Mrozowski et al. 1996), the Massachusetts Mills Agent's House (Beaudry and Mrozowski 1987b), and the Lawrence Manufacturing Company Overseers' block (Mrozowski 2000, 2006), the archaeology of Lowell has explored the growth of working-class and middle-class cultural consciousness, the changing face of capitalism, and its spatial and biological expressions.

CLASS CONSCIOUSNESS
Much of the archaeological research in Lowell has concentrated on recovering evidence of both working-class and middle-class cultural consciousness. In his early work in Lowell, Robert Schuyler sought to recover the archaeological deposits located in the yards of the workers' housing at the Merrimack Manufacturing Company. Schulyer was successful in recovering what he considered to be primary deposits dating to some of the earliest periods of Lowell's history (ca. 1830–50). The results of much of the work Schuyler carried out in Lowell has not been extensively reported upon (Schuyler 1974, 1976), however his work pointed to Lowell's potential as an archaeological laboratory for examining American urban industry and the class-based society it helped to create.

Larger-scale investigations were conducted in the 1980s and 1990s at the Boott Cotton Mills Boarding Houses, the Massachusetts Mills Agent's House, and the Lawrence Manufacturing Company's Overseers' Block. Between these three sites, archaeologists have been able to compare artifact assemblages from four different classes of Lowell's workers. At the Boott Mill Boarding House residential units for both unmarried mill common workers, often primarily women, and skilled workers, almost exclusively men, and their families presented an interesting point of contrast. By comparing the results from the Boott Mills with those from excavations carried out in the Massachusetts Mill agent's yard and those from several overseers' units at the Lawrence Manufacturing Company, it was possible to examine the material expressions of class in some detail.

The overall conclusion drawn from these comparisons is that although differences between the various households were evident, there was also evidence of common behaviors. This was particularly true of alcohol consumption. Despite the rhetoric of the temperance movement, a cultural battle with strong class connotations, evidence of heavy alcohol use was found at all of the households. Evidence of liquor bottles being secreted in the privy of the skilled laborers unit at the Boott Mills also points to just one method that allowed workers to overcome the strictures against drinking maintained by Lowell's various companies.

Other evidence of class lines being blurred came from faunal and material culture analyses. These results suggest a reliance on similar cuts of meat among all of the households investigated, but differences existed in the presentation of food. The latter came in the form of the more extensive use of more expensive transfer-printed pearlwares and whitewares at both the agent's house and overseers' blocks as compared to common undecorated white wares at the Boott boarding houses.

Class differences were most evident in the biological evidence from the various households. Evidence of rodent infestations like those found at the boarding houses was not found at either the agent's house or the overseers' block. And despite calls from Lowell's board of health for the companies to end the use of privies in the 1880s, they were still in use at the boarding houses almost forty years later. Archaeological evidence of an extensive new drainage system dating to the 1880s was found at the overseers' block, whereas evidence from the boarding houses confirms that privies were in use until 1918, when the influenza pandemic killed millions across the earth. Apparently the pandemic got the attention of the companies.

THE ARCHAEOLOGY OF URBAN SPACE

One of the most fascinating aspects of the archaeological research carried out in Lowell focused on the manner in which space was apportioned by the various companies along class lines. Mill operatives and skilled workers, for example, were provided housing that had only rear yards. Archaeological investigations of those yards found pollen and plant macrofossil evidence that indicates that they were maintained well into the nineteenth century. The housing blocks supplied by the Lawrence Company for its overseers included rear yards and small front yards. Archaeological investigations of the front yards indicate that they served primarily as ornamental spaces. The same was true of the Massachusetts and Boott Mills duplex that served as home to the agents for each company. Here archaeological and environmental evidence points to both front and side yards that only served as ornamental space,

while evidence from the rear yard suggests they were used for activities that included the slaughtering of animals. Soils analysis from various households also found evidence that lead poisoning would have been a peril for the young children who lived in the boarding houses and overseers' block but not the agent's dwelling, pointing to another biological measure of class differences.

The interdisciplinary character of the archaeological investigations carried out in Lowell points to the many ways in which class differences and commonalities can be explored. Whether through the use of biological evidence to explore class differences or material culture analysis to examine contrasting or commonly shared class sensibilities, the archaeological analyses of this early industrial center point to the multifaceted character of class formation and expression.

Further Reading: Beaudry, Mary C., and Stephen A. Mrozowski, eds., *Interdisciplinary Investigations of the Boott Mills, Lowell, Massachusetts, Vol. I: Life at the Boardinghouses*, Cultural Resources Management Study No. 18, Division of Cultural Resources (Boston: North Atlantic Regional Office, National Park Service, United States Department of the Interior, 1987a); Beaudry, Mary C., and Stephen A. Mrozowski, eds., *Interdisciplinary Investigations of the Boott Mills, Lowell, Massachusetts, Vol. II: The Kirk Street Agent's House*, Cultural Resources Management Study No. 19, Division of Cultural Resources (Boston: North Atlantic Regional Office, National Park Service, United States Department of the Interior, 1987b); Beaudry, Mary C., and Stephen A. Mrozowski, eds., *Interdisciplinary Investigations of the Boott Mills, Lowell, Massachusetts, Vol. III: The Boardinghouses System as a Way of Life*, Cultural Resources Management Study No. 21, Division of Cultural Resources (Boston: North Atlantic Regional Office, National Park Service, United States Department of the Interior, 1989); Beaudry, Mary C., and Stephen A. Mrozowski, "Cultural Space and Work Identity in the Company City: Nineteenth Century Lowell, Massachusetts," in *The Archaeology of Urban Landscapes: Explorations in Slumland*, edited by Alan Mayne and Tim Murray (Cambridge, UK: Cambridge University Press, 2001), 118–131; Gordon, Robert B., and Patrick M. Malone, *The Texture of Industry: An Archaeological View of the Industrialization of North America* (New York: Oxford University Press, 1994); Mrozowski, Stephen A., "The Growth of Managerial Capitalism and the Subtleties of Class Analysis in Historical Archaeology," in *Lines That Divide: Historical Archaeologies of Race, Class, and Gender*, edited by James A. Delle, Stephen A. Mrozowski, and Robert Paynter (Knoxville: University of Tennessee Press, 2000), 276–305; Mrozowski, Stephen A., *The Archaeology of Class in Urban America* (Cambridge, UK: Cambridge University Press, 2006); Mrozowski, Stephen A., Grace H. Zeising, and Mary C. Beaudry, *Living on the Boott Historical Archaeology at the Boott Mills Boardinghouses, Lowell, Massachusetts* (Amherst: University of Massachusetts Press, 1996); Schuyler, Robert L., "Lowellellian Archaeology," *Society for Industrial Archaeology Newsletter*, supplementary issue no. 7 (1974): 3–4; Schuyler, Robert L., "Merrimack Valley Project: 2nd Year," *Society for Industrial Archaeology Newsletter*, supplementary issue no. 8 (1976): 7–8.

Stephen A. Mrozowski

SALEM MARITIME NATIONAL HISTORIC SITE

Salem, Massachusetts

The Archaeology of Late-Eighteenth- and Early-Nineteenth-Century Commerce and Trade

The site of Salem was known as Naumkeag to Native Americans, meaning "the fishing place." Trade in fish and other products of the sea were to contribute to the rise of Salem as one of New England's most important colonial and post-colonial seaports. Salem participated in a complex web of sea-trade patterns that involved the export of fish, livestock, wood products, and rum to markets in the West Indies and Europe, the movement of slaves from Africa to the New World, and British manufactured goods from Europe to New England. Generations of families such as the Derbys and Crowninshields helped to establish some of these trade routes and, in so doing, their own family fortunes. The story of Salem's national importance in trade is told at Salem Maritime National Historic Site, a 9-acre park established in 1938 that includes eighteenth- and nineteenth-century wharves; a variety of historic structures, such as the 1675 Narbonne House, the 1762 Derby House, the 1780 Hawkes House, the 1819 Custom House and Public Stores, the 1909 St. Joseph Hall, the replica vessel *Friendship*; and archaeological sites associated with many of these. Archeology tells us about the shifting importance of consumer goods to families of average means at the Narbonne House, and tells us about the different systems of wharf construction at both Derby Wharf and Central Wharf.

THE NARBONNE HOUSE

The Narbonne House is a rare survival of a modest, two-story seventeenth-century house and lot close to the Salem waterfront. Archeological investigations conducted in the long, narrow yard to the rear of the house revealed dense archaeological deposits that document the changing material lifestyle of Salem's tradespeople during the transition of Massachusetts from colony to commonwealth.

The Narbonne House was built in 1675 by Thomas Ives, a "slaughterer." The original house plan consisted of a one-room, end-chimney structure with two stories and a steeply pitched roof situated directly on Essex Street. The house remained static architecturally for nearly a century during which time it was occupied by Deacon Simon Williard and several boarders. Between 1750 and 1780 the house belonged to Captain Joseph Hodges, who did not occupy the structure but improved it with a gambrel-roofed addition. In 1780 Hodges sold the house to the tanner, Jonathan Andrews. Upon his death the following year, Andrews left the house to his family, including his widow, Mary Andrews, herself the

daughter of a wealthy Salem merchant. Mary occupied the modest house until her death in 1820.

Archaeological testing in the Narbonne House yard conducted by the National Park Service in 1973 revealed a service yard containing a well and possible dairy in addition to a cobble-paved driveway. However, the most astonishing discovery consisted of an abandoned privy pit and a trash pit filled with ceramics and other household items dating to the period of the Andrews' occupation. The privy alone contained more than 10,000 artifacts, many of them local ceramics but also an astonishing array of English wares. These included Leeds-type molded creamwares dating between 1765 and 1780, shiny black lead-glazed Jackfield-type wares dating between 1740 and 1780, and banded or annular pearlware. There were five teapots in these pottery types in addition to "rosso antico" and "black basalt" stoneware.

The point has been made by archaeologist Geoffrey Moran that the American passion for English ceramics was as strong after the Revolutionary War as before. Since the excavation of the Narbonne site from 1973 to 1975, a large number of early-nineteenth-century pottery and glass dump sites have been discovered in other New England seaports, including Portsmouth, New Hampshire. It is possible that these dumps signal transitional phases in households as would result from tenants moving or even the death of an individual. Another theory proposes that British ceramic manufacturers unloaded an enormous stockpile of inexpensive ceramic tablewares on the American market at the conclusion of the War of 1812. This might have allowed Mary Andrews to discard her outmoded eighteenth-century ceramics and replace them with more stylish wares at modest cost.

DERBY WHARF

Derby Wharf is a restored stone-faced wharf that extends almost 2,100 feet into Salem Harbor in front of the Custom House. It represents an outstanding feat of marine engineering undertaken by the Derbys, the town's most prominent merchant family. The core of the wharf was built by Richard Derby in 1762 and lengthened in 1806. By 1812, fifteen warehouses were situated along the entire length of the wharf. Such a wharf allowed ships to off-load cargo directly onto the wharf instead of using an earlier, more labor-intensive method of off-loading cargo onto

View of the rear of the Narbonne House and yard in Salem.   [Steven R. Pendery]

lighters and barges from ships at anchor in deep water. Recent archeological investigations and earlier repairs have revealed the details of Derby Wharf construction.

The original timber bulkhead system involved construction using horizontal members and vertical supports or piles. Tie-backs were used, which consisted of horizontal timbers locked into the vertical wharf face to maintain its position as the structure was backfilled with clay, stone, and sand fill. Constant contact with moisture preserved the wooden wharf components, which typically consisted of Eastern white pine and spruce. This differs from crib wharves that consisted of wooden cribs constructed elsewhere and floated into place. Because the docking side of any wharf must periodically be dredged of silt that tends to accumulate in this type of environment, archaeological evidence for cargo may not be plentiful. However, the fill contained within the wharves may yield well-preserved archaeological evidence from the period of wharf construction.

The Derby family was involved in trade with the southern colonies, the West Indies, Russia, India, and China. New England goods included furniture and other wood products, livestock, and rum, which were traded for a vast array of luxury items that made Salem one of the wealthiest ports in the new republic. Jefferson's Embargo of 1807 and the War of 1812 brought trade to a halt and prompted transfer of New England capital to support domestic manufacturing. For much of the nineteenth century the wharf serviced bulk cargoes and finally fell into decline in the twentieth century.

CENTRAL WHARF

Central Wharf lies due west of Derby Wharf on the Salem waterfront. The 800-foot-long wharf evolved under the ownership of different individuals, including Simon Forrester, John Bertram, Michael Shepard, and Augustus Brooks. It appears to vary in construction type from Derby Wharf and includes cob crib components. Similar to Derby Wharf, it served as the foundation for several nineteenth-century warehouse structures. Archaeological testing has not been as extensive as has been conducted at Derby Wharf, and several questions about its evolution remain to be answered.

View of Derby Wharf and the *Friendship* from Central Wharf.   [Steven R. Pendery]

Further Reading: Moran, Geoffrey P., "Trash Pits and Natural Rights in the Revolutionary Era," *Archaeology*, 29(3) (1976): 194–202; Moran, Geoffrey P., Edward F. Zimmer, and Anne E. Yentsch, *Archeological Investigations at the Narbonne House, Salem Maritime National Historic Site*, Cultural Resource Management Study No. 6 (Boston: Division of Cultural Resources, North Atlantic Regional Office, National Park Service, 1982); National Park Service, *Salem: Maritime Salem in the Age of Sail*, Handbook 126, (Washington, DC: National Park Service, U.S. Department of the Interior, 2002); Salem Maritime National Historic Site, National Park Service Web site, http://www.nps.gov/sama/ (online October 2006).

Steven R. Pendery

HARPERS FERRY NATIONAL HISTORIC PARK

Harpers Ferry, West Virginia

The Archaeology of Early American Manufacturing

INTRODUCTION

Industrial development at Harpers Ferry, West Virginia, began in 1794 when the United States Congress decided to establish armories for the manufacture and storage of arms. Harpers Ferry has a long and complex history where labor struggled with capital, and corruption derailed mass manufacturing. Although government officials often declared the facility as inefficient and a drain on federal resources, Harpers Ferry is the place where interchangeable parts were first perfected. This process became known as the "American

Manufacturing System" throughout the world, and other industries rushed to imitate the practice. Although industrial development in Harpers Ferry proceeded in a turbulent atmosphere, it also impacted the daily life of the community. Most of Harpers Ferry is now part of a national historical park, and the history and archaeology provide a complex picture of industrial life in a manufacturing town.

HARPERS FERRY: A PLACE IN TIME
During the 1790s the United States found itself in a precarious situation with unfriendly neighbors. Spain claimed Florida and the Louisiana Territory, and England controlled the entire northern border with its Canadian possession. In 1794 England and the United States signed a treaty of peace, although France claimed that it violated the Franco-American alliance of 1778. Tensions grew between France and the United States, and Congress prepared for new hostilities. Because the U.S. government obtained its weapons from France, and in anticipation of imminent hostilities, President Washington supported the construction of two U.S.-funded armories, one in Harpers Ferry and the other in Springfield, Massachusetts. Construction of the Harpers Ferry armory began in 1799, and armorers produced the first guns by 1801.

Skilled craftsmen characterized production at the armory during the first several decades of the facilities' operations. This task-oriented production entailed a high degree of manual skill and knowledge on the part of the armory worker. The armorers believed that their task consisted of making the complete gun—lock, stock, and barrel—and they perceived the introduction of labor-saving machinery as a threat to their way of life.

The factories developed in a rather haphazard fashion with little attention to the ideals of mass production. Both management and armory workers resisted any forms of a division of labor. However, the U.S. government contracted with John Hall, an inventor and manufacturer from Maine, to establish workshops and develop a breech-loading rifle composed of interchangeable parts. Hall's manufacturing ideas endangered what remained of craft production and threatened to change armory workers from skilled craftsmen to wage laborers who tended machines. Despite several setbacks, an 1826 inspection report of Hall's rifles described that he had successfully completed the first fully interchangeable weapon ever made in the United States. The manufacturing was completed with unskilled labor. Hall's innovations revolutionized industry on a global scale to the point where manufacturing with interchangeable parts became known as the "American Manufacturing System."

While Hall perfected interchangeable parts, many armory workers resisted changes in their work practices. Thomas Dunn's appointment in 1829 as superintendent pleased most members of the Ordnance Department. The manufacturing community believed that he could establish a work discipline at the facility. Dunn enforced a number of rules, such as forbidding loitering, gambling, and consuming alcoholic beverages on armory premises. He also held armory workers personally responsible for the damage or destruction of tools.

Unaccustomed to these new regulations, armorers protested by harassing Dunn outside of the armory gates. On January 30, 1830, a released worker named Ebenezer Cox approached the superintendent's office and shot and killed Dunn at point-blank range. Although executed for his crime, Cox became a folk hero among the armorers. Whenever subsequent managers tried to impose factory discipline, Cox's name was always mentioned to the armory officials.

While Harpers Ferry developed, Virginius Island developed as a small industrial community adjacent to the federal town. The community began as a small industrial complex with over a dozen small crafts and industries owned by various individuals. Owners and craftsmen placed their small industries at strategic points on the landscape to access the waterpower available from the adjacent Shenandoah River. They did not follow an overall systematic development plan, and one local newspaper described the industrial complex as a "little Pittsburgh."

By the 1850s one person, Abraham Herr, owned most of the Virginius Island, and unlike the previous owners, he subscribed to the model of paternalistic oversight. Controlling workers' living space by standardizing the built environment appears to have been part of Herr's ideal for an industrial community. Herr constructed a row house for his workers that consisted of a standardized façade, much like the row houses found in northeastern industrial communities, such as Lowell, Massachusetts, and Manchester, New Hampshire. Herr built his family's dwelling on the other side of the railroad tracks from his mill and the workers' housing, keeping both places within close eyesight.

While Herr developed private industry on Virginius Island, the armory underwent major revisions in its layout and labor system. In 1841 a military superintendent replaced the civilian management system and proceeded to enforce a more intricate division of labor. A clock was installed in the armory, and all workers were forced to labor to standardized time. Rules and regulations reinforced factory discipline found at many of the middle Atlantic and New England industrial enterprises. In order to easily accommodate the change in work habits, it was necessary to change the work environment. Most of the armory buildings were unsuited for the implementation of a division of labor, because they lacked architectural and functional unity. The Harpers Ferry facilities contrasted sharply with the orderly layout of other factory systems.

Therefore, in 1844 Superintendent Major John Symington, an engineer, redesigned the town by imposing a grid system over the existing town plan. Armory workers protested the introduction of new time-saving machinery and the implementation of wage labor. The armorers went on strike, rented a canal boat, and marched to U.S. President John Tyler. The president explained that he was sympathetic to the worker's cause but told them that they must "hammer out their own salvation."

The new armory buildings were of a unified Gothic architectural style, and they contrasted sharply with the almost randomly placed earlier armory buildings. Work spaces were reorganized to create a more efficient and compliant workforce. Because of John Hall and many others, interchangeable manufacturing was well under way, and armorers who once considered themselves craftsmen now tended machines, following the rhythmic motions dictated by industry.

In 1854, because of local political pressure, Congress ordered the removal of the military system, and a civilian armorer, Henry Clowe, became the next superintendent. Armory workers reverted to their old habits, the payroll increased, and arms manufacturing dropped to its lowest level since 1845. For the next several years the facility was mired in corruption, and the Ordnance Department once again struggled to change management practices.

Harpers Ferry served as a catalyst for the Civil War. John Brown attacked the town with the hope of creating a slave insurrection. Capturing Harpers Ferry was important for Brown's plan because the arsenal stored over 10,000 guns. These weapons could be used to overthrow the slaveholders and liberate enslaved African Americans. Although Brown and his men were captured, convicted, tried, and hanged, tensions at the facility remained high for the next two years. After the bombardment of Fort Sumter in 1861, Virginia seceded from the Union. Seizing the armory and arsenal at Harpers Ferry became a major objective for the Confederacy. Lieutenant Roger Jones, stationed at Harpers Ferry with fifty regulars and fifteen volunteers, feared that an advancing force of 360 Confederates would capture the town. Before these forces arrived on April 18, 1861, Jones set fire to the federal factory buildings and abandoned the town.

Some of the buildings were saved by the townspeople in order to salvage their livelihood. Immediately after the Civil War, some Harpers Ferry citizens were optimistic about the prospect of revitalizing the armory, since a small operation had been reestablished in August 1865. However, General Grant reported in 1867 to the secretary of war that the United States no longer required the Harpers Ferry grounds and recommended against rebuilding the armory. With no economic base, the town was described as "next to dead" and a "village of paupers."

Industry never fully revitalized in Harpers Ferry, although Virginius Island showed some signs of redevelopment. The cotton mill on Virginius Island was converted to a flour mill, and entrepreneurs Child and McCreight struggled to make their enterprise profitable. After the 1870 flood, the flour mill was the only major industry operating in the community. In the 1880s William Savery from Delaware purchased the armory grounds on the Potomac River and Upper Halls Island on the Shenandoah River, and established two pulp mills. While Child and McCreight's flour mill discontinued operations in the late 1880s, the pulp mills existed into the twentieth century. Harpers Ferry never regained the economic prominence it had during the 1840s and 1850s.

ARCHAEOLOGY OF INDUSTRY AND INDUSTRIAL LIFE IN VIRGINIUS ISLAND

Archeologists have worked in Harpers Ferry National Historical Park since the 1960s rediscovering the community's rich cultural history. Many of the early excavations concentrated on the early nineteenth-century gun manufacturing industry and supporting commerce. In 1959 and 1960 archaeologist Edward Larabee uncovered the foundations of the arsenal, an important armory building located in a visible place on the landscape. Because the town is prone to flooding, the top of the historical foundation's walls are now about 3–5 feet below the present surface. Portions of the walls uncovered by these excavations are now exposed and in view along Shenandoah Street.

Edward Larabee also performed the initial excavations on Halls Island and located some foundations belonging to the U.S. Rifle Works. The island originally contained Hall's Rifle works, where interchangeable parts were first developed in the 1820s. However, when the armory facilities were redesigned in the 1840s, the U.S. government constructed a new set of buildings upon this earlier enterprise. Using a resistivity and seismic survey, Hamilton Carson located anomalies on Halls Island. Excavations, in the form of trenches, found 2.5–4-foot-wide shale walls of the 1840s U.S. Rifle Works at about 6 feet beneath the current ground surface. Carson also uncovered a headrace and channel that led to a 9-foot wide turbine pit. The turbine pit is still exposed and visible when walking through the island on a nature trail.

David H. Hannah produced the first assessment of archaeological resources on Virginius Island in the mid-1960s and briefly described above-ground historical features. From 1966 to 1968, he directed a Job Corps project to uncover the foundation walls of the large cotton-mill ruin, and he opened part of the raceway on the north side of the mill. This work exposed three basement chambers within the mill. Within the narrow center chamber sits four well-preserved, in situ Leffel turbines positioned in a wooden floor. Flour-milling machinery parts also were recovered near the base of the excavations. The walls of these buildings have recently been stabilized and partially restored, and the turbines still survive in their original location. This structure, along with other industrial ruins on Virginius Island, is visible along a walking trail through the island.

Recent excavations on Virginius Island focus on several sites whose inhabitants crosscut the social, cultural, and economic structure of the island community. One is the residence of Lewis Wernwag Sr. and his household, which included enslaved men and women. Wernwag, an internationally known bridge builder and inventor, constructed the island saw mill and machine shop. He was well connected with Harpers Ferry's upper echelon through politics and civic activities. Although Lewis Sr. died in 1843, his son continued to live on the island and operate the machine shop until the 1870 flood. The Wernwag house served as the McCreight family home during the 1870s and possibly 1880s. Excavations at this lot indicate that the Wernwags participated in the new and growing consumer society. While living in a secluded industrial setting nothing stopped the family from buying the most recent and up-to-date consumer goods. Tablewares and teawares appear to be divided between plain and decorated vessels. This assortment of decorated wares reflects the norms associated with the bourgeois family rituals, whereas the plainer wares would suggest that other options for dining existed.

Craftsman Jesse Scofield and his family lived on Virginius Island from the mid-1830s to the mid-1850s. Documentation exists of Scofield's activities and partnership with Wernwag. After Scofield sold his island property, the house probably was rented to factory employees in the 1850s and to other working-class households after the Civil War. Excavations at this lot indicate that the Schofield household had fewer alcoholic beverage bottles than other contemporary working-class sites, although the proportion of medicinal bottles is comparable to the other sites. This observation might indicate that there were similar working-class approaches to health maintenance and hygiene as well as access to professionalized health care. One of the most impressive findings at the site was the collection of 6,398 blackberry and raspberry seeds from the rear yard near the house. Archaeologists believe that it may have been a repository for the dumping of chamber pots.

Archaeologists also excavated a tenement structure built in 1850 by Abraham Herr, the flour mill owner. An 1857 lithograph shows that these new structures were built in a standardized architectural form. Because of the poor preservation of records, only gross generalizations can be made about the demographic composition of the building's occupants based on the area's census data. Generally they were landless laborers, and some may have been immigrants from England or of English ancestry from the New England area. They worked either in Herr's Flour Mill or for the Harpers Ferry and Shenandoah Manufacturing Company's cotton factory in the 1850s. In the 1860s and 1870s, the inhabitants worked in another island flour mill, and from the 1880s through the turn of the twentieth century the occupants most likely worked in a pulp mill. Excavations at a tenement site provide a significant amount of information about an often-understudied class of people: the laborers and their families. The most striking observation is in the number of remains of wild species relative to domestic species in this assemblage, suggesting that the family still relied on hunting to supplement their diet. Flotation samples from the yard indicate that raspberry plants also existed in the immediate area. The assemblage contained

a relatively large proportion of alcoholic beverage bottles. There is an increasing use of alcohol at the domestic site, and it is probably related to the rise of the temperance movement in Harpers Ferry and the negative connotations that grew with drinking in public places.

ARMORY WORKER HOUSEHOLDS

Other archaeological work at Harpers Ferry has focused on understanding the impact of industrialization on everyday life. Studies have occurred at armory workers' houses, a hotel, boardinghouses, stores, and at dwellings of private citizens.

One project examined the house of the master armorer, the person who oversaw the daily production of guns in the factory. Archaeological evidence of the household indicates that the families eagerly participated in the new industrial order by purchasing the newest and most fashionable commodities transported into town by rail and canal. However, not all households welcomed these changes in everyday life in the same way. Evidence of the persistence of craft and home industry is apparent in some of the excavations of armory workers' domestic lots. In one context dating to the 1820s through 1830s, a comparatively large quantity of gun parts and tools was found in association with the worker's dwelling. Since armorers were often employed in a craft or piece-work situation until 1841, these tools and gun parts may be proof that piece-work manufacturing was done on the armorers' home lots. Factory discipline was only in its most rudimentary form in Harpers Ferry; however, in 1841 the military took control of the armory and enforced strict work regulations. After 1841 gun parts and tools were no longer found in the archeological assemblage. This change in the assemblage is linked to the change in management practices.

The alteration in landscape, dietary habits, and consumer orientations is also telling of the changing industrial life. The earlier industrial landscape appears to be more groomed and reflects an attitude of the harmonious nature between the machine and the garden (or industry and nature). The earlier residents of the workers' houses tended to purchase and dispose of ceramics that were fashionable for the era. They also consumed higher proportions of pre-cut meats. After 1841 the families acquired, used, and disposed of consumer goods that were fashionable several generations earlier. An analysis of the faunal assemblage shows that they also ate a higher proportion of wild animals after 1841. In all likelihood, the post-1841 residents purchased products and reverted to a way of life when they believed they had some control over their daily lives—a time when they were not part of the industrial machine. Economic constraints may be one explanation for this phenomenon, but much in the same way that residents adhered to their craft occupation, this consumer pattern may be an expression of worker's desire for the preindustrial order. This story of armory workers' lives and some of the tools used by workers in their home is explained in more detail in one of the museum buildings in Lower Town Harpers Ferry.

BOARDINGHOUSES

Boarders traditionally tend to be the landless, mobile laborers of industrial society. Examination of a late nineteenth-century boardinghouse privy and its comparison to an entrepreneur household's assemblage illuminates the differences in material wealth and health conditions between classes in an industrializing society. Generally, the boarders lacked variety in their diet and had a relatively high disease rate (i.e., intestinal roundworm and whip worm). One of the town's major entrepreneurial families living adjacent to the boardinghouse had a significantly greater variety of foods as well as a much higher rate of parasites. Other stereotypes of wealth held true when comparing these two assemblages. The entrepreneur's household had a greater diversity of higher-cost ceramics whereas the boarders used common "thrasher's china." About 76 percent of the containers found at the boardinghouse were medicine-related, as compared to only 20 percent at the entrepreneur's house. The boarders also had a substantially greater proportion of painkillers and medicines for digestive disorders. These differences are a major indicator of the contrast between laborers', and nonlaborers' health and medicinal treatments.

The archaeology work at Harpers Ferry contributes significant information to the Park's story about life in an early historic period American industrial town. The town's industrial development affected work and domestic life as well as the landscape and the built environment. As time discipline increasingly drove individuals' lives, residents chose to either participate in these new cultural patterns, attempt to alter them, or withdraw from them. The archaeology at Harpers Ferry provides some ways to think about how people reacted to the new industrial order.

PUBLIC EDUCATION AND ACCESS TO THE SITE

There are many industrial-era sites located within the boundaries of Harpers Ferry National Historical Park, and they are fully accessible to the general public. Interpretive trails wind through the industrial and domestic ruins on Virginius Island. The remains of the cotton/flour mill, another cotton mill, and the head gates of a canal system are easily visible. Domestic sites are also adjacent to trails. The Wernwag foundations lay in ruins along Wernwag Street. The location of the Schofield house sits to the south of Wernwag Street and is buried under flood sediments. The outline of the west row-house foundation is faint but visible from Wernwag Street. A map of the island is stationed at a bridge before entering the island, and it provides a general guide of the historic landscape. Future interpretive walks may describe the lives of entrepreneurs and working-class families who lived on this land.

The armory worker's house along Shenandoah Street, the only existing armory worker's house still standing in the national park, is painted white, and the ghost outline of another building is on its east wall. The associated foundation is outlined adjacent to the structure. Lower Town Harpers Ferry has several museum exhibits that use archeological materials to interpret the town's history. The industry exhibition contains some of the machinery that could have been used in the armory, and on the opposite wall is an exhibit of Virginius Island's industries with some industrial-related artifacts associated with the community. Across the street is an exhibition entitled Harpers Ferry: A Place in Time. The exhibits use archaeological materials from the armory worker's house to provide an overview of work and everyday life in the antebellum town. Another display uses archaeological materials to show life in a late nineteenth-century boardinghouse.

Also along Shenandoah Street is an exhibition in one of the buildings that describes the concepts of stabilization, rehabilitation, and reconstruction. Historic foundations from an earlier period are exposed on the interior of the building, and visitors can read about the different options available in the preservation of sites and buildings. Along the same street there are exposed foundations related to the armory. Unfortunately, these are not interpreted to the public. There is also a new path by the railroad berm that provides access to the old armory grounds. All of these places are open and accessible to the public. There is a shuttle bus that moves people from the parking lot to Lower Town Harpers Ferry. Once off the bus the visitor has the option to head toward Virginius Island and experience the industrial ruins or journey into town and visit the various exhibitions.

Further Reading: Barry, Joseph, *The Strange Story of Harpers Ferry with Legends of the Surrounding Country*, reprint of 1903 edition (Shepherdstown, WV: Shepherdstown Register, 1988); Gilbert, Dave, *A Walker's Guide to Harpers Ferry, West Virginia* (Harpers Ferry, WV: Harpers Ferry Historical Association, 1992); Gilbert, Dave, *Waterpower: Mills, Factories, Machines & Floods at Harpers Ferry, West Virginia, 1762–1991* (Harpers Ferry, WV: Harpers Ferry Historical Association, 1999); Harpers Ferry National Historical Park, Archeology at the U.S Armory, Harpers Ferry NHP Web site, http://www.nps.gov/history/archeology/sites/npSites/harpersFerry.htm (online October 2007); Moyer, Teresa, and Paul A. Shackel, *"To Preserve the Evidences of a Noble Past": Harpers Ferry and the Making of a National Historical Park* (in preparation); Palus, Matthew, and Paul A. Shackel, *"They Worked Regular": Craft, Labor, Family and the Archaeology of an Industrial Community* (Knoxville: University of Tennessee Press, 2006); Shackel, Paul A., *Culture Change and the New Technology: An Archaeology of the Early American Industrial Era* (New York: Plenum Publishing, 1996); Shackel, Paul A., *Archaeology and Created Memory: Public History in a National Park* (New York: Kluwer Academic/Plenum Publishing, 2000); Smith, Merrit Roe, *Harpers Ferry Armory and the New Technology: The Challenge of Change* (Ithaca, NY: Cornell University Press, 1977).

Paul A. Shackel

THE ROBINSON HOUSE SITE

Manassas National Battlefield Park, Virginia
The Archaeology of a Free Black Family in Virginia

The Robinson House site is located on land that became part of Manassas National Battlefield Park in the 1930s. The park was established near Manassas, Virginia, to commemorate the two battles that were fought here during the American Civil War. This area of Piedmont Virginia was first cleared and developed in the early eighteenth century, when a plantation economy was established using enslaved labor to produce mass quantities of tobacco. The site was home to James "Gentleman Jim" Robinson and his family from the 1840s through 1936. The Robinson House was in the midst of fighting during the first battle of Manassas in 1861 and was used as a headquarters as well as a field hospital during the second battle in 1862. In addition to interpreting the site for its role in these Civil War battles, the archeological investigations at the Robinson House represent a trend on Civil War battlefields to discuss the role enslavement had in the Civil War and to recognize a larger social history of African American families before, during, and after this event. Investigations at the site also represent the interdisciplinary approach of historical archeology and the usefulness of studying late-nineteenth- and early-twentieth-century material culture for insight into the struggles of African American families through the Reconstruction period.

James Robinson was born free in 1799, and oral tradition claims that his father was Landon Carter, a wealthy white landowner and slave owner and the grandson of Robert "King" Carter of Westmoreland County, Virginia. The Robinson family traces their lineage to Carter and an enslaved woman from his plantation Pittsylvania, located in the Manassas area. Historical documentation also shows that James Robinson was "bound out," or indentured for a period of time in a Virginia tavern, where he earned the $484.94 needed to purchase 170 acres of land near the town of Manassas.

James Robinson and his companion, an enslaved woman named Susan Gaskins, had six children. Because of Susan's enslaved status, by law she could not marry, and her children were born into enslavement. James and Susan's first two children were sold and taken to Louisiana. Susan and the other four children were the property of John Lee, a local white landowner. From the Robinson papers we know that James Robinson purchased his son Tasco from Lee for 30 dollars. Eventually, James Robinson purchased another of his sons and indentured one of his daughters. The remainder of his family was entrusted to him in John Lee's last will and testament. These documents are reminders of the lengths to which African Americans would go to maintain their family ties. The

documents also show that Robinson owned his farm and was a trusted and respected member of his community, and he conducted business with many prominent families.

On July 21, 1861, the first battle of Manassas raged, and by noon had reached the ground immediately around the Robinson House. The family left their home prior to the fighting. The house escaped major damage. Only a year later, in August of 1862, the house served as a hospital for the Union during the second battle of Manassas. On September 11, 1862, this description was printed in the *Charleston Daily Courier*: "The Robinson House is used as a Yankee hospital. In a visit there this morning, I found 100 of them [Yankees] packed in the rooms as thick as sardines . . . the wounds of the majority were undressed, the blood had dried upon their persons and garments, and altogether there the most horrible set of beings it has been my lot to encounter."

Minié balls and other Civil War artifacts recovered at the site tell the story of these battles, while other artifacts found at the site tell another story—one of survival. By the mid-nineteenth century, James Robinson was the third wealthiest African American in Prince William County. Although his property was damaged during the Civil War, the perseverance of the Robinson family returned this land to a prosperous farm.

The original 1840 house built by James Robinson is believed to have been completely removed in 1926 when a section of the house was rebuilt. The 1926-era Robinson House stood until 1993, when arsonists burned the structure. Rather than rebuild the house, the National Park Service, in consultation with local descendants of James Robinson, decided to concentrate efforts on research, including archeological investigations, architectural studies, historical research, and oral-history interviews.

During the architectural fabrics study, the National Park Service made an incredible discovery. Wedged behind insulation in an attic wall were dozens of Robinson family accounts, letters, receipts, and other documents now known as the Robinson papers. Dating from 1827 to the 1850s, the documents are an invaluable record of James Robinson's financial transactions. They provide significant information for studying the Robinson family and the negotiation of their difficult social and economic position before and after the Civil War.

Archaeological excavations were performed at the Robinson House in 1995 and 1996. Several significant features were located during these excavations, including the base and portion of a hearth to the 1840s Robinson House chimney, a Civil

"Rallying the troops of Bee, Bartow, and Evans, behind the Robinson House." Caption and illustration from *The Battle of Bull Run*, by G. T. Beauregard in *The Century*, November 1884.   [Library of Congress]

War–era barn, a possible root cellar or privy, foundations to an unidentified outbuilding, and the remains of an icehouse, later used as a trash pit by the family. Because the icehouse feature was used as a trash pit over several generations, a large number of artifacts was recovered.

Artifacts recovered from the Robinson house are reflective of the continuity of their African identity. Colonoware, or low-fired, unglazed earthenware known to be produced by Native Americans and African Americans, was recovered from the Robinson House site. Because no Native American groups inhabited this area at the time of Robinson's occupation, it is believed that the colonoware found here was produced by African Americans as part of a traditional African potting method. Mancala gaming pieces were also recovered from the excavations at the Robinson House. Still played today, mancala is thought to be one of the world's oldest games. The versatile and portable game is played with gaming pieces, often made from pebbles, shells, or smoothed shards of glass and ceramics, with a gaming board fashioned from wood or merely a series of small holes dug in the ground. African peoples brought variations of the game with them to the United States during the seventeenth and eighteenth centuries.

The products we buy and use, or our consumer behavior, reflects not only the time period in which we live but also our cultural and ethnic identities and the ways in which we perceive ourselves. Archaeologists at the Robinson House used the recovered artifacts to study the consumer behavior of the family to gain insight into how the Robinsons expressed their identity and negotiated their position in the community both before and after emancipation.

A study of ceramics recovered at the site showed that, like other families, the Robinsons may have followed dominant material dining standards in which consumers assembled sets of matching or similar wares in lieu of large set purchases. Because the Robinsons were farmers, it is not unusual that canning and other food-storage containers made up a large percentage of the total glass assemblage. Home food preservation allowed the Robinsons to avoid a consumer marketplace that may have been racially exclusive under some circumstances while living a relatively self-sufficient and resourceful lifestyle. However, the glass collection also reflects the family's participation in the consumption of mass-produced goods and brand-name items. This type of consumer behavior may be indicative of an avenue that could have evaded local or community merchants' opportunity to provide lower-quality goods or misweighed products. Some examples of mass-produced goods from the site include Listerine, Noxema, Sloan's Liniment, Vick's Vaporub, Smith Brothers cough syrup, Lysol, Pepsi Cola and other sodas, and McCormick and Company Extract and Spices.

Like consumer behavior, the use of space may also help us understand cultural and ethnic identities. The landscape of the Robinson farm, defined by the features recorded in the archaeological investigations and architectural study, showed that the Robinson House was small, although as many as nine people lived there during the nineteenth century. Although this choice may be governed in part by socioeconomic factors, ideas about what constituted a proper house and the use of outdoor space may have been just as important. Later, when the family had the means to expand their house, they did not. It is believed that this was a conscious

This photo shows the small size of the Robinson House prior to 1870. The porch on the rear shows the family's desire for privacy. [Library of Congress]

choice in order to remain unobtrusive and guard their privacy in a largely white community.

A study of the backyard and more private areas around the Robinson farm shows that these spaces were used as an extension of the house where family members could interact with others in the African American community. In this way, ties with other African Americans were made stronger, and their sense of community reinforced.

Today only the stone foundation of the 1926 Robinson House remains easily visible on the site, although it stands as a steadfast symbol of African American heritage. The site is open to the public as part of Manassas National Battlefield, and some of the artifacts from the excavations are on display in the Manassas National Battlefield Visitor Center.

Further Reading: Martin Seibert, Erika K., and Mia T. Parsons, "Battling Beyond First and Second Manassas," in *Archaeological Perspectives on the American Civil War*, edited by Clarence Geier and Stephen Potter (Tallahassee: Florida University Press, 2001), 270–286; Martin Seibert, Erika K., "The Third Battle of Manassas: Power, Identity and the Forgotten African-American Past," in *Myth, Memory, and the Making of the American Landscape*, edited by Paul A. Shackel (Tallahassee: University Press of Florida, 2001), 67–84; Martin, Erika K., Mia T. Parsons, and Paul A. Shackel, "Commemoration of a Rural African-American Family at a National Battlefield Park," *International Journal of Historical Archaeology* 1(2) (1997): 157–178; Manassas National Battlefield Park Web site, http://www.nps.gov/mana/index.htm (online April 2005); The Robinson House, A Portrait of African American Heritage, National Park Service Web site, http://www.nps.gov/history/archeology/robinson/index.htm (online April 2005).

Erika K. Martin Seibert and Mia T. Parsons

MANASSAS, ANTIETAM, MONOCACY, AND PETERSBURG

Maryland and Virginia

The Archaeology of the Civil War in Virginia and Maryland

The American Civil War is perhaps the most studied and controversial episode in our country's history. Volumes have been written on nearly every detail of the war, covering every battle and every general from both armies. But what is often ignored is the physical evidence left behind by the soldiers. Only recently have systematic archaeological surveys been undertaken of many Civil War sites. The results have greatly increased our understanding of how this conflict was fought, as well as of the individuals fighting.

Archaeologists have utilized a number of methods to survey Civil War sites. Two of the most common survey techniques in archaeology are pedestrian walkover surveys and the excavation of shovel test pits. Both of these methods are frequently used at Civil War sites, particularly when a site was utilized as a long-term camp. At these camps, soldiers would often construct semi-permanent huts and other shelters, usually to wait out the winter months. These camps leave a considerable archaeological footprint that is often identifiable through traditional survey techniques.

Another common method for identifying and exploring archaeological sites from the Civil War is a systematic metal detector survey. For decades, metal detectors have been used by relic hunters who have used them to locate artifacts, some of which can be sold for high prices in today's market. Artifact detection and removal by relic hunters often is illegal and always is destructive of the archaeological record. If artifacts are removed from the ground without their locations being recorded precisely, the *context* in which they are set has been erased. Archaeologically, they have lost much, if not all, of their value as sources of information about the past. For this reason, metal detectors as an archaeological tool have often been avoided by professional archaeologists.

In recent years, many archaeologists have overcome this aversion and begun to conduct systematic metal-detector surveys that include the careful and detailed recording of artifact locations and contexts of our nation's battlefields. The following examples illustrate a variety of effective methods for identifying archaeological resources at Civil War battlefields. Some of the most successful of these surveys have been conducted on National Park Service lands in Maryland and Virginia. These surveys have identified a range of archaeological sites associated with the Civil War, including the homes of wealthy planters and enslaved African Americans, the camps of soldiers, and the fields on which they fought.

ANTIETAM NATIONAL BATTLEFIELD

The Battle of Antietam, fought on farm fields 70 miles northwest of Washington, D.C., is known as the bloodiest day in American history. The 120,000 soldiers engaged in this fight left a considerable archaeological footprint—one that survives despite the decades of relic and souvenir hunting that began almost immediately after the battle. Because more and more lands associated with the battle have been preserved by the National Park Service, there now exists a unique opportunity to study this entire landscape of conflict.

Beginning in 1994, an extensive professional archaeological metal detector survey of Antietam National Battlefield was launched that included portions of the West Woods, the North Woods, the Mumma Orchard, the East Woods, and the Piper Orchard. These surveys resulted in the precise recording and recovery of thousands of artifacts, many of which were military in nature and could be linked to the Battle of Antietam. These artifacts were carefully mapped and analyzed for clues about the

battle. In many cases, the archaeological evidence supported historical accounts of the battle. For example, the artifacts recovered in the East Woods included not only the expended ammunition that was common throughout all of the surveys but also a multitude of personal items and accoutrements. These included military buttons, belt buckles, and gun parts. Because the East Woods was the scene of some of the fiercest fighting at the Battle of Antietam, the mix of ammunition and personal items may represent the carnage and confusion that took place on this small portion of the battlefield.

In addition to broad surveys of parts of Antietam National Battlefield, some specific finds have been investigated as well. For example, in 1988 a group of relic hunters were legally searching for Civil War artifacts on the privately owned Roulette Farm, adjacent to the National Park Service boundary. They discovered what at first appeared to be an abandoned knapsack and accoutrements, but soon began to discover fragments of human bone. This discovery was reported to Antietam National Battlefield, and that summer, an archaeological investigation was undertaken. Four shallow, partial graves were identified and the remains recovered. This excavation provided tantalizing clues about the four Union soldiers who had been hastily buried shortly after the battle. After careful examination of the archaeological evidence, forensic clues, and the historical record, the National Park Service was able to offer potential identifications for these soldiers. At the conclusion of the survey, and exactly 127 years after their deaths, these men from the famed Irish Brigade were buried with honors in the Antietam National Cemetery.

MANASSAS NATIONAL BATTLEFIELD PARK

Located just 25 miles west of Washington, D.C., the fields of Manassas National Battlefield Park are only a handful of those in the nation that saw not one but two major Civil War Battles. In the first major battle of the Civil War on July 21, 1861, and during the larger battles of August 28–30, 1862, almost 27,000 men were killed, wounded, or captured. Both battles resulted in Confederate victories and sent panic to the nearby Union capital. The huge numbers of troops who fought on this ground left considerable archaeological evidence of their movements throughout the battles, and archaeologists have conducted a number of surveys on these fields over the last twenty years.

Although several portions of the battlefield have been explored through the use of systematic metal detector surveys, the Brawner Farm serves as an example of a location where both metal detecting and traditional excavation units were utilized to explore the fierce fighting that took place around the house. Heavy action took place here on the opening day of the battle of second Manassas in the early evening of August 28, 1862. After acquiring the Brawner Farm in 1985, the National Park Service conducted archaeological surveys of the house area. The initial survey consisted of excavation units immediately adjacent to the house and in the nearby surrounding yard area. The purpose of this work was to differentiate between the existing Brawner house and the foundation for the earlier house that stood during the Civil War. Not only did these excavations successfully locate several foundation features of the original (ca. 1820) house, but also they identified one of the best possible scenarios of Civil War archaeology—a sealed archaeological context.

After the Brawner family returned to their heavily damaged home following the second battle, they found the yard strewn with the debris of battle. Rather than attempting to remove this waste, they utilized Virginia bluestone gravel from a quarry just 500 yards to the north of their home. This gravel was spread about the yard and effectively sealed the battle-related debris beneath the surface. Throughout the remainder of the war, Union troops would pass through the property and camp around the Brawner house, each time leaving behind evidence of their occupation. But this later camping debris remained separated from the earlier remnants of battle. When archeologists explored this property 125 years later, the layer of gravel would essentially serve as a time capsule. Detailed evidence was obtained about types of ammunition used by individual Union and Confederate regiments, allowing archaeologists to piece together information about the men who fought around the house in 1862.

In 1994 archaeologists returned to the Brawner Farm to conduct a complete metal-detector survey of the adjacent field in an area measuring 200 by 220 feet. Despite earlier relic hunting prior to National Park Service ownership of the property, additional detailed clues were obtained that supported historical accounts of the battle. For example, the exact position of the battle line of the Nineteenth Indiana Infantry could be identified through a long line of dropped .58-caliber ammunition and other equipment. This metal-detector survey complemented the earlier excavation units that had been placed about the house and greatly expanded the understanding of the fighting on the Brawner Farm.

Also at Manassas National Battlefield Park archaeological investigations and interpretation have been conducted at the Robinson House site, another family farm that existed before and following the battles (see the essay in this encyclopedia by Siebert and Parsons).

MONOCACY NATIONAL BATTLEFIELD

Although a relatively small battle compared to the others discussed in this chapter, the battle of Monocacy is singularly important because of its role in delaying the approach of Confederate forces to Washington, D.C., in the summer of 1864. Known as the "The Battle That Saved Washington," the battle of Monocacy pitted a large Confederate force, led by General Jubal Early, against a much smaller force of battle-seasoned veterans and recently recruited militia under the command of General Lew Wallace. Although the battle resulted in an eventual rout of the Union troops, Confederates suffered severely enough that their arrival at Washington was delayed until after its defenses had been occupied by federal reinforcements.

Although Monocacy National Battlefield was legislatively mandated in 1934, the majority of the lands that constitute this park were not acquired until the last quarter of the twentieth century. As a result, the battlefield was extensively hunted and artifacts removed unsystematically and without recording by relic collectors. However, professional scientific archaeological surveys of the Best Farm portion of the battlefield, which began in 2001, resulted in the identification of a high concentration of battle-related artifacts.

In addition, evidence of several short- and long-term encampments was uncovered along the much-traveled Georgetown Pike. This road was utilized by both sides throughout the conflict for troop movements related to such campaigns as Antietam, Gettysburg, and the 1864 march through the Shenandoah Valley. Tens of thousands of soldiers camped along the Pike, particularly in the vicinity of the Baltimore and Ohio Railroad Station at Monocacy Junction. Although battle-related debris typically took the form of fired bullets and exploded artillery shells, evidence of these campsites included melted lead, coins, and an array of military accoutrements. Perhaps one of the most unique artifacts was a federal canteen spout inscribed "LT. HART. 128." Research identified a Lieutenant Ambrose B. Hart of the 128th York Infantry who had encamped with his regiment at Monocacy Junction between August 5 and August 7, 1864, on the march to the Shenandoah Valley.

In addition to exploring these short-term encampments, archaeologists identified a major winter encampment of union troops adjacent to the battlefield. Camp Hooker, which was built and occupied by the Fourteenth New Jersey Volunteer Infantry in 1862, protected the strategically important Monocacy railroad junction. Although extensively relic-hunted, a systematic metal detector survey identified the bounds of the camp as well as numerous archaeological features.

PETERSBURG NATIONAL BATTLEFIELD

The siege of Petersburg resembled the battles of Europe during World War I more so than those of the American Civil War. Beginning in June 1864, Robert E. Lee's besieged Army of Northern Virginia dug in around the strategic Confederate transportation center of Petersburg, Virginia. For the next nine months, General Ulysses S. Grant's Union Army waged a campaign of numerous attacks that variably attempted to pierce Lee's lines or to extend them to the point that they were so thin they would eventually break. This was the case in April 1865, when Union forces were finally able to end the stalemate and take charge of the city. The American Civil War would end one week later.

Due to the sheer numbers of troops involved and the length of the Petersburg campaign, miles of archaeological sites relating to the siege were created across the landscape. Over the years, much of this has been destroyed by modern development, not to mention by struggling Southern farmers attempting to return their besieged lands back into fruitful fields. Only a handful of the miles of trenches and earthen forts survive, largely under the protection offered by Petersburg National Battlefield. One such feature preserved by the National Park Service is the Crater, a gaping pit formed on July 30, 1864, when Union engineers exploded a mine beneath the Confederate lines. Despite fierce attacks by federal troops, including members of the United States Colored Troops, the attack was repulsed, and the Confederate line held until the close of the siege. However, this portion of the lines remained hostile for the entire siege, with the opposing forces being located just 70 yards from one another.

One of the many questions plaguing researchers is what life was like in the trenches around Petersburg. To address this question, the National Park Service has engaged in two excavations of the picket lines in advance of the Crater. The Confederate picket line was excavated first in 1978, because its location could be easily determined from the surviving earthworks adjacent to the Crater. Evidence of bullet casting as well as supplies abandoned by Confederate soldiers left clues as to life in the trenches. The Union picket line, on the other hand, was not identified until 1999. Although it had once proven to be a formidable entrenchment, all above-ground features of this line had been destroyed by farming in the late-nineteenth and twentieth centuries. However, careful archaeological exploration with metal detectors resulted in its discovery, and beneath the plowed soils, the base of the trench was found to be much as it would have been in 1864.

RICHMOND NATIONAL BATTLEFIELD PARK
Perhaps the most contested city of the American Civil War, Richmond, Virginia, saw numerous battles and campaigns take place at its doorstep. Today, the National Park Service preserves portions of a number of these battles, including Gaines Mill, Cold Harbor, Malvern Hill, and Drewry's Bluff. During the 1862 Peninsula Campaign and the 1864 Overland Campaign, these battles played a pivotal role in deciding the fate of the Confederate capital.

However, much of the focus of recent archaeology at Richmond National Battlefield Park has not been on battle tactics but rather on the cross section of the war that is preserved at its sites. That is, not only do these sites preserve archaeological evidence of battles, but they contain information about the people who lived on and worked this land during the Civil War. At the Malvern Hill Unit of Richmond National Battlefield Park, archaeologists have searched for the remnants of two plantations that stood at the time of the battle. Historical evidence painted two different pictures of life at these sites. At the West Plantation, enslaved African Americans lived in a group of buildings that resembled small, single-family dwellings. This finding provides valuable information about the social structure of the community, where slaves may have lived in family units. Just a short distance away at the Crew Plantation, mostly young-adult slaves lived in two dormitory-like structures separated by sex.

In 2001 archaeologists used remote sensing techniques in an effort to locate these structures and to learn about the lives of those men and women who were held at these plantations. Electronic resistivity surveys measure the resistance of materials to electrical current between two points. Features such as buried foundations can often be detected in this manner. Magnetometry detects changes in the magnetic fields of subsurface features, such as burned soils, hearths, and large metal objects. Using these methods, archaeologists identified subsurface anomalies that were then ground-truthed, that is, physically checked using traditional archaeological field techniques. These surveys met with mixed results, with no trace of the West Plantation slave village being identified, and with some traces of the Crew Plantation being found to survive. The combination of the historical record and the limited archaeological data has enabled the park to better interpret the lives of those who lived on the Malvern Hill Battlefield during the Civil War.

Although much of the focus of archaeological explorations at Richmond National Battlefield Park have been on the domestic side of the Civil War, frequent looting has required significant stabilization and mitigation through archaeology. All federal lands are protected by the Archaeological Resources Protection Act (ARPA), which prohibits the taking of artifacts without a research permit. When looters rob National Parks of their archaeological resources, an ARPA investigation must be undertaken to document the illegal activity and to assess the extent of the damages. Nearly half of all archaeology conducted at the various units of Richmond National Battlefield Park is in support of ARPA investigations. It is important that these resources be preserved so that future generations may learn the multitude of stories they can tell us about the American Civil War.

Further Reading: Beasley, Joy, ed., *Archaeological Overview and Assessment and the Identification and Evaluation Study of the Best Farm, Monocacy National Battlefield, Frederick, Maryland*, Occasional Report No. 18 (Washington, DC: National Capital Regional Archeological Program, 2005); Geier, Clarence R., and Stephen R. Potter, *Archaeological Perspectives on the American Civil War* (Gainesville: University Press of Florida, 2000); Geier, Clarence R., David G. Orr, and Matthew B. Reeves, *Huts and History: The Historical Archaeology of Military Encampment during the American Civil War* (Gainesville: University Press of Florida, 2006); Monocacy National Battlefield Park, *Best Farm Visitor's Guide 2007*, Western Maryland Interpretive Association by Monocacy National (available at Monocacy National Battlefield Visitor Center), National Park Service Web site, http://www.nps.gov/mono/historyculture/index.htm; Reeves, Matthew B., *Dropped and Fired: Archaeological Patterns of Militaria from Two Civil War Battles, Manassas National Battlefield Park, Manassas, Virginia*, Occasional Report No. 15 (Washington, DC: National Capital Regional Archeological Program, 2001); Richmond National Battlefield Park, Malvern Hill Unit, Historical trail with multiple wayside markers that discuss the archaeological investigations.

Brandon S. Bies

THE USS *MONITOR* SHIPWRECK SITE

The USS *Monitor* National Marine Sanctuary, Atlantic Ocean
The Archaeology of the First Union Ironclad

The *Monitor* National Marine Sanctuary contains the remains of the famous Union ironclad warship USS *Monitor*. On March 9, 1862, early in the American Civil War, the ironclad warships USS *Monitor* and CSS *Virginia* fought to a draw at Hampton Roads, Virginia. The battle of Hampton Roads marked the first encounter between vessels of this new type, and its effects reached far beyond Virginia, resulting in the rapid abandonment of conventional wooden, sail-powered ships-of-the-line and an escalation of naval weaponry and armor. On December 31, 1862, the *Monitor* sank off Cape Hatteras, North Carolina, in 235 feet (72 m) of water, where it lay for more than a century before its discovery during a research expedition. The *Monitor* was soon listed on the National Register of Historic Places and later became a National Historic Landmark. On January 30, 1975, the *Monitor*'s remains were designated America's first National Marine Sanctuary, to be protected and managed by the National Oceanic and Atmospheric Administration (NOAA), an agency of the U.S. Department of Commerce.

EMERGENCE OF AMERICA'S FIRST IRONCLAD WARSHIPS

The *Monitor* was designed and built by the brilliant but controversial Swedish-American inventor John Ericsson. The U.S. Navy awarded Ericsson a contract primarily because he guaranteed the remarkably rapid delivery of an ironclad capable of countering the threat posed by the Confederate ironclad *Virginia* (ex-USS *Merrimack*), already under construction at the Gosport Navy Yard in Portsmouth, Virginia. Employing a radical design and innovative construction methods, Ericsson delivered the new vessel in less than four months. The *Monitor* was commissioned at the Brooklyn (New York) Navy Yard on February 25, 1862, barely a week after the commissioning of the *Virginia*.

The *Monitor* was strikingly different from any other vessel afloat. A radical departure from conventional high-sided wooden warships, the *Monitor*'s hull was almost completely submerged, presenting enemy ships an exceptionally small profile. *Monitor*'s only superstructure was a gun turret amidships and a small raised pilothouse forward; its armored deck was less than 2 feet (60 cm) above the waterline. The *Monitor* was the first warship to employ an armored, rotating gun turret that could train its guns on a target regardless of the heading of the ship itself, which was a significant advancement in naval gunnery. Instead of a conventional battery of cannons

lined along one or more gun decks, the *Monitor*'s armament consisted only of two 11-inch (28-cm) Dahlgren smooth bore guns, mounted side-by-side in its turret.

The *Monitor*'s keel was laid on October 25, 1861, and the completed vessel was launched on January 30, 1862. After very rushed and abbreviated sea trials, she arrived in Hampton Roads on the evening of March 8, 1862. Incredibly, earlier that day the CSS *Virginia* had made its maiden voyage into Hampton Roads and wreaked havoc on the Union fleet. Two warships were sunk and a third was run aground and heavily damaged, while the *Virginia* suffered only superficial damage. A receding tide was all that intervened between the remaining Union ships and the Confederate ironclad.

Early on March 9, 1862, the *Virginia* steamed back into Hampton Roads, prepared to finish off the Union fleet. The *Monitor* steamed out to intercept its iron counterpart, thus commencing one of the most celebrated sea battles in history. The *Monitor*'s design proved to be effective, but the four-hour battle ended in a draw, with neither ship being able to significantly damage the other.

The repercussions of this battle were felt worldwide. Although other ironclad warships had been built in Europe, they were untried in battle against similar foes. The battle of Hampton Roads brought about the rapid abandonment of conventional wooden warships. In the United States, the *Monitor* gave its name to an entirely new family of low-freeboard, turreted vessels. By the end of the American Civil War sixty monitors of various classes had been completed or were under construction. Although these monitors had all the characteristics of the first, each successive class incorporated design modifications. The USS *Monitor*, the prototype, was wholly unique.

LOCATION, PROTECTION, RESEARCH, AND MANAGEMENT

The *Monitor* lay undisturbed, its exact location unknown, until August 1973 when it was discovered off Cape Hatteras by a scientific team aboard Duke University's R/V *Eastward*. The wreck lies approximately 16 nautical miles (25.8 km) south-southeast of Cape Hatteras Lighthouse. The USS *Monitor* had long been considered one of the most famous and significant warships in the history of the United States Navy—indeed, in terms of naval technology, one of the most important ships in the world. Therefore, *Monitor*'s discovery generated widespread interest and excitement, but also serious concern.

The first problem faced by researchers and historic preservation managers was how to protect this important historic vessel. Because its location was outside the territorial waters of the United States, and because the U.S. Navy had officially abandoned the *Monitor* in 1953, no simple means of protection was apparent. However, it was soon recognized that recent federal legislation, the Marine Protection, Research, and Sanctuary Act of 1972, could be used to protect a significant shipwreck such as the *Monitor*. Therefore, on January 30, 1975, the secretary of commerce designated the *Monitor* America's first National Marine Sanctuary. Since then the *Monitor* has been protected and managed by the National Marine Sanctuary Program, a part of NOAA.

The *Monitor*'s inaccessibility is a major factor influencing protection, management, and research. *Monitor* lies on a flat, featureless, sandy seabed at a depth of nearly 240 feet (73 m). Water depth places it out of reach of most scuba divers. The wreck lies near the confluence of two major ocean currents, the cold southerly flowing Labrador Current and the warm Gulf Stream. These currents compete for dominance in the vicinity of the *Monitor*, creating confusing and often violent currents that can create tremendous stresses on the *Monitor*'s hull and carry away parts of the hull and its contents. The *Monitor*'s hull and contents have been influenced by three principal factors: damage that occurred at the time of sinking, deterioration caused by more than a century of exposure within a dynamic seawater environment, and damage resulting from human activities. Some researchers have postulated that *Monitor* was inadvertently depth-charged during World War II, resulting in severe damage to the lower hull and, possibly, to the stern armor belt. In addition, illegal anchoring and fishing activities have damaged the wreck in recent years.

Since 1975 NOAA has gathered a considerable amount of data at the sanctuary. The unique characteristics and location of the site have made it the object of studies by a wide range of specialists, including archaeologists, geologists, oceanographers, biologists, corrosion and structural engineers, and marine salvors. From archaeological and engineering studies, we know that the *Monitor* rolled over as it sank, allowing its turret to pull free and sink to the bottom, upside down. The hull then settled to the seabed, still inverted, where it landed on the turret. The inverted hull now rests partially buried in sediment with the stern port quarter held above the bottom by a series of supporting structures installed by U.S. Navy divers as part of a multi-year stabilization and recovery program.

NOAA conducted the first diving expedition to the *Monitor* in 1977, when commercial divers from the Harbor Branch Oceanographic Institution explored the site from the Johnson-Sea-Link submersible, recovering a signal lantern and a sample of hull plate for analysis. In 1979 NOAA conducted a major archaeological expedition, headed by Gordon Watts, North Carolina State Underwater Archaeologist and co-discoverer of the wreck. The month-long expedition permitted three archaeologists to conduct mapping and recovery

activities at the site, watched over by professional divers from Harbor Branch. Even today, this remains one of the deepest archaeological excavations personally conducted by trained archaeologists. Additional expeditions were conducted in 1983, 1985, and 1987, documenting corrosion rates and state of preservation of the wreck. By 1990 NOAA had determined that preservation of the *Monitor* would require development and implementation of an aggressive management plan that considered various stabilization and recovery options.

NOAA conducted brief site surveys in 1990, 1991, and 1992 to collect additional site data needed for development of management options. Then in 1993 NOAA conducted the *Monitor* Archaeological Research and Structural Survey (MARSS) Expedition. The goals of this major expedition were to map and videotape the *Monitor*'s hull deploy a permanent mooring; recover exposed, threatened artifacts; and conduct test excavations and mapping of the *Monitor*'s turret in order to assess the feasibility of recovery. Two years later NOAA conducted the 1995 *Monitor* Archaeological Research, Recovery, and Stabilization Mission (MARRS'95). This time the primary goal was to help stabilize the *Monitor*'s deteriorating hull and recover its propeller and shaft. For this major undertaking, NOAA enlisted the assistance of several organizations, including the U.S. Navy, the USS *Edenton* (ATS-1), the Mariners' Museum, the National Undersea Research Center at the University of North Carolina at Wilmington (NURC/UNCW), and Key West Diver, Inc. Although Hurricane Felix and two lesser storms interrupted the expedition, both NOAA and the U.S. Navy conducted successful dives on the *Monitor*. During 1996 and 1997 NOAA conducted two mapping surveys utilizing laser-line scanning devices.

In April 1998 NOAA submitted to Congress a report and recommendations for long-term preservation of the *Monitor*'s remains, "Charting a New Course for the *Monitor*: A Long-Range, Comprehensive Plan for the Management, Stabilization, Preservation, and Recovery of Artifacts and Materials from the *Monitor*." The plan reviewed a matrix of stabilization and recovery options and concluded that complete recovery of the *Monitor* was not feasible, due to the advanced state of deterioration of the hull. The plan therefore recommended that NOAA pursue a plan of hull stabilization along with selective recovery of the most significant components, including the propeller, engine, and, especially, the famous revolving gun turret and guns. The plan included sections on major component recovery, conservation, curation, and exhibition as well as archaeological documentation and recovery.

STABILIZATION AND RECOVERY

From 1998 through 2002, NOAA, the U.S. Navy, and the Mariners' Museum conducted a series of large-scale expeditions that resulted in the stabilization of *Monitor*'s hull and the recovery of some of *Monitor*'s most significant components, including the propeller, shaft, engine, and, in 2002, the famous gun turret itself, which was recovered with the guns, carriages, over 100 artifacts, and the remains of two crewmen. These expeditions were complex, requiring four to six weeks on-site and involving more than 100 divers and support personnel. Funding was provided by NOAA, the U.S. Navy, and the Department of Defense Legacy Resources Management Fund.

CONSERVATION, EXHIBITION, AND REPORTING

All objects recovered during these expeditions were transported to the Mariners' Museum, where conservation began in a unique setting that allowed museum visitors to watch the conservation work in progress. Temporary exhibits displayed conserved artifacts, provided visitors with the *Monitor*'s history, and described the massive recovery operations. The USS *Monitor* Center opened at the Mariners' Museum in 2007 interprets the *Monitor* within the broader context of the American Civil War, with emphasis on advances in naval technology and the importance of naval actions during that conflict.

Further Reading: Arnold, J. Barto III, G. Michael Fleshman, C. E. Peterson, G. P. Watts, Clark P. Weldon, and W. Kenneth Stewart, "USS *Monitor*: Results from the 1987 Season," in "Advances in Underwater Archaeology," special issue, *Society for Historical Archaeology*, 26(4) (1992): 47–58; Broadwater, John D., "Managing an Ironclad: Recent Research at the *Monitor* National Marine Sanctuary," in *Ships of War, Vol. 2* (Oxford: Oxford University Press, 1984); Miller, Edward M., *U.S.S.* Monitor: *The Ship That Launched a Modern Navy* (Annapolis, MD: Leeward Press, 1978); Mariners' Museum's USS *Monitor* Center Web site, http://www.monitorcenter.org; *Monitor* National Marine Sanctuary Web site, http://monitor.noaa.gov; Watts, Gordon P., Jr., "The Location and Identification of the Ironclad USS *Monitor*," *International Journal of Nautical Archaeology and Underwater Exploration* 4(2) (1975): 301–329; Watts, Gordon P., Jr., "Deep-Water Archaeological Investigation and Site Testing in the USS *Monitor* National Marine Sanctuary," *Journal of Field Archaeology* 12 (1985): 315–332.

John D. Broadwater

Southeast Region

KEY FOR SOUTHEAST REGIONAL MAP

1. Dust Cave
2. Sloan
3. Windover
4. Hardaway
5. Mulberry Creek
6. Icehouse Bottom
7. Watson Brake
8. Poverty Point State Historic Site
9. Horr's Island shell ring
10. Copena sites: Cave Springs, Hampton Cave, Walling Mound, and Florence Mound
11. Marksville State Historic Site
12. Pinson Mounds State Archaeological Park
13. Hiwassee Island
14. Lubbub Creek Archaeological Complex
15. Tunacunnhee
16. McKeithen
17. Bynum Mound
18. Kolomoki Mounds State Historic Park
19. Key Marco
20. Lake George
21. Moundville Archaeological Park
22. Winterville
23. Ocumulgee National Monument
24. Calusa sites: Mound Key and Pineland
25. Toltec Mounds Archeological State Park
26. Etowah Indian Mounds Historic Site
27. Lake Jackson Mounds State Archaeological Site
28. Harlan
29. Spiro Mounds Archaeological Park
30. Town Creek Mound State Historic Site
31. Coosa (Little Egypt)
32. Fatherland (Grand Village of the Natchez Indians)
33. Hillsborough Archaeological District
34. Tatham Mound
35. Governor Martin
36. Santa Elena and Charlesfort
37. Parkin Archeological State Park
38. Santa Catalina de Guale
39. St. Augustine
40. Mission San Luis de Apalachee
41. Fort St. Louis and Spanish Presidio La Bahia
42. La Belle shipwreck
43. Arkansas Post National Memorial
44. Early Historic period Tunica sites, general area
45. Chota and Tanasee
46. Chalmette Battlefield
47. Shiloh National Military Park
48. CSS *Hunley* shipwreck
49. Andersonville National Historic Site
50. Topper
51. Page-Ladson
52. Eva
53. Rollins shell-rings
54. Stallings Island
55. Submerged Aucilla River valley ancient sites
56. 1554 Spanish Fleet shipwrecks, off Padre Island National Seashore
57. USS *Hatteras* Civil War shipwreck
58. SS *Robert E. Lee* and U-166 German submarine World War II shipwrecks
59. Pensacola
60. Fig Island shell ring complex
61. Sapelo shell ring complex
62. Fort Center
63. Camden Revolutionary War site
64. Fort Fisher
65. Ninety-Six National Historical Site
66. Horseshoe Bend National Military Park

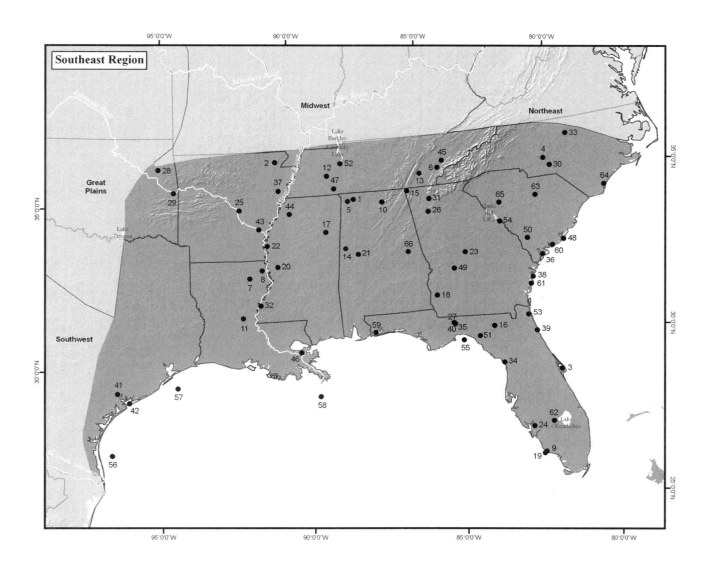

Southeast Region

Midwest

Northeast

Great
Plains

Southwest

INTRODUCTION

This section of *Archaeology in America* includes essays about archaeological sites in the Southeast region of North America. This region is defined roughly by the northern borders of North Carolina, Tennessee, and Arkansas. The region includes some sites in eastern Oklahoma (Spiro and Harlan), then the boundary generally falls south to and along the Texas Gulf of Mexico coast (one essay covers historic shipwrecks and formerly terrestrial ancient sites now beneath the gulf's waters). The region stretches along the Texas gulf coast to include essays about sites related to the seventeenth-century French explorer La Salle and historic Spanish shipwrecks off Padre Island. The states of Mississippi, Alabama, Georgia, South Carolina, and Florida constitute the remainder of the region.

The region encompasses the southern Atlantic coastal plain and piedmont, and the southern Appalachian Mountains. The Gulf of Mexico coastal plain and the lower half of the wide Mississippi River valley are prominent physiographic features of the region. The lush and resource-rich tropical and subtropical environments of the southern Atlantic and Gulf of Mexico coasts were the locations for the development of complex cultures during ancient times. The lower Mississippi River valley and river valleys of the interior Southeast, such as the Tennessee, Tombigbee, Black Warrior, Coosa, and Etowah, also saw the rise of complex cultures with many substantial earthen architecture and engineering structures at major settlements (e.g., Watson Brake, Poverty Point, Moundville, Atlantic Coast Shell Ring sites, Key Marco, and Spiro).

The archaeological sites described and interpreted in these essays extend in time from the earliest human settlements, sites that were occupied even while glaciers covered much of northern North America during the maximum extent of glaciation at the end of the Pleistocene to the mid-twentieth century. Readers can follow the cultural developments throughout the Southeast, from the relatively simple social organization of small groups among the earliest human inhabitants (e.g., Dust Cave, Sloan, and Windover) to the much more complex hierarchical political and social organization of later times, including the construction of special structures to serve as the residences of high-status individuals and mound complexes specialized for ritual uses.

Several essays describe sites where European explorers and Native Americans first encountered each other in Florida and the subsequent developments that grew out of this contact of cultures (e.g., the Governor Martin site, the Santa Elena and Charlesfort sites, St. Augustine, and Santa Catalina de Guale). The horrific outcome of these cultural encounters for many of the Native American cultures is described, as are the desperate and deadly clashes between expeditions of different European countries as represented at sites along the Atlantic coast from South Carolina to northern Florida. The essays describe Revolutionary War, War of 1812, and Civil War sites, including the recovery and conservation of the Confederate States submarine the *Hunley* in Charleston, South

Carolina. Other historic shipwreck sites are described, from the earliest French and Spanish era (the *La Belle*) to a World War II U-boat and its final merchant victim.

We have focused these essays on the most important and interesting archaeological sites and topics in the Southeast region. Readers can learn more about these sites, and others as well, by using the sources of information and references in the last section of each essay. Many of the sites can be visited as part of national, state, or local public parks.

The articles in the Southeast section of *Archaeology in America* include eleven general essays on various topics that cover ancient or historic time periods. The general essays are followed by 50 essays on specific archaeological sites or related groups of sites in a particular region. The more specific essays are arranged in roughly chronological order.

ENTRIES FOR THE SOUTHEAST REGION

THE EARLIEST INHABITANTS AND SITES IN THE SOUTHEAST

When people first arrived in the area now known as the southeastern United States is unknown, but it was at least 13,000 years ago, as indicated by the first evidence for widespread settlement across the region in the form of sites and assemblages characterized by highly distinctive Clovis projectile points and an array of other tools of stone, bone, and ivory. These first peoples have come to be known as Paleoindians since they are assumed to be the ancestors of the Native peoples encountered by European explorers on the North American mainland in the sixteenth century.

By scholarly convention, Paleoindian occupations are assigned to the Pleistocene epoch, or the Ice Age, which ended about 11,500 years ago with the conclusion of the last major cold phase of the most recent glaciation—a time known as the Younger Dryas, from around 12,850 to a little more than 11,500 years ago. Ice sheets in the Northern and Southern hemispheres advance and retreat over cycles of about 110,000 years. The most recent glaciation reached its maximum about 21,000 years ago, but global temperatures began warming and ice began to retreat dramatically shortly after 15,000 years ago, with occasional reversals to colder climate. The last of these colder intervals within a general warming pattern is known as the Younger Dryas period. The end of the Younger Dryas marks the onset of the modern era or the Holocene, a time of comparatively warm and stable interglacial climate.

The Late Pleistocene Southeast had a dramatically different natural environment than at present, occupied by a wide array of plant and animal species of kinds and in combinations not seen in the modern world. The presence of ice sheets to the north, even retreating ones late in the period, meant that plant and animal communities accustomed to colder weather extended much farther south. Coniferous forests were present into the mid-South, while mixed hardwood forests occurred further to the south. Much of the currently submerged continental shelf was exposed due to the massive amounts of water locked up in the northern ice sheets. As these ice sheets melted after 15,000 years ago, the seacoast moved slowly inland, flooding terrain formerly habitable for animals and people alike. In addition to modern animal species, much larger or more unusual animals were prominent on the southeastern landscape, including mammoth, mastodon, bison, elk, giant ground sloths, tortoises, beavers,

and fearsome predators like the dire wolf, the saber-toothed tiger, and the giant short faced bear. Many of these species went extinct at the end of the Pleistocene, before or during the time of the Younger Dryas. The reasons remain unknown, although the dramatically changing climate, the widespread appearance of human populations, and a great many other factors—such as introduced disease or fire, and even a comet impact—have all been suggested as possible contributing factors.

Human beings arrived in the New World, and in the Southeast, sometime during the last glacial period, perhaps well before the ice sheets began to retreat some 15,000 years ago. Paleoindian sites in the Southeast are typically placed into one of three periods by archaeologists, depending on their age and the kind of artifacts and other materials found on them. These are the pre-Clovis or Early Paleoindian period, prior to about 13,500 years ago and extending back to whenever first entry occurred, something still unknown; the Clovis or Middle Paleoindian period, from about 13,500 to 12,850 years ago; and the post-Clovis or Late Paleoindian period, from 12,850 to 11,500 years ago. Conveniently, the two latest periods can be identified by common and readily identifiable artifacts, such as Clovis and post-Clovis projectile point forms, while sites of the earliest period are currently much more difficult to find and recognize.

A number of sites dating to the Early Paleoindian period have been found in recent years. These include Cactus Hill in southern Virginia, where a number of stone tools, chipping debris, and two small triangular points were found in deposits dating to about 17,000–18,000 years ago, stratigraphically below a Clovis assemblage. Also in Virginia, at Saltville, stone flakes and a probable modified bone tool were found in deposits about 15,000 years old. In the Southeast, at Page-Ladson in Florida, an underwater site in the Aucilla River, a cut elephant tusk and a number of pieces of debitage were found in deposits some 14,500 years old. At the Topper site in South Carolina, probable chipped-stone artifacts have been found at depths of up to several meters below a well-defined Clovis assemblage, in deposits dating from 16,000 to as far back as 50,000 years ago. Topper is a major chert (a very fine-grained stone often used for chipped-stone tools) quarry, which would have long attracted human populations looking for workable stone for their tools. Other possible Early Pale-oindian sites in the region include Johnson near Nashville, where hearths dating to about 14,000 years ago have been found eroding from a river bank; and Little Salt Springs in Florida, where an apparently butchered giant tortoise was found in underwater deposits in a sinkhole dating to about 14,500 years ago.

Early Paleoindian sites are extremely rare in the Southeast, suggesting that only small numbers of people were present. Given the widely varying ages of the sites that have been found, some of these groups may well have died out, with permanent sustained settlement not coming until the end of the period or in the ensuing Middle Paleoindian period. A generalized foraging adaptation is assumed to have been in place, with peoples using a wide range of plant and animal species, and perhaps occasionally targeting larger animals. Projectile points appear to have been made by some of these peoples, as indicated by the early triangular points found at Cactus Hill. Other probable Early Paleoindian points have been found at Meadowcroft Rockshelter in Pennsylvania, and at Page-Ladson and other sites in Florida. None of these points exhibit the fluting that is the hallmark of subsequent Middle Paleoindian Clovis points. Unfortunately, some of these points, like the early triangular points from Cactus Hill, resemble much later point types found in the region, making them hard to recognize in artifact collections. That is, while we have already undoubtedly found Early Paleoindian artifacts in surface and other contexts, we don't know how to recognize them for what they are yet.

Middle Paleoindian sites and artifacts are much more common across the Southeast and are identified by the presence of Clovis projectile points and some of the specialized stoneworking debris from their manufacture. Clovis points are lance-like in shape and up to several inches long, with parallel to slightly expanding bodies, a flat to slightly indented base, and, most characteristic, one or more wide flake scars running upward from the base a third or more the length of the blade. Because these flake scars resemble the grooves, or flutes, in classical Greek and Roman columns, they have come to be known as fluted points. Sites producing Clovis points have been dated across North America to between 13,500 and 10,800 years ago, although most sites appear to date to a much a narrower time range, between about 13,100 and 10,850 years ago. These peoples or at least their technology appears to have emerged somewhere and spread rapidly over the landscape, moving long distances in a short time.

In western North America Clovis points have been found with the killed and butchered remains of large animals like mammoth or mastodon. As a result, Clovis peoples are assumed to have targeted large game animals, although how much of their diet actually came from hunting, much less from large game, is unknown. In the Southeast no large animal kill sites have been found associated with Clovis points, although tools of bone and ivory from a number of now extinct Late

Pleistocene species have been found, primarily in Florida's springs, sinks, and rivers. Some level of exploitation of large game is thought to have occurred, even if these peoples were for the most part generalized foragers, eating whatever plants and animals were readily available.

Clovis points have been found in large numbers across the Southeast, particularly along the major interior river systems or near major stone sources, leading a number of archaeologists to suggest that the technology and associated culture may have arisen in the region or perhaps in the nearby southern plains. Many points occur as isolated finds or in small numbers, perhaps representing sites where short-term activities, visits, or hunting incidents took place. The largest Clovis sites and assemblages found to date occur at outcrop or quarry/workshop sites, where suitable stone, typically the highest quality to be found in a given area, was gathered and worked into points and tools. Major Middle Paleoindian sites in quarry/workshop settings in the Southeast include Carson-Conn-Short, Nuckolls, and Wells Creek Crater in Tennessee; Topper in South Carolina; Hardaway in North Carolina; and Thunderbird and Williamson in Virginia. At these locations, not only was stone mined and worked, but it is likely that the peoples remained for appreciable periods of time; if not permanent residents, they regularly revisited these locations as their movements took them elsewhere.

Middle Paleoindian peoples in the Southeast did sometimes range up to several hundred miles from the locations where they quarried stone. They probably did this for a number of reasons, such as to find new sources of food, stone, and other useful materials, and also to find other people with whom they could exchange information and obtain marriage partners from outside their local group. Given that populations were still small and widely scattered over the landscape, a great deal of effort likely needed to be invested in maintaining ties between human groups over large areas. Meetings between differing groups were likely planned rather than fortuitous, and probably took place at resource-rich areas such as major stream crossings or at quarries, where materials critically important to the manufacture of their tools could be obtained. The well-made tool kit of the Clovis peoples—and especially the elaborate fluting on their projectile points, requiring a kind of stoneworking expertise never seen in the subsequent human occupation of the Americas—was undoubtedly a critically important and shared aspect of Middle Paleoindian culture across the region and beyond. As such, the impressive Clovis tool kit not only was of functional utility, but also almost certainly helped to promote ties between groups by demonstrating common values about what was considered an appropriate level of craftsmanship in the tools they used.

The Late Paleoindian period, from 12,850 to 11,500 years ago, witnessed the appearance and replacement of an array of cultures across and in different parts of the Southeast. The period closely corresponds with the Younger Dryas cold episode, and its sudden onset and its cold and somewhat variable climate is thought to be linked, in some way, to the ending of Clovis culture, the final extinction of Late Pleistocene megafauna, and the diversification of cultures that occurred about this time. Archaeological cultures extending over no more than a few hundred miles are recognized in a number of areas, primarily from the restricted occurrence of distinctive projectile point types. These are assumed to reflect areas within which people sharing a common stone tool manufacturing technology and style were in fairly regular interaction, leading to the manufacture of similar tool forms. Conversely, these peoples seem to have less interaction with those in areas where different projectile point types were being made. We don't really know, of course, how closely these different point forms matched different cultures or adaptations. Their restricted distribution does indicate, however, that group ranges or territories, and the amount of interaction over long distances, were apparently decreasing over time.

Fluting like that employed on Clovis points continued for a few centuries into the Late Paleoindian period, with a new emphasis on the production of flutes running the entire length of the blade, in some areas on points with more deeply indented or fishtail-shaped bases. Over time these more fully fluted forms, known by names such as the Barnes, Cumberland, Folsom, Gainey, or Redstone types, gave way to a range of nonfluted points, some with narrow bases and expanding blades, and others more traditionally lance-like in shape. These include the Beaver Lake, Hinds, Simpson, Suwannee, and Quad types. With their appearance, fluting disappeared from the region, never to return. These initial nonfluted forms were themselves replaced within a few centuries, and certainly by 12,000 years ago, by notched Dalton points, many of which were regularly and extensively resharpened from their use as both projectile points and knives. A great variety of Dalton point types or varieties, or closely related forms like the San Patrice, occur all across the Southeast during the last part of the Late Paleoindian period, and probably for a short time into the ensuing Holocene period. By the very end of the period, about 11,500 years ago, side-notched point types were becoming increasingly common in some parts of the region. The appearance of notching, coupled with the extensive resharpening indicated on many points, probably reflects an increasing concern for their use as durable, multipurpose tools, involved in not only the killing but also the butchering of game animals and the processing of their hide, bone, and antler.

The Late Paleoindian period is more, however, than the story of changes in projectile point morphology. Although sea level and vegetational communities would not approximate those of the present for several thousand more years, these were the first peoples in the Southeast to exploit an essentially modern flora and fauna, albeit under the colder and more varied climatic conditions of the Younger Dryas. While there is some evidence for a population decline across the

region at the start of the period, indicated by the fact that there are far fewer immediate post-Clovis than Clovis point forms in most parts of the region, by the time fluting disappears populations appear to have rebounded. The increasing numbers of points and sites, in fact, indicate that populations were growing markedly over the region. While human adaptation to and familiarity with the resources of the Eastern Woodlands was assumed to occur slowly and gradually over the course of several thousand years during the subsequent Archaic period, it is now believed that much of this adjustment occurred during the Late Paleoindian period.

During the Late Paleoindian period, the first extensive use of cave entrances and rockshelters as living places occurs in the Southeast, and it is at this time that cemeteries appear in some areas, notably among the Dalton culture peoples of the central Mississippi valley and, apparently, in ponds and sinks in parts of Florida. People were becoming settled, living in smaller areas for longer periods of time, as reflected in the increasingly localized appearance of many tool forms and the increased use of readily available, lower-quality stone sources in tool manufacture. They may have still moved their residences a fair number of times over the course of a year, but these moves were within ever smaller and more socially bounded areas.

The end of the Younger Dryas marks the end of the Paleoindian period. By convention geologists and climatologists place the onset of the Holocene, and archaeologists the beginning of the Archaic period, a little after the end of the Younger Dryas, at 10,000 radiocarbon years before the present. We now know that this age calibrates to about 11,500 calendar years ago in real time. Radiocarbon dates typically become progressively younger than they should be with increasing age, although it has only been in the last decade that the amount of offset between radiocarbon and calendar ages during Paleoindian times has been documented. Anyone interested in understanding the changes occurring the Paleoindian era in the Southeast, or indeed anywhere in North America, must become adept at converting between one time scale and the other, and must note when radiocarbon years, as opposed to calendar years, are being used in the discussion.

Further Reading: Anderson, David G., "Paleoindian Occupations in the Southeastern United States," in *New Perspectives on the First Americans*, edited by B. T. Lepper and R. Bonnichsen (College Station: Texas A&M University Press, 2004), 119–128; Anderson, David G., "Pleistocene Human Occupation of the Southeastern United States: Research Directions for the Early 21st Century," in *Paleoamerican Origins: Beyond Clovis*, edited by R. Bonnichsen, B. T. Lepper, D. Stanford, and M. R. Waters (College Station: Texas A&M University Press, 2005), 29–42; Anderson, David G., and Kenneth E. Sassaman, eds., *The Paleoindian and Early Archaic Southeast* (Tuscaloosa: University of Alabama Press, 1996); Fiedel, Stuart J., "Older Than We Thought: Implications of Corrected Dates for Paleoindians," *American Antiquity* 64 (1999): 95–116; Goodyear,

Albert C., "The Early Holocene Occupation of the Southeastern United States: A Geoarchaeological Summary," in *Ice Age Peoples of North America*, edited by R. Bonnichsen and K. Turnmire (Corvallis, OR: Center for the Study of the First Americans, 1999), 432–481; Goodyear, Albert C., "Evidence for Pre-Clovis Sites in the Eastern United States," in *Paleoamerican Origins: Beyond Clovis*, edited by R. Bonnichsen, B. T. Lepper, D. Stanford, and M. R. Waters (College Station: Texas A&M University Press, 2005), 103–112; Walker, Renee B., and Boyce N. Driskell, eds., *Foragers of the Terminal Pleistocene in North America* (Lincoln: University of Nebraska Press, 2007); Webb, S. David, ed., *First Floridians and Last Mastodons: The Page Ladson Site in the Aucilla River* (Dordrecht, The Netherlands: Springer, 2006).

David G. Anderson

ANCIENT EARTHEN AND SHELL ARCHITECTURE

Between 500 and 6,000 years ago, Native peoples in the Southeast built thousands of mounds from earth and shell. These were used as cemeteries; monuments; effigies; and platforms for domestic structures, elite residences, and ritual and ceremonial activities. Larger earth and shell works may contain numerous structures built by forming earth or shell into architectural features, such as individual mounds of various shapes and sizes, rings and other enclosures, walls, ramps, causeways, and elevated plazas, as well as excavated features such as borrow pits, ponds, canals, moats, cisterns, sunken plazas, and water courts.

Not all Southeastern groups constructed large-scale earth and shell architecture. It first appeared in the Southeast at points where migratory hunter-gatherers settled in one place and developed complex social organizations to manage their resources. Management strategies included marking territory and symbolizing kinship and historic authority with mounds, while other large-scale utilitarian architecture supported the mound complex. The forms this architecture took varied across the landscape and through time.

ARCHAIC PERIOD (4000–1000 BC)
In the lower Mississippi River valley, Archaic hunter-gatherers periodically met at riverine environments where subsistence resources were sufficiently abundant to support large aggregations of people. At least fifty Archaic mound sites are spread across the lower Mississippi valley at these points. These are among the earliest mounds in the Southeast, and most outwardly resemble the conical burial mounds of the Woodland and Mississippian cultures that would follow. However, few human remains have been found that would support the use of these early mounds for burials. Of these, perhaps the best case for funerary use is the 5-meter-high, 6,000-year-old Monte Sano mound in Louisiana, where the remains from a possible human cremation were identified below the mound.

While most early sites contain a single conical earth mound, some have multiple mounds. Among the earliest sites, at around 5,500 years ago, is Watson Brake in north Louisiana. There hunter-gatherers built ten earthen mounds surrounding a central plaza 350 meters in diameter. Measuring between 1 and 6 meters high, the mounds were connected by an earthen ridge. Toward the end of the Archaic period at Poverty Point, the largest and most complex architecture of its time was constructed. Built across a 400-acre expanse, Poverty Point comprises conical mounds, a 20-meter-tall bird effigy mound, a series of parallel mounded "house" ridges, and a ball court. Equally famous for the abundance of exotic trade items, the site's existence is linked to its centralized location within a far-flung trading network. No earthen mound architecture of its size would be built again for another 2,000 years in the Southeast.

In Florida, distinctive Archaic mound-building cultural traditions arose, some of which included funerary functions. Around 5,400 years ago, along the St. Johns River, 175 burials were placed on a prepared surface beneath a low-lying sand mound at Tick Island. Similar sand burial mounds up to 2 meters high are found upriver at the Thornhill Lake and Orange sites. Common to the period, bannerstones (carved stones used as weights for *atl atls*, or throwing sticks) and numerous marine shell beads and tools were associated with these burials, indicating relations with nonlocal people. The limited number of exotic lithic items suggests that these cultures lay on the margins of Southeastern exchange networks.

Twenty miles east of the St. Johns River, another Archaic group built an extensive complex consisting of six earthen mounds along the Atlantic coast at around 2600 BC. These mounds also contained bannerstones and human remains. Unlike the burials at Tick Island, however, the remains were scattered rather than placed in prepared grave pits below the mound. However, subsequent to the mound construction, pits were dug into the mound and human remains placed in them.

Elsewhere in Florida and South Carolina, similarly shaped conical mounds are found at coastal shell ring sites. These mounds differ from those at Tomoka in that they are made predominantly of oyster shell. At the Bonita, Horr's Island, and Fig Island sites, the shell mounds served as cappings to smaller sand mounds. Although no evidence yet exists that these mounds were built for human burials, subsequent cultures used them as cemeteries.

Horr's Island, Florida, shell works with ceremonial ringed village, mound, and adjacent habitation area.   [Martin Pate / National Park Service]

Different kinds of shell mound constructions are found at large midden mounds along the St. Johns River and north Atlantic coast of Florida. Occasionally conical, these mounds are more commonly irregularly shaped as they follow the shoreline for hundreds of meters. Frequently multicomponent, their great initial volumes deposited during the Archaic were increased substantially by subsequent cultures. The presence of hearths as well as pottery and other everyday artifacts indicates that during the Archaic period the mounds served as places of habitation. But the occasional presence of scattered human remains and exotic artifacts also suggests social and symbolic significance. The height of these shell mounds could reach 5 to 10 meters. As such, they likely served as markers of kin and other social identities, much like the smaller conical burial mounds. Some of the mounded middens, like the more formally planned shell ring coastal sites, were probably feasting sites, as evidenced by large episodic deposits of shell (e.g., coquina and oyster).

Shell rings are the most widespread and recognizable type of Archaic mounds found along the Atlantic and Gulf coasts from South Carolina to Mississippi. Made almost exclusively of oyster shell, they represent formal ceremonial feasting sites, some of which were occupied year-round. These sites also represent the first recognizable "shell works," with the larger rings accompanied by shell causeways, ramps, trails, mounds, and multiple, connected rings.

WOODLAND PERIOD (1000 BC–AD 1000)
Around 3,000 years ago, the widespread mound-building traditions of the Archaic disappeared. Perhaps retreating sea levels or other climatic conditions caused a collapse of the coastal and riverine resources vital for supporting the populations and social organizations necessary for constructing large-scale public works.

Mound traditions began to reappear during the Early Woodland period. The Tchefuncte cultures in Mississippi and Louisiana began constructing low, conical mounds around 2,500 years ago. Some of them contained burials. Low sand burial mounds were being constructed at early Deptford (the name used for an Early Woodland culture in the area) sites

Raffman Site, Louisiana, Late Woodland, Coles Creek earthen mound complex and associated habitation areas. [Martin Pate / National Park Service]

along the coast of Georgia between 1,700 and 2,000 years ago. Similar small conical burial mounds are sporadically located up into North Carolina and into the piedmont and summit regions of the Appalachian Mountains.

Some Woodland mounds, including Deptford burial mounds, contained trade goods, demonstrating connections with the mound-building Adena culture in the Midwest. At Crystal River, Florida, a large mound complex begun during this period consisted of multiple sand mounds. One burial mound was surrounded by a ring of shell that also contained burials. Later during the Middle Woodland, Crystal River represented the southernmost ceremonial complex of Swift Creek–related cultures, which originated in and spread across southern Georgia into southwest Alabama and northern Florida. As Swift Creek changed into the Late Woodland Weeden Island cultures, distinct pottery types were added and mound use expanded.

Among the largest Weeden Island sites on the interior coastal plain are Kolomoki, Letchworth, and McKeithen. These regional centers are characterized by multiple earthen

mounds, both conical and platform types, that served as the foundation for wooden structures. The mounds reached heights of 18 meters and surrounded large plazas with habitation and midden deposits found between the mounds. The presence of both village deposits and mounds indicates both sacred and secular functions, a phenomenon first identified at many Archaic mound sites.

Coastal manifestations of Weeden Island mound architecture took on a different form. These are found most prominently along the Florida panhandle, such as at Third Gulf Breeze, and as far south as Weedon Island on Tampa Bay. Unlike the structures at interior sites, coastal mounds and circular rings surrounding plazas are made of shell piled up to 3 meters high, although many rings are lower and represent accretional, that is, gradually built up, rather than purposeful architectural deposits. Exotic goods and distinct pottery in the mounds suggest sacred ancestor worship. Lying on the edges of the Weeden Island world, these coastal sites and mounds never attained the size or regional importance found at the ceremonial/trade centers of the interior.

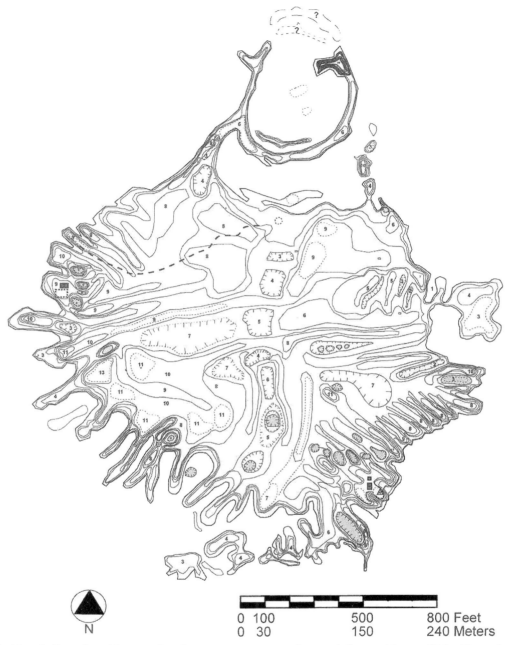

Russell Key, Florida, shell works with mounds, plazas, water courts, ring, and finger ridges.   [John Beriault / National Park Service]

In Louisiana, Marksville mounds contained exotic goods and other evidence of burial ceremonialism linking them to the Hopewellian traditions of the Midwest. Although most Marksville sites contained only one burial mound, the larger earthworks included platform and conical earthen burial mounds often surrounded by extensive earthen ridges measuring up to 2 meters high and 1,000 meters long. Marksville burials may be found in log-lined vaults. The largest burial

mound was found at the Crooks site, where over 1,000 interments were uncovered. In contrast, the Baytown cultures that followed Marksville in the region have relatively few exotic artifacts and, rarely, low conical earthen burial mounds, suggesting an end to the earlier tradition of Hopewellian-influenced mound burial ceremonialism.

Perhaps among the most unusual Hopewell-influenced earthen architecture in the Southeast is that found in south

Florida around Lake Okeechobee. At the best-known site, Fort Center, most of the thirteen mounds served as house foundations; only one contained burials. But a pond contained preserved wooden statuary associated with charnel activities. Mounded earthen rings with radiating and other linear embankments were built at these sites, in part to raise land above flood level. The unusual shapes of these earthworks held symbolic significance and, at the same time, allowed crops to be grown above the frequently flooded surrounding Everglades.

Middle Woodland settlements followed many of the mounding traditions of earlier Woodland cultures. In Tennessee, earthen enclosures and mounds characterize many sites. At Pinson, fifteen mounds served ceremonial purposes. Earthen ramps and orientation to cardinal directions were important architectural features. One mound was enclosed by an elevated earthen ridge. This feature is duplicated at several sites, including Old Stone Fort, where a unique earthen and stone wall encompassed 50 acres of flat habitation area and mounds. This arrangement of village/mound and multiple mound sites is characteristic of many Middle Woodland cultures and can also be found at Pharr, with eight mounds, and Bynum, with six mounds and a village.

By the Late Woodland (AD 700 to 1050), the use of burial mounds was in decline, yet the tradition of mound building persisted among some cultures. Boyd Mounds in Mississippi is one of the best-preserved burial sites of this period. Meanwhile, in central Arkansas, the Plum Bayou culture constructed the Toltec mound complex. There a 3-meter-tall earthen enclosure was located on a relic river shoreline. Inside, the complex consisted of sixteen mounds, the tallest of which stood 15 meters tall. Its enclosure and location isolated Toltec physically and symbolically from the outside rural communities, for which it served as a political and religious center.

At the Ocmulgee site on the Macon Plateau in Georgia, initial construction of seven large mounds began in AD 900. A large village grew at the site. The Great Temple Mound, the largest mound, today still stands 17 meters high. Four conical mounds served as earthen lodges with room for up to forty-seven individuals. These undoubtedly functioned as places of ritual and ceremony. Similar constructions were common at the time among other cultures. In Louisiana, for example, Coles Creek cultures constructed large platform mounds as foundations for residences or public structures. Most famously, at Troyville, the tallest mound in the enclosed complex once stood 25 meters tall.

Along the Atlantic coast and the parallel St. Johns River of eastern Florida, the St. Johns cultures were prolific mound builders. Conical sand burial mounds, usually just over a meter high, are ubiquitous and yield artifacts indicative of contact with Hopewell and Swift Creek cultures. But it is the shell midden mounds that often reach monumental proportions. Placed atop earlier Archaic shell mounds, Woodland shell midden mounds reached tens of meters in height and ran hundreds of meters along shoreline. The shell ramps and causeways built for accessing the tops of these massive mounds continued a tradition of shell works construction begun during the Archaic.

But the most complex and expansive of all shell architecture is found at the coastal sites of southwest Florida. There, Woodland architectural features include conical and platform mounds; ramps and causeways; protective seawalls; canals, water courts, and ponds; plazas and courtyards; and shell crescents, rings, ridges, and effigy constructions.

Large shell works are common in Charlotte Harbor, Estero Bay, and the Ten Thousand Islands on offshore mangrove keys, where village and mound structures covered sites between 20 and 125 acres in size. The Pineland, Mound Key, Fakahatchee Key, and Dismal Key sites are among the largest and most complex shell works, with platform and conical shell mounds 5 to 10 meters in height. To access these and the village interiors canals were built, taking into account daily tides, which flushed waste and freshened water courts, fish traps, and aquacultural ponds. On Russell Key, over a dozen water courts, more than two dozen finger ridges or wharfs, two large mounds, three large plazas, and a shell ring were constructed across the 60-acre site.

In form, size, and location, these complex sites represent a type of patterned shell works that include platform mounds housing important individuals, finger ridges that served as docking areas and/or habitation locales, mounds for sacred functions that were isolated from the main settlement, and a variety of infrastructural constructs that supported the settlement, such as canals, ponds, and seawalls. The size and regular spacing of these sites along the coast suggest that they were regional centers. Their complexity reflects the high level of social organization needed to construct and manage them.

Other large sites hold similar mounded structures, which may have also represented totemic effigies. At Big Mound Key, for example, four shell platform mounds arranged in a rectangle, an isolated shell mound, two canals, and a rectangular pond made up the center of the site, much like at other large shell works. But a set of nine low, concentric, curvilinear shell ridges suggest that a crab or spider form was the symbolic motivation behind their construction (similar concentric ridges are found at the Poverty Point and Fig Island sites).

Other shell works in southwest Florida suggest use as tribute-based villages or processing centers focused on fishing or shellfishing. These sites lack many of the shell architecture features of the more architecturally complex regional centers, but they do contain large and extensive mounds. At the 30-acre Turner River site, multiple rows of conical shell mounds extend linearly for a quarter-mile along the river. Nineteen individual steep-sided shell mounds reach heights of 5 to 6 meters and are more than 20 meters in diameter, with plazas occasionally interspersed among the mounds.

Narrower, low areas between any two mounds may have served as canoe landings or, perhaps, locations of domiciles placed on elevated wooden platforms. This site type is little studied, but some variation of it may also be found at the southernmost known shell works. The 40-acre Johnson's Mound lacks canals and finger ridges but contains extensive shell mounds ranging from 4 to 6 meters high.

MISSISSIPPIAN TO HISTORIC CONTACT (AD 1000–1700)

Around AD 800, earthen architecture in the Southeast got bigger. As agriculture provided sustainable resources and populations increased, societies built large mounds to symbolize the power of their groups and leaders. Large platform mounds were residential foundations for important community members and locations for high-status rituals. Multiple mounds, both platform and burial, surrounded large plazas, which were venues for large-scale public ceremony. The largest of these mound complexes likely represented important political centers; smaller ones may have been local centers, perhaps under the political control of rulers who resided at the larger sites. The dominance of these Mississippian mound-building traditions was widespread, with major mound centers found in every state in the Southeast.

The largest Mississippian mound center was located at Moundville, Alabama, where twenty-six to twenty-nine earthen mounds, the tallest at 18 meters, covered 300 acres and held over 1,000 inhabitants between AD 1000 and 1450. Up to 10,000 people lived in rural homesteads surrounding the center—a centralized pattern typical of Mississippian settlement. The site functioned under a tribute-based economy, with the countryside population providing the bulk of the subsistence resources that supported the center. The nobility received a wide range of exotic items such as mica, copper, galena, and marine shell, which ultimately accompanied them to their interments.

Etowah in north Georgia was another large mound center occupied from AD 1000 to 1550. One of three mounds that demarcate a central plaza was a 19-meter-high platform mound that had a log-lined stairway leading to its top. Home to as many as several thousand people, the overall site contained six earthen mounds, a village area, barrow pits, and a defensive ditch. Like many Mississippian mound sites, Etowah was encircled by a defensive palisade.

The contemporary Parkin site on the St. Francis River in Arkansas was originally protected by an encircling moat and log palisade. Agricultural fields lay outside the protected area. Today, out of perhaps an original seven mounds, only one large ceremonial mound remains. It provided the foundation for a large structure (chief's house?) with an attached apron that supported attendant structures. The site once was home to a 17-acre village/mound complex. Its population of over 1,000 was supported by as many as twenty-five surrounding hamlets. In addition, the Parkin site is believed to

be the village where de Soto and members of his expedition raised a cross on one of the mounds.

Emerald Mound in southwestern Mississippi is the largest single mound in the Southeast. Constructed between AD 1250 and 1700, this platform mound, shaped like a parallelogram, covers 8 acres, measures 235 by 135 meters, and stands nearly 11 meters high. On top sit two (formerly six) additional platform mounds at either end, the tallest extending an additional 3 meters skyward. The massive structure functioned primarily as a ceremonial center, with its extensive flat top serving as a plaza. A few burials have been recovered from the secondary mounds. Emerald Mound represents one of the few preserved mounds of the Natchez Indians, whose historic accounts provide the knowledge base for Mississippian social organization and settlement patterns—chiefdoms, large mounds, and surrounding hamlets.

The mounds described above are found in the heartland of the Mississippian culture area. Frontier settlements on the peripheries of the Mississippian world differed somewhat. On the western edge, in Oklahoma, the 80-acre Spiro site comprises twelve mounds (one burial, two platform, and nine house mounds), ceremonial plazas, and villages. The site, occupied from AD 850 to 1450, was home to leaders, who directed laborers from outlying villages to build the mounds. Six mounds encircle an oval plaza on the western side of the site. In the early twentieth century, treasure hunters recovered basketry, feather capes, and cloth from mound looting. These were discarded for more "valuable" objects, such as copper from the Great Lakes, shell beads from California, and decorated whelk shells from Florida. The quantity and variety of these exotic trade items remain unparalleled in any other part of the Mississippian world, largely because of the unusual conditions of preservation. As with the earlier Poverty Point site, Spiro's strategic location facilitated trade between distinct culture areas, accounting in part for its great size and wealth.

On the opposite side of the Mississippian world, in southern North Carolina, sits the Town Creek mound and village site. The ramped platform mound provided the foundation for a large wooden structure, but there is no evidence of burial or elite residence. This mound, in turn, was surrounded by a variety of other wooden structures, many of which had palisades and contained burials in their earthen floors. Burial artifacts from Town Creek link it to Cahokia, Spiro, and other Mississippian sites, but the site is not particularly large by the standards of its time. The single mound measures less than 4 meters high. Some think these characteristics are due to the site's marginal location on the easternmost edge of the Mississippian world, where, faced with threats posed by local non-Mississippian populations the inhabitants could not prosper.

Lake Jackson in north Florida was perhaps the southernmost true Mississippian center. It consisted of one burial and six platform mounds, the largest of which stood 11 meters high. Occupied between AD 1000 and 1250, burial and trade objects indicate full participation in the Mississippian traditions. Artifacts include copper breastplates, necklaces, bracelets, anklets, and cloaks.

Further south and east along the St. Johns River in Florida, mound-building cultures at Mt. Royal and Mill Cove/Shield Mound participated in the Mississippian trade network, but they lay outside the Mississippian world proper. In part, archaeologists exclude them from the Mississippian tradition because their resource base relied on fishing rather than agriculture. But the mound architecture at these sites also differed. Platform mounds made mostly of sand, with shell in lesser amounts, rose 6 meters high. But at both Mt. Royal and Shields Mound, extensive raised "roadways" up to 1 meter high and 6 meters wide radiated from the mounds. At Mt. Royal, these raised tumuli bounded a sunken plaza measuring 50 meters wide and 1,200 meters long that had been built between the mound and a man-made pond—the probable source of material for the mound itself. Caches of unworked whelk shell, a coastal resource, have led some to suggest that the site was a likely trade nexus for the extensive shell artifacts found at distant Mississippian sites, such as Cahokia and Spiro.

The large shell midden mounds along the St. Johns River and east Atlantic coast of Florida, begun in the Archaic and Woodland periods, reached their greatest volumes in the Mississippian period as shell continued to be added to the mounds of past cultures. A number of these sites reached heights up to 15 meters and lengths of hundreds of meters (e.g., Turtle Mound). But the most extensive and complex shell works of the period continued to be built along the coastal mangrove swamps of southwest Florida. There, sites begun in the Woodland, such as Pineland, Mound Key, Russell Key, and Turner River, continued to be occupied into the Mississippian and historic contact periods. Some are identifiable as the centers of known historic chiefdoms.

Further Reading: Anderson, David G., and Robert C. Mainfort Jr., eds., *The Woodland Southeast* (Tuscaloosa: University of Alabama Press, 2002); Gibson, Jon L., and Philip J. Carr, eds., *Signs of Power: The Rise of Cultural Complexity in the Southeast* (Tuscaloosa: University of Alabama Press, 2002); Marquardt, William H., and Claudine Payne, eds., *Culture and Environment in the Domain of the Calusa* (Gainesville: University of Florida, Institute of Archaeology and Paleoenvironmental Studies, 1992); Mathis, Mark A., and Jeffrey J. Crow, eds., *The Prehistory of North Carolina: An Archaeological Symposium* (Raleigh: North Carolina Department of Cultural Resources, Division of Archives and History, 1983); Milanich, Jerald T., ed., *Famous Florida Sites: Crystal River and Mount Royal* (Gainesville: University Press of Florida, 1999); Perry, I. Mac, *Indian Mounds You Can Visit: 165 Aboriginal Sites on Florida's West Coast* (St. Petersburg, FL: Great Outdoors, 1998); Pluckhahn, Thomas J., *Kolomoki: Settlement and Status in the Deep South, A.D. 350–750* (Tuscaloosa: University of Alabama Press, 2003); Sassaman, Kenneth E., ed., "Archaic Mounds in the Southeast," *Southeastern Archaeology* 13 (1994): 89–186.

Michael Russo and Margo Schwadron

ANCIENT SITES AND ARCHITECTURE ON THE ATLANTIC AND GULF COASTS

For the first millennia that hunter-gatherers lived in North America their economic preoccupations centered on daily searches to meet basic family needs for food, clothing, and shelter. In these small, mobile bands, each family benefited equally in, and depended upon, the success of other families. Sharing was a unifying ethic and effectively leveled the status of individuals within each band; individual accumulation of wealth or power would have been considered selfish and harmful for the community as a whole. This equitability principle extended among bands of families as they periodically aggregated to share seasonally abundant resources, exchange stories, trade materials, and to maintain old and establish new social relationships, including marriages. At the end of these meetings, bands would separate and continue with their mobile subsistence pursuits.

By 6,000 years ago, along river and ocean shorelines in the Southeast, the interface of wetland and woodland environments was sufficiently productive to support year-round occupations. At these places, a number of Archaic period bands altered their seasonally mobile foraging strategies and settled for extended periods, or even permanently, in one spot. Through the hosting of ceremonies and feasts, these groups continued their relationships with their more mobile contemporaries and developed new relationships with other, nearby settled people. The most successful settlements grew in size and importance in their respective regions.

With increasing populations and permanent settlements, communities developed new technologies, social relations, and organizing principles to acquire sufficient food to meet their growing needs. As they had been doing for millennia,

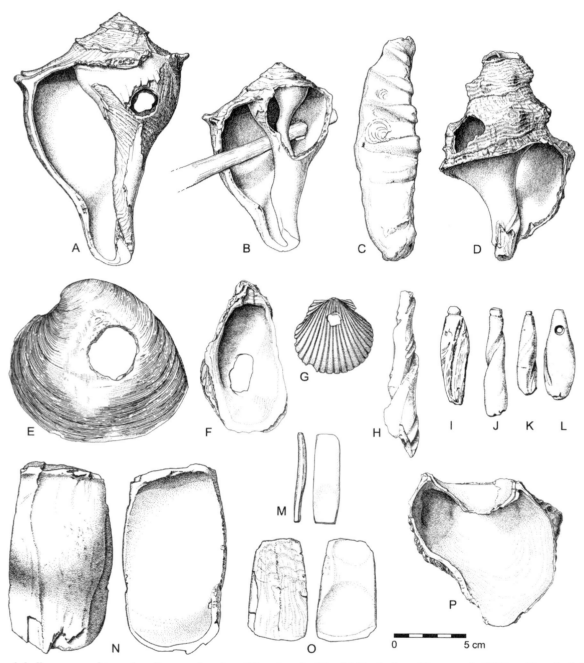

A variety of shells were used to make all sorts of tools. [Drawings by Merald Clark, from Marquardt, William H., ed. *Culture and Environment in the Domain of Calusa*. Gainesville: University of Florida Institute of Archaeology and Paleoenvironmental Studies, Monograph 1, 1992. Courtesy of William H. Marquardt.]

people were still largely reliant on chipped- and ground-stone tool technologies for use in hunting and in gathering plants. But now, tethered to their settlements, hunters were limited in the distances they could travel to kill game. To compensate, they expanded technologies geared to acquiring fish and other wetland resources. Along the coasts, they lacked suitable raw stone, so they used marine shell for many tools, including fish hooks, net gauges, gouges, axes, adzes, chisels, hammers, anvils, knives, scrapers, needles, ladles, spoons, cups, and

bowls. Most of the Archaic cultures that settled the coasts permanently were also the first in their regions to invent or adopt pottery, which was used to prepare food for daily meals as well as to contribute to ceremonial feasts, where ostentatious displays may have contributed to greater prestige.

While the manufacture of small tools and pottery operated on a family or individual level, other aspects of the new wetlands-centered economies required leadership and community support. Specialized knowledge and many laborers

DeBry engraving of Native Americans digging out a canoe, ca. 1590.   [Library of Congress]

were needed to manufacture dugout canoes, fish weirs, and large fish nets. Without canoes, access to areas of exploitable shellfish and fish was limited to the edges of mainland rivers, shallow marshes, and swamps. Canoes were essential for travel along interior rivers and among the myriad marshes and mangrove islands in coastal estuaries.

Large-net fishing also required community participation both to make the nets and to manipulate them once in the water. Positioning fish weirs across critical spots in rivers and tidal creeks called for both planning expertise and construction and maintenance labor that were beyond the scope of individuals or single families. The management of these corporate structures must have been directed by skilled or otherwise enterprising individuals who persuaded or compelled people to action for the benefit of the community. In return for their efforts, these situationally influential leaders received the respect and support of their communities. They could then potentially parlay that support into other aspects of village life, such as hosting ceremonies and feasts, thereby gaining the benefits of greater prestige and power.

Ceremonies were parts of daily social and sacred life among these hunter-gatherers. Spirits and ancestors were honored and entreated for help through rituals that often included food and other material offerings. When these ceremonies involved the entire community or neighboring groups, their presentation went beyond the scope of single individuals or families. In these times, respected and enterprising

individuals probably took responsibility for supporting and feeding guests, compelling individuals to work toward the success of the ceremony. So the prestige and power associated with hierarchical leadership probably was earned and accepted, despite the persistence of an egalitarian ethic in other aspects of social life. Among growing Archaic period populations, large feasts were vehicles for bonding community members, for appeasing enemies or establishing defensive alliances, and for inducing others into intercommunity affiliations through marriage or other kinship relations. Large feasts would also have served as "insurance policies." They incurred social and material obligations from guests, ensuring that future subsistence needs would be met in times of shortage or through reciprocal feasts. The increasingly complex social relationships among communities and the individuals who took on leadership roles in ceremonies and feasts are evident in the archaeological record in the layouts of permanent settlements, the varied size and importance of neighboring settlements, differential access to material goods and the spiritual world, and large-scale public architecture at key sites.

EARLY LOWER MISSISSIPPI VALLEY MOUND SETTLEMENTS

Some of the first definitive evidence that societies were organizing differently in terms of increased complexity in social relations is found at early earthen architecture mound sites in

Mound D, located on Horr's Island, stands 4 meters tall.   [Michael Russo]

the lower Mississippi River valley. There over fifty Archaic mounds were built along river edges between 3,000 and 6,500 years ago. Among the earliest are multiple-mound sites with individual mounds reaching up to 9 meters high, such as at Watson Brake in Louisiana. These large mounds and mound complexes indicate forms of social organization previously unseen on the Archaic cultural landscape.

Considerable planning and direction was needed to prompt community members to invest labor into non-subsistence-oriented, public-architecture projects such as these mounded platforms. At these mound sites, economies had expanded from those limited to immediate subsistence needs to ones that included the generation of enough food to permit occasional hosting of events related to wider kin and political relationships. As at earlier hunter-gatherer sites, where people seasonally aggregated for largely social reasons, the mound sites functioned as meeting places for widely distributed bands. However, they also were likely places where incipient tribes featuring greater numbers of people were forming, based on existing kin relations. Population increase is reflected in both site size and density, which suggest that societies in many places had moved beyond simple bands to related groups acting in their members' common interest. One measure of that transformation is the construction of large-scale public works in the form of mounds. Common interest, however, did not mean equal interest, and differences in

power among mound builders are observable in the mounds, which vary greatly in height and volume. Through their ability to obtain greater food surpluses and socially obligated labor, certain groups built grander mounds and mound complexes than others.

Aside from the mounds themselves, little differentiation of status among individuals or groups can be identified in the archaeological record. At Monte Sano in Louisiana, hierarchical distinctions are suggested by a large structure and possible burials beneath a big earthen mound. But, in general, burial and structural remains—key markers of social disparity—are absent at early mound sites. And this holds true even toward the end of the Archaic period, when the massive and architecturally complex Poverty Point site in Louisiana was, without a doubt, the largest mound complex in North America. The planning and labor required for its construction suggests that, at least at this one site, complex social relations existed on a scale previously unseen in the Southeast. But little in the form or burials or structures from the mounds has been identified to suggest that hierarchical social relations existed among community members.

Poverty Point and related sites do differ from earlier mound sites in the region insofar as their artifact assemblages are characterized by an abundance of exotic trade items. Some, such as various stones, were brought to Poverty Point as raw materials to be transformed into more valued lapidary objects.

Whether these items were used at the site as status symbols or traded outward, they mark an extensive industry absent at other early mound sites and represent surplus production beyond the subsistence economy. Typically among complex societies such as chiefdoms, extensive surplus production is used to finance elite projects, for example, territorial expansion, elaborate architectural monuments such as mounds, or warfare. But in the absence of definitive data illustrating social stratification—for example, elaborate burials indicating a social elite—archaeologists have been understandably reluctant to identify Poverty Point as a chiefdom. Thus, despite the surpluses, the surplus production and management of valued lapidary objects is seen as family based.

Despite the ambiguity still present in Poverty Point interpretations, most scholars agree that great numbers of people contributed to the massive mounds that reinforced the history, land rights, and power of the community. Also, in terms of sedentism and social organization, the site is clearly more permanent and complex than any that preceded it, or any that followed it over the next 2,000 years.

SOUTH FLORIDA RING AND MOUND COMMUNITIES

Nearly a thousand miles away, along the coast of south Florida, other Archaic period groups were showing signs of increased social complexity. Between 4,000 and 5,000 years ago, at least four shell ring sites appeared among what had been, at best, sparsely populated mangrove swamps. Initially these sites were seasonal aggregation points for hunter-gatherer bands from the interior Florida peninsula. But rather quickly, some bands came to settle along the coast year-round. The south Florida ring sites served as the base communities for multiple families and, perhaps, multiple kin groups. The largest communities built plazas, used both for daily living activities and for larger ceremonies and feasts. The primary component of feasts was oysters, and refuse shell was mounded to construct massive U-shaped rings that surrounded plazas.

Shell rings served multiple purposes, both secular and sacred. On a practical level, they were places for refuse. Habitation and ceremonies occurred within the ring plaza, and the proximity of the ring reduced the labor involved in transporting the shell to dump sites. As with much of the early mounding in the Southeast, rings also functioned as territorial and symbolic markers. Contiguous and encircling rings may have symbolized village unity, while the height of ring walls separated insiders from outsiders.

Faunal and plant remains indicate year-round food collection by those living in the ring villages. Intensive settlement is also evident in the size of rings, some measuring up to 250 meters long and 5 meters deep. Horr's Island is unique among shell ring sites, revealing evidence of numerous house structures on the inside of the ring along the plaza edge, with most located at the closed end of the ring. Constructed of saplings and of uniform size, the houses were circular and

about 3 meters in diameter, large enough to accommodate a nuclear family. Pits and hearths are found both within and without the structures. Outside the Horr's Island shell ring were two other living areas defined by deep, linear oyster shell middens, each 200 meters long. Posts and limestone-lined hearths indicate that daily maintenance activities were also associated with these middens.

All three living areas at Horr's Island—the ring and two linear middens—were associated with their own conical mounds. At the end of the shell ring's north wall, Mound A rises 6 meters high. It was constructed as a small sand mound placed on a prepared and ritually burned ground surface. That mound was then capped with alternating layers of shell and sand. The midden ridge called area B supports Mound B, which was similarly made from sand and shell but measures only 1 meter high. At the other midden ridge, 1-meter-high Mound C was made only of shell.

These mound, midden, and plaza features together constitute the Horr's Island village. Because the two linear shell ridges hold less evidence of houses (fewer posts) and less shell, they appear to have been less intensively occupied. It is unclear if the groups associated with them resided permanently at the site or were perhaps only seasonal visitors or guests at ceremonial events. But the existence of separate living areas, each with its own mound, suggests three distinct kin or other social groups. The group associated with Mound A clearly held more power, at least in terms of obligated labor, as evidenced by its greater size, tall mound, and its having the only living area containing a ring and plaza. The plaza served double duty as a public area for daily activities of the ring inhabitants and as a sacred arena for all three groups during ceremonies. Set atop a large sand dune, a rarity in the otherwise low-lying mangrove swamps, Mound A reached 15 meters above the nearby gulf waters. No other feature in the region surpasses this height, save for yet another mound on Horr's Island, isolated 400 meters east of the village. Four-meter-tall Mound D, placed on a 12-meter-high dune, was unassociated with any midden areas. Its elevation and isolation suggest a special significance.

Horr's Island sits atop a unique parabolic sand dune surrounding an embayment up to 2 miles in diameter. Elsewhere along this dune other, smaller habitation areas have been found that probably represent foraging camps or rural hamlets that articulated with the large Horr's Island village. Other than these sites, however, Archaic settlements were rather dispersed. To the north of Horr's Island, occupants at the Bonita and Hill Cottage sites constructed even larger shell rings and mounds. Unfortunately, the Hill Cottage mounds were destroyed before archaeological investigations could be conducted. At over 250 meters in length, the Reed site on the Atlantic Ocean is the largest south Florida ring. But other than these large sites, Archaic period sites along the more than 800 kilometers (500 miles) of south Florida coastline are rare.

The sparsity of coastal Archaic sites suggests relatively small populations. It also is puzzling because it is unclear what compelled the ring builders to settle, claim, and mark their territories with large-scale public architecture at so few points along a long and seemingly wide-open coastline. The answer may lie, in part, in the corporate investment needed to exploit dense mangrove environments. These zones are marked by relatively few areas of dry land. Horr's Island, for example, sits on an unusually high dune that rises some 10 to 12 meters above sea level at the northern end of an otherwise unbroken expanses of mangrove swamps, euphemistically termed the Ten Thousand Islands. The site was likely a base for logistical foraging, it being easier to settle than to invest the labor necessary to build dry land amid the mangrove swamps that were closer to food resources. During the later Woodland and Mississippian time periods, more populous cultures did indeed make their own lands amid the mangroves, but Archaic period peoples apparently chose not to do so.

CAROLINA BIGHT SHELL RING COMMUNITIES

Other shell ring–building cultures were more densely populated. Between 3,000 and 5,000 years ago along a coastal region called the Carolina Bight, from South Carolina to northeast Florida, three distinct cultural groups are identifiable. Whereas northeast Florida groups built rings similar in size (up to 250 meters) and shape (U-shaped) to those in south Florida, the Georgia and South Carolina rings averaged only 50 meters and were circular. Yet the shell ring sites in these more northern areas were densely distributed, often being part of multiple-ring sites. Over ten times as many shell rings were built along the 240-kilometer (150-mile) bight as were built along the much longer south Florida coast, indicating higher population densities.

In the more temperate climate of the Carolina Bight, rings were placed in mainland and island hardwood hammocks found among extensive coastal lowland marshes. Access to, and settlement on, the numerous islands were logistically and technologically easier than in the mangrove forests of south Florida, but also required corporate investment to make dugouts for water transportation. As in south Florida, most rings were settled throughout the year. Evidence of daily living, while sometimes present, is not apparent at all sites. Most rings are made of massive piles of shell, indicating that many rings were principally arenas for large-scale feasting rather than daily living.

Some of the larger ring sites, such as Fig Island in South Carolina and Sapelo in Georgia, were not solely ceremonial. They contain several rings, including the largest in their regions, measuring from 80 to over 100 meters across. The multiple rings at these sites vary in both size and function. At Fig Island, one ring contains layers of crushed shell suggestive of pedestrian traffic associated with daily living; another is made up of uncrushed, large piles of "clean" shell, suggesting episodic and quick deposits after mass feasting. The

upper levels of the largest shell ring known in the Southeast (6 meters tall) are made of shell mined from elsewhere and brought to the site to construct a conspicuous monument. Attached to the large ring is the only Archaic mound found in South Carolina. The 4-meter-high mound and the large ring, in particular, are evidence of the site's complex design, as well as of the complex social organization behind the multiple-ring/mound village. As at Horr's Island, the association of the largest ring with a mound indicates prestige and power unmatched at Fig Island or any other South Carolina ring site. At Fig Island, the varied uses of its six rings and mound indicate both a sacred and secular site where ceremonial and spiritual needs were manifest through public architecture that required planning, direction, and community involvement to an extent previously unknown in the region.

Fig Island and most other South Carolina ring builders produced a style of pottery referred to as Thom's Creek pottery, a sand-tempered ware; ring builders in Georgia made a different type, Stallings fiber-tempered wares. Fig Island, the largest site in the region, was centrally located among the Thom's Creek shell rings, while the large three-ring Sapelo complex was centrally located among Stallings coastal sites. Their large sizes, multiple rings, central locations, and separate pottery traditions suggest that these sites served as incipient tribal political centers. Differences in the size and shapes of Stallings and Thom's Creek rings and associated pottery, along with those of the adjacent St. Marys region in northeast Florida, further indicate that the Late Archaic was a time of expanding and increasingly complex politics. Distinct tribes arose and sought to separate and distinguish themselves from their neighbors through their architecture and aspects of material culture, such as pottery styles.

ORANGE SETTLEMENTS

Some of the most densely populated and socially complex sites during the Archaic were found on the central east coast of Florida. Here scores of settlements were spread along 400 kilometers (250 miles) of Atlantic coast and 325 kilometers (200 miles) of the adjacent freshwater St. Johns River and marshlands. Largely spring-fed from a deep aquifer, the St. Johns River valley was less affected by the climate fluctuations that characterized much of the Southeast during the mid-Holocene. As sea level rose, internal hydrostatic pressure forced artesian spring waters to breach the surface land and flood the valley, creating expansive freshwater wetlands in Florida around 6,000 years ago (the first ones following the Ice Age). Human inhabitants quickly settled in this rich environment, exploiting the fish and other natural resources and constructing mounded middens of earth and shell (freshwater snail and mussel). They buried their dead in sand mounds. One mound, Tick Island, was built around 5,500 years ago. The community was largely egalitarian, as evidenced by more than 175 burials with no extravagant burial furniture. Social distinctions are nevertheless indicated by differential inclusion of artifacts in burials and the restriction of mound burials to those old enough to have attained a social standing. Differences are also seen in burial methods. A few individuals were interred in a large grave pit associated with a structure that was subsequently capped by a sand mound. Many bodies were placed in extended positions in separate graves, and the remains of other individuals were buried as bundled bones or in flexed positions after long-term storage.

Mound burials were also found on the adjacent coast at Tomoka. Dating to 4,600 years ago, this minimally investigated site consisted of a complex of nine or more conical sand burial mounds rising up to 3 meters in height, a possible mortuary pond, and an extensive shell midden spread across 15 hectares along a small tidal stream. The largest mound contained scattered human remains and caches of rare artifacts, including bannerstones, suggesting special status for the buried individuals and the mound itself.

By 4,000 years ago, settlers along the St. Johns River and the coast had universally adopted fiber-tempered, Orange-period pottery. Populations had increased dramatically, as indicated by permanent rather than seasonal occupations in both coastal and riverine zones, and by a site density over twelve times that found during the previous pre-ceramic Archaic period along the river. Along the coast, scores of Late Archaic Orange sites were occupied, where few pre-ceramic sites had been known. The common use of the same pottery and the absence of shell rings separate the Orange region culture from the ring-building cultures to the north and south. While permanent settlements indicate that societies were no longer organized in simple bands, but rather in more complex kin or tribal formations, the great number of and distances between Orange sites suggest that a rather loose tribal association linked the communities.

ARCHAIC PERMANENT SETTLEMENT AND SOCIAL COMPLEXITY

During the Middle and Late Archaic periods in the Southeast, abundant wetland resources, settled and rising populations, and increased site density were critical factors leading certain groups to develop more complex social organization than had been exhibited by their strictly mobile foraging ancestors. Such organization was necessary, in part, to manage wild foods, which, however abundant, could be overexploited due to the fact that more people were occupying the same areas throughout the year. Managing the increasing number and complexity of social relations both within the community and between corporate groups required a more intricate organization than was found among earlier bands.

Of course, not all Archaic groups achieved the level or kinds of complex organization that mound and ring builders did. In particular, mobile foragers of the interior uplands continued to manage their subsistence economies based on seasonal hunting and gathering, largely as they had for thousands of years. What differed in some cases among these mobile foragers, however, was their range of seasonal movement. With more settled populations occupying river and coastal shorelines, the traditionally unrestricted seasonal forays to these resources were now limited. or cut off altogether. To obtain their accustomed food and other resources, such as good stone for making tools, mobile hunter-gatherers had to deal with the people who now claimed ownership of these places. New social relations were manifest through ceremony and trade, and individuals skilled in managing these relations earned prestige and power in their communities. The presence of large-scale mounded architecture during the Archaic is certainly evidence that social organization was becoming more complex among certain, settled societies. But, in turn, this complexity required that the more mobile groups attain new levels of social interaction. Unfortunately, evidence for increasing complexity among mobile foragers, who had to limit their material culture and maintain low population levels, is not easily visible in the archaeological record.

Most scholars view Middle and Late Archaic Southeast societies as egalitarian, exhibiting no evidence of permanent social stratification in which certain categories of people held more power than others. But social complexity takes many forms and is apparent among all societies, even aggressively egalitarian ones. Such actions as individual ownership, wealth accumulation, and food hoarding are actively and often ruthlessly discouraged in hunter-gatherer societies. In such low-production economies, significant differences in wealth or social obligation from which status distinctions can arise may simply not be possible given the limited means of production. Nonetheless, interpersonal hierarchies do arise and, in fact, often characterize hunter-gatherer economies. A few individuals can incur social obligations from their peers through sharing food; controlling children and, often, women; and managing skilled tasks, such as horticulture, warfare, and large-scale community projects. During the Archaic in the Southeast, such changing social relationships resulted in new technologies and architectural construction that set the stage for subsequent mound-building tribal and chiefdom societies.

Further Reading: Aten, Lawrence E., "Middle Archaic Ceremonialism at Tick Island, Florida: Ripley P. Bullen's 1961 Excavations at the Harris Creek Site," *Florida Anthropologist* 52 (1999): 131–200; Gibson, Jon L., and Philip J. Carr, eds., *Signs of Power: The Rise of Cultural Complexity in the Southeast* (Tuscaloosa: University of Alabama Press, 2002); Marquardt, William H., ed., *Culture and Environment in the Domain of the Calusa*, Institute of Archaeology and Paleoenvironmental Studies Monograph 1 (Gainesville: University of Florida, 1992); Sassaman, Kenneth E., ed., "Archaic Mounds in the Southeast," *Southeastern Archaeology* 13 (1994): 89–186; Sassaman, Kenneth E., and David G. Anderson, eds., *Archaeology of the Mid-Holocene Southeast* (Gainesville: University Press of Florida, 1996).

Michael Russo

COMPLEX ANCIENT SOCIETIES IN THE LOWER MISSISSIPPI VALLEY AND FLORIDA

The early development of complex Native American societies on the coastal plain of the Gulf of Mexico has long intrigued archaeologists. Two regions in particular, the lower Mississippi valley (LMV) and peninsular Florida, are distinguished by enormous architectural monuments of earth and shell, elaborate material culture, and long-distance trade. These products and activities suggest complex social organization that enabled coordinated labor, creation and planned use of food surpluses, and relatively unequal or non-egalitarian societies. Some of the later archaeological sites in these regions are arranged in such a manner as to suggest centralized political, economic, and religious organization. Perhaps most striking has been the *absence* of evidence for agriculture, as well as the surprisingly early dates for many sites. Social complexity in the LMV and Florida pre-dates the adoption of agriculture by at least several centuries and persists alongside contemporaneous agricultural societies of the Mississippi period (about AD 1000–1700).

Intensive agriculture based on domesticated plants such as maize has been a hallmark of most complex societies, integral to the origins of the earliest cities and states of Mesoamerica and chiefdoms in eastern North America. Complexity is associated with vertical or hierarchical leadership but also involves statuses and inequalities that are horizontal or unranked, including ethnic diversity. Agriculture provided the surpluses required for specialization in non-subsistence-related tasks, political and religious hierarchies, and social stratification. Yet cultural complexity cannot simply be equated with agriculture. Archaeological and ethnographic evidence for complex, non-agricultural societies from around the world demonstrates that people long ago discovered and pursued alternative paths to social and political complexity. More precisely, insufficient ecological potential for food collection and production brings *external constraints* to the creation and expansion of complex societies, constraints that in some instances were surpassed through ingenuity, political influence, and persistent effort.

Extraordinarily productive fishing, hunting, and gathering provided the economic base that was central to the emergence of complex societies in the LMV and Florida, but provide only part of the explanation. The origins of complexity can now be traced back thousands of years to affluent, foraging societies of the Middle and Late Archaic periods (about 6000–500 BC). Consideration of the timing, scale, or intermittent rise and fall of complex societies should also take into account the ways in which *internal* social constraints were negotiated and overcome. Archaeologists have only begun to describe and understand the histories of these pre-Columbian societies and disagree as to whether or not such non-agricultural communities qualify as "chiefdoms" comparable to Mississippian culture. Due to a

relative lack of corresponding evidence for individual wealth and status, the focus has shifted to corporate or family-based leadership and strategies in the establishment of political-religious authority. One thing is certain, however: numerous politically integrated societies or regional polities of the LMV and peninsular Florida achieved uniquely indigenous forms of social differentiation and complexity without agriculture. Archaeologists refer to these societies using general cultural labels such as Coles Creek, Belle Glade, and Caloosahatchee.

ARCHAIC PERIOD ANTECEDENTS
Corresponding trajectories of foraging societies in the LMV and peninsular Florida provide a comparative perspective of emergent complexity on the gulf coastal plain of southeastern North America. The indigenous origins of complexity in the LMV of present-day Louisiana and western Mississippi are deeply buried in alluvial sediment deposited over millennia by the Mississippi River and its tributaries. The remains of earthworks planned and constructed in ancient times are the largest and today the most visible representation of complex Native American societies. An enormous, bird-shaped mound and six concentric, crescent-shaped earthen rings at the Poverty Point site in northeastern Louisiana were recognized by the middle of the twentieth century as likely evidence its builders had benefited from agriculture. The largest of the mounds towers 70 feet (21 m) over Maçon Ridge, and the entire site is estimated to cover more than 1.2 square miles (3 square kilometers [km²]). Early archaeological research produced unanticipated interpretive problems when the earthworks were determined to have been constructed between 3,550 and 3,250 years ago (1600 and 1300 BC), long before the inception of agriculture. Exquisite crafts such as bird pendants, figurines, and stone gorgets, and evidence for widespread exchange of resources such as chert, shells, galena, quartz crystal, and copper indicate economic relationships on an extensive scale that would not be surpassed for over a millennium. The deliberate planning, organization, and massive expenditure of labor needed to create the earthen architecture at Poverty Point challenges conventional understanding of cultural evolution, pre-dating not only agriculture, but the widespread adoption of pottery, sedentary villages, and more complex social organization. Poverty Point and sites associated with Poverty Point culture remained somewhat enigmatic to archaeological understanding until the final decade of the twentieth century, signifying uncharacteristically early, non-agricultural, complex mound-building societies in the LMV.

A major shift in professional viewpoints commenced in the 1990s, by which time archaeological investigations and systematic radiocarbon dating had provided a series of break-throughs in the interpretation of Archaic period mounds and mounded middens. Michael Russo (in Sassaman and Anderson, 1996) distinguishes ceremonial mounds from mounded earth and shell middens, all of which are now known to date as early as 5,700 years ago (3750 BC). Russo estimates that at least sixty mound sites dating from the Middle to Late Archaic are located in the LMV and Florida. Horr's Island, on the southwest gulf coast of peninsular Florida, stands out as a major Middle to Late Archaic age site with extensive midden deposits up to 16 feet (5 m) deep and three mounds constructed from sand and shell, thought to date to 4,400 and 5,900 years ago (2450–3950 BC). Aquatic resources such as oyster, other shellfish, and marine fish constitute the majority of subsistence remains and, along with architectural evidence, indicate a relatively sedentary or permanent pre-ceramic settlement. Dense shell middens representing the residues of shellfish consumption, deposited in circular and semicircular rings, are also known to date from the Middle and Late Archaic periods in Florida and northward along the Atlantic coast. Russo (in Gibson and Carr, 2004) suggests that inequalities are represented in the spatial distribution and volume of shell, which correspond to ritual feasting among higher-status groups or households in societies with both simple and complex or trans-egalitarian organization.

Frenchman's Bend, Hedgepeth, Monte Sano, and Watson Brake are among the numerous Middle Archaic ceremonial mounds now known in Louisiana, the most impressive being Watson Brake. Watson Brake consists of an enormous oval ridge connecting eleven conical mounds, the largest of which is over 23 feet (7 m) high. As at Poverty Point, despite the obvious need for communal organization of labor, there is no evidence for agriculture. Aquatic resources such as freshwater drum and catfish provided a substantial proportion of subsistence needs, along with deer, various species of small mammals, turkey, and aquatic birds. Hickory, acorn, and pecan provided abundant nut harvests in the fall. In contrast to the case at Poverty Point, little evidence exists for long-distance exchange at Middle Archaic sites in the LMV or Florida peninsula. Middle Archaic ceremonial mounds in the LMV foreshadow the subsequent Poverty Point mound-building tradition by 2,000 years. The Poverty Point site is certainly still the largest among early monumental earthen architecture, but it is by no means the earliest.

Underlying commonalities among pre-ceramic mound, mounded midden, and shell ring sites in the LMV and Florida exist in the ecological potential for the development of social complexity among affluent foragers in riverine and coastal environments, what Jon Gibson (in Sassaman and Anderson, 1996) refers to as "logistical based sedentism." Resource abundance and accessibility did not simply "cause" social complexity, however, as the distribution of sites with ceremonial mounds and mounded midden do not uniformly correspond with aquatic resource availability. Prosperous communities of fisher-hunter-gatherers proliferated and achieved repeated political and economic success during the Middle and Late Archaic time periods. Competition may have heightened inequalities and conflict as populations increased in size and challenged existing territorial boundaries. Distinct bands were likely drawn together through ritual feasting, ceremonialism, supernatural beliefs, and underlying cultural connections such as language and kinship, to create expansive, even more complex communities such as those that built and inhabited Poverty Point and Watson Brake. A majority of communities in the LMV and Florida remained small-scale foragers, however, practicing seasonal, residential mobility with little discernible evidence of differential distribution of resources. Archaeologists continue to debate the degree of sedentism or sedentary settlement represented by Watson Brake, Horr's Island, and other Archaic sites, and whether the ancient Americans who constructed the earthworks and middens were organized as hierarchical, ranked, egalitarian, or trans-egalitarian societies. One thing is becoming clearer, however: monumental construction was intentional, thoroughly designed, and punctuated, not fortuitous, accidental, or accretional.

LOWER MISSISSIPPI VALLEY

Post-Archaic period, pre-Columbian complexity among non-agricultural societies in the LMV is represented by numerous regionally distinct cultures and phases, suggesting a high degree of social differentiation analogous to historically documented tribal variation. Following the decline of Poverty Point exchange and mound building, archaeologists have distinguished a sequence of specific cultural groups in the region that seem to have carried on the complex social organization and architectural construction of earlier times. These are referred to as Tchefuncte (about 800–200 BC), Marksville (about 200 BC–AD 400), and Baytown-Troyville (about AD 400–700) components. The more widespread production and use of ceramic vessels at Tchefuncte sites, subsequent technological improvements and stylistic diversification during Marksville times, and communal burials in cemeteries and mounds are generally characteristic of cultural development associated with the Woodland time period. Early and Middle Woodland societies in the LMV otherwise continued to focus on acorn, hickory, other wild plant foods, and aquatic resources, especially along the coast. Although earthen construction is associated with each of these traditions, notably conical burial mounds and the initiation of truncated or flat-topped pyramidal mounds, the more restricted spatial distribution of sites, generally smaller size of mounds, and decline in long-distance exchange have been used to infer the existence of relatively egalitarian tribal societies, occasionally made more conspicuous by the aggrandizing achievements of high-profile individuals in opportunistic pursuit of status.

The sites of Marksville and Troyville stand out in this regard, with substantial monumental architecture, encircling earthen embankments, and, in the case of Marksville, artifactual evidence for indirect Hopewellian connections or long-distance exchange with Middle Woodland societies in the Midwest. Along with interregional interaction, the construction of ceremonial mound centers and elaborate interments in sub-mound tombs are interpreted as evidence of increased complexity among competing lineages or corporate groups during the Middle Woodland. It is noteworthy that the inhabitants of Marksville and Troyville did not rely on the cultivation of starchy seed plants associated with Woodland period plant domestication in the Midwest, nor did they pursue horticulture in any meaningful sense. As more becomes known about affluent fisher-hunter-gatherers and logistically based sedentism of the Archaic period, archaeologists will undoubtedly arrive at fresh perspectives on the origins and development of social complexity during the Middle Woodland.

The culmination of complex, non-agricultural societies in the LMV is without a doubt associated with the more geographically extensive Coles Creek culture of the Late Woodland, Coles Creek period (about AD 700–1200), first identified by James Ford in the 1930s. Once characterized based on ceramic evidence as relatively static in contrast to Mississippian culture, with which it overlaps by two centuries, Coles Creek is now thought to have consisted of affluent foragers who achieved a remarkably high degree of sedentary village life with social formations described as ranked, hierarchical, elite, and complex. As in the case of Poverty Point, the layout and enormous size of many Coles Creek mounds led some archaeologists to infer that maize agriculture produced the subsistence surpluses necessary to sustain communal labor. Yet Coles Creek peoples flourished on a profusion of fish and shellfish, supplemented with acorn, wild seeds, fruits such as persimmon, deer, and small mammals. Starchy seed crops were adopted in the northern LMV but, like maize, do not appear in the southern LMV until late Coles Creek times. Reliance on wild plant foods persisted in the southern LMV and along the gulf coast, where aquatic resources remained important. Coastal and northern variants of Coles Creek have consequently been identified, but in both instances agricultural production seems to have remained inconsequential until the infusion of Mississippian ideas and peoples.

Coles Creek material culture included small, triangular projectiles, correlated with the widespread adoption of the bow and arrow, and relatively plain, grog-tempered (tempered using crushed fragments of ceramics) pottery with rectilinear incising. In comparison to previous Marksville and subsequent Mississippian cultures, there is a paucity of elaborate craft items and status or prestige goods, and diminished long-distance exchange. Nor were Coles Creek mounds built as lavish mortuaries or burial places for prominent men and their lineages. Earthen platforms were instead primarily constructed as substructures for ceremonial buildings and residences, with occasional later interments. Interpretation of Coles Creek mound sites as political-religious centers is largely based on these substructural mounds and hierarchical or centralized settlement patterns. Small sites, with typically three mounds, are more numerous than larger, multi-mound sites with centrally located plazas, and both are outnumbered by outlying villages or non-mound sites.

The Greenhouse site in the lower Red River valley and Lake George in the Yazoo basin are among the best-known Coles Creek mound centers. Greenhouse consisted of three large platform mounds and four smaller mounds or low rises laid out around an unoccupied plaza. Circular and rectangular buildings on several of the mounds served as residences of the elite and possible mortuaries or temples that housed the remains of venerated ancestors. Lake George is characterized by platform mounds surrounding two largely vacant plazas, but it soon emerged as the largest Coles Creek center. At least twenty-five mounds were constructed beginning in the Baytown period and concluding with the Lake George phase of the Mississippi period. Mound A, the largest and centrally positioned mound at the site, was no less than 55 feet (17 m) high and contained architectural evidence of a ceremonial structure on the summit. Burials in Mound C with apparent human sacrificial interments hint at the elite status of certain individuals. Lake George is also unique among Coles Creek mound centers in having been fortified by a surrounding palisade and moat.

Stephen Williams and Jeffrey Brain argue for Mississippian influence on late Coles Creek culture at Lake George, beginning with attenuated contacts after AD 1000 and culminating in the cultural hybridization of the Plaquemine variant of Mississippian culture after AD 1200. Coles Creek and subsequent Plaquemine components in the southern LMV exhibit less evidence of Mississippian contacts, especially in coastal areas south of Baton Rouge. The indigenous origins of Coles Creek mound construction can be traced through earlier Troyville and Marksville traditions, with comparatively little interregional interaction. Increased numbers of Coles Creek mound and non-mound sites in the alluvial Mississippi valley and its many tributaries indicate long-term population growth based on the localized intensification of fishing, hunting, and gathering. The scale of Coles Creek political integration never encompassed a major portion of the LMV but was instead punctuated by the overlapping if not independent consolidation and decline of numerous regional polities. Some Coles Creek centers may have been the exclusive residences of the elite, with a majority of the population living in dispersed villages. Political and religious authority thus became increasingly exclusionary, centralized, and hierarchical among regionally integrated communities of complex foragers. Four centuries later, Native American descendants who survived European disease epidemics and colonization were documented as various historic tribes of the LMV, such as the Chitimacha tribe of Louisiana.

PENINSULAR FLORIDA

Following the Middle Archaic time period in south Florida there are no known societies comparable to Poverty Point culture, which is locally represented at contemporaneous sites in the northwest Florida panhandle. Indigenous histories of fisher-hunter-gatherers in peninsular Florida are comparable to those associated with the LMV, however, in that abundant aquatic resources enabled the development and maintenance of complex social formations without reliance on agricultural production. The Archaic period derivation of these communities is apparent in long-standing traditions of producing and shaping shell rings, mounded middens, and ceremonial earthen mounds. Coastal and inland wetland resources remained significant throughout peninsular Florida for millennia, with an enormous variety of salt- and freshwater fish, shellfish, turtle, alligator, aquatic birds, and small mammals. Belle Glade and Caloosahatchee are among the best known non-agricultural, complex cultures of peninsular Florida.

Maize agriculture was adopted between AD 750 and 1000 among contemporaneous societies in northwest, north central, and east Florida, the latter associated with historic Timucuan villages encountered by Europeans. St. Johns culture of north central and east Florida, the forerunner of Timucuan society, nonetheless retained a broad reliance on productive fishing, hunting, and gathering. Ceramic evidence indicates that St. Johns culture in turn derived from Late Archaic Orange culture at sites in the St. Johns River drainage. Hopewellian influence or interaction has been found after AD 100 at late St. Johns I period (about 500 BC–AD 750) sites, including conical burial mounds with mica, galena, and copper artifacts. Subsequent Mississippian influence during the St. Johns II period (about AD 750–1565) is associated with the integration of communities into simple chiefdoms engaged in maize agriculture, but to a lesser extent than contemporaneous Mississippian communities of northwest Florida. Late Woodland period Weeden Island culture (about AD 300–1200) of northwest Florida and the peninsular Gulf Coast apparently followed a similar trajectory in the adoption of maize agriculture after about AD 750, represented by regional variants such as Wakulla in the northwest, Cades Pond in north central Florida, and Manasota around Tampa Bay. Early Weeden Island I mound centers such as McKeithen in north Florida indicate considerable achieved status, mortuary ceremonialism, and emergent social complexity well prior to the advent of agriculture.

Non-agricultural social complexity is arguably best represented at sites associated with Belle Glade culture in south Florida. Named after the Belle Glade site and recognized at sites throughout Lake Okeechobee Basin and the Kissimmee River drainage, Belle Glade culture is characterized by monumental earthworks dating as early as 1000–500 BC, when Archaic peoples apparently migrated into the region. Belle Glade is divided into four periods, spanning 500 BC to AD 1700, with evidence for sustained population growth and increased complexity among communities of fisher-hunter-gatherers. Sites with circular ditches, mounded middens, residential mounds, and mortuary platform mounds prior to AD 1000 were subsequently enlarged with the addition of linear embankments and attached earthen mounds. Fort Center is the best known and largest Belle Glade mound center, covering approximately one square mile and consisting of mounds, linear embankments, ditches or moats, and artificial ponds. The latter preserved a wooden mortuary platform and wide array of carved wooden artifacts. The mortuary compound included a charnel house on the summit of a platform mound and encircling embankment. Smaller sites with residential mounds and mounded middens are also found throughout the Okeechobee basin, as are canals ostensibly constructed to facilitate transportation. Along with the earthworks and mounded middens, these expansive projects indicate a high degree of planning, community organization, and expenditure of labor. Based on maize pollen recovered at Fort Center, Sears (1982) has suggested that the ditches and linear embankments were utilized for maize agriculture. This isolated occurrence has not been corroborated through additional archaeobotanical evidence, however, and purported maize agriculture at Belle Glade sites remains in doubt.

Caloosahatchee culture is known from sites along the rivers, bays, and estuaries south of Charlotte Harbor on the southwest gulf coast west of the Okeechobee basin and north of the Everglades. Caloosahatchee society consisted of complex fisher-hunter-gatherer communities organized around the abundant marine resources of the Charlotte Harbor region. Material culture from Caloosahatchee and Glades sites such as Key Marco indicate a high degree of complexity related to subsistence and ceremonialism. Besides ceramics, shell, bone, and wood artifacts rarely preserved at archaeological sites were commonly utilized due to the scarcity of knappable stone. Material culture from Key Marco includes a profusion of well-preserved wood artifacts, including bowls, cups, trays, tablets, mortars and pestles, amulets, masks, animal and human figurines, throwing sticks, clubs, canoes, and paddles.

The Caloosahatchee chronology is generally subdivided into five periods spanning roughly 500 BC to AD 1700, culminating with the historically documented Calusa. Shell middens and mounds are found along the coast, as well as on offshore islands such as Cayo Costa and Pine Island, with smaller sites located further inland and along interior rivers. As in the Glades region to the south, larger ceremonial and residential sites are located along the coast, indicating a wide-ranging and long-standing orientation to marine resources in south Florida. Caloosahatchee shell middens are generally more extensive and massive, however, and many sites include large causeways, canals, and platform mounds. The latter supported buildings used for political and religious ceremonies. Randolph Widmer (1988) makes a case for the evolution of non-agricultural chiefdoms by AD 800 based on long-term population growth and competition over resources. Complex social formations were likely produced earlier, as reflected in monumental architecture and mounded midden dating as early as the Late Archaic. Regardless, communities formed hierarchical regional polities with higher population densities based on the intensification of long-established traditions of fishing, hunting, and gathering. These politically integrated and centralized societies mobilized substantial communal labor and undertook large-scale construction projects that inspire awe among cultural tourists even today.

Further Reading: Gibson, Jon L., and Philip J. Carr, eds., *Signs of Power: The Rise of Cultural Complexity in the Southeast* (Tuscaloosa: University of Alabama Press, 2004); Kidder, Tristram R., "Coles Creek Period Social Organization and Evolution in Northeast Louisiana," in *Lords of the Southeast: Social Inequality and the Native Elites of Southeastern North America*, edited by Alex W. Barker and Timothy R. Pauketat, Archaeological Papers of the American Anthropological Association No. 3 (1992), 145–162; Kidder, Tristram R., "Woodland Period Archaeology of the Lower Mississippi Valley," in *The Woodland Southeast*, edited by David G. Anderson and Robert C. Mainfort, Jr. (Tuscaloosa: University of Alabama Press, 2002), 66–90; Milanich, Jerald T., *Archaeology of Precolumbian Florida* (Gainesville: University Press of Florida, 1994); Milanich, Jerald T., *Florida's Indians from Ancient Times to the Present* (Gainesville: University Press of Florida, 1998); Sassaman, Kenneth E., and David G. Anderson, eds., *Archaeology of the Mid-Holocene Southeast* (Gainesville: University Press of Florida, 1996); Sears, William H., *Fort Center: An Archaeological Site in the Lake Okeechobee Basin* (Gainesville: University Press of Florida, 1982); Widmer, Randolph J., *The Evolution of the Calusa: A Non-Agricultural Chiefdom on the Southwest Florida Coast* (Tuscaloosa: University of Alabama Press, 1988).

Mark A. Rees

THE ORIGIN AND DEVELOPMENT OF SOUTHEASTERN CHIEFDOMS

For more than 500 years prior to their first contact with Europeans, Native peoples across much of the Southeast and lower Midwest lived in politically organized units that archaeologists refer to as chiefdoms. Societies classified as chiefdoms are known from several parts of the world. They are, in general, regional in scale, organizing different communities, towns, and villages under the authority of a central person, or chief. Because chiefdoms lack permanent armies and large bureaucracies, the real authority of most chiefs is limited, so they usually depend on a broader consensus, such as the advice of councils, in making decisions. The population of most chiefdoms ranges from a few hundred to as many as 10,000 people, and most occupy a territory that rarely exceeds 50 kilometers (km), or 30 miles, in diameter. In chiefdoms, various kinship relations usually have much to do with a person's social standing, which means that one's position within society may be fixed from birth and political offices such as chief can be inherited. Finally, most chiefdoms have economies based on farming and rely on the production of agricultural surplus, or harvesting more food than is needed for immediate consumption. These extra harvests or surpluses can then be stored for use in emergencies (if next year's crop fails, for example) or put toward political ends such as hosting a feast for friends and allies. Not all chiefdoms make surpluses by farming—some exploit rich fishing grounds—but all need to produce surplus in one form or another.

The people of most Southeastern chiefdoms practiced maize agriculture, built flat-topped mounds of packed earth as platforms for their temples and the houses of their chiefs, and created open plazas in the centers of their towns for public ceremonies. Archaeologists generally use the term "Mississippian" when referring to these chiefdoms, a term denoting societies that share certain archaeologically visible characteristics, including particular kinds of artifacts and architecture, that date to the period of about AD 1000–1600. Mississippian chiefdoms flourished across much of the Eastern Woodlands, as far north as Illinois and southern Wisconsin, as far west as eastern Oklahoma, as far east as the Carolinas and Georgia, and south to Florida and the gulf coast. However, not all Southeastern chiefdoms are considered Mississippian in terms of how archaeologists classify societies based on pottery styles, building construction methods, the presence and form of mounds, dietary practices, and the like. The Powhatan chiefdom of coastal Virginia, for example, grew maize but did not build mounds, while the Calusa of southern Florida built mounds but based their economy on fish rather than maize. Moreover, not all Mississippian people who grew maize and built mounds and plazas lived in chiefdoms; some lived independently in towns and communities that were not tied to any larger political unit. In this essay, the focus will be on Mississippian chiefdoms, from their origins around AD 1000 through their demise after the mid-sixteenth century in the aftermath of entanglements with European colonial powers.

ORGANIZATION OF MISSISSIPPIAN CHIEFDOMS

A Mississippian chiefdom typically consisted of a large central town or village surrounded by smaller subject towns, villages, or communities of dispersed farmers. The larger central town was the seat of the regional chief and was usually characterized by greater labor investments in civic and ritual architecture, such as mounds and plazas, although most subject communities had their own leaders and public spaces. Mississippian settlements, large and small, were usually located on or near the floodplains of major river valleys. These rich locales offered access to a range of wild plants and animals, especially fish, while also providing the best soils for agriculture. Mississippian farmers practiced a form of agriculture called shifting cultivation. In shifting cultivation, a plot of land is farmed for several years until it is no longer fertile, at which point it is abandoned (or left fallow) and a new plot cleared and prepared for planting. Eventually, the fallow plot recovers its capacity to produce a surplus and may be planted again. While maize was the most important crop to Mississippian farmers, they grew it alongside crops of beans and squash, and so these three plants are often referred to as the Three Sisters.

In Mississippian chiefdoms, subject communities were obligated to give some portion of their food surplus to the regional chief as a kind of tribute. Only rarely, however, did the chief hold absolute power over his or her subjects, who may have recognized a regional authority only during special, ceremonial occasions. This potential for conflict between a regional center and its subjects was a source of instability in Mississippian chiefdoms, many of which lasted for less than three or four generations (100–150 years) before splintering into their constituent parts. In time, a leader from one of the formerly subject communities could rise to regional prominence and begin anew the process of chiefdom formation. David G. Anderson has denoted this waxing and waning of chiefdom formation, decline, and reorganization as "chiefdom cycling."

Warfare was very important in Southeastern chiefdoms. Many Mississippian towns were surrounded by deep moats or enclosed by defensive palisades—tall fences made of thick, upright wooden posts—and many towns had both palisades and moats. Most palisades were equipped with round or square bastions along the walls—elevated platforms where sentries could stand watch or fire arrows down upon attackers. The bow and arrow was introduced to the Southeast about AD 700 and with it came the need for such innovative forms of defense as palisades and moats. Throughout the Southeast, chiefdoms were often separated by vast tracts of uninhabited woodland that archaeologists call buffer zones. Buffer zones served as a kind of no-man's-land between warring chiefdoms, but were also places where Mississippian hunters sought wild game such as whitetail deer.

Religion had a significant role in the organization of Mississippian chiefdoms. The most ubiquitous evidence of Mississippian religion consists of the thousands of platform mounds erected from AD 1000 to 1600. Although the practice of building mounds has a history that stretches back many thousands of years in eastern North America, it is during the Mississippian period that it reached its zenith both in the number and distribution of mounds. Platform mounds carried a rich symbolic load that went far beyond their obvious function as the foundation for temples or the houses of chiefs. Mississippian

people periodically dismantled the temples atop their mounds and then covered the old mound surface with new layers of soil that over time buried the original mound far below. Thus, many of the mounds that we see today have many levels of construction history that are hidden by their green, grassy surfaces. Vernon J. Knight has proposed that platform mounds symbolized the earth and its fertility, and that the ceremonial act of burying the old mound surface beneath a new one enacted a metaphorical cycle of destruction and rebirth, like the cycle of the seasons.

Ancestor veneration was also common in Mississippian religion. Ancestors were deceased kin honored and remembered by their living descendents, in return for which they were believed to bestow good fortune and fertility, both to families and crops. Many of the temples atop platform mounds were mortuaries that held the bones of important people, particularly dead chiefs and their families. Ancestors were a prevalent theme in Mississippian art and were often depicted in statues made of stone, clay, or wood, or materials like bone that resist rot and decay. Some of the most spectacular examples of Mississippian art—the famous engraved shell cups and gorgets from the Spiro site in Oklahoma and the embossed copper plates from Georgia's Etowah site—illustrate the deeds of powerful ancestors and culture heroes. Unlike platform mounds, which seem to have had a strong communal emphasis, owning objects such as these was probably beyond the reach of all but the most elite members of Mississippian chiefdoms.

ORIGINS OF MISSISSIPPIAN CHIEFDOMS

The origins of Mississippian chiefdoms are indelibly linked to the increasing significance of maize agriculture in much of the lower Eastern Woodlands from AD 800 to 1000, a time known to archaeologists as the Late Woodland period. Maize was not native to the Eastern Woodlands, having first been domesticated in what is now central Mexico by about 6000 BC. Archaeologists have recovered small quantities of maize from Middle Woodland (Hopewell) contexts dating to the first two centuries AD, illustrating the plant's long history of use in eastern North America. Its consumption during the Middle Woodland period, however, was probably limited to special occasions, and nowhere did it contribute significantly to Hopewell diets. Rather, Middle Woodland people subsisted both by hunting and gathering and by cultivating several starchy seed crops that were native to the Eastern Woodlands.

In the Late Woodland period, as human populations increased over much of eastern North America, people began to recognize certain benefits that maize provided over domesticated native seed plants, such as maygrass, sunflower, and sumpweed. First, maize offered a higher-yield crop than any of the native domesticated plants, and it had a much higher caloric value. These benefits were important, for as the human population of any region grew, people living there became more tightly packed, so that the territory available for hunting and gathering decreased. Maize allowed people to intensify their food production within these smaller territories, even though the clearing and maintenance of maize fields required higher investments of labor. Just as important, maize is more readily harvested and stored than earlier native seed crops. Given the ease of picking maize cobs from their stalks, increasing populations meant more hands available at harvest time, as well as for clearing new land for fields. Thus, this shift to maize agriculture created a clear benefit—up to a point—for having access to more people and their potential labor. Finally, since maize can be easily stored for long periods, people had more incentive to produce surpluses.

The relationship between labor and surplus—the fact that more labor could produce more surplus—was an essential part of the social context in which chiefdoms began to form after about AD 1000. As competition for the rich, floodplain locales intensified, so too did competition for people both to clear and farm such places and to defend them from others. That is, the leaders of groups that claimed desirable locales actively sought to attract new people to their groups. More people translated to larger surpluses and better defense. Also, attracting new people could create debt relationships, as families new to a particular locale likely found that the better soils for farming were already claimed by other families. Many newcomers therefore found themselves periodically dependent on their more affluent neighbors in times of want. They could repay their debt by working in their benefactors' fields or by giving up a portion of their own surplus during times of plenty. Such debt relations, particularly when passed from one generation to the next, planted the seeds of inequality and hereditary status, two of the defining aspects of chiefdoms. Such relations extended to the regional scale, as those communities situated in rich locales attracted more people than those in less desirable areas. The larger communities enjoyed an obvious military advantage over their smaller neighbors, but also had more labor and surplus to invest in social activities such as building mounds and hosting feasts. Maize did not produce chiefdoms, but an increasing reliance on maize—a productive and easily stored source of food—created the conditions that made chiefdoms possible.

MISSISSIPPIAN FLORESCENCE

After AD 1000, a number of large farming communities emerged in the Southeast and lower Midwest. One of the first regions where the various social factors related to chiefdom development came together was the American Bottom area of southwestern Illinois, the floodplain located across the Mississippi River from the modern-day city of St. Louis, Missouri. Here, at about AD 1050, the great Mississippian center of Cahokia began to coalesce in a rapid burst of social action. Cahokia was a large settlement for more than a century prior to this date, but by AD 1100—in less than fifty years—it had grown to become the largest of all Mississippian towns, home to several thousand people (by some estimates as many as 10,000).

Indeed, it was by far the largest prehistoric center north of Mexico. At its height, Cahokia boasted at least 100 earthen mounds spread across an area of 10 square kilometers (km²) (about 4 square miles [mi²]). The archaeological site is dominated by Monks Mound, which rises to a height of 30 meters (100 ft) above the main plaza and is the largest earthen platform ever built in native North America. Within just a few miles of Cahokia were the second and fourth largest of all Mississippian sites: the St. Louis and East St. Louis mound groups, both of which are now mostly lost to modern development. Across the lower Eastern Woodlands, several other Mississippian centers emerged between AD 1000 and 1200, a time that archaeologists refer to as Early Mississippian. These include the Shiloh and Obion sites in Tennessee, Kincaid in southern Illinois, and Macon Plateau in Georgia, among many others.

Shortly after AD 1200, Cahokia began a steep and rapid decline, the causes of which are still contested among scholars. During the next two centuries, however, many new Mississippian centers emerged in the southeastern United States. This time from AD 1200 to 1400, known as the Middle Mississippian period, witnessed a florescence of Mississippian society. Some of the most important chiefdom centers from this period include Moundville in Alabama, Etowah in Georgia, Oklahoma's Spiro Mounds, Florida's Lake Jackson site, Winterville and Lake George in Mississippi, and Angel Mounds in Indiana. The regional exchange of exotic raw materials and finely crafted objects reached its apex at that time. Especially important were whelk shells traded from the northern gulf coast, which skilled artisans crafted into beautifully engraved cups and gorgets, and native copper from the Great Lakes area, which was worked into thin, embossed copper plates. These are among the most beautiful and striking objects ever made in Native North America, and their discovery at many of the above-named sites serves as direct testimony to the far-reaching influence of these centers' chiefly elites.

MISSISSIPPIAN DECLINE AND THE DEMISE OF SOUTHEASTERN CHIEFDOMS

After AD 1400, there was a significant decline in mound building throughout the Eastern Woodlands. Long-distance exchange of rare and exotic materials also declined, as did the skilled crafting of ritual objects in shell and copper. Many important Middle Mississippian centers were abandoned or underwent major transformations in scale and regional power. Archaeologists have proposed several explanations for this decline, but none is universally accepted. Perhaps the onset of the Little Ice Age in the previous century—a period of cooler temperatures across most of the Northern Hemisphere—so disrupted agricultural cycles that many of the Middle Mississippian chiefdoms collapsed. Mississippian chiefdoms were always unstable, and such a dramatic change might have been sufficient to unravel the threads of their organization. Or perhaps the rituals and religious values that made the Mississippian movement attractive to new adherents simply ran out of steam and were no longer enough to hold the chiefdoms together. It is important to remember, however, that this process was under way during the century prior to European contact, so that the causes of the Middle Mississippian decline were probably internal and cannot be explained by the introduction of external agents such as European settlers and their diseases.

This decline, however, does not mean that chiefdoms disappeared across the Eastern Woodlands. Instead, many new chiefdoms emerged during the time from AD 1400 to 1600, referred to as the Late Mississippian period. Although the leaders of these chiefdoms did not build mounds as large as those of their predecessors, or support as many of the specialists who crafted beautiful objects in copper and shell, many do appear to have wielded authority over considerable distances. These later chiefdoms are best known from the written accounts provided by early European explorers, and particularly from accounts of the Hernando de Soto expedition, which ventured across much of the American Southeast from 1539 to 1543. Chiefdoms with names like Apalachee, Cofitachequi, Chiaha, Coosa, Tascaloosa, Chicasa, Casqui, and Pacaha leap from the de Soto accounts and offer important insights into Late Mississippian society.

These accounts, however, would open one of the last historical windows into the world of the Southeastern chiefdoms. On the heels of Spanish and later French and English explorers came devastating infectious diseases, such as measles and smallpox, against which the people of these Late Mississippian chiefdoms had no natural resistance. Moreover, new European colonies introduced a market-style economy to the Eastern Woodlands, in which native people traded hides and slaves to European merchants for manufactured goods such as cloth, glass beads, brass pots, and guns. This combination of factors—the loss of life from disease and a new economic system—undermined the Mississippian economy based on maize. Within a century of European contact, the Mississippian world had largely disappeared, though its legacy would live on—and lives on today—in the peoples of the Creek, Chickasaw, Choctaw, Cherokee, Catawba, Ponca, Osage, and other Indian nations.

Further Reading: Anderson, David G., *The Savannah River Chiefdoms: Political Change in the Late Prehistoric Southeast* (Tuscaloosa: University of Alabama Press, 1994); Beck, Robin A., "Consolidation and Hierarchy: Chiefdom Variability in the Mississippian Southeast," *American Antiquity* 68 (2003): 641–661; Blitz, John, *Ancient Chiefdoms of the Tombigbee* (Tuscaloosa: University of Alabama Press, 1993); Butler, Brian, and Paul Welch, eds., *Leadership and Polity in Mississippian Society* (Carbondale: Southern Illinois University, Center for Archaeological Investigations, 2006); Earle, Timothy K., *How Chiefs Come to Power: The Political Economy in Prehistory* (Stanford, CA: Stanford University Press, 1997); Knight, Vernon J., "The Institutional Organization of Mississippian Religion," *American Antiquity* 51 (1986): 675–687; Milner, George R., *The Cahokia Chiefdom: The Archaeology of a Mississippian Society* (Washington, DC: Smithsonian Institution Press, 1998); Milner, George R., *The Moundbuilders: Ancient Peoples of Eastern North America* (London: Thames & Hudson, 2004); Muller, Jon, *Mississippian Political Economy* (New York: Plenum Press, 1997); Pauketat, Timothy, *Ancient Cahokia and the Mississippians* (Cambridge: Cambridge University Press, 2004); Smith, Bruce, ed., *The Mississippian Emergence* (Washington, DC: Smithsonian Institution Press, 1990).

Robin A. Beck

ANCIENT VILLAGE LIFE IN THE SOUTHEAST

Villages during ancient times in the Southeast were communities where a number of family groups lived for much or all of the year, practicing a sedentary way of life. Initial occupation of the Southeast during the Late Pleistocene and Early Holocene, before village life was established, was by hunter-gatherer groups that in most areas appear to have been highly mobile, moving their residences a number of times a year in the scheduled pursuit of new resources, as those around their campsites became depleted. These groups or bands were typically small, no more than a few families totaling between twenty-five to fifty individuals, and people likely came together in large numbers only for short periods when resources were plentiful in a given area and could support the rendezvous of two or more bands.

The presence of remains of plants and animals available only during specific times of the year is widely used by archaeologists to identify the season or seasons when sites were occupied.

In the Southeast, the earliest unequivocal evidence for people living year-round in one location dates to the Middle Holocene, about 5,000 years ago, at the Horr's Island site in southwest Florida. This site, a massive midden composed mainly of shellfish and other subsistence debris, is located on the coast in an area rich in marine and estuarine food resources. Numerous postholes were found at the base of the midden, indicating that structures were present, although what they looked like is unknown. In the warm south Florida climate these buildings would not have to have been substantial, although, as was the case in later occupations in this region, some were characterized by elaborate woodworking that included representations of real and mythic animals, intended to convey status and ceremonial meaning and to impress visitors.

Middens containing large quantities of subsistence debris appear in a number of coastal and interior riverine settings across the Southeast during and after the Middle Holocene.

The remains within them, where they have been examined by specialists, indicate that many of these sites were occupied seasonally or for longer periods. Most of those that have been carefully examined do not, however, appear to have been occupied year-round. During one or more seasons, populations are thought to have dispersed away from these sites, to take advantage of resources available in other areas. Some of these middens were truly massive accumulations, and some also appear to have been intentionally built in a ring or "U" shape, with the location, amount, and kinds of debris in specific segments or portions, perhaps reflecting the arrangement, size, and status of individual families or lineages within the community. The open areas within the circles or the U's, furthermore, may have had the same function as more formally prepared plazas or open areas surrounded by mounds or earthworks that appear widely across the region over the following millennia.

The first evidence for the construction of substantial domestic structures also occurs during the Middle Holocene. Structures with posts and other large construction members, prepared floors and dug-out foundations, and thick wattle-and-daub, hide-covered, or woven/thatched roofs and walls require appreciable effort to build, and attest to the likelihood that group mobility was minimal during the periods these structures were occupied, which was likely over one or more seasons. The more substantial walled and roofed structures were likely used as residences during cold weather, a theory supported in some cases by the presence within them of hearths or seasonal biotic indicators. Substantial domestic structures in the Southeast have been found in a number of areas dating back at least 4,000 more years, including at the Bailey site in Tennessee, at the Mill Branch and Lover's Lane sites in eastern Georgia, and at several midden mound sites with substantial prepared clay floors or platforms in the Tombigbee River valley of northeast Mississippi.

Human burial in marked cemeteries is an additional indicator of extended settlement in a given area and at specific locations. Cemeteries are created when people are buried in specific locations over a period of years or generations, perhaps in marked graves and family groupings. Such behavior marks the location as one in which the group has a substantial personal history and investment. The earliest marked cemeteries in the Southeast occur during the Paleoindian period with the Dalton culture of the central Mississippi Valley, as represented by the numerous clusters of human bone and elaborate, well-made artifacts found at the Sloan site in northeast Arkansas, and during the Late Paleoindian and Early Holocene periods in parts of Florida, as represented by burials submerged in sinks or ponds, such as at Little Salt Spring or Windover. At least one Dalton site from northeast Arkansas, the Lace site, had a substantial midden, but the site was destroyed by land leveling before thorough excavations could be conducted to determine whether structures were present.

Aside from these early and somewhat isolated examples, archaeological cultures characterized by sites with substantial domestic structures, dense midden deposits, and marked cemeteries, suggesting a mainly sedentary way of life, do not appear widely in the Southeast until the Late Holocene, about 5,000 years ago, and after. At this same time evidence for monumental construction also appears, in the form of mound and earthwork building, in the lower Mississippi River valley, at sites like Watson's Brake, Frenchman's Bend, and Caney. Given the lack of evidence for extended occupation, it is assumed that these mound centers were occupied for short periods of time, during intermittent episodes of ceremony, festival, and construction, by groups dispersed over the surrounding landscape much of the year. The presence of these mound centers, produced by collective short-term labor for ceremonial purposes, is a pattern that occurs over and over again in the millennia to come. It is also yet another indication that at least some of the peoples of the Southeast were becoming permanently invested and attached to specific parts of the landscape. The increasingly territorial behavior reflected by the occurrence of middens, mounds, and cemeteries was a part of the process leading to sedentary life and permanent village communities on the landscape.

By the Woodland period, from 3,000 to 1,000 years ago, evidence of fairly substantial domestic structures appears in many parts of the Southeast, and mounds were being built in many areas, most typically dome-shaped earthen edifices that covered and commemorated burials placed within and under them, and less commonly truncated pyramids or platforms whose tops were likely used for public ceremonies, and less commonly as bases for temples, charnel houses, or other structures. Whether permanently occupied communities were present is less certain in most areas, particularly until late in the period, and many Woodland groups are thought to have been residentially mobile at least part of the year. Many of the mounds and earthworks that are hallmarks of the period, in fact, are thought to have been built by populations dispersed much of the time and, as a result, used only intermittently. Where residential structures are found on Woodland period sites, evidence for large-scale storage, in the form of pits or storerooms capable of holding great quantities of food, sometimes appears in and around these structures, again suggesting more permanent settlements.

Toward the end of the Woodland period, after about AD 700, the bow and arrow appears in the Southeast, and evidence for warfare increases dramatically. Intensive maize agriculture also appears in some areas soon after, and by the Mississippian period, after about AD 1100, maize was grown widely across much of the region. Communities that were unquestionably occupied most or all of the year appear in many areas, with the extended settlement likely facilitated by the increased crop yields and surpluses. Fortified communities first appear during the Late Woodland period, often tightly packed arrangements of houses surrounded by palisades and ditches. Social organization changed to accommodate the demands of increased population and interaction, extended settlement, and agricultural productivity, with hereditary groups or elites emerging and controlling public ceremony, warfare, and construction, in part through the use of crop surpluses. Many of the larger permanently occupied Mississippian communities—besides serving as the centers of elite households, temples, and public ceremony—were, if fortified, refuges that outlying populations could retreat to in times of warfare.

Warfare was directed at controlling land, crops, and agricultural surplus and obtaining and maintaining prestige and prerogatives. It took two distinct forms: attacks on individuals or small parties away from settlements, or large-scale attacks on the settlements themselves. Evidence for the destruction of communities and the massacre of inhabitants soon follows the establishment of permanent communities in the region, with the ruins of suddenly destroyed settlements themselves somewhat paradoxically providing archaeologists with some of their best evidence for village life. In communities that were abandoned more gradually or peacefully, in contrast, most evidence for household life was removed as the people departed, with the buildings themselves pulled apart or left to gradually decay in the region's damp climate.

What went on in the village communities of the Southeast over the thousands of years that they existed? Family life, for the most part, including food preparation and cooking, tool manufacture, and the fabrication of items of everyday life. In many communities the dead were buried under or near the houses they lived in, while in others, or when the people were of special status, the deceased might be placed in special charnel houses, mounds, or temples. More public interaction, such as games or ceremonies involving larger numbers of people, took place in the open areas between residences, or in the larger communities in the formal plazas that were typically surrounded by houses, mounds, or earthworks. During the last millennia prior to contact, village boundaries in many areas were defined by fortification lines, as warfare became more common.

Not everyone lived this way. In some areas, communities were more dispersed, with households scattered over the landscape, along stream or river margins. What is meant by a "community" or a village in the Southeast thus varies, and care must be taken to avoid assuming that they all looked alike or were comparable in size. Some communities, particularly during the Archaic period, were little more than scattered households. Over time larger groupings of houses occurred, sometimes with associated plazas, earthworks, and mounds—but, again, not everywhere in the region. Even during the Woodland many people lived in dispersed households and may have moved one or more times a year. Although increasing investment in facilities such as mounds, cemeteries, and structures occurred, only with the appearance of intensive agricultural food production were communities occupied year-round, true villages as we tend to think of the term, in large parts of the region.

Further Reading: Anderson, David G., and Robert C. Mainfort Jr., eds., *The Woodland Southeast* (Tuscaloosa: University of Alabama Press, 2002); Anderson, David G., and Kenneth E. Sassaman, "Early and Middle Holocene Periods, 9500–3750 B.C.," in *Smithsonian Handbook of North American Indians*, Southeast vol., edited by Raymond D. Fogelson (Washington, DC: Smithsonian Institution, 2004), 87–100; Gibson, Jon L., and Philip J. Carr, eds., *Signs of Power: The Rise of Cultural Complexity in the Southeast* (Tuscaloosa: University of Alabama Press, 2004); Milner, George R., *The Moundbuilders: Ancient Peoples of Eastern North America* (New York: Thames and Hudson, 2003); Pauketat, Timothy R., *Ancient Cahokia and the Mississippians* (Cambridge: Cambridge University Press, 2004); Pauketat, Timothy R., *Chiefdoms and Other Archaeological Delusions* (Lanham, MD: AltaMira Press, 2007); Sassaman, Kenneth E., *People of the Shoals: Stallings Culture of the Savannah River Valley* (Gainesville: University Press of Florida, 2006); Sassaman, Kenneth E., and David G. Anderson, eds., *The Archaeology of the Mid-Holocene Southeast* (Gainesville: University Press of Florida, 1996); Sassaman, Kenneth E., and David G. Anderson, "Late Holocene Period, 3750 to 650 B.C.," in *Smithsonian Handbook of North American Indians*, Southeast vol., edited by Raymond D. Fogelson (Washington, DC: Smithsonian Institution, 2004), 101–114; Smith, Bruce D., "The Archaeology of the Southeastern United States: from Dalton to de Soto, 10,500–500 B.P.," *Advances in World Archaeology* 5 (1986): 1–92; Smith, Bruce D., *Rivers of Change: Essays on Early Agriculture in Eastern North America* (Washington, DC: Smithsonian Institution Press, 1992).

David G. Anderson

DE SOTO'S EXPEDITION AND OTHER EARLY EUROPEAN-INDIAN ENCOUNTERS

The contact between different cultures has been a central focus of anthropological interest since the discipline's inception. This has been especially true for historical archaeology, which has the unique ability to examine the topic from both a historical (documents) and an archaeological (material objects) perspective. The resulting analyses have contributed to the understanding of patterns of adaptation by both colonizing and indigenous peoples.

The archaeological perspective concerning the cultural contact human experience has changed through time. Early assessments of European-Indian contact tended to focus on how indigenous peoples acculturated and assimilated into European-derived society, while later studies stressed the frequently tragic, sometimes genocidal consequences of contact on the natives. By the end of the twentieth century, the discussion had shifted to encompass the changes incurred by both cultures. "Creolization" is the term applied to processes resulting in a hybrid culture adapted to the new social and natural environments. Creolization studies are particularly pertinent to the southeastern United States, where the earliest sustained contact between indigenous cultures and exploring Europeans took place in North America.

It is impossible to talk about the European-Indian encounters in the Southeast without at least mentioning Columbus's voyages of discovery to the New World. There was at least one such encounter preceding this event (the Vikings 500 years earlier at L'Anse aux Meadows in Newfoundland), but it did not have the lasting impact that the Spaniards would have upon the Americas. So although whether or not Columbus "discovered" America is debatable; the fact that he set into motion forces that would profoundly change both the Old World and the New is not.

Columbus, himself, was not the first Spaniard to set foot on North American soil. Indeed, he probably never saw the North American mainland as he sailed from one Caribbean island to the next. That distinction is claimed by Juan Ponce de Léon, who in 1513 made landfall somewhere along the northeast coast of Florida, claiming all of *La Florida* for Spain. However, there is historical and archaeological evidence suggesting that the Spaniards had been conducting slaving raids along the Florida peninsula prior to de Léon's arrival. This may account for the hostile reception he received when he led an expedition to southwestern Florida in 1521. This initial colonizing attempt ended before it began when Ponce de Léon was shot in the neck with an arrow shortly after debarking to establish his settlement. Five years would pass before the Spaniards next attempted to settle *La Florida*.

In 1526 Lucas Vázquez de Ayllón received the royal *asiento* (charter) to settle *La Florida*. His colony, San Miguel de Guadalupe, which is believed to be located somewhere along the coast of South Carolina or Georgia, lasted only a matter of months before being abandoned by its settlers after the death of their leader. No archaeological evidence of this short-lived settlement as been found. The seemingly cursed *asiento* then passed to Pánfilo de Narváez, whom the historian Samuel Eliot Morrison characterized as the most incompetent of all those who sailed for New Spain in this era.

The relationship with the natives scarcely improved with Pánfilo de Narváez. His expedition, which began in the vicinity of Tampa Bay in 1528, was plagued by conflict throughout the length of the Florida peninsula. What Narváez lacked in diplomacy he made up for in brutality, precluding any assistance he might have received from the local inhabitants. In a desperate attempt to return to Spanish holdings in Mexico, Narváez's men built rafts by melting down their armor to make nails and provisioned their voyage by killing their horses. The sad details of this catastrophic failure are known from the writings of one of the expedition's four survivors, Alvar Nunez Cabeza de Vaca, who was finally rescued six years after the expedition began. Although no definitive archaeological evidence related to the expedition has been recovered, the account by Cabeza de Vaca has been instrumental in our understanding of the sixteenth-century inhabitants of coastal *La Florida*. Certainly they gave his successor, Hernando de Soto, an idea of what to expect when the *asiento* passed to him.

Hernando de Soto assembled an incredibly ambitious, well-equipped expedition for his assault on *La Florida*. In May 1539 he landed on the west coast of Florida with over 600 men (and at least two women), 299 horses, a drove of swine, and equipment and craftsmen to establish several towns. The exact location for the landing and initial encampment has yet to be found, although the De Soto National Memorial was established in Bradenton, Florida, to commemorate the landing. The exact location has been intensely debated by archaeologists, with the majority favoring the Tampa Bay vicinity, though Charlotte Harbor, to the south, has also been proposed.

The *entrada* ventured north in search of gold and glory. Archaeological investigations throughout peninsular Florida have failed to turn up much evidence of the de Soto army's depredations upon the local peoples. However, excavations at Tatham Mound, in Citrus County, have uncovered Indian burials accompanied by a wealth of sixteenth-century European material culture, including glass beads, iron armor fragments, and objects made from silver and copper coins. It is unclear, however, whether these artifacts were obtained from the de Soto or earlier Narváez expedition, since the two went through the same area and were only eleven years apart. Also not clear is the exact nature of the contact, since these artifacts were clearly in a secondary context (as these objects were in a mound, they must have been in the hands of Indians for some time before being buried).

In any event, by October the de Soto expedition was still intact, but without direction. De Soto made the decision to winter at the captured Apalachee capital of Anhaica (in modern-day Tallahassee), consolidate his forces, and decide where to go next. After five months under virtual siege by guerrilla attacks, de Soto broke camp to pursue rumors of gold to be found to the north. During the resultant four-year odyssey, de Soto and his army crossed ten states and impacted scores of Native societies. Many of the events that took place were recorded in four separate narratives. In 1543 the bedraggled remnant of the expedition, which had been reduced by half, finally struggled into a Spanish outpost near Tampico, Mexico. Dozens of scholars have read the chronicles associated with the expedition and for over a century have searched for evidence of it on the ground. However, it was not until 1987 that a de Soto campsite was located archaeologically.

Though sixteenth-century Spanish artifacts had occasionally been found at Indian sites, these were in contexts (e.g., Tatham

Mound) suggesting that they had been obtained through trade or the salvage of shipwrecks. De Soto's 1539–40 winter camp—the Governor Martin site, named for a former Florida governor whose mansion overlooks the site—was fortuitously discovered prior to the construction of a new office complex in downtown Tallahassee. Subsequent archaeological investigations confirmed that the site was indeed de Soto's winter encampment.

The location of the Governor Martin site does not contradict any of the documents associated with the expedition and falls within the approximate distances to geographic features mentioned in those narratives. One of the aboriginal structures excavated at the site shows evidence of European construction (sawn posts and wrought nails) and there is evidence of burning mentioned in the narratives. Excavations uncovered several hundred chain mail links, early-style Spanish olive jars, sixteenth-century majolica fragments, a dozen glass chevron beads, a crossbow point, and five copper coins dating to the early sixteenth century. The aboriginal material also dates to this time period (known archaeologically as the late Fort Walton period).

The most definitive evidence for a de Soto occupation, as opposed to that of another sixteenth-century explorer (e.g., Narváez), is a fragment of a pig jaw. The burned piece of maxilla was found in a pit containing late Fort Walton ceramics and a Nueva Cadiz bead. It is recorded that de Soto brought a herd of pigs with him to serve as a mobile larder, in hopes of avoiding the fate of his predecessor. Pigs are not native to the southeastern United States.

Although no additional, definitive evidence of de Soto's trek has been recovered, there is evidence for subsequent sixteenth-century Spanish contact in the Southeast. The site of another Spanish explorer has been located in western North Carolina. Shortly after Pedro Menendez d'Avilés founded St. Augustine (about 1565) in northeastern Florida, he sent Juan Pardo to explore the interior of the Southeast and establish several outposts. The Berry site, in the foothills region of North Carolina, is believed to be the village of Joara where Pardo established Fort San Juan in 1567. Excavations have revealed several burned structures exhibiting both Native and European influences, as well as a wealth of sixteenth-century Spanish artifacts.

The impacts of these expeditions have been debated for over a century. The transitory nature of the encounters might seem to argue for little lasting effect on the Native population beyond the adoption of a few European trade items. However, many have argued that the largest impact came not from material culture, but rather from the disastrous effects of Spanish-introduced diseases on the native inhabitants against which they had no immunity. Several scholars have made compelling cases for precipitous aboriginal depopulation in the Southeast based on both historical accounts and archaeological evidence. This pandemic hypothesis was accepted as fact by most archaeologists and historians during the 1980s and early 1990s, and still is widely cited today.

However, more recently, other scholars have come to believe that these diseases would have spread irregularly into the Southeastern interior. If this were the case, some populations would have been hit hard while others would have been missed, at least for a time. Furthermore, a reanalysis of the archaeological evidence of the sixteenth century suggests that what at first appears to be population decline may actually be population dispersal due to environmental and political factors. Epidemic disease is not easily documented in the archaeological record and may not have been the sole, or even primary, cause of cultural change everywhere during the period of initial contact. It did, though, become an increasingly important factor when the Europeans began developing permanent settlements.

The first permanent settlement in *La Florida* was St. Augustine. Continuously occupied since 1565, it served as an administrative and defensive focal point for Spain's nascent colony. It was the only settlement of the sixteenth century to succeed in the long run. Indeed, it outlasted the Spanish colony itself and retains some of its Spanish character to this day, as exemplified by the impressive Castillo de San Marcos. The Castillo, built with forced Indian labor, and other structures in the town have seen much archaeological research. Some of these were explicitly architectural studies or involved spatial patterning, while others focused on the activities of the colonists and their interactions with the natives through the mission system.

With the completion of decades of ongoing research, it has been possible to undertake the study of an entire community. Such a study is a logical outgrowth of accumulated interdisciplinary research; as James Cusick states, "It shares, with historical ethnography, a concern for in-depth analysis of people and culture in social context; it deals, like many analyses in historical archaeology, with issues of ethnicity, acculturation and social structure; and its research strategy requires the comparison of household level data." St. Augustine in particular has proven amenable to such an approach.

At the western end of Florida is Pensacola, which also claims to be the oldest U.S. city, though the original settlement did not last. In 1559 Tristán de Luna founded a colony on Pensacola Bay. Immediately beset by natural calamities and loss of supplies, the colony struggled and was abandoned in 1561. There was little interaction with the natives, which might account in part for its lack of success. Over 130 years would pass before the Spaniards attempted another settlement in the area. This one would remain, though it would be won, and lost, by both the French and the British over the ensuing centuries.

A colonial outpost that has witnessed a great deal of archaeological research, mostly under the direction of Stanley South, is Santa Elena. Founded just after St. Augustine, Santa Elena was originally intended to be *La Florida*'s capital and briefly served in that capacity. It had a population of several hundred before being abandoned in favor of St. Augustine in 1587. Located on the U.S. Marine Corps base on Parris Island, South Carolina, it was the site of the Spanish fort San Marcos. South worked at the site for nearly twenty years, during which time he discovered the main settlement of Santa Elena and the earlier Spanish fort San Felipe. Excavations in each of them yielded information on the lifestyles of the early settlers as well as data on the status differences within the settlement and interactions with the native inhabitants.

The preceding sites provided ample data for archaeologists to determine a pattern in the interaction between the Spaniards and the native peoples they encountered. Kathleen Deagan, conducting research in St. Augustine, studied the processes related to the formation and development of the Hispanic-American cultural tradition in Florida—specifically, which elements of the native culture the Spaniards adopted as part of their adaptation to this New World colony. As a result of her archaeological investigations, Deagan concluded that acculturation in eighteenth-century St. Augustine was undertaken largely by Indian women in mixed Spanish, or *mestizo*, household units, within a primarily male-oriented (military) cultural setting. So the Spanish colonial adaptation pattern incorporated native elements into low-visibility, subsistence activities while maintaining a Spanish flavor in the highly visible and socially important areas of clothing, tablewares, religion, and the like. That is to say, a European veneer was maintained over a Native American infrastructure. Based on the archaeological evidence accumulated from more than a decade of fieldwork, Deagan suggested that the processes involved in the formation of the Hispanic-American tradition in St. Augustine were common to much of the Spanish New World.

But what of the English in North America? For most of the sixteenth century, England settled for trying to pirate the wealth that Spain was extracting from its New World colonies. Though they may have preferred to go to the source of the gold and silver, Spain's grip on the Caribbean was sufficient during the sixteenth century to make the English look elsewhere to establish a foothold in the New World. The ill-fated first colony in the 1580s at Ft. Raleigh—the so-called Lost Colony at Roanoke in North Carolina—represents England's initial bid to challenge Spain in *La Florida*. Were their interactions with the local inhabitants any different from those of the Spaniards?

To address this one must first answer the question, why did the colony fail? Conventional wisdom has it that the colonists were poorly supplied and too inexperienced to sustain a viable colony. Others point to bad relations with the local Indians, which made settlement impossible. However, dendrochronological studies focusing on the widths of bald cypress tree rings (distinguishing good and bad growing years) suggest that the English tried to found a colony during the worst drought in at least 800 years along the Carolina coast. Rather than ineptitude, it was the environment that caused crops to fail and led to competition for scarce resources, the root of conflict between the European colonists and the Indians.

The struggles of the Roanoke colonies would be repeated twenty years later with the England's first "successful" colony at Jamestown. The same conflicts with the native inhabitants and lack of supplies would result in the "starving time" and near decimation of the colony by hunger and Indian attack. This would be overcome only with the discovery of a viable trade commodity: tobacco. Thus, the fate of the native inhabitants was sealed once the Europeans discovered there was something in the Southeast worth dying for.

So what was the role of the native peoples in the face of European contact? The Spanish sent the message that they were not to be trusted, with their raids on the continent for slaves, gold, and, later, land. The natives resisted or collaborated, depending on their circumstances and perceptions about what best suited their interests. Yet, ultimately, they were overcome by technology, biology, and, eventually, the sheer numbers of settlers arriving to claim their share of the American dream.

Further Reading: Clayton, Lawrence, Vernon J. Knight, and Edward Moore, *The De Soto Chronicles: The Expeditions of Hernando de Soto to North America in 1539–1543* (Tuscaloosa: University of Alabama Press, 1993); Dawdy, Shannon, "Creolization," *Historical Archaeology* 33 (2000); Deagan, Kathleen, "Accommodation and Resistance: The Process and Impact of Spanish Colonization in the Southeast," in *Columbian Consequences*, edited by David H. Thomas (Washington, DC: Smithsonian Institution Press, 1990), 297–314; Ewen, Charles, "Continuity and Change: De Soto and the Apalachee," *Historical Archaeology* 30 (1996): 41–53; Ewen, Charles, and John Hann, *Hernando de Soto among the Apalachee: The Archaeology of the First Winter Encampment* (Gainesville: University Press of Florida, 1998).

Charles R. Ewen

NATIVE AMERICAN POPULATION DECLINE AND EUROPEAN CONTACT

With the arrival of Europeans in the southeastern United States, Native American populations diminished considerably. Numerous factors were responsible for the devastating decrease in Native American numbers, including Old World diseases, superior European weaponry, and the disruption and collapse of traditional social orders, subsistence patterns, and settlement organization. The earliest known European contact in the Southeast was recorded in 1513, when Ponce de Léon landed on the east and southwest coasts of the Florida peninsula. A series of other Spanish contacts followed quickly after this, including in 1521, when the Spanish slave traders Francisco Gordillo and Pedro de Quejo landed on the South Carolina coast. These relatively brief encounters were soon followed by other Spanish explorers—Hernando de Soto in 1539–43, Tristan de Luna in 1559–61, and Juan Pardo in 1566–68—whose expeditions took them deep into the Southeast. The expeditions of Hernando de Soto, for example, began in Florida and continued through the present-day states of Georgia, South Carolina, North Carolina, Tennessee, Alabama, Mississippi, Arkansas, Texas, and Louisiana. During their explorations, the Spanish came into direct contact with many Native American villages, introducing new diseases and fighting for supplies.

A French expedition, headed by Jean Ribault, arrived in the Southeast in 1562. The small fort, called Charles Fort or Charlesfort, that this group built on what is now Parris Island, South Carolina, was abandoned soon after its construction and the colonists sailed back to France. A second expedition in 1564 established a small colony, Fort Caroline, located near the mouth of the St. Johns River in Florida, which was massacred by the Spanish in 1565. The French did not attempt to resettle in the region until Robert La Salle sailed down the Mississippi River in the 1680s. The English arrived in the Southeast over a hundred years later, marking the beginning of the deerskin trade in the region. By the time the English arrived, the remaining Native Americans were the descendants of groups who had suffered mass depopulation due to Spanish contact. Prior to founding Charles Town (present-day Charleston, South Carolina) in 1670, early English settlers in Virginia had developed a slave trade that already extended into the Southeast. Native American slave trappers ventured into the area, killing men and capturing women and children to be sold as slaves (Martin 1994).

Archaeologists are very interested in discovering the Native American sites visited by Europeans. Charles M. Hudson, an ethnohistorian, has reconstructed de Soto's trek in the Southeast, detailing the hardships that the Native Americans experienced (Hudson 1997; Hudson and Tesser 1994). The most direct evidence for contact is the presence of European artifacts at a site. One of the areas best documented for Spanish contact is associated with the Coosa chiefdom in northwest Georgia. Archaeologist Marvin T. Smith (2000) has recorded Spanish artifacts dating from 1540–60 at numerous sites in the Coosa region.

Comparing pre-epidemic and post-epidemic Native American population sizes is one method for estimating disease casualties. Pre-contact numbers are difficult to verify, as the earliest census information is available only through European observers. This problem has led scholars to use a variety of methods to gauge pre-contact population size, including estimating the carrying capacity of the environment, extrapolating from modern population studies, archaeological evidence, historical accounts, and even calculating the number of individuals who occupied Native American houses. Consequently, population estimates at contact vary considerably. For example, estimates for North America north of central Mexico range from 900,000 to 18,000,000 people. Similar discrepancies in population esti-

mates occur for the Southeast. Douglas H. Ubelaker (1988, 1992) has conducted a detailed study of historical records and estimated that there were around 204,400 people in the Southeast at contact, and 1,894,350 in all of North America. Ubelaker's estimates for the Southeast are similar to those made by John R. Swanton (1979 [1946]) in an earlier study. Henry E. Dobyns (1983) combined ecological factors and modern population studies to produce an estimate exceeding 700,000 for the late prehistoric Florida Timucuan speakers alone. His estimates are consequently much higher than others proposed for the Southeast and for North America as a whole.

Similar measures are used to record population decline. Ubelaker estimates that population size in the Southeast declined from 204,400 in 1500 to 157,400 in 1600, and eventually to 60,370 in 1800, a population decrease of 71 percent over 300 years. In contrast, Dobyns estimated a reduction of 95 percent for the Tumucuan speakers between 1500 and 1617.

Other Southeastern archeologists have relied on site size and numbers to document decline. One problem following depopulation was the breakdown of political and social organization. In the lower Mississippi valley, archaeologist Ann Ramenofsky (1987) used settlement pattern data to document a great decrease in group size and considerable population movement following the Spanish arrival. Following de Soto's journey through the area, rapid depopulation ensued, large towns were abandoned, survivors combined to form smaller settlements, and people moved to other areas. Marvin Smith (1987) also used archaeological data to document significant population decline in the interior Southeast during the sixteenth century. This rapid population loss prompted the breakdown of the geographically large and dominant Coosa chiefdom into smaller political entities.

During the contact period, Native Americans suffered greatly from Old World diseases, which are considered the leading cause of the demographic collapse that occurred. Among the deadliest diseases introduced to the New World at that time were smallpox and measles. Other European-introduced diseases, including influenza, also affected the native populations, killing many.

Human skeletal collections have been associated with three major contact period provinces of Spanish Florida: Timucuan, Guale, and Apalachee. The Timucuans were a number of tribes that inhabited central and north Florida and southeastern Georgia; their first contact with Europeans was in the mid-1500s. Based on archaeological and historical findings, the Timucua and Guale who experienced sustained early Spanish contact were the first to suffer dramatic population losses through disease and overwork. The third group, the Apalachee, also experienced stress that led to their eventual demise, but that occurred somewhat later because of their isolation relative to the other two groups.

Several diseases that are spread directly from one person to another, most notably smallpox and measles, triggered widespread epidemics; however, the various settlement patterns known to exist throughout the southern landscape probably contributed to groups being affected differently. Chiefdom populations were at greater risk for massive casualties since diseases such as measles will spread rapidly through densely settled groups. Population decline appears to have started early in the sixteenth century as members of the de Soto expedition noted what might be presumed to have been victims of Old World disease piled in houses at Cofitichequi, a large chiefdom site located in South Carolina. Social breakdown would have been far more disastrous when an illness struck the majority of a population at once. Interference with work efforts could have reduced food production, resulting in famine and malnutrition. In contrast to the populous chiefdoms, mobile and small groups were to some extent buffered from diseases transmitted through direct human-to-human contact since infections were more likely to burn themselves out before they could be transmitted to the next group.

During their expeditions, the Spanish chronicled large areas of uninhabited land between the Native American communities they encountered. Spatial scattering of settlements would safeguard individuals from direct disease contact. Extensive trade networks established prehistorically in the Southeast, however, could have contributed to the wide dissemination of diseases, even into areas not directly contacted by the Spanish.

Unfortunately, there is limited skeletal evidence for diseases introduced by the Spanish because measles does not affect bones and smallpox rarely does. Therefore, scientists who study skeletal remains, or human osteologists, cannot easily identify diseases as the cause of depopulation. Osteologists, however, can identify bone damage caused by metal weapons such as those used by the Spanish. At Tatham Mound in Florida, for example, Dale Hutchinson identified cut marks created by metal weapons on a right scapula and a left humerus. Evidence for Spanish contact at Tatham Mound was documented by the presence of hundreds of early-sixteenth-century European artifacts. At Mission San Luis, in northern Florida, Larsen and others identified an individual with a gunshot wound. This Spanish mission site dates between 1656 and 1704.

The collapse of Native social and political systems in the Southeast led to other changes in health. Following the Spanish settlement at St. Augustine by Pedro Menéndez de Avilés in 1565, missions were organized along the coast and into northwest Florida. The missions were established to increase control of Native Americans and to use them for labor to support Spanish needs, especially food. One example is Mission San Luis, founded in the densely populated and environmentally rich Apalachee chiefdom.

Several scientists have studied skeletons discovered at early mission sites. Clark Spencer Larsen and Christopher Ruff examined the skeletons at Mission Santa Catalina de Guale, located on St. Catherine's Island off the Georgia coast. The Guale Indians were forced into heavy labor, including food production for the mission priests and military, carrying loads, and construction. As a result of this workload, the contact period Guale showed increased bone size compared with pre-contact groups. Additional research

evaluating stress related to mission life and Spanish contact, conducted by Larsen and others, has focused on populations associated with Mission San Luis de Apalachee and Mission Patale, both located in Florida. Poorer nutrition and greater stress, in part caused by infectious diseases, during the developing years were found to cause small tooth size in children. Similar findings were observed in the skeletons of children from Mission Santa Catalina de Guale.

RELATED SITES AND MUSEUMS

There are a number of parks and museums throughout the Southeast that relate to the contact period and sites occupied during that historic time. Information about several of these is summarized here.

Parkin Archaeological State Park, Parkin, Arkansas (www.arkansasstateparks.com/parkinarcheological)

Many scholars believe the Parkin site is the village Casqui visited by the de Soto *entrada* in 1541. This National Historic Landmark has an onsite research laboratory established by the Arkansas Archeological Survey and an interpretive museum, and provides site tours and other educational programs. The park, occupied by Native Americans between AD 1000 and 1550, covers 17 acres and has a moated village and a large platform mound.

Florida Museum of Natural History, Gainesville, Florida (www.flmnh.ufl.edu)

Located at the University of Florida Cultural Plaza in Gainesville, this museum contains artifacts excavated from numerous sites of the Spanish-Indian contact period, including the Tatham Mound (8CI203), located near the Withlacochee River in Citrus County. Spanish artifacts discovered at the mound include metal beads and pendants, Nueva Cadiz and other glass beads, and metal artifacts including armor fragments. Artifacts recovered from the Indian Pond Site (8CO229) are housed at the museum. Spanish artifacts also were discovered at this seventeenth-century site, thought to have been first visited by Hernando de Soto.

Fort Caroline National Memorial, Jacksonville, Florida (www.nps.gov/timu/historyculture/foca.htm)

The National Park Service manages this ecological and historical preserve, which memorializes the French presence in Florida during the sixteenth century. The fort was founded by 200 soldiers and artisans in 1564 under the direction of Rene de Goulaine de Laudonniere. Timucuan Indians, led by Chief Saturiwa, assisted in the construction of the fort. After driving out the French only a year after the colony was founded, the Spanish imposed tribute on the Timucuans and forced them into missions. Only an estimated 550 Timucuans were alive in 1698. The park contains a fort exhibit that recalls the life and deaths of sixteenth-century French colonists and provides trails for exploring the natural habitats of the Timucuans.

Mission San Luis, Tallahassee, Florida (www.missionsanluis.org)

Mission San Luis is a National Historic Landmark site and represents the only re-created seventeenth-century mission community in the Southeast. The site offers tours and demonstrations of the tasks that sustained the mission centuries ago. Reconstructed Apalachee and Spanish structures that can be explored at the site include a ball plaza where traditional ball games were played, an Apalachee village council house, and Spanish structures.

St. Augustine, Florida

In the territory inhabited by Timucuan Indians at contact, Pedro Menéndez de Avilés founded St. Augustine in 1565. This was the first permanent Spanish settlement and the oldest continuously occupied community in the present-day United States. Fort Matanzas National Monument is located 15 miles south of the historic district of St. Augustine, marking the spot where the Spanish battled with French Huguenots for control of Florida, destroying them and their colony.

St. Catherines Island, Georgia

St. Catherines Island was registered as a National Historic Landmark in 1970 and is the location of the lost Mission Santa Catalina, Georgia's oldest known church. The church was founded in 1566, when the Spanish began developing mission programs in the Guale province, under the command of Governor Pedro Menendez de Aviles of St. Augustine. The church was destroyed by fire in 1597, but, following a period of abandonment, Santa Catalina was reconstructed on the previous site. It was later abandoned after the British siege of 1680. The island is now a wildlife refuge and can be accessed by private boat from Colonel's Island. David H. Thomas excavated the site in the 1970s for the American Museum of Natural History.

Fernbank Museum of Natural History, Atlanta, Georgia

Collections recovered from Mission Santa Catalina de Guale are currently housed here. Items from the collections may be on display to illustrate Native interactions with the Spanish.

Ocmulgee National Monument, Macon, Georgia

This National Park Service site has a museum with displays of archaeological artifacts dating from 10,000 years ago to a 300-year-old European sword. Visitors can explore preserved earthen mounds and a reconstructed earth lodge containing an original 1,000-year-old floor.

Los Adaes State Historic Site, Robeline, Louisiana (www.crt.state.la.us/siteexplorer)

This eighteenth-century site was the capital of Spanish Texas for over forty years and had a fort and mission. Here the Spanish interacted and traded with the Caddo Indians as well as the French. Guided tours of the grounds and archaeological labs are available, and historic demonstrations are offered throughout the year.

Grand Village of the Natchez Indians and Emerald Mound, Natchez, Mississippi (http://www.mdah.state.ms.us/hprop/gvni.html)

The Natchez Indians inhabited this area near the Mississippi River from 700 to 1730. French explorers visited the Grand Village of the Natchez in the late 1600s. Following several decades of a peaceful existence, conflicts began between the French and the Natchez, which eventually led to the Natchez leaving the area. The 128-acre site includes a museum accredited by the American Association of Museums, a reconstructed Natchez Indian house, and three ceremonial mounds. The Emerald Mound is located nearby on the Natchez Trace Parkway. This site was occupied from 1200 to 1600 and is the second largest ceremonial earthwork in the United States.

Frank M. McClung Museum, University of Tennessee, Knoxville

Exhibits trace the last 12,000-15,000 years of Native American life in Tennessee, including the historic period. Video presentations document the history of archaeology in the state and discuss archaeological methods.

Further Reading: Dobyns, Henry F., *Their Numbers Become Thinned: Native American Population Dynamics in Eastern North America* (Knoxville: University of Tennessee Press, 1983); Hudson, Charles M., *Knights of Spain, Warriors of the Sun: Hernando de Soto and the South's Ancient Chiefdoms* (Athens: University of Georgia Press, 1997); Hudson, Charles, and Carmen Chaves Tesser, eds., *The Forgotten Centuries: Indians and Europeans in the American South 1521–1704* (Athens: University of Georgia Press, 1994); Hutchinson, Dale L., and Lynette Norr, "Late Prehistoric and Early Historic Diet in Gulf Coast Florida," in *In the Wake of Contact: Biological Responses to Conquest*, edited by Clark Spencer Larsen and George R. Milner (New York: Wiley-Liss, 1994), 9–20; Larsen, Clark Spencer, ed., "The Archaeology of Mission Santa Catalina de Guale: 2. Biocultural Interpretations of a Population in Transition," *Anthropological Papers of the American Museum of Natural History* 68 (1990); Larsen, Clark Spencer, Hong P. Huynh, and Bonnie G. McEwan, "Death by Gunshot: Biocultural Implications of Trauma at Mission San Luis," *International Journal of Osteoarchaeology* 2 (1996): 42–50; Larsen, Clark Spencer, and George R. Milner, eds., *In the Wake of Contact: Biological Responses to Conquest* (New York: Wiley-Liss, 1994); Larsen, Clark Spencer, and Christopher B. Ruff, "The Stresses of Conquest in Spanish Florida: Structural Adaptation and Change before and after Contact," in *In the Wake of Contact: Biological Responses to Conquest*, edited by Clark Spencer Larsen and George R. Milner (New York: Wiley-Liss, 1994), 19–34; Martin, Joel W., "Southeastern Indians and the English Trade of Skins and Slaves," in *The Forgotten Centuries: Indians and Europeans in the American South 1521–1704*, edited by Charles Hudson and Carmen Chaves Tesser (Athens: University of Georgia Press, 1994), 304–324; Mooney, James, *The Aboriginal Population of America North of Mexico* (Washington, DC: Smithsonian Miscellaneous Collections, 1928); Ortner, Donald J., *Identification of Pathological Conditions in Human Skeletal Remains* (New York: Academic Press, 2003); Ramenofsky, Ann F., *The Vectors of Death: The Archaeology of European Contact* (Albuquerque: University of New Mexico Press, 1987); Smith, Marvin T., *Archaeology of Aboriginal Culture Change* *in the Interior Southeast: Depopulation during the Early Historic Period* (Gainesville: University of Florida Press, 1987); Smith, Marvin T., *Coosa: The Rise and Fall of a Southeastern Mississippian Chiefdom* (Gainesville: University Press of Florida, 2000); Stojanowski, Christopher M., Clark Spencer Larsen, Tiffiny A. Tung, and Bonnie G. McEwan, "Biological Structure and Health Implications from Tooth Size at Mission San Luis de Apalachee," *American Journal of Physical Anthropology* 132 (2007): 207–222; Swanton, John R., *The Indians of the Southeastern United States* [1946] (Washington, DC: Smithsonian Institution Press, 1979); Thomas, David H., "The Archaeology of Mission Santa Catalina de Guale: 1.

Search and Discovery," *Anthropology Papers of the American Museum of Natural History* 63 (1987); Ubelaker, Douglas H., "North American Indian Population Size, A.D. 1500–1985," *American Journal of Physical Anthropology* 77 (1988): 289–294; Ubelaker, Douglas H., "North American Population Size: Changing Perspectives," in *Disease and Demography in America*, edited by John W. Verano and Douglas H. Ubelaker (Washington, DC: Smithsonian Institution Press, 1992), 169–176; Verano, John W., and Douglas H. Ubelaker, eds., *Disease and Demography in America* (Washington, DC: Smithsonian Institution Press, 1992).

S. Homes Hogue

ST. AUGUSTINE AND OTHER EARLY EUROPEAN COLONIAL SETTLEMENTS

Spanish Europeans began to explore the southeastern United States within two decades of Christopher Columbus's first voyage to the West Indies. Both the French and Spanish established substantial settlements on the lower Atlantic coast well before the English settled farther north at Roanoke and Jamestown. These early incursions into *La Florida*, represented today by archaeological sites in South Carolina, Georgia, and Florida, significantly influenced the course of historical events that followed. Intensive archaeological study of several key sites, ranging from explorer period encampments to early urban centers, has contributed vital perspective on many issues.

Spain was the dominant European presence in the Southeast until early in the eighteenth century. Historical documents assign the first landfall to Juan Ponce de Léon in 1513, near present-day St. Augustine. In slightly more than another decade, serious colonizing efforts were attempted. The best known is that of Lucas Vasquez de Ayllon in 1526 on the South Carolina and Georgia coasts. Soon after, in 1528, Panfilo de Narváez unsuccessfully attempted to settle a colony in northern Florida. Hernando de Soto launched his three-year *entrada* about a decade later, touching ground near Tampa Bay and concluding a circuitous 4,000-mile path across coastal lowlands, piedmont, and mountains at the Mississippi River. In his wake, during the 1560s, Tristan de Luna explored inland from the gulf coast and Juan Pardo probed the interior from Santa Elena on the south Atlantic coast.

French ambitions in the region led them to establish two forts, Charlesfort at Port Royal Sound in South Carolina (1562) and Fort Caroline in extreme northeastern Florida (1564). Spanish claims to the area were defended in 1565, however, with removal of the French and replacement of them with their own installations, named Santa Elena and St. Augustine. Santa Elena served as the regional capital until it was abandoned in 1587, at which time St. Augustine became the administrative and religious center of *La Florida*.

Through the seventeenth century a network of Catholic missions was established across northern Florida and along coastal Georgia. During the middle part of the same century a provincial administrative center was founded at Apalachee near present-day Tallahassee. English-sponsored raids and pirates plagued the Spanish holdings from the 1660s and culminated with sieges and the burning of St. Augustine in 1702 and 1704. Spain temporarily forfeited control of the region to England in 1763–84, and then permanently in 1821.

St. Augustine was an obvious location for the earliest serious archaeological investigation of Spanish sites in the southeastern United States. It is unique in its collection of extant colonial structures, including the fort named Castillo de San Marco. A program of systematic research has been ongoing at sites in and around St. Augustine since the 1970s. A complementary program of long-term excavation at Santa Elena on Parris Island, South Carolina, the first Spanish capital town, was initiated in 1979 by Stanley South and continues today under joint oversight with Chester DePratter. Early interest in the exploratory period of the early sixteenth century was generated in association with the 1939 observance of Hernando de Soto's trek through the region, but the federal commission appointed to assemble available information had only sparse archaeological results to work from. Quietly and gradually, a richer body of evidence accumulated over the next forty years, and by 1980 Charles Hudson and his students were in a position to combine documentary and archaeological clues and propose a refined interpretation of de Soto's route. Publication of their work spurred efforts to confirm the route against concrete archaeological findings. Prominent among these were the investigation of Soto's winter encampment (the Governor Martin site) in Tallahassee, and the more recent study of the Berry site in western North Carolina. Research at Spanish mission sites also accelerated in the 1970s and 1980s, to some extent in anticipation of the Columbus quincentenary.

Several of the numerous Franciscan missions of coastal Georgia and northern Florida were thoroughly investigated.

EPHEMERAL SITES OF THE EXPLORATION PERIOD

Trade items indicative of sixteenth-century Spanish exploration, such as glass beads, iron tools, and weaponry, have been reported from numerous Native American sites in the region. These occurrences have been used to anchor competing proposals for the paths of de Soto, de Luna, and Pardo through the interior, and on occasion to make the case for even earlier expeditions such as those of Ayllon (1526) and Narváez (1528). Most of this material represents fortuitous discovery and even in the best cases is seldom regarded as absolute evidence of a Spanish presence, mainly owing to the highly portable nature of the artifacts. However, the general correspondence between the location of such finds and documentary sources is often very good. With the joining of archaeological and documentary records, an especially compelling case has been made for the location of the Indian province of Coosa in northern Georgia and adjacent areas of Tennessee and Alabama.

Solid evidence for the location of de Soto's 1539–40 winter encampment has been excavated at the Governor Martin site (8LE853B) at Tallahassee. An unusually wide array of early Spanish artifacts occurs with material characteristic of the indigenous Apalachee Indian community that grudgingly hosted the *entrada*. Telltale discoveries include distinctive glass beads, coins, pottery, fragmentary weapons and armor, and pig bones. Work resumed at the site in 2007 to expand on the initial study of 1987.

The location of de Soto's Joara village has come to light at the Berry site (31BK22) in a mountain valley of western North Carolina, where there is also evidence of Fort San Juan, established by Juan Pardo in 1567. Distinctive artifacts include majolica and olive jar ceramics, glass and metal beads, and iron tools. Wrought nails and spikes point to the presence of Spanish buildings. Overall the European material constitutes a uniquely domestic kind of assemblage for a remote, sixteenth-century site. Much evidence has also been recovered from structures associated with the ancient Joara community of Native Americans. Work at this site was begun in 1986 and is ongoing.

TOWNS AND FORTIFICATIONS

St. Augustine has been a focal point of archaeological investigation of the Spanish colonial experience in North America since the 1930s, and systematic scientific research has been under way since the 1970s. The effort has involved excavation of many sites representative of a continuous occupation since 1565. By design, the study has examined locations associated with a cross section of activities, socioeconomic sectors, and ethnic groups. The results reveal the process by which a distinctive Creole culture developed at this relatively isolated colonial center.

Since Stanley South of the University of South Carolina's Institute of Archaeology and Anthropology confirmed the site of Santa Elena in 1979, beneath the golf course at Parris Island Marine Base, work has continued largely uninterrupted at *La Florida*'s first capital. Excavations have revealed evidence of the original town as well as two forts that protected it at different times. Both forts San Felipe and San Marcos were surrounded by large moats and were more apparent than the town site between them. Although portions of each fort were lost to erosion, remarkable features remained well preserved within their walls. Obvious evidence of fortified houses was recorded and barrel wells produced a trove of well-preserved remains. Artifacts within the forts reveal aspects of both domestic and military activities, including vestiges of the earlier French Charlesfort (1562) beneath Fort San Felipe. Excavation at the town site has been rewarded by discovery of informative deposits in features such as daub pits, the outlines of domestic structures, and the residues of specialized activities, including pottery production.

The site of mission San Luis de Talimali in northwest Florida was excavated in the 1980s and is now a public historic site operated by the state of Florida. Established in 1656, the town-like community also served as the provincial capital until 1704. In addition to the mission, Apalachee included the residence of the provincial governor and headquarters for a garrison of soldiers. Outside of St. Augustine, San Luis was unique in seventeenth-century Florida by serving such diverse roles. Among the initial archaeological discoveries was a large, circular Indian council house situated across a plaza from the complex of mission buildings. In addition to the mission precinct with its church and friary, one Indian and one Spanish building were identified adjacent to the plaza, presumably for important households. Elsewhere the community's fort was identified as a blockhouse surrounded by a palisade. In an area serving the Spanish community both wattle-and-daub and plank houses have been excavated. Archaeological investigations of this site allow for a revealing view of the kind of existence led at a prosperous provincial center by Native Americans, Spaniards, and people of mixed blood. The unusual constellation of political, economical, and social activities at San Luis are manifest in its well-documented archaeological record.

MISSIONS

After a rocky start under Jesuit efforts, Franciscan Catholic missions became the dominant feature of the Spanish colonial landscape in the Southeast until the network collapsed under the English attacks of 1702 and 1704. By the middle of the seventeenth century up to forty Franciscan missions were active in eastern Georgia and northern Florida. Many mission sites have been archaeologically investigated since the 1940s, about a dozen of them very thoroughly. Mission archaeology in the Southeast since the 1970s emphasized the two-way consequences of culture contact and raised the question of whether a single model explains the physical and documentary evidence from mission sites of the region.

One of the best documented of these sites is Santa Catalina de Guale on St. Catherines Island, Georgia. Mission buildings were discovered and excavated by David Hurst Thomas of the American Museum of Natural History in the 1980s. Three structures common to most such sites, a church, friary, and kitchen, were revealed, as were two wells and the mission cemetery in the floor of the church. Santa Catalina, situated within Guale Indian territory, was occupied from about 1576 until 1680 and represented the northernmost Spanish settlement on the Atlantic coast after Santa Elena was abandoned in 1587. An unusually rich archaeological assemblage, especially from church burials, is revealing of the important food production and religious roles played by this site in the Guale province.

The site at Amelia Island, Florida, where Santa Catalina was relocated in 1686 was excavated by the University of Florida from 1985 to 1990. The work revealed traces of a second, slightly earlier mission church believed to be that of Santa Maria de Yamasee. At the Santa Catalina location evidence for a church (with a cemetery), kitchen, and friary was documented. Those discoveries were compared with an unusually detailed architectural drawing of the site prepared in 1691. Deviations from that idealized plan illustrate the value of archaeological evidence as a source of refined information and perhaps betray inevitable tension between military and religious interests.

The mission site closest to St. Augustine, in the Timucua Indian province, was called Nombre de Dios (8SJ34). It was the first mission established in North America and among the longest-lived, having functioned well into the eighteenth century. Only the cemetery and a portion of the Indian village associated with this site have been firmly identified, based mainly on archaeological excavations in the 1930s. Many European artifacts of diverse kinds were associated with the burials.

In north central Florida excavation at the Fig Springs site (8CO1) provides information about one of the remote Timucua mission enclaves believed to represent mission San Martin de Timucua. It is significant for having been minimally disturbed prior to investigation. Although the usual triad of buildings and a cemetery were documented, the architectural scale and artifactual evidence contrast with that of more mainstream missions. The church, for example, was apparently rather small and possibly even an open-air structure. Also, cemetery burials were not distinguished by notable quantities of grave goods.

Studies of the San Pedro y San Pablo de Patale site (8LE152) in the Apalachee province augment findings from San Luis with evidence from the early mission period of that area. The location of the mission church is firmly established by the discovery of the cemetery. Some suggestive evidence exists for a friary adjacent to the church.

Bioarchaeological analyses of large Native American burial populations, often from mission cemeteries, have contributed significantly to modern understanding of the conditions of Spanish colonialism in the Southeast. Pioneered by Clark Larsen, this research charts a pattern of physiologic and dietary change wrought by the conditions of contact. Intensification of maize farming, consolidation of settlements, and a draft labor system all contributed to a general decline in Native American health.

The archaeology and history of Spanish *La Florida* are interpreted for the public in numerous locations. Public sites abound in the vicinity of St. Augustine, including Fountain of Youth Park, Castillo de San Marcos, numerous colonial houses in the Spanish Quarter, and living history programs. Near Tallahassee, the site of mission San Luis de Tamali features reconstructed mission buildings, exhibitions, and interpretive programs. Exhibitions at the Florida Museum of Natural History in Gainesville give a thorough overview of relevant archaeology and history. In Georgia, the Fort King George historic site is located at the former site of a Franciscan mission.

Further Reading: Florida Museum of Natural History, "St. Augustine, America's Ancient City," http://www.flmnh.ufl.edu/staugustine/unit5.htm; Friends of Mission San Luis, Inc., "Mission San Luis," http://www.missionsanluis.org; Hann, John H., and Bonnie G. McEwan, *The Apalachee Indians and Mission San Luis* (Gainesville: University of Florida Press, 1998); Hudson, Charles M., *Knights of Spain, Warriors of the Sun: Hernando de Soto and the South's Ancient Chiefdoms* (Athens: University of Georgia Press, 1997); Larsen, Clark Spencer, "Reading the Bones of La Florida," *Scientific American* (June 2000): 80–85; McEwan, Bonnie G., *The Spanish Missions of La Florida* (Gainesville: University of Florida Press, 1993); Milanich, Jerald T., and Susan Milbrath, *First Encounters: Spanish Explorations in the Caribbean and the United States, 1492–1570* (Gainesville: University of Florida Press, 1991); South Carolina Institute of Archaeology and Anthropology, "Santa Elena, Charlesfort," http://www.cas.sc.edu/sciaa/staff/depratterc/newweb.htm.

Dennis B. Blanton

SUBMERGED TERRESTRIAL SITES AND SHIPWRECKS IN THE GULF OF MEXICO

INTRODUCTION AND SETTING
The Gulf of Mexico is the ninth largest ocean basin in the world. It is bounded on the northeast, north, and northwest by the gulf coast of the United States, on the southwest and south by Mexico, and on the southeast by Cuba. It connects with the Atlantic Ocean through the Florida Straits between the United States and Cuba, and with the Caribbean Sea through the Yucatan Channel between Mexico and Cuba. The gulf

101   103   104   108   109   114   122   202   203   201

110-1   110-2   111   113   204

115   116   102   205   117   119   120   118   121

* broken bottles 106, 107, and 112 are not pictured.

A selection of artifacts recovered from the *Mardi Gras* wreck in 4,000 feet of water.   [Amy Borgens]

basin is approximately 615,000 square miles, measuring approximately 995 miles (1,601 km) from east to west and 560 miles (901 km) from north to south. Almost half of the basin is shallow intertidal waters. The waters of the continental shelf and continental slope vary in depth between 656 and 9,842 feet (200–3,000 m) and represent nearly half (42 percent) of the gulf's area. Very deep, abyssal areas beyond 9,842 feet (3,000 m) make up 20 percent of the area. At its deepest it is 14,383 feet (4,384 m) at the Sigsbee Deep, an irregular trough more than 300 nautical miles (550 km) long.

Water enters the gulf through the Yucatan Strait, circulates as the Loop Current, and exits through the Florida Strait eventually forming the Gulf Stream. Portions of the Loop Current often break away, forming eddies that affect regional current patterns.

Thirty-three major river systems and 207 estuaries drain into the Gulf of Mexico, including the Mississippi River. During the months of June through November, the gulf is frequently subjected to the ravages of powerful cyclonic storms known as hurricanes, which have contributed significantly to both the formation and destruction of submerged archaeological sites.

Submerged archaeological sites in the Gulf of Mexico can take one of two forms, either historic period shipwrecks or prehistoric sites dating from the Pleistocene or early Holocene, when much of the continental shelf was exposed as dry land. Lowered sea level was a response to the expansion of glacial ice sheets. By the time of maximum glaciation, the freezing of water as glacial ice resulted in a lowering of sea level to approximately 450 feet (129 to 137 m) below the

The sinking of the USS *Hatteras* by the CSS *Alabama*.   [Courtesy U.S. Navy Historical Center]

present high stand. This maximum sea level recession occurred between 20,000 and 18,000 years ago, at the end of the Pleistocene time period; most of the continental shelf was exposed as dry land at this time.

SUBMERGED PREHISTORY

One of the most active current debates among archaeologists and others interested in ancient America relates to the peopling of the New World. Since the 1960s archaeologists have argued that people had crossed from Asia to the New World over a land bridge at the Bering Straits that was exposed at the end of the last Ice Age, some 14,000 years ago. According to this theory, they then spread southward along ice-free corridors through North America between 10,800 and 11,500 years ago. This hypothesis neatly explained the widespread appearance of a culture that produced an elegantly flaked and fluted stone spear point known as the Clovis point, named after the site in New Mexico where it was first discovered. The "Clovis first" model has now crumbled under a preponderance of evidence that people have lived in the Americas for at least 16,000 years and possibly more than 30,000 years. Discoveries of "pre-Clovis" artifacts have been reported from the

Meadowcroft Rockshelter site in Pennsylvania and the Cactus Hill site in Virginia, and even the Monte Verde site in southern Chile. It is probable that the New World was populated in multiple waves originating from many parts of Eurasia.

Prehistoric archaeological sites now being discovered on the submerged continental shelf of the Gulf of Mexico offer some hope of contributing to the debate over how and when the New World first was populated. Two areas in particular have yielded cultural material dating from before the last sea level rise: the drowned Aucilla River valley off the panhandle of eastern Florida and the relict Sabine River valley offshore of the present border between Texas and Louisiana. Although very different geologically, these two areas have been shown to have preserved sites from the scouring effects of rising sea level.

APALACHEE BAY, FLORIDA

Florida State University's work both in the present Aucilla River and in drowned remnants of the river offshore in Apalachee Bay has yielded dozens of submerged prehistoric sites and thousands of chipped-stone artifacts up to 9 miles (14 km) from the current shoreline. Of the sites discovered, one of the more productive is the Econfina Channel site

The 37-mm aft deck gun of the U-166. [Courtesy Minerals Management Service, U.S. Dept. of the Interior]

(8TA139), where chipped-stone artifacts were found on the margins of what is interpreted to be the ancient channel of the Econfina River. The site is thought to represent the remains of a small Middle Archaic period camp. The site is located 2.9 miles (4.7 km) seaward from the mouth of the modern Econfina River and probably dates from between 6500 and 5500 BP. The inhabitants of the Econfina Channel site were people who made Marion- or Putnam-style projectile points/knives and knapped chert from nearby outcrops, possibly sharpening some chipped stone tools locally. Local outcrops of chert were identified in the field.

Discovered in 1988, the Fitch Site (8JE739), located 6.2 miles (10 km) from the mouth of the modern Aucilla River in 17 feet (5.2 m) of water, appears to be the remains of a large quarry for stone tool making of unknown age. There was substantial evidence of stone tool manufacture in the remains of stone chipping debris, but no examples of a finished product. The site is probably older than 7,500 years, based on its depth and on what is known of the sequence of sea level changes. The techniques used to flake the stone tools suggest an earlier, possibly Paleoindian or Early Archaic age.

The J&J Hunt site (8JE740) has been a major focus of attention since its discovery in 1989 at a distance of 3.5 miles (6 km) from the mouth of the modern Aucilla River in 12 to 15 feet (3.7–4.6 m) of sea water. This single site has yielded nearly 2,000 artifacts dating from around 7,000 years ago.

HISTORIC SHIPWRECKS
The Spanish Entrada

The northern gulf coast has a long history of maritime activity following European entry into the Americas. The Spanish learned soon after their conquest of Mexico in 1521 that the quickest route from the Mexican port of Veracruz to Havana, the jumping-off point for the trip home to Spain, was not a straight line but instead took advantage of the prevailing currents and winds that ran offshore of Texas and Louisiana. One of the first recorded accounts of Spanish explorers along the gulf coast is Alvar Nuñez Cabeza de Vaca's 1528 account of the ill-fated expedition led by Pánfilo de Narváez. After exploring the interior of Florida, the expedition tried to make their way across the gulf to Mexico in four sailing barges, which they constructed for the voyage. All four vessels were lost, most of them along the coast of Texas. Out of a party of 400, only Cabeza de Vaca and three other survivors reached Mexico. Spanish treasure fleets regularly sailed through gulf waters transporting gold and silver from Mexico back to Spain. Three vessels from the 1554 fleet, *Santa María de Yciar*, *Espíritu Santo*, and *San Estebán*, wrecked off Padre Island, Texas, in a violent storm. One of the wrecks, believed to be the *Espíritu Santo*, was found by a private, out-of-state salvage firm in 1967. Suit was filed by the Texas attorney general's office to halt the salvage operation and gain custody of the recovered artifacts. After a prolonged legal battle, custody of the artifacts was eventually awarded to the state.

The Texas Antiquities Committee, a branch of Texas's historic preservation office formed in response to the Antiquities Bill passed by the Texas legislature in 1969, began investigations at the site of another 1554 wreck, identified as the *San Estebán*, in 1972 with a detailed magnetometer survey. Magnetometer "hits" indicating the presence of iron were tested using a "blower" device similar to a prop-wash deflector that forced a jet of water straight to the shallow bottom, blowing away the 5-foot (1.5-m) overburden of sand and shell. The artifacts were exposed lying on a dense deposit of Pleistocene clay, where they had adhered together in mass "conglomerates," due to corrosion and chemical interactions since the shipwreck, in which individual artifacts could be recognized only after the conglomerates were X-rayed. Several large conglomerates were recovered during the first season, together with a number of isolated artifacts and small conglomerates. In 1973 investigators returned to the site with an underwater archaeological field school from the University of Texas. In addition to extensive excavations at the site, a surface survey of the island opposite the wreck sites was carried out to locate evidence of the survivors' or salvagers' camps. During the 1973 season, the remaining major artifact conglomerates were recovered, along with many small conglomerates and isolated artifacts. The two seasons of excavation recovered over 13 tons (12,000 kilograms [kg]) of encrusted artifacts. Meanwhile, an archival research team recovered and translated over 1,000 pages of original documents from Spanish archives.

Of the hundreds of artifacts recovered from the *San Estebán*, the most significant for interpretation of the ship

itself was the aft section of the keel with part of the sternpost. This is the only major fragment of the ship that survived, but it was sufficient to permit an estimation of the size of the ship, which was thought to be something just under 97 feet (30 m) long and with a cargo capacity of 286 tons. Also recovered were wrought-iron anchors, a "built-up" cannon formed of welded iron bars, crossbows, astrolabes, tools, ship's fittings and fastenings, and silver coins and bullion. Several items of Native American manufacture were recovered, including a mirror made from a polished iron pyrite nodule and prismatic blades of obsidian. The silver coin and bullion and a small amount of gold bullion made up the greatest part of the fleet's cargo, but such perishable items as cochineal, hides, and wool also were being shipped to Spain. The collection from the *San Esteban* and the *Espíritu Santo* is housed in the Corpus Christi Museum of Science and Technology. The third wreck, the *Santa María de Yciar*, was destroyed in the 1950s when the Port Mansfield Channel was dredged.

Five years after the loss of the 1554 fleet, Spanish explorer Don Tristan de Luna de Arellano arrived in Pensacola, Florida, with a colonizing force of 1,500 men. Before Luna had even unloaded his vessels, they were struck by a devastating hurricane on the night of September 19, 1559. Seven of his ships were destroyed, most of their supplies were lost, and many people lost their lives. The enterprise was doomed by the disaster, and the few survivors eventually trickled back to Mexico.

In 1992 the remains of one of Luna's ships were discovered by a team from the Florida Bureau of Archaeological Research. The lower hull of the wreck was found to be surprisingly well preserved, and over 3,000 artifacts were recovered from the site, dubbed the Emanuel Point shipwreck. Among the unique finds discovered on the wreck were an iron breastplate and a wooden model of a Spanish ship carved by one of the crewmen. A major exhibit featuring the Emanuel Point ship is housed at the J. Earle Bowden Building in the Pensacola Historic District. Jointly sponsored by Historic Pensacola, Inc., and the Fiesta of Five Flags Association, Inc., the exhibit traces the heritage of Pensacola through its five cultural periods. The centerpiece of the new attraction is a full-scale replica of the stern section of the shipwreck site in a diorama setting that includes many of the original artifacts.

The Colonial Period

By the end of the seventeenth century, the French turned their attention to the Gulf of Mexico. In 1685 the French explorer La Salle received a royal commission to establish a colony near the mouth of the Mississippi River. The Spanish captured one of four vessels; while in route, two of the remaining ships wrecked at Matagorda Bay, Texas, and the expedition ended in failure. One of La Salle's ships, the *La*

Belle, one of the most important shipwrecks ever discovered in North America, was excavated inside a cofferdam by the Texas Historical Commission. Many of the artifacts are displayed in the Bob Bullock Texas State History Museum in Austin, and others will be exhibited in museums around Matagorda Bay.

In 1699 the French sent Pierre le Moyne, Sieur de Iberville, to colonize the lower Mississippi Valley. Iberville established a French settlement at Biloxi Bay in 1699. After 1701, the settlement was moved to Mobile Bay. In 1718 Iberville's brother, Jean Baptiste le Moyne, Sieur de Bienville, established a colony at New Orleans. Four years later, the seat of French government was transferred from Biloxi to New Orleans. In 1762 the French ceded control of Louisiana to Spain. As Spain's interests in the gulf increased, Spanish naval and merchant vessels became more numerous along the coast. The remains of the Spanish colonial merchant vessel *El Nuevo Constante*, which wrecked off the Louisiana coast in 1766, were discovered in 1979 by a group of shrimpers, who initially attempted to recover artifacts from the wreck using a mechanical dredge. The would-be treasure hunters eventually informed the state government of Louisiana, which contracted a team of professional archaeologists to investigate the site in 1980. Hundreds of artifacts were recovered from the vessel and the well-preserved remains of its lower hull were carefully mapped, despite the remarkably poor diving conditions and near-zero visibility. Among the more interesting finds was a rich array of small ceramic "knick-knacks" bound for sale in Europe. The muddy, anaerobic (with little or no oxygen) conditions also preserved a substantial portion of the ship's perishable cargo, including annatto (an orange dye made from the seeds of a shrub), indigo, and dyewood. Artifacts from the site are permanently curated at the Division of Archaeology in Baton Rouge, with a selection included in a traveling exhibit that circulates around Louisiana. A second vessel of the fleet, *Corazón de Jesús y Santa Bárbara*, was lost during the same storm. The remains of the *Santa Bárbara* have not yet been discovered.

A New Nation Emerges

In 1800 Louisiana was secretly returned to France, and Thomas Jefferson feared that Napoleon's control of the Mississippi outlet could mean serious trouble for U.S. shipping in the gulf. Jefferson dispatched Robert Livingston to Paris, where Livingston in April 1803 negotiated the sale of the Louisiana Territory to the United States. The boundaries of the territory were left vague, giving the United States a strong claim to Texas and "West Florida." The period from 1803 to 1821 was a time of intensive expansion in the Gulf of Mexico region. Centered on the port town of New Orleans, the region saw pirates and patriots jostle for positions of power within New Orleans and, later, the barrier islands of the Gulf of Mexico. In addition, while privateering exploded as an occupation, the port of New Orleans grew as a commercial center. Upriver trade brought commodities such as cotton, flour, rope yarn,

lead, whiskey, tobacco, pork, hides, and furs. European manufactured goods were imported and moved up the Mississippi River to markets in distant towns. Coastal trade between New Orleans and British-held East and West Florida also grew.

Growing tensions during the first years of the nineteenth century led to a major conflict between Great Britain and the United States in 1812. The impetus for this conflict was the British Royal Navy's practice of stopping American merchantmen on the high seas and impressing American sailors to serve aboard its ships. Great Britain also continued to maintain military ports on American soil, blockaded American ports, and incited Native Americans to raid and destroy American settlements. In the Gulf of Mexico, between 1805 and 1812, the British Navy and privateers blockaded and patrolled the mouth of the Mississippi River, seizing prizes going to and from the port of New Orleans. This had a huge impact on the local economy of New Orleans and the Gulf of Mexico region. British warships and privateers caused serious difficulties for the trade routed south from New Orleans. New Orleans merchants sending cargoes to and receiving cargoes from Santo Domingo, Cuba, Veracruz, Campeche, and other colonial ports suffered severe losses from British seizures. These events, combined with British aggressions perpetrated along the eastern seaboard of the United States, culminated in Great Britain and the United States going to war.

Three shipwrecks dating from this turbulent period of American history have been discovered recently during oil and gas surveys in the deep gulf on the approaches to the Mississippi River. The deepest of the three, found in over 4,000 feet (1,219 m) of water, was partially excavated by a team of archaeologists from Texas A&M University and the Minerals Management Service (MMS) of the U.S. Department of the Interior in May 2007 using a remotely operated vehicle (ROV). The team recovered a cannon dating from 1797, a rare ship's stove, English creamware and other ceramics, glass bottles, navigational instruments, and hundreds of gunflints and musket balls. The artifacts are being cleaned and stabilized at Texas A&M and eventually will be returned to Louisiana for permanent display. None of the three ships has, as yet, been positively identified.

By 1812 most waterborne commerce in the central part of the gulf took place in New Orleans. On January 10, 1812, the first steamship arrived at New Orleans from Pittsburgh. Soon after the introduction of steam vessels, maritime commerce in the Gulf of Mexico increased dramatically. Before the outbreak of hostilities during the Civil War, several major steamship lines were servicing New Orleans. The growth in maritime activity led to a proportionate increase in ship losses. Salvers located a mid-nineteenth-century steam vessel off High Island, Texas; the MMS investigated the wreck site and identified the vessel as the side-wheeler *New York*, which operated between New Orleans and Galveston and was lost in September 1846.

Civil War

Although most Civil War naval battles took place in inland waters, the Gulf of Mexico was a theater of conflict for Union blockaders, Confederate blockade runners, and Southern "commerce raiders" or privateers. Just as Bermuda was an important staging area for blockade runners in the Atlantic, Havana, Cuba was an important port for blockade runners operating in the Gulf of Mexico. Early in the war U.S. President Abraham Lincoln ordered a blockade of Southern ports. Confederate President Jefferson Davis responded to this action by issuing *Letters of Marque* to Confederate privateers allowing them to attack U.S. shipping.

The Civil War in the gulf is defined by the Northern blockade of Southern ports and the daring attempts by Confederate vessels to run this blockade. A number of important Civil War vessels have been located in state waters, such as the Confederate ironclads CSS *Louisiana* in Plaquemines Parish, Louisiana, and the *Huntsville* and *Tuscaloosa* in the Mobile River. The remains of the Union ironclad *Tecumseh*, whose sinking by a Confederate mine prompted Farragut's famous order "Damn the torpedoes, full speed ahead!" are well known off Fort Morgan, Alabama.

Only one U.S. warship, however, was sunk at sea in the gulf. This important shipwreck, the USS *Hatteras*, has been the subject of repeated investigations by the MMS, the Texas Historical Commission, and Texas A&M University at Galveston. Constructed in 1861 by the Harlan and Hollingsworth Company of Wilmington, Delaware, for the Charles Morgan line of gulf coast steamships, the vessel was originally known as the *St. Mary*. An iron-hulled steamer of 1,450 tons, the side-wheeler was purchased by the U.S. Navy in September 1861 and converted to a gunboat. The vessel was armed with four 32-pounder cannons (a 20-pounder rifled cannon was added later) and renamed *Hatteras*. After distinguished service in the South Atlantic Blockading Squadron, the vessel was transferred to the Gulf Blockading Squadron on January 26, 1862. In less than a year, *Hatteras* captured seven Confederate blockade runners off Vermilion Bay, Louisiana. Early in 1863 she was ordered to join the squadron under Rear Admiral David Farragut, who was attempting to retake the key Texas port of Galveston, Texas.

As the blockading squadron lay off the coast on the afternoon of January 11, 1863, a set of sails was sighted just over the horizon, and *Hatteras* was ordered to give pursuit. She chased the intruder for four hours, closer and closer to shore, and farther and farther from her supporting fleet. Finally, as dusk was falling, the *Hatteras* came within hailing distance of the square-rigged, black-hulled vessel. Commander Homer C. Blake demanded to know the identity of the ship. "Her Britannic Majesty's Ship *Vixen*," came the reply. Blake ordered one of *Hatteras*'s boats launched to inspect the "Britisher." Almost as soon as the boat was piped away, a new reply came from the mystery ship, "We are the CSS *Alabama*!" A broadside from the *Alabama*'s guns punctuated the reply. Within thirteen minutes, *Hatteras*, sinking rapidly, surrendered.

The USS *Hatteras* today rests in 58 feet (17 m) of water about 20 miles (32 km) off Galveston. Her 210-foot (64-m) iron hull is completely buried under about 3 feet (1 m) of sand. Only what's left of her 500-horsepower walking-beam steam engine and her two iron paddle wheels remain exposed above the seafloor. Although the wreck site has been identified, it remains largely unexplored.

The Early Twentieth Century

After the Civil War, stern-wheelers began to increase in frequency, and throughout the last half of the century a variety of sailing craft, such as schooners, clippers, and "New Orleans" luggers, also were in use along the northern gulf coast. With the beginning of oil production in Louisiana and Texas at the onset of the twentieth century, the need for steam propulsion decreased. By 1910 to 1920, diesel engines and screw propellers began to replace steam engines and paddle wheels.

World War II

Soon after America's entry into World War II, some twenty-four German U-boats operated in the Gulf of Mexico. *U-507*, under the command of Korvettenkapitän Harro Schacht, claimed the first vessel sank in gulf waters when on May 4, 1942, she torpedoed the freighter *Norlindo* just off Key West, Florida. Other U-boats soon joined the onslaught in the gulf, including *U-166*, commanded by Kapitänleutnant Hans-Günther Kühlmann. *U-166* took up position off the mouth of the Mississippi River to lay mines and attack merchant shipping. Kühlmann sank the passenger freighter SS *Robert E. Lee* approximately 45 miles (72 km) southeast of the Mississippi River on July 30, 1942. *PC-566*, the naval vessel escorting the freighter, in turn sank the *U-166*. In all, seventeen U-boats sank fifty-six ships in the Gulf of Mexico and damaged fourteen others over the course of approximately a year, with only one U-boat lost. The remains of the lost U-boat, *U-166*, along with its last victim, *Robert E. Lee*, were discovered during a gas pipeline survey in 2001 in over 5,000 feet (1,524 m) of water. These sites, along with several other casualties of the war discovered in the deep gulf, were investigated by an expedition jointly funded by the MMS and the National Oceanographic and Atmospheric Administration under the National Oceanographic Partnership Program in 2004.

Further Reading: Arnold, J. Barto, and Richard J. Anuskiewicz, "USS *Hatteras*: Site Monitoring and Mapping," in *Underwater Archaeology Proceedings from the Society for Historic Archaeology Conference*, edited by Paul Forsythe Johnston (Washington, DC: Society for Historical Archaeology, 1995), 82–87; Arnold, J. Barto, III, and Robert S. Weddle, *The Nautical Archeology of Padre Island: The Spanish Shipwrecks of 1554* (New York: Academic Press, 1978); Bruseth, James E., and Toni S. Turner, *From a Watery Grave: The Discovery and Excavation of La Salle's Shipwreck, La Belle* (College Station: Texas A&M University Press, 2005); Church, R. D. Warren, R. Cullimore, L. Johnson, W. Schroeder, W. Patterson, T. Shirley, M. Kilgour, N. Morris, and J. Moore, *Archaeological and Biological Analysis of World War II Shipwrecks in the Gulf of Mexico: Artificial Reef Effect in Deep Water*, OCS Study MMS 2007-015 (New Orleans, LA: U.S. Department of the Interior, Minerals Management Service, 2007), http://www.gomr.mms.gov/PI/PDFImages/ESPIS/4/4239.pdf

(online August 2007); "Emanuel Point Shipwreck," http://www.fl heritage.com/archaeology/projects/shipwrecks/emanuelpoint/ (online August 2007); Faught, Michael K., "Geophysical Remote Sensing and Underwater Cultural Resource Management of Submerged Prehistoric Sites in Apalachee Bay: A Deepwater Example, Site Predictive Models, and Site Discoveries," http://www.gomr.mms.gov/homepg/ whatsnew/papers/2002%20ITM%20Archaeology%20Session.pdf (online August 2007); Irion, Jack, and David A. Ball, "The *New York* and the *Josephine*: Two Steamships of the Charles Morgan Line," *International Journal of Nautical Archaeology* 30(1) (2001): 48–56; "Mardi Gras Shipwreck," http://www.flpublicarchaeology.org/mardigras/ (online August 2007); Pearson, Charles E., and Paul E. Hoffman, *The Last Voyage of El Nuevo Constante: The Wreck and Recovery of an Eighteenth-Century Spanish Ship off the Louisiana Coast* (Baton Rouge: Louisiana State University Press, 1995); Pearson, Charles E., and Paul E. Hoffman, *El Nuevo Constante: Investigation of an Eighteenth-Century Spanish Shipwreck off the Louisiana Coast*, 2nd ed. (Baton Rouge, LA: Department of Culture, Recreation, and Tourism, 1998), http://www.crt.state.la.us/archaeology/NUEVO/NUEVO.HTM (online August 2007); "Unterseeboot U-166," http://www.pastfoundation.org/ U166/index.htm (online August 2007).

Jack B. Irion

HISTORIC PERIOD MILITARY SITES IN THE SOUTHEAST

From coastal Civil War fortifications to backcountry Revolutionary War battlefields, hundreds of archaeological sites reveal the Southeast's rich military past. Military sites include battlefields, defensive works (forts, batteries, redoubts, trenches), camps, landscapes, ships and shipwrecks, and cemeteries—anywhere armies, soldiers, warriors, or armed citizenry marched, lived, camped, maneuvered, or fought. These sites are the special interest of military site archaeologists, who focus on reaching a broader understanding of conflict and war through archaeological research. Military site archaeologists assert that the study of military sites (1) provides a different perspective on conflict from that provided by historic documents, (2) substantiates or refutes standard interpretations of war and warfare, (3) is sometimes the only method of documenting unrecorded events associated with conflict and warfare, and (4) provides tangible evidence of the impact of conflict and warfare on society. Although military site archaeology focuses on sites associated with the historic period, archaeological evidence of conflict is not necessarily restricted to the documented past. Military site archaeologists recognize the importance of understanding evidence of prehistoric, protohistoric, and contact period armed conflict, although these topics are more often encompassed under the study of the anthropology of warfare (for example, the work of David H. Dye for the Southeast).

Military site archaeology is synonymous with battlefield archaeology; however the latter rubric overemphasizes just one aspect of military site archaeology—the field of conflict—at the expense of other critical sites, such as campgrounds, that can provide insights into soldier life and morale. On the other hand, the mere presence of a military occupation or artifacts at a site being investigated does not constitute military site archeology, unless the project focus is on understanding the military experience or warfare.

The development of military site or battlefield archaeology as distinct subdiscipline is still in its infancy. The earliest excavations in the Southeast were almost exclusively at prominent, visible fortifications. These and subsequent efforts have been largely site specific and descriptive of military architecture and artifacts. Beginning in the 1990s broader anthropological perspectives have led to examinations of soldier life; cultural interaction between soldiers, civilians, and Native Americans; cultures in conflict; and behavioral aspects of battle. These studies have provided some of the first theoretical-level research at battlefields, informed by a battlefield model introduced by Richard A. Fox Jr. and Douglas D. Scott at the Little Big Horn Battlefield, Montana. Fox and Scott asserted that just as other human behavior is patterned, so is battlefield maneuvering. These patterns can be revealed by recording the locations of fired and unfired ammunition and other military artifacts. The model is predictive of depositional patterns based on cultural aspects of the combatants, such as training, nationality, and morale. In the Southeast, Scott has demonstrated this technique at the Civil War battlefield of Monroe's Crossroads in North Carolina.

Scott's contribution to military site archaeology was not only important to the development of anthropological perspectives; he also made respectable an important field technique—the use of a metal detector for controlled systematic battlefield survey. Relic collectors have used metal detectors at battlefields and campsites across the Southeast since World War II. As a result most archaeologists came to associate metal detecting with looting and refused to use the technology, despite countless examples of battlefields and campgrounds being overlooked when archaeologists relied solely on the traditional shovel test method of survey. One of the early exceptions was Roy Dickens. A pioneer in Southeastern archaeology, Dickens was also a pioneer in the use of metal detectors at battlefields, having first used them at Horseshoe Bend National Military Park, Alabama, in the 1970s. However, it was Scott's work that clearly demonstrated that in the hands of a professional archaeologist, a metal detector could be used effectively as an archaeological tool to gain anthropological insights. Today, metal detectors are widely used at battlefields and other military sites, and some state historic preservation offices are beginning to suggest their routine use in cultural resource management projects when the presence of former battlefields or military camps is suspected in the project area.

Meanwhile, relic collecting has had devastating effects on the archaeological manifestations of military sites across the Southeast, often to the degree that information is available only from private collections. Recognizing this reality, Christopher T. Espenshade, Robert L. Jolley, and James B. Legg have called for the combined use of metal detectors and collector interviewing as an essential method in the archaeological study of military sites. James B. Legg and Steven D. Smith have taken this one step farther at the South Carolina Revolutionary War battle of Camden site, interviewing over a dozen Camden battlefield collectors, inventorying their collections, and conducting site visits with collectors in an attempt to reconstruct artifact locations. With the interviewing of multiple collectors, patterns have emerged at the Camden battlefield despite the loss of this information from past collecting. Relic collectors have also been used as volunteers on archaeological projects. National Park Service archaeologist John E. Cornelison has conducted such projects at the Chickamauga and Chattanooga national military parks in Georgia and Tennessee, and the Kings Mountain Military Park in South Carolina.

Clarence R. Geier has also made significant contributions to military site archeology with the publication, with a host of co-authors, of three edited volumes on Civil War archaeology: *Look to the Earth: Historical Archaeology and the American Civil War* (1994), *Archaeological Perspectives on the American Civil War* (2000), and *Huts and History: The Historical Archaeology of Military Encampment during the American Civil War* (2006). These works exemplify the development of Civil War archaeology over the last two decades. Specifically, they have greatly advanced the study of the Civil War and have demonstrated the value of an anthropological approach to that conflict, which, as Smith asserts in the first volume, is the only means by which archaeology can make a relevant contribution to the understanding of an already thoroughly studied war.

Others who have made impressive contributions to military site archaeology in the Southeast are Lawrence E. Babits at Eastern Carolina University, North Carolina; Samuel D. Smith at the Tennessee Division of Archaeology; Daniel T. Elliott at the Lamar Institute in Georgia; Scott Butler at the Flank Company, Georgia; and Chad O. Braley of Southeastern Archaeological Services, Georgia.

FORTIFICATIONS

As noted, military site archaeology in the Southeast began with the investigation of fortifications most often under the auspices of state and national parks. Initially these efforts were ancillary to restoration and reconstruction efforts, and the archaeology was usually confined to uncovering architecture and collecting artifacts for display. Notable examples in which both preservation and archaeology were important include Stan South's 1960 excavations at Civil War Fort Fisher, North Carolina, and 1970 investigations in Revolutionary War Star Fort at the Ninety-Six National Historical Site, South Carolina; National Park Service studies at Fort Sumter and Fort Moultrie in Charleston, South Carolina; and Lee Hanson's investigations of the Civil War Water Battery at Fort Donnelson, Tennessee, in 1968.

Excellent efforts in the 1980s include Karl Kuttruff's excavations at British Fort Loudon (1756), in Tennessee, and the British Fort of Pensacola, Florida (1763–81), by Judith A. Bense in 1989. More recent examples include Elliott's excavations at Georgia forts Argyle (1733) and Hawkins (1806) and the Revolutionary War Spring Hill redoubt in Savannah. Babits has conducted several field seasons at the French and Indian War Fort Dobbs in North Carolina, and Butler recently discovered the lost Confederate Fort Albert Sidney Johnson in Mobile, Alabama. These are just a few examples of numerous studies of military fortifications across the Southeast.

In addition to the above, site-specific examples, broader examinations of Civil War fortification in terms of strategy and tactics include Robert J. Fryman's 1997 study of Confederate military engineering in the Atlanta, Georgia, Campaign and Christopher O. Clement, Steven D. Smith, and Ramona M. Grunden's 2000 study of the Confederate defense of the Charleston-to-Savannah railroad in South Carolina. Both studies used Global Positioning System (GPS) data collection and Geographic Information System (GIS) analysis to unearth past military landscapes from the remnants of field fortifications. In Tennessee Samuel D. Smith, Benjamin C. Nance, and Fred M. Prouty have made sweeping statewide surveys inventorying Civil War, Revolutionary War, and World War II sites across the state. Such work serves as the foundation for future research.

BATTLEFIELDS

Battlefield archaeology has grown exponentially since archaeologists began to use the metal detector as a survey tool in combination with GPS technology. Diagnostic military items such as ammunition, buttons, and arms are largely metal objects. Locating these artifacts and pinpointing their locations across the landscape using GPS data-gathering instruments not only is efficient, but also reveals battlefield maneuver and unit behavior. In addition to the battlefields already mentioned, successful battlefield studies using metal detectors as the main means of survey include Butler's discovery of the two Revolutionary War battlefields Fishdam Ford and the Waxhaws in South Carolina. Elliott also has used these techniques at a survey of the Nash Farm battlefield in Georgia. Elliott's work at Sunbury, Georgia, demonstrated the power of a multi-disciplinary approach combining metal detecting, traditional shovel testing, and ground-penetrating radar in a battlefield survey. Smith and Legg (2007) used metal detector survey at the site of the Revolutionary War siege of Fort Motte, in South Carolina, to define battle positions and camp features. They have conducted similar work at the South Carolina Revolutionary War battlefields of Blackstock's Plantation and Huck's Defeat.

National Park Service archaeologist David Lowe advocates another analysis technique, which when used in conjunction with metal detecting is proving to be a powerful method for battlefield archaeology. Lowe's system of battlefield analysis is based on nineteenth-century historian Hans Delbrück's concept of inherent military probability. That is, the battlefield is viewed with a military eye that predicts the likelihood of unit placements and maneuvering during battle. By means of this military terrain analysis the landscape is studied to identify key terrain, observation and fields of fire, concealment and cover, obstacles, and avenues of approach (KOCOA). These locations can then be targeted using metal detector and GIS technology to reveal the archaeological manifestation of a military unit's presence during the battle. The presence or absence of evidence of military occupation provides an explanatory framework for battlefield research.

CAMPS

Another fruitful area of military site archaeology has been the excavation of campsites, both long-term and temporary. It is through the excavation of encampments that archaeologists can gain insights into soldier life, including subsistence, health, morale, and resource exploitation. Whereas battlefields are representations of human behavior under short-term conditions of stress, campgrounds provide a perspective on the common soldier. Furthermore, in contrast to battlefields, the archaeological expression of a campground is of a more dense concentration of military features such as huts, sinks, and wells. At campsites, archaeologists not only can apply new techniques such as metal detecting, but also can return to more traditional forms of archaeology, such as block excavation and ground-penetrating radar, to reveal campsite patterns or to locate graves and other features. It is important to note that military sites developed within a closed cultural system that operated under strict rules. Archaeologists studying campsites know the expected patterns or the imposed patterns, and can observe variations in those patterns from the archaeological record as revealing morale levels or perhaps even variations in status and ethnicity.

The focus on campsites has increased as the discipline has developed. Early Southeastern examples include Legg and Smith's 1987 excavations of the Civil War 55th Massachusetts camp and cemetery on Folly Island, South Carolina, and Camp Baird, the impressive complete regimental camp of the 32nd United States Colored Infantry at Hilton Head, South Carolina, excavated by Legg and Espenshade in 1990. Scott Butler has excavated an 1812 U.S. camp at Point Peter, St. Mary's, Georgia. Guy Prentiss

revealed the stockade walls of the Civil War Andersonville Prison in Georgia and amazingly uncovered an escape tunnel.

UNIQUE APPROACHES TO MILITARY SITE ARCHAEOLOGY

Not all battlefield archaeology requires metal detecting or even traditional excavation techniques to gain knowledge about conflict and war. Lawrence E. Babits's provocative study of the Revolutionary War Cowpens battlefield in South Carolina, titled *A Devil of a Whipping: The Battle of Cowpens*, combined intensive historical research of unit rosters, personal diaries, pension records, reenactment experience, experimental archaeology with period weaponry, and field survey methodology to provide a new and innovative perspective on the battle. Elsa Heckman conducted a computer-generated viewshed analysis of the Lookout Mountain battlefield in Tennessee, attempting to determine the Confederate and Union forces' visibility during the battle and how their view affected their decisions.

Underwater investigations in the Southeast have been some of the most exotic applications of military site archaeology. The Mariners Museum in Newport News, Virginia, displays artifacts from the Union ironclad USS *Monitor*, discovered off the coast of North Carolina. That long-term discovery and research project is matched only by the raising of the Confederate submarine *H.L. Hunley*, found just outside Charleston Harbor, South Carolina, and its subsequent laboratory excavation and conservation in Charleston.

Military site archaeology is new but long overdue. A body of anthropological theory is needed to take the subdiscipline beyond the descriptive and site-specific stage. However, military site archaeologists are also in a race against time as relic collecting and development intrude upon the remaining battlefields and campsites, few if any of which remain untouched by these destructive practices. In the 1930s laborers at battlefields across the Southeast literally shoveled out artifacts in their effort to reconstruct Civil War entrenchments and batteries. Today, many of these sites are nearly archaeologically invisible, their artifacts removed by collectors and their parapets leveled by development.

Further Reading: Babits, Lawrence E., *A Devil of A Whipping: The Battle of Cowpens* (Chapel Hill: University of North Carolina Press, 1998); Dye, David H., "Warfare in the Sixteenth Century Southeast: The De Soto Expedition in the Interior," in *Columbian Consequences*, Vol. 2: *Archaeological and Historical Perspectives on the Spanish Borderlands East*, edited by David H. Thomas (Washington, D C: Smithsonian Institution Press, 1990), 211–222; Elliott, Daniel T., *Sunbury Battlefield Survey*, prepared for American Battlefield Protection Program, National Park Service, Washington, DC (Box Springs, GA: LAMAR Institute, 2006), http://shapiro.anthro.uga.edu/Lamar/PDFfiles/Publication%2064.pdf); Espenshade, Christopher T., Robert L. Jolley, and James B. Legg, "The Value and Treatment of Civil War Military Sites," *North American Archaeologist* 23(1) (2002): 39–67; Geier, Clarence R., David G. Orr, and Matthew

B. Reeves, *Huts and History: The Historical Archaeology of Military Encampment during the American Civil War* (Gainesville: University of Florida Press, 2006); Geier, Clarence R., and Stephen R. Potter, *Archaeological Perspectives on the American Civil War* (Gainesville: University of Florida Press, 2000); Geier, Clarence R., and Susan E. Winter, eds., *Look to the Earth: Historical Archaeology and the American Civil War* (Knoxville: University of Tennessee Press, 1994); Legg, James B., and Steven D. Smith, *"The Best Ever Occupied . . .": Archaeological Investigations of a Civil War Encampment on Folly Island, South Carolina* (Columbia: South Carolina Institute of Archaeology and Anthropology, 1989); Luckett, William W., R. L. Comstock Jr., and Horace Sheely Jr., *Fort Sumter Excavations,* *1951–1959* (Tallahassee, FL: Southeastern Archeological Center, National Park Service, 1962); Scott, Douglas, Lawrence Babits, and Charles Haecker, eds., *Fields of Conflict: Battlefield Archaeology from the Roman Empire to the Korean War,* 2 vols. (Westport, CT: Praeger Security International, 2007); Smith, Steven D., James B. Legg, Tamara S. Wilson, and Jonathan Leader, *"Obstinate and Strong": The History and Archaeology of the Siege of Fort Motte* (Columbia: South Carolina Institute of Archaeology and Anthropology, 2007); South, Stanley A., *Palmetto Parapets: Exploratory Archeology at Fort Moultrie, SC, 38CH50* (Columbia: University of South Carolina, Institute for Archeology and Anthropology, 1974).

Steven D. Smith

PALEOINDIAN SITES IN THE SOUTHEAST

Tennessee to Florida

Ancient Immigrants Adapt to Different Environments

The earliest widespread culture in the Southeast is known as Clovis and dates from about 13,350 to 12,900 years ago. Clovis people were hunter-gatherers who lived in environments with a wide variety of now extinct animal species, as well as species that survive today, such as whitetail deer. The extinct animals they hunted, referred to collectively as "megafauna" because of their large size compared with modern forms, included mastodon, mammoth, llama, horse, tapir, ground sloth, giant bison, giant beaver, and giant tortoise. The fossilized remains of many of these now extinct animals have been found at many locations across the Southeast, including Big Bone Lick in Kentucky, the Kimmswick site in Missouri, and Page-Ladson in Florida, to name just a few. Sites where early Paleoindian stone tools occur in association with bones of extinct mammals have been documented in the Southeast, but they are very rare and are discussed below.

Southeastern forests were dominated by hardwood and mixed hardwood-pine during the Paleoindian period. Pollen analysis by Hazel and Paul Delcourt suggests that the late Ice Age environment for most of the Southeast in the temperate latitudes hosted a cool, moist, hardwood forest dominated by beech and hickory. Summer temperatures in this zone were on average cooler than today, with less seasonal variation compared to the modern era. The climate and vegetation of the area south of 33 degrees latitude, the subtropical zone, was similar to today's, with forests dominated by oak, hickory, sweetgum, and pine. The water table was lower than today due to a lower sea level and decreased rainfall. Remains of Late Pleistocene animals also provide clues to help in reconstructing the environment. Theories advanced to explain the mass extinction of large faunal species include overhunting by humans, changes in climate and vegetation patterns, and epidemic diseases, possibly introduced by humans and/or dogs from the Old World. Whatever the cause, it is evident that more than thirty taxa of large terrestrial animals were extinct by about 12,900 years ago, coincident with the cold snap known as the Younger Dryas climatic episode.

Perishable materials have rarely survived in most Paleoindian period sites, so archaeologists rely heavily on the stone artifacts from these early hunting-gathering cultures to reconstruct their lifestyles. Paleoindians preferred fine-grained, silica-rich rocks such as chert or flint, agatized dolomite, agatized coral, and silicified sandstone. They practiced a core tool technology; this involved striking the edge of a large cobble of silica-rich stone (a core) to detach stone flakes large enough to use after further modification as spear points or knives, or tools such as scrapers. One type of core common in the Paleoindian tool kit is called a bifacial core. A bifacial core could be chipped and shaped to make a spear point.

The fluted point is the hallmark of the Clovis period. The flute is actually a relatively long, narrow flake removed from the base of a bifacial core. Scores of fluted bifaces have been found at sites across the Southeast, including Adams and the Little River complex sites of Kentucky, Wells Creek and Carson-Conn-Short in Tennessee, and Topper and Big Pine Tree in South Carolina. The scar formed from detaching the flute allows the point to fit snugly inside a handle or spear shaft, thus allowing for use of the point as both a knife and a projectile. Tools such as spear points, foreshafts, burnishers, billets, and shaft straighteners were made of ivory, bone, and antler. This evidence indicates that animals were hunted not only for food but also for a variety of materials to make into

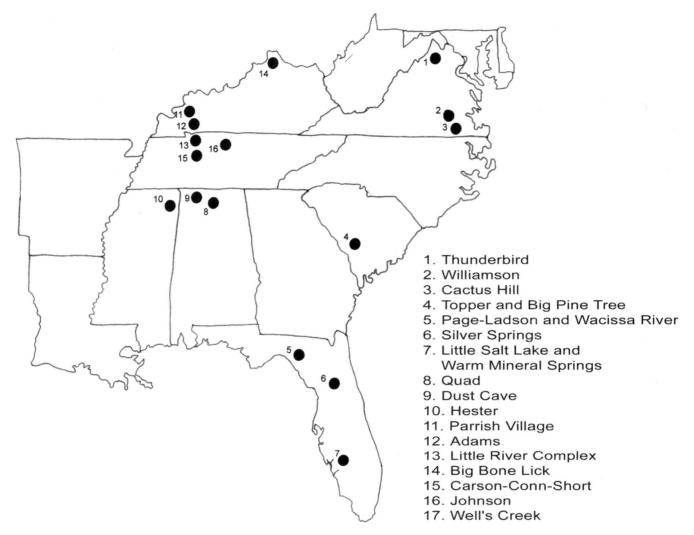

1. Thunderbird
2. Williamson
3. Cactus Hill
4. Topper and Big Pine Tree
5. Page-Ladson and Wacissa River
6. Silver Springs
7. Little Salt Lake and
   Warm Mineral Springs
8. Quad
9. Dust Cave
10. Hester
11. Parrish Village
12. Adams
13. Little River Complex
14. Big Bone Lick
15. Carson-Conn-Short
16. Johnson
17. Well's Creek

Paleoindian sites in the Southeast.   [Juliet E. Morrow]

tools and other items. Some of the best evidence for use of late Ice Age animals comes from freshwater springs, rivers, and sinkholes in Florida. One notable discovery is a complete foreshaft made of mammoth ivory recovered from Sloth Hole in the Aucilla River. Experiments demonstrate that proboscidean (i.e., mammoth, mastodon, elephant) ivory is easiest to work with while it is still fresh or "green." So it is likely that Paleoindian hunters were preying on live animals and not simply scavenging old carcasses. Comparatively little is known about the entire stone tool repertoire of post-Clovis Paleoindians, but it is assumed that at least some of the same chipped-stone tools continued to be made and used.

Given the available evidence, terrestrial game would have been the primary food source for Paleoindians. There is little empirical evidence for Paleoindian use of plants, although there is some evidence that people may have consumed fleshy fruits, such as grapes and berries, as well as nuts. Research on modern hunter-gatherers indicates that the hunting of large

mammals is often more efficient in terms of calories produced than is plant collecting. There are over twenty-two sites, mostly in the western United States, where Clovis people dispatched a mammoth, mastodon, bison, or other megafaunal species. The fact that these hunting sites are elusive in the Southeast may be due to geological processes rather than to a major difference in subsistence orientation between Paleoindians living east and west of the Mississippi River. Clovis people had over thirty additional large animal species to hunt than did their descendents. After the Ice Age extinctions, about 10,800 years ago, the largest prey animals available to post-Clovis Paleoindian groups in the Southeast were modern bison, elk, deer, and bear. On the margins of the Southeast, there is a well-preserved Clovis site near Kimmswick, Missouri. There archaeologists excavated the remains of a mastodon cow and calf and various species of small mammals, whitetail deer, amphibians, turtles, and other aquatic fauna. These animal remains were found in a layer of sediment that also contained Clovis points and chipped-stone debris from making and resharpening stone tools. Ground sloth remains recovered from the Kimmswick site suggests that a hide from such an animal may have been brought to the site as a piece of clothing or possibly as part of a temporary shelter.

Florida is legendary for its Late Pleistocene faunal deposits. Perhaps the most direct piece of evidence for the hunting of Late Pleistocene megafauna comes from the Wascissa River, where a diver found a *Bison antiquus* skull with the tip of an unknown type of chert spear point embedded in its skull. A radiocarbon date of about 13,000 years ago places this extinct bison skull exactly within the Clovis period. A faunal assemblage containing aquatic, avian, and small mammal species is associated with a variety of Late Paleoindian and Early Archaic stone tool styles—for example, Cumberland, Quad, Beaver Lake, and Dalton—and debris at Dust Cave, Alabama.

Paleoindian societies likely had a band-type social structure in which the primary social groups consisted of a dozen to perhaps several dozen individuals. Based on evidence from outside the Southeast, they probably aggregated into larger groups during seasons when food was plentiful. The sparse number of artifacts recovered from excavations of Paleoindian campsites such as Cactus Hill and Thunderbird in Virginia and Kimmswick in Missouri suggests that Paleoindians did not live in year-round, permanent settlements. The occurrence of exotic cherts made into tools and left at Paleoindian campsites hundreds of miles from their geologic source is evidence of long-distance movement during their migration to the New World and possible trade once they became more settled in specific regions. The fact that even Clovis fluted points themselves vary slightly from region to region suggests that settlement of groups in specific regions or territories probably occurred fairly rapidly as they expanded throughout the continental United States.

The Paleoindian period in the Southeast can be divided into three sub-periods: pre-Clovis, Clovis, and post-Clovis. The sub-periods are well represented in the Southeast on the basis of stone tools found on the surface of farm fields and on river gravel bars, as well as from archaeological excavations of buried sites, where artifacts are sometimes discovered in their original context. The Clovis period is identified with the Clovis spear point, and the post-Clovis period is represented by a succession of fluted and nonfluted spear points. In the Southeast, the Paleoindian period ended about 10,500 years ago (8500 BC) as the culture evolved into a variety of regionally based cultures of the Early Archaic period, such as Dalton, Hardaway, Bolen, Taylor, and Thebes/St. Charles.

Although there are claims of pre-Clovis cultural remains, convincing evidence for antiquity is generally lacking. The recently excavated Cactus Hill site in Virginia has produced convincing evidence for a pre-Clovis occupation. Cactus Hill is a stratified site in a 1.8-meter-thick sand dune above the Nottoway River. The site contains cultural material from the eighteenth century to the Paleoindian period within the upper 1.0 meter of the dune. The Clovis occupation at Cactus Hill is

represented by fluted points and other stone tools commonly recovered from Clovis period sites. A sample of pine charcoal from a hearth provided a radiocarbon date of 10,920 ± (plus or minus) 250 years ago. The pre-Clovis component of the site consists of a number of quartzite artifacts from the manufacture or maintenance of chipped-stone tools at a level slightly beneath the Clovis tools. Pine wood charcoal associated with the pre-Clovis quartzite artifacts provided a radiocarbon date of 15,070 ± 70 years ago. Additional excavations exposed another area containing clusters of quartzite flakes debitage, one of which was associated with a hearth-like feature. Soil from the hearth-like feature produced a radiocarbon date of 16,670 ± 730 years ago. To confirm the pre-Clovis occupation, the types of artifacts and artifact distributions observed at Cactus Hill must be identified at additional sites in the region. In the Southeast, the search for early sites is advancing through the application of geological methods and the study of landscape evolution.

Clovis is a name for a culture, a time period, and a particular variety of fluted stone spear point or knife. The name derives from Clovis, New Mexico, which is located near the site Blackwater Draw Locality No. 1. Excavations in 1932 at Blackwater Draw found Clovis fluted points with extinct megafauna in Ice Age gravel deposits. Another tool type specific to the Clovis period is a long, narrow blade detached from a specially prepared core. Unmodified blades could be used to cut, score, and skin, but often the blades were modified into end scrapers or other tools. Clovis stone tools tend to be large, multifunctional, highly portable, and durable. Clovis points have been found throughout the Southeast, with notable concentrations in areas associated with chert or flint tool stone, springs, salt licks, and karst topography. These Clovis concentrations include the Interior Low Plateau of northern Alabama, Tennessee, and Kentucky; the confluence region of the Illinois, Mississippi, and Missouri rivers of greater St. Louis; and the Aucilla River in Florida. Buried, stratified sites with Clovis occupations are very rare in the Southeast. Cactus Hill and the Thunderbird site, both in Virginia, produced Clovis artifacts from buried deposits.

The period following Clovis, after about 10,900 years ago, and preceding the Early Archaic period, about 10,500 to 8,000 years ago, is termed the post-Clovis period. The post-Clovis occupations of the Southeast are represented by a variety of fluted spear point types known as Gainey/Sedgwick, Redstone, and Cumberland; Pelican (fluted and nonfluted); and nonfluted types known as Beaver Lake, Quad, Coldwater, Suwanee, and Simpson. Each of these spear point types has a unique geographic distribution. The name Gainey derives from a post-Clovis site in Michigan, but points of this style (having a deep basal concavity, a well-defined midline ridge, and well-expressed flutes) can be found at least as far south as Arkansas and as far west as Oklahoma and Texas. Sedgwick is a name for a small version of Gainey-like points often made from small cobbles of Crowley's Ridge chert that are common in northeast Arkansas. Redstone points seem to be most common in the Mid-south region (Kentucky, Tennessee, and northern Alabama) and the south Atlantic region. Suwannee and Simpson points are common in Florida but also occur in adjacent states. These geographic variations in projectile point type may indicate that human groups were narrowing the spatial ranges in their settlement systems.

One of the most important stratified sites dating to the Paleoindian period is the Thunderbird site. Located among the Jasper quarries of the middle Shenandoah River valley in Virginia, it is one of only a few sites where there is a buried, stratified Paleoindian through Early Archaic cultural sequence (Clovis-Dalton/Hardaway-Kirk/Palmer). The Thunderbird site was excavated in the early 1970s by a team led by William Gardner. A detailed final report has not yet been published, but a great deal of information is available from preliminary field reports and theses. The site is located on a terrace of the south fork of the Shenandoah River where the maximum depth of the deposits was approximately 3.5 feet. All of the classic Clovis tools were recovered during the excavation, but the majority of cultural material recovered included debitage from manufacturing chipped-stone tools.

The Johnson site in Tennessee is a Clovis period, quarry-related workshop excavated by Mark Norton and John Broster. The site consists of an 8-meter-thick sequence of stratified sediments and cultural material evident in the cutbank of the Cumberland River in the Nashville basin. A wide range of Early Archaic spear points along with Clovis points were recovered from the eroding cutbank. The base of a Clovis point preform was recovered from the lowest cultural stratum at the cutbank, and 30 centimeters away from this diagnostic artifact a sample of wood charcoal produced a radiocarbon date of 11,700 ± 980 years ago. In the upper portion of this stratum two basin-shaped features were identified. One of the features consisted of ash, charcoal, burned bone, and chert debitage and was radiocarbon dated to 12,660 ± 970 years ago. The other feature produced a radiocarbon date of 11,980 ± 110 years ago. Twenty of the twenty-six Clovis point preforms recovered from the site were found in situ. Three Clovis points were recovered from the beach below the cutbank.

Located on Kentucky Lake, the Carson-Conn-Short site is another significant Clovis period, quarry-related workshop site investigated by Broster and Norton. This site is one of the largest known Clovis sites in the Southeast. It consists of seven distinct areas on terrace ridges near the Pleistocene channel of the Tennessee River; it is close to a source of high-quality tool stone. Investigations at the site have produced predominantly Clovis points, preforms, and flake tools along with a few Cumberland artifacts. Paleoindian artifacts were generally found between 30 and 55 centimeters below the ground surface. Clusters of fire-cracked chert suggest the possibility that Paleoindians camped long enough at the site to make fire hearths. Of the thousands of tools recovered from the site only a small number are definitively post-Clovis.

Several Clovis quarry-related workshop sites in Allendale County, South Carolina, have been investigated by Al Goodyear. Buried by alluvium from flooding of the Savannah River, the Big Pine Tree site is a multi-component stratified site containing a succession of Woodland, Archaic, and Paleoindian occupations. Clovis preforms along with side scrapers, end scrapers, gravers, prismatic blades, blade cores, and other stone artifacts were found 115 to 135 centimeters beneath the surface, below a stratum containing Dalton-style artifacts. Charcoal and bone were not preserved in the Clovis stratum, and radiocarbon dating was not successful. At the Topper site, ongoing excavations are revealing discrete activity areas where chert was being made into Clovis points and other tools.

The Silver Springs site in Florida is a stratified, multi-component site in an eolian dune deposit that was being used to supply sand. In the 1960s Silver Springs was one of a very few sites in the eastern United States where fluted points occurred below an Archaic period occupation. Excavations totaling roughly 500 square feet by Wilfred Neill in the 1950s revealed a stratified sequence of Woodland through Paleoindian deposits within a 2.4-meter-thick zone of the sand dune. The Paleoindian stratum was situated below a culturally sterile zone, between 2.2 and 2.4 m below the surface. Two possible preforms, two basal fragments of Suwannee points, and one fluted point blade fragment were retrieved from this stratum. A complete "waisted" fluted point (having a constricted haft element) and a classic Western-style Clovis point were recovered from borrowed sand deposits. A few other non-diagnostic Paleoindian tools were also found. In 1973 Thomas Hemmings re-excavated the site and described the geology. His investigation confirmed Neill's stratigraphic sequence and recovered a midsection of a fluted point from 1.5 m below the ground surface, well above the Paleoindian stratum.

Located on a scarp overlooking a swamp east of Tampa, the Harney Flats site was a multi-component site excavated prior to construction of Interstate 75. The site revealed a substantial Suwannee, Simpson, and Early Archaic Bolen occupation zone located at a depth of 1.0 to 1.6 m below the surface. The majority of artifacts were recovered from the upper half of this stratum. No radiocarbon dates are available for this site, but Bolen side-notched points have been dated elsewhere to between 10,000 and 9,500 years ago. Deposition of sediments between the Suwannee and Bolen occupations was evidently not sufficient to allow stratigraphic separation of these components.

The Page-Ladson site consists of two contiguous inundated sinks in the Aucilla River of northwestern Florida. The site contains stratified Paleoindian and Early Archaic cultural deposits that have been investigated using underwater archaeological methods since 1983. At a depth of 4 m within a test pit (6 m below the water surface), chert debitage, adze fragments, and an Early Archaic Bolen-style point were associated with a buried A soil horizon or stable surface. Radiocarbon dating on charcoal from this soil layer resulted in dates of about 10,000 and 10,280 years ago, respectively. The oldest cultural stratum yet recognized at Page-Ladson lies just below the Bolen stratum. Known as zone D, it contains a variety of extinct fauna (mastodon, camel, horse, and giant armadillo) as well as chipped-stone debitage and a bola stone. Clovis, Suwannee, and Simpson points as well as worked megafaunal bone and ivory artifacts have been found in eroded contexts near the site; however, no time-diagnostic artifacts have been recovered from zone D. Radiocarbon dates on zone D range from 10,529 ± 90 to 13,130 ± 200 years ago, so there is a high probability that pre-Clovis, Clovis, and post-Clovis period artifacts will be found.

Further Reading: Anderson, David G., "Paleoindian Occupations in the Southeastern United States," in *New Perspectives on the First Americans*, edited by Bradley Lepper and Robson Bonnichsen (College Station, TX: Center for the Study of the First Americans, 2004); Goodyear, Albert C., "The Early Holocene Occupation of the Southeastern United States: A Geoarchaeological Summary," in *Ice Age Peoples of North America: Environments, Origins, and Adaptations of the First Americans*, edited by Robson Bonnichsen and Karen Turnmire (Corvallis: Oregon State University Press, 1999); Haynes, Gary A., *The Early Settlement of North America: The Clovis Era* (Cambridge, UK: Cambridge University Press, 2002).

Juliet E. Morrow

DUST CAVE

Tennessee River Valley, Alabama

Analysis of an Ancient Deeply Stratified Intact Archaeological Deposit

Dust Cave (1Lu496) is one of many small caves located in the limestone escarpment overlooking the north side of the Tennessee River just downriver from the present-day city of Florence, Alabama. Beginning as a cultural resource management (CRM) project, initial explorations within the entrance chamber of this small cave revealed nearly 5 meters of remarkably well-preserved strata containing archaeological remains from the Late Pleistocene through the Early to Middle Holocene (Sherwood et al. 2004; Walker et al. 2006). The complexity of the stratigraphy is shown by the east profile of the entrance trench.

Threatened by occasional flooding from the impounded Pickwick Lake, excavation of most of the deposits within the entrance chamber was undertaken by field schools over twelve seasons from 1989 through 2002, supported by the Tennessee Valley Authority, the Alabama Historical Commission, the National Science Foundation, IBM, the National Geographic Society, the University of Alabama, the University of Tennessee, Skidmore College, and Middle Tennessee State University. In all, students and scientists from over two dozen universities were involved in the fieldwork at Dust Cave. Researchers have utilized innovative ways to interpret the ways of life of the cave's prehistoric occupants from the sedimentary record, from organic remains preserved by means of the cave's protective environment, and from the artifacts excavated during their investigations.

The sedimentary record has been examined in several ways, including its depositional history (Goldberg and Sherwood 1994), the magnetic characteristics of the sediments (Gose 2000; Collins et al. 1994), the structural characteristics of sediments, and the contents and chemical signatures of features (Homsey and Capo 2006).

Through forty-three C-14 (radiocarbon) dates and numerous thin-section samples from cave deposits, the depositional history is fairly well understood. The cave was choked with Tennessee River alluvium during the Late Pleistocene (Collins et al. 1994), but these sediments were mostly flushed from the entrance chamber by about 13,000 years ago. About 10,650 BC (Sherwood et al. 2004), humans first used the cave entrance chamber. Five important archaeological components, named after stylistically distinctive point types, were identified: Quad/Beaver Lake/Dalton (10,650 to 9200 BC), Early Side Notched (10,000 to 9000 BC), Kirk Stemmed (8200 to 5800 BC), Eva/Morrow Mountain (6400 to 4000 BC), and Benton (4500 to 3600 BC) (Driskell 1994, 1996; Sherwood et al. 2004).

Around 3600 BC, headroom apparently became so restrictive that the cave was finally abandoned. Additional detritus from the bluff and cave roof accumulated on the talus slope and cave floor, concealing and protecting the archaeological deposits from natural destruction and vandalism.

Excavators found a variety of pit features (depressions dug into the cave floor to store materials or for another use) and fire hearths in the cave (Homsey and Capo 2006). Prepared red clay surfaces, lightly fired, are an intriguing feature within the Dust Cave deposits that seem to date from the earliest to latest use of the cave (Sherwood and Chapman 2005). Basketry-impressed surfaces occur in some of these features, indicating that baskets or mats—probably made of grasses or reeds, which were removed after use or subsequently decomposed—were used in the features. While their function is mysterious, these features may have been used for roasting or drying foods, as early as the Late Pleistocene. Similar features with prepared and fired clay surfaces have been found at early sites elsewhere in the eastern United States (Sherwood and Chapman 2005).

Because of the protection provided by the cave environment, the deposits within the entrance chamber are remarkable for the

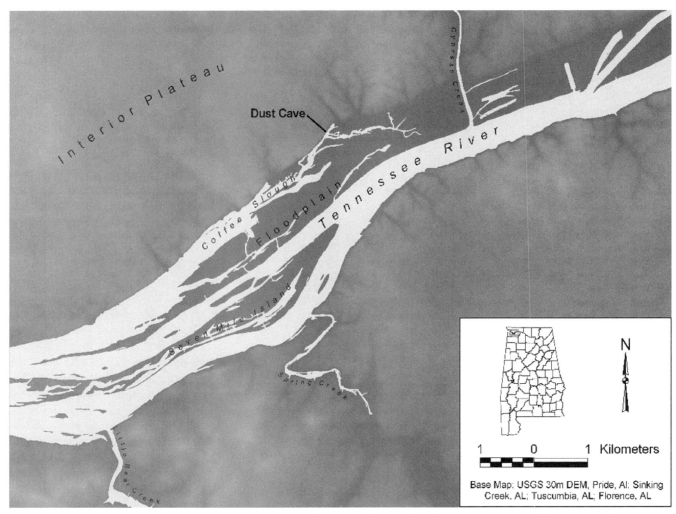

Location of Dust Cave. (This digital elevation model is modified from Sherwood et al. 2004: Figure 1.) [Reproduced by permission of the Society for American Archaeology from *American Antiquity*, Vol. 69, no. 3, 2004]

preservation of organic remains. The archaeological deposits throughout the sequence contain ash and charcoal in thin strata, discrete lenses, and dispersed within the general matrix. Animal bones are numerous in the deposits, and bone preservation is excellent, providing an unusual opportunity to examine small and fragile remains, even fish scales, not usually preserved in most sites in the Southeast (Grover 1994; Walker 1997, 2002). Charred plant remains, as well as phytoliths, are numerous in features and the general matrix (Gardner 1994). Articulated dog remains (Morey 1994; Walker et al. 2005) are present, and freshwater mussels (Parmalee 1994) and gastropods occur in large numbers. About two dozen human burials, dating to the Middle Archaic, have been investigated and described (Hogue 1994).

Subsistence studies have been a major area of inquiry (Driskell and Walker 2001; Walker et al. 2001). Animal bones (Grover 1994; Walker 1997) suggest that aquatic species, particularly waterfowl, were very important to the earliest (Late Pleistocene) inhabitants of the cave. In addition to bone tools and food waste, a cache of goose humeri was found in an early

context (Walker and Parmalee 2004). Results contrast with faunal profiles from other Late Pleistocene and Early Holocene sites in the eastern United States, where large mammals, particularly deer, predominate. Perhaps the excellent preservation in Dust Cave resulted in a more reliable sampling of early hunter-gatherer animal use. Alternatively, Dust Cave may have been a special-function site, so that the refuse is not a good indicator of overall subsistence economies.

In a study of plant macrofossils from Dust Cave and several other early sheltered sites in the region, Hollenbach (2007) found that subsistence activities changed little from the Late Paleoindian to the Early Archaic. A major focus on nut mast (particularly hickory) exploitation is indicated from the earliest (Late Pleistocene) times, a regional subsistence trend previously thought to have developed much later, in the Middle Holocene. Considering both plant and animal remains, Hollenbach concluded that subsistence and settlement were organized around plants that were plentiful and easily collected. Early hunter-gatherers of the area exploited upland nut

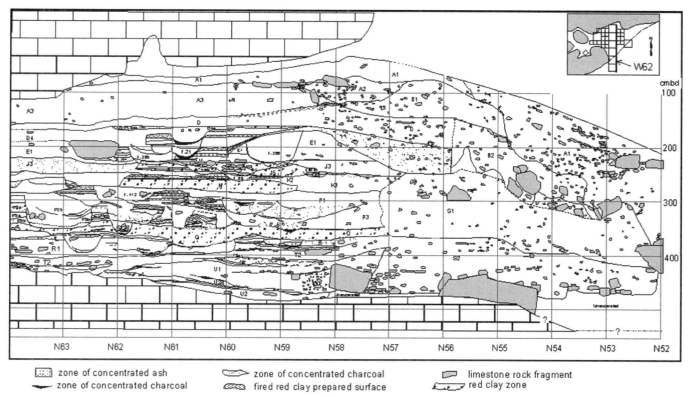

Stratigraphy revealed in the entrance trench at Dust Cave. (Profile W62 after Sherwood 2001: Figure 8.3, and Sherwood et al. 2004: Figure 3.) [Reproduced by permission of the Society for American Archaeology from *American Antiquity*, Vol. 69, no. 3, 2004]

mast and nearby animal/floral resources in the fall, seeds in early winter, floodplain resources including aquatic resources in the winter and spring, and fruits in the summer. Hollenbach points out that prey animals were often attracted to the same plant resources (young shoots, mature seeds, nut mast) as their human predators, reinforcing the notion that hunting was mostly embedded in the collecting cycle, and not the reverse.

Bone tools, described in Goldman-Finn and Walker (1994), are well represented for an early site, again because of the good preservation in a cave environment. A few ground-stone tools complement the large assemblage of chipped-stone tools, most made from a locally available, high-quality stone, the blue-gray Ft. Payne chert (Johnson and Meeks 1994). Biface tools and production debris dominate the chipped-stone assemblage (Meeks 1994, 2000). Blades were produced during the Late Paleoindian period, but this technology disappears during the Early Archaic. Although not yet studied in detail, the role or roles of blade tools may have been increasingly filled by bifacial tools or expedient tools made on flakes. Functional studies of Dust Cave stone tools are just beginning (Walker et al. 2001, 184–189), but examinations of small numbers of tools suggest that most were used to work bone or wood, or were used in hunting or butchering.

Dust Cave was first occupied by Paleoindian hunter-gatherers who apparently used the cave as a campsite in the fall (and perhaps also in the spring), when people focused on the nearby aquatic resources of the wide Tennessee River floodplain. Nut mast was available on nearby slopes, and a relic prairie with sinkholes and sinkhole lakes was present atop the bluff over the cave. Climate change during the Late Pleistocene is punctuated by the Younger-Dryas, a cold period in which the peoples of Dust Cave practiced a foraging lifeway similar to their successors in spite of harsher climatic conditions and their impact on nearby plant and animal resources.

Further Reading: Collins, M. B., Wulf Gose, and Scott Shaw, "Preliminary Geomorphological Findings at Dust and Nearby Caves," *Journal of Alabama Archaeology* 40 (1994): 34–55; Driskell, Boyce N., "Stratigraphy and Chronology at Dust Cave," *Journal of Alabama Archaeology* 40 (1994): 17–34; Driskell, Boyce N., "Stratified Late Pleistocene and Early Holocene Deposits at Dust Cave, Northwest Alabama," in *The Paleoindian and Early Archaic Southeast*, edited by David Anderson and Kenneth Sassaman (Tuscaloosa: University of Alabama Press, 1996), 315–330; Driskell, Boyce N., and Renee Walker, "Late Paleoindian Subsistence at Dust Cave, Northwest Alabama," in *On Being First: Cultural Consequences of First Peopling*, edited by Jason Gillespie, Susan Tupakka, and Christy de Mille (Calgary: Chacmool Archaeological Association of the University of Calgary, 2001), 409–425; Gardner, Paul, "Carbonized Plant Remains from Dust Cave," *Journal of Alabama Archaeology* 40 (1994): 189–207; Goldberg, Paul, and Sarah Sherwood,

"Micromorphology of Dust Cave Sediments: Some Preliminary Results," *Journal of Alabama Archaeology* 40 (1994): 56–64; Goldman-Finn, Nurit, and Renee Walker, "The Dust Cave Bone Tool Assemblage," *Journal of Alabama Archaeology* 40 (1994): 104–113; Gose, Wulf A., "Palaeomagnetic Studies of Burned Rocks," *Journal of Archaeological Science* 27 (2000): 409–421; Grover, Jennifer, "Faunal Remains from Dust Cave," *Journal of Alabama Archaeology* 40 (1994): 114–131; Hogue, S. Homes, "Human Skeletal Remains from Dust Cave," *Journal of Alabama Archaeology* 40 (1994): 170–188; Hollenbach, Kandace D., "Gathering in the Late Paleoindian Period: Archaeobotanical Remains from Dust Cave, Alabama," in *Foragers of the Terminal Pleistocene in North America*, edited by Renee B. Walker and Boyce N. Driskell (Lincoln: University of Nebraska Press, 2007), 132–147; Homsey, Lara K., and Rosemary C. Capo, "Integrating Geochemistry and Micromorphology to Identify Feature Function at Dust Cave, a Paleoindian through Middle Archaic Site in Northwest Alabama," *Geoarchaeology* 21(3) (2006): 237–269; Johnson, Hunter, and Scott Meeks, "Source Areas and Prehistoric Use of Fort Payne Chert," *Journal of Alabama Archaeology* 40 (1994): 65–76; Meeks, Scott C., "Lithic Artifacts from Dust Cave," *Journal of Alabama Archaeology* 40 (1994): 77–103; Meeks, Scott C., *The Use and Function of Late Middle Archaic Projectile Points in the Midsouth*, University of Alabama Office of Archaeological Services, Report of Investigations No. 77 (Moundville, AL: 2000); Morey, Darcy F., "*Canis* Remains from Dust Cave," *Journal of Alabama Archaeology* 40 (1994): 160–169; Parmalee, Paul, "Freshwater Mussels from Dust and Smith Bottom Caves, Alabama," *Journal of Alabama Archaeology* 40 (1994): 132–159; Sherwood, Sarah C., and Jefferson Chapman, "Identification and Potential Significance of Early Holocene Prepared Clay Surfaces: Examples from Dust Cave and Icehouse Bottom," *Southeastern Archaeology* 24(1) (2005): 70–82; Sherwood, Sarah C., Boyce N. Driskell, Asa R. Randall, and Scott C. Meeks, "Chronology and Stratigraphy at Dust Cave, Alabama," *American Antiquity* 69(3) (2004): 533–554; Walker, Renee B., "Late Paleoindian Faunal Remains from Dust Cave, Alabama," *Current Research in the Pleistocene* 14 (1997): 85–87; Walker, Renee B., "Early Holocene Ecological Adaptations in North Alabama," in *Culture, Environment, and Conservation in the Appalachian South*, edited by Benita J. Howell (Urbana: University of Illinois Press, 2002), 21–41; Walker, Renee, Kandace Detwiler, Scott Meeks, and Boyce Driskell, "Berries, Bones, and Blades: Reconstructing Late Paleoindian Subsistence Economy at Dust Cave, Alabama," *Midcontinental Journal of Archaeology* 26(2) (2001): 169–198; Walker, Renee B., Boyce N. Driskell, and Sarah C. Sherwood, "The Dust Cave Archaeological Project: Investigating Paleoindian and Archaic Lifeways in Southeastern North America," in *Seeking Our Past: An Introduction to North American Archaeology*, edited by Sarah W. Neusius and G. Timothy Gross (Oxford: Oxford University Press, 2006), 83–94, Student CD, D-5; Walker, Renee B., Darcy F. Morey, and John H. Relethford, "Early and Mid-Holocene Dogs in Southeastern North America: Examples from Dust Cave," *Southeastern Archaeology* 24(1) (2005): 83–92; Walker, Renee B., and Paul W. Parmalee, "A Noteworthy Cache of *Branta canadensis* at Dust Cave, Northwestern Alabama," *Journal of Alabama Archaeology* 50(1) (2004): 18–35.

Boyce C. Driskell

THE SLOAN SITE

Northeastern Arkansas

The Late Paleoindian Dalton Culture in the Southeast

The Sloan site is the most famous among hundreds (over 750 in Arkansas alone) of sites throughout the Southeast where Dalton-style points have been found. The Dalton-style point is based on the same kind of chipped-stone technology as earlier fluted points, such as the Clovis point type. Dating to between 10,500 and 9,900 years ago, Dalton-style points, in addition to being lance shaped, are substantially modified by chipping along the edges. Dalton-style points are found throughout the southeastern United States, but especially in a region known as the Mid-south, stretching from south of Memphis, Tennessee, to north of St. Louis, Missouri, and from east of Carbondale, Illinois, to west of Columbia, Missouri. "Dalton" derives from the name of Judge S. J. Dalton, who with Carl Chapman, then a professor at the University of Missouri, noted this distinctive artifact type in a deeply buried archaeological deposit near Jefferson City, Missouri, in 1948. Their observation was particularly important because they detected a deeply buried soil layer that contained lanceolate points and end scrapers in a highway construction excavation. Confirmation of an early date was made during the next two years from controlled archaeological excavations at the Graham Cave site, located west of St. Louis, with Dalton points found at the base of deep excavations. By around 1960 investigators had identified Dalton points from sites throughout the southeastern United States.

THE SLOAN SITE

The Sloan site, in northeastern Arkansas, named after the landowners, was small—11 × 12 meters—and was completely excavated in 1974. Sloan is interpreted as the earliest known cemetery in the New World, although only small fragments of human bone were recovered (Morse 1997). The excavation and analysis confirmed the sophistication of the Late

Paleoindian artifact assemblage produced and used by the site's creators. These early inhabitants of the Mid-south area took advantage of a rich Pleistocene environmental setting. Braided stream channels provided oak-hickory forest edge ecotones ideal for whitetail deer, ducks, and other fauna.

In 1970, just prior to the Sloan investigations, another Dalton period site known as the Brand site, located almost 65 kilometers to the south of Sloan, was excavated. The Brand investigations confirmed the bulk of the Dalton tool kit in intact deposits. Brand is interpreted as a deer hunting campsite because it contains artifacts that appear to have been used for butchering deer and other animals and includes debris generated in the refurbishing of stone tools (Goodyear 1974).

The investigations at the Sloan site and subsequent analysis expanded the understanding of the Dalton culture considerably. Sloan was located at the top of a stabilized sand dune. Caches of artifacts and their systematic locations indicated the presence of approximately thirty extended burials oriented east-west, although the preservation of the skeletal remains was very fragmentary. A total of 211 bone fragments indicated that both adults and children had been interred here. The 439 artifacts recovered were exclusively tools. In contrast to Brand, no evidence of Dalton tool manufacture or maintenance in the form of lithic debris and waste flakes was found in the undisturbed cemetery horizon, about a meter deep. Nearby was another site of the same period, discovered in 1962 and now largely destroyed, which probably was the settlement where the people buried at Sloan lived and worked. Stone resources containing the lithic raw material used for the tools found with the Sloan site burials existed in the nearby uplands of Crowley's Ridge where the Cache River watershed extended and in the Ozark highlands 75 kilometers to the southwest. Other very fine chert utilized to make some of the Sloan artifacts was available in the Burlington outcrops near St. Louis, 300 kilometers to the northeast. Many of the stone artifacts recovered exhibited no wear from use and had been manufactured or resharpened before burial. Green and red paint on at least one artifact and red ocher in graves indicate complex graveside ceremonies.

THE SLOAN ARTIFACTS
Uncovered at Sloan were 146 fluted points, 42 adzes, 95 other bifaces, 35 abraders, 1 edge-abraded cobble, 33 hafted end scrapers, 68 other unifaces, and 19 other stone artifacts.

The Dalton point is a fluted lanceolate biface. Normally it is serrated. After its manufacture, it functioned as a projectile point and as a knife since it was probably mounted on a foreshaft to be propelled by an *atl atl* or spear thrower. Impact scars found on the tips of recently manufactured points but usually not on resharpened ones indicate that the resharpened points functioned mainly as knives. When resharpened because of wear or breakage, the point usually acquired a beveled edge while the knapper minimized the loss of point width. Resharpening also created a shoulder at

the base, which lessened its effectiveness as a projectile. Use-wear studies indicate that the point was used mostly to cut meat. In contrast to the Clovis point from which it was derived, the Dalton point has a shortened ground (for strength) base, maximizing the area left for cutting. Recycled worn-out or broken points were often made into handheld skewers (to puncture skins) and burins (for engraving wood and bone).

The Dalton adze is one of the earliest known true hand adzes in the world. The adze exhibits a pointed, gouge-like working edge and is ground over the entire butt end, which would have been fit into a haft and handle. Use wear analyses indicate the adze was used on charred and seasoned wood. It was hafted in a combination of wood, leather, and antler. Possibly, there was a wood (or antler) handle with leather straps and an antler (or wood) wedge. The Dalton hand adze likely was used to make cypress tree trunks into dugout boats, wood masks, and possibly even grave posts.

A very large biface, called the Sloan point, is thought to have been used as a handheld object during dancing. Hafted end scrapers were used to scrape skins. A variety of other unifaced artifacts, mostly scraping and cutting tools, were also handheld. One specialized concave-edged hafted scraper is unique to the Dalton culture and, although not identified as to its specific use, would have been ideal for foreshaft (a wooden handle that attaches to a spear and can detach from the spear shaft) manufacturing. There were also small distinctive hammer stones and abraders used to manufacture tools. Besides striated cobbles that were probably used to prepare edges for knapping, there were two types of ironstone abraders. One type was grooved on one face; it is inferred that the groove was used to grind the edges and surfaces of adzes. Another type was notched on the edges and is thought to have been used to grind the bases of points. An edge-abraded cobble was probably used to grind foods such as berries, roots, or nuts. In addition to adze preforms—that is, stones roughly shaped to serve as adzes, but without the final modifications to create the finished tool—other bifaces, which have not yet been interpreted as to function, were recovered. They were too small to be point preforms. A *piece esquillee* (a small wedge-shaped stone artifact) was discovered to have been used to cut meat; normally these are interpreted as exhausted cores or wedges to split wood or bone.

Further Reading: Goodyear, Albert C., *The Brand Site: A Techno-Functional Study of a Dalton Site in Northeast Arkansas*, Research Series, No. 7 (Fayetteville: Arkansas Archeological Survey, 1974); Goodyear, Albert C., "The Chronological Position of the Dalton Horizon in the Southeastern United States," *American Antiquity* 47(2) (1982): 382–395; Morse, Dan F., *Sloan: A Paleoindian Dalton Cemetery in Arkansas* (Washington, DC: Smithsonian Institution Press, 1997); Morse, Dan F., and Phyllis A. Morse, *Archaeology of the Central Mississippi Valley* (New York: Academic Press, 1983).

Dan F. Morse

THE WINDOVER SITE

Titusville, Florida

A 7,400-Year-Old Burial Pond with Remarkable Preservation

Windover (8BR246) was discovered accidentally in 1982 during road construction on the southwest side of Titusville, Florida (Doran 2002). It is a charnel pond, one of only four known from the Florida Early to Middle Archaic periods. All of these charnel ponds date to before 6,000 years ago, although Windover is the oldest, with a date of around 7,400 years ago. In these sites the dead were intentionally interred in peat deposits in small freshwater ponds in central and south Florida. In some cases the bodies were held in place by wooden stakes, mostly pine with a few being oak, driven into the peat.

Windover is the only charnel pond that has been the subject of a detailed and focused multi-year investigation by different specialists. Charnel ponds, because of their saturated and near neutral pH, provide near optimum preservation of many organic materials, including human bones. Installation of an extensive well pump drainage system installed at the site allowed for controlled excavation beginning in 1984 and continuing each fall through 1986.

In all, the well-preserved remains of at least 168 individuals, 91 containing preserved brain tissue, were found. These remains constitute one of the largest burial inventories, if not the biggest one, of this antiquity in the New World. The bones of some burials were commingled, possibly as a result of their initial discovery with a backhoe in 1982, while others were intact and accompanied by a variety of artifacts. These materials include one of the oldest *Lagenaria siceraria* (white-flowered bottle gourd) north of Mexico, with a direct date of about 7,290 years ago. Other rare plant offerings associated with burials include a prickly pear pad, drilled sabal palm seed beads, and a cane snare trigger.

There were 67 samples of hand-woven fabrics from 54 adult and subadult burials. Fabrics were more commonly associated with juveniles and females. Manufacturing techniques include four types of close twining, and single forms of open twining and plaiting. Items include flexible fabrics, bags, and mats and represent a very early, highly sophisticated fiber arts inventory. The finest specimens have a "thread count" of ten strands per centimeter. Some items may have been specifically manufactured for burial with the dead. The twined and plain weave items are the oldest in North America, and perhaps even in the New World. Cortical surfaces of the woven materials had been removed by mastication and abrasion. Species are difficult to identify but are most likely either sabal palm or saw palmetto.

Wooden artifacts, many from oak, include a double-ended grinder, a mortar and pestle, burial stakes, and spear shaft fragments. The wood of *atl atl* handles was predominantly (*n* = 3) from the pecan hickory group, although one handle was dogwood. One antler point had wood residues from holly within the bore. Deer bone and antler were common raw materials, but other tools were fashioned from the bones of manatee, Canidae, and Felidae (most likely dog and bobcat). Perishable artifacts also include an array of antler projectile points, a shaft straightener, barbed bone points, flaking tools, *atl atl* spurs or hooks and handles, engraved bone tubes, punches, pins, gorges, and awls. Several shark's teeth, some drilled for hafting, and a small number of marine shells were also recovered.

One stone biface and several of the tools made from teeth still had mastic residues, indicating they were hafted. The entire lithic tool inventory consists of four bifaces (three Florida Stemmed Archaic and one Kirk serrated–type projectile points), a biface tip, and one thinning flake. This lack of lithics attests to the importance of organic artifacts in daily life as well as to the scarcity of lithics resources in this part of Florida. In general, artifacts were more commonly placed with adult male burials.

Seeds and fleshy fruit remains, either as part of offerings or as gut contents, were from a number of species, including grape, elderberry, hackberry, holly, nightshade, cherry, and wax myrtle. These and other species were probably used as food as well as in medicinal and ritual functions. Most of the burial-associated material suggests late summer to fall burial.

Ancient DNA (aDNA) analysis has been of limited success and suggests that the most likely mitochondrial DNA (mtDNA) haplogroup at Windover is X. The aDNA analysis has been more frustrating than informative but continues. Isotopic analysis more strongly suggests a riverine/marsh terrestrial subsistence orientation with a limited marine component and is very similar for males and females.

Males and females are equally represented, and approximately half the sample is less than 17 years of age. Males were slightly healthier than females. Females show a greater frequency of cribra orbitalia, porotic hyperostosis, and infectious lesions. Degenerative joint disease is most apparent in the vertebrae and is slightly more common in males than in females and is somewhat higher than in many other groups regardless of antiquity. This could reflect a higher number of older individuals in the Windover series. Based on fracture patterns, most injuries, though not all, appear accidental.

Roughly 50 percent of the site is unexcavated. The landowner, Jim Swann of EKS, Inc., who brought the site to archaeologists' attention, encouraged and financially supported the project, and in 2002 donated the site to the Preservation and Education Trust, Inc. The site is listed on the National Register of Historic Places.

Further Reading: Doran, Glen H., ed., *Multidisciplinary Investigations of an Early Archaic Florida Cemetery* (Gainesville: University Press of Florida, 2002).

Glen H. Doran

THE HARDAWAY SITE

Along the Yadkin River, East Central North Carolina
A Rare Stratified Site with a Long Sequence of Archaeological Deposits

The Hardaway site is located along the Yadkin River in east central North Carolina. Excavations at Hardaway during the mid-twentieth century, along with work at the nearby Doerschuk and Gaston sites along the Roanoke River, revealed archaeological deposits representing relatively discrete cultural periods stacked in a layer-cake fashion that was unprecedented in the state. Today we know that the occupations represented at Hardaway span some 12,000 years of North Carolina prehistory. Hardaway is still one of the few stratified archaeological sites known in the state.

In particular, Hardaway is noted for remains associated with the Late Paleoindian through Archaic periods, about 4,000 to 11,000 years ago. Thus, Hardaway's intermittent occupations span the end of the last full glacial period in North America (known as the Ice Age) through the beginnings of modern climatic conditions, including the transition to modern plant and animal communities. Accordingly, humans in North Carolina, as well as elsewhere in North America, adapted to the changing landscape, living in bands composed of small family groups that relied on hunting and gathering forest animals and plants. Generally speaking, bands probably exhibited seasonal movements over fairly large territories, living in short-term camps. Although Hardaway represents an example of one such camp, it likely had a unique role in the settlement system.

Hardaway is located on a hilltop high above the Yadkin River. The site was named for the Hardaway Construction Co., builder of a dam across the river that provided electricity for an aluminum manufacturing plant built in Stanly County in 1917 by the Carolina Aluminum Company (now Alcoa). Today, the site is owned and protected by Alcoa, which has landscaped the property. About 0.4 hectares (about 1 acre) in size, the area now shows little physical evidence of the site, other than an occasional stone artifact that might be seen through the grass.

Herbert M. Doerschuk, a local artifact collector who worked for the Carolina Aluminum Company, discovered the site in the 1930s and brought it to the attention of Joffre L. Coe, then director of the Research Laboratories of Anthropology (now Research Laboratories of Archaeology) at the University of North Carolina at Chapel Hill (UNC). Archaeologists subsequently undertook excavations at the site in 1948–59 and 1975–80. The former period resulted in the landmark publication by Coe titled "The Formative Cultures of the Carolina Piedmont," which established the prehistoric cultural sequence for the region. Unfortunately, this publication also alerted relic hunters to the significance of the site. Despite the best efforts of Alcoa and UNC to protect the site, irreparable damage was done by indiscriminate digging for artifacts.

The entire collection of material from Hardaway comprises more than 1.5 million artifacts, including stone spear points, scrapers, and other tools. Flaking debris resulting from the manufacturing of stone tools constitutes a large part of the collection. Other material includes animal bone fragments and pottery shards. Along with the waste from tool manufacture, the wide range of conditions in which stone tools are found at Hardaway—from early production failures to heavily used or broken specimens—provides important insights into prehistoric tool technologies. What is more, the incredible density of stone tool manufacturing debris indicates tool production was an important activity at the site.

More recent research by I. Randolph Daniel Jr. on portions of the Late Paleoindian/Early Archaic (about 10,500–9,000 years ago) material excavated during 1975–80 explored the question of site function and settlement adaptations at Hardaway. Indeed, the location of the Hardaway site is no accident. The site is uniquely situated along the Yadkin River near the southern end of the Uwharrie Mountains to take advantage of abundant natural outcrops of rhyolite—a stone well suited for making stone tools. Rhyolite is a metamorphosed volcanic rock that caps much of the Uwharrie Mountains and exhibits a quality necessary for producing chipped-stone tools—that is, it can be flaked relatively easily, because it has good conchoidal fracture properties. Few stone types in North Carolina can be worked as well as rhyolite, and virtually no other location contains the quality and abundance of rhyolite as do the Uwharrie Mountains. In fact, the Uwharrie Mountains contain numerous prehistoric stone quarries and were probably an important resource for tool stone throughout prehistory.

The vast majority of stone artifacts came from the quarries located in the Uwharries, and Late Paleoindian/Early Archaic artifacts made from Uwharrie rhyolite exhibit a wide geographic distribution, being found as much as 200 kilometers from Hardaway. Moreover, Hardaway played a distinctive role in Early Archaic settlement adaptations. That is, at least a portion of a group's stay at Hardaway was to be used to acquire stone to replenish tool kits depleted through foraging activities elsewhere in their settlement range. While group movement was probably quite variable across the region, bands still needed to schedule trips to the Uwharrie Mountains to retool. It may be that small bands with shifting territories were "tethered" to Uwharrie rhyolite sources throughout the Early Archaic period.

In 1990 Hardaway was designated a National Historic Landmark. In 2005 Alcoa Foundation officially donated the Hardaway collection to UNC and awarded the university a grant for outreach programs to educate North Carolina schoolchildren and the public about the site. The grant supports a variety of programs, including an Archaeology Days event at local museums, a traveling exhibit on the state's first peoples, a public television program, and education materials for teachers that include lesson plans on Hardaway. In particular, a portion of the grant will be used to help renovate a permanent home for the Hardaway collection on the UNC campus.

Further Reading: Coe, Joffre L., *Formative Cultures of the Carolina Piedmont*, Transactions 54 (Philadelphia: American Philosophical Society, 1964); Daniel, I. Randolph Jr., *Hardaway Revisited: Early Archaic Settlement in the Southeast* (Tuscaloosa: University of Alabama Press, 1998); 1999 Uwharries Lithic Conference, Asheboro, North Carolina, http://www.arch.dcr.state.nc.us/uwharrie/framesmain.html; North Carolina Archaeological Society Web site, http://rla.unc.edu/ncas/Links/index.html; Ward, H. Trawick, and R. P. Stephen Davis Jr., *Time Before History: The Archaeology of North Carolina* (Chapel Hill: University of North Carolina Press, 1999).

I. Randolph Daniel, Jr.

THE MULBERRY CREEK AND EVA SITES

Middle and Lower Tennessee River, Alabama and Tennessee

Ancient Settlements and Grave Sites

People have lived along the Tennessee River valley for thousands of years. The present valley was formed as water and sediment poured southward from melting glaciers at the end of the last Ice Age in North America, about 14,000 years ago. Ancient artifacts, such as Paleoindian spear points found throughout the Tennessee River valley, indicate humans have lived here for the last 11,000 years. Thousands of archaeological sites have been recorded, many of which have been scientifically studied, and some can be visited. Archaeologists have reconstructed prehistoric life based on excavations at these sites, and their interpretations provide an important scientific perspective of prehistoric human occupation of the valley from earliest times to its abandonment around AD 1400.

The archaeology of the Tennessee River valley has been of interest to its inhabitants and visitors for over 150 years. Systematic and intensive research by University of Alabama archaeologists as part of the federal work relief programs of the Great Depression uncovered large numbers of ancient camps along the middle Tennessee River. Researchers from the universities of Tennessee and Kentucky, also associated with Depression-era programs, found habitation sites in the lower Tennessee River valley.

By 8,000 years ago, the human presence in the middle and lower valley was widespread and extensive. Projectile points, among other artifacts, document increasing numbers of people and their campsites. During the early period of settlement, local groups of hunters and gatherers moved seasonally from the river floodplain to the adjacent uplands. By 7,000 years ago, people were leaving large quantities of debris that accumulated over the years. Shells from gathering freshwater mollusks and snails, chert flakes from tool manufacture, animal bone and charred plant remains from cooking, ash from campfires, and a variety of stone and bone tools make up the deposits of these sites. These remains are found throughout the Tennessee valley,

Progress picture of Eva Site, Direction North. Eva Site (40BN12), Benton Co., Tennessee. Progress picture of site down N-S test trench showing cross trench (E-W) after trenching. Direction north. Photo courtesy Frank H. McClung Museum, The University of Tennessee, Knoxville.

but are most commonly seen near areas of extensive, shallow shoals. Some archaeologists believe permanent settlement was the norm by 7,000 years ago, with hunters and gatherers regularly trekking into the uplands from their base camps for game animals, such as deer and turkey, and wild plant foods, including nuts, fruits, and acorns.

THE MULBERRY CREEK SITE, CHEROKEE, ALABAMA

The Mulberry Creek site, a large shell midden located in north Alabama, was the focus of substantial settlement beginning at least 8,500 years ago. "Shell midden" refers to a large accumulation of shell and other cultural and natural remains that result from repeated human activities or occupation of a particular spot. Native Americans at Mulberry Creek hunted a wide variety of game, gathered many wild plants, and fished in the river and its tributaries.

Mulberry Creek represents the largest excavated shell midden in the mid-continent of North America. People lived intermittently at the confluence of Mulberry Creek and the Tennessee for more than 7,000 years, leaving an astonishing record of human habitation. The site is located on the banks

of the Tennessee River (now Pickwick Reservoir) near Cherokee, Alabama.

People utilized the Mulberry Creek site between approximately 8,500 and 600 years ago, with peak use between 5,000 and 3,300 years ago. The earliest inhabitants visited the locale intermittently for 1,500 years or so, perhaps as one stop in a seasonal movement throughout a large foraging territory. Between 7,000 and 5,000 years ago, the Mulberry Creek site was first used as a campsite for gathering shellfish, manufacturing flint tools, and burying the dead. The inhabitants were small groups of hunters and gatherers—perhaps only a few families.

Mulberry Creek provides some of the earliest evidence in eastern North America for warfare, some 6,800 years ago. The resident family groups engaged in an intermittent, but bitter struggle over the use of the shoal area, as evidenced by some burials with multiple embedded spear points. The conflict abated during the period from 5,000 to 3,500 years ago, despite an increase in site use and population size.

The deep shell mound runs along the south bank of the Tennessee River for some 300 feet, and up Mulberry Creek for about 200 feet. Over 18 feet of alternating layers of alluvium are interspersed with deposits of shell, stone, and

Early archaeologists explore Mulberry Creek.   [University of Alabama Museums, Tuscaloosa, Alabama]

bone artifacts, as well as graves left by the ancient inhabitants.

The site was excavated by the University of Alabama under the field supervision of archaeologist James R. Foster from July 1936 to February 1938 as part of the federal Works Progress Administration program. The excavations ended prematurely when the floodgates to Pickwick Lock and Dam were closed in February 1938, virtually inundating the site. No further excavations have been carried out at the site since the WPA research. The artifacts and human remains have been studied over the intervening years by archaeologists and physical anthropologists. The site is not accessible, but an interpretation of the site and some of its artifacts may be seen at Mound State Monument, located near Moundville, Alabama.

THE EVA SITE, CAMDEN, TENNESSEE

Another concentration of ancient activity and settlement is the area around the mouth of the Duck River, near Camden, Tennessee, in the lower Tennessee valley. Many archaeological sites here date between 11,000 and 600 years ago. A number of them were scientifically excavated in the late 1930s and early 1940s as part of federal work relief programs before the Tennessee Valley Authority dams flooded much of the valley.

The Eva site was one such early campsite that was excavated. The site, occupied from about 8,500 to 5,900 years ago, has one of the best archaeological sequences for early hunters and gatherers in the lower Tennessee valley.

Eva is located on the east bank of an old, abandoned course of the Tennessee River. Based on skeletal remains and associated artifacts found at the site, the inhabitants were egalitarian hunting, fishing, and gathering people who may have lived at the site for most of the year. Some 180 human remains and 18 dog burials were excavated in the relatively small excavation area at the site. Most of the dog burials, 4 interred with humans, date from 7,900 to 6,600 years ago. Dogs may have been important to these hunters and gatherers for hunting, carrying packs, and protecting the camp from strangers.

Excavations under the supervision of archaeologist Douglas H. Osborne took place from September to November 1940 by the University of Tennessee, with funds from the Tennessee Valley Authority and labor provided by the Works Progress Administration. The midden was about an acre in extent. The occupation in the center of the site measured about 6 feet thick and became much thinner at the edges of the site. The site has been completely destroyed as a result of rampant looting and wave action from the current reservoir. Interpretation of the early hunters and gatherers of the lower Tennessee valley and artifacts from Eva may be seen at the University of Tennessee's McClung Museum in Knoxville.

Further Reading: Dye, David H., "Riverine Adaptation in the Midsouth," in *Of Caves and Shell Mounds*, edited by Kenneth C. Carstens and Patty Jo Watson (Tuscaloosa: University of Alabama Press, 1996), 140–158; Lewis, M. N., and Madeline Kneberg, "The Archaic Culture in the Middle South," *American Antiquity* 25 (1959): 161–183; Lewis, M. N., and Madeline Kneberg Lewis, *Eva: An Archaic Site* (Knoxville: University of Tennessee Press, 1961); Webb, William S., and David L. DeJarnette, *An Archeological Survey of Pickwick Basin in the Adjacent Portions of the States of Alabama, Mississippi and Tennessee*, Bureau of American Ethnology Bulletin 129 (Washington, DC: Smithsonian Institution, 1942).

David H. Dye

THE ICEHOUSE BOTTOM SITE

Lower Little Tennessee River Valley, Eastern Tennessee

A Deeply Stratified Archaic Period Site with a Series of Ancient Deposits

Icehouse Bottom (40MR23) is the largest and most intensely investigated of seven buried Archaic period sites in the lower Little Tennessee River valley excavated prior to inundation by the Tellico Reservoir. Arranged into a layer cake of prehistory, 7 feet (2.1 m) of stratified Early Archaic (8000–6000 BC) and 3 feet (0.9 m) of Middle Archaic (6000–4000 BC) occupation layers yielded artifacts and features that now define the phases and patterns of these two periods in the Mid-south.

Over the 7,000 years that comprise the Archaic period in eastern Tennessee (roughly 8000–1000 BC), gradual changes came to pass in Native culture. In general, these people were hunters and gatherers who were organized into bands of thirty to fifty related individuals. Each band occupied a residential base, such as Icehouse Bottom, situated in areas of maximum environmental diversity and/or adjacent to raw material

sources, such as chert. Close to these sites were riverine resources, sloughs, backwaters, creeks, broad floodplains, valley slopes, and uplands. These base sites, in turn, probably articulated with a number of field camps where plants and animals were collected and processed for food. The whitetail deer was the principal food animal, supplemented by a wide array of mammals, fish, birds, and freshwater mussels. The gathering of wild plants was as important as hunting. Of primary importance were hickory nuts and acorns. Toward the end of the Archaic, sunflowers were domesticated, and the gathering of herbaceous plants such as chenopodium and sumpweed intensified, leading to their domestication in the first millennium BC. The Archaic period in Tennessee was pre-ceramic, with containers made of basketry, hides, wood, and—in the Late Archaic—soapstone.

Excavations at Icehouse Bottom.   [Jefferson Chapman]

In some areas of Tennessee, Late Archaic societies became less egalitarian as some degree of social stratification developed. Certain kinship groups were accorded more power and prestige than others. Archaeological evidence for this comes from increased burial ceremonialism and marked differences in the way some individuals were treated. Closely related to social stratification was the increase in interregional exchange of status objects, such as gulf and Atlantic marine shells and Lake Superior copper.

Icehouse Bottom was excavated as part of the archaeological salvage excavations from 1967 to 1979, prior to the creation of Tellico Reservoir by the Tennessee Valley Authority. Between 1969 and 1971, excavations focused on the Middle Woodland period occupation, where ceramic and lithic artifacts indicated that the occupants of the site had trade relations with the Hopewell people of Ohio. Investigations at the Rose Island site in 1973–74 revealed that Early Archaic period occupations were buried deep within the alluvial sediments. Postulating that this phenomenon was likely repeated at sites on the alluvial floodplains adjacent to the river, excavators began testing for buried occupations in 1975, using a backhoe. Four were located that field season, and excavations were carried out at Icehouse Bottom in an area upstream from the earlier work. The success of the Rose Island and Icehouse Bottom investigations ultimately led to the discovery and testing of two other buried Early Archaic period sites (Bacon Farm and Calloway Island), a buried

Middle Archaic site (Howard site), and two buried Late Archaic sites (Iddins and Bacon Bend). The presence of sixty buried sites was noted in a backhoe testing survey of the valley in 1977.

The excavation at Icehouse Bottom was by arbitrary 0.2–0.3 foot (6–9 centimeters [cm]) levels within the natural stratigraphy. Approximately 1,300 square feet (121.8 m²) of Middle Archaic strata and 1,800 square feet (167.2 m²) of Early Archaic strata were excavated. All soil was water-screened through 1/4-inch (6.5-millimeter [mm]) mesh, and artifacts were piece-plotted—that is, the location of each artifact was recorded individually on the site map as it was excavated.

Because 11 feet of alluvium preserved occupation layers spanning 2,500 years, a clear record existed of changes in material culture. The projectile point sequence confirmed that observed at sites in North Carolina and West Virginia—corner-notched points with serrated blades (Palmer, Kirk types) followed by stemmed points with notched/bifurcated bases (St. Albans, LeCroy, Kanawha types), stemmed serrated points (Kirk Stemmed type), broad-bladed stemmed points (Stanly type) and lanceolate with contracted stem (Morrow Mountain type). An array of other cutting, chopping, scraping, grinding, and shredding tools were also part of the lithic assemblage. *Atl atl* weights in the Middle Archaic strata attest to the use of the spear thrower. Due to the acidity of the soil, no bone or shell was found. However,

Artist's depiction of an Early Archaic period base camp.   [Jefferson Chapman]

based on sites elsewhere in Tennessee, bone artifacts probably also were an important part of the tool kit. A total of 113 soil samples were taken from features and excavation layers and screened through fine mesh using a technique known as flotation. Subsequent analysis of the plant remains suggests a narrow subsistence focus on hickory nuts and acorns.

Outcrops of fine-grained chert nodules occur on the valley slopes adjacent to Icehouse Bottom, and this stone was probably one of the reasons people were attracted to the site. Abundant debris from tool manufacture was found at the site, and the majority of the Early Archaic chipped-stone artifacts were manufactured from local cherts.

No evidence of postholes was observed at Icehouse Bottom or at any of the buried Archaic period sites in the valley. Apparently, whatever shelters were used by the site occupants left no visible remains. The most common

features (167 were found during excavations) at the site were prepared hearths—circular clay surfaces about 1.5–2.0 feet (46–61 cm) in diameter, made from reddish brown clay brought from the valley slope, placed on the alluvial sandy loam ground surface, and fired. On twenty-nine of these hearths, there remained textile impressions. These impressions were made by vegetal-fiber textiles and basketry, including both large globular bags and rectangular mats made by open simple twining and Z-twist wefts. They are the earliest well-dated evidence of basketry and textile east of the Mississippi River. The use of prepared hearths continued through Early and Middle Archaic components at the site, although the impressed hearths were restricted to the early occupations, 7500–6900 BC. It is possible that the fired surfaces functioned as griddles.

The Icehouse Bottom site was inundated by the Tellico Reservoir in 1979. Many of the artifacts can be seen in the

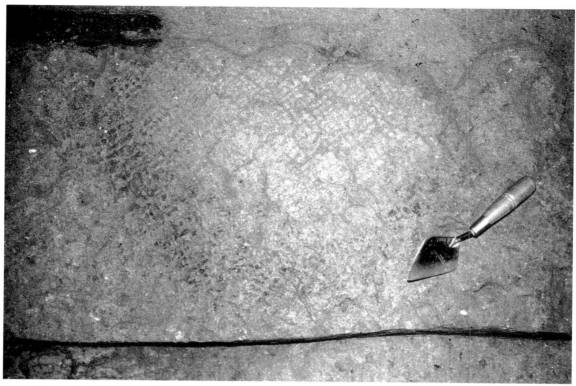

Textile impressed hearth.   [Jefferson Chapman]

permanent exhibition Archaeology and the Native Peoples of Tennessee, at the Frank H. McClung Museum, University of Tennessee, Knoxville.

Further Reading: Chapman, Jefferson, *Tellico Archaeology: 12,000 Years of Native American History*, rev. ed. (Knoxville: University of Tennessee Press, 1994); Chapman, Jefferson, *Archaic Period Research in the Lower Little Tennessee River Valley*, Department of

Anthropology Report of Investigations No. 18 (Knoxville: University of Tennessee, 1977); Chapman, Jefferson, "Archaeology and the Archaic Period in the Southern Ridge-and-Valley Province," in *Structure and Process in Southeastern Archaeology*, edited by Roy S. Dickens and H. Trawick Ward (Tuscaloosa: University of Alabama Press, 1985), 137–153; Frank H. McClung Museum Web site, http://mcclungmuseum.utk.edu.

Jefferson Chapman

WATSON BRAKE

Northeast Louisiana

Large and Complex 5,500-Year-Old Earthen Architecture

Watson Brake is a 5,500-year-old earthen mound group in northeast Louisiana. It is the largest and most complex earthwork of the fifteen Middle Archaic (7,000–4,000 years ago) mound sites identified in North America. Hunter-gatherers constructed eleven mounds and connecting ridges that form an apparently planned oval earthwork 300 meters (m) in diameter.

SITE SETTING

The site is in the Mississippi valley west of the Tertiary Uplands, along the edge of a Pleistocene terrace, above a small tributary of the Ouachita River that flows west to east from the swamp known as Watson Brake. The placement of the site provided direct access to upland, floodplain, and riverine resources used by the hunters and gatherers who lived at Watson Brake. Alluviation at the confluence of the Watson Brake drainage and the Ouachita River altered the flow pattern of the tributary, a change that may be related to either the occupation or the abandonment of the site.

THE EARTHWORKS

Eleven mounds and eight ridge segments form a 300-meter oval oriented to the northwest-southeast. The largest mound is conical and over 7 meters high. The second-largest mound is dome-shaped and is 4.5 meters high. The other nine mounds range in height between 0.5 and 3.5 meters, and all are dome-shaped. The ridges are symmetrical in cross section and vary between 0.25 and 2.5 meters in height.

The mounds and ridges along the terrace escarpment were constructed in multiple stages. Mound A was built in seven stages; Mound B in four stages; Mounds D, I, and J in three stages; and Mound C in two stages. The ridges usually are two-stage structures. The interior mounds and ridges (Mounds E, F, G, and H) are single-stage structures.

Thick sub-mound and sub-ridge middens along the terrace edge attest to the use of the site long before mound construction began. With the exception of Mound E, the interior mounds and ridges lack sub-mound middens. Although the reason for variability in mound and ridge composition is not known, sub-mound/sub-ridge radiocarbon dates indicate that their placement fit a preconceived plan.

SITE USE

Domestic activities took place on the mounds and ridges. Artifacts associated with processing and cooking plants and animals were recovered from the surface of each stage of the mounds and ridges, with the exception of conical Mound A. A probable bead-making workshop was located on Mound D and a biface production area on ridge K/A. Very few artifacts have been found in the oval enclosure, with just a light scatter observed on the natural rises.

Site use around the exterior of the enclosure appears to have been limited. Surveys in the adjoining uplands and swamps have also failed to locate campsites. Thus, the limited data now available suggests that food procurement activities were adjacent to Watson Brake, and that the resources were transported directly to the site, the place of residence.

SUBSISTENCE AND ECONOMY

The setting, adjacent or nearby to several different kinds of environments, provided an abundance of resources, foremost of which were riverine. Main channel (drum, bass, buffalo, and catfish) and backwater fish (crappie, bream, and bass) make up over 50 percent of the faunal remains from excavations. Turtles, amphibians, reptiles, migratory fowl, snails, and mussels were also important components in the diet. Upland resources included small game and deer.

Plant remains included the mast crop hickory. Evidence for goosefoot, marsh elder, grape, and hackberry was present, although seeds occurred in small numbers and none showed evidence of domestication.

Perhaps one of the most important resources for the Watson Brake people was the availability of river cobbles for hot-rock cooking. In the absence of ceramic vessels, food was either roasted or baked, steamed, or boiled with hot cooking stones. Heating and cooling shatters cobbles into fragments of so-called fire-cracked rock. These broken rocks were the most abundant kind of artifact from the earthworks (347 kg, about 763 lb).

River cobbles also provided the raw material for chipped-stone tools. Evidence of trade for nonlocal chert was nonexistent. The Watson Brake folk made projectile points, bifaces, scrapers, and microdrills, but the relatively small number suggests these artifacts were probably taken from the site.

MATERIAL CULTURE

The distinctive Evans projectile point style is associated with Middle Archaic sites in Louisiana and southern Arkansas. The distribution of this style of projectile point does not extend to the east side of the Mississippi River, suggesting that the river was a cultural boundary about 5,000 years ago. Interestingly, effigy stone beads have been found at other, roughly contemporaneous sites, but they have not been found at Watson Brake, even though the technology necessary for their production was present. The most distinctive Middle Archaic artifacts are simple ceramic cubes, blocks, and spheres averaging about 4 centimeters in size. They consistently date to about 5,300 years ago. Interestingly, these objects occur only in four northeast Louisiana parishes, and they have yet to be observed on Middle Archaic sites to the south. Their function is not known.

Although two Poverty Point–style artifacts are in the Watson Brake collections, there is no evidence for cultural continuity between the two. Artifact style and lithic technology differ between the two cultures. For some reason, Middle Archaic mound building abruptly ended around 5,000 years ago. It then reappeared over 1,000 years later with the emergence of the Poverty Point culture.

ACCESSIBILITY

Watson Brake is not accessible to the public. To arrange tours of the site, contact the regional archaeologist at the University of Louisiana at Monroe. Additional information on the site is available through the Division of Archaeology in Baton Rouge, Louisiana.

Further Reading: Jones, Reca, "Archaeological Investigations in the Ouachita River Valley, Bayou Bartholomew to Riverton, Louisiana," *Louisiana Archaeology* 10 (1985): 103–69; Sassaman, Kenneth E., and Michael J. Heckenberger, "Crossing the Symbolic Rubicon in the Southeast," in *The Rise of Cultural Complexity in the Southeast*, edited by J. L. Gibson and P. J. Carr (Tuscaloosa: University of Alabama Press, 2004), 214–233; Saunders, Joe, "Are We Fixing to Make the Same Mistake Again?" in *Signs of Power: The*

Rise of Cultural Complexity in the Southeast, edited by J. L. Gibson and P. J. Carr (Tuscaloosa University of Alabama Press, 2004); Saunders, Joe, Thurman Allen, and Roger T. Saucier, "Four Archaic? Mound Complexes in Northeast Louisiana," *Southeastern Archaeology* 13 (1994): 134–153; Saunders, Joe W., Reca Jones, Kathryn Moorhead, and Brian Davis, "An Unusual Artifact Type from Northeast Louisiana," *Southeastern Archaeology* 17 (1998): 72–79; Saunders, Joe W., Rolfe D. Mandel, C. Garth Sampson, Charles M. Allen, E. Thurman Allen, Daniel A. Bush, James K. Feathers, Kristen J. Gremillion, C. T. Hallmark, H. Edwin Jackson, Jay K. Johnson, Reca Jones, Roger Saucier, Gary L. Stringer, and Malcolm F. Vidrine, "Watson Brake, A Middle Archaic Mound Complex in Northeast Louisiana," *American Antiquity* 70(4) (2005): 631–668; Saunders, Joe W., Rolfe D. Mandel, Roger T. Saucier, E. Thurman Allen, C. T. Hallmark, Jay K. Johnson, Edwin H. Jackson, Charles M. Allen, Gary L. Stringer, Douglas S. Frink, James K. Feathers, Stephen Williams, Kristen J. Gremillion, Malcolm F. Vidrine, and Reca Jones, "A Mound Complex in Louisiana at 5400–5000 Years B.P.," *Science* 277(5333) (1997): 1796–1799.

Joe Saunders

POVERTY POINT STATE HISTORIC SITE

Poverty Point, Northeastern Louisiana
Ancient Massive Earthen Architectural Complex and Trade Center

The Poverty Point archaeological site represents the most spectacular product of the so-called Poverty Point culture, located in the lower Mississippi River valley during the Late Archaic period (2000–500 BC). This massive earthen architectural and archaeological complex, constructed and occupied about 1700–1100 BC, includes six mounds; six concentric, semi-elliptical earthen ridges; and a plaza. The site also served as the center of a major exchange network; large amounts of exotic raw materials, including steatite (soapstone), sandstone, hematite, magnetite, galena, copper, and a variety of different kinds of cherts were brought in from as far as 1,600 kilometers away, with some being redistributed to related sites throughout the lower Mississippi valley. Poverty Point was, without question, the largest and most culturally elaborate settlement of its time in North America. That it was supported by a hunting-gathering economy makes Poverty Point truly exceptional.

The site is situated on the eastern edge of Macon Ridge in West Carroll Parish, northeast Louisiana. A low, almost level, elevated, terrace-like geological feature, Macon Ridge extends for nearly 100 miles north to south along the western edge of the Mississippi alluvial valley. At Poverty Point, Macon Ridge is about 9 meters above the floodplain, providing a dependably dry spot overlooking what was likely a wet and swampy, yet very productive, environment. Today, part of the site is in mature hardwood forest, but limited pollen analyses suggest grasses dominated the local vegetation during its prehistoric occupation.

Although some of the mounds were recognized prior to the twentieth century as ancient earthen architecture, the ridges went unrecognized, mostly because of their magnitude. The concentric ridges are so large that their true dimensions and spatial configuration are not easily perceived at ground level. In fact, it was not until 1953, when archaeologist James Ford examined a series of aerial photographs for the lower Mississippi valley, that the geometric arrangement of ridged earthworks was noticed.

The six earthen ridges form a C-shaped enclosure, with the bluff edge of Macon Ridge "closing" the opening. The diameter of the ridged enclosure at the outermost ridge (Ridge 6) is roughly 1.2 kilometers, and at the innermost ridge (Ridge 1), it is about 600 meters. Straightened out and laid end to end, the ridges would stretch over 12 kilometers. These ridges, which some believe to have served as living areas, stand 1–2 meters high. In the southern part of the site, the height of these ridges has likely been reduced through roughly 140 years of cultivation. They are separated by depressions, or swales, 40 to 60 meters wide, created by the removal of sediments for ridge construction. Each ridge is divided into sectors by as many as five depressed alleyways, or aisles, and they are all connected by a raised causeway in the southwest sector.

A 35-acre plaza is defined by the innermost constructed ridge and the bank of Macon Ridge. The plaza appears today as a large, flat expanse that one might assume was the natural topography of Macon Ridge. Soil cores and excavations, however, have revealed that considerable filling and leveling was undertaken to create and maintain this level area.

Five of the six mounds are located within the boundary of the Poverty Point State Historic Site. Three mounds (A, B, E) are outside and two (C, D) are inside the ridged enclosure. A privately owned sixth mound, Motley Mound, is located about 2 kilometers north of the rest of the mounds and ridges.

Standing roughly 23 meters tall with a base about 216 meters by 195 meters, Mound A is the largest mound at Poverty Point. In fact, it is the second-largest earthen

1946 aerial photograph of the Poverty Point site, showing the earthen ridges (light rings) and swales (dark rings). Mound A, covered with trees, is easily seen west of the enclosure. Scale 1:1923.76. [Courtesy of U.S. Army Corps of Engineers, Vicksburg District]

structure in North America (after Monks Mound at Cahokia). It is frequently referred to as the Bird Mound, because its unusual cross shape reminds some of a bird in flight; however, no empirical evidence supports such an intended symbolism. Motley Mound has been identified as a smaller, unfinished version of Mound A.

Mound B is a conical mound roughly 6.5 meters high and 55 meters in diameter. Mound C is an oval mound about 70 meters long; due to erosion, its original width is

unknown. The top of the mound rises only about 2 meters above the plaza, but it extends about 1.2 meters below the current plaza ground surface. Mound D is a Late Woodland construction, about 2,000 years younger than the other earthworks at the site. It is a small, flat-topped, rectangular mound, built on the southeast end of Ridge 2, and it measures roughly 40 meters by 35 meters by 2 meters high. Mound E is a flat-topped, semi-rectangular mound, about 4 meters tall, that originally had basal dimensions of about 100 meters by 100 meters; it is a prehistoric

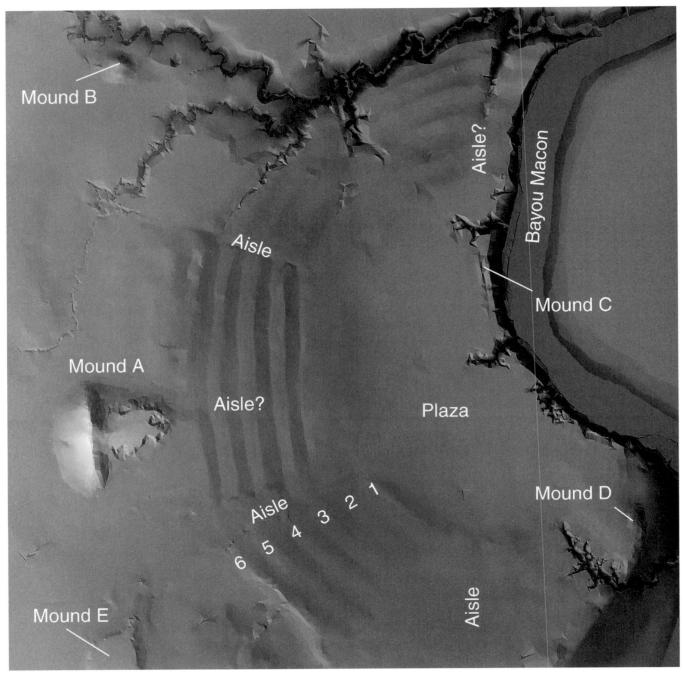

Surface topography of Poverty Point State Historic Site, with earthen architectural features labeled. [Courtesy of Division of Archaeology, Office of Cultural Development, Department of Culture, Recreation and Tourism, State of Louisiana]

construction of unknown affiliation. There is no clear evidence regarding the functions of these mounds.

Archaeologists have estimated that about 750,000 cubic meters of dirt were moved during mound and ridge construction. Landscape preparation and maintenance probably required an equivalent amount of earth movement. The dirt for this work had to come from somewhere, and in addition to the swales, there are huge topographic depressions on the site

that are likely borrow areas created during mound construction.

Artifact assemblages (the variety and amount of artifacts recovered from the site) acquired in the archaeological excavation of and surface collection at the site further reinforce the notion that Poverty Point was not the product of a typical Late Archaic culture. The sheer quantity of exotic raw materials, from both near and distant sources, is staggering. The manner in which these materials were acquired is not at all clear; no trade items from Poverty Point have been identified at sites near the sources. Also interesting is that the exotic materials do not appear to have been restricted in use or in distribution. They were used to make both utilitarian tools and ornamental items, and all segments of the population appear to have used them.

Although the populations at Poverty Point and related sites are not alone in making and using such artifacts, this group of sites is particularly well known for polished stone artifacts: plummets, which are teardrop-shaped objects made of hematite or magnetite and are believed to be fishing net weights; *atl atl*, or spear thrower, weights of various materials and designs; pendants of both geometric and zoomorphic forms (of which the pot-bellied owl is the most renowned); and beads of various shapes.

The ceramic-artifact assemblage at Poverty Point is also unusual. The ubiquitous finger-molded baked loess/clay balls (also known as Poverty Point objects, or PPOs) are of particular interest. Because stones for cooking were not readily available in the local environment, the occupants of Poverty Point manufactured artificial rocks from sediments at the site. To be sure, the PPOs were used at other Late Archaic sites in eastern North America, but nowhere are they as plentiful or as diverse in form as at Poverty Point. There are shards from ceramic vessels, the oldest in the lower Mississippi valley, at Poverty Point, but they are rare; steatite and sandstone vessel fragments are found far more often.

Although the area has been farmed historically—the archaeological site takes its name from the Poverty Point plantation established there sometime prior to 1843—the people who built the earthworks were not farmers. Animal and plant remains from Poverty Point and related sites indicate these people supported themselves by hunting, fishing, and gathering wild plants. Many archaeologists believe that nearby food resources were sufficiently plentiful that people were able to live at Poverty Point year-round.

Poverty Point has been important in the history of American archaeology particularly because of the site's uniqueness—early on, archaeologists recognized that it did not fit into existing culture historical schemes for the Southeast. Poverty Point is an impressive site, with monumental architecture and an abundance of nonlocal raw materials, and with a refined lapidary industry that lacked both an agricultural subsistence base and a well-developed ceramic technology. As such, the site represented an explanatory problem for archaeologists who subscribed to a model of progressive cultural evolution. How could the site be as old as it appeared, yet so amazingly complex?

Over the years, archaeologists have established that there were Middle Archaic precedents for mound construction and the lapidary technology. While Poverty Point takes mound building to a new height, it no longer appears to have come seemingly out of thin air. At the same time, archaeologists have been forced to rethink some of their traditional assumptions about people who built monumental architecture. Although Poverty Point's place in the lower Mississippi valley cultural sequence is now accepted, a challenge remains: explaining how and why Late Archaic hunter-gatherers so transformed their landscape.

Poverty Point was acquired by the state of Louisiana in 1972, and since that time, efforts have been focused on preserving and protecting the site while making it accessible to visitors. The Poverty Point State Historic Site has a museum, a well-developed public education program, a self-guided pedestrian hiking trail, and a paved driving route (used for both interpretive ranger-guided tram and self-guided car tours). The site is open to visitors from 9:00 am to 5:00 pm daily, except on Thanksgiving, Christmas, and New Year's Day.

Further Reading: Ford, James A., and Clarence H. Webb, *Poverty Point: A Late Archaic Site in Louisiana*, Anthropological Paper 46 (New York: American Museum of Natural History, 1956); Gibson, Jon L., *The Ancient Mounds of Poverty Point: Place of Rings* (Gainesville: University Press of Florida, 2000); Gibson, Jon L., *Poverty Point: A Terminal Archaic Culture of the Lower Mississippi Valley*, 2nd ed., Anthropological Study Series No. 7 (Baton Rouge, LA: Department of Culture, Recreation and Tourism, 1999); Louisiana Office of State Parks, Poverty Point State Historic Site, www.lastateparks.com/poverty/pvertypt.htm; Webb, Clarence H., *The Poverty Point Culture*, 2nd ed., Vol. XVII of *Geoscience and Man* (Baton Rouge: Louisiana State University School of Geoscience, 1982).

Diana M. Greenlee

ANCIENT SHELL RING SITES

Coastal South Carolina, Georgia, and Florida
Early Architecture for Ceremonial and Political Uses

Shell rings are generally circular piles of shell surrounding level areas or plazas. They were built beginning about 4,600 years ago, during a time period that archaeologists call the Late Archaic. These shell ring constructions present the first evidence for large-scale public architecture arising out of increasing social complexity developed by egalitarian hunter-gatherer bands as they permanently settled parts of the coast of what is now the southeastern United States.

Aerial photo of the Fig Island shell ring complex.   [Michael Russo]

Shell rings were always constructed in the vicinity of predictable and abundant supplies of oyster along mouths of rivers, barrier islands, marshes, and mangrove swamps. Although the remains of other species of shellfish, fish, and other marine life are present, oyster shell makes up the greatest volume in all extant rings. Today, forty-five Archaic shell ring sites comprising sixty-five individual rings are found within estuaries from South Carolina to Mississippi, with most located in South Carolina, Georgia, and Florida.

Eight Late Archaic groups of coastal shell rings are distinguishable by their geographic locales and varied uses of ceramics and shell tools; shell ring builders were the first in

their regions to invent or adopt pottery specific to their cultural needs. The kinds of shell rings these groups built also serve to distinguish their cultural identities. Among these groups, shell rings range in size from 30 to 250 meters across and 1 to 6 meters in height. Their shapes can be circular, semicircular, or hexagonal; some are U-shaped or of irregular forms that defy easy description.

Among the Thoms Creek cultural groups in South Carolina, who also produced early fiber-tempered pottery, shell rings are typically C-shaped or circular, with most measuring 50 to 60 meters across. The largest rings are found at the multiple-ring Fig Island complex (2100–1700 BC). The

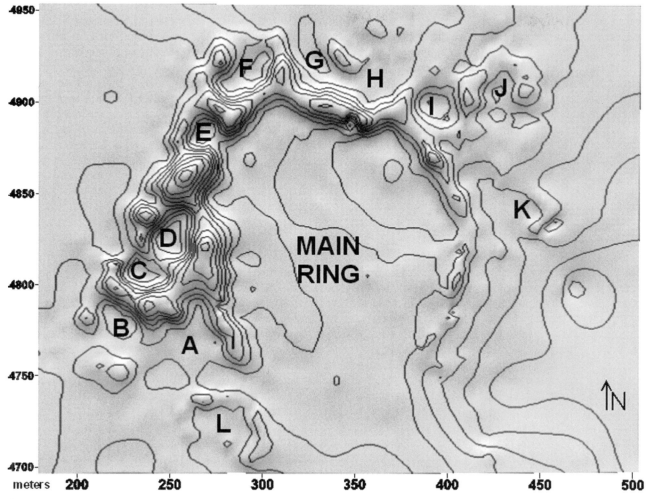

Rollins shell ring complex, with attached and nearby rings.   [Michael Russo]

2-meter-high hexagonal Fig Island 2 ring spans 82 meters. Fifty meters to its east stands an even larger mounded shell monument, Fig Island 1. This continuous shell work contains four attached rings and their attendant plazas, a mound, and a causeway connecting the mound to the largest ring. The largest ring on Fig Island 1 is 100 meters in diameter, rising nearly 6 meters above its plaza.

In Georgia the Stalling Island cultural groups also produced fiber-tempered pottery and constructed C-shaped and circular shell rings, with most ranging between 30 and 60 meters across. It is likely, however, that the smaller of these rings are merely remnant portions of grander rings that have been reduced in size by erosion. The largest rings are found at the Sapelo ring complex (2200–1700 BC), which includes three rings. Ring 1 stands nearly 3 meters high and measures 80 meters in diameter.

Only three shell rings are found in northeast Florida, but these are substantially larger and differ in shape from those in Georgia and South Carolina. The earliest of the three, Oxeye, was constructed around 4,600 years ago (2600 BC), before pottery was adopted in the southeast United States. Oxeye, the only circular ring in Florida, spans 160 meters.

Nearly 1,000 years after Oxeye was built, the use of fiber-tempered pottery had been widely adopted for centuries in the region. People used this pottery for ceremonial display as well as food preparation at a massive ring complex they built nearby on Fort George Island at the Rollins shell ring (2100–1600 BC). Extending 250 meters across, the site consists of a 3-meter-tall U-shaped ring with twelve other rings attached to its outside walls, making it the largest shell ring of its time. Thirty-five miles south of Rollins, the contemporaneous (1800–1500 BC) Guana ring was much less ambitious in form and height—a simple U-ring at a little over a meter tall—but still more extensive than any Stalling Island and Thoms Creek rings.

Four other rings are known farther south, in peninsular Florida. The 250-meter long Reed ring (1500–1300 BC) lies over 200 miles (322 km) south of Guana and was built by yet another founding pottery-producing culture whose unique wares included spicule-tempered and sand-tempered pottery. Across the peninsula, on the gulf coast, the Bonita and Horr's Island U-shaped shell rings were constructed around 4,000 (2300–1800 BC) and 4,500 (2600–2000 BC) years ago, respectively—before the local adoption of pottery. The Bonita ring measures 230 meters long, while Horr's Island is 160 meters. However, at nearly a kilometer in length, the Horr's Island complex includes the ring and plaza, four mounds, and associated living areas, making it the most extensive shell ring complex.

One hundred miles to the north, construction on another ring, Hill Cottage, began around the same time as Horr's Island (2600–1600 BC). But occupation at Hill Cottage continued for centuries after Horr's Island had been abandoned. As at Horr's and Bonita, the pottery had not been adopted at Hill Cottage when construction of the ring was initiated. But unlike the case at those other two sites, pottery was introduced midway through ring construction. This indicates that the use of pottery was not necessary for the gathering and processing of large quantities of shellfish used to build rings, but was used for such once introduced.

When shell rings were first identified in the 1800s, their circular shape intrigued investigators. They speculated that the rings served as fish traps, forts, and prisons for captured enemies. Now that more rings have been identified, it is known that circles are among the least common shapes in which rings were built. Their unique shapes, however, are key to understanding their functions.

The shapes of shell rings reflect the organization of the societies that built them. As the wide differences in shapes, sizes, and artifacts suggest, shell rings likely served diverse purposes. In South Carolina and Georgia, ring sites are closely spaced, averaging one every 7 to 10 miles (11–16 km). The smaller, single rings served as village and ceremonial sites for local kin groups. Here the shell used in ring construction comes from both daily meals and periodic, small-scale ceremonial feasts. As shellfish were consumed, their shells were discarded underfoot or next to houses, and the rings began to accumulate. The plaza served as an area where periodic ceremonial activities and public discourse occurred, while the plaza edges were where small houses were constructed and daily cooking and maintenance activities took place. Few of the smaller rings were wide enough on top to accommodate such living activities, and no evidence of houses has ever been identified on top of the rings.

The larger ring sites, such as Fig Island in the Thoms Creek region and Sapelo in the Stallings region, were centrally located political and ceremonial centers. The individual shell rings at these multiple-ring sites served different purposes. Some of the ring sites were primarily residential, as evidenced by artifacts related to daily living activities within and along the inside edges of the rings. Other rings were primarily ceremonial, as indicated by construction episodes resulting from large-scale feasting on oysters and the general absence of everyday artifacts and living floors within the ring or plaza. Oysters were consumed in large quantities during periodic ceremonial events at these rings, and the shells of those feasts were deposited in massive piles to form the rings. With each subsequent feast, the shell deposition resulted in contiguous and progressively higher ring walls. In contrast, the largest rings and mounds at these complexes may have been built as public projects with much or all of the shell taken from quarries at distant shell middens rather than being from feasts held at these sites.

As in Georgia and South Carolina, large shell rings in Florida served as regional political and ceremonial centers. The larger sizes of the Florida rings, however, indicate that they accommodated up to ten times as many guests. Their larger size was, in part, due to the greater geographic areas and populations that the Florida rings served. In Florida, the distances between rings held a wider range, from 35 to 200 miles (55–322 km). In south Florida, in particular, populations were generally low along the coast and widely dispersed. Except for ring sites themselves, few contemporary sites are known, and these are relatively small. Large coastal ring sites were host to ceremonies and feasts for these rural coastal communities, as well as for widely dispersed migratory hunter-gatherers from the interior.

The reason Florida rings are generally U-shaped while Georgia and South Carolina rings are generally circular or C-shaped is probably due to the differing social organizations of each group. Common to all rings is the central plaza, which served the necessary and functional purposes for both habitation and ceremony at ring sites. The plazas provided group members a view of each other that assured sharing of resources, facilitated communication, and provided an arena for display and ceremony. Ethnographically, U-shaped settlements around a central plaza allow two kin or other social groups to live with their closest kin and alliances on one side of the U, opposing themselves to less related groups on the other. In these settlement plans, temporary or permanent leaders are placed at the closed end of the group to facilitate communication and mitigate conflicts between opposing members. Circular and C-shaped arrangements can similarly align opposing groups, but also more easily facilitate multiple alignments—for example, two distinct moieties in either side of the ring with separate clans aligned within each moiety. The circular shape symbolizes unity and bonds the greater group together, even though it is made up of potentially opposing factions.

Because of historical circumstances, not all shell rings are the same size or shape. As guests fed on the enormous numbers of oysters at shell rings during ceremonies, their social and economic obligations to their hosts deepened. The guests would come away from these feasts owing their hosts a reciprocal feast, promises of marriage or other alliances, support in battle, labor, or some other form of repayment. These social debts created unequal standings between the shell ring hosts and their guests. Other ring communities remained beholden until they reciprocated. But smaller, dispersed groups lacked the natural resources, manpower, or managerial skills to host equally extravagant feasts themselves and were perpetually indebted.

One result of inequalities arising out of differential abilities in hosting feasts can be seen in differences in the size and number of shell ring sites within a given region. Fig Island represented the largest ring site along a coast that was densely packed with lesser ring communities. Its preeminence in hosting feasts and imposing social obligation on others is reflected in its monumental architecture, which includes the 6-meter Fig Island 1 complex, with an attendant mound that likely served as the residence or resting place of high-status individuals. The building of such large-scale architecture required leadership and labor otherwise unavailable from the typical family-level subsistence economies of the region. A political economy in which food surpluses were used to obtain the necessary social will and labor for the construction of shell rings had to arise before such monuments began appearing on the coast.

The sizes and forms of the Horr's Island mounds and ring indicate that social relations were also complex and unequal. At the shell ring, the position of prestige and power is marked at the closed end, where the ring reaches its greatest height and volume. But two other distinct living areas lie outside the ring, each associated with its own small mound. These indicate that other groups—less prolific than the ring-building community, as judged by their more moderate shell constructions—also lived at the site. These groups lacked, or otherwise lay outside, the social organization capable of constructing their own rings or large mounds.

Shell ring builders were remarkably different from their mobile foraging, hunting-gathering ancestors. Among the varied rings, inventions of new shell and ceramic technologies, the establishment of permanent settlement, and the appearance of incipient social stratification are evident in the shell architecture and monuments the ring builders left behind.

Further Reading: Russo, Michael, "Measuring Shell Rings for Social Inequality," in *Signs of Power: The Rise of Cultural Complexity in the Southeast*, edited by Jon L. Gibson and Philip J. Carr (Tuscaloosa: University of Alabama Press, 2004), 26–70; Russo, Michael, and Gregory Heide, "The Joseph Reed Shell Ring (8Mt13)," *Florida Anthropologist* 55(2) (2002): 67–88; *Sapelo Shell Rings*, http://www.lostworlds.org/sapelo_shell_rings.html; Saunders, Rebecca, "The Stratigraphic Sequence at Rollins Shell Ring: Implications for Ring Function," *Florida Anthropologist* 57(4) (2004): 249–268; *Shell Rings of Southeastern North America*, http://www.nps.gov/history/seac/shellrings/index.htm; Trinkley, Michael B., "The Form and Function of South Carolina's Early Woodland Shell Rings," in *Structure and Process in Southeastern Archaeology*, edited by Roy S. Dickens Jr. and H. Trawick Ward (Tuscaloosa: University of Alabama Press, 1985), 102–118; Waring, Antonio J., Jr., and Lewis H. Larson, "The Shell Ring on Sapelo Island," in *The Waring Papers: The Collected Works of Antonio J. Waring, Jr.*, edited by Stephen Williams, Papers of the Peabody Museum of Archaeology and Ethnology No. 58 (Cambridge, MA: Harvard University, 1968), 263–278.

Michael Russo

COPENA SITES

Tennessee River Valley, Northern Alabama
Middle Woodland Mortuary Mounds and Artifacts

Copena is a Middle Woodland time period mortuary complex (a distinctive set of cultural traits found in burials from this time period and geographic area) dating from approximately 100 BC to AD 400. Copena sites are found throughout the Tennessee River drainage of northern Alabama and immediately adjacent areas of Mississippi and Tennessee. The name "Copena" combines "copper" and "galena," two imported raw materials used in the

Copena mound 40Hn4 being staked for excavation. [Tennessee Valley Authority and the University of Alabama Museums]

Copper artifacts from 40Hn4. [Tennessee Valley Authority and the University of Alabama Museums]

manufacture of artifacts typically found at Copena mortuary sites.

The name "Copena" was first applied to Copena mounds, small burial mounds scattered throughout the area. Copena mounds were excavated and reported by early-twentieth-century archaeologists such as Clarence B. Moore and—slightly later—Gerard Fowke. A number of Copena mounds were excavated during relief-era projects in advance of the creation of the Pickwick, Wheeler, and Guntersville lakes on the Tennessee River. Burial caves showing similar artifacts were excavated at this time, and these too were called Copena. More recently, Copena has been used as the name for the entire cultural system that produced the mounds and caves.

We now know, however, that several separate and distinct Middle Woodland societies were responsible for the creation of Copena mortuary sites. The Copena mortuary complex represents a set of shared beliefs that created and reinforced social ties among these groups. These social ties were further reinforced and extended by the exchange network that provided the specialized artifacts found in the mounds and caves. Copena is best understood, then, as a distinctive regional mortuary complex and interaction sphere that in turn participated, at some level, within the greater Hopewellian interaction sphere, which was centered in the Midwest, of the same time period.

MORTUARY MOUNDS

Copena mortuary mounds are small, accretionary (gradually built up) mounds averaging about 6 feet in height and 50 feet in diameter. They occur singly or in groups of as many as five and are usually located well away from any habitation area. Copena mounds ordinarily began as burial areas with no evidence of mound building. At some point, a simple earthen mound was constructed over these precedent burials. This mound fill could contain additional, inclusive burials. Yet more graves, intrusive burials, could be excavated into the fill. Some mounds have a final cap of clay and sand with no

further burials. Small accretionary mounds such as these do not require large amounts of labor and could have been constructed over time by a small kinship-based group. Radiocarbon dates suggest that a single mound could have been in use for 200 years or more.

The ways in which individuals were buried in Copena mounds were highly variable. Bodies can be found in an extended or flexed position. Burials of disarticulated remains—that is, partial bodies or skeletons—and cremated remains were sometimes included. Any of these burial types can be found in the initial burial group, subsequent burials, or intrusive burials. Any of these burial types can be found with or without mortuary artifacts.

Copper artifacts found in Copena mounds include reel-shaped gorgets, beads, ear spools, celts, breastplates, and cut sheets. The most numerous artifacts are beads, with about 1,000 examples. All other artifacts total just about 150. Galena is almost always found as ground nodules, some weighing over 10 pounds. Ground galena is a shiny, glitter-like material and may have been used in pigments or similar applications. A few galena beads have been found. Greenstone celts and digging tools are commonly found with burials and as inclusions in the mound fill. Greenstone, like copper and galena, is a nonlocal resource. Other artifacts include marine shell cups and beads, mica, pigment-producing minerals, and projectile points. Strangely, pottery vessels are not included, although they are a prominent aspect of just about every other Middle Woodland mortuary mound complex.

MORTUARY CAVES

Caves and sinkholes are common features in the limestone formations of the Tennessee valley. Several of these caves show evidence of use as Copena mortuary sites. Some of these caves show only minor evidence of use for burials. Rockhouse

Ground galena nodules from 40Hn4. [Tennessee Valley Authority and the University of Alabama Museums]

Spring Cave in Limestone County, Alabama, for example, contained the apparent remains of a single individual about 150 feet back from the entrance.

At Cave Springs in Morgan County, eighteen Copena burials were found in three areas approximately a quarter mile into the dark zone of the cave. The constantly moist atmosphere in Cave Springs resulted in the preservation of materials not found in mounds. The burials were wrapped in fabric and matting. Other artifacts in association with these burials included a coil of rope, a mass of powdered red ocher, four marine shell cups, and a bow with five cane arrows. The wet, powdery condition of all of the organic materials, however, prohibits their removal from the cave. No definitive Copena artifacts were found in the cave, but small copper stains with some burials indicate the former presence of copper artifacts. The other artifacts are also consistent with a general Copena association. One projectile point found with a burial dates to this time. Most significantly, the only Middle Woodland platform pipe ever found in a Copena-related context was found at Cave Springs. The pipe was deliberately broken into several pieces and scattered over an area away from the burials.

Hampton Cave, located just outside Guntersville, Alabama, was excavated in 1939 prior to the creation of Guntersville Lake. It is clear that a great many individuals were interred in Hampton Cave. The burial area was located in a small room about 65 feet from the mouth of the cave and consisted of a deposit of cremated human remains and ashes 4 feet thick. Typical Copena mortuary artifacts, all also burned, were mixed with the bone and ash. A description of the cave in 1890 describes the deposit as 4 feet thick at that time, but adds that much of the deposit had been removed over the years and spread on surrounding fields for fertilizer.

PLATFORM MOUNDS

Investigators over the past few years have discovered that at least two platform mounds were constructed by Copena peoples. The first of these was the Walling Mound, located along the Tennessee River south of Huntsville, Alabama. The Walling site complex includes the mound, a large contemporaneous Middle Woodland village, and two smaller mounds about half a mile to the east. One of these smaller mounds is a Copena mound. The second mound is of a size and shape consistent with its being a second Copena mound. The upper levels of the Walling Mound date to much later, Mississippian times. Recent excavation, though, has revealed that the three initial mound stages date to the Copena period. Features, artifacts, and plant and animal remains from the summit of Stage 2 of the mound, the most well-preserved level, indicate that activities such as feasting and other communal rituals took place here. At least some of these rituals included the display or other use of exotic materials and artifacts.

The second known Copena platform mound is the Florence Mound. The mound is a rectangular mound that measures 40 feet high, with steep sides. Steps have been built on the north side, but early descriptions note remnants of a ramp on the east side and an arcuate embankment surrounding the mound at a distance of 275 feet. No trace of the ramp or embankment can be seen today. As at the Walling Mound, a minor Mississippian occupation on the mound summit and the shape of the mound led to a presumed Mississippian age for the mound. Recent test excavations, however, have shown that the Florence Mound was entirely constructed during the Middle Woodland. We have no information relating to the mound's function during the Middle Woodland. The Florence Mound is located at Indian Mound Museum in Florence, Alabama, and it is the only Copena mound or cave available for public visitation.

Further Reading: Cole, Gloria G., *The Murphy Hill Site (1Ms300): The Structural Study of a Copena Mound and Comparative Review of the Copena Mortuary Complex*, Office of Archaeological Research, Research Series No. 3 (Tuscaloosa: University of Alabama, 1981); Walthall, John A., "Hopewell and the Southern Heartland," in *Hopewell Archaeology: The Chillicothe Conference*, edited by David S. Brose and N'omi Greber (Kent, OH: Kent State University Press, 1979), 200–208; Webb, William S., *An Archeological Survey of Wheeler Basin on the Tennessee River in Northern Alabama*, Bulletin 122, (Washington DC: Bureau of American Ethnology, 1939); Webb, William S., and David L. DeJarnette, *An Archeological Survey of Pickwick Basin in the Adjacent Portions of the States of Alabama, Mississippi and Tennessee*, Bulletin 129 (Washington DC: Bureau of American Ethnology, 1942); Webb, William S., and Charles G. Wilder, *An Archaeological Survey of Guntersville Basin on the Tennessee River in Northern Alabama* (Lexington: University of Kentucky Press, 1951).

Eugene M. Futato

MARKSVILLE STATE HISTORIC SITE

Marksville, Louisiana

A Rare Middle Woodland Mound Complex in the Lower Mississippi Valley

The Marksville site, which spreads across 100 or more acres, includes two earthen embankments, seven earthen mounds, and up to several dozen smaller earthworks. Construction began by AD 1, and the site was used until at least AD 350. The physical layout of this ceremonial center and the styles of its artifacts tie the local Marksville culture to the contemporaneous Hopewell culture in the midwestern United States. The site is one of only three known mound and embankment complexes dating to the Hopewell period in the lower Mississippi River valley.

Marksville was constructed by people whose ancestors had lived in the region for generations. Just over 2,000 years ago, the ideas that archaeologists recognize as the Hopewell culture began to develop. The people in central Louisiana interpreted these ideas in the context of their own culture, and a combination of the two is much in evidence at Marksville. The site was a center for ceremonial events and activities, although the exact nature of those events remains a mystery. Burial of high-status members of the community was certainly important, based upon the cemetery in Mound 4, but archaeologists have not identified the purpose and function of the other mounds and earthworks.

The Marksville people continued a centuries-old pattern of hunting and gathering plants and animals for use as food, tools, and construction materials. Analyses of food remains indicate very few changes in economy over the 5,000–7,000 years leading up to Marksville. There is no evidence for the domestication of native seed plants, as occurred in contemporary midwestern societies. Stone tool technology remained similar to that of earlier periods. The *atl atl* and dart were the primary hunting tools, with popular stone point styles being of the straight and contracting stem varieties. Fish and turtles were captured with nets, but hook-and-line fishing was done as well. Archaeologists have found impressions of split-cane baskets and woven mats at the Marksville site. Pottery vessels were primary containers for storage and cooking. Pots that were used for domestic activities are often plain, while those found in ceremonial contexts at Marksville are beautifully decorated. The decorations include stylized bird and plant motifs, as well as complicated rectilinear and curvilinear designs.

The heart of the site consists of a C-shaped embankment, referred to as Enclosure A, that measures 1,000 meters long, with the open side overlooking an old river channel. The embankment varies in height from 0.5 meters to 2.5 meters; the different heights created an artificial horizon for observers inside the enclosure watching celestial events in the night sky. Within Enclosure A lie six mounds. The site is laid out on a geometric grid, with the mounds positioned to mark alignments pointing to important celestial events. Mounds 2 and 6 are the largest mounds at the site and lie at opposite ends of the central plaza. Mound 2 has been partially modified by modern activities, and its original shape is difficult to discern. It probably had a large, flat platform on its north end, with a taller, dome-shaped southern end. Mound 6 is a circular mound built as two platforms stacked on top of one another, like a wedding cake. The lower platform is largely hidden below the modern ground surface, leaving the second platform visible today. Flat surfaces may have allowed this mound to serve as a stage for ceremonies seen by people gathered in the plaza.

Mounds 4 and X lie on the east and west sides of the central plaza. Mound 4 was the cemetery for a select few of the Marksville community. The burial surface is a 1.5-meter-high rectangular platform. On this platform, a series of tombs were excavated, and bodies were placed in them. The tombs contain the remains of adults, children, and infants, indicating burial in the mound was reserved for members of certain-families or clans. Two dogs were also buried on this platform. Eventually, the platform was covered with a thick layer of earth, forming the final conical shape. Mound X has been severely altered by modern activities, and its original size and shape are unknown.

Mounds 3 and 5 are low domes of white earth. This earth can be found at the site, but very large areas would have had to be stripped to gather enough soil to build the mounds. While color was an important element of these two mounds, its meaning is unknown. The purpose of these mounds also is unknown, although they are positioned on a true north-south axis, so they may mark this alignment. Mound 5 appears to be the primary location for astronomical observations. On the south side of Enclosure A, two gateways lead to a raised causeway crossing the ditch outside the embankment to a circular ridge of soil 0.6 meters high and 98 meters in diameter.

This circular embankment and causeway may represent a ceremonial entrance to the site whose position reflects the position of the Milky Way and sun on the solar equinoxes and solstices.

The Marksville site also contains numerous small, circular earthworks, and all but one of these earthworks lie between the two large enclosures. Each earthwork is 10–30 meters in diameter, with a small ditch lying outside of a low embankment. Inside the embankment, the ground was dug out to create a sunken floor up to 0.5 meters below the surface. The central area of the sunken floor was then excavated to create a deep pit up to 2 meters below the surface. This deep pit was the location of repeated large fires. Archaeologists do not know what purpose these small earthworks served, although they are believed to be ceremonial facilities.

Several hundred meters north of Enclosure A lies a second enclosure and mound complex. No archaeological investigations have been conducted in this area; it is assumed this embankment and mound are part of the Marksville site.

Gerard Fowke of the United States National Museum (part of the Smithsonian Institution) was the first archaeologist to visit Marksville in 1926. His excavations into mounds 3 and 4 produced the first artifacts suggesting the Hopewell influence at the site. During the 1930s, the Federal Emergency Relief Administration (FERA) and the Works Progress Administration (WPA) funded large projects at the site. In 1933 the FERA project completed the excavation of Mound 4, explored mounds 5 and 6, and selected areas along the bluff edge. The subsequent WPA project in 1939 excavated a series of trenches around Mound 2. Unfortunately, a report has not been completed for either project. Limited excavations in 1971, 1993, 1998, 2000, 2001, and 2002

have explored several of the small, circular earthworks, placed soil cores across each mound to determine its internal structure, and examined the embankment, causeway, and outer circle.

The Marksville site is the largest and most complex mound and earthwork site of the Hopewell period in the lower Mississippi valley. The Marksville people chose to participate in the Hopewell culture to a greater degree than most of their neighbors, although archaeologists today are still trying to understand why they did so. The spatial organization of the site represents a sophisticated understanding of geometry and astronomical knowledge. Although the site is organized on a regular grid, individual mounds are positioned to create sightlines to important celestial events. So the site was a place where the timing of important ceremonial and ritual events could be predicted and measured. While that much is clear, the precise nature and meaning of the ceremonies performed within the main enclosure and in the small, circular earthworks remain a mystery.

Further Reading: Fowke, Gerard, "Archaeological Investigations II," in *Forty-fourth Annual Report of the Smithsonian Institution Bureau of American Ethnology* (1928), 399–540; Jones, Dennis, and Carl Kuttruff, "Prehistoric Enclosures in Louisiana and the Marksville Site," in *Ancient Earthen Enclosures of the Eastern Woodlands*, edited by Robert C. Mainfort Jr. and Lynne P. Sullivan (Gainesville: University Press of Florida, 1998), 31–56; McGimsey, Chip, Katherine M. Roberts, H. Edwin Jackson, and Michael L. Hargrave, "Marksville Then and Now: 75 years of Digging," *Louisiana Archaeology* 26 (2005): 75–98; Toth, Alan, "Archaeology and Ceramics at the Marksville Site," Anthropological Papers No. 56 (Ann Arbor: University of Michigan, Museum of Anthropology, 1974).

Chip McGimsey

PINSON MOUNDS STATE ARCHAEOLOGICAL PARK

Near Jackson, Tennessee

A Middle Woodland Ceremonial and Mortuary Mound Center

The largest Middle Woodland period (dating to about 200 BC–AD 300) archaeological site in the Southeast, Pinson Mounds, is located about 80 miles east of Memphis, Tennessee, near the town of Jackson on the south fork of the

Forked Deer River. Within an area of approximately 400 acres, the site includes at least twelve mounds, an earthen geometric enclosure, and associated ritual activity areas. Of these mounds, five are large, rectangular platforms ranging in height from 8 to 72 feet (Mainfort 1986, 1988; Mainfort and McNutt 1996). The largest, Sauls Mound, is the biggest Middle Woodland mound in the Southeast.

Archaeological excavations conducted on Ozier Mound (Mound 5) in 1981 provided the first unequivocal, well-dated (about AD 100–200) evidence for the construction of rectangular platform mounds during the Middle Woodland period. Such mounds had earlier been thought to be confined to the Mississippi period (post–AD 1000).

This ramped earthwork, approximately 33 feet tall, was constructed in at least six stages, with the summit of each stage covered by a thin layer of pale yellow sand. Copper, mica, and microblades of nonlocal chert were associated with the uppermost mound summit, linking Ozier Mound with ritual activity areas elsewhere at the site. Ozier Mound's size and the repeated renewal of the earthwork by additional construction stages are comparable to characteristics found in later Mississippian flat-topped mounds that supported structures.

Only three burial mounds have been identified at Pinson Mounds. By far the largest of these, the Twin Mounds (Mound 6), are a pair of large, intersecting conical mounds, each about 23 feet tall and 80 feet in diameter. Partial excavation of the northern Twin Mound provided a rare view of a large, undisturbed Middle Woodland burial mound.

At the base of the northern Twin Mound, four log- and/or fabric-covered tombs containing the remains of sixteen adults were found. All human remains were from primary burials; there is no evidence that the excavated tombs served as crypts where bodies were reduced to bones, then removed for reburial. One tomb contained the remains of at least eight relatively young women covered with a large quantity of Marginella beads. Several of these individuals wore fiber headdresses decorated with copper ornaments, as well as necklaces of freshwater pearls. A pair of engraved rattles cut from human skull and decorated with a bird motif in the widespread Hopewellian style were found at the knees of an elderly man. Each rattle contained small quartzite river pebbles. Also found with the burials were a small mica mirror, a schist pendant, and a finely crafted boatstone of green speckled schist.

Constructed between about AD 100 and 200, the northern Twin Mound is the product of a complex sequence of construction events. First a layer of puddled clay (moistened to a thick liquid consistency) was placed over tombs and associated ritual features. A circular, flat-topped primary mound, covered with alternating bands of multicolored earth and sand, was then constructed where the tombs were located. Many sharpened wooden poles were driven into the surface of the primary mound at intervals of about 2 feet. Neither the function nor the significance of these poles is known, but they would have presented annoying obstacles during subsequent mound construction. Separated from the primary mound by a narrow walkway was a low, sand-covered berm that supported a number of large, outslanting posts. Several distinctive layers of soil were then added, covering the primary mound, the

walkway, and the circular berm and raising the northern Twin Mound to its final height.

Off-mound excavations at Pinson Mounds have documented several ritual activity areas, characterized by the presence of large, roughly circular, bent-pole structures—and, in several instances, mortuary features. These include the Cochran site (west of Ozier Mound), the Twin Mounds sector (south of the Twin Mounds), and the Mound 12 sector (northeast of Mound 12). Various nonlocal materials, including copper, mica, galena, and Flint Ridge chert microblades, are associated with these localities, strengthening the case for their use within the ritual sphere rather than for domestic purposes. Excavations in the Duck's Nest sector uncovered no structural remains, but produced portions of forty-seven individual ceramic vessels, at least ten of which are stylistically nonlocal.

Like most large Middle Woodland ceremonial sites, Pinson Mounds was not built by the residents of a single small village or group of villages. The variety of stylistically distinctive pottery types suggests that individuals from as far away as southern Georgia and Louisiana participated in rituals at Pinson Mounds. For example, among the nonlocal pottery shards found in the Duck's Nest sector are examples of Swift Creek Complicated Stamped (a southern Georgia pottery type), McLeod Simple Stamped (pottery commonly found in the Mobile Bay area), limestone-tempered pottery wares (characteristic of the Tennessee River valley to the east), and several other pottery types with no known local counterparts. The presence of nonlocal pottery is expected, since the size and importance of Pinson Mounds was undoubtedly known to Native American groups throughout the Southeast.

The earthen enclosure at Pinson Mounds is one of the few Middle Woodland geometric embankments recorded in the Southeast. Although large expanses of virtually flat topography are present within the earthwork complex, the enclosure (particularly the western half) occupies some of the most precipitous terrain in the area. For approximately 140 degrees of its circumference, the embankment describes a nearly perfect circle with a diameter of about 590 feet, but the remainder of the embankment lies well inside the projection of the implied circle. Mound 29, a ramped platform mound about 10 feet tall and constructed in at least two stages, is located in the southeastern quadrant of the enclosure.

Pinson Mounds has been designated a National Historic Landmark and is managed by the state of Tennessee as an archaeological park. On-site facilities include a visitor center with exhibits and a theater, a large archaeological laboratory, and a collections storage area. Over 6 miles of hiking trails provide access to most major mounds, and an elevated boardwalk offers a view of bottomland ecology.

Further Reading: Anderson, David G., and Robert C. Mainfort Jr., eds., *The Woodland Southeast* (Tuscaloosa: University of Alabama Press, 2002); Kwas, Mary L., "Antiquarians' Perspectives on Pinson

Mounds," *Tennessee Anthropologist* 21 (1996): 83–123; Kwas, Mary L., "Politics and Prehistory: The Making of Pinson Mounds State Archaeological Area," *Tennessee Anthropologist* 22 (1997): 52–71; Mainfort, Robert C., Jr., "Middle Woodland Ceremonialism at Pinson Mounds, Tennessee," *American Antiquity* 53 (1988): 158–173; Mainfort, Robert C., Jr., "Pinson Mounds and the Middle Woodland Period in the Midsouth and Lower Mississippi Valley," in *A View from the Core: A Synthesis of Ohio Hopewell Archaeology*, edited by Paul J. Pacheco (Columbus: Ohio Archaeological Council, 1996),

370–391; Mainfort, Robert C., Jr., and Charles H. McNutt, "Calibrated Radiocarbon Chronology for Pinson Mounds and Middle Woodland in the Midsouth," *Southeastern Archaeology* 23 (2004): 12–24; Pinson Mounds park Web site, www.tennessee.gov/environment/parks/PinsonMounds; Walling, Richard, Robert C. Mainfort Jr., and James Atkinson, "Radiocarbon Dates for the Bynum, Pharr, and Miller Sites, Northeast Mississippi," *Southeastern Archaeology* 10 (1991): 54–62.

Mary L. Kwas and Robert C. Mainfort, Jr.

THE HIWASSEE ISLAND SITE

Southeastern Tennessee

Site of Early Studies at an Important Ancient and Historical Center

Hiwassee Island is in Meigs County at the confluence of the Hiwassee and Tennessee rivers in southeastern Tennessee, about 20 miles north of Chattanooga. Major excavations on the island were conducted from April 1937 to April 1939 by Works Progress Administration (WPA) crews under the direction of archaeologists from the University of Tennessee. These efforts were in conjunction with construction of the Tennessee Valley Authority's (TVA) Chickamauga Dam and Reservoir on the Tennessee River. Hiwassee Island was one of thirteen sites investigated throughout the reservoir area. Thomas M. N. Lewis, an apprentice of W. C. McKern at the Milwaukee Public Museum, was the principal investigator for the project.

In 1938, Madeline D. Kneberg, a physical anthropologist and student of Faye-Cooper Cole at the University of Chicago, joined the team as supervisor of the main laboratory in Knoxville (Sullivan 1999). She became highly influential in the analytical work and in 1946 co-authored with Lewis the report of investigations titled *Hiwassee Island: An Archaeological Account of Four Tennessee Indian Peoples*. Their report was innovative for its time period, because they attempted not only to describe the archaeological deposits and artifacts, but to link these to patterns of human behavior. The report also provides one of the most comprehensive examples of the use of McKern's Midwest Taxonomic Method. Although certainly dated by today's standards, the Hiwassee Island report was a landmark for its time.

The archaeological deposits on Hiwassee Island also provided one of the first regional chronologies in the Southeast, thus laying the foundation for future work in the Tennessee valley and a comparative base for other areas. A significant part of this chronology was based on the stratigraphic

sequence of the large platform mound in the 7- to 8-acre Mississippian-period town on the island. This sequence allowed division of the Mississippian time period into the Hiwassee Island and Dallas phases. The earlier was named for the Hiwassee Island site itself, and the later for the Dallas site, another Mississippian town in the Chickamauga basin. The distinction between these phases still is recognized today as the major division between the Early and Late Mississippian occupations in the upper Tennessee valley, but several refinements have been made in the regional chronology since the WPA work. The dates for the Mississippian phases in the region now are as follows: Martin Farm, AD 900–1100; Hiwassee Island, AD 1100–1300; and Dallas, AD 1300–1550, with the Mouse Creek phase on the Hiwassee River overlapping the latter part of the Dallas phase.

Also noteworthy is the WPA-era investigators' definition of three prehistoric pottery types from shards found on the island, named by archaeologists as Hiwassee Island Red Filmed, Hiwassee Island Red-on-Buff, and Hiwassee Island Complicated Stamped. Hiwassee Island Red on Buff pottery is one of the very few prehistoric ceramic wares from the eastern United States that is painted with colored (red) designs.

THE CULTURAL CONTEXTS OF THE HIWASSEE ISLAND SITE

Late prehistoric occupations from at least the Late Woodland period (AD 600–900) to the historic period, although not continuous, are known to be represented on Hiwassee Island. In general, mounds and mound centers in the Chickamauga basin, like the one on Hiwassee Island, show patterns of use

Excavations of the main, Mississippian period platform mound at Hiwassee Island. Note the multiple summits, building patterns including clay platform, and stepped ramps. [The University of Tennessee Press and the Frank H. McClung Museum, University of Tennessee]

and disuse. The relatively small excavations in residential areas on the island, as opposed to mounds, make it difficult to interpret the extent and nature of those areas through time. A second, possible platform mound in the area of the Mississippian period town also was not investigated. A stockade surrounded the town, but it is not clear when in the town's history it was constructed.

During the Late Woodland period, native people built conical mounds that were used as burial places. At least fifteen were constructed on Hiwassee Island. These burial mounds initially were thought by archaeologists to date solely to the Late Woodland period. Scholars consequently were puzzled by the lack of burials dating to the subsequent Hiwassee Island phase. Radiocarbon dates obtained in the 1970s showed that the burial mounds were used until about AD 1200 (Schroedl et al. 1990). These burial mounds thus were used for several centuries that span the Late Woodland and Early Mississippian periods.

The use of Hiwassee Island during the Martin Farm phase is unconfirmed. During the tenth and eleventh centuries,

native people in the region began building platform mounds. They also made pottery in new shapes that became characteristic of the Mississippian period, but they continued to use limestone tempering in the pottery clay, which was characteristic of the Woodland period.

Construction of the large platform mound began by the twelfth century, as demonstrated by a radiocarbon sample that yielded an early-thirteenth-century date from the fifth major mound construction stage (Sullivan 2007b). This date also indicates that the Hiwassee Island phase component in the mound now dates to the earlier portion of this phase (twelfth though early thirteenth centuries AD) because this mound stage is where Lewis and Kneberg defined the break between the Hiwassee Island and Dallas phases. The Hiwassee Island mound is an excellent example of the elaborate platform mounds native peoples built as substructures for important buildings at this time. The mound included multiple summits with multiple buildings. As during earlier periods, native peoples hunted and collected a diversity of local flora and fauna for food, but their increasing use of

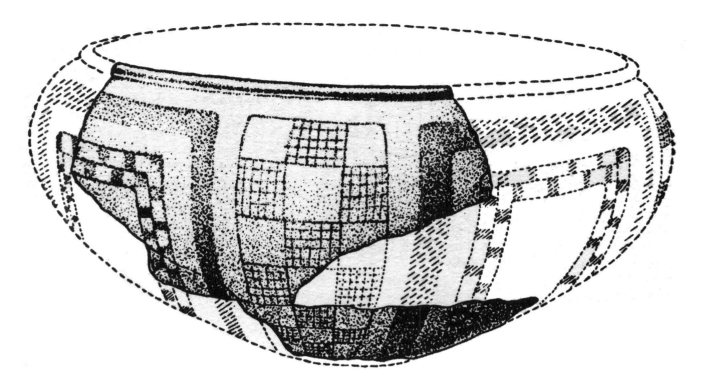

A Hiwassee Island Red on Buff pottery bowl.   [The University of Tennessee Press and the Frank H. McClung Museum, University of Tennessee]

maize likely fueled population growth. Potters began to use shell tempering almost exclusively in pottery, as opposed to the earlier limestone temper. Motifs on complicated stamped pottery from this time period (Hiwassee Island Complicated Stamped) suggest interactions with groups in what is now northern Georgia.

The later part of the Hiwassee Island phase, from the early thirteenth to the fourteenth century AD, is not represented in the Hiwassee Island mound, and there is little other evidence from the site to suggest intensive use at this time. During this phase in the Chickamauga basin, several small mound centers were followed by fewer centers with larger mounds that may have served as focal points for political consolidation of a dispersed population. The Hiwassee Island mound may have fallen into disuse as part of this process. The late Hiwassee Island phase was a time of marked change, characterized by a shift from the conical burial mounds to interments in platform mounds, a marked increase in the use of Hiwassee Island Red Filmed and Red-on-Buff pottery, and the probable predominance of wall trench architecture, as well as a marked increase in elaborate objects once associated with the Southern Cult or Southeastern Ceremonial complex—such as engraved shell gorgets, monolithic axes, and copper ornaments and head-

dresses. None of these elaborate objects were found in the Hiwassee Island mound, and the only shell gorgets found on the island date to the later Dallas phase. The Hixon site, another mound site in the Chickamauga basin, dates primarily to the later part of the Hiwassee Island phase (Sullivan 2007a). The Hixon mound is known for its stratigraphic sequence of a large number of shell gorgets. The nature of interregional relationships among native peoples at this time especially is intriguing and suggests intensified relationships with other regions, as evidenced by trade items (especially marine shell) and iconography.

Use of the Hiwassee Island mound resumed in the early fourteenth century AD, corresponding with the early part of the Dallas phase. Changes at this time were again quite dramatic. The island's residents altered the platform mound to a single summit. Burials were placed in the mound and around and in dwellings in the town below. People also experimented with new pottery styles, including the use of new decorations, such as incising, strap handles, and effigy motifs (referred to as Dallas Decorated). Later during the Dallas phase and elsewhere in the region, people built structures that were supported by large posts; the use of small posts, set in trenches or singly, became obsolete. Only the structures on the uppermost summits of the Hiwassee Island mound were of this style.

It is not clear when the Mississippian-period town was abandoned for the last time. A fifteenth-century Mouse Creek phase occupation is unconfirmed, although Lewis and Kneberg suggested that the pottery found at the very top of the platform mound might date to this phase. Several large towns of this time period were located a few miles farther up the Hiwassee River. These towns included central plazas flanked by large buildings that were not built on mounds, but served as public meeting places or council houses. The historically known Cherokee occupied similar towns until the early nineteenth century.

During the historic period, several Native American burials were interred in the Hiwassee Island mound. The island was last inhabited by native peoples in the late eighteenth and early nineteenth centuries by a small group of Cherokee families. Sam Houston, the famous nineteenth-century politician, lived on the island for a time with Chief John Jolly's (Oolooteeskee) family.

THE EXCAVATIONS AT HIWASSEE ISLAND

Charles Nash, Wendell Walker, and Charles Fairbanks were the supervisory field archaeologists at Hiwassee Island, under Lewis's direction. They provided the daily supervision of the large WPA crews, which sometimes numbered up to 100 workers. A survey and records search of archaeological localities on the island by the WPA team identified at least fifteen conical mounds, several small midden areas, and—on the north end of the island—a large village area with two substructure mounds. The team excavated five of the conical mounds, but the majority of their attention was devoted to investigations of sections of the large Mississippian village—and in particular, the excavation of the entire main substructure mound.

The nature of large southeastern mounds was incompletely understood in the 1930s (Fairbanks 1970, 40–45). The idea that these mounds supported buildings was new, and techniques for excavating this type of mound were being developed. The Hiwassee Island mound was one of the first, if not the first, mounds in North America to be dug using a horizontal-stripping technique. This technique exposed entire summits complete with building patterns, so that it was possible to reconstruct how the mound appeared at various points in time. Plans of multiple buildings on the various summits were exposed, photographed, and mapped. Crews also kept detailed notes and records of artifact proveniences and other features, such as burial and pit features.

THE HIWASSEE ISLAND SITE TODAY

Hiwassee Island is now part of the Hiwassee Wildlife Refuge (http://www.southeasttennessee.com/www/docs/700.1770), where each year thousands of migrating sandhill cranes can

be viewed, as well as highly endangered whooping cranes. In February, the refuge hosts the Annual Cherokee Heritage and Sandhill Crane Days, where attendees can hear lectures about local cultural and natural history (http://www.southeast tennessee.com/www/docs/801.2337/cherokee-heritage-sandhill-crane-days.html).

Adjacent to the refuge is Blythe's Ferry Cherokee Removal Memorial Park (http://www.cherokeeheritage trails.org/redclay_places.html), where thousands of Cherokee emigrants crossed the Tennessee River during the Trail of Tears deportation. Visitors can view outdoor exhibits that chronicle the Cherokee experience. An overlook atop a bluff provides a vista of the former ferry crossing, Chickamauga Lake, Hiwassee Island, and the Hiwassee River Wildlife Refuge. The park is located at the old Tennessee 60 crossing (bypassed by a new bridge installation) of the Hiwassee River, between Cleveland and Dayton, Tennessee.

The collections from the WPA and TVA investigations of Hiwassee Island are curated by the Frank H. McClung Museum at the University of Tennessee. A few artifacts are exhibited in the museum's permanent exhibit, Archaeology and native Peoples of Tennessee (http://mcclungmuseum.utk.edu). Photographs curated by the museum of the WPA excavations can be viewed in an online archive maintained by the University of Tennessee libraries (http://diglib.lib.utk.edu/wpa/index.htm).

Further Reading: Fairbanks, Charles H., "What Do We Know Now That We Did Not Know in 1938?" *Southeastern Archaeological Conference Bulletin* 13 (1970): 40–45; Lewis, Thomas M. N., and Madeline Kneberg, *Hiwassee Island: An Archaeological Account of Four Tennessee Indian Peoples* (Knoxville: University of Tennessee Press, 1946); Lewis, Thomas M. N., Madeline Kneberg Lewis, and Lynne P. Sullivan, comps., eds., *The Prehistory of the Chickamauga Basin in Tennessee*, 2 vols. (Knoxville: University of Tennessee Press, 1995); Schroedl, Gerald F., C. Clifford Boyd Jr., and R. P. Stephen Davis Jr., "Explaining Mississippian Origins in East Tennessee," in *The Mississippian Emergence*, edited by B. D. Smith (Washington DC: Smithsonian Institution Press, 1990), 175–196; Sullivan, Lynne P., "Madeline D. Kneberg Lewis: Leading Lady of Tennessee Archaeology," in *Grit-Tempered: Early Women Archaeologists in the Southeastern United States*, edited by Nancy M. White, L. P. Sullivan, and Rochelle Marrinan, Florida Museum of Natural History, Ripley P. Bullen Series (Gainesville: University Press of Florida, 1999), 57–91; Sullivan, Lynne P., "Dating the Southeastern Ceremonial Complex in Eastern Tennessee," in *Chronology, Iconography, and Style: Current Perspectives on the Social and Temporal Contexts of the Southeastern Ceremonial Complex*, edited by Adam King (Tuscaloosa: University of Alabama Press, 2007a), 88–106; Sullivan, Lynne P., "Archaeological Time Constructs and the Construction of the Hiwassee Island Mound," in *75 Years of TVA Archaeology*, edited by Erin Pritchard and Todd Ahlman (Knoxville: University of Tennessee Press, 2007b).

Lynne P. Sullivan

THE TUNACUNNHEE SITE

Northwest Georgia

Middle Woodland Period Mortuary Architecture and Artifacts

The Tunacunnhee site (9Dd25), a Middle Woodland mound complex and habitation area, is located along Lookout Creek, a tributary of the Tennessee River, in far northwestern Georgia. The mounds were constructed on a slightly elevated limestone outcrop at the base of Lookout Mountain. The associated habitation area is on the Lookout Creek floodplain, several hundred meters southwest of the mound group.

The 1973 University of Georgia Tunacunnhee excavations yielded important information on Middle Woodland mortuary ritual, social organization, and regional exchange and interaction. Artifacts associated with many of the mound burials indicated that local Middle Woodland groups participated in far-reaching regional social networks that involved the exchange of exotic objects (smoking pipes, ear spools, breastplates) and materials (copper, silver, mica) from distant sources. These artifacts are diagnostic of what archaeologists have traditionally called the Hopewell interaction sphere. Investigation of the nearby habitation area disclosed features and artifacts suggesting that some mortuary-related activities took place away from the mounds, reinforcing the idea that the study of mortuary ritual must extend far beyond the actual place of interment.

The Tunacunnhee mound complex consisted of four conical earth and stone mounds and at least two mortuary features placed between them. The mounds ranged from 4 to 12 meters in diameter and from 1 to 2 meters in height. Three mounds (mounds C, D, and E) had earthen cores covered by a mantle of limestone rocks. In contrast, the fourth and largest mound (Mound A) was constructed entirely of limestone rocks. It is difficult to determine the exact number of individuals interred in the four Tunacunnhee mounds, but the total probably falls somewhere between thirty and forty. Uncalibrated radiocarbon dates suggest that mound construction started about AD 100 and continued for 100–200 years.

Construction of the four mortuary structures was a very complex process. The early stages of ritual activity at all four mounds focused on centrally placed submound tombs excavated into the clay subsoil. The best example of this feature type was a rectangular tomb in Mound E that measured approximately 3.1 meters by 2.3 meters and extended about 0.8 meters into the ground. Stains in the tomb wall suggest that once the body was placed in the tomb, it was sealed with logs, then covered with earth.

People buried in the central tombs were usually placed in an extended position and accompanied by a variety of exotic artifacts. Items associated with the Mound E burial included three copper panpipes, two copper ear spools, a polished stone platform pipe, and a very large stone celt. Other central tomb burials were accompanied by numerous copper items, including a silver-covered copper panpipe, breastplates, and ear spools. Also present were a cache of smoking pipes, shark teeth, mica, and a quartz crystal biface.

Many of the burial goods were made from materials that originated far from northwest Georgia. For example, most of the copper came from the Lake Superior region, and the silver originated in Ontario, Canada. The shark teeth came from the Gulf or Atlantic coasts. Based on the energy spent in grave construction and the type, number, and diversity of associated burial goods, people buried in central tombs were probably socially prominent individuals in local or regional Middle Woodland society.

Other people were interred at Tunacunnhee during subsequent stages of mound construction and use. In at least one of the mounds, burials had been placed in shallow pits constructed around its outside margin. Some pits contained the remains of several individuals. Exotic artifacts were occasionally associated with these burials, but not usually in the quantity or variety found with central-mound interments.

Additional burials were placed in the mound fill, along with individual skeletal elements, including an isolated cranium. These individuals had no associated exotic artifacts. In what appears to be the final episode of mortuary activity at Mound C, a stone-lined pit was excavated into the top of the mound.

Excavation between the Tunacunnhee mounds revealed that Middle Woodland people also constructed limestone-filled mortuary features outside the mounds. These pits contained the remains of several individuals. Some had associated burial items, but unlike in many of the mound burials, they appeared to be utilitarian objects, including small stone celts, chert bifaces, and bone awls, made from locally available materials.

Field investigations in the nearby habitation area revealed typical cultural remains expected from a Middle Woodland habitation area—many stone artifacts (flaked and ground) and limestone- and grit-tempered pottery (simple stamped and cord marked). In addition, excavations revealed indications of ritual activity probably associated with mound ceremonialism. This evidence, including both artifacts and features, suggests that some of the activities related to preparing both the dead and the living for the coming mound rituals took place in the habitation area. For example, the remains of a small, circular structure with a central rock-filled hearth appear to represent a sweat lodge. Nearly two thousand years later, some Southeastern Native American groups, like the Creek, used similar kinds of structures for ritual purification, a common practice after dealing with the dead. Also, several pits near the structure yielded small quantities of copper, mica, quartz crystal flakes, and prismatic blades resembling those found with the mound burials.

Mortuary activities that may have taken place in off-mound locations include making ritual objects for placement with the deceased, processing the body before burial, and ritual feasting. Residents and ritual participants may have used the possible sweat lodge for self-purification during and after mortuary rituals.

Study of the Tunacunnhee artifacts has helped provide a clearer picture of the social and economic relationships that existed between Lookout Valley Middle Woodland groups and those that lived in nearby and distant places. The variety of exotic materials represented at Tunacunnhee indicates that the groups that buried their dead in the mounds participated in social networks with ties extending throughout much of eastern North America. Archaeologists have speculated about the meaning of these connections for decades without coming up with a definitive explanation. What is demonstrated is that Lookout Valley groups actively participated in these far-reaching networks and shared ideas about ritual behavior—and probably many other cultural traits—with other nearby and distant societies.

Part of the explanation for why these materials ended up at Tunacunnhee may have to do with the site's location. Tunacunnhee is strategically situated near the juncture of several trail systems that were important avenues of communication and transportation during the early Historic period. The social and economic significance of these trails, as well as the nearby Tennessee River, probably extended far into the past. Middle Woodland groups that lived near this area would have had access to the goods and ideas of people from distant lands as they traveled throughout the Southeast and Midwest along these routes, which later became today's interstate highways. In fact, a modern highway, southbound from Chattanooga, passes near Tunacunnhee shortly after crossing into Georgia. Similar kinds of artifacts and materials found at contemporary sites elsewhere in the southern Appalachian region suggest that many, but not all, Middle Woodland societies also participated in these complex social networks.

Further Reading: Jefferies, Richard W., *The Tunacunnhee Site: Evidence of Hopewell Interaction in Northwest Georgia*, Anthropological Papers of the University of Georgia No. 1 (Athens: University of Georgia, Department of Anthropology, 1976); Jefferies, Richard W., "The Tunacunnhee Site: Hopewell in Northwest Georgia," in *Hopewell Archaeology: The Chillicothe Conference*, edited by David S. Brose and N'omi Greber (Kent, OH: Kent State University Press, 1979), 162–170; Jefferies, Richard W., "Death Rituals at the Tunacunnhee Site: Middle Woodland Mortuary Practices in Northwestern Georgia," in *Recreating Hopewell*, edited by Douglas K. Charles and Jane E. Buikstra (Gainesville: University Press of Florida, 2006), 161–177.

Richard W. Jefferies

THE McKEITHEN SITE

Northern Florida

A Woodland Period Ceremonial and Mortuary Mound Center

The McKeithen site (8CO17) is a Weeden Island–culture mound and village complex in north Florida that dates back to the Middle to Late Woodland period. McKeithen was an important ceremonial center in North Florida related to, although much smaller than, the impressive Kolomoki site in southwest Georgia. Weeden Island sites in north Florida and adjacent parts of the Southeast shared common socioreligious practices, as inferred from mound-related ceremonialism. But Weeden Island sites are perhaps best recognized through a diverse suite of pottery styles characterized by unusual vessel

shapes and diverse and often intricately incised, punctuated, and red-painted decorations. The McKeithen site is no exception, and this site is one of few such Weeden Island sites to have been systematically excavated in modern times.

McKeithen, dated to AD 150–750, is located in western Columbia County, in the thickly forested Middle Florida Hammock Belt. Subsistence was based on making use of rich plant and animal resources of the hammocks and nearby aquatic habitats. Although no evidence of maize horticulture was identified, the site represents an example of a pre-Mississippian

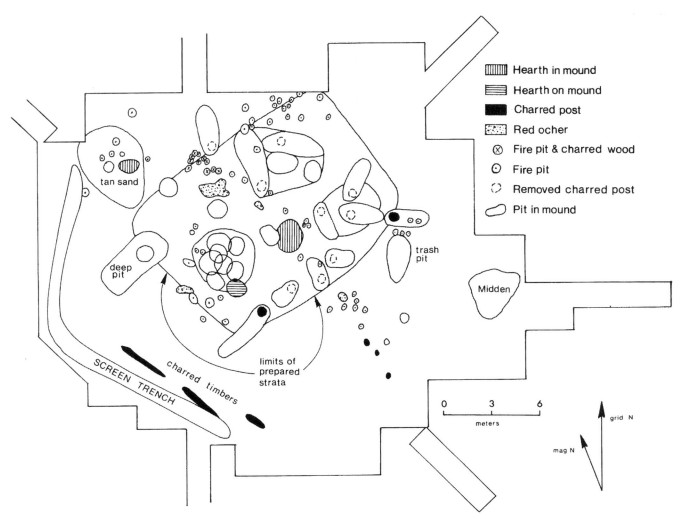

McKeithen Mound A plan showing features. [The Florida Museum of Natural History]

society having a sociopolitical organization between true egalitarian and ranked chiefdom levels.

The site consists of three earthen mounds arranged in an isosceles triangle that is partially encircled by a horseshoe-shaped village midden. This mound-midden arrangement surrounds a plaza area nearly devoid of cultural material. The triangular arrangement of mounds, with Mound B at its apex, may have some significance in terms of astronomical phenomena and for observing the rising sun during the summer solstice. The entire site covers an area of nearly 20 hectares (approximately 50 acres); it was partly excavated in the late 1970s by Jerald T. Milanich and students. Tim Kohler excavated in the village for his Ph.D. dissertation and formulated a three-phase chronology for its occupation. Other dissertations, master's theses, or student papers contributed to the body of data on McKeithen and north Florida Weeden Island in general—for example, Brenda Sigler-Lavelle on settlement

patterning; Ann Cordell on the McKeithen pottery; G. Michael Johnson on lithics; and Vernon J. Knight on symbolism of the pottery iconography.

Milanich's excavations revealed that the three mounds—two platform mounds (A and B) and one burial mound (C)—were contemporaneous and had different functions. Mound A was a platform mound with numerous randomly placed large postholes and pits, a central hearth, many smaller fire pits, two refuse deposits containing hundreds of shards from at least twenty-seven vessels, and pieces of deer bone. Most of the pottery represents utilitarian wares, with stamped and relatively simple incised or punctated decorations. Milanich and colleagues interpreted the mound as a locus for charnel activities in which the dead were macerated and prepared for burial. An alternative explanation is that Mound A functioned as a platform for community gatherings and ritual feasting rather than mortuary activities. This interpretation is based on more

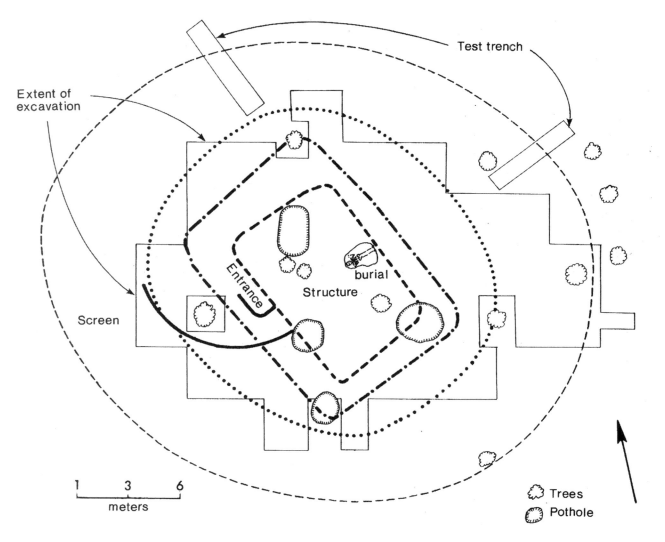

McKeithen Mound B plan.   [The Florida Museum of Natural History]

recent excavations of similar Middle Woodland platform mounds in the Southeast.

Mound B was also a platform mound, but it contained remnants of a structure believed to have been the residence of an important woman in the community, a religious specialist or big-man—big-woman in this case. She was interred in a shallow grave dug into the house floor. The house floor also yielded several interesting Weeden Island zoned red plate forms and a pottery bird head. This zoned red painted pottery is included among types (along with intricately incised and punctated styles) that are considered prestige wares on the basis of the time and effort expended in making them, and because some pots were made of clays that were not local to McKeithen and the north Florida region.

Mound C was a conical burial mound. While badly disturbed by looters, it retained evidence of a charnel structure on top, a bundled interment of at least thirty-six people, and an east side cache of Kolomoki-style effigy pots and prestigious, intricately decorated Weeden Island incised pots with appliquéd bird heads. The unusual animal effigy forms, often red slipped or painted, are considered cult or mortuary wares, as they occur exclusively in mortuary contexts. The animals depicted are believed to have ritual significance as symbols of proper behavior, impropriety, and mediation in life and death.

Radiocarbon dates place the time of construction and use of the McKeithen mounds between about AD 350 and 475. This coincides with Kohler's middle phase of village occupation, AD 250–550. At McKeithen, Cordell's analysis involving direct comparison with local clay samples has shown that

Weeden Island Zoned Red pottery from Mound B (FLMNH accession 80-12).   [The Florida Museum of Natural History]

most of the utilitarian pottery and some of the zoned red painted and slipped prestige and mortuary ceramics were made locally.

Evidence for some degree of ranking or status differentiation at McKeithen during this time is inferred from the abundance and nonrandom distribution of prestige pottery and nonlocal lithics in the village, as well as the special treatment given to the woman buried in the structure on Mound B. This individual would likely have been in charge of coordinating ritual and mortuary activities carried out at Mounds A and C. She was in her early to mid-thirties when she died. A small stone arrow point was found embedded in her hip bone. She is thought to have been shot with the arrow at least several months before her death, based on the amount of bone reaction in the vicinity of the injury. Her importance at McKeithen is supported by skeletal isotopic data that distinguishes her from the local north Florida population. Carbon and oxygen

stable isotope analyses of teeth from this individual and others from Mound C indicate that she was an immigrant to McKeithen, probably as a young adult. The isotopic signature from Mound C skeletons is consistent with a subsistence regimen proposed for the region. In contrast, the Mound B woman appears to have come from an area where maize and/or marine foods played a greater role in the diet.

Excavations at McKeithen culminated in the 1984 publication of the McKeithen Weeden Island volume, which was republished as *The Archaeology of North Florida* in 1997. The site and its artifacts are still of great interest to researchers studying Woodland mounds, settlement and exchange patterns, and the emergence of social complexity. Although the site is not open to the public, the pottery and other excavated artifacts are stored at the Florida Museum of Natural History (http://www.flmnh.ufl.edu/flarch), University of Florida, Gainesville.

Mound C vessels: Weeden Island Red turkey vulture effigy with incising and cut-outs (upper left; FLMNH A-20086); Weeden Island Plain four-headed effigy (upper right; FLMNH A-10952); Weeden Island Incised "wing-nut" pot with appliquéd roseate spoonbill heads (lower; FLMNH A-20094).   [The Florida Museum of Natural History]

Further Reading: Cordell, Ann S., *Ceramic Technology at a Weeden Island Period Site in North Florida*, Ceramic Notes No. 2, Occasional Publications of the Ceramic Technology Laboratory (Florida State Museum, 1984); Knight, Vernon James, "Feasting and the Emergence of Platform Mound Ceremonialism in Eastern North America," in *Feasts: Archaeological and Ethnographic Perspectives on Food, Politics, and Power*, edited by Michael Dielter and Brian Hayden (Washington DC: Smithsonian Institution Press, 2001), 311–333; Kohler, Tim A., "The Social and Chronological Dimensions of Village Occupation at a North Florida Weeden Island Period Site," Ph.D. diss. (University of Florida, 1978); Milanich, J. T., A. S. Cordell, V. J. Knight Jr., T. A. Kohler, and B. J. Sigler-Lavelle, *McKeithen Weeden Island: The Culture of Northern Florida A.D. 200–900* (New York: Academic Press, 1984), reprinted with new foreword as *Archaeology of Northern Florida A.D. 200–900: The McKeithen Weeden Island Culture* (Gainesville: University Press of Florida, 1997); Pluckhahn, Thomas J., *Kolomoki: Settlement, Ceremony, and Status, AD 300–750* (Tuscaloosa: University of

Alabama Press, 2003); Turner, Bethany L., John D. Kingston, and Jerald T. Milanich, "Isotopic Evidence of Immigration Linked to Status During the Weeden Island and Suwannee Valley Periods in North Florida," *Southeastern Archaeology* 24 (2005): 121–136; Willey,

Gordon R., *Archaeology of the Florida Gulf Coast*, Smithsonian Miscellaneous Collections, No. 113 (Washington, DC: Smithsonian Institution, 1949).

Ann S. Cordell

BYNUM MOUNDS SITE

Natchez Trace Parkway, Northeastern Mississippi
Middle Woodland Mortuary Mounds and Village Complex

Located in the Pontotoc Hills of northeastern Mississippi near a minor tributary of the Tombigbee River, the Bynum mound group is one of several important Middle Woodland period (about 200 BC–AD 300) mortuary sites in the upper Tombigbee drainage. Included within an area of roughly 20 acres were six conical burial mounds ranging in height from about 1.5 to 4.2 meters, as well as an extensive early Middle Woodland occupation area. Five mounds were excavated in the late 1940s, two of which (Mounds E and F) had been largely destroyed and yielded little information.

The remains of several roughly circular bent-pole houses, as well as numerous post molds and pits, were identified in excavations of the 7-acre village area, and it is clear that many others were at least partially exposed. The large size of these structures, which had diameters of greater than 20 meters, as well as the lack of associated hearths and storage pits, indicates that they represent specialized buildings associated with ritual activities, not domestic houses. Supporting this interpretation was the discovery of a small piece of copper, several lumps of galena, and a fancy pottery vessel (Marksville Stamped style) decorated with a raptorial bird motif in the occupation area.

Mound A, which measured slightly over 3 meters in height, covered a low, earthen platform that had been substantially damaged by a modern house cellar. At the base of the mound, below the platform, were two burned, parallel oak logs flanking the extended skeleton of an adult female with a bicymbal copper ear spool at both wrists. Also associated with this grave were three human cremations—two slightly flexed adults and a child—represented by only fragments of bone.

Mound B, with a height of 4.2 meters and a diameter of approximately 20 meters, was the largest of the Bynum earthworks. At the base, excavations exposed the remains of a mortuary house with a sunken floor, measuring approximately 11.5 meters by 9.1 meters. The exterior of the depressed floor was lined with small saplings. Sixteen large posts were identified within the depression, but their shallow depth makes it unlikely that they supported a heavy roof. Within the ashes on the pit floor were horizontal log molds, interpreted as a rectangular framework. A shallow pit with a burned interior, perhaps used for cremations, was located near the center of the building.

An L-shaped row of twenty-nine polished greenstone celts (ax heads) and three secondary human cremations were located on top of the ash deposits, while the remains of an adult male, buried in an extended position, were found near the eastern edge. Also associated with the structure floor were two pairs of copper bicymbal ear spools, two fragments of whelk shell (*Busycon perversum*) from the gulf coast, and nineteen Gibson- or Norton-type projectile points that appear to be imported from the Illinois River valley. All of them were placed within the remains of the structure after it had burned. A piece of galena was found below the exterior saplings, outside the sunken floor of the mortuary house. Mound stratigraphy suggests that construction was completed as a single event. Radiocarbon dating indicates that Bynum Mounds A and B were roughly contemporary and dated to the second century BC.

Mound D, a small, conical earthwork measuring about 1.8 meters tall, covered a small mortuary facility consisting of a sunken rectangular floor with a fired circular pit near the center and four large posts outside the structure floor. Several fragments of human tooth enamel were found just below the rim of the pit. Associated artifacts included a copper ear spool, a rolled copper bead, and a greenstone celt. The structural remains probably represent a rectangular canopy covering the fire pit.

The Bynum Mounds site is located on the Natchez Trace Parkway, about 30 miles southwest of Tupelo, Mississippi. The site is open to the public daily at no charge. The two largest mounds have been rebuilt for viewing.

Further Reading: Anderson, David G., and Robert C. Mainfort Jr., eds., *The Woodland Southeast* (Tuscaloosa: University of Alabama Press, 2002); Bynum Mounds Web site, www.cr.nps.gov/nr/travel/mounds/byn.htm; Cotter, John L., and John M. Corbett, *The*

Archaeology of the Bynum Mounds, Mississippi, Archaeological Research Series No. 1 (Washington, DC: United States Department of the Interior, National Park Service, 1951); Mainfort, Robert C., Jr., "Pinson Mounds and the Middle Woodland Period in the Midsouth and Lower Mississippi Valley," in *A View from the Core: A Synthesis of Ohio Hopewell Archaeology*, edited by Paul J. Pacheco (Columbus: Ohio Archaeological Council, 1996), 370–391; Mainfort, Robert C., Jr.,

and Charles H. McNutt, "Calibrated Radiocarbon Chronology for Pinson Mounds and Middle Woodland in the Midsouth," *Southeastern Archaeology* 23 (2004): 12–24; Walling, Richard, Robert C. Mainfort Jr., and James Atkinson, "Radiocarbon Dates for the Bynum, Pharr, and Miller Sites, Northeast Mississippi," *Southeastern Archaeology* 10 (1991): 54–62.

Robert C. Mainfort and Mary L. Kwas

KOLOMOKI MOUNDS STATE HISTORIC PARK

Southwestern Georgia

A Large Woodland Period Village and Earthen Mound Complex

Kolomoki is one of the largest prehistoric mound complexes in the eastern United States. The site is located in southwestern Georgia, on a small tributary of the Chattahoochee River. Most of the site is now protected as part of Kolomoki Mounds State Historic Park, operated by the Georgia Department of Natural Resources.

The Smithsonian Institution conducted excavations at Kolomoki in the late 1800s. Large-scale excavations were led by archaeologist William Sears from 1948 to 1953. Sears believed that the site dated to the Mississippian period (AD 1000–1600), when flat-topped structures such as Kolomoki's Mound A were built throughout the Southeast. However, recent work by Thomas Pluckhahn has validated the long-held suspicion that the main occupation at Kolomoki actually dates to the preceding Woodland period. At the time of its highest development during the Middle and Late Woodland periods, from around AD 350 to 750, Kolomoki was perhaps one of the most populous settlements north of Mexico.

The Kolomoki site includes eight preserved mounds. The largest of these, Mound A, is a flat-topped pyramid about 56 feet in height. Limited archaeological excavations on the summit and flanks of Mound A failed to divulge its function. There was no definitive evidence that the mound supported a structure like a temple or chief's residence, as was the case for similar mounds from later periods.

Immediately to the west of Mound A is a large, open plaza. Recent test excavations indicate that this area was kept free of debris, probably for use in ceremonies. The plaza at Kolomoki would have been large enough to accommodate hundreds of people.

Mounds B and C, which flank Mound A to the south and north (respectively), each consist of small, dome-shaped constructions. Excavation in Mound C revealed the remnants of large wooden posts that were probably used in religious ceremonies. Mound B appears to have been constructed of sweepings from the plaza.

Mounds D and E stand opposite Mound A, forming a line to the west. These mounds served as burial repositories. Each of the two mounds included large caches of ceramic vessels, some elaborately decorated in the forms of animals and people. The ceramic caches were deposited on the eastern sides of the mounds, presumably during mortuary rites. Mound D contained the remains of nearly 100 individuals, including extended burials in rock-lined graves, cremations, and isolated crania (skulls). Several of the burials in Mounds D and E included artifacts associated with the Hopewell culture of the Midwest, including copper and meteoric iron discs. Mica ornaments, shell beads, and stone celts also accompanied some of the burials.

Finally, Mounds G, F, and H are small, flat-topped mounds. Excavations in the latter two mounds indicated that they served as platforms or stages, probably for ceremonial occasions. Mound G was used as a cemetery during the nineteenth century and has never been investigated archaeologically.

Historical accounts suggest that several more mounds were formerly present at Kolomoki. In addition, there are descriptions of a low, discontinuous earthen embankment encircling the site. Such earthen enclosures, presumably constructed for ritual rather than defensive purposes, are common on Hopewell sites in the Midwest, but relatively rare in the Southeast. The enclosure at Kolomoki, as well as these other mounds mentioned in historical accounts, appears to have been plowed away during the late nineteenth and early twentieth centuries, when the site was extensively cultivated.

Archaeological investigations indicate that Kolomoki was the location of an extensive settlement. During the first half of the occupation, from around AD 350 to 550, the village took the form of a large oval, centered on the plaza and roughly continuous with the reported enclosure. Based on the size of the village, a population in the range of 200 to 400 has been estimated. In the second half of the occupation, the

View to the east of mounds D (lower left foreground) and A (center background) at Kolomoki.   [Thomas J. Pluckhahn]

village was smaller and less formally defined. The population may have been only half that of earlier phases. By around AD 750, Kolomoki was abandoned.

Kolomoki Mounds State Historic Park is open year-round. A small museum shows the interior of Mound E as it was left after excavation. Interpretive exhibits provide background information on the site.

Further Reading: Pluckhahn, Thomas J., *Kolomoki: Settlement, Ceremony, and Status in the Deep South, A.D. 350 to 750*

(Tuscaloosa: University of Alabama Press, 2003); Milanich, Jerald T., et al., *McKeithen Weeden Island: The Culture of Northern Florida, A.D. 200–900* (New York: Academic Press, 1984); Sears, William H., *Excavations at Kolomoki: Final Report* (Athens: University of Georgia Press, 1956); Trowell, Christopher, "A Kolomoki Chronicle: The History of a Plantation, a State Park, and the Archaeological Search for Kolomoki's Prehistory," *Early Georgia* 26(1) (1998): 12–81; Williams, Mark, and Daniel T. Elliott, eds., *A World Engraved: Archaeology of the Swift Creek Culture* (Tuscaloosa: University of Alabama Press, 1998).

Thomas J. Pluckhahn

THE KEY MARCO SITE

Ten Thousand Islands, Southwest Florida Coast

Early Archaeological Investigations and Spectacular Artifact Finds

The Key Marco site is one of the most important archeological discoveries ever found in North America. Located on a small mangrove island at the northern end of the Ten Thousand Islands in southwest Florida, the site was inadvertently discovered in 1896, when locals, digging in a mangrove pond for garden muck, unearthed unusually well-preserved prehistoric wooden artifacts. The artifacts attracted the attention of Frank Hamilton Cushing, an archaeologist at the Bureau of American Ethnology at the Smithsonian Institution, who proceeded to the site, conducted excavations in the muck, and recovered a unique and artistically rich assemblage of objects that have astounded scientists for generations.

Typically, organic materials, including wood, decay quickly and are not preserved in archaeological deposits. However, within the anaerobic (lacking atmospheric oxygen) muck pond of Key Marco, beautifully carved and painted wooden ceremonial and utilitarian objects, rope, netting, cordage, and fishing nets with float pegs survived in excellent condition. Along with shell tools and ceramics, this archeological assemblage is one of North America's most complete and well-preserved collections and has provided scientists an invaluable opportunity to study a rarely seen prehistoric material culture.

Cushing's expedition to Key Marco brought him by boat along the southwest Florida coast, where he explored many of the remote keys, describing them as "artificial shell islands" because they contained enormous, complicated shell work sites on islands completely built of shell. Along other parts of the coast of the southeastern United States, such human-made shell enclosures and mounds also are found. Cushing noted that many of these shell work sites consisted of similar layouts and features, including water courts, canals, and mounds.

Upon reaching Key Marco, he described the key as an isolated island situated in open water, containing complex, architectural arrangements of shell deposits, including numerous mounds, canals, court-like landings, water courts, ponds, elevated walkways, and protective seawalls. The site contained a central canal dividing the site, as well as an 18-foot-high flat-topped mound that probably supported a chiefly residence or a temple that housed the bones of important ancestors. Many of these prehistoric features were depicted in a detailed topographic map of the site produced by Wells Sawyer, the expedition's artist and photographer.

Over two seasons Cushing excavated the central muck pond of the site, naming it the Court of the Pile Dwellers after recovering the remains of wooden pilings around shell benches extending into the muck. Cushing thought these piers were from structures such as scaffold dwellings or foundations for pile-supported quays that held long, narrow, low thatched houses. The central muck pond was believed to have been a water court filled via an inlet canal. The numerous shell benches surrounding the water court functioned as canoe landings, docks, or structures related to scaffold dwellings. Over and around these shell benches, Cushing recovered many household articles, as well as other construction materials, including thatch roofing material and timbers. Based on finding groups of utilitarian artifacts together, along with bundles of ceremonial objects and housing material, Cushing thought that the scaffold buildings must have collapsed into the pond during a destructive storm or fire, devastating the site in one catastrophic event.

Through Cushing's excavations, many rare and unusual prehistoric artifacts were uncovered—mostly wooden utilitarian

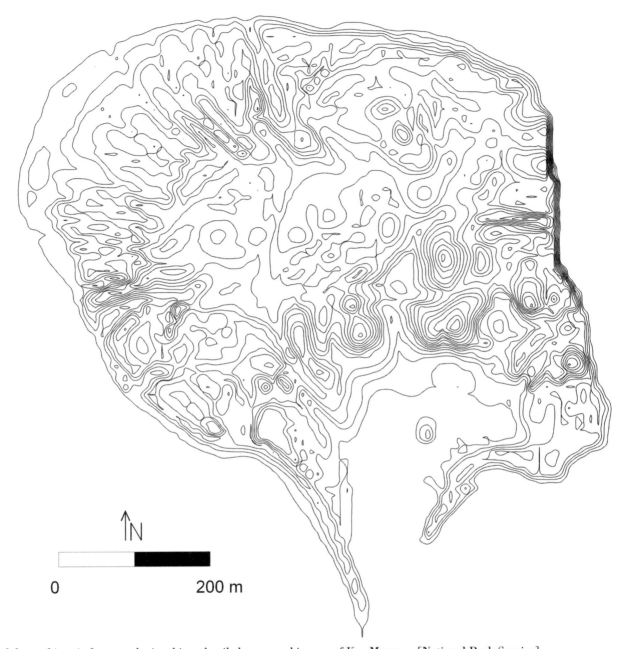

Many of the prehistoric features depicted in a detailed topographic map of Key Marco.   [National Park Service]

objects, such as wood bowls, mortars and pestles, cups, benches, and clubs, as well as ceremonial items, such as wooden masks. Many objects were painted with black, white, grayish blue, and brownish red pigments. Once the intricately painted wooden objects were exposed to air, they often deteriorated rapidly, although fortunately many of them were photographed and painted by Sawyer.

Cushing's 1896 excavation only covered a small part of the whole Key Marco site. Unfortunately, most of the Key Marco site has since been destroyed by modern development in the years since his discovery. However, portions of the site remain partially intact, buried underneath the modern streets and buildings of Marco Island. Additional work over the years has also added to our interpretation of the ancient inhabitants of Key Marco and when and how they constructed such complex shell work sites and crafted such beautiful artifacts.

Not all archaeologists agree about the exact date of the Key Marco occupation. Mostly this is because the site was not excavated using modern archaeological methods, so there are questions about the provenience of artifacts from the muck pond. Nevertheless, prehistoric ceramics, as well as several radiocarbon dates, suggest that the site was occupied by a Woodland culture referred to as Glades, which dates between AD 110 and AD 1670. This was a nonagricultural culture with broad adaptive strategies for the subtropical wetlands and coasts of south Florida. The members of the Glades culture took advantage of the wild plant and animal foods in their natural environment for sustenance and to create their tools, crafts, and artwork.

At the time of historic contact, all of south Florida was dominated by the Calusa tribe, a sedentary, socially stratified, and complex nonagricultural chiefdom whose subsistence was based solely on marine resources. The Calusa chiefs had influence over some fifty to seventy towns in south Florida, all of which paid tribute to the tribe, whose political center was north of Key Marco. Although the Calusa were the dominant tribe over south Florida at the time of contact, it is not known whether the Ten Thousand Islands sites, including Key Marco, were part of the Calusa chiefdom or were a separate but affiliated tribe.

Key Marco, like other large shell work sites in the Ten Thousand Islands region, was likely a Woodland period regional center. These sites typically contain platform mounds for the houses of important individuals, finger ridges that served as docking areas or habitation locales, plazas for public meetings or rituals, mounds isolated from the main settlement and reserved for sacred functions, and a variety of canals, ponds, and seawalls. Key Marco, as well as other such sites in southwest Florida, suggests a high level of social complexity, based on the great construction efforts and organized leadership necessary for planning and executing large public works.

The artifacts from Cushing's investigation are preserved and curated at three museums: the Smithsonian Institution's National Museum of Natural History, the University Museum of the University of Pennsylvania, and the Florida Museum of Natural History.

Further Reading: Cushing, Frank H., *Exploration of Ancient Key-Dweller Remains on the Gulf Coast of Florida* (Gainesville: University Press of Florida, 2000); Gilliland, Marion S., *Key Marco's Buried Treasure: Archaeology and Adventure in the Nineteenth Century* (Gainesville: University of Florida Press, 1975); Gilliland, Marion S., *The Material Culture of Key Marco, Florida* (Port Salerno: Florida Classics Library, 1989); Kolianos, Phyllis E., and Brent R. Weisman, *The Florida Journals of Frank Hamilton Cushing* (Gainesville: University of Florida Press, 2001); Kolianos, Phyllis E., and Brent R. Weisman. *The Lost Florida Manuscript of Frank Hamilton Cushing* (Gainesville: University Press of Florida, 2005); Widmer, Randolph J., *The Evolution of the Calusa* (Tuscaloosa: University of Alabama Press, 1988).

Margo Schwadron

THE LAKE GEORGE SITE

The Yazoo River Basin, West Central Mississippi
The Development of a Large Earthen Mound Center

The Lake George site is a late prehistoric multi-mound center that is located at the western edge of Yazoo County, in the Yazoo basin region of west central Mississippi. The Yazoo basin is an alluvial floodplain of the Mississippi River and is acknowledged as one of the richest agricultural areas in the entire country. It is also exceedingly rich in prehistoric archaeological sites. The largest of these sites is Lake George, which was built during the peak of aboriginal development in the basin.

The general vicinity of the Lake George site reveals a long sequence of prehistoric occupations. Beginning at least by 2000 BC, peoples of the Poverty Point culture had taken up residence in the area. This widespread culture is distinguished by the fine lithic technology utilized by its members, who often made use of exotic stones from distant sources, and by a system of food preparation that utilized fired clay balls that they heated for cooking. Pottery was introduced shortly thereafter, about 2,500 years ago, as part of the Tchefuncte culture, and these people also briefly occupied the site. Shortly after that, about 2,000 years ago, the Marksville variation of the famous Hopewell culture made an appearance. That variation was, in turn, followed by components of a local culture known as Baytown.

Although there may have been some movement of earth at the site earlier, the first real mound building at Lake George occurred about AD 800, when people of a strong, new, local cultural development, referred to as Coles Creek by archaeologists, began their occupation. The earliest mound was a platform that supported a structure on its summit. This was the beginning of the late prehistoric temple mound tradition in

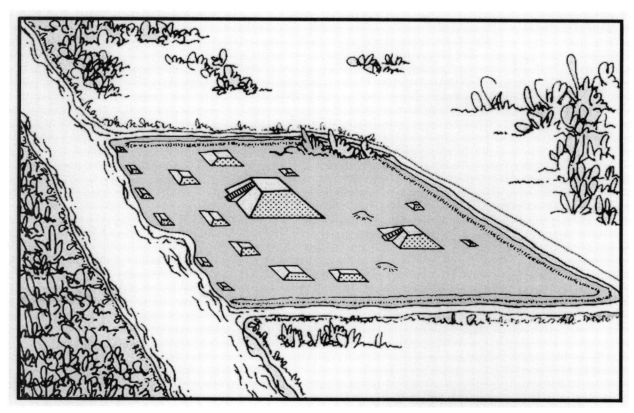

The Lake George site, ca. AD 1400.   [Jeffrey P. Brain]

this part of the Mississippi valley. Throughout the last centuries of the first millennium AD, several additional mounds were constructed around a central plaza. The site covered only a few hectares (one hectare equals 2.471 acres) and the mounds were relatively small; none more than a half dozen meters in height. Not all of the buildings placed on top of these mounds were temples. Some of the buildings atop the mounds may have been used for other public functions, while some were residences for the elite elements of society. Otherwise, few people lived at Lake George.

The Coles Creek peoples practiced a corn-based agriculture supplemented by the rich natural food resources of the Mississippi valley. There is some debate among archaeologists familiar with this period of time about whether natural food resources were supplemental or the main source of food, supplemented by the corn. In any case, the people of the Coles Creek culture clearly had achieved a comfortable existence that was finely tuned to their environment. Their material culture was characterized by a plain clay pottery and few stone artifacts.

This modest development, however, changed around AD 1200. New influences suddenly appeared at the site, and a program of large-scale public works in the form of earthen architecture was initiated. Within a generation, or two at most, dozens of additional mounds were built around a double plaza

dominated by a huge central mound that was twenty meters high and covered a couple of hectares. The entire site grew to more than 20 hectares and was surrounded by a palisaded embankment on three sides (the fourth fronted a natural lake). The staggering amount of earthwork construction and emphasis on a great focal mound represented a major departure from the native Coles Creek ceremonial center. It was, however, characteristic of a dynamic new development influencing most of the midwestern and southeastern United States at this time, called Mississippian.

Mississippian actually was not a unified culture, but a series of innovations in ways of life, including subsistence, social and political structure, economic and trade relations, and probably ceremonial activities. These are manifested in an intensive corn-bean-squash agriculture, the political and social control to effect large public-works programs, the exchange of exotic materials and finished artifacts over great distances, and new religious symbols. Many local peoples adopted these innovations and participated in what might be called the Mississippian co-prosperity sphere during the last 500 years or so before European contact. The Coles Creek people at Lake George participated in this new Mississippian world.

What prompted the strong Mississippian influence of local populations can, in this instance, even be identified. During the twelfth century, the greatest Mississippian site—in fact, the largest prehistoric site in all of the United States—was Cahokia, in west-central Illinois near the confluence of the Mississippi and Missouri rivers. This center had some form of contact with distant peoples, and its influences were felt far and wide, even into the southern part of the Mississippi valley and the Yazoo basin. We can be certain of at least some contact with Cahokia, because stone and pottery artifacts distinctive of that center and its environs have been found in archaeological excavations at Lake George and nearby sites—for example, the Winterville site—dating to about 1200, just at the beginning of the great program of mound construction.

Lake George flourished for another two centuries and was certainly the center of a large population descended from the local Coles Creek peoples. In keeping with the earlier tradition, however—and quite different from other contemporary Mississippian sites, such as Cahokia—the Lake George site had only a small resident population; hence, it remained a largely vacant ceremonial center used periodically by people living in smaller settlements in the immediately surrounding area.

By the middle of the fifteenth century, Lake George was abandoned. In its place, several smaller mound sites scattered around the Yazoo basin assumed whatever functions it had fulfilled. It is not known why this change occurred, but it was not due to population collapse, for the Yazoo remained one of the most densely inhabited regions in the country well into the sixteenth century.

Further Reading: Brain, Jeffrey P., "Late Prehistoric Settlement Patterning in the Yazoo Basin and Natchez Bluffs Regions of the Lower Mississippi Valley," in *Mississippian Settlement Patterns*, edited by Bruce D. Smith (New York: Academic Press, 1978), 331–368; Williams, Stephen, and Jeffrey P. Brain, *Excavations at the Lake George Site, Yazoo County, Mississippi, 1958–1960*, Peabody Museum of Archaeology and Ethnology Papers, Vol. 74 (Cambridge, MA: Harvard University, 1983).

Jeffrey P. Brain

THE WINTERVILLE SITE

The Yazoo River Basin, Mississippi

Ancient Earthen Mound Complex with Wide Cultural Connections

The Winterville site is a late prehistoric multi-mound center located in the Yazoo basin of Mississippi in the county of Washington. It is 6.5 kilometers north of the city of Greenville, 1.5 kilometers south of the small village of Winterville, and 5 kilometers east of the present channel of the Mississippi River.

Winterville was first settled during the eleventh century by peoples of the Coles Creek culture. Coles Creek had developed in the southern part of the lower Mississippi valley during the later centuries of the first millennium AD. This culture practiced corn agriculture, which was supplemented by the rich aquatic and terrestrial resources of the Mississippi River and its valley. A secure subsistence base enabled the Coles Creek people to employ some of their communal energies in the construction of regional ceremonial centers, which dramatically impacted the landscape with one or more earthen mounds. These were platform mounds—that is, they were primarily used as platforms on top of which buildings were constructed. This was the beginning of the temple mound tradition. It is probable that not all the buildings on top of the mounds were temples in the usual sense, however. Some of these buildings may have been used for such standard religious purposes as to sacrifice or pray to supernatural beings, while others may have been charnel houses, where the remains of revered ancestors were kept. Some were almost certainly houses for the living social elite. The latter may well have had priestly functions, and so it is reasonable to conclude that all of the activities at the centers revolved around ceremonial matters.

The mounds averaged a few meters in height; when there were more than one, they were arranged around a plaza, thus defining the ceremonial center. The entire site was rarely more than a few hectares (one hectare equals 2.471 acres) in extent. The most common artifacts found at these centers and at Coles Creek hamlets and farmsteads are pottery shards from a well-made ware exhibiting very simple decoration. Stone and bone tools are present, but relatively uncommon. No Coles Creek burials have been found at Winterville, but at other contemporary sites, mortuary practices include human burials in mounds (perhaps those atop which charnel houses were built). Skeletal remains found in these mounds sometimes are articulated in formal burials; other times individual bones are disarticulated and are rarely accompanied by grave goods.

The Winterville site, AD 1400.   [Jeffrey P. Brain]

The Coles Creek people who settled Winterville in the eleventh century were pioneers. They represented the northernmost outpost of the Coles Creek culture within the lower Mississippi valley. In this exposed position, they were strongly influenced by a new cultural tradition, the Mississippian, that had been developing in the central Mississippi valley and was centered at the great site of Cahokia. Cahokia was the largest mound site in prehistoric America north of Mexico. At its height of development, in the twelfth century, Cahokia was in contact with broad reaches of the continent, and it greatly influenced much of the midwestern and southern portions of the present United States. During the later twelfth century, those new influences penetrated the lower Mississippi valley and began to impact the Coles Creek culture. Because of its location, Winterville would have received the brunt of Cahokia contact and would have been among the first to be affected.

Around AD 1200, Winterville manifested a series of changes related to contact with Cahokia that transformed the site. The most obvious change was a commitment to major earthen architecture projects. The modest Coles Creek mounds were buried beneath thick, new mantles of earth and served as foundations for larger earthen structures, and many new mounds and other earthworks were added to the site.

These were arranged around a double plaza, at the intersection of which was placed a great mound that was more than fifteen meters in height. This emphasis upon a large central mound as the focal point of the site is distinctly different from the Coles Creek pattern but quite characteristic of the Mississippian tradition.

The source of this inspiration is manifested by pottery and stone artifacts from Cahokia or its environs that have been found at Winterville. Also introduced at this time was the use of ground mussel shell as a tempering agent in the manufacture of pottery, which was decorated with many new techniques and more elaborate designs than had been characteristic of the Coles Creek culture. It is probable that the already naturally rich subsistence base was augmented by new domesticated resources—perhaps superior varieties of corn.

In spite of all the new influences and activities, Winterville remained essentially a vacant center in the Coles Creek sense. That is, it seems that few people actually lived at the site, and presumably those continued to be an elite segment who were responsible for the proper functioning of the society and its ceremonial activities. As before, some of these people were interred in the mounds, but an important change in mortuary customs is evident, as the burials were accompanied by pottery vessels, tools, and other personal effects.

The people of Winterville were also interacting closely with their neighbors to the south, in the Yazoo basin. Most important of these was the nearly identical site of Lake George, which was undergoing a similar transformation at this same time. Both sites were at the height of their development in the thirteenth and fourteenth centuries and were clearly the centers for a large and prosperous population. At this time, the resident elites at Winterville and Lake George were in contact with other regions in the Mississippi valley and beyond. Evidence of contact with Cahokia, however, disappears, as that great site had fallen into decline. Then, early in the fifteenth century, Winterville and Lake George were abandoned. Their place was taken by many smaller mound centers, which may indicate a fragmentation of power. The population of the Yazoo basin remained strong, however, and continued to participate in late prehistoric developments within and beyond the Mississippi valley.

Further Reading: Brain, Jeffrey P., "Late Prehistoric Settlement Patterning in the Yazoo Basin and Natchez Bluffs Regions of the Lower Mississippi Valley," in *Mississippian Settlement Patterns*, edited by Bruce D. Smith (New York: Academic Press, 1978), 331–368; Brain, Jeffrey P., *Winterville: Late Prehistoric Culture Contact in the Lower Mississippi Valley*, Archaeological Report No. 23 (Jackson: Mississippi Department of Archives and History, 1989); Williams, Stephen, and Jeffrey P. Brain, *Excavations at the Lake George Site, Yazoo County, Mississippi, 1958–1960*, Peabody Museum of Archaeology and Ethnology Papers, vol. 74 (Cambridge, MA: Harvard University, 1983).

Jeffrey P. Brain

MOUNDVILLE ARCHAEOLOGICAL PARK

West Central Alabama
The Second-Largest Ancient Mound Complex North of Mexico

Moundville, the second-largest mound center north of Mexico, was the capital of a Mississippian chiefdom. The site is spread over 300 acres on a high terrace overlooking the Black Warrior River roughly 14 miles south of Tuscaloosa, Alabama. The heart of this impressive community is a 185-acre mound-and-plaza architectural complex.

For some 400 years (AD 1050–1450), a small number of hereditary chiefs and their retainers living at Moundville held political and religious authority over a much larger population of commoners living along a 25-mile stretch of the Black Warrior valley. The chiefdom was supported by a flourishing agricultural economy. While most people were farmers, some were craft specialists. Moundville is famous for its distinctive black-filmed engraved pottery, greenstone celts, carved stone palettes, and shell and copper ornaments.

HISTORY OF MOUNDVILLE AND ITS PEOPLE

People lived on the river valley terrace at Moundville for 700 years. Over the centuries, the community grew to great prominence, then faded from view as its political fortunes changed. The terrace was first settled about AD 900 by a small village of Native American farmers. Insofar as we know, there were few economic and social differences among the village residents. A century and a half later (about AD 1050), people built two mounds on the terrace. It is at this time that we see the beginnings of social stratification related to hereditary ranking and differential access to wealth and prestige. The early mounds were the locations of public activities and perhaps for the houses of the first chiefs. Most people, however, lived on farmsteads consisting of a household or two scattered among their fields on the terrace and nearby floodplain.

Moundville as we see it today was built between AD 1200 and 1250. The layout of the mound-and-plaza complex was planned carefully. People abandoned the earlier mounds, even demolishing one to make way for the new constructions. Low spots in the terrace were also filled to provide a level surface. The new complex had at least twenty-nine mounds, although some of the smaller ones are no longer discernible. The core of this planned community consists of fifteen mounds (Mounds B and E to R) that form a rough rectangle around a large central plaza. People built the mounds in pairs, alternating burial mounds with ones that had structures on their summits. The mound-top structures served as homes for nobles and locations for public activities. The largest mounds are on the northern edge of the plaza. The mounds get progressively smaller as one moves from north to south around either side of the plaza. Archaeologists think that the mound pairs were associated with clans, and that the positions and sizes of the mounds reflect the ranking of the clans. A large, low mound (Mound A) in the center of the plaza was likely the location of public ceremonies. The functions of the two small mounds (Mounds S and T) on the eastern edge are

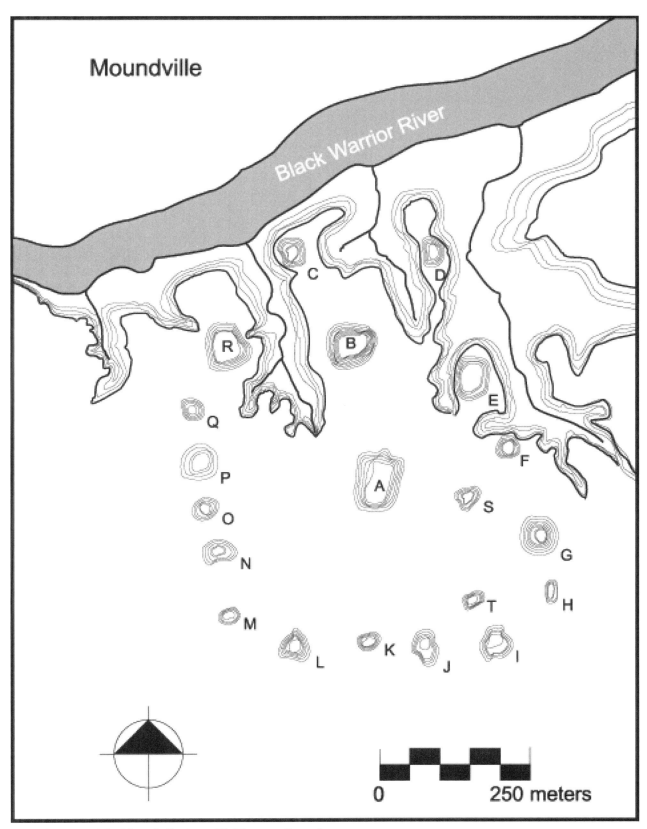

Moundville

Black Warrior River

A topographic map of the Moundville site.   [C. Margaret Scarry]

not known. Mound B, the largest mound, has two ramps leading up steep slopes to a summit 58 feet above the plaza. Presumably the chief lived atop this mound. Mounds C and D, which sit on ridges on the extreme northern edge of the terrace, were burial mounds for nobles.

For a century after it was built, the mound-and-plaza complex was surrounded by a palisade. During this time, ordinary people lived in houses located between the outer periphery of the mound group and the palisade. Houses were arranged in neighborhoods that suggest extended families lived together. The resident population of Moundville at this time is estimated to have been 1,000 people.

Shortly after AD 1300, the palisade was torn down. At the same time, most commoners moved away from Moundville to rural farmsteads elsewhere in the Black Warrior Valley. Moundville itself remained the home for the chief and other high nobles. While the living population at Moundville declined dramatically, the mound-and-plaza complex became a resting place for the dead.

More than 3,000 burials have been excavated at the site, most of which were interred after AD 1300. Some graves contain elaborate mortuary goods, including such items as copper ear spools and pendants, shell gorgets, and carved stone palettes. Variations in the locations and contents of these finely furnished graves suggest at least two levels of status among the elite. Many of the dead, however, were interred with no grave goods or with only a ceramic vessel or two. It seems that while few commoners lived at the site, their families brought them to Moundville for burial when they died.

After AD 1450, the power of the Moundville chiefs waned. Activities continued for a time on a few mounds, but the chiefdom seems to have collapsed. During this time, commoners moved from their scattered farmsteads to nucleated villages (clusters of dwellings, often brought together for self-defense) in which there is little evidence for ranking among clans or individuals. By the time the first Europeans ventured into the interior Southeast, Moundville's chiefs had lost their political and economic hold over the Black Warrior valley. In AD 1540, de Soto's army made its way across the Southeast by traveling from one chiefdom to the next. The Spaniards passed through the Moundville area without stopping, as they surely would have done if they had arrived when the Moundville chiefs were in power. Because the chiefdom disintegrated before the first Europeans arrived, we have no written descriptions of its people. We do not know the identities of the descendants of this once-vibrant community.

POLITICAL AND ECONOMIC ORGANIZATION OF THE MOUNDVILLE CHIEFDOM

By the time the mound-and-plaza complex was built in the thirteenth century, the Moundville chiefs ruled over a territory that encompassed the floodplain of the Black Warrior valley,

from 15 miles north to 10 to 20 miles south of their capital. Throughout Moundville's tenure as a political and religious center, the high chiefs and their retainers lived at the capital. Lesser chiefs lived at several single-mound sites at strategic locations along the river. These district chiefs governed the commoners living within their territories. At the height of the chiefdom, there were seven single-mound centers. Most commoners lived on farmsteads surrounded by their fields. Clusters of farmsteads formed communities tied to the single-mound centers.

The Moundville chiefdom was supported by an economy based on extensive maize agriculture. Commoner families grew large crops of maize, beans, and squash. They supplemented their harvests by gathering hickory nuts, acorns, and wild fruits. They obtained meat by hunting—especially for deer—and fishing. Based on practices of later Native American communities in the Southeast, women probably did most of the agricultural labor, while men cleared land and hunted. Rural families paid tribute to their chiefs in the form of agricultural products and portions of game. Chiefs used some of the food given as tribute to host feasts. Much of the tribute, however, supported the activities and households of the nobles and their retainers.

HISTORY OF EXCAVATIONS AT MOUNDVILLE

Moundville has a long and distinguished history of excavation. In 1869, Nathaniel Lupton drew a map of the site that depicts twenty-nine mounds, including the central prominent mounds and a number that are barely distinguishable today. In 1905 and 1906, Clarence B. Moore spent several months working at Moundville. He sank test holes in the summits of the mounds and excavated several off-mound areas. Moore's excavations are responsible for much of what we know about the elite burials and material culture of Moundville. Between 1930 and 1941, David DeJarnette and Maurice Goldsmith conducted excavations for the Alabama Museum of Natural History using Civilian Conservation Corps labor. These Depression-era excavations targeted the path of a roadway subsequently built encircling the plaza, as well as the locations of the administration and museum buildings. DeJarnette and Goldsmith's excavations revealed numerous structures and burials and produced tens of thousands of artifacts.

Since World War II, excavations at Moundville have been smaller in scale. Field schools conducted by the University of Alabama (initially directed by DeJarnette, more recently by Vernon James Knight and John Blitz) have explored both mound and off-mound areas. A University of Michigan Museum of Anthropology project directed by Christopher Peebles explored areas north of Mound R and on the northwest riverbank. Additional work on the northwest riverbank was conducted by the University of Alabama Office of Archaeological Services.

As a result of over a century of work at the site, we have a detailed chronology for the site and considerable understanding of mound use, domestic life, and mortuary practices.

MOUNDVILLE TODAY

Moundville is a National Historic Landmark and a state park. Located just off Highway 69 South, roughly 14 miles south of Tuscaloosa, it is easily accessible to visitors. The park is operated and maintained by the University of Alabama Museums. Visitors to Moundville can watch a video that gives the history of the site, view museum exhibits, walk or drive around the central mound-and-plaza complex, and hike nature trails. A campground offers tent pads, electrical hookups, and shower facilities. Entry and camping fees are low. More information about Moundville Archaeological Park can be found at http://moundville.ua.edu.

Further Reading: Knight, Vernon J., ed., *The Moundville Expeditions of Clarence Bloomfield Moore* (Tuscaloosa: University of Alabama Press, 1996); Knight, Vernon J., and Vincas P. Steponaitis, eds., *Archaeology of the Moundville Chiefdom* (Tuscaloosa: University of Alabama Press, 2006 reprint).

C. Margaret Scarry

LUBBUB CREEK ARCHAEOLOGICAL COMPLEX

Tombigbee River Valley, West Central Alabama

Modern Studies Illuminate Ancient Village Development

The Lubbub Creek archaeological locality was defined spatially by a tight bend in the Tombigbee River that was to be bisected by a barge canal, a part of the Tennessee-Tombigbee Waterway constructed in the 1970s. The area that was to be disturbed by construction of the canal and associated spoil areas comprised slightly more than 250 acres (100 hectares). The task assigned to archaeologists working with the waterway construction program was to identify, evaluate and save as much as possible of a Mississippian period site that was located somewhere within the project area before it was destroyed by construction. The existence of a major late prehistoric site in the midst of the project area came as a surprise to the U.S. Army Corps of Engineers. Because the site was clearly eligible for inclusion on the National Register of Historic Places, time was of the essence: the dredge contract has already been signed, and it carried significant penalties if that work were delayed by archaeological mitigation.

The archaeological research, which had adequate funding but little time, encompassed several notable features. This was perhaps the first large project to use a real-time computer database to keep track of all aspects of excavation, including mapping, subsequent laboratory analysis, production of the museum catalog, and publication of the results. It used a judicious sampling program to define the limits of archaeological resources within the project area and subsequently to choose areas where mitigation of the impact to the archaeological site by construction could be attained through excavation, which would save important archaeological data before the site was destroyed. It was, and remains, one of the few projects to include biological anthropologists, archaeozoologists, paleoethnobotanists, and geologists in every phase of the research, from first excavation through the writing of the final report. Finally, the time it took to excavate, process, and analyze each archaeological unit was recorded, and these time-task measures were reported for each unit, by class of unit (e.g., pits or post molds) and in aggregate for the project as a whole.

To summarize a very complex piece of fieldwork, a first phase sample of 1 percent, by volume, was excavated in the 100 hectares of the archaeological locality (1,153 test units). In addition to earlier, small Archaic and Woodland period components, a late prehistoric Mississippian settlement of approximately 57 acres (23 hectares) was defined. Following the analysis of the first phase results, the decision was made to save and preserve the eastern half of that village (and a number of earlier components) and to excavate a 20 percent sample of the western half. The basic unit in this second phase was a 10×10–meter (m) test unit that was expanded, as necessary, to include all the features that were present in the original sample unit. In the end, 187 test units and a total of more than 25,000 square

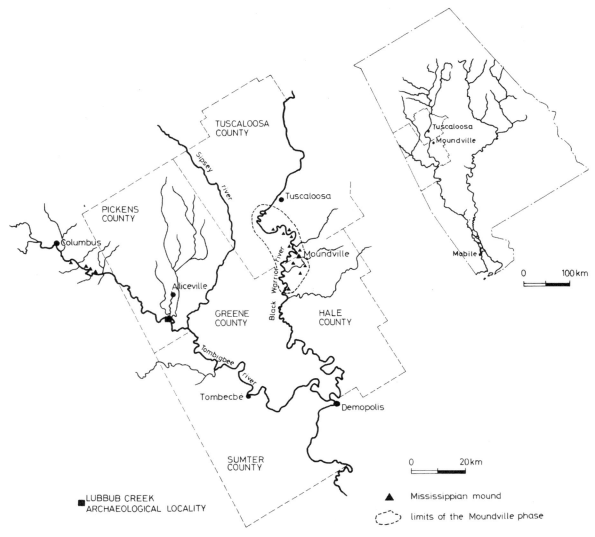

Location of the Lubbub Creek archaeological locality and its relationship to Moundville and sites of the Moundville phase. [Christopher S. Peebles]

meters (m²) were excavated. The field and preliminary laboratory component on this project took a bit more than a year. All told, from initial testing through the final report, approximately 85,000 person-hours were devoted to the project.

The sample statistics from the testing and the excavation are important in the analysis and summary of the history of this prehistoric settlement. They were used in the first instance to predict the total population of archaeological features and their distribution within the archaeological locality. Then they were used to characterize the size and extent of the several settlements that were located there sequentially during the centuries that the site was occupied. For the 1153 test units, expressed as density per 100 m², there were 0.42 burials ($s = 1.23$; s, here and in the following comparison, equals the standard deviation, an estimate of the precision of the average density; this and the other density frequencies given here are average values useful for comparisons among different kinds of archaeological remains excavated, not actual amounts of material found in each and every 100 m² area within the site), 0.10 structures ($s = 0.53$), and 1.03 pits ($s = 2.42$). For the 187 major excavations units—again expressed as density per 100 m²—there were 0.39 burials ($s = 1.19$), 0.06 structures ($s = 0.08$), and 1.15 pits ($s = 1.21$). As even the most cursory comparison shows, there are no significant differences between the predicted density from the testing (based upon the estimates from the test pits) and the actual density

Aerial view of the Lubbub Creek archaeological locality in November 1979. The excavation units and dragline constructing the levee to contain the spoil from the dredge are clearly visible.   [Christopher S. Peebles]

recovered in the excavation of 20 percent of the western half of the village. These sample statistics, plus a solid ceramic, stratigraphic, and radiocarbon chronology, provide the foundations for writing a prehistoric narrative of this settlement.

The initial Mississippian village (designated the Summerville I phase) was founded about AD 1100; it covered approximately 20.5 acres (8.5 hectares). Sequential pairs of public buildings were erected on the spot where the focal pyramidal mound would be built. This village was set within a palisade that enclosed 47 acres (19 hectares). During its occupation, there were as few as ten houses and as many as thirty-one houses in this village, which had a population of between 50 and 100 people.

In the middle phase (designated Summerville II and III phases), perhaps between AD 1250 and 1500, the palisade was demolished, the mound given final form, and the village, which comprised approximately 18 houses for perhaps 100 people, spread over 28 acres (11.3 hectares).

At a point near AD 1500 (the Summerville IV phase), a kilometer-long ditch was dug around the village, and a palisade was likely erected on top of the berm formed by soil removed from the ditch. The village within this fortification comprised from seven to ten houses and from 50 to 100 people.

As a cross-check on the various sample statistics and estimates of population, if the standard floor-area estimate is used for the Mississippian period as a whole (that is, the total floor area for all periods is summed across 300 years of occupation), then a total of 905 people lived there throughout the occupation. If the total number of burials, taken as lives lived, is estimated for the site as a whole, then approximately 1,000 Mississippians called the Lubbub Creek archaeological locality home over a span of a bit more than 300 years. These two estimates are sufficiently close to give additional weight to the adequacy of the sampling strategy.

Based on the analysis of the skeletal remains that were excavated, the health of this population was good throughout

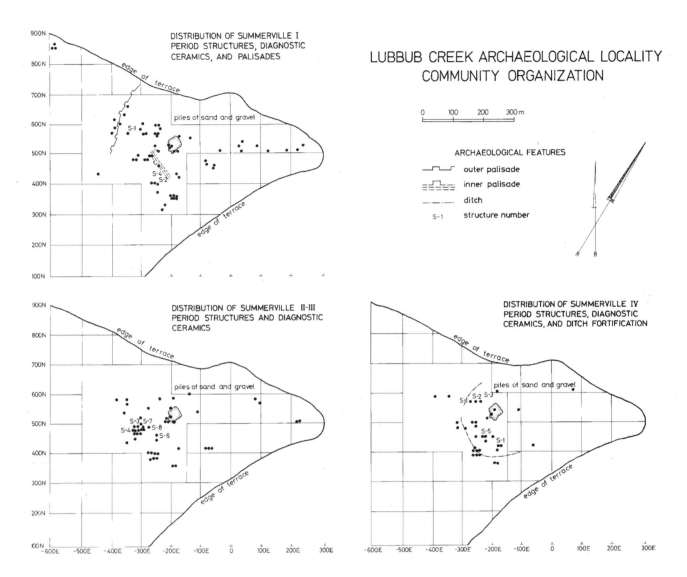

Distribution of diagnostic archaeological features through time in the Lubbub Creek archaeological locality.   [Christopher S. Peebles]

the occupation of the Mississippian village. The inhabitants were consummate farmers, and through their selection the phenotypic diversity of corn decreased. The Lubbub Creek farmers seem to have selected certain kinds of corn to continue planting and to have discontinued the use of other kinds of corn from the earliest occupation of the site to its most recent occupation. Conversely, the diversity of gathered and hunted foods increased. In each period, a relatively undifferentiated village was spread out around the mound, which served as a focus for the settlement. Although there was some social differentiation of space beyond the obvious contrast between mound and village at Lubbub, it is neither as marked

nor as dynamic as that at Moundville, their nearest large Mississippian neighbor.

Further Reading: Blitz, John H., *Ancient Chiefdoms of the Tombigbee* (Tuscaloosa: University of Alabama Press, 1993); Jenkins, Ned J. and Richard A. Krause, eds., *The Tombigbee Watershed in Southeastern Prehistory* (Tuscaloosa: University of Alabama Press, 1986); Knight, Vernon J., and Vincas P. Steponaitis, eds., *Archaeology of the Moundville Chiefdom* (Washington DC: Smithsonian Institution Press, 1998); Peebles, Christopher S., "The Rise and Fall of the Mississippian in Western Alabama: The Moundville and Summerville Phases," *Mississippi Archaeology* 22 (1987): 1–31.

Christopher S. Peebles

OCMULGEE NATIONAL MONUMENT

Macon, Central Georgia

Site of Early Archaeological Study and Earthen Architecture Complex

The Ocmulgee National Monument, located near the present-day city of Macon, Georgia, was the scene of one of the first and largest federal archaeological projects initiated during the Great Depression. There were many of these federal archaeological investigations used as a means of putting unemployed individuals back to work (Jennings 1994; Kelly 1940; Lyons 1996). Excavation of sites located within the monument and nearby laid the groundwork for much of the archaeological research conducted in Georgia and elsewhere in the Southeast over the next several decades. Many of the questions raised by this early archaeological work are still relevant today—and in some cases have yet to be answered satisfactorily.

The Ocmulgee National Monument is located on the Ocmulgee River where it crosses the fall line separating the Piedmont and Coastal Plain physiographic provinces. The term "Ocmulgee" derives from the Ocmulgee tribe of Native Americans, their old fields, and the river that flowed by those fields. It is often used to refer to any federal relief program archaeological investigations that took place in the vicinity of Macon. The monument, where most of these investigations occurred, includes two geographically separate tracts of land: one located in the broad floodplain below the fall line and containing the Lamar site (9BI2); and the other, located 3 kilometers to the north on the Macon Plateau, a relatively flat area of Piedmont uplands, and containing the Macon Plateau site and the Macon Trading Post site (9BI1).

The first accurate description of archaeological remains at Ocmulgee was published by Charles C. Jones in 1873. No professional excavations were undertaken in the area, however, until the beginning of the federal relief program in December 1933. Administered by the National Park Service and funded by several agencies—in particular, the Works Progress Administration (WPA)—the federal program continued until 1941 and employed at its peak in 1935 almost 800 workers. Many of the leading archaeologists of the mid-twentieth century were involved in the program as employees or students, including J. Lawrence Angel, Charles H. Fairbanks, James A. Ford, Jesse D. Jennings, Arthur R. Kelly, Walter W. Taylor, and Gordon R. Willey (e.g., Jennings 1994).

The greatest amount of fieldwork occurred at the Macon Plateau site, where portions of eight mounds and more than a mile of exploratory trenches were excavated. Excavations at the Lamar site were limited in scope and included a test trench in Mound A, a 100-square-foot unit in the habitation zone, and testing to trace the outline of the defensive palisade surrounding the site. A number of sites outside the boundaries of the monument were also investigated, with the most extensive excavations occurring at the Middle Woodland–period Swift Creek site (9BI3) and the Mississippian-period Brown's Mount (9BI5) and Stubbs Mound sites (9BI12).

Aboriginal occupation of the Macon Plateau site ranges from the Paleoindian and Early Archaic periods to the early eighteenth century. The major component, however, is the Early Mississippian Macon Plateau phase that dates to the eleventh century AD. There is much about Macon Plateau culture, as currently known, that is enigmatic. To begin with, the ceramic assemblage (the types and range of pottery found at the sites)—which consists almost exclusively of undecorated vessels, use of shell temper, and vessel forms (such as jars with handles and gourd-effigy bottles)—is very different from the Late Woodland pottery that precedes it in time and the Mississippian pottery that is roughly contemporary with it elsewhere in central Georgia. Less than a dozen Macon Plateau phase sites are known, and all are located within an 8-kilometer stretch of the Ocmulgee River below Macon. These data suggest that Macon Plateau culture represents a Mississippian group that migrated into central Georgia from the Tennessee valley or the lower Chattahoochee valley. Not all archaeologists, however, accept this interpretation.

The Macon Plateau site is also unusual in its size and topography. Its eight earthen mounds are distributed over an area measuring approximately 1,000 meters by 660 meters, making the site one of the largest known Mississippian mound groups. Surface elevation across the site drops 20 meters from north to south, and some mounds are separated by 5- to 10-meter-deep swales containing intermittent streams. All of this suggests that the site consists of several mound-and-plaza groups that the ancient designers and builders intended to be separate, rather than a single integrated mound-plaza arrangement, as is typical of Mississippian mound complexes elsewhere in the Southeast.

The structure known as the Macon Earth Lodge (Mound D-1 Lodge) is perhaps the most widely known architectural feature at the site but is also controversial. This circular

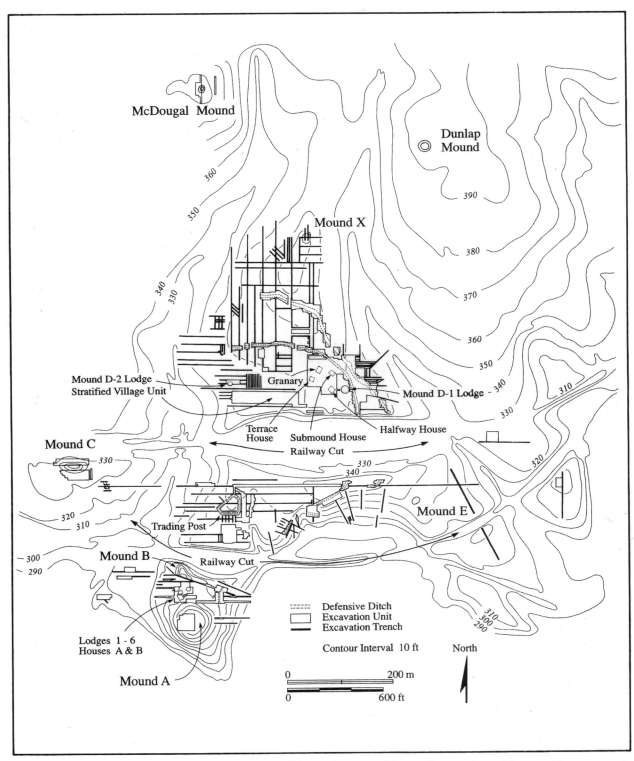

Topographic map of the Macon Plateau showing location of the trading post, Macon Plateau site architectural features, and excavation units.   [University of Georgia Press]

structure, which measures 12 meters in diameter, was identified at the time of excavation as an earth lodge of the type characteristic of plains agricultural societies, such as the Hidatsa and Mandan. More recently, archaeologists have suggested it was an earth-embanked structure with clay plastered on the underside of the roof, perhaps as a fire prevention measure.

Also enigmatic are two ditch-like features, referred to as dugouts, that extend across the northern part of the site for distances of 335 meters and 370 meters. They are usually identified as defensive ditches, but variation in depth and the fact that they do not extend across the entire site argues for a different function. There is at present no satisfactory explanation for their existence.

The Late Mississippian Lamar site, about 3 kilometers south of the Macon Plateau and on the Ocmulgee River floodplain, covers approximately 16 hectares (about 40 acres) and had a palisaded perimeter, two large earth mounds, and a habitation zone. Occupied into the later half of the sixteenth century, it may have been the capital for the chiefdom of Ichisi, which was visited by the de Soto expedition in 1540 as it traveled eastward across central Georgia.

The latest archaeologically known occupation at the Ocmulgee National Monument is the English trading house (Macon Trading Post) and associated aboriginal Ocmulgee Fields culture, which dates to the 1690–1715 period. The trading house is represented by a pentagonal stockade enclosing at least two buildings and probably was constructed by traders from Charleston, South Carolina, to serve the trade of the Creek tribe. The Ocmulgee Fields occupation is known from building posthole patterns, pits, and burials located in the vicinity of the trading house. It shares some ceramic features with the mid-sixteenth-century Lamar site culture, but its closest ceramic affiliation is with the seventeenth-century Blackmon phase on the lower Chattahoochee River. The Ocmulgee Fields inhabitants were apparently Hitchiti-speaking Lower Creeks who moved to central Georgia in the late seventeenth century to gain better access to the trading house.

The Ocmulgee National Monument is located on the southeastern edge of Macon, Georgia, off Interstate 16. Additional information on the monument and driving directions can be found at www.nps.gov/ocmu.

Further Reading: Fairbanks, Charles H., *Archaeology of the Funeral Mound, Ocmulgee National Monument, Georgia*, Archaeological Research Series No. 3 (Washington, DC: USDI National Park Service, 1956); Hally, David J. (ed.), *Ocmulgee Archaeology: 1936–1986* (Athens: University of Georgia Press, 1994); Jennings, Jesse D., "Macon Daze," in *Ocmulgee Archaeology 1936–1986*, edited by David J. Hally (Athens: University of Georgia Press, 1994), 47–50; Kelley, Arthur R., "Archaeology in the National Park Service," *American Antiquity* 5 (1940): 274–282; Lyon, Edwin A., *A New Deal for Southeastern Archaeology* (Tuscaloosa: University of Alabama Press, 1996).

David J. Hally

THE CALUSA

Southwest Florida Coast

A Rich Ancient Culture in the Estuaries of the Florida Gulf Coast

In the sixteenth century, Calusa Indian people controlled much of south Florida from their capital town of Calos on the southwest Florida coast near present-day Fort Myers. They exerted influence as far away as Cape Canaveral and received tribute from client towns as distant as Lake Okeechobee, present-day Miami, and the Florida Keys. During the 1560s their domain included at least fifty towns. By the early 1600s the Calusa controlled more than sixty towns, and many others paid them tribute.

Divided into nobles and commoners, the Calusa supported an elite military force. They built earthworks, engineered substantial canals complete with water control structures, and traded widely. Their belief system involved daily offerings to their ancestors, a trinity of deities, and a concept of afterlife. Elaborate rituals included processions of masked priests, animal impersonations, synchronized singing by hundreds, and human sacrifice. Their painted, engraved, and carved objects are among the most renowned of all Native American artworks.

All of this was achieved without the benefit of staple crop agriculture. The Calusa were principally a fishing society, with supplementary gathering, hunting, and gardening. Only in the past twenty-five years have the remarkable accomplishments of these Native Americans become fully appreciated by archaeologists, historians, and other scholars, and only in the past decade have the Calusa attracted public interest beyond their traditional homeland.

Although many Calusa sites have been lost to development, well over 100 remain today. Many are on, in, or near the bountiful estuaries of Pine Island Sound, Charlotte Harbor, or

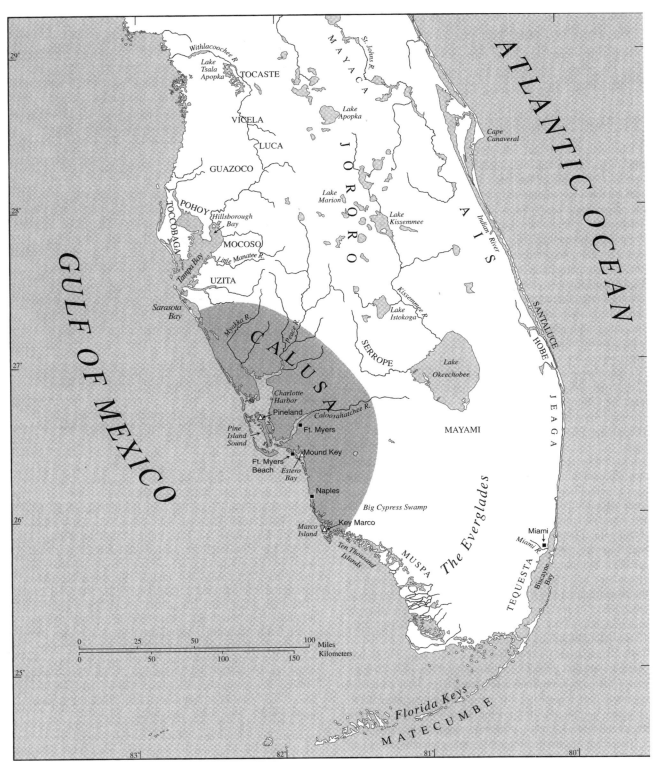

Calusa territory in the sixteenth and seventeenth centuries.   [Map created by Daniel G. Cole. Source: *Handbook of North American Indians*, National Anthropological Archives, Smithsonian Institution.]

Large numbers of fish were caught as one of the main staples in the Calusa diet.   [Courtesy of William H. Marquardt, Florida Museum of Natural History]

Estero Bay. Archaeological sites of the two largest historic Calusa towns, Mound Key and Pineland, are open to the public. Of the two, Pineland is the better studied and more easily accessible.

Florida gulf coastal fishing societies were present by 6,000 years ago, but it is not known whether they were directly ancestral to the Calusa. Artifacts known from southwest Florida changed only gradually after about AD 500, leading most archaeologists to infer that the historic Calusa descended from people who had lived on the southwest Florida coast for at least 1,000 years. In short, the Calusa were an indigenous south Florida people, not migrants from Mexico or the Caribbean.

The rich estuarine habitats available to the Calusa were important to their prosperity. By extending their influence across the vast interior wetlands and flatlands of the southern Florida peninsula, the Calusa also guaranteed themselves ample and varied foods throughout the year. In the Calusa heartland, the group's success at fishing and shellfish gathering was the result of a combination of freshwater from the Peace, Myakka, Caloosahatchee, and Estero rivers; the protection of coastal barrier islands; and shallow, grassy estuaries of extraordinary year-round productivity. Rich in sea grasses and surrounded by mangrove forests, the estuaries

were home to over fifty fish species and more than twenty kinds of mollusks and crustaceans that could be exploited by the Calusa. The daily staple was fish, caught in great numbers with nets, traps, and weirs. Large fish were also caught on hook and line. Numerous wild plants were used for food, medicine, and fuel. Gourd-like squash (*Cucurbita pepo*) and papaya (*Carica papaya*) were harvested and probably cultivated by about 2,000 years ago.

In addition to food, medicine, and firewood, plants provided raw materials for tools, handles, containers, clothing, thatching, mats, weapons, canoes, fishing gear, and cordage for line and fishing nets. The Calusa fashioned lightning whelk and other mollusk shells into hammering, pounding, perforating, and cutting tools. They made robust mollusk shells into fishing gear such as sinkers, net weights, net mesh gauges, and anchors. The metapodial (lower leg) bones of deer were fashioned into pins, points, fishing gorges, and parts of compound fishhooks. They made beads from certain shells and bones, and shaped turtle carapaces into net mesh gauges. Shark teeth were used for cutting, engraving, carving, and grating tasks. From wood and fiber they built fish traps, weirs, and corrals. They carved wood into bowls, boxes, planks, canoes, paddles, and pounding and grinding implements, as well as a wide range of ceremonial and decorative items, such

Several artifacts found by Cushing at the Key Marco site.   [Catalogue No. 240915, Department of Anthropology, Smithsonian Institution. Courtesy of the Smithsonian Institution.]

as masks, ear ornaments, and figurines. They chose natural dyes, latex, and oils to make paints for decorating art objects as well as their bodies. Local clays and sands were used to make coiled utilitarian pottery for cooking and storage.

The Calusa inhabited the coastal zone, often favoring places away from the gulf coast yet near their estuarine food sources. Calusa houses were said to be on "little hills," probably midden mounds or linear or curvilinear ridges. At least

some of the people lived in large, communal, thatched houses. In the 1690s there were sixteen such houses in the main Calusa village on Mound Key, each apparently accommodating several dozen people. One structure described in 1566, called the "king's house," was large enough for 2,000 to stand inside "without being very crowded." Such a structure would have occupied over 600 square meters. Ritual specialists performed rites in a special building that had benches and an altar or central mound and masks covering the walls. Some south Florida coastal people probably lived in thatched houses built on pilings over the water, as was observed in the seventeenth century near present-day Miami.

South Florida natives used several kinds of canoes, including seagoing vessels, small cargo canoes, and barges made of platforms connecting two canoes. Artificially constructed canals connected major coastal towns to interior watercourses and facilitated movement into and out of large villages. Some canals, such as the one on Pine Island, ran for miles and were as much as 30 feet (9 meters [m]) wide. Such widths might have been necessary to accommodate some of the larger trading and tribute vessels, which are described as two canoes lashed together with a platform on top. When the Calusa king traveled, he had his own special double canoe, with a sheltered platform on which he sat. As many as twelve canoes accompanied him.

Both men and women wore only scant clothing made of hide and woven mat coverings. Personal adornment included body paint, especially on ritual occasions, and it was said to have spiritual significance. The Calusa king wore his hair long and stained himself black on his face and body. The art of the Calusa is world renowned, principally because of the Key Marco site, excavated by Frank Cushing in 1896. Strictly speaking, Key Marco is somewhat south of the Calusa heartland, and the materials excavated by Cushing may be over 1,000 years old. Whatever their age, Key Marco's artifacts are unsurpassed in diversity and quality of organic preservation. Cushing unearthed wooden items such as tools, handles, containers, pestles, arrows, weapons, and canoe paddles. He also found a number of carved and painted masks and figureheads, as well as a 6-inch-high wooden feline figurine.

Calusa nobles did not work, nor did warriors at the command of the Calusa king. Nobles ate certain foods denied to commoners. Spiritual specialists and healers received special treatment and compensation. The trappings of leadership were highly visible. The paramount leader sat on a special stool and was fanned with incense by the chief priest. Client towns provided a bride to the paramount leader to cement political ties.

The principal leaders were the hereditary paramount leader, or "king," a war captain, and a head priest. The king's role was to mediate between the secular and sacred realms, ensuring the health and prosperity of the people and the continued productivity of the environment. The war captain waged war on behalf of the Calusa and commanded military specialists and a militia that could be mobilized at the request of the king. The head priest maintained the temple and its idols, had the power to summon storms, and probably coordinated or conducted important rites of passage, including death rituals and human sacrifice.

The Calusa believed one had three souls: in one's shadow, in one's reflection, and in the pupil of one's eye. The soul in the eye was thought to survive after death. Another belief was that at the moment of death, the human soul enters a smaller animal or fish, and upon the death of that animal, it passes on to an even smaller one, and so on, until it disappears altogether. The Calusa respected the dead and placed food, herbs, and tobacco offerings as well as animal skulls on mats at the burial places. They also consulted with the dead in order to foretell the future or to learn of activities happening elsewhere.

Indian people of south Florida had surely learned of Columbus's landfall in the late fifteenth century and knew of early Spanish slaving expeditions around south Florida in the early 1500s. Following the devastation of Cuban natives between 1510 and 1514, the Calusa king permitted some Cuban refugees to settle in southwest Florida. Thus, it is no surprise that the Calusa greeted Juan Ponce de León's June 1513 arrival near their capital town less than enthusiastically. They attacked the Spaniards with arrows and sent warriors in eighty canoes to engage them. When Ponce de León's expedition returned in 1521, the Calusa attacked again, injuring many, including Ponce de León himself, whose wound proved fatal.

Forty-six years later, Spanish Jesuits began a mission effort at the Calusa capital town of Calos, but were unsuccessful. Spanish soldiers assassinated two Calusa kings between 1567 and 1569, yet the Calusa remained politically powerful. They still inhabited their coastal towns as late as 1697, when Franciscans from Cuba attempted to establish a mission. The Franciscans were banished when they insisted that the Calusa give up their rituals and beliefs.

Well aware of the English presence north of the Florida peninsula, Spanish forts and missions in north Florida, and Spanish settlements in Cuba, the Calusa leadership chose an isolationist policy at the turn of the eighteenth century. This left them powerful in their own territory, but without the benefit of firearms. By 1704 the English had breached Spanish defenses in north Florida, neutralizing the Spanish presence that had buffered the Florida peninsula from warring European factions farther north.

The English thirst for slave labor fueled the demise of the Calusa and other south Florida native peoples. Between 1704 and 1711, heavily armed Uchise Creek and Yamasee Indians forced south Florida native people from their traditional lands and waters, killing many and capturing others for sale as slaves in the Carolina colony.

In 1711 Spaniards living in Cuba transported some refugee south Florida Indian people to Cuba, but most soon died of typhus and smallpox. Among the deceased were the king and the war captain of the Calusa. Calusa society faded from the historical record in the eighteenth century. Any direct descendants of the Calusa and other south Florida native people will likely be found in Cuba.

The Calusa are not related to cultures of the greater southeastern United States, such as those that dealt the final blow to Calusa sovereignty in the early 1700s. The Uchise and

Yamasee were part of an allied assortment of native peoples whom the English called "Creeks." Composed of the Muskogee-speaking Upper Creeks and Hichiti-speaking Lower Creeks, these people came from the present-day Georgia and Alabama area, centered on the Coosa and Chattahoochee rivers.

The later "Spanish Indians," who worked in southwest Florida fisheries in the late 1700s and early 1800s and in some cases married Spanish fishermen, descended from Creek people who migrated into south Florida. Seminole and Miccosukee peoples who live in south Florida today also descend from these Creek-related groups who once lived north of present-day Florida, not from the indigenous Calusa.

MOUND KEY ARCHAEOLOGICAL STATE PARK

The historical capital of the Calusa nation at the time of European contact was Calos, located in a bay known as Escampaba. Protected as a state park, the island is today known as Mound Key, situated in Estero Bay near Fort Myers Beach. The site is listed in the National Register of Historic Places. Native Florida Indian people, Spanish fisher folk, and twentieth-century Europeans all made their homes there, altering the landscape in their own ways.

In the sixteenth century Calos was the largest Calusa town, with more than 1,000 inhabitants. Archaeological deposits occupy most of the 125-acre (51-hectare) island, although some parts of the island have been reduced by dredging and modern habitation. Still visible are substantial mounds (the largest over 32 feet [9 m] high), a large artificial canal, and both midden ridges and burial mounds. Only limited mapping and testing of the site has been accomplished, but based on available evidence it is believed that the island was inhabited by at least AD 100.

Mound Key is open from 8 am to sundown every day of the year and is accessible by boat. Private crafts are allowed to land, or visitors may patronize one of several tour boat companies that travel regularly to the site. An unimproved path with interpretive signs traverses the island, leading the hiker through the main canal trench and up and over the highest mound. There are no docks or facilities.

THE RANDELL RESEARCH CENTER
AT PINELAND

The Pineland site complex is located on the northwestern shore of Pine Island in coastal southwest Florida, near Fort Myers. First inhabited about 2,000 years ago, Pineland was the second largest of the historic Calusa towns, remaining occupied until 1710. The site was partially damaged in the twentieth century by the removal of portions of some mounds for road material and fill dirt, and by the filling of low areas, including much of the ancient canal. Nevertheless, enormous shell mounds still overlook Pine Island Sound, and remains of many centuries of Indian village life blanket the old pastures

and groves. Remnants of the Pine Island Canal, a waterway that reached 2.5 miles (4 km) across Pine Island, are still visible. A sand burial mound and numerous midden mounds still stand. Native plants and animals characteristic of coastal hammocks, pinelands, wetlands, and shell mounds are abundant. The site is listed in the National Register of Historic Places.

In addition to its midden mounds, Pineland includes buried, waterlogged deposits of considerable research potential. Pineland is also internationally known to climate researchers due to its demonstrated importance in the study of past human-climate relationships. Pineland is the most systematically tested and extensively studied of all known Calusa sites. Excavations undertaken there by the Florida Museum of Natural History (FLMNH) since 1988 form the most comprehensive systematic material record of the extinct Calusa culture.

Thanks to a grant of land from Donald and Patricia Randell and funds raised from donors, agencies, and foundations, the FLMNH has established the Randell Research Center at the Pineland site as a permanent program of archaeological and environmental research. The site is open to the public every day except Thanksgiving and Christmas. Visitors can experience the Calusa Heritage Trail, a 3,700-foot walking path (about 0.7 miles, or 1,128 m) that winds among and over the mounds, wetlands, and canal. The trail includes museum-quality interpretive signs and wayside benches, as well as stairways to the tops of both primary shell mounds, observation platforms atop the tallest mound, and a bridge and boardwalk over low-lying areas. Also available are public restrooms, a picnic area, and a teaching pavilion featuring interpretive materials and a bookshop.

Further Reading: Brown, Robin C., *Florida's First People* (Sarasota, FL: Pineapple Press, 1994); Cushing, Frank H., *Exploration of Ancient Key-Dweller Remains on the Gulf Coast of Florida* (Gainesville: University Press of Florida, 2000); Gilliland, Marion S., *The Material Culture of Key Marco, Florida* (Gainesville: University Presses of Florida, 1975); MacMahon, Darcie A., and William H. Marquardt, *The Calusa and Their Legacy: South Florida People and Their Environments* (Gainesville: University Press of Florida, 2004); Marquardt, William H., "The Emergence and Demise of the Calusa," in *Societies in Eclipse: Eastern North America at the Dawn of European Colonization*, edited by D. Brose, C. W. Cowan, and R. Mainfort (Washington, DC: Smithsonian Institution Press, 2001), 157–171; Marquardt, William H., ed., *The Archaeology of Useppa Island*, Institute of Archaeology and Paleoenvironmental Studies Monograph 3 (Gainesville: University of Florida, 1999); Marquardt, William H., and Karen J. Walker, eds., *The Archaeology of Pineland: A Coastal Southwest Florida Village Complex, ca. A.D. 50–1710*, Institute of Archaeology and Paleoenvironmental Studies Monograph 4 (Gainesville: University of Florida, 2007); Mound Key Archaeological State Park Web site, www.floridastateparks.org/moundkey/default.cfm; Randell Research Center at Pineland Web site, www.flmnh.ufl.edu/RRC/; Southwest Florida Archaeology and Ethnography, Florida Museum of Natural History Web site, www.flmnh.ufl.edu/sflarch; Walker, Karen J., "The Material Culture of Precolumbian Fishing: Artifacts and Fish Remains from Coastal Southwest Florida," *Southeastern Archaeology* 19 (2000): 24–45; Walker, Karen J., Frank W. Stapor Jr., and William H. Marquardt, "Archaeological Evidence for a 1750–1450 BP Higher-than-Present

Sea Level along Florida's Gulf Coast," in *Holocene Cycles: Climate, Sea Levels, and Sedimentation*, edited by C. W. Finkl Jr. *Journal of Coastal Research*, Special Issue No. 17 (1995): 205–218.

William Marquardt

TOLTEC MOUNDS ARCHEOLOGICAL STATE PARK

Near Little Rock, Arkansas

A Mississippian Political and Ceremonial Mound Center

The Toltec Mounds site was the largest ceremonial center of Plum Bayou culture in the lower Mississippi valley. Situated near the Arkansas River, it was one of the largest sites in the Mississippi River valley 1,100 years ago. The site had at least eighteen mounds surrounded by an earthen embankment and ditch that enclosed 100 acres. The mounds were built and used as platforms for religious ceremonies by people who lived in the surrounding countryside. Only a few people lived at the site.

The Toltec name is the result of a mistaken but common belief in the mid-1800s that the mounds of the eastern United States had been built by ancient peoples who migrated to Mexico before the Indians moved into the area. Investigations of sites during the 1880s uncovered evidence to conclude that the mounds, in fact, had been built and used by the ancestors of the local Indians, not the Toltecs or Aztecs of Mexico. Nevertheless, the name Toltec was given to a local railway station and village, and now to the state park preserving the site as well.

Native Americans lived on the Arkansas River floodplain and adjacent uplands for thousands of years. The earlier people hunted and gathered and moved seasonally to obtain food. By about 500 BC, they began farming and settled into villages. The way of life of the people who built Toltec Mounds developed out of the local farming cultures of the Arkansas floodplain and is called the Plum Bayou culture. Radiocarbon dates place most of the mound construction between about AD 700 and 1050, but the use of the site began earlier. Plum Bayou culture cannot be identified with any modern Native American people who were in Arkansas at the time of contact with the Hernando de Soto expedition in 1541. The oral tradition of the modern Quapaw tribe relates that they had recently migrated to the Arkansas River, which was where French explorers encountered them in the 1670s.

The Toltec Mounds site was located on a lake that was an ancestral channel of the Arkansas River 3 miles east of the active river. The Arkansas River formed a broad floodplain, extending from the modern city of Little Rock eastward to the Mississippi River. The Ouachita Mountains and Ozark plateaus are west of Little Rock, with the Arkansas River and its tributaries draining these uplands. The Plum Bayou people obtained a wide variety of resources from the uplands and floodplain. The Toltec Mounds site did not have a large population but was a religious and social center for people who lived in nearby small villages and farmsteads. They cultivated domesticated plants, such as little barley, maygrass, Poaceae, knotweed, chenopod, squash, and maize. The most common seed is a grass of the Poaceae family, which has not been identified to the species level. They hunted white-tailed deer, gray squirrel, turkey, passenger pigeon, and other animals with the bow and arrow. Hickory nuts, acorns, wild fruits, and various kinds of fish also were important in the diet. They obtained a variety of rocks to make tools from river gravel deposits and from the uplands. Local clays were used to make pottery for cooking, serving, and storage. Houses and household items were made of wood and river cane.

The site was large and impressive, with two prominent mounds that were 49 feet (Mound A) and 39 feet (Mound B) high. A third mound was about 12 feet high, and fourteen additional mounds were between 2 and 5 feet high. The mounds were positioned in two rectangular arrangements bordering open spaces, or plazas, used for public ceremonies. Most of the mounds were square to rectangular in shape, with a flat top. One side of the site was on the bank of the lake, and the other sides were enclosed by the embankment, which was over a mile long and 8 to 10 feet high. The embankment had at least two openings. It did not, apparently, support a wooden stockade. Soil to build the embankment and mounds had been scraped up from the adjacent ground.

Excavations conducted between 1977 and 1993 by the Arkansas Archeological Survey under the direction of Martha A. Rolingson sampled various areas of the site, including six mounds. Excavation in the plaza produced few artifacts, an indication that this area was kept clean, as are central areas for community activities in modern southeastern Native American villages. The larger mounds at Toltec were placed in the positions of the sun on the horizon at sunrise and sunset on the equinoxes and summer solstice. The mounds were built over a period of 300 years, and only toward the end of this period would all of the mounds have been visible, as they are today. The tallest mound has not been excavated. Mound B, the second highest, was in use throughout the period. It was built in stages, with the upper surface of each stage used for some time before more soil was added to the top, increasing the height of the mound over time.

Across the plaza from Mound A was one of the smallest mounds. It has been badly damaged by modern farming, but apparently was once two to three feet high and built in a single stage about AD 750 to 800. The surface of this mound had an extensive trash deposit on it containing plant remains, animal bones, tools to butcher the animals, and cooking and serving containers. Also present were bones from species such as hawk, eagle, bear, and fox. These animals were not normally consumed as food by southeastern Native Americans, but they were important in rituals. Minerals that were ground to make paint pigment were present, as was a thin sandstone artifact with red pigment on one surface. These and other artifacts are evidence that this deposit was not ordinary domestic trash; instead, it apparently resulted from feasts served to people who came to the site to participate in ceremonies.

At the south end of the plaza, the fourth-largest mound was not built until about AD 950. It was built in stages, but it was enlarged to increase the area covered, rather than to add height. It too had extensive trash deposits on the stage surfaces. It may have had a residence on it that would probably have been the dwelling of a chief or priest.

Only one burial mound is known on the site. It was briefly excavated by the University of Arkansas Museum in 1966. Two burials were uncovered, neither of which had elaborate grave goods. In the 1880s, a shaft was sunk in the center of this mound but did not encounter burials. Single pottery bowls were exposed in both of these excavations, perhaps placed on the mound with offerings. Based on this limited information, and also from other related sites, burial practices were apparently simple even at the ceremonial center. Most people were probably buried near their houses in the villages and farmsteads.

Nineteenth-century landowners Mary Eliza and Gilbert Knapp were fascinated by the mounds and reported the site to the Smithsonian Institution in the 1870s. As a result, the site was visited and excavated in the 1880s and included in a massive study of mound sites conducted by Cyrus Thomas. The site had a reputation of not producing whole artifacts or items that could be used in museum exhibits and was therefore largely ignored. When the Arkansas Department of Parks and Tourism purchased the site in 1975, the Arkansas Archeological Survey initiated a major research program that continues today.

Toltec Mounds Archeological State Park is maintained by the Division of Parks, with a visitor center, exhibits, park trails, educational programs, tours, and special events. The Arkansas Archeological Survey is responsible for research on the site and maintains a laboratory and research station at the park visitor center.

Further Reading: Nassaney, Michael S., "The Historical and Archaeological Context of Plum Bayou Culture in Central Arkansas," *Southeastern Archaeology* 13 (1994): 36–55; Rolingson, Martha Ann, "Plum Bayou Culture of the Arkansas-White River Basin," in *The Woodland Southeast*, David G. Anderson and Robert C. Mainfort Jr., eds. (Tuscaloosa: University of Alabama Press, 2002), 44–65; Rolingson, Martha Ann, *Toltec Mounds and Plum Bayou Culture: Mound D Excavations*, Research Series No. 54 (Fayetteville: Arkansas Archeological Survey, 1998); Rolingson, Martha Ann, "Toltec Mounds site" and "Plum Bayou Culture" entries in *The Encyclopedia of Arkansas History & Culture*, http://encyclopediaofarkansas.net, 2006; Thomas, Cyrus, "Report on the Mound Explorations of the Bureau of Ethnology," *Bureau of Ethnology Annual Report 12, 1890–1891* (Washington, DC: U. S. Government Press, 1894), 3–742, reprint (Washington, D C: Smithsonian Institution Press, 1994).

Martha Ann Rolingson

THE ETOWAH SITE

Northwest Georgia

An Ancient Native American Town and Earthen Mound Complex

Etowah is a Mississippian period (ca. AD 1000–1600) mound town located on the Etowah River floodplain in northwestern Georgia. Several impressive earthen platform mounds were constructed at the site, and many of its most important residents were buried with finely crafted art objects associated with a widespread symbolic complex known as the Southeastern Ceremonial Complex. The builders of Etowah were the ancestors of the Creek people, whose descendants

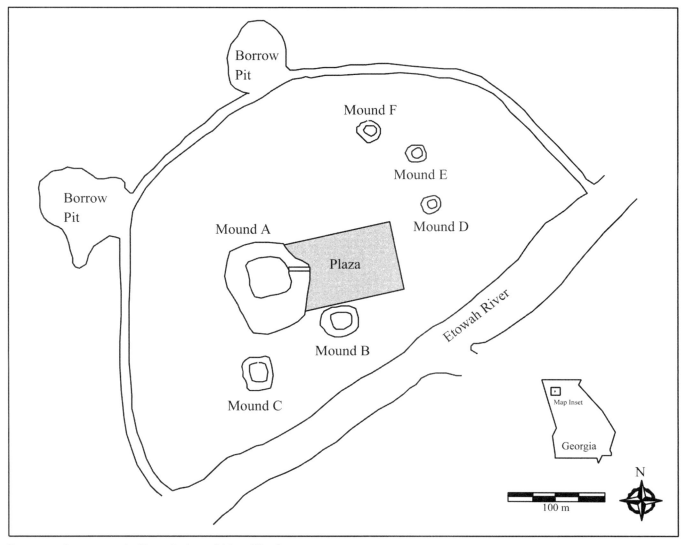

Important features at the Etowah site.   [Adam King]

live in the Southeast and in Oklahoma, where some were forced to move in the early nineteenth century.

Etowah served as the capital of prehistoric chiefdoms for over five centuries, and during the fourteenth century was the most important center in northern Georgia and adjoining states. The site rose to prominence during the Mississippian period, when most social groups in the Southeast were corn farmers living in settled villages, hamlets and farmsteads. Communities were organized into larger social units that anthropologists call chiefdoms. These societies consisted of up to a few thousand people administered by a centralized decision-making structure headed by a hereditary chief. Social ranking, where some people were born into families more important and influential than others, was an integral part of the fabric of these chiefdom societies.

One of the reasons Etowah is so well known is that it is a big and impressive place. During the course of the site's history, at least six large platform mounds were constructed from earth. The largest of these mounds, Mound A, stands over 19 meters tall and has a prominent ramp projecting from its eastern side as well as a lower terrace on its southern side. Mounds B and C are each large, flat-topped pyramidal mounds measuring 7 and 6 meters tall, respectively. Of the two, only Mound C originally had a ramp, which also projected from its eastern flank. The smallest mounds at the site (D, E, and F) are rectangular to oblong platforms that stand about 3 meters high each. To the south, the site is bordered by the Etowah River, but its other sides are surrounded by borrow pits connected by a large ditch. This ditch encloses approximately 22 hectares (one hectare equals 2.471 acres) and reportedly extended to the river on both sides before it was partially filled for agricultural purposes. A palisade with bastions located just inside of the ditch once surrounded the site, fortifying it for a period of time.

During the Early Mississippian period (AD 1000–1200), when chiefdoms were just beginning to form across the Southeast and Midwest, Etowah emerged as one of the earliest centers in northern Georgia. When Etowah was first occupied, around AD 1000, the site was a modest town containing at most one small mound (the initial phase of construction of Mound A), a series of large public buildings, and possibly a small plaza. At this time, only two other chiefdom centers are known to have existed in all of Georgia. A century later, other centers had emerged throughout the region, and even though a second mound was started at Etowah, it remained a modest chiefdom. By AD 1200, Etowah and the other, similar centers in the Etowah valley were abandoned, suggesting that the valley saw a significant, but at this point unexplained, population exodus.

By AD 1250, people had returned to Etowah, and the site experienced a florescence, reaching its peak of influence in the region. From that point to about AD 1375, there was a boom in monument construction. Mound B was significantly enlarged, and most of the huge Mound A was constructed. It is of particular significance that this is the period when Mound C was constructed. Mound C served as the final resting place of the most important members of Etowah's society. Membership in the elite stratum was at least in part symbolized by the possession of and burial with finely crafted objects made of native copper, local and nonlocal stone, and marine shell. Many of those objects bear elaborate decorations and took considerable skill to make. Some of them are comparable to art objects from other time periods and parts of the world. The artifacts recovered from Etowah have long been recognized to be part of a pan-Mississippian artistic tradition called the Southeastern Ceremonial Complex.

Sometime after AD 1325, the area east of Mound A was converted to an open plaza and paved with a thick layer of red clay, and the entire site was surrounded by the ditch and palisade. The ditch connects a series of borrow pits used to collect construction material for the mounds. The palisade was constructed of posts 12 to 18 inches in diameter set into a trench, creating a formidable wall 12 feet tall that had rectangular bastions positioned at regular intervals along its perimeter. The labor invested in these fortifications suggests a clear concern for defense.

Before the end of the fourteenth century, Etowah and all other mound centers in the valley were abandoned, suggesting yet another valley-wide collapse of chiefdoms. In the archaeological record of Etowah, there are a few clues as to how or why this second abandonment came about. First, it appears that the defensive palisade was burned. While it is possible to envision an accidental burning of the palisade caused by lightning or Etowah's inhabitants, it seems more plausible that the palisade was burned intentionally—possibly as part of an attack.

The final burial activities at Mound C provide more details about this series of events. One of the last burials in the mound was a large, log-lined tomb that contained two marble statues of a man and a woman. Similar statues are generally considered to be representations of chiefly ancestors, in some cases even representing the founders of chiefly lineages. If this is the case at Etowah, then their burial marks a symbolic end to the site's ruling lineage. As the excavator described the burial, the statues were jumbled one on top of the other and the human remains and grave goods were scattered about the floor of the tomb. It is as if the statues were buried in a hurry, perhaps under duress from the threat of attack.

Stratigraphically above the burial containing the statues, excavators found a scatter of human remains and burial objects that continued up the face of Mound C's ramp to the summit. Historical accounts include descriptions of invading armies sacking sacred temples, or charnel houses, that held the bones of illustrious ancestors. The materials found on the ramp at Mound C could very well be the remains of one such rampage. Thus, it appears that Etowah, at its peak of influence, might have met with a violent end.

People did not return to Etowah until the end of the fifteenth century, just before the coming of Hernando de Soto—the first European to traverse the interior Southeast. During this occupation of Etowah, three small mounds (D, E, and F) were built and the summit of Mound B was reused. At this time, Etowah comes into written history, referred to as the town of Itaba, which de Soto visited in August 1540. Evidence of that visit includes such European items as an iron celt, an iron spike, fragments of chain mail, a sword hilt, and portions of a European-style rotary quern found in archaeological deposits at the site. De Soto had little to say about Itaba, except that it was a subject town in the larger Coosa paramount chiefdom.

The depopulation and social disruption caused by the initial Spanish incursions and later attempts to colonize the Southeast fundamentally altered the native political and social landscape. By the close of the sixteenth century, Mississippian chiefdoms had disappeared from the Etowah valley for the last time. Populations in northwestern Georgia, decimated by disease, appear to have coalesced and moved down the Coosa drainage into Alabama, and they ultimately became part of the Creek Confederacy.

Today Etowah is preserved as a park operated by the state of Georgia, and it also is listed in the National Register of Historic Places and as a National Historic Landmark. The park is open to visitors all year, except Sundays and major holidays.

Further Reading: Kelly, A. R., and L. H. Larson, "Explorations at the Etowah Indian Mounds Near Cartersville, Georgia: Seasons 1954, 1955, 1956," *Archaeology* 10(1) (1957): 39–48; King, Adam, *Etowah: The Political History of a Chiefdom Capital* (Tuscaloosa:

University of Alabama Press, 2003); Larson, Lewis H., Jr., "Archaeological Implications of Social Stratification at the Etowah Site, Georgia," in *Approaches to the Social Dimensions of Mortuary Practices*, edited by J. A. Brown, Society for American Archaeology, Memoir 25 (1971), 58–67; Larson, Lewis H., Jr., "The Etowah Site," in *The Southeastern Ceremonial Complex: Artifacts and Analysis*, edited by P. Galloway (Lincoln: University of Nebraska Press, 1989), 133–141; Moorehead, W. K., ed., *The Etowah Papers* (Andover, MA: Phillips Academy, 1932); Thomas, C., *Report on the Mound Explorations of the Bureau of Ethnology*, Smithsonian Institution, Bureau of Ethnology, Twelfth Annual Report (Washington, DC: 1894).

Adam King

LAKE JACKSON MOUNDS STATE ARCHAEOLOGICAL SITE

Lake Jackson, Northwest Florida

A Late Prehistoric Political and Ceremonial Mound Center

The Lake Jackson site is a large Mississippian mound center in northwest Florida just north of Tallahassee. Between AD 1250 and 1500 it was the capital of an important chiefdom that archaeologists call the Lake Jackson phase. At its peak, the site included six or seven earthen mounds, cleared plazas, and a residential area. Mound 2, the largest at the site, is approximately 36 feet high and measures about 275 feet by 310 feet at the base. The other mounds range in height from 3 feet (Mound 7) to 16 feet (Mounds 3 and 4) and have basal measurements of 65 by 65 feet (Mound 7) to 160 feet by 180 feet (Mound 4).

The leaders of the Lake Jackson chiefdom ruled over a territory that encompassed much of what is now Leon, Jefferson, and Wakulla counties, an area of about 2,000 square kilometers. The population of the chiefdom numbered in the thousands, with a high estimate by early Spanish missionaries of 30,000 people. The Lake Jackson site appears to have been abandoned shortly before the first European explorers entered the area, but the descendents of the people who constructed Lake Jackson, the historic Apalachee, remained and continued to be influential to the end of the seventeenth century.

The people of the Lake Jackson phase were farmers who raised corn, beans, and squashes. They rounded out their diets with meat from deer and other mammals, fish, and shellfish. Most people lived in small hamlets and farmsteads, but there was also a sizable residential population at Lake Jackson. Extrapolating from mission period accounts, the hamlets and farmsteads formed dispersed communities that coordinated occasional moves made necessary by soil depletion and firewood shortages. The members of a community cooperated in the preparation of fields in the winter and spring, as well as in communal hunts coupled with field clearing.

Most members of the Lake Jackson chiefdom were commoners. They farmed the land and were largely self-sufficient, making their own tools and producing food for their families. Social relations were based on kinship ties and membership in local communities. A small number of high-status individuals occupied positions of authority in this society. These individuals had ties to other societies, access to exotic goods, and power that commoners did not.

The highest-ranked people of the Lake Jackson phase, those buried in Mound 3, were treated very differently from commoners. Their funerals were occasions for public rituals and civic construction projects. They were buried with items of value and with material symbols of status and position, including copper and stone axes, elaborate beaded costumes, engraved shell gorgets, and repoussé copper plates. Many of these items were manufactured outside the Lake Jackson chiefdom and would have been difficult to obtain.

During the first half of the sixteenth century, two Spanish expeditions entered the Apalachee territory in north Florida. The accounts of these expeditions do not mention the presence of mounds, so we assume that the Lake Jackson site was abandoned before 1528. That is consistent with radiocarbon dates from Mound 3 at Lake Jackson, although abandonment of the site occurred not long before the Spaniards' appearance. The apparent short interval between Lake Jackson's abandonment and earliest European accounts of the Apalachee and material culture similarities argue that the historic Apalachee were the descendents of the peoples who built Lake Jackson. This continuity allows us to carefully use historic accounts of the Apalachee to augment the archaeological data on the prehistoric Lake Jackson chiefdom.

After their encounters with the Narvaez and De Soto expeditions, the Apalachee maintained their independence for several generations. The Spaniards finally established a permanent presence in Apalachee territory in 1633 when they established numerous missions and a garrison at San Luis mission. There are numerous historical accounts of the Apalachee that date from the mission period. They were effectively destroyed as a group in 1704 following attacks by English colonists and their Creek Indian allies. Survivors were incorporated into the Creek or fled to St. Augustine, Pensacola, and Mobile.

Lake Jackson has received less attention from archaeologists than is the case for other large Mississippian centers such as Moundville or Etowah. Fortunately, the investigations that have been conducted allow us to discuss the site's general chronology and organization as well as the role its leaders played in the larger Mississippian world.

In the early 1940s, Gordon Willey and Richard Woodbury conducted the first scientific excavations at Lake Jackson. Their work was limited, but they were able to identify the major occupation as dating to the Mississippian period. Based on comparisons to earlier sites in the region, Willey argued that the pattern of settlement for the late prehistoric societies reflected a shift from small-scale community and kin-based groups to larger societies with centralized leadership based at a few large mound centers. Lake Jackson is one example of the latter. Subsequent research has borne out Willey's insights.

In the late 1940s, John W. Griffin conducted salvage excavations in a residential area of the site in anticipation of the creation of a small pond. Griffin found evidence of what were presumably domestic structures and a cleared area or plaza. His work helped refine our picture of the organization of the Lake Jackson community.

In the mid-1970s, B. Calvin Jones of the Florida Bureau of Archaeological Research conducted rescue excavations of Mound 3, which was being mined for top soil. Jones's excavations revealed that the mound had served as a mortuary facility for the most important members of Lake Jackson society. Jones uncovered over ten construction stages, each of which had a building on its summit. Periodically, graves dug through the floors of the mound summit and a new construction stage was added to the mound. Many graves contained skeletons accompanied by material symbols of rank and position. John Scarry analyzed the mortuary patterning in Mound 3 and argued that there appeared to have been two offices, one marked by axes that men had access to and one marked by copper plates that was open to both men and women.

In the early 1990s, Claudine Payne conducted test excavations to gain additional information on the dating of other mounds and on the extent and organization of the residential zone. Payne also incorporated information from other excavations at the site to produce a rough picture of the spatial organization of the site.

From an archaeological standpoint, Lake Jackson is important because of the information it has provided about relationships among Mississippian chiefdoms and the exchange of symbolically charged objects between the elites of different chiefdoms. These distinctive objects are often referred to as being part of a Southeastern Ceremonial Complex. The stratigraphy of Mound 3, coupled with radiocarbon dates, has helped refine the dating of these widely shared objects. Stylistic and technological analyses of the materials from Mound 3 have also helped refine pictures of the kinds of objects exchanged among the leaders of Mississippian chiefdoms and the sociopolitical relationships they maintain among themselves.

A portion of the site containing three of the mounds forms the core of the Lake Jackson Mounds Archaeological State Park. The park, which also contains a nineteenth-century gristmill, is open from 8:00 am to sunset. There is an admission fee. The park entrance is located on Indian Mounds Road.

Further Reading: Jones, B. Calvin, "Southern Cult Manifestations at the Lake Jackson Site, Leon County, Florida: Salvage Excavation of Mound 3," *Midcontinental Journal of Archaeology* 7 (1982): 3–44; Payne, Claudine, "Fifty Years of Archaeological Research at the Lake Jackson Site," *Florida Anthropologist* 47 (1994): 107–119; Payne, Claudine, and John F. Scarry, "Town Structure at the Edge of the Mississippian World," in *Mississippian Towns and Sacred Places*, edited by R. Barry Lewis and Charles Stout (Tuscaloosa: University of Alabama Press, 1998), 22–48; Scarry, John F., "Elite Identities in Apalachee Province: The Construction of Identity and Cultural Change in a Mississippian Polity," in *Material Symbols*, edited by John Robb, Occasional Paper No. 26 (Carbondale: Southern Illinois University Center for Archaeological Investigations, 1999), 342–361.

John Scarry

THE HARLAN SITE

Eastern Oklahoma

A Late Prehistoric Mound Center

The Harlan site is a Mississippian-period mound center in eastern Oklahoma overlooking the Fourteen Mile Creek valley, near the margin between the western prairies and the eastern woodlands. The site was an important regional center, used primarily between AD 900 and 1200. It was part of a network of mound centers, including the Spiro site, and local communities in northeast Oklahoma and northwest Arkansas that were culturally linked as part of the Northern

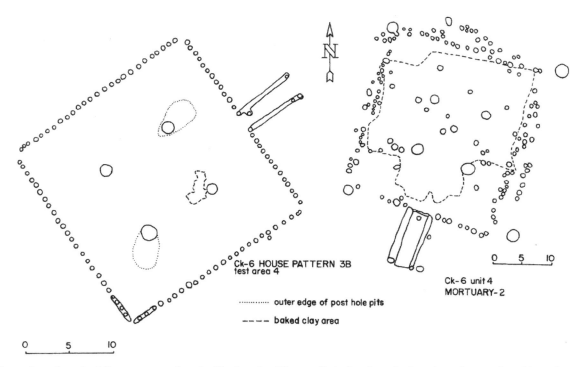

The floor plan of two buildings excavated at the Harlan site. The small circles show the location of posts placed into the ground to form the walls and support the roof.   [Courtesy of Academic Press]

Caddoan tradition. The site was not a village but instead served as a ceremonial and civic center, consisting of five mounds and several buildings used as mortuaries surrounding an open plaza. Near the time the site was abandoned, another mound center known as the Norman site was established nearby. Other mound centers in the region related to the Harlan site include Cavanaugh, Eufaula, Ewing Chapel, Collins, Goforth-Saindon, Hughes, Huntsville, Lillie Creek, Loftin, Parris, Pineville, Reed, Skidgel, and Spiro.

The people who built and used the Harlan site lived in individual or small groups of houses dispersed along the Grant River and Fourteen Mile Creek valleys. Most houses were square with a mean floor area of 46 square meters. Houses had thatched roofs with walls constructed of mud plastered over sticks woven between poles placed vertically in the ground. The economy was based on hunting, fishing, gathering, and agriculture. Although maize was grown, it was not a major part of the diet until around AD 1100. Trade was also important, with evidence for artifacts and raw materials from sources in the southwestern United States and several places east of the Mississippi River. The range of objects placed with burials provides evidence for significant status differences and identifies Harlan as the center of a chiefdom.

Harlan covers an area of about 20 acres (about 8.5 hectares). The largest mound at the site was 14 feet tall, with a rectangular base and a flat top. It was used as a platform for important buildings. The site also included a conjoined burial mound (Unit 1) composed of three cones, similar to Craig Mound at the Spiro site. Two other mounds marked the locations of buildings used as mortuaries where the remains of individuals were kept, often for years. Periodically these remains were transferred to the mound and covered by a new layer of soil. Some individuals placed in the mound were also cremated. Grave offerings in the mound include beads, stone and wood earspools, clay and stone pipes, copper, conch shells, pottery, and a variety of stone tools.

Before constructing the Fort Gibson reservoir, salvage excavations directed by Robert E. Bell of the University of Oklahoma were conducted at Harlan in 1949, 1950, and 1958. Today the site is largely inundated and is not accessible to the public.

Further Reading: Bell, Robert E., *The Harlan Site, Ck-6, A Prehistoric Mound Center in Cherokee County, Eastern Oklahoma*, Memoir 2 (Norman: Oklahoma Anthropological Society, 1972); Bell, Robert E., ed., *Prehistory of Oklahoma* (New York: Academic Press, 1984); Oklahoma Archeological Survey Web site, http://www.ou.edu/cas/archsur/counties/cherokee.htm (online January 2006).

J. Daniel Rogers

SPIRO MOUNDS ARCHAEOLOGICAL PARK

Spiro, Eastern Oklahoma

An Earthen Architecture Mound Complex with Spectacular Artifacts

Near the western margin of the eastern forests where they turn into the grasslands of the Great Plains lies Spiro Mounds. Spiro was a great civic and religious center of a chiefdom of the cultural tradition archaeologists call Mississippian. The societies of this tradition dominated the eastern woodlands between AD 900 and 1600. The Spiro site is composed of a series of mounds built as burial places and platforms for temples and other public buildings. Some mounds are cone shaped, whereas others are shaped like a truncated pyramid. Perhaps the single most remarkable thing about Spiro is the huge quantity of rare artifacts originally placed with the dead. Also found at the site are the remains of large and small buildings scattered between the mounds. Rather than the center of a dense village or town, Spiro was at the heart of a large dispersed community that stretched along the Arkansas River.

Spiro includes twelve mounds and was the largest site with mounds in a region encompassing western Arkansas and eastern Oklahoma. The site was connected culturally to many others in a region that also includes eastern Texas and northwestern Louisiana. Together, all of these sites are part of the widely dispersed Mississippian tradition and specifically part of the Northern Caddoan regional tradition. The people who lived in this region shared a cultural heritage and spoke related languages. Beyond the Caddoan region, the people at Spiro formed most of their ties with cultures to the south and east, sometimes making trade connections as far away as the Great Lakes or Florida.

HISTORY, CULTURE, AND PEOPLE

The Spiro site has a long history of use beginning around AD 700 and continuing until AD 1450. During this period Spiro developed as a cultural and political center, although even from its beginning it was a place with a special significance. The first known use of the site was as a cemetery. Later the site grew to include mounds, plazas, and temple, residence, and mortuary buildings. As Spiro expanded, so did the concentration of people living in the area. By the time Spiro had become a significant place, it was also the center of a chiefdom, that is, a hierarchically organized society lead by a hereditary chief drawn from a prominent lineage. Although there are several other mound centers in eastern Oklahoma and western Arkansas, such as the Harlan site, all of these sites are smaller and have less evidence for the presence of high-status individuals. The political rise of the Spiro elite

took place between about AD 850 and 900. By that time there is evidence for large buildings where chiefs and priests lived and where rituals pertaining to the dead were carried out.

The society that built Spiro was organized into social statuses that included commoners, possibly slaves, and a separate elite class of chiefs and priests. By the time Spiro reached its greatest size (around AD 1250) it had become a place set apart from everyday activities. It was reserved for social and political gatherings, the activities of the elite, and a place for the burial of important people.

Although very few, if any, commoners lived at Spiro, they did live in nearby communities consisting of small clusters or individual houses scattered along the edges of the Arkansas River valley. Houses were made by placing poles vertically in the ground and then plastered over with mud to construct the walls. Long grasses were collected to make the thatched roofs. Early houses were usually square with an extended entryway. Later houses were typically rectangular and smaller. The decrease in house size over time provides evidence for changes in family size.

Scattered between the houses were gardens of maize, squash, maygrass, little barley, knotweed, and sunflower. Although maize is the best-known of these plants, it was not a significant part of the diet until after AD 1100. At Spiro, maize was never as important as it was at contemporary sites further to the south and east. Besides cultivating plants, people practiced extensive hunting, fishing, and gathering of wild plants. Deer was the most important game animal, although rabbits, turkeys, beavers, squirrels, and many other animals, including an occasional bison, were part of the diet.

DESCRIPTION OF THE SITE

The Spiro site includes two clusters of mounds, referred to as the floodplain and uplands groups. These two groups of mounds were built and used over a period of 750 years. The floodplain group consists of Ward Mounds 1 and 2 and Craig Mound, also referred to as the Great Temple Mound. The Ward Mounds are low circular mounds, each constructed over the remains of a building that once stood on the spot. Somewhat later the mounds were used as burial places for at least thirty-one individuals.

The other mound, Craig Mound, in the floodplain group deserves special consideration because it is where the most important people were buried along with many incredible artifacts. Craig Mound itself consisted of four conjoined

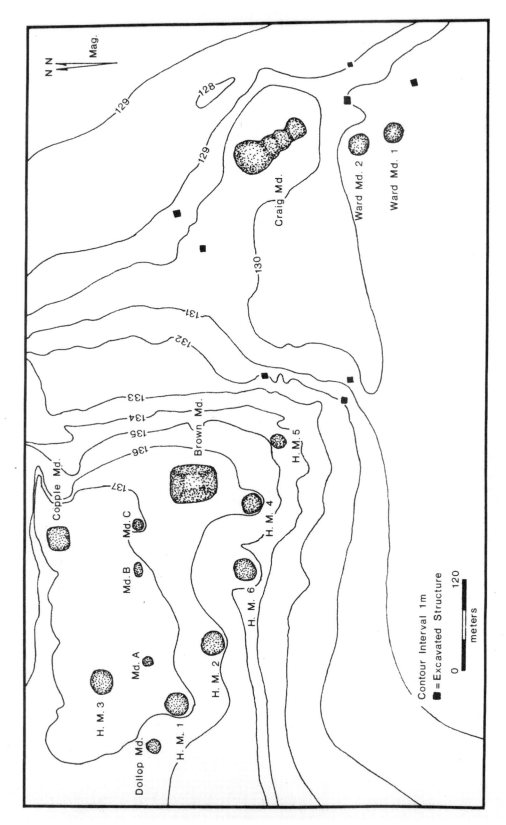

Map of the Spiro site, showing the locations of twelve major mounds and three minor mounds (A, B, and C). Small squares mark the locations of buildings excavated in the 1930s. [Copyright © 2008 by the Southeastern Archaeological Conference]

Craig Mound during excavation in January 1937. The oval cavity near the bottom center of the mound marks the location of the Great Mortuary, where many artifacts were found.   [Sam Noble Oklahoma Museum of Natural History]

circular mounds built up over the course of hundreds of years by adding layer after layer of soil. Craig Mound probably started as four separate mounds adjacent to each other. As layers were added, the mounds began to overlap one another. The four mounds were not built at the same rate, nor were they used for the same purpose. For instance, the northernmost cone served as a series of platforms for large buildings used as mortuaries and possibly elite residences. In a cycle repeated many times, each successive building was used, cleared out, destroyed, and covered with a layer of soil. As part of this cycle, other burials were also placed in the mound. In one instance, referred to as the Great Mortuary, the contents of one of the buildings were not cleared out. Discovered on the floor were the remains of high-status burials with many rare and exotic artifacts, including numerous marine whelk shells with elaborately carved decorations. Burials were also being placed in the lesser cones of the mound, along with other major features, such as a crematory basin made of baked clay with steps leading down into it.

The upland group of mounds characterizes the main early history of Spiro. This group of mounds consists of Brown Mound, Copple Mound, Dollop Mound, and House Mounds 1 through 6. All of the mounds are positioned to form a rough oval, referred to as the Plaza. Brown Mound, the largest in the upland group, was a truncated pyramid, a style common among contemporary Mississippian societies to the east. Brown Mound was primarily not a burial mound but instead served as a platform for important buildings. Excavations revealed the intricate nature of its construction, including the

careful layering of alternating soil colors. Copple Mound is the second largest in the upland group. Like Brown Mound, it was a platform with an intricate history of construction that involved adding soil in and around a partially dismantled building. Although mound construction proceeded in episodes, its construction can be thought of as edge, periphery, and center. House Mounds 1–6 were also not burial mounds but were instead relatively small mounds built over the remains of special buildings. Like many of the other mounds at the site, the building of the mounds was closely tied to commemorating the spot where a building was intentionally dismantled. Except for Brown Mound, the mounds in the upland group were not used after about AD 1250.

Much of the information about Spiro comes from archaeological excavations. The history of excavations is a long and dramatic story beginning with Joseph Thoburn, a historian with the Oklahoma Historical Society, who excavated one of the Ward mounds in 1916–17. The most remarkable and tragic part of the story begins in the 1930s, during the height of the Great Depression, when mounds, including the Craig Mound, were leased to men whose sole interest was acquiring artifacts to sell on the open market. The flood of rare and unusual artifacts that came from their excavations resulted in major media coverage, prompting one newspaper to compare the Craig Mound discoveries to those of King Tutankhamen's tomb in Egypt. Among the finds were thousands of shell beads, freshwater pearls, hundreds of engraved whelk shells, many copper tools and decorations, hundreds of stone tools, maces, pipes, stone and wood sculptures, baskets, and textiles. Many of them were sold without being recorded by photographs, drawings, or written descriptions. Worse, these objects were removed from their archaeological context without any recording of their positions within the mound or what other artifacts or materials they were associated with. Much potential information about the objects, the site, and ancient America was lost due to this lack of recording.

By 1936, professional archaeologists had raised enough public concern that a law was passed in Oklahoma that required a state permit for excavations. The era of pothunting was over, and archaeologists from the University of Oklahoma began a systematic study of the site with support from the Works Progress Administration (WPA), one of Franklin D. Roosevelt's New Deal relief programs. Although excavation techniques of the 1930s were far less precise than those in current use, for the first time reliable information was obtained to assess the context and meaning of the remarkable discoveries in the Craig Mound. Archaeological work halted at the beginning of World War II in 1941.

Following the work of the 1930s, Spiro slipped into obscurity. It was not until 1970 that the state of Oklahoma and the U.S. Army Corps of Engineers took up the challenge of opening the site to the public as an archaeological park. Craig Mound was reconstructed, and a five-year research program was begun to refine the site's chronology, collect evidence on diet and technology, and verify the location of nearby sites in the area.

In 1978 a visitors' center was opened to the public. The Spiro Mounds Archaeological Center houses interpretive exhibits and offers a variety of public programs throughout the year. The 90-acre park includes a series of paths leading to each mound. Interpretive signs describe the mounds, along with the history and culture of the people who built and used Spiro.

Further Reading: Bell, Robert E., ed., *Prehistory of Oklahoma* (New York: Academic Press, 1984); Brown, James A., *The Spiro Ceremonial Center: The Archaeology of Arkansas Valley Caddoan Culture in Eastern Oklahoma*, 2 vols., Memoirs of the Museum of Anthropology, No. 29 (Ann Arbor: University of Michigan, 1996); Brown, James A., Bell, Robert E., and Wyckoff, Don G., "Caddoan Settlement Patterns in the Arkansas River Drainage," in *Mississippi Settlement Patterns*, edited by Bruce D. Smith (New York: Academic Press,1978), 169–200; Early, Ann M., "Prehistory of the Western Interior after 500 B.C.," in *Handbook of North American Indians*, Vol. 14 (Washington, DC: Smithsonian Institution, 2004), 560–573; Oklahoma Archeological Survey Web site, http://www.ou.edu/cas/archsur/counties/leflore.htm (online January 2006); Rogers, J. Daniel, Wyckoff, Don G., and Peterson, Dennis A., eds., *Contributions to Spiro Archaeology: Regional Perspectives and Mound Excavations*, Studies in Oklahoma's Past, No. 16 (Norman: Oklahoma Archeological Survey, 1989).

J. Daniel Rogers

THE TOWN CREEK MOUND STATE HISTORIC SITE

Southern Piedmont, North Carolina

A Native American Town and Ceremonial Center

The Town Creek site is located in the Pee Dee River valley on the Little River in the southern Piedmont of North Carolina. Town Creek was an important place for nearly 10,000 years, with artifacts indicating that the site was used at least intermittently from the Early Archaic through Historic periods (8000 BC–AD 1700) (Boudreaux 2005; Coe 1995, table 10.1). Most of the archaeological deposits at Town Creek date to the Mississippian period (AD 1050–1400), when the site was a regionally important town and ceremonial center (Boudreaux 2005). Today, the site is preserved as the Town Creek Indian Mound State Historic Site, the only state-run park in North Carolina devoted exclusively to the interpretation of Native American culture (Ward and Davis 1999, 123). It consists of a museum, an area for living-history displays, and archaeologically based reconstructions of a mound, palisade, wooden enclosure, and three buildings (Carnes-McNaughton 2002; Coe 1995, 29–41; South 1995).

Town Creek has an interesting history of scientific investigation. The site is distinctive within southeastern archaeology for several reasons, one of which is because fieldwork took place there intermittently for approximately fifty years (1937–83). The long-term excavations produced a valuable research collection and made Town Creek one of the most extensively excavated sites in the region (Boudreaux 2005; Coe 1995). Unlike other sites in the southeast that were excavated by large crews in a short period of time (e.g., some of the Depression-era "make work" excavations described in Lyon 1996), Town Creek was excavated by relatively small crews over a long period of time. Prior to World War II, crews of fewer than fifteen dug almost the entire mound (today's mound is a reconstruction), the surrounding area, and an area along the Little River. Work conducted after the war was undertaken by two- or three-person crews focusing on one or two 10 by 10 ft units at a time. The cumulative result of this approach over the course of five decades was extraordinary, resulting in the exposure of approximately 100,000 square feet of archaeological deposits and the documentation of virtually an entire Mississippian town.

Although tens of thousands of features were mapped at Town Creek, only slightly more than half (55 percent) were excavated (Boudreaux 2005, 23). Consequently, deposits were preserved for future research. Finding the precise locations of thousands of undisturbed features has been likened to having an X-ray of the entire site, facilitating the development of future problem-specific research designs (Ferguson 1995, xvi).

THE MISSISSIPPIAN COMMUNITY AT TOWN CREEK

Although Town Creek had been used at least intermittently for thousands of years, the most intense period of occupation occurred between AD 1050 and 1400 (Boudreaux 2005). While the form and function of the structures within the community would change significantly throughout its history, the town's layout was established at the outset and remained relatively unchanged from that point onward. Public buildings and monuments were placed along a central east-west axis, and corporate-group buildings were constructed to the north and south of this axis.

Beginning around AD 1050, Town Creek consisted of a large, oval plaza surrounded by buildings. The center of the plaza was occupied by a large monument consisting of a 112-foot-diameter circular enclosure made of wooden posts with several massive posts near its center. Rectangular public buildings were constructed on the west side of the plaza—beneath where the mound would later be built—and a number of circular houses surrounded the rest of the plaza. People were buried in the floors of public and domestic buildings. Based on ethnohistoric accounts and evidence from other archaeological sites, public buildings were places where leaders met to discuss important community issues that probably included political affairs, internal disputes, and relations with other communities (Hudson 1976; Swanton 1979).

Significant changes occurred across Town Creek beginning around AD 1250. A platform mound was built on the western side of the plaza over the community's earlier public buildings. The mound was built in at least four stages, and each stage appears to have supported several rectangular public buildings. Mound construction and use continued for at least 100 years (Boudreaux 2005, 153). Architectural and ceramic vessel data suggest that the mound's summit may have been the site of communal gatherings. At the same time the mound was built, a rectangular enclosure was built across the plaza next to the river. Several buildings and a number of burials were located within this enclosure.

Dramatic changes occurred in the site's domestic sphere after the mound was built. It seems that former house sites were then encircled with an enclosure of wooden posts and used as cemeteries. Although people were no longer living in these locations, at least four former house sites were maintained as cemeteries, probably by corporate groups (possibly extended families or lineages) that occupied them before the mound was built. Each circular, enclosed cemetery appears to have been paired with a large, rectangular structure. It is possible that each structure pair represents public buildings—a cemetery and adjacent area for large-group gatherings—associated with one of the several corporate groups in the Town Creek community.

Some burials on the mound and within the enclosure were associated with a distinctive suite of artifacts suggesting that these people participated in community rituals. These probable ritual artifacts include the remains of rattles and ornaments made of nonlocal materials such as marine shell, exotic stone, copper, and mica. Although unusual artifacts were generally not present in the corporate-group areas north and south of the plaza, certain burials within these areas were distinguished in another important way. One centrally located burial in each house and two burials in each enclosed cemetery were distinctive because they were buried in extended positions. It seems likely that the individuals represented by these centrally placed, extended burials were important members of their household and family groups.

Town Creek was no longer occupied by AD 1450. No one knows for certain why this occurred, but it has been argued that a number of communities in the region were abandoned at approximately AD 1450 due to climatic changes that negatively affected crop production (Anderson et al. 1995). Although it was no longer a formal town, Town Creek continued to be an important place for Native Americans after this time. The presence of European trade goods indicates that the mound and two cemetery areas were used in the 1500s and 1600s.

CONCLUSION

Town Creek has played a major role in archaeology and public education in North Carolina for decades. For countless visitors since the 1950s, Town Creek has been their introduction to the study of prehistoric ways of life. For archaeologists, there are numerous possibilities for future studies at Town Creek. Significant research potential remains in the collections from the site, and thousands of documented features are preserved for future research.

Further Reading: Anderson, David G., David W. Stahle, and Malcolm K. Cleaveland, "Paleoclimate and the Potential Food Reserves of Mississippian Societies: A Case Study from the Savannah River Valley," *American Antiquity* 60(2) (1995): 258–286; Boudreaux, Edmond A., "The Archaeology of Town Creek: Chronology, Community Patterns, and Leadership at a Mississippian Town," unpublished Ph.D. diss. (Department of Anthropology, University of

North Carolina, Chapel Hill, 2005); Carnes-McNaughton, Linda F., "The Nature of Public Archaeology at Town Creek Indian Mound," in *The Archaeology of Native North Carolina: Papers in Honor of H. Trawick Ward*, edited by Jane M. Eastman, Christopher B. Rodning, and Edmond A. Boudreaux III, Special Publication No. 7 (Biloxi, MS: Southeastern Archaeological Conference, 2002), 12–17; Coe, Joffre L., *Town Creek Indian Mound: A Native American Legacy* (Chapel Hill: University of North Carolina Press, 1995); Ferguson, Leland G., "Foreword," in *Town Creek Indian Mound: A Native American Legacy*, by Joffre L. Coe (Chapel Hill: University of North Carolina Press, 1995), xiii–xx; Hudson, Charles, *The Southeastern Indians* (Knoxville: University of Tennessee Press, 1976); Lyon, Edwin A., *A New Deal for Southeastern Archaeology* (Tuscaloosa: University of Alabama Press, 1996); South, Stanley, "Reconstruction of the Town House on the Mound," in *Town Creek Indian Mound: A Native American Legacy*, by Joffre L. Coe (Chapel Hill: University of North Carolina Press, 1995), 282–300; Swanton, John R., *The Indians of the Southeastern United States*, Bureau of American Ethnology Bulletin No. 137 (Washington, DC: U.S. Government Printing Office, 1946), reprint (Washington, DC: Smithsonian Institution Press, 1979); Ward, H. Trawick, and R. P. Stephen Davis Jr., *Time before History: The Archaeology of North Carolina* (Chapel Hill: University of North Carolina Press, 1999).

Edmond A. Boudreaux, III

THE SITE OF COOSA OR LITTLE EGYPT

Northwest Georgia

The Archaeology of a Powerful Mississippian Chiefdom

Coosa was the name of a powerful Mississippian chiefdom that exercised some degree of political control over at least half a dozen other chiefdoms located in northwestern Georgia and adjacent portions of Alabama and Tennessee in the mid-sixteenth century. Both the de Soto and Luna expeditions traveled to Coosa in response to its fame and reputed wealth. The ceremonial and political center for the chiefdom, also named Coosa, is known to archaeologists as the Little Egypt site (9MU102). Little Egypt consists of two flat-topped earth mounds, a large plaza, and a surrounding habitations zone.

Little Egypt (9MU102) is located on the Coosawattee River at the point where it crosses the Great Smokey Fault that separates the Blue Ridge Mountains from the Great Valley section of the Valley and Ridge physiographic province. The site covers an area measuring approximately 360 by 180 meters on the south bank of the river at the mouth of Talking Rock Creek. In recent times, plowing and overbank flooding have reduced Mounds A and B to low rises, measuring respectively 3 meters and 2 meters in height. Artifacts dating to the Early Woodland period (perhaps as early as 3,000 years ago), the subsequent Mississippian time period, and eighteenth- and nineteenth-century Cherokee are present at the site, but the major occupations date to the fifteenth and sixteenth centuries.

The first professional investigation of Little Egypt was undertaken by Warren K. Moorehead in 1925. The site had recently been scoured by floodwaters from Talking Rock Creek and the Coosawattee River, and Moorehead excavated a number of exposed burials as well as a large 30- by 40-foot pit in the summit of Mound A. University of Georgia investigations began in 1969 and spanned four field seasons through 1972. Research focused on delineating site boundaries, identifying mound configuration and construction stages, and excavating a random sample of domestic structures. The site was inundated in 1974 when the Army Corps of Engineers completed construction of the Carters Lake reservoir.

Occupation deposits dating to the Little Egypt phase (beginning about AD 1400) are limited to the northern third of the site. Mound A construction began at this time, and through four building stages grew to height of at least 2.75 meters. The summit of the Stage 3 platform, the last relatively intact construction stage, measured approximately 20 meters square and was surmounted by a single square structure measuring 9.1 meters on each side.

The Barnett phase occupation (dated to about AD 1500) covers an area measuring approximately 275 by 180 meters. Mound B was constructed in two stages at this time, and at least two construction stages were added to Mound A. By this time, Mound A consisted of a central platform flanked by raised terraces on at least two sides. Architectural evidence on the summit of the central platform has been destroyed by plowing, but the terrace located on its southeastern flank supported a 9.8 by 9.1–meter structure. Abundant domestic pottery, lithic tools and debitage, animal bone, and charred plant remains on the floor demonstrate that it was a domestic residence.

Three Barnett phase domestic structures, including the building on the southeast terrace of Mound A, were excavated during University of Georgia investigations. These buildings were square and were erected in shallow basins measuring

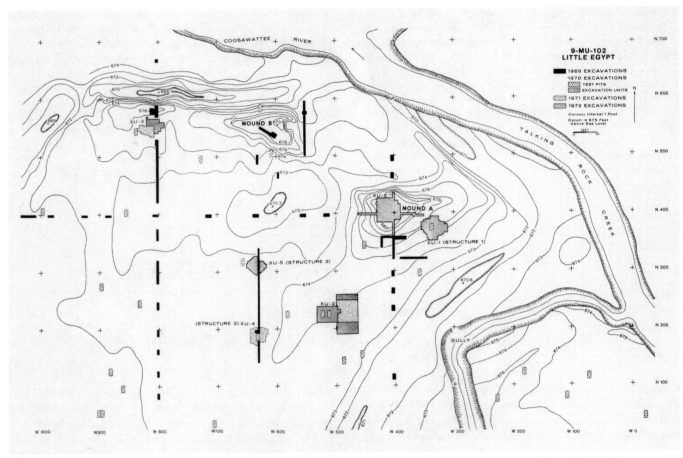

Map of the Little Egypt site showing floodplain configuration, Mounds A and B, and excavation units.   [David J. Hally]

approximately half a meter deep. Exterior walls were constructed with individually set posts and had earth banked against their exterior surface to a height of perhaps 1 meter. Peaked roofs, covered with thatch or bark shingles, were supported by these walls and four interior posts. The central floor contained a hearth, and the outer floor was divided by low walls into compartments for sleeping, storage, and craft activities. Analysis of floor debris from the three structures indicates that this type of building was used primarily during the colder months of the year. Nearby corn cribs, elevated a number of feet off the ground, may have protected outdoor work areas from sun and rain during the summer.

Little Egypt is one of seven large Barnett phase towns along a 19-kilometer stretch of the Coosawattee River below the Great Smokey Fault. These sites range from 2 to 5 hectares and are spaced on average about 3 kilometers apart. Similar clusters of between four and seven large towns, dating to the mid-sixteenth century, are known from the Coosa, Etowah, Hiwassee, Tennessee, and Little Tennessee rivers in northwestern Georgia and adjacent portions of Alabama and Tennessee. In each case, there is evidence that one town had

one or more platform mounds. These site clusters represent politically centralized chiefdoms, administered by a chief who resided at the town with mounds.

Several iron artifacts recovered by Moorehead from a burial in Mound A and a Nueva Cadiz glass bead found on the site surface in 1972 have been dated by Marvin T. Smith to AD 1540–60. Similar types of artifacts have been found by amateur archaeologists in burials at three other towns in the Coosawattee River site cluster as well as four towns in site clusters on the Coosa and Etowah Rivers. Smith's dates for these artifacts suggest that they were obtained from the de Soto and Luna expeditions of 1540 and 1560, respectively.

Charles Hudson and his colleagues have reconstructed the routes of the de Soto and Luna expeditions through the Southeast using a variety of evidence, including daily travel distances, geographical features such as rivers and mountains, the location of known sixteenth-century mound centers, and the geographical distribution of sites with mid-sixteenth-century Spanish artifacts. According to their reconstruction, Little Egypt is the town of Coosa and the capital of the Coosa chiefdom.

De Soto first heard about the powerful chiefdom of Coosa during his march eastward across central Georgia in the spring of 1540. After crossing the Blue Ridge Mountains east of Ashville, North Carolina, the expedition headed southwest along the eastern edge of the Great Valley, reaching Coosa in mid-July. Members of the expedition were impressed with the wealth of Coosa; one chronicler, the gentleman of Elvas, stated that it was densely populated with a number of large towns separated by planted fields.

A contingent of soldiers from the Luna expedition, led by Mateo del Suarez, traveled to Coosa in the summer of 1560 in search of food for the starving colony. During their several-week stay, Suarz and his men joined warriors from Coosa in a military expedition against a chiefdom located near present-day Chattanooga, Tennessee, that had formerly paid tribute to the Coosa chief.

It is clear from the chronicles of the two Spanish expeditions that the chief of Coosa at one time controlled a half-dozen or so chiefdoms in the region. This paramount chiefdom appears to have stretched for approximately 400 kilometers along the eastern edge of the Great Valley from north of Knoxville, Tennessee, to the vicinity of Childersburg, Alabama.

Accounts from the Luna expedition suggest that the power of Coosa had begun to decline by 1560. By 1600, the Coosawattee, Etowah, and Coosa River valleys in northwestern Georgia were abandoned. The remnant populations of Coosa and the region's other chiefdoms had begun a gradual movement down the Coosa River to the vicinity of Talladega, Alabama, where they rejoin written history in the eighteenth century as part of the Creek confederacy.

The Little Egypt site lies at the foot of Carters Dam and Lake near the visitors' center. The basin in which the site is situated, and occasionally the mounds themselves, can be viewed from the visitors' center located adjacent to the dam. For directions, go to http://carters.sam.usace.army.mil.

Further Reading: Hally, David J., *Archaeological Investigation of the Little Egypt Site (9MU102), Murray County, Ga., 1969 Season*, Laboratory of Archaeology Series, Report No. 18 (Athens: University of Georgia, 1979); Hally, David J., *Archaeological Investigation of the Little Egypt Site (9MU102), Murray County, Georgia, 1970–72 Seasons*, Laboratory of Archaeology Series, Report No. 40 (Athens: University of Georgia, 2007); Hally, David J., Marvin T. Smith, and James B. Langford Jr., "The Archaeological Reality of De Soto's Coosa," in *Columbian Consequences*, Vol. 2 of *Archaeological and Historical Perspectives on the Spanish Borderlands East*, edited by David Hurst Thomas (Washington, DC: Smithsonian Institution Press, 1990), 121–138; Hudson, Charles, *Knights of Spain, Warriors of the Sun: Hernando de Soto and the South's Ancient Chiefdoms* (Athens: University of Georgia Press, 1997); Hudson, Charles, Marvin Smith, David Hally, Richard Polhemus, and Chester DePratter, "Coosa: A Chiefdom in the Sixteenth-Century Southeastern United States," *American Antiquity* 50 (1985): 723–737; Smith, Marvin T., *Coosa: The Rise and Fall of a Southeastern Mississippian Chiefdom* (Gainesville: University Press of Florida, 2000).

David J. Hally

THE FATHERLAND SITE

Southwest Mississippi

The Archaeology of the Grand Village of the Natchez

The Fatherland site, now known as the Grand Village of the Natchez Indians, is a National Historic Landmark owned by the state of Mississippi and administered by the Mississippi Department of Archives and History. The site is significant due to numerous French colonial accounts of the Natchez Indians' use of the mounds and plaza that correlate with archaeological findings. The site's name is somewhat misleading: the Grand Village was a ceremonial center with only a few important members of the tribe in permanent residence. Most people lived on family farms in settlement districts dispersed over approximately 140 square miles.

Colonial observations of Natchez ceremonial activities at the Grand Village have been widely used to interpret late prehistoric mound sites across the Southeast and Midwest. Early eighteenth-century European writers who described the site include Pierre LeMoyne d'Iberville, André Pénicaut, Jacques Gravier, Pierre-François-Xavier de Charlevoix, Dumont de Montigny, and Le Page du Pratz. Following René-Robert Cavelier de La Salle's initial contact with the tribe in 1682, visits by European missionaries, soldiers, and traders culminated in the establishment of a French colony among the Natchez in 1716. By the 1720s, the influx of Europeans and Africans into the Natchez colony to develop commercial tobacco plantations led to increasing friction with local Indians. The Grand Village was an important contact point between the Natchez and the French during the years leading

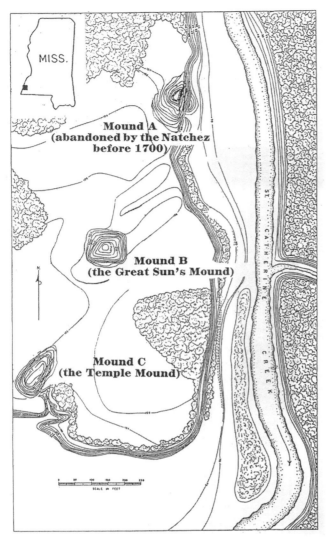

The Fatherland site (the Grand Village of the Natchez). [Mississippi Department of Archives and History]

up to the disastrous Natchez rebellion against the French in 1729. The site became a battleground, and was abandoned shortly thereafter.

Archaeological investigations at the Grand Village/Fatherland site commenced in 1924, and the site was designated a National Historic Landmark in 1965. The state of Mississippi acquired the site for preservation and interpretation in 1971. Administered by the Mississippi Department of Archives and History, the Grand Village of the Natchez Indians museum and archaeological park opened to the public in 1976.

NATCHEZ CULTURE HISTORY
Twentieth-century archaeological studies in the lower Mississippi Valley link the historic Natchez Indians with the prehistoric Plaquemine culture, which lasted from around

AD 1200 until the late seventeenth century. A group of archaeologists known as the Lower Mississippi Survey (LMS), founded in 1939 by Philip Phillips, James A. Ford, and James B. Griffin, spearheaded this work. The LMS archaeological investigations continued in the region during the last half of the twentieth century, led by Stephen Williams, Jeffrey P. Brain, Ian W. Brown, Vincas P. Steponaitis, and others.

The Natchez are probable descendants of the powerful Quigualtam chiefdom encountered by the Hernando De Soto expedition in 1542–43. In the late seventeenth century, the tribe's strategic position on the Mississippi River drew the Natchez into the struggle between France and England for supremacy in the lower Mississippi Valley. In 1716 Jean-Baptiste Le Moyne, sieur de Bienville established Fort Rosalie about 3 miles northwest of the Grand Village on the bluff overlooking the Mississippi River. Clashes between Indians and French in 1722 and 1723 disrupted the nascent French colony at Natchez, presaging the Natchez Rebellion of 1729. The rebellion erupted in November of that year with the massacre of the small French community. Some of the colony's enslaved Africans joined the Natchez in the surprise attack, which resulted in the deaths of over 200 men, women, and children. Within months, a combined French and Indian army retaliated, eventually driving the Natchez from their homeland. By the mid-1730s, the Natchez had become refugees, many eventually adopted by the Chickasaws, Creeks, and Cherokees. Today, Natchez descendants are recognized in Oklahoma and South Carolina.

The eighteenth-century Natchez have frequently been portrayed as a single ethnic group; however, they were a combination of at least four groups: Natchez, Koroa, Grigra, and Tiou. The last three groups, usually classified as Tunican speakers, probably joined the Natchez for protection during the chaotic and dangerous decades that accompanied European intrusion into the Southeast. The language spoken by the Natchez is classified as an isolate, that is, it is unrelated to others once spoken in the lower Mississippi Valley. However, two other tribes in the region, the Taensa and Avoyelle, are tentatively classified as Natchez speakers as well.

Natchez society was based upon a matrilineal kinship system, which determined an individual's membership in one of two ranks known as nobility and commoners. At the head of the nobility was the Sun family, lead by the hereditary chief called the "Great Sun." Recent analysis of Natchez social structure indicates that the two ranks were probably moieties, two halves of the tribal society that performed support services for each other. Although the European colonists routinely believed the Great Sun controlled the entire Natchez tribe, the Natchez were in fact a confederation of autonomous villages or settlement districts, each under the influence of a chief who may, or may not, have been related to the Sun family.

Maize agriculture, besides being a major source of food, played a prominent ceremonial role in the lives of the Natchez

Indians during the Little Corn feast in early summer and the Great Corn feast in autumn. The Natchez also hunted deer and other game, speared and trapped fish, and gathered wild plants.

SITE DESCRIPTION

The first archaeological work at the site was Warren K. Moorehead's limited testing in 1924. In the 1930s, archaeologists Moreau B. C. Chambers and James A. Ford identified the Fatherland site (named for a nineteenth-century cotton plantation) as the place mentioned frequently in the French colonial records as the "Grand Village of the Natchez." Chambers led the first extensive archaeological excavations in 1930 for the Mississippi Department of Archives and History. In 1962 and 1972 Robert S. Neitzel carried out further archaeological investigations for the department, which eventually led to the state's acquisition of approximately 126 acres along St. Catherine Creek.

The site's three mounds have been designated A, B, and C. French colonial descriptions focus on the Great Sun's Mound (Mound B) and the temple mound (Mound C). Mound A was evidently not in use during the French colonial period. Excavations at Mounds B and C revealed that they were built incrementally, and radiocarbon dates from all three mounds indicate this occurred between AD 1200 and historic contact. Unfortunately, very little remained of the archaeological footprint of the last structure atop Mound B, which would have been the chief's house seen by Europeans who visited the site.

The identification of Mound C as the temple mound is based upon its location and twenty-six human burials, recalling French colonial accounts of burial activity in and around the temple building. Neitzel documented a significant portion of the historic Natchez temple's archaeological footprint atop Mound C. The temple's floor plan reveals a two-roomed structure with a smaller northern portico adjoining a larger southern (or rear) enclosure, with the whole building being about 60 feet long and 42 feet wide.

In addition to the structures on the mounds, European visitors to the Grand Village mentioned the presence of a few dwellings near the mounds and ceremonial plaza. Neitzel's 1972 excavations uncovered evidence of four off-mound building locations. In 1983 a fifth building location came to light during excavations connected with an erosion-control project. Neitzel also found the remnants of a siege trench dug by the French military during the final confrontation at the Grand Village in February 1730.

PUBLIC EDUCATION AND ACCESS

The Grand Village of the Natchez Indians is located within the city limits of Natchez at 400 Jefferson Davis Boulevard. The grounds are open daily from dawn to dusk. The museum offers exhibits about the Natchez Indians and the French colonial period and is open Monday–Saturday from 9:00 am to 5:00 pm and Sunday from 1:30 to 5:00 pm, except for Labor Day, Thanksgiving, Christmas, and New Year's Day. Admission is free. The site also features a reconstructed Natchez Indian house and outdoor interpretive signs. The museum staff offer educational programs to school and adult groups. Annual public events include the Natchez Powwow, lacrosse games, educational day camp, and archaeology lecture series. For information call (601) 446-6502 or visit the site's Web page at http://mdah.state.ms.us/hprop/gvni.html.

Further Reading: Antoine Simone Le Page Du Pratz, Gordon Sayre, trans., *Histoire de la Louisiane* (originally published in three volumes, Paris: De Bure, Delaguette, Lambert 1758), http://www.uoregon.edu/~gsayre/LPDP.html; Barnett, James F., Jr., *They Became Invisible: A History of the Natchez Indians to 1735* (Jackson: University Press of Mississippi, 2007); Neitzel, Robert S., *Archaeology of the Fatherland Site: The Grand Village of the Natchez* Vol. 51, Part 1 (New York: Anthropological Papers of the American Museum of Natural History, 1965); Neitzel, Robert S., *The Grand Village of the Natchez Revisited: Excavations at the Fatherland Site, Adams County, Mississippi, 1972*, Archaeological Report No. 12 (Jackson: Mississippi Department of Archives and History, 1983); Swanton, John R., *Indian Tribes of the Lower Mississippi Valley and Adjacent Coast of the Gulf of Mexico* (Mineola, NY: Dover, 1998).

James F. Barnett, Jr.

THE HILLSBOROUGH ARCHAEOLOGICAL DISTRICT

The Piedmont, North Carolina

Native American Villages Before and During European Contact

The Hillsborough archaeological district contains a group of archaeological sites that has been instrumental in furthering our understanding of Native American history in Piedmont North Carolina during the late pre-contact and contact periods from AD 1000 until the early 1700s. The district, situated within a 25-acre bend in the Eno River, is located where the historic Great Trading Path crossed the river and near the early colonial town of Hillsborough, established in

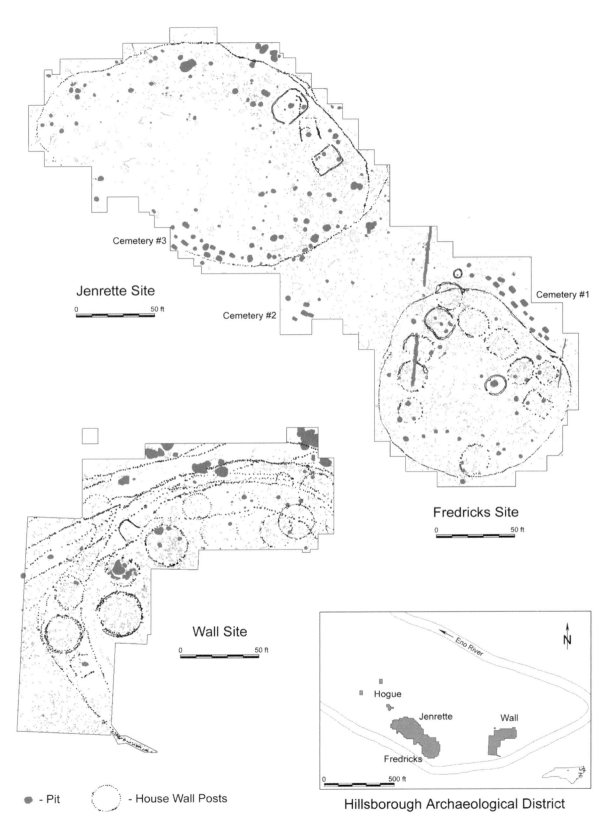

Cemetery #3

Jenrette Site

0   50 ft

Cemetery #2

Cemetery #1

Fredricks Site

0   50 ft

Wall Site

0   50 ft

● - Pit   ⬚ - House Wall Posts

Hogue

Eno River

Jenrette

Wall

Fredricks

0   500 ft

N

Hillsborough Archaeological District

Excavation plans for the Wall, Jenrette, and Fredricks sites.   [R. P. Stephen Davis, Jr.]

the mid-1700s. Artifacts found in the district indicate a long history of intermittent occupation by Native Americans that dates back 12,000 years; more permanent settlements, occupied sequentially after AD 1000, are represented by the Hogue, Wall, Jenrette, and Fredricks sites. These villages document the period during which native people in the region first came in contact with Europeans, and they have been the focus of intensive research by archaeologists from the University of North Carolina at Chapel Hill interested in understanding the impact of European colonization upon Native Americans. Interaction with Europeans, primarily traders and explorers, fundamentally altered native Piedmont societies and ultimately brought about their demise through disease, warfare, and slaving.

Throughout most of human history in Piedmont North Carolina, native peoples were hunters and gatherers who lived in small bands and moved seasonally as new food resources became available. They were strongly dependent upon white-tail deer and various nut crops, including acorns and hickory nuts. Archaeologically, this way of life is characterized by the remains of numerous small campsites scattered across the landscape. These sites typically are not well preserved due to centuries of agricultural plowing and are represented by scatters of discarded projectile points and other stone tools, chipping debris from making these tools, and, for later periods, fragments of broken pottery. Such artifacts in excavations within the Hillsborough archaeological district indicate this area was occupied by hunter-gatherers over many millennia prior to the advent of settled village life and agricultural food production.

THE HOGUE SITE

The initial shift toward more settled life is represented at the Hogue site, a small, semi-permanent community established during the early centuries of the Haw River phase culture (AD 1000–1400) of the Late Woodland period. Sites of the Haw River phase have been identified along the streams and small rivers of the north-central Piedmont in North Carolina. Food remains at these sites indicate the diet was based on a mix of hunting and gathering as well as the growing of corn, squash, sunflower, and (later) beans. Like other Haw River sites, the Hogue site reflects a community of scattered households and probably was one of several such communities dispersed along the upper Eno River valley.

The Hogue site was first identified in 1984 and is the least studied of the Hillsborough sites. Subsurface testing using soil augers identified three localities within a 3-acre site area where midden-filled pits were preserved, and in 1989 excavation blocks totaling 2,330 square feet were excavated in each of those areas. Each block revealed a cluster of postholes representing an ancient dwelling and several associated pits that had been filled in with midden soil or refuse. The pits included a large, cylindrical storage facility that had been filled in with broken pottery fragments, discarded stone tools,

and food remains (i.e., animal bones and charred seeds), as well as several basin-shaped pits and human burials. The burials were clustered in a small cemetery near one of the dwellings. The graves were shallow and contained flexed skeletons, none of which were accompanied by funerary objects.

Artifacts from Hogue include triangular chipped-stone arrow points, chipped hoes, ground-stone celts, and numerous pottery fragments. These potsherds represent large, undecorated, conical jars (probably cooking pots) with straight or slightly constricted necks. Most jars had net-impressed exterior surfaces and were typical of pottery made elsewhere during the Haw River phase and the preceding Uwharrie phase. The continuity of this ceramic trait suggests that the people who lived at Hogue are descended from earlier Woodland peoples in Piedmont North Carolina.

THE WALL SITE

The Wall site is an example of a permanent, compact, stockaded village of the Hillsboro phase (AD 1400–1600). It was first investigated in 1938, and at the time was thought to be an Occaneechi town visited by the English explorer John Lawson in 1701. Extensive excavations, totaling more than 12,000 square feet, were conducted in 1940 and 1941. These revealed several circular alignments of postholes where houses once stood, evidence for multiple defensive walls (called stockades) surrounding the village, and dense deposits of refuse within a thick midden at the northern edge of the site. Very little evidence, however, was found to indicate the village was occupied into the historic era (after about AD 1650), and no European-made artifacts were found within the undisturbed midden.

In 1983 excavations resumed at Wall to clarify the site's age and presumed association with the Occaneechi. In addition to providing new information about the village layout, these excavations obtained radiocarbon samples from house and stockade postholes. These samples indicated the site was occupied sometime during the fifteenth and sixteenth centuries and not during the early eighteenth century. Thus, the Wall site represents a native community occupied just prior to the establishment of permanent English settlements in Virginia and the Carolinas. This site provides important baseline information for understanding what native societies were like before the social upheavals that accompanied prolonged European contact.

Additional excavations at Wall were conducted between 1984 and 2002 and, together with the earlier investigations, total about 20,500 square feet, or about one-third of the entire site. These excavations, which exposed the remains of more than a dozen houses, are of sufficient extent to provide a clear picture of this Hillsboro phase village. When first established, the village consisted of a ring of circular houses surrounding an open plaza. These houses were circular and about 25 feet in diameter. The lack of central support postholes and daub suggests that they were of bower, not wattle-and-daub, construction (i.e., like a wigwam). Just beyond the houses was a tall stockade that encircled the village. As the population grew and the village expanded, the stockade was torn down and rebuilt. This is indicated by at least five palisade alignments. In some instances houses were rebuilt; in others they were repositioned to make way for new houses. It is estimated that, at its maximum size, this village covered about 1.25 acres and was occupied by 100–150 people.

Despite Wall's relatively long and complex settlement history, comparatively few burials were found, which suggests a much lower mortality rate when compared to later historic sites such as Fredricks and Upper Saratown. Burials usually were located within or adjacent to houses and were placed within shaft-and-chamber graves. This type of grave is common at later sites associated with historic Siouan-speaking tribes such as the Shakori, Sissipahaw, and Sara. It was formed by digging a deep, cylindrical shaft and then, at the bottom, scooping out a chamber off to one side. The body was placed in the chamber, often accompanied by shell ornaments and a small pot that may have contained food. The chamber was then sealed with large rocks. Finally, the shaft was refilled with dirt from the original excavation of the grave.

Excavations of the midden and several large pits at the village periphery have provided ample evidence of material culture as well as subsistence practices during the Hillsboro phase. Plant remains indicate that fields surrounding the Wall site were used to grow corn, squash, and beans; these were supplemented by wild berries and fruits as well as hickory nuts, walnuts, and acorns. A variety of animals—including wild turkey, passenger pigeons, turtles, fish, and many small mammals—are represented in the abundant faunal sample; however, whitetail deer were clearly the predominant source of meat. In fact, the extremely large quantity of deer bones recovered indicates that this animal was quite plentiful when the Wall site was occupied.

The pottery found at Wall and other Hillsboro phase sites suggests a cultural discontinuity with the preceding Haw River phase. Whereas earlier vessels were constructed by the paddle-and-anvil method using cord- or net-wrapped paddles, Hillsboro vessels were built using carved paddles—a method with a long history in the Southeast but heretofore largely absent in the north-central Carolina Piedmont. Most Hillsboro vessels had exterior surfaces that were simple stamped (i.e., made using paddles with parallel grooves cut into the tool surface); other vessels had check-stamped surfaces (made by paddles with two sets of grooves cut perpendicular to one another), smoothed or burnished surfaces, and occasionally corncob-impressed surfaces. These surface treatments are accompanied by a variety of vessel forms and decorative treatments absent in earlier pottery assemblages. In fact, Hillsboro pottery differs so dramatically from Haw River phase pottery that the two phases are thought to represent distinct, unrelated populations. Overall similarities in

material culture between Wall and the Jenrette, Fredricks, and Mitchum sites suggest that the Hillsboro phase is ancestral to the historic Shakori, Occaneechi, and Sissipahaw tribes, respectively.

THE JENRETTE SITE

Jenrette was a stockaded village of the Jenrette phase (AD 1600–80) and was occupied during the second half of the seventeenth century. It is thought to be the Shakori town of Shakor, which was visited by the German explorer John Lederer in 1670. Jenrette is one of the earliest contact-era sites excavated in Piedmont North Carolina; contact with Virginia traders is indicated by glass beads and brass ornaments in small quantities. Charred peach pits also were found, but these likely have a Spanish origin and were introduced earlier than, and independent of, the English trade. The small quantity of trade goods found at Jenrette suggests that contact with the Virginians was both intermittent and indirect. This may explain why, unlike later native village sites such as Fredricks, few burials were found, suggesting that European-introduced diseases did not ravage the Jenrette village.

University of North Carolina archaeologists discovered the site in 1989, and over the next ten years excavated an area of almost 27,000 square feet to expose the village in its entirety. These excavations revealed that Jenrette was much smaller than Wall, covering only about half an acre, and the population size presumably was proportionately smaller. Given a lack of archaeological evidence for rebuilding houses and the stockade, as well as less substantial refuse deposits, Jenrette also appears to have been occupied for a much shorter period of time.

The basic village pattern at Jenrette was similar to that of Wall: a ring of houses surrounded an open plaza and was, in turn, enclosed by a stockade. As many as a dozen houses are represented by concentrations of postholes, numerous refuse-filled storage pits, and basin-like cooking pits. The Jenrette houses were substantially smaller than those at Wall and were constructed differently. Two of the three houses that could be clearly delineated are roughly rectangular and were constructed by digging trenches to erect the wall posts. Each had a corner entrance, indicated by a gap in the wall trench nearest the plaza, and deep cylindrical storage pits were dug into the floors. Whereas the houses at Wall covered 300–500 square feet, the two Jenrette house floors were only 220–300 square feet.

The pottery at the site was used to define the Jenrette ceramic series, and it is very similar to pottery from the nearby Mitchum site, a probable Sissipahaw village of the same period. The Jenrette pottery mostly consisted of jars with either smoothed or simple-stamped exteriors; other vessels were either brushed or cob impressed. Decorated cazuela bowls and check-stamped jars, well represented at the Wall site, are absent at Jenrette. Still, similarities are strong enough to indicate that the people who lived at Jenrette are likely descendents of the population represented at the Wall site.

Other artifacts from Jenrette reflect a variety of native-made tools and other items of material culture that were soon replaced by European goods obtained through the developing deerskin trade. Rhyolite, often scavenged as waste flakes from earlier Archaic time period campsites, was used to chip small triangular arrow points, drills, perforators, gravers, and scrapers. Other metamorphic and igneous rock was used to fabricate hoes, celts, and large milling stones. Animal bones were cut, split, and ground smooth to create hide scrapers, awls, and needles; freshwater mussel and marine shells were used to make finely notched scrapers and small disk beads; and clay was used to create smoking pipes. Other clay pipes of both English and of native origin were obtained through trade. The faunal and botanical remains found at Jenrette indicate the persistence of traditional subsistence practices based on hunting whitetail deer; capturing a diverse range of other terrestrial and aquatic species; cultivating corn, beans, bottle gourd, and sumpweed; and collecting acorns, hickory nuts, and walnuts during the fall.

THE FREDRICKS SITE

The Fredricks site is believed to represent Achonechy Town, an Occaneechi village visited by John Lawson in 1701. During the mid-1600s, the Occaneechi occupied an island of the same name on the Roanoke River, just below the confluence of the Staunton and Dan rivers, where they acted as middlemen in the developing trade between the Virginia colony and native tribes of the Carolina and Virginia backcountry. In 1676 their control of trade was broken due to an attack by a frontier settler militia during Bacon's Rebellion. Sometime before 1700 they migrated south and established a village along the Eno River; by the early 1710s they had moved back to the Virginia frontier under the protection of the Virginia colonial government.

The identification of Fredricks as an Occaneechi settlement is based on John Lawson's description of the town's location and the age of European trade artifacts found at the site. According to his journal, published in 1709, Lawson traveled the Great Trading Path, or Occaneechi Path, through much of Piedmont North Carolina. He encountered the Achonechy town on the north side of the Eno River near the trail's crossing point. This crossing, along with the placement of the Occaneechi village, is depicted on a 1733 map of North Carolina by Edward Moseley. Modern reconstructions of the trading path route place its crossing at the Hillsborough archaeological district. European artifacts found at Fredricks, including kaolin pipe fragments, wine bottles, and glass beads, indicate that the site was occupied sometime between about 1690 and 1710. Finally, native earthenware pottery similar to that from Fredricks was found during excavations at Fort Christanna, Virginia, where the Occaneechi are known to have resided during the 1710s.

The Fredricks site was excavated in its entirety between 1983 and 1986. A total excavation area of about 18,500 square feet revealed a small, circular, stockaded town that covered about one-quarter of an acre and consisted of about a dozen houses around an open plaza. Some houses were represented by oval alignments of individual wall posts, similar to the structures at Wall, whereas other houses were built similarly to Jenrette houses where trenches were dug for wall posts. At the edge of the plaza was a small building interpreted as a communal sweat lodge. It was represented by an oval wall-trench pattern about 10 feet in diameter and contained a large central fire pit. Numerous cylindrical, refuse-filled storage pits were located in the floors of some houses and adjacent to others.

Just outside the stockade was a small cemetery that contained thirteen graves. Two additional cemeteries containing twelve graves were later found while excavating at the Jenrette site, located adjacent to Fredricks. One of these cemeteries was aligned to the Jenrette site stockade, indicating that this structural feature was still visible when this cemetery was created. It also suggests that the Jenrette village may have been occupied when the Fredricks village was established. Graves within all three cemeteries were arranged in small clusters, each containing an adult female and one or more juveniles. These burials have been interpreted as representing family units.

The stockade and houses at Fredricks show no evidence of rebuilding or extensive repairs, and this evidence suggests that the town was likely occupied for fewer than ten years. Fredricks also is the smallest historic-era Indian settlement identified in Piedmont North Carolina and was probably occupied by no more than seventy-five people. Despite a small population, at least twenty-five burials can be attributed to its brief occupation. This archaeological evidence clearly reflects the general conditions, described by early explorers such as Lawson, that Piedmont tribes faced at the beginning of the eighteenth century. Disease, warfare, and slaving together brought about rapid population disruption and decline, resulting in smaller, more mobile societies with smaller settlements used for briefer periods of time.

Trade also affected native societies in many ways, but the most archaeologically visible consequence was the acquisition of novel goods not previously available. At Fredricks, European-made artifacts were found in much greater quantity and variety than at earlier contact-era sites. Trade artifacts were particularly abundant as funerary objects. In addition to numerous glass beads and brass ornaments commonly found at earlier contact-era sites, Fredricks graves and refuse-filled pits contained metal knives, axes, hoes, scissors, and spoons as well as a flintlock musket, numerous gun parts, lead shot, a brass kettle, pewter porringers, wine bottles, thimbles, bells, and kaolin pipes.

Despite the influx of European goods and ideas, many aspects of Occaneechi life remained traditional. Animal and plant remains from Fredricks indicate a subsistence pattern very similar to that at Jenrette and Wall, even as more effort was directed toward trade in pelts and native people learned about new foods from English traders. Occaneechi hunters, armed with more efficient weapons, no doubt spent more time away from the village and traveled farther from home; however, the villagers' diet continued to rely on corn, beans, squash, venison, and meat from a variety of other small terrestrial and aquatic animals. Numerous peach pits were found, but evidence for other Old World plant and animal species was rare, consisting of a single pig bone, a horse bone, and a watermelon seed.

The pottery used at the Fredricks site was exclusively of local manufacture and is largely represented by two types: Fredricks Plain and Fredricks Check-Stamped. Vessels consisted of small- to medium-sized jars with slightly flaring rims and small, simple bowls. Jar rims occasionally were notched. The check-stamped pottery is reminiscent of that found at the Wall site; however, simple-stamped pottery—the predominant ware at both Wall and Jenrette—is almost entirely absent at Fredricks. Small jars and bowls were found in several of the Fredricks graves, and the overall uniformity of these and other vessels suggests that they were made by only a few potters.

Other traditional technologies are less well represented. Little evidence was found of working either shell or bone, and the assemblage of chipped-stone tools appeared to rely heavily upon items (e.g., arrow points, drills, perforators, scrapers, and large flakes) scavenged or recycled from earlier nearby sites.

Within a few years after John Lawson's visit, the Occaneechi abandoned the Eno valley. Other neighboring Siouan tribes including the Shakori, Sissipahaw, Eno, Adshusheer, Keyauwee, and Sara, also left the North Carolina Piedmont and sought refuge among the Catawba to the south or Virginia's protection at Fort Christanna. Within thirty years, the first English settlers arrived in the Eno valley, where they established farms and created the frontier town of Hillsborough. Today, a full-scale replica of the Occaneechi village, built by members of the Occaneechi Band of Saponi Nation, is located adjacent to the Hillsborough archaeological district near downtown Hillsborough. It is open to the public.

Further Reading: Davis, R. P. Stephen Jr., "The Cultural Landscape of the North Carolina Piedmont at Contact," in *The Transformation of the Southeastern Indians, 1540–1760*, edited by Robbie Ethridge and Charles M. Hudson (Jackson: University Press of Mississippi, 2002), 135–154; Davis, R. P. Stephen, Jr., Patrick C. Livingood, H. Trawick Ward, and Vincas P. Steponaitis, *Excavating Occaneechi Town: Archaeology of an Eighteenth-Century Indian Village in North Carolina*, CD-ROM (Chapel Hill: University of North Carolina Press, 1998), Web edition (2003), http://ibiblio.org/dig; Driscoll, Elizabeth M., H. Trawick Ward, and R. P. Stephen Davis Jr., "Piedmont Siouans and Mortuary Archaeology on the Eno River, North Carolina," in *Archaeological Studies of Gender in the Southeastern United States*, edited by Jane M. Eastman and Christopher B. Rodning (Gainesville: University Press of Florida, 2001), 127–151; Lawson, John, *A New Voyage to Carolina*, edited with introduction and notes by Hugh T. Lefler (Chapel Hill: University of North Carolina Press, 1967); Ward, H. Trawick, and R. P. Stephen Davis Jr., "The Impact of Old World Diseases on the Native Inhabitants of the North Carolina Piedmont," *Archaeology of Eastern North America* 19 (1991): 171–181; Ward, H. Trawick, and R. P. Stephen Davis Jr., *Indian Communities in the North Carolina Piedmont, A.D. 1000–1700*, Research Laboratories of Anthropology Monograph Series No. 2 (Chapel Hill: University of North Carolina, 1993); Ward, H. Trawick, and R. P. Stephen Davis Jr., *Time Before History: The Archaeology of North Carolina* (Chapel Hill: University of North Carolina Press, 1999); Ward, H. Trawick, and R. P. Stephen Davis Jr., "Tribes and Traders on the North Carolina Piedmont, A.D. 1000–1710," in *Societies in Eclipse: Archaeology of the Eastern Woodlands Indians, A.D. 1400–1700*, edited by David S. Brose, C. Wesley Cowan, and Robert C. Mainfort Jr. (Washington, DC: Smithsonian Institution Press, 2001), 125–141.

R. P. Stephen Davis, Jr.

THE TATHAM MOUND SITE

Citrus County, Florida

Ancient and Early Historic Burial Mound

In 1984 archaeologists searching for the site of one of famed Seminole leader Osceola's camps stumbled upon the Tatham Mound in a dense swamp in Citrus County, Florida. Pottery fragments found on the surface and its geographical location suggested that the mound might have been constructed by people who encountered the Spanish expedition of Hernando de Soto in 1539. Excavations carried out in 1985 and 1986 revealed that it was a burial mound built in two stages. The prehistoric lower part contained the remains of at least 28 people, while the later upper level yielded the bones of at least 339 individuals. Abundant beads and other pre-1550 Spanish artifacts were also excavated from the upper stratum (many accompanying individual burials), clearly indicating contact with the de Soto expedition.

The mound was constructed in two stages, several centuries apart, by people who lived in small settlements in the swamps near the Withlacoochee River. These people were part of what archaeologists call the Safety Harbor Culture, which was the dominant group that inhabited the region in west-central Florida from about AD 900 until 1700. They were some of the first people in what is now the United States to encounter Spanish explorers. Although they were undoubtedly in contact through trade with Mississippian groups elsewhere in the Southeast, their environment was not conducive to large-scale agriculture. The population lived in widely scattered settlements and fished, hunted, and gathered wild resources.

The undisturbed nature of the Tatham Mound prompted archaeologists from the Florida State Museum (now the Florida Museum of Natural History) to seek funding to carry out a thorough excavation. Much to their surprise, famed science-fiction/fantasy author Piers Anthony agreed to fund the bulk of the project to its completion. He then wrote a novel based on the findings.

Among the bones in the upper part of the mound were several that had wounds produced by edged metal weapons, like swords. None of the wounds showed evidence of healing, suggesting that these people died from their injuries. Although there is no way to prove that the metal weapons were wielded by Spanish soldiers (as opposed to Native Americans who had obtained metal weapons by trade or salvage), it is likely that the people buried in the mound had direct and sometimes violent contact with members of the de Soto expedition. In addition, nineteen burials were accompanied by early sixteenth-century Spanish artifacts, mostly metal or glass beads.

The accounts of the de Soto expedition say little about this part of Florida, although several small Native American towns are noted in passing. The writers mention several instances of capturing local people, as well as a number of skirmishes where both Native Americans and Spaniards were killed. The people buried in the Tatham Mound would have had several opportunities for contact with de Soto's men since the bulk of the expedition, heading north, passed through the area in the summer of 1539. Several months later, a contingent of Spanish cavalry was sent back along the same route to instruct the supply ships anchored near Tampa Bay to travel north to unload supplies. Part of this force then traveled north again through the Tatham Mound area. These trips provided ample opportunities for both violent and peaceful contact, and the beads

and other artifacts may have been given directly to people or left in the area as gifts.

The excavations showed that twenty-five to thirty people were buried in at least two (or possibly more) rows. Many of these individuals were wearing European beads or other artifacts, and they included people of both sexes. They ranged in age from infants to elderly adults. None of these burials showed evidence of violent death. Although not all archaeologists agree, some have suggested that these people were all buried within a short time period and may have died from disease accidentally introduced by the Spaniards. Some of the Spanish explorers may have had viral diseases such as influenza or measles, or had other maladies that were not considered life-threatening in Europe. The Native Americans, however, had never been exposed to Old World pathogens, and hence had no natural immunity to them. Such new diseases could be lethal, and it is possible that many of the people in the Tatham Mound were victims of such illnesses.

Tatham Mound yielded 153 glass beads and 320 European metal artifacts. Of the metal artifacts, 299 were beads (most of silver but also a few of gold, brass, and bronze). There were also two iron or steel chisels, an iron spike, some decorative items of silver and gold, and a plate from Spanish armor. These artifacts constitute the largest collection of early sixteenth-century Spanish artifacts from any North American archaeological site.

The spectacular nature of the post-contact upper layer of the mound often overshadows the lower, earlier part. This smaller sand mound, which was completely covered by the later post-contact one, contained the remains of at least twenty-eight people. Bone preservation was not good, but several artifacts of native copper were found, indicating that these people may have been powerful or wealthy. One person wore a copper ear ornament and had an elaborate copper plume ornament (carefully embossed with raised lines indicating the shaft and rays of a feather) at the back of the head. The plume, originally about 9 or 10 inches (23 cm) long, was probably attached to the hair. Bone preservation was too poor to tell whether this person was male or female. Immediately next to this person was a circular copper plate, about 9 inches (23 cm) in diameter, with small raised dots around the edges. Beneath the plate was the skeleton of an infant. A nearby burial of an adult female had a copper-covered cypress wood baton in her chest area. One end of this baton had a carved peg with hair or plant fiber tied around it, probably as a tassel. Several other people were accompanied by celts (stone ax heads) made of stone not found in Florida, and large numbers of shell beads made from saltwater mussel shells.

The lower mound was radiocarbon dated to around AD 950, based on a date from the copper-covered baton. The small number of people buried there, along with the exotic copper and stone artifacts, makes it likely that the mound was constructed to bury important people, possibly religious or political leaders and their relatives.

The Tatham Mound is not accessible to the public. It is located deep in swamps on protected state of Florida property managed by the Southwest Florida Water Management District.

Further Reading: Anthony, Piers, *Tatham Mound* (New York: Morrow, 1991); Hutchinson, Dale L., *Tatham Mound and the Bioarchaeology of European Contact: Disease and Depopulation in Central*

Gulf Coast Florida (Gainesville: University Press of Florida, 2006); Mitchem, Jeffrey M. "Redefining Safety Harbor: Late Prehistoric/ Protohistoric Archaeology in West Peninsular Florida." Ph.D. dissertation, University of Florida, 1989; Mitchem, Jeffrey M., "The Ruth Smith, Weeki Wachee, and Tatham Mounds: Archaeological Evidence of Early Spanish Contact," *Florida Anthropologist* 42(4) (1989): 317–339; Mitchem, Jeffrey M., and Jonathan M. Leader, "Early Sixteenth Century Beads from the Tatham Mound, Citrus County, Florida: Data and Interpretations," *Florida Anthropologist* 41(1) (1988): 42–60.

Jeffrey M. Mitchem

THE GOVERNOR MARTIN SITE

Tallahassee, Florida
De Soto's First Winter Encampment

In October of 1539, Hernando de Soto and his expedition of just over 600 Spaniards established a winter base camp at a native village in the vicinity of modern-day Tallahassee, Florida. Coming less than fifty years after Columbus's first voyage of discovery, it was the first winter spent on the longest, and ultimately disastrous, inland reconnaissance of North America during the sixteenth century. The expedition occupied what is now known as the Governor Martin site until early March 1540 before continuing north. The exact location of this camp was lost to modern researchers until it was fortuitously discovered in the spring of 1987.

THE EXPEDITION
The de Soto *entrada* set sail from its staging point in Havana on May 18, 1539, and made landfall off the west coast of Florida a week later. Over 600 men and at least 2 Spanish women are recorded on the expedition roster. Also present were over 200 horses, a drove of swine, and specially trained war dogs. By early October, the army was in the territory of the Apalachee chiefdom (the Florida panhandle). Although they encountered stiff resistance, the Spaniards were eventually able to gain possession of the principal village of Anhaica Apalache. Since he had neither found the gold he expected nor had any idea where it might be found, de Soto decided that his army should stop, regroup, and plan its future journey. By the following spring, the Spaniards were ready to resume their quest.

Anhaica Apalache did not cease to exist when de Soto's army decamped. The Apalachee returned to reoccupy their

violated homes, while de Soto's men marched to their fate. When the Spaniards returned nearly a century later—this time in the guise of Franciscan missionaries—they encountered a society probably very similar to the one de Soto saw. The village of Anhaica apparently remained a community of such importance that in 1633 one of the first missions in Apalachee was established in its midst: San Luis de Xinyaca.

THE SEARCH FOR DE SOTO
The route of the de Soto *entrada* and the site of his first winter encampment have been sought by cartographers, historians, and archaeologists for nearly three centuries. The pioneering attempts of Guillaume de l'Isle in 1718 began the serious pursuit (both scholarly and popular) of de Soto's path, and this work resulted in several possible routes. One of the earliest studies, produced during the eighteenth century, was undertaken by Spain to show its prior claim to territory then held by the English.

By the early twentieth century, the first winter camp's location in the vicinity of Tallahassee was so well established that John R. Swanton, chair of the United States De Soto Expedition Commission, referred to the area as one of the route's "datum points." His certainty about Tallahassee was based on documentary data (i.e., the geographic descriptions of Apalachee in the de Soto narratives and the distances the Spaniards reported as traveling from place to place). Nevertheless, the exact location of Anhaica continued to elude detection.

DISCOVERY

Like much of Florida in recent decades, Tallahassee was experiencing rapid commercial and residential development in 1987. That was when an office complex planned for downtown provided an opportunity for archaeologists to investigate a patch of ground that remained relatively intact. The first test pit produced shards of Spanish olive jar and burned clay daub, both characteristic of seventeenth-century mission sites, causing the excavators to initially conclude that a mission had been located.

In the weeks that followed, however, archaeologists were unable to locate any of the other expected mission-related artifacts or features. Native ceramics consisted mainly of incised, late Fort Walton–period varieties (a Native American style pottery dated to AD 1450–1633) that tended to predate the seventeenth century, rather than stamped Jefferson ceramics usually found on mission sites. Furthermore, the tin-glazed Spanish polychrome majolicas that characterize Spanish missions in northwest Florida were largely missing from the collection. Instead a few fragments of an unusual yellow-glazed European pottery turned up. This would later be identified as Melado ware, a sixteenth-century Spanish type. An extensive dig, lasting ten months, was eventually able to assemble sufficient evidence to identify the site as Anhaica.

EVIDENCE

The identification of the site as de Soto's winter encampment is compelling, if not conclusive. Its location does not contradict any of the four narratives associated with the expedition. Prominent geographic features, such as mounds, rivers, or lakes, that might have occasioned comment are not present either in the narratives or at the site. The Governor Martin site falls within the approximate distances from Anhaica to various other landmarks (e.g., the Aucilla River and the Gulf of Mexico) as recorded in expedition accounts. The site has evidence of burning, as mentioned in the documents, and there are signs of European improvement (sawed posts, wrought nails) to a structure.

Aboriginal artifacts account for most of the material assemblage from the Governor Martin site. The majority of the ceramics are late Fort Walton types. A survey of the surrounding area indicated that the excavated portion of the site was just a small part of a large Apalachee village.

Spanish ceramics consist mainly of olive jar fragments. Chronologically identifiable rim fragments can be classified as the early type dating from around AD 1490 to 1650. Also found were such sixteenth-century majolica types as Columbia Plain (AD 1492–1650), including a pre-1550 green variant, and Caparra Blue (AD 1492–1600). European beads are recorded as being part of the inventory brought by de Soto, and they were found in the excavation. A faceted amber bead, a dozen faceted chevron beads, and a single Nueva Cadiz bead from Governor Martin are good sixteenth-century marker artifacts, and they have also been found at other sites associated with the expedition. Wrought nails of various sizes and types are present in the material assemblage. Many of these are associated with a burned sixteenth-century structure on the site, and they may represent evidence of European modification of an aboriginal structure. A crossbow quarrel is the only example of sixteenth-century weaponry recovered. Another example of military hardware that was obsolete by the Mission period was chain-mail armor. Over 2,000 links of iron mail were recovered, as well as 20 links of brass mail. Five copper coins, Spanish maravedis and Portuguese ceitils, date to the late fifteenth and early sixteenth centuries, a narrow window of time consistent with early European contact.

All of these items place the site in the early sixteenth century, but they cannot distinguish between the expedition of Pánfilo de Narváez in 1528 and that of Hernando de Soto eleven years later. Fortunately, just before the close of the 1987 field season, a burned maxilla fragment from a domestic pig (*Sus scrofa*) was unearthed when digging a sixteenth-century structure. This bone is significant because de Soto brought a herd of swine with him to avoid the same fate as the earlier Narváez expedition. Narváez and his men found little food in the southern reaches of Apalachee province and were eventually reduced to eating their horses to survive.

SIGNIFICANCE

It appears that a century of searching for de Soto's first winter encampment has finally succeeded. The *New York Times* (May 19, 1987) referred to it as "the crowning achievement of recent scholarly efforts to determine more precisely the route of the de Soto expedition." However, identifying the site, or even the route of the expedition, is not terribly important in itself. The significance lies in the picture it gives us of native life at contact. It allows us to calibrate our ceramic sequence and, eventually, to correlate archaeological assemblages with the villages recorded by de Soto. Indeed, it represents an important step toward a sixteenth-century archaeological geography of the southeastern United States, the beginning of a tumultuous period that eventually ended with the removal of Indians from much of the Southeast.

Further Reading: Clayton, Lawrence, Vernon J. Knight Jr., and Edward C. Moore, eds., *The De Soto Chronicles*, Vols. 1 and 2 (Tuscaloosa: University of Alabama Press, 1993); De Soto National Memorial Web site, http://www.nps.gov/deso/ (online January 2007); Ewen, Charles, and John Hann, *Hernando de Soto Among the Apalachee: The Archaeology of the First Winter Encampment* (Gainesville: University of Press of Florida, 1998).

Charles R. Ewen

PARKIN ARCHEOLOGICAL STATE PARK

Parkin, Northeastern Arkansas

A Fortified Mississippian Site Visited by the de Soto Expedition

The Parkin site is a 17-acre fortified Mississippian village site in Cross County in northeast Arkansas. Outside the modern small town of Parkin, the site is located on the east bank of the St. Francis River, with a moat-like ditch surrounding it on the other three sides. It is the "type site" used by archaeologists to define the Parkin phase, a group of about twenty-five fortified village sites situated along the St. Francis and Tyronza rivers that began to be occupied about 600 years ago. Early-sixteenth-century Spanish artifacts excavated at the Parkin site in the 1960s and the 1990s indicate it was occupied in 1541, when the expedition of Hernando de Soto passed through the region. The site's configuration and geographical location indicate that it is probably the town of Casqui described in the written accounts of the expedition.

Most Parkin phase sites appear to have been founded around AD 1350, but some evidence suggests the beginning date may be at least a century earlier. Spanish artifacts from the Parkin site indicate that some of them were still occupied in 1541, but there is no way to determine the date of their final demise. Based on the de Soto expedition accounts, some archaeologists have suggested that the Parkin phase sites were all part of a single chiefdom, ruled by a powerful chief who lived at Parkin. In 1541 the ruling chief was named Casqui, and the smaller villages in the area were under his dominion. He was at war with another ruler who lived to the northeast, and this probably explains why all Parkin phase sites were fortified with ditches and palisades (stockade-like walls).

The Parkin phase people were primarily farmers who grew crops in the fertile soil along the rivers. Corn (maize) was their main crop, but archaeological excavations have revealed that they grew and collected a wide range of plants, seeds, and nuts. Deer and fish were their main sources of meat, supplemented by a wide variety of other animals from the adjacent river and forests. The fertile soil and abundant game allowed large populations to be maintained, and at its peak the Parkin site may have housed more than 1,500 people.

The site has long been known to archaeologists and artifact collectors. Sponsored by the Peabody Museum at Harvard University, Edwin Curtiss dug in several small mounds at the site (then known as Stanly Mounds) in 1879–1880. The collection he amassed is now at Peabody Museum. Clarence B. Moore, the indefatigable digger of mounds in the Southeast, spent only a single day at the site in 1910 but noted its renown among artifact collectors. In the first half of the twentieth century a sawmill was located to the south, and most of the mill workers lived on the site. Many of these people dug for pottery and other artifacts during their spare time. The site became well known for the elaborately decorated pottery found there, especially the realistic human-head effigy vessels.

In the 1960s, archaeologists and local residents began discussing preservation of the site and the possibility of turning it into a state or federal park. To address concerns about whether the site contents were still relatively intact, Charles R. McGimsey III of the University of Arkansas Museum directed test excavations for nine days in 1965. The crew for this project consisted of Arkansas Archeological Society members. The research yielded evidence of houses, human burials, and undisturbed archaeological deposits in several parts of the site. Returning the next year, McGimsey taught a University of Arkansas field school at Parkin, with similar results.

One artifact found on the surface during the 1966 work was a European glass bead. This seven-layer bead is a distinctive type known as a faceted chevron bead. This style of bead was made for a relatively short time, and was brought to the New World by Spanish explorers between AD 1492 and 1550. Earlier in the 1960s, a local man excavated a small brass bell that accompanied the burial of a child. This type of bell, known to archaeologists as a Clarksdale bell, was likewise only brought to the New World by Spanish explorers and settlers in the 1500s. These two artifacts had to have come from the de Soto expedition, which traveled through the area in the summer of 1541.

With evidence of intact archaeological deposits and undeniable artifacts relating the site to the de Soto expedition, the Arkansas legislature designated the site a state park in 1967. Although a substantial portion of the site was donated to the state, there were many small residences and an active church on the site, all owned by different people. Funding for acquisition and development did not materialize until the late 1980s. The Archaeological Conservancy, Inc., was instrumental in helping to acquire these various parcels, negotiating with landowners and solving title problems.

In 1990, funding was provided to develop a state park and to create an Arkansas Archeological Survey Research Station. A station archaeologist was hired, and construction started on a visitor information center with exhibits, offices, a laboratory, and artifact storage space. Parkin Archeological State Park opened to the public in 1994.

Research station archaeologists carried out extensive excavations in the 1990s, investigating prehistoric structures and other features. One area on the site's eastern edge revealed that the defensive ditch at that spot was more than 26 meters (about 85 ft) wide and 1.9 meters (about 6.25 ft) deep, measured from the modern ground surface. These excavations also found postholes from a heavy defensive palisade wall, with at least one bastion (or guardhouse). These excavations showed that the site deposits are more than a meter (about 3.5 ft) thick. A radiocarbon date from a burned house at the bottom of the deposits showed that it was destroyed sometime between AD 1000 and 1250.

Excavations in a different part of the site uncovered additional Spanish artifacts, including two fragments of Clarksdale bells and two lead shot from matchlock arquebuses (early musket-like rifles) carried by de Soto's men. Although these small artifacts do not prove that the expedition was at Parkin, they leave no doubt that the site was still occupied in 1541.

Parkin Archeological State Park is open Tuesday through Sunday. It is closed on Mondays, Christmas Day, and Thanksgiving Day. State park staff arrange tours and other activities for school classes and other groups. Interpretive displays are adjacent to a walking trail on the archaeological site. The visitor information center includes permanent artifact exhibits and an introductory film.

Further Reading: Arkansas Archeological Survey, Parkin Archeological State Park Web site, http://www.uark.edu/campus-resources/archinfo/parkin.html (online March 2003); Davis, Hester A., "An Introduction to Parkin Prehistory," *Arkansas Archeologist* 7(1–2) (1966): 1–40; Mitchem, Jeffrey M., "Mississippian Research at Parkin Archeological State Park," in *Proceedings of the 14th Annual Mid-South Archaeological Conference*, edited by Richard Walling, Camille Wharey, and Camille Stanley, Special Publication No. 1 (Memphis: Panamerican Consultants, 1996), 25–39; Morse, Phyllis A., "The Parkin Archeological Site and Its Role in Determining the Route of the de Soto Expedition," in *The Expedition of Hernando de Soto West of the Mississippi, 1541–1543*, edited by Gloria A. Young and Michael P. Hoffman (Fayetteville: University of Arkansas Press, 1993), 58–67; Morse, Phyllis A., *Parkin: The 1978–1979 Archeological Investigations of a Cross County, Arkansas Site*, Research Series No. 13 (Fayetteville: Arkansas Archeological Survey, 1981); Scarry, C. Margaret, and Elizabeth J. Reitz, "Changes in Foodways at the Parkin Site, Arkansas," *Southeastern Archaeology* 24(2) (2005): 107–120.

Jeffrey M. Mitchem

THE SANTA ELENA AND CHARLESFORT SITES

Parris Island, Coastal South Carolina

Sixteenth-Century French and Spanish Colonial Settlements

Santa Elena, a Spanish colonial settlement located on Parris Island, South Carolina, was occupied for twenty-one years in the second half of the sixteenth century. For nearly a decade after its founding, it was the capital of Spanish Florida. After its abandonment in 1587 it was never reoccupied.

From the time of Columbus, the Spanish claimed all of the New World except for that part carved out for Portugal in the Treaty of Tordesillas (1494). The portion later named *La Florida* by Juan Ponce de Léon was the subject of several exploratory expeditions (Pánfilo de Narváez, Hernando de Soto, and Tristán de Luna) in the first half of the sixteenth century, but only the unsuccessful effort by Lucas Vásquez de Ayllón (1526) actually landed colonists along what is today the southeastern coast of the United States. With the failed 1559–61 effort by Tristán de Luna y Arrelano, viceroy of New Spain (Mexico), to settle parts of *La Florida*, including the Atlantic coastal area known as Santa Elena, King Phillip II of Spain decided that it was time to curtail further efforts in Spanish Florida. This changed when a small French expedition arrived on the Florida coast early in 1562 and established Charlesfort on Parris Island, near present-day Beaufort, South Carolina.

Charlesfort was abandoned in 1563 due to lack of resupply, but a second, larger French settlement was established on the St. John's River near present-day Jacksonville, Florida, in 1564. This new settlement, *La Caroline*, consisted of several hundred colonists and soldiers. Upon learning of this new French intrusion, Phillip II appointed his most trusted military commander, Pedro Menéndez d'Avilés, to mount an expedition to drive the French from *La Florida*.

Menéndez arrived on the Florida coast in August 1566 with a large military contingent. He established St. Augustine as a base of operations, and then he moved against the French colonists at *La Caroline* (or Fort Caroline). He captured the fort, and, in the weeks that followed, he tracked down and killed those who had escaped his attack.

One of the block excavations opened beside the Parris Island Recruit Depot Golf Course, revealing clues as to the 1566–87 occupation of Spanish Santa Elena.   [Stanley South]

The excavated northwest bastion of Fort San Felipe, designed to protect the Spanish town of Santa Elena.   [Stanley South]

A large block excavation showing the excavated Spanish postholes for a structure and the adjacent pits filled with Spanish refuse. [Stanley South]

With the French colony eradicated, Menéndez moved to consolidate his hold on Florida. He established several small forts around the Florida peninsula, including one at Santa Elena, to prevent the French from reoccupying the coastline where Charlesfort had been. When a large group of reinforcements were sent to Florida by the king, Menéndez sent 250 soldiers in the company of Captain Juan Pardo to Santa Elena. In 1566 and 1567, Pardo led contingents of soldiers into the interior in an unsuccessful effort to find an overland route to Mexico.

Early in 1569, nearly 200 settlers were sent to Santa Elena, and in that year the town became the seat of government and capital of Spanish Florida. Menéndez was recalled to Spain in 1574, and he died while there. His two sons-in-law each led the small colony for a year after his death, but they were not successful in dealing with Native American groups in the area. In 1576 the Native Americans rose up against the Spaniards and drove them from Santa Elena, forcing a withdrawal to St. Augustine and Cuba.

Pedro Menéndez Marques, the new Governor of Florida, reoccupied Santa Elena in 1577, and he spent the next three years subduing the surrounding Native American communities. These attacks were in part retaliation for the forced evacuation of 1576 but were also due to the fact that crewmen from a French shipwreck (*La Prince*) had sought refuge among the Indians in the year the Spanish were gone.

Santa Elena was occupied by a garrison of approximately seventy-five soldiers until 1587, when the settlement was again abandoned as a result of the attacks against Spanish holdings by Englishman Francis Drake. Included among the towns Drake destroyed was St. Augustine. He intended to attack Santa Elena as well, but he could not find the entrance to its harbor. Santa Elena was simply too far from St. Augustine and Havana for it to be successfully supplied and defended, so in the end the Spaniards decided to abandon it and focus effort and resources on St. Augustine.

Following its abandonment in 1587, the site was subsequently occupied by a group of Yamasee Indians in the seventeenth century, by plantations to the time of the Civil War, and by freedmen after the war. The U.S. Marine Corps purchased Parris Island in 1918, and the Santa Elena site was part of the "Maneuver Grounds" used to train marines for service in France during World War I. A golf course was constructed on the site in 1947, and it continued in use until 2000.

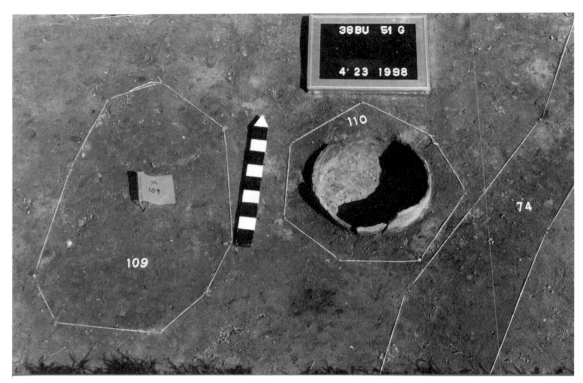

Detail of some of the archaeological features revealed, marked, and mapped before final excavation is undertaken.   [Stanley South]

Archaeologist Chester DePratter, pointing to the bottom of the profile of the moat of Spanish Fort San Felipe. To the right, James Legg points to the bottom of the shallower French Charlesfort moat cut into by the later Spanish fortification ditch.   [Stanley South]

One of the wooden barrels placed to serve as well liners by the Spaniards at the town of Santa Elena.   [Stanley South]

ARCHAEOLOGICAL EXCAVATIONS

In 1923 Marine Corps Major George Osterhout excavated in a fort that he thought was French Charlesfort. More recent research has shown that fort to be Spanish Fort San Marcos (II), which was occupied from about 1582 to 1587. No further excavations were conducted on the site until Stanley South began work there in 1979. Since that initial work, South and Chester DePratter, assisted by James Legg and others, have conducted more than forty field seasons of work there.

Testing programs implemented by South and DePratter indicate that the Santa Elena town site covers approximately 15 acres (6 ha). A portion of the site has been lost to erosion by storms and the nearby tidal creek. To date, remains of two Spanish forts—Fort San Felipe (I) occupied from 1566 to 1570, and Fort San Marcos (II) used from about 1582 to 1587—have been identified and excavated (at least in part). At least two other Spanish forts have been the subject of searches, but they have not yet been found. Excavations in 1997 uncovered the remains of Charlesfort buried beneath Fort San Felipe (I).

Excavations in the town have focused on two lots that were occupied by Governor Gutierre de Miranda from 1580 to 1587. These excavations have revealed that the governor's house was 22 feet square and may have been two stories tall. A smaller, D-shaped hut (perhaps for a servant) was found on the same lot as the main house, and two other structures were present on an adjacent lot. To date, five barrel-lined drinking-water wells have been found on the two lots belonging to the governor. Remains of several other structures in the town have been partially exposed, but none have been totally excavated.

Shovel testing beyond the edge of the town proper led to the discovery of a pottery kiln that was used during the last few years of the town's occupation. This small updraft kiln was apparently used by a potter trying out local clays, since none of the many vessels fired in the kiln were glazed as they would have been for everyday use. Near the kiln was a work shed with the wheel pit and pivot stone for a potter's wheel still sitting in place just in front of it. More recent work has uncovered the potter's house and well, but that well has not yet been excavated.

Recent work on the site has focused on site stabilization in conjunction with the U.S. Army Corps of Engineers and other small projects associated with site interpretation. The site is accessible to visitors through walking trails and interpretive signage. There is an extensive exhibit of Santa Elena artifacts at the Parris Island Museum on the marine base.

Further Reading: DePratter, Chester B., Santa Elena/Charlesfort, South Carolina Institute of Archaeology and Anthropology Web site, http://www.cas.sc.edu/sciaa/staff/depratterc/newweb.htm; DePratter, Chester B., and Stanley South, "Discovery at Santa Elena: Boundary Survey," South Carolina Institute of Archaeology and Anthropology, Research Manuscript No. 221 (Columbia: University of South Carolina, 1995); Lyon, Eugene, *The Enterprise of Florida: Pedro Menéndez d'Avilés and the Spanish Conquest of 1565–1568* (Gainesville: University Presses of Florida, 1976); Paar, Karen L., "To Settle Is to Conquer: Spaniards, Native Americans, and the Colonization of Santa Elena in Sixteenth Century Florida," Ph.D. diss. (University of North Carolina, Chapel Hill, 1999; South, Stanley, *Archaeology at Santa Elena: Doorway to the Past*, South Carolina Institute of Archaeology and Anthropology, Popular Series, No. 2 (Columbia: University of South Carolina, 1991); South, Stanley, Russell Skowronek, and Richard Johnson, *Spanish Artifacts from Santa Elena*, South Carolina Institute of Archaeology and Anthropology, Anthropological Studies, No. 7 (Columbia: University of South Carolina, 1988).

Chester B. DePratter and Stanley South

ST. AUGUSTINE

The North Florida Coast

The Oldest Continuously Occupied European Settlement in the United States

St. Augustine is the oldest continuously occupied European settlement in the United States. Spanish colonists, led by Pedro Menéndez d'Avilés, established the settlement as a private venture in 1565 after routing the French from nearby Fort Caroline. The city served as the seat of colonial government in Spanish Florida from 1587 until 1763, and again between 1784 and 1821 when Spain regained control from the English. Research at St. Augustine has been a model for historical archaeology worldwide. At least thirty-three archaeological sites have been investigated, most under the auspices of a continuing research program. The history and archaeology of St. Augustine are interpreted for the public at numerous sites in and around the city.

Even as a governmental and religious administrative center St. Augustine was regarded as a backwater community. The city still maintained a distinctly Hispanic character by virtue of its dependence upon a government subsidy and its ongoing military mission. Yet the challenges of isolation, including unreliability of official support, necessitated a resourcefulness that fostered a unique and culturally diverse colonial society. Interest in how that society developed and functioned over the course of two centuries has been a leading concern of archaeological studies.

Florida was visited and named by Spanish subjects as early as 1513. It was explored and sporadically occupied over the next five decades but not permanently settled until 1565. Establishment of a visible presence was mainly a response to construction of forts on the southeastern Atlantic coast by France. The first capital of *La Florida* was founded at Santa Elena in 1566 (at present Parris Island, South Carolina) with St. Augustine serving as a separate military post. Within a year, the first Spanish fort at St. Augustine was moved from a Timucua Indian village to an alternative location nearby.

In 1572 the settlement moved again to its final location. The small fortified enclave became an official colony of the government in 1576, a change in status that hastened its emergence as a viable town. The enduring value of St. Augustine to Spain was its strategic mission. The site was close enough to critical shipping lanes to afford protection for the Spanish fleet, to provide a buffer with the English in the north, and to offer a haven for shipwreck victims. The early town consisted of simple wattle-and-daub structures, and most of the buildings housed soldiers and their families. After Franciscan missionaries arrived in 1573, areas were developed for a mission compound, a convent, and parish churches. Throughout the last quarter of the sixteenth century the small, isolated colonial town was severely tested by Indian attacks, epidemics, hurricanes, and English raids.

From the beginning, the circumstances of the community fostered emergence of an increasingly rigid social order. Status was largely defined by ethnicity, origin, and income, and those distinctions influenced the way the city developed. People of Spanish origin dominated the privileged class. A middling status was usually afforded criollos of Spanish heritage and many mestizos of mixed blood, mostly of Spanish and Indian ancestry. Indians and Africans occupied the lower rungs of St. Augustine society. Although these social distinctions defined a code of privilege, the city's population routinely functioned at a level of integration profoundly apparent in archaeological evidence. From the beginning Spanish men regularly married Indian women, and Indians and Africans filled essential, albeit subservient, roles. Franciscan missionaries exerted significant influence through most of the seventeenth century because St. Augustine served as the administrative hub for the mission network.

A more formal city plan was implemented by the seventeenth century, organized by a grid of streets radiating from a main plaza. This scheme defined residential, business, and government precincts that were to persist for nearly two centuries. Historical and archaeological evidence documents how proximity to the main plaza correlated closely with socioeconomic status. Growth remained handicapped by erratic financial support from the provincial government, but a reasonably stable local society developed.

With establishment of the English colony at Charleston in 1670, Spanish dominance in the region faced mounting challenges. To protect its strategic position, St. Augustine responded with construction of a massive stone fort, the Castillo de San Marcos. The effort of constructing and outfitting the fort fueled new growth well into the eighteenth century. Sturdy styles of architecture that used stone and cement-like tabby were indicative of the maturing urban environment. The city's population was also expanded by an influx of refugees, mainly Indians, from mission settlements plagued by English-sponsored raids and pirate attacks. In this environment the unique cultural flavor of St. Augustine society was only enriched. Ironically, illicit commerce with English privateers and Indian traders blossomed. The result was improvement in quality of life for at least some residents, even in the face of severe constraints.

Contraction of Spain's hinterland settlement network had been underway since the 1660s and culminated with a general retreat to St. Augustine following the English attacks of 1702 and 1704. Spain eventually ceded St. Augustine and all of Florida to the English in 1763. Although Spain resumed control of Florida from 1784 to 1821, St. Augustine had forever been changed.

St. Augustine is celebrated as a place of landmark research in historical archaeology. Excavations since at least 1934 have sampled a cross section of sites representative of every historical period, of all socioeconomic dimensions, and of diverse cultural affiliations. Since the 1970s, under the direction of Charles Fairbanks and Kathleen Deagan, an explicitly interdisciplinary, anthropological research design has guided systematic studies. The archaeological program at St. Augustine also pioneered the integrated study of ecological context and subsistence. Results from investigation of several dozen sites are published in numerous scholarly and popular works.

The cumulative outcome of long-term research is a vivid portrayal of how a creole culture developed in America's oldest city. Indigenous Indian traditions strongly influenced the colonizing Hispanic population from the beginning. As the city evolved from a small, isolated military garrison to the regional presidio, these diverse ethnic strains fused to create a uniquely adapted, wholly new cultural pattern.

Numerous deposits and features representing the founding era of the sixteenth century have been identified and excavated. Excavations at Fountain of Youth Park (8SJ31) have produced evidence of the first fort and settlement in the form of a moat, a well, the outlines of large buildings, and a lime kiln. At the permanent city site a prominent source of information is material deposited in barrel wells regularly spaced on the town grid. Archaeological evidence reveals a relatively impoverished existence for inhabitants in the earliest period. Architectural debris is indicative of ephemeral wattle-and-daub or plank buildings. Ceramics of both Hispanic and Indian origin dominate the artifacts, and most are classified as utilitarian wares. Compared with Santa Elena, the capital of the early period, St. Augustine's household sites produced fewer nonutilitarian items, less-exclusive types of pottery, and lower diversity of possessions overall.

Sites of the seventeenth century are representative of they city's initial growth phase. They include Josef Lorenzo de Leon (SA26-1) and Ximinez-Fatio House (SA34-2), where remains of structures and house lot activities were documented. Early houses of post-and-thatch construction were later replaced by tabby. Archaeological evidence from this middle period reflects a time of relative stability and increasing self-reliance. Spanish American and Indian ceramics largely replaced types imported from Spain, a burgeoning subsistence economy provided local foods, and the occurrence of items from other European sources reveals an active contraband trade. At the site of mission Nombre de Dios (8SJ34), artifacts with Timucua Indian burials reveal the influence of Franciscan missionaries on the native culture.

Eighteenth-century sites associated with the second period of expansion also received significant attention, owing in part to the rich documentary record and to public consciousness of them in the modern city. By this time, many more buildings were made of oyster-shell tabby. Rich archaeological deposits on house lots include still-pervasive wells but also discrete trash pits. One exemplary site is the de Hita site (SA7-4), which is representative of the criollo majority in the city during this period. Extensive excavation revealed aspects of a fully formed Spanish American cultural tradition. Among the socially intermediary but dominant criollo population, status was publicly represented with objects of European origin, especially Hispanic, while ordinary household activities were commonly represented by objects derived from the indigenous Indian culture. Criollo diet was diverse, with both domestic mammal and native foods well represented. The important mestizo element of the city was examined through study of the de la Cruz site (8SA16-23), among others. Compared with da Hita and other criollo sites, material evidence at de la Cruz clearly betrayed a lower socioeconomic standing. Most obvious was the low incidence of objects of Hispanic origin, a proportionally greater occurrence of British goods, and a distinct dominance of Native Indian–influenced material. Mestizo diet was distinguished by heavy representation of local foodstuffs such as fish and much less of large domesticated mammals. Investigation at Fort Mose (8SJ40) illuminates important aspects of the free black population and its role in defense of the Spanish colony.

Beyond traditional scholarly contributions, a remarkable legacy of the St. Augustine archaeology program is its educational achievements. Hundreds of university students have received basic field training, and for more than one generation it has been a graduate school proving ground. The educational program extends to the public realm as well. Active excavations are often open for viewing and interpreted to visitors, and many exhibitions have been created to communicate findings. The ongoing commitment to public education is to be found throughout the Spanish Quarter, through a virtual Web-based exhibit, and in a research collection and exhibitions at the Florida Museum of Natural History. The modern city of St. Augustine also coordinates construction activities with a full-time archaeology staff.

Further Reading: Chaney, Edward, and Kathleen A. Deagan, "St. Augustine and the La Florida Colony: New Life-styles in a New Land," in *First Encounters: Spanish Explorations in the Caribbean and the United States, 1492–1570*, edited by Jerald T. Milanich and Susan Milbrath (Gainesville: University of Florida Press, 1991), 166–182; Deagan, Kathleen A., *Spanish St. Augustine: The Archaeology of a Colonial Creole Community* (Gainesville: University of Florida Press, 1983); Deagan, Kathleen A., ed., *America's Ancient City, Spanish St. Augustine, 1565–1763* (New York: Garland Publishing, 1991); Florida Museum of Natural History, St. Augustine, America's Ancient City Web site, http://www.flmnh.ufl.edu/staugustine/unit5.htm; Hoffman, Kathleen, "Cultural Development in *La Florida*," *Historical Archaeology* 31 (1997): 24–35.

Dennis B. Blanton

THE SITE OF SANTA CATALINA DE GUALE

St. Catherines Island, Georgia

Archaeology of an Early Spanish Mission

St. Catherines Island lies 10 miles off the Georgia coast, blanketed with dense forests, briar patches, and sometimes impenetrable palmetto thicket. Only a single person lives here today, but 300 years ago 1,000 people lived and worked at Mission Santa Catalina. For a century, this was the northernmost Spanish settlement along the Atlantic seaboard.

The Guale (pronounced "wally") people of St. Catherines Island and elsewhere along the Georgia coast were among the first indigenous peoples met by Europeans exploring north of Mexico. Beginning in 1566, the Guale were exposed to a long, intensive period of Spanish missionization. Because the Spanish colonists were few in number, they employed the missions as an agency to occupy, hold, and settle the Georgian frontier. As

Father Pareja, stationed for years in these missions, put it, "we are the ones who are conquering and subduing the land."

Mission Santa Catalina survived until 1680, when Captain Francisco de Fuentes rallied his Spanish soldiers and Guale musketeers to protect the mission from attack by hundreds of British officers and Yuchi Indians. Although Fuentes, the missionaries, and the Guale converts put up a gallant struggle, they soon abandoned Mission Santa Catalina. The fall of Mission Santa Catalina signaled the waning of Spanish control in the American Southeast and set the stage for British domination of the American colonies.

Shortly after the Spanish retreat, the British Captain Dunlop commanded a small British force to the battle scene:

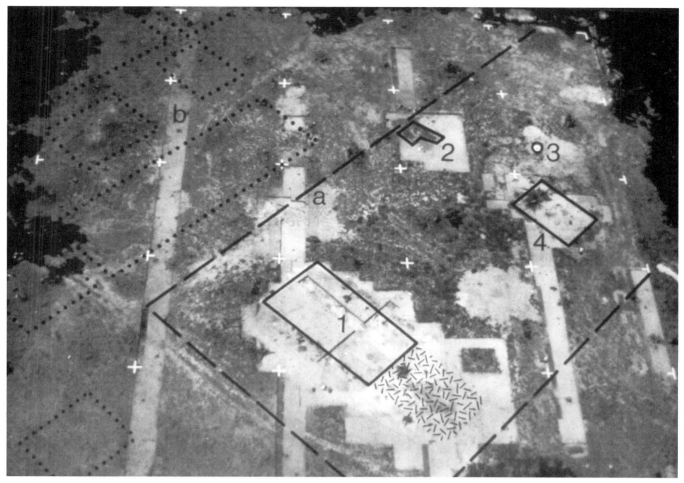

This aerial photograph, covering 1 hectare, shows the town plan of Mission Santa Catalina de Guale (Georgia); the white tick marks are placed every 20 meters. Building 1 is the mission church (convento), structure 2 is the kitchen (cocina), item 3 is the early mission well, and building 4 is the friary (convento). The dashed line (*a*) denotes the fortification protecting the "sacred" precinct of Mission Santa Catalina. The dotted line (*b*) shows the distribution of Guale Indian houses throughout the pueblo part of the mission compound. [David Hurst Thomas]

"We came about noon to the North/East of St. Catherina . . . where the great setlement was we see the ruins of severall houses which we were informed the Spanish had deserted for ffear of the English about 3 years ago; the Setlement was Great." This is the last recorded account of Mission Santa Catalina. The Franciscan church, the barracks, and the rest of the "great setlement" fell beneath hurricane-tossed soil and the roots of stately live oaks, encrusted with Spanish moss.

SEEKING SANTA CATALINA

Established less than seventy-five years after Columbus first set foot on New World soil, Mission Santa Catalina has much to tell about America's past, especially the head-on collisions between Native American and European culture.

In 1680 Santa Catalina de Guale was a mission abandoned, and within a few decades it became a mission lost. For the next 300 years, antiquarians, historians, and archaeologists speculated about the whereabouts of Mission Santa Catalina de Guale. The combined French, English, and Spanish historic documentation available in the late 1970s supplied little more than general geographic clues. The limited archaeological evidence suggested only that—if any mission structures remained intact—they were likely to be buried somewhere near the southwestern marsh on St. Catherines Island.

In 1977 the American Museum of Natural History began looking for Mission Santa Catalina, combining randomized island-wide archaeological surveys with geophysical prospection (employing proton magnetometry, soil resistivity survey, and ground-penetrating radar analysis). After a five-year search, the archaeological expedition finally found the long-lost Franciscan mission on St. Catherines Island.

The American Museum of Natural History excavated for fifteen years at Mission Santa Catalina de Guale. The entire mission complex and the Guale pueblo that surrounded it followed a rigid grid system, in which the long axis of the church was oriented 45 degrees west of magnetic north. The central plaza was rectangular, with the church defining the western margin of the central plaza, and the *cocina* (kitchen) and one or more *conventos* (the residence for the friars; usually translated as monastery, convent, or friary) fringing the eastern margin.

THE CHURCH (*LA IGLESIA*)

The two churches at Santa Catalina were completely exposed during the archaeological investigation and, except for the eastern wall (preserved as a witness section), the entire church deposit was excavated. The late-sixteenth-century *iglesia* was destroyed by fire, probably in September 1597.

After a period of abandonment, Santa Catalina was resettled by the Spanish in 1604, and the mission church was reconstructed following a single nave plan, lacking both transept and chancel. The symbolic separation between nave and sanctuary was emphasized by a composite construction technique. The sanctuary end of the church, constructed entirely of wooden planking, was apparently elevated above the lateral wattle-and-daub walls of the nave. Some evidence suggests that the interior of the sanctuary may have been decorated with a reredo—several decorative metal panels that were apparently not removed before the church was abandoned.

A clearly demarcated sacristy was built on the Gospel side of the church (the left-hand side of the sanctuary as one faces the altar). This room was presumably used for storage of vestments, linens, candles, processional materials, and other ritual paraphernalia essential to celebration of the Mass. Inside, we found a cache of charred wheat, which was probably destined to be baked into the "host," flatbread used in the Eucharist. Although wheat never had assumed great dietary importance to Spaniards living in *La Florida*, this inglorious cache inside the sacristy underscores the effectiveness of the Franciscan Order in obtaining the supplies necessary for the proper conduct of Church ritual—even on the most remote northern frontier of the Guale province.

Fronting the church at Santa Catalina is a square shell-covered subplaza, probably a low-walled enclosure demarcating the public entrance to the church. Ubiquitous features of the New World religious architecture, such churchyards served not only as a decorous entryway into the church but also variously functioned as outdoor chapels, areas to contain overflow congregations, and sometimes as cemeteries.

THE CEMETERY (*EL CAMPO SANTO*)

The only known cemetery at Santa Catalina was found inside the church, where we encountered a minimum of 431 individuals buried beneath the floor of the nave and sanctuary. The *campo santo* at Santa Catalina also contained an astounding array of associated grave goods, including nearly three dozen crosses, Franciscan medallions, small medals, so-called "Jesuit" finger rings (with unique sculpted Sacred Heart castings), and a cast figurine depicting the

infant Jesus with a cross in one hand and the other raised in a gesture of blessing. Additional grave goods in the *campo santo* include complete imported majolica vessels, several projectile points, a chunky stone, a rattlesnake shell gorget in the Tellico style, two complete glass cruets, two mirrors, hawks bells, one rosary, eight shroud pins, two copper plaque fragments, and one large piece of shroud cloth.

The cemetery also contained 70,000 glass trade beads. Most were embroidery beads sewn onto clothing and sashes; other beads were portions of jewelry and ornaments. Rosary beads were commonly found accompanying burials. The others are aboriginal shell beads and lapidary beads.

THE FRIARY (*EL CONVENTO*) COMPLEX

Eastward across the plaza stood the *convento* and *cocina* complex. The *convento* comprised one or more subsidiary buildings in which friars and lay brothers lived cloistered lives according to the rules of their Franciscan Order.

At least two superimposed *conventos* exist at Santa Catalina. The earlier structure was probably built in the late 1580s, shortly after the Franciscans arrived. Construction was entirely of rough wattle and daub (considerably coarser than that employed in building the church). The kitchen and refectory were probably housed inside the sixteenth-century *convento*, the other rooms were probably used for living quarters and storage. Kitchen debris and table scraps were tossed out the back door, where a fringe of shell midden accumulated against the rear wall—well out of sight from the church. A clearly incised drip line demonstrates that the sixteenth-century convento had eaves extending about 1 meter beyond the rear wall.

This building was probably burnt by rebellious Guale in the fall of 1597. When Fray Ruiz supervised the reconstruction in 1604, he apparently separated sacred from secular, because a distinct *cocina* was erected 20 meters to the north of the new *convento*. The detached kitchen was also a common feature within urban St. Augustine, Florida.

Set into the clay floor of the central room was a curious floor feature: a rectangular clay foundation, standing 25 centimeters above the floor, scooped out to receive an oval, metallic receptacle. Although this floor font might have held holy water, this feature was more likely employed for personal hygiene, perhaps as a foot bath.

Immediately outside the back of the *convento* was a concentration of nearly four dozen bronze bell fragments (other fragments have been found haphazardly scattered about Santa Catalina). Several pieces show punch and axe marks, indicating that the bells were deliberately destroyed; at least four different bells are represented. The mission bell always held a special significance, at times symbolizing the entire mission enterprise. Like all sacred vessels of the church, bells were consecrated and blessed, this status continuing even after the breaking of a bell. The fragments found behind the seventeenth-century *convento* were probably from bells broken by rebellious Guale during the uprising of 1597. Friars who returned to Santa Catalina some years later undoubtedly came upon some of these fragments, and the broken bells found behind the *convento* may be a deliberate cache of still-consecrated fragments, perhaps intended for recycling into new bells.

THE KITCHEN (*LA COCINA*)

The new friary was about 15 percent smaller than its predecessor, but this size differential was more than counterbalanced by the new *cocina* built 20 meters to the northwest. These walls were supported by squared-off pine posts, placed in pits. The southern end of the kitchen was apparently left open, presumably to facilitate both access and ventilation.

The cooking for the friars was probably shifted to this new structure early in the seventeenth century. Although most kitchen debris was discarded some distance away (probably outside the walled mission compound), some midden accumulated in pits near the *cocina*, and occasional smaller pieces of garbage were trampled underfoot, being thus incorporated in the kitchen floor.

THE MISSION WELLS

Two wells were found on the eastern side of the plaza. The first, initially located by the magnetometer survey, was a simple barrel well, consisting of seven decomposing iron rings above the well-preserved remains of an oak casing. The construction pit was relatively small, perhaps 1.5 meters in diameter, with the much smaller barrel well located inside. Relatively little was found in the construction pit and well fill (some olive jar and majolica shards, plus a metal plate). This well obviously had a relatively short use life, and archaeologists think it likely dates from the sixteenth century.

A second, much larger well was encountered later, directly between the *cocina* and the *convento*. When first recognized, the large circular construction pit was more than 4 meters in diameter, with a dark largely circular stain in the middle. As we excavated downward, the construction pit narrowed, with distinct "steps" on both sides; a seventeenth-century cave-in is recorded in the southern sidewall, where one of the sand steps apparently collapsed. Although the well and its contents are still being analyzed, some details are now available.

The well was originally much smaller, having been first constructed with standard barrels. It was subsequently renovated using a casement constructed of two U-shaped cypress logs that were lowered into the construction pit and then nailed together. This later handmade well casing was at least 2 meters in diameter, considerably larger than any of the mission period wells encountered elsewhere in Spanish Florida. Clearly crosscutting surrounding features, this well was one of the last features built at the mission and was probably in use until the final mission abandonment in the 1680s.

The Spanish friars dispatched to frontier missions such as Santa Catalina de Guale profoundly influenced the religious and social conduct within the colony of *La Florida*. They were the primary agents in establishing new settlements, determining the nature of defensive installations, and formulating agrarian policy. But the *micos* of Guale—the native power brokers—also exerted a huge influence, negotiating the details and nuances of daily life along the Georgia coast. Although the missions of Spanish Florida are largely invisible today, they had a lasting effect on the cultures of its native peoples—and on the course of early colonial history.

Further Reading: Larsen, Clark Spencer, "The Archaeology of Mission Santa Catalina de Guale: 2. Biocultural Interpretations of a Population in Transition," *Anthropological Papers of the American Museum of Natural History* 68 (1990); Thomas, David Hurst, "The Archaeology of Mission Santa Catalina de Guale: 1. Search and Discovery," *Anthropological Papers of the American Museum of Natural History* 63(2) (1987); Thomas, David Hurst, "Saints and Soldiers at Santa Catalina: Hispanic Designs for Colonial America," in *The Recovery of Meaning in Historical Archaeology*, edited by Mark P. Leone and Parker B. Potter (Washington, DC: Smithsonian Institution Press, 1988), 73–140; Thomas, David Hurst, *St. Catherines: An Island in Time*, Georgia History and Culture Series (Atlanta: Georgia Endowment for the Humanities, 1988).

David Hurst Thomas

THE SITE OF MISSION SAN LUIS DE APALACHEE

Tallahassee, Florida

The Archaeology of an Early Spanish Mission in Florida

Mission San Luis was the western capital of Spanish Florida in the seventeenth century, serving as the military, administrative, and religious counterpart to St. Augustine in the east. It was one of the first Franciscan missions established in Apalachee province in 1633. At that time, the community was known by the name Anhaica Apalache, and it had been the capital when the Pánfilo de Narváez and Hernando de Soto expeditions first explored the region in 1529 and 1539, respectively. The ancestor village of San Luis is one of the first native communities in North America to be described in several de Soto expedition accounts over a five-month period, between October 6, 1539, and March 3, 1540. In 1656 Spanish authorities selected a hilltop location for their capital, and San Luis was relocated to its present location. Thus, Mission San Luis was simultaneously the paramount Apalachee village and Spanish western capital.

Most early missions in the Southwest and California have at least some standing colonial remains, and many are still active parishes. By contrast, most Florida missions were destroyed during a 1702–04 British advance into the area, thus vanishing from sight and public awareness. Mission San Luis is one of only two Franciscan missions in Spanish Florida whose location was never lost; the other is Nombre de Dios in St. Augustine. Research at San Luis has focused on the nature of Spanish and Indian social life at the western capital, and the effects of missionization on both cultures.

The first major excavations were conducted on a large Apalachee building identified as a council house. These kinds of structures are well documented as seats of native governance and centers of social, political, and ritual native life. In 1675 Bishop Calderón described them as "the great lodge, made of wood, round in form, covered with thatch, and built with a very large opening or skylight in the center of the roof." The council house at Mission San Luis was located on the southeastern edge of the plaza. It measured over 120 feet in diameter, making it the largest historic Indian building identified to date in the Southeast. It was supported with eight major posts and furnished with two concentric rows of benches under which corncob-filled smudge pits smoldered to provide insect control. The scale of this building—it was up to five stories high and held as many as 2,000–3,000 people—speaks to the importance of San Luis as an Indian village and of the power of its chief. Materials from the council house included many stone projectile points, debitage (small pieces of flint knapping debris), and thousands of pottery shards. The seeds of *Ilex vomitoria*, used for the brewing of the traditional *cacina*, or native tea, were identified from the large central hearth. This black drink induced vomiting, hence the plant's scientific name, and was widely used in the Southeast during rituals and the like. On the whole, the structural remains and artifacts indicate that the traditional architectural forms and native activities associated with council houses, such as preparing *cacina*, flint knapping, and hide preparation, continued during the mission period.

The same is true of the chief's house identified through excavations just west of the council house. It, too, was a conical, thatched building measuring 70 feet in diameter (almost half the diameter of the council house and approximately three times the size of commoners' homes). It had a single row of benches along the interior wall and a central hearth. Materials from the chief's house were similar to those from the council house in that they were primarily native in origin,

with very few European artifacts. One unusual aspect of the assemblage was the large number of quartz crystal beads and pendants, which were likely related to the dual political and religious roles of native leaders. Interestingly, there is very little historical or archaeological evidence for common people living on the hilltop. Most Apalachees appear to have maintained a pre-contact settlement pattern, living in dispersed farmsteads and hamlets close to their fields.

Spaniards, on the other hand, believed that "civilized" people lived in fixed, orderly communities. All Spanish residences at Mission San Luis were clustered on the east side of the plaza and followed a common vernacular architectural plan. Most were small rectangular dwellings with a center divider separating public from private space. Archaeologists believe there were at least fifty houses, based on demographic estimates of several hundred Spaniards residing at Mission San Luis.

Two Spanish features rounded out the rest of the community: the religious and military complexes. Excavations revealed that the church was a large, rectangular building measuring 110 by 50 feet. It had a thatched roof and plank walls. The spacing of interior support posts showed that the nave was divided into a series of bays, following the proportional system known as the golden section, or *sectio aurea*, a common feature of Gothic and Renaissance buildings in Europe. Among the most fascinating archaeological discoveries was the cemetery in the church floor. Based on initial sampling, it is estimated that between 700 and 900 Christianized Apalachee Indians are buried in the nave, as was the custom in many European churches during the colonial era. Just north of the church was the friary, or *convento*, with its detached kitchen. The *convento* was a wattle-and-daub structure 40 by 70 feet that contained a large public room that served as the friars' private chapel and classroom, as well as cloistered areas including the refectory (dining room), cells used for sleeping and storage, and a pantry where thousands of pottery fragments were found. The remains were almost exclusively aboriginal in origin and suggest that the Franciscans maintained their vows of poverty and had few personal possessions.

El Castillo de San Luis is the only structure for which a drawing and detailed description exists. These were prepared in 1705, the year after Mission San Luis was burned and abandoned by the Spaniards and their Apalachee allies, just two days before a British-instigated attack force arrived. The military complex consisted of a two-story blockhouse and large parade ground, enclosed with a wooden palisade and moat. The term *castillo* means "castle," and refers to medieval fortifications built to protect surrounding residents against attacks from other European powers. Since soldiers were able to return home when not on duty, the amount of household refuse was limited. Remains from the excavations were primarily building materials, as well as weaponry and cooking implements.

Archaeology at Mission San Luis has revealed a distinct approach to Spanish colonization in North America. Both Spaniards and Apalachees had well-defined concepts of community layout and architecture; Mission San Luis reflects both. As noted earlier, most Apalachees lived in the surrounding countryside and came to the hilltop for church services, meetings and festivities in the council house, and ballgames.

Spaniards, however, lived within close proximity to one another in a tight-knit neighborhood. In keeping with European and native traditions, the town was anchored by a large central plaza. However, rather than a square or rectangular Hispanic-style plaza, the plaza at Mission San Luis was round (410 ft in diameter), in keeping with Apalachee tradition, and was used for their ballgames. Both cultures located the most important buildings and residences close to the plaza. At Mission San Luis, the Apalachee council house and Franciscan church are situated across the plaza from each other, as are the chief's house and deputy governor's house. Because Spaniards were such a small minority living within a powerful centralized chiefdom, there was a remarkable degree of accommodation and integration of cultural elements at this site.

Although Spaniards and Apalachees successfully blended these aspects of their lives, their respective architectural forms, as well as many activities, remained distinct. The greatest changes in social life included religion among the Apalachees and intermarriage for both populations. The introduction of Catholicism brought about the integration of the Christian God within the natives' worldview. The most profound expression of this is found in the cemetery where Apalachees chose to be buried inside the church, and in a Christian manner. Another profound change was the integration of Indian women into Hispanic households as wives and servants, documented archaeologically by the abundance of native pottery throughout the Spanish village at Mission San Luis. This practice had a remarkable impact on this and other Spanish colonial communities. These women and their offspring (who, as mestizos, were exempt from manual labor) formed the foundation of Hispanic American culture in North America.

Mission San Luis is a National Historic Landmark and the 2006 Presidential Preserve America award winner. Much of the Mission has been reconstructed and is open to the public Tuesday–Sunday, 10:00 am–4:00 pm. The site is closed on Mondays and on Thanksgiving and Christmas Day. Mission San Luis is handicap accessible. There is also a visitors' center and gift shop, El Mercado. For more information, please visit the Web site, http://www.missionsanluis.org, or call (850) 487–1791.

Further Reading: Hann, John H., *Apalachee: The Land between the Rivers* (Gainesville: University of Florida Press, 1988); Hann, John H., and Bonnie G. McEwan, *The Apalachee Indians and Mission San Luis* (Gainesville: University of Florida Press, 1998); McEwan, Bonnie G., "Apalachee and Neighboring Groups," *Handbook of North American Indians, Southeast* 14 (2004): 669–676; Wenhold, Lucy, trans., "A Seventeenth-Century Letter of Gabriel Díaz Vara Calderón, Bishop of Cuba, Describing the Indians and Indian Missions of Florida," *Smithsonian Miscellaneous Collections* 95(16) (1936): 13.

Bonnie G. McEwan

FORT ST. LOUIS AND SPANISH PRESIDIO LA BAHÍA

Central Texas Coast

La Salle's 1684 and Later Spanish Attempts to Claim Territory

In 1684 the famous French explorer Robert Cavelier, Sieur de La Salle sailed to the New World to establish a colony at the mouth of the Mississippi River. He missed his mark by some 400 miles, and instead made landfall in January 1685 along what is today the central Texas coast. After several months of searching, La Salle found a suitable location some thirty miles inland from the Gulf of Mexico, where he began construction of a small settlement that became known as Fort St. Louis. The fledgling colony lasted only four short years before the hostile neighboring Karankawa Indians wiped out the last remaining colonists. The site remained unoccupied for thirty-three years before tensions between France and Spain would lead the Spanish to establish Nuestra Señora de Loreto Presidio de la Bahía, commonly referred to today as Presidio La Bahía, atop the remains of Fort St. Louis. The second Spanish settlement was intended to thwart any future French attempt to reestablish a presence along the northern Gulf of Mexico.

Present among the approximately 180 original French colonists was La Salle's friend and confidant, Henri Joutel. Joutel kept a detailed journal beginning with the expedition's departure from France in 1684 and continuing through to the

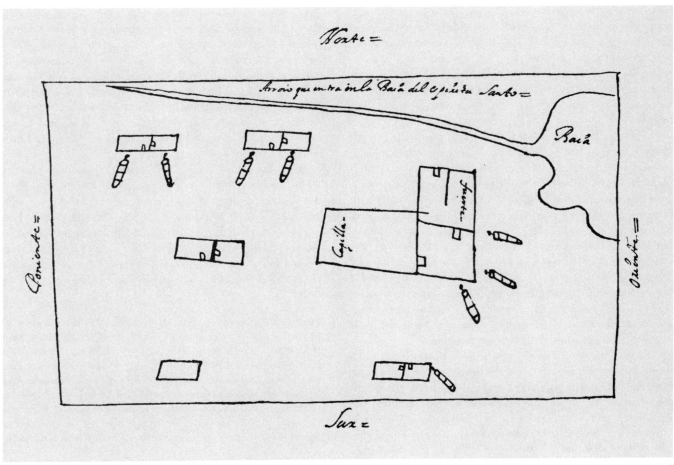

Spanish map of La Salle's Fort St. Louis made in 1689 and showing eight cannons used to guard the settlement.   [James E. Bruseth]

murder of La Salle by his own men in 1687. Joutel's diary provides us with one of the earliest accounts of local Texas plants, animals, Native American tribes, everyday life at the settlement, and the disastrous events that took place during the French attempt to establish a colony along the gulf coast.

Utilizing timbers salvaged from one of his ships, l'Aimable, which was lost along the Texas coast, La Salle's men constructed a two-story structure that served as lodging for La Salle and his officers as well as a stronghold in case of attack by the local Karankawa Indians. Later a small chapel was constructed adjacent to the stronghold. Housing for the remainder of the colonists consisted of small huts built of upright poles with thatch roofs. Around the settlement the colonists fenced in a small garden and pens to hold domestic animals transported from France.

For over two years the colony struggled while La Salle explored the vast regions to the south and north on foot. In 1687 La Salle lost his only remaining ship, La Belle, during a storm in Matagorda Bay. The ship had recently been loaded with many of the colony's supplies and trade goods in anticipation of relocating the settlement to the mouth of the Mississippi River. Distraught over this loss, La Salle left the settlement with sixteen men to seek help from French settlements along the Great Lakes and in eastern Canada. Only a few days into the journey, La Salle was murdered near modern-day Navasota, Texas, by his own men, who had become disgruntled with his leadership. Joutel and five men survived the ordeal and made their way to Canada and eventually back to France. The remaining colonists were massacred in late 1688 or early 1689 when the Karankawa Indians attacked the settlement. Several children were spared and later rescued by the Spanish.

At the time of La Salle's settlement, this part of the New World was claimed by Spain. When the Spanish Crown learned about the attempts by King Louis XIV of France to establish a colony along the northern Gulf of Mexico, Spain initiated a massive search for La Salle's colony to counter the threat. After numerous unsuccessful attempts to find La Salle, the Spanish general Alonso de León finally located the French settlement in the spring of 1689. He found the fort

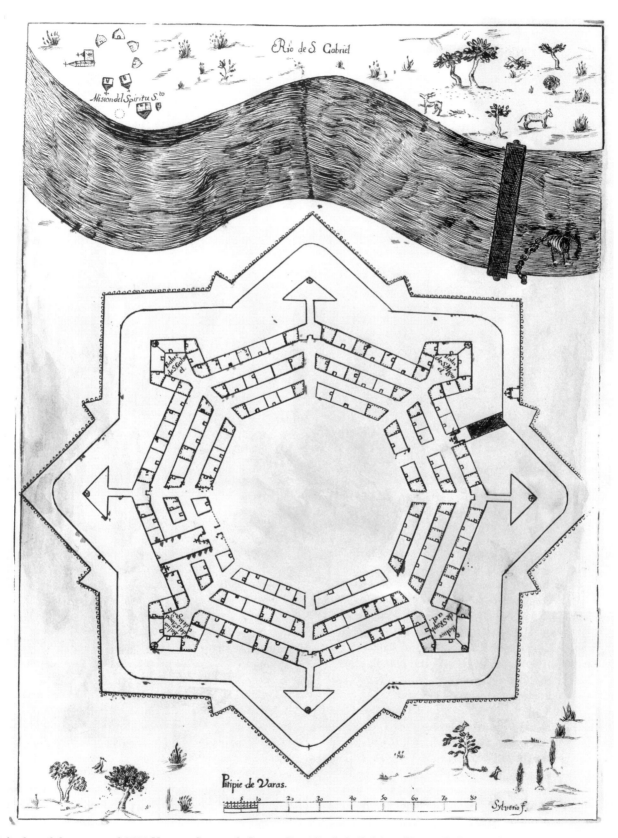

Spanish plan of the proposed 1722 Nuestra Señora de Loreta Presidio de la Bahía.   [James E. Bruseth]

Eight iron cannons excavated at Fort St. Louis.   [James E. Bruseth]

ransacked and abandoned. General de León's party buried the remains of three French colonists and eight iron cannons belonging to the French colony. The Spanish also made a crude map of the settlement before returning the following year to burn what remained of it. The Spanish came back to the site in 1722 to build Presidio La Bahía, an elaborate fortification in the shape of a sixteen-point star, shown on archival maps with an inner octagonal arrangement of room blocks and an interior plaza. Presidio La Bahía was occupied until 1726, when it was moved several miles inland.

The location of Fort St. Louis has been debated by historians, archaeologists, and local residents for over a century. In 1950 the Texas Memorial Museum conducted the first excavations at the site. Although French and Spanish artifacts were found, the results were inconclusive. In 1996 the Texas Historical Commission was contacted when part of a cannon was exposed at the site. Remarkably, all eight French iron cannons were recovered in the exact location where the Spanish had buried them in 1689. Following the discovery of La Salle's cannons, the Texas Historical Commission

began archaeological investigations to confirm the location of La Salle's Fort St. Louis and the overlying Spanish Presidio La Bahía.

The archaeological work has confirmed much of what is depicted in the archival documents of both the French and Spanish occupations. Numerous artifacts, a total of 157,726 of them, were recovered, of which approximately 70 percent are Spanish colonial, 20 percent are native Karankawa, and about 10 percent are French.

Portions of the French stronghold, chapel, and several smaller house foundations were exposed beneath the surface. In addition, the remains of three French colonists were exposed, undoubtedly the individuals massacred during an attack by the Karankawa Native Americans. Remote sensing investigations and excavations have confirmed much of the presidio's layout, as shown on the Spanish drawings and maps, with the exception that only a single row of inner room blocks was constructed. A much richer archaeological record for the Spanish occupation accords well with the archival record, which indicates that the presidio was resupplied from

Mexico on occasion, and that the Spanish had a more established interaction with local Indians.

To bring the story to the public, seven museums in six Texas coastal counties jointly created the La Salle Odyssey, a trail of exhibits that together tell the extraordinary story of La Salle's ill-fated expedition and the remarkable discovery and excavation of the *La Belle* and Fort St. Louis 300 years later. The museums include the Corpus Christi Museum of Science and History, Corpus Christi; the Texas Maritime Museum, Rockport; the Texana Museum, Edna; Calhoun County Museum, Port Lavaca; Museum of the Coastal Bend, Victoria; Matagorda County Museum, Bay City; and the Palacios Area Historical Museum, Palacios.

Further Reading: Bruseth, James, *The La Salle Projects*, Texas Historical Commission, Archeology Division, www.thc.state.tx.us (online 1999–2007); Bruseth, James E., Jeffery J. Durst, Tiffany Osburn, Kathleen Gilmore, Kay Hindes, Nancy Reese, Barbara Meissner, and Mike Davis, "A Clash of Two Cultures: Presidio La Bahía on the Texas Coast as a Deterrent to French Incursion," *Historical Archaeology* 38 (2004): 78–93; Bruseth, James E., and Toni S. Turner, *From a Watery Grave: The Discovery and Excavation of La Salle's Shipwreck* La Belle (College Station: Texas A&M University Press, 2005); Foster, William C., ed., *The La Salle Expedition to Texas: The Journal of Henri Joutel, 1684–1687* (Austin: Texas State Historical Association, 1998).

Jeffrey J. Durst, James E. Bruseth, and Maureen J. Brown

LA BELLE SHIPWRECK

Matagorda Bay, Texas
1686 Shipwreck from La Salle's Colonization Attempt

The excavation and study of the shipwreck of *La Belle* has provided new information about the seventeenth-century French explorer Robert Cavelier, Sieur de La Salle's effort to colonize the Gulf of Mexico at the mouth of the Mississippi River. *La Belle*, discovered in 1995 in Matagorda Bay, was excavated inside a steel cofferdam, which allowed seawater to be removed and the wreck to be treated much like an archaeological site on land. More than one million artifacts were found that show the range of materials La Salle thought necessary to establish his New World colony.

La Belle was one of four ships that sailed from France in 1684 to establish a colony at the mouth of the Mississippi River. During the journey, one of the ships, a small ketch called the *St. Francois*, was captured by pirates in the Caribbean. Due to inaccurate maps and the inability to accurately calculate longitude in the seventeenth century, La Salle's three remaining ships overshot their intended destination and landed along the coast of what is now Texas. After making landfall, another ship, *l'Aimable*, was lost along with much of its cargo. A third vessel, *Le Jolly*, sailed back to France after unloading its passengers. By 1685, only the *La Belle* was left to explore the coast or, if the need arose, to seek help from French settlements in the Caribbean.

A small land fortification, called Fort St. Louis, was built on the coast to serve as a temporary camp for the colonists until the Mississippi River could be found. Assuming that the river was only a short distance to the northeast, La Salle loaded *La Belle* with his remaining cargo, sailed it to the northeastern end of Matagorda Bay, and began an overland search for the river. His plan was to find the Mississippi, return to where *La Belle* lay anchored, and then sail to the river to establish his colony. La Salle never found the Mississippi. He returned to Matagorda Bay to find *La Belle* lost—this occurred during a violent storm in February 1686—and his colonial plans ruined.

The modern search for the wreck of *La Belle* began during the late 1970s with marine surveys on Matagorda Bay, which was where the ship was thought to have been lost. Marine surveys continued periodically until *La Belle* was finally located in 1995. Confirmation of the wreck's identity came with the recovery of a bronze cannon decorated with the crest of the seventeenth-century French king Louis XIV and the crossed-anchor insignia of Le Compte de Vermandois, Admiral of France in the 1680s.

The ship's discovery generated extensive debate about how to salvage the wreck. *La Belle* had lain undetected for more than three centuries, despite oil exploration and canal dredging in Matagorda Bay. The ship lay only a few hundred meters from the Gulf Intracoastal Waterway canal, an artificially deepened shipping channel used by large boats and barges. Though protected by the Texas Antiquities Code, the site lay 20 kilometers offshore in a remote part of the coast where damage could easily occur without archaeologists learning about it. So it was decided that the entire ship and its cargo would be excavated.

Although the water over the wreck was only 4 meters (m) deep, visibility was very poor and on many days near zero. Archaeologists call such investigations dark-water excavations.

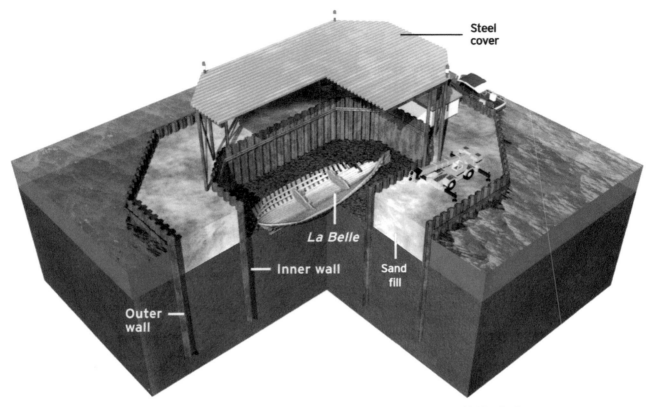

Cutaway view showing the internal structure of the cofferdam.   [Fort Worth Star-Telegram/Clif Bosler]

They are routinely done, but even the most experienced under-water archaeologists can miss small artifacts and inadvertently damage fragile items. To reduce this risk, *La Belle* was excavated as if it were a dry land site by building a steel cofferdam around the wreck and pumping the water out. This was the first time this method of shipwreck excavation would be attempted in the Americas, although it had been done in Europe. The benefits of the cofferdam were that a large crew could fully excavate the site within a single season, and all artifacts, whether small or fragile, could be carefully collected.

The cofferdam consisted of two parallel rows of sheet piling encircling the wreck. Each sheet of steel piling was 18.3 meters long and 0.92 centimeters (cm) wide. The pilings were driven down 13 meters into the bed of Matagorda Bay, continued through 4 meters of water, and extended 1.3 meters above the water. The space between the inner and outer rows of sheet piling, a gap of about 10 meters, was filled with sand to form the cofferdam's wall. The interior dimensions of the completed cofferdam were 18 meters by 28 meters.

Excavation of *La Belle* took place from September 1996 through April 1997 under the direction of the author of this article with assistance from several other archaeologists at the Texas Historical Commission. A crew of twenty people labored seven days a week to excavate the contents of the wreck and the hull. More than one million artifacts were recovered, mostly found in eighty-five casks and ten wooden boxes packed into the cargo holds.

The most common objects recovered from the wreck site were trade goods intended for barter with local Native Americans. These artifacts include at least 790,000 small glass seed beads. Other trade items included brass pins, brass needles, bells, Jesuit finger rings, axe heads, and straight and folding knives. The large quantity of trade goods shows the magnitude of the commercial portion of La Salle's enterprise. These objects had been personally acquired by La Salle and his men to be traded with Native Americans for fur and hides that would be exported back to France for sale.

A number of weapons were recovered, including two ornately decorated bronze cannons, exactly like the one found in 1995. Other weapons include a deck-mounted swivel gun, an estimated thirty flintlock muskets (poor preservation of some guns

Excavation inside the cofferdam as *La Belle* is just beginning to be uncovered.   [Photograph by Robert Clark]

made a precise count difficult), iron shot for the cannons, and lead shot and gunflints for the muskets. Gunpowder was also found, still contained in small casks. Several pole arms of the halberd, spontoon, and partisan types were excavated.

Many of the artifacts were intended for daily use by the colonists. Ceramic containers stored and served food and drink and held medicines. Pewter bowls, porringers, cups, and plates also held food for storage and serving. Glass bottles contained liquids, most likely wine or brandy. The myriad other items include writing instruments, whistles, measuring weights, coiled brass wire, iron bar stock, carpentry tools, coiled rope, religious items such as a crucifix and rosary beads, leather shoes, smoking pipes, buttons, pieces of cloth from uniforms, buckles, and jewelry.

The hull of *La Belle* was dismantled timber by timber. Study of the hull remains, together with preserved rigging elements, tell us that *La Belle* was a sleek, three-mast sailing ship with a draft of about 8 feet.

All of the cargo and the hull remains were conserved by the Conservation Research Laboratory at Texas A&M University.

This work includes painstaking cleaning, documentation, and preservation of the artifacts using a wide variety of techniques, including immersion in polyethylene glycol. To bring the story to the public, seven museums in six Texas coastal counties jointly created the La Salle Odyssey, a trail of exhibits that together tell the extraordinary story of La Salle's ill-fated expedition and the remarkable discovery and excavation of the *La Belle* and Fort St. Louis 300 years later. The museums include the Corpus Christi Museum of Science and History, Corpus Christi; the Texas Maritime Museum, Rockport; the Texana Museum, Edna; Calhoun County Museum, Port Lavaca; Museum of the Coastal Bend, Victoria; Matagorda County Museum, Bay City; and the Palacios Area Historical Museum, Palacios. Other artifacts are on display at the Bob Bullock History Museum in Austin, and the remaining objects are stored at the Corpus Christi Museum of Science and History.

La Salle's colony failed, ultimately due to the loss of the *La Belle*, and the French presence in Texas disappeared. This early arrival of the French in Texas, however, awakened

Spain to the fact that its northeastern frontier of New Spain was being challenged by a rival European power. Consequently, missionaries and soldiers were sent to build missions and presidios, and in so doing imprinted a Hispanic legacy for Texas.

Further Reading: Bruseth, James, *The La Salle Projects*, Texas Historical Commission, Archeology Division, www.thc.state.tx.us (online 1999–2007); Bruseth, James E., and Toni S. Turner, *From a Watery Grave: The Discovery and Excavation of La Salle's Shipwreck*, La Belle (College Station: Texas A&M University Press, 2005).

James E. Bruseth

ARKANSAS POST NATIONAL MEMORIAL

Near Stuttgart, Arkansas
The Earliest Surviving French Site West of the Mississippi River

In the spring of 1686, French explorer Henry de Tonti stopped at the Quapaw village Osotouy on his way down the Mississippi River in search of Robert Cavelier de la Salle, whose expedition to the Mississippi River valley was missing. Tonti and La Salle had visited the Quapaw village of Kappa, above the mouth of the Arkansas River four years earlier, and found the Quapaws friendly to French overtures. The Arkansas was also one of the few rivers in the American midcontinent that provided access from the Mississippi into the lands to the west.

On the 1686 trip, Tonti left a few men to establish an outpost and trade center. Arkansas Post thus became the first French settlement to survive west of the Mississippi. Undermanned, isolated, and underfunded, survival at this outpost was a grave concern for most of the subsequent century. For many decades, its greatest advantage was the close and interdependent relationship between European and African inhabitants and the Quapaws who resided nearby. By the time that the Louisiana Purchase brought Arkansas Post and the Quapaws under American control, residents in and around the post had forged a multi-racial, multi-ethnic society.

One serious problem that plagued post residents was the unstable landscape. Flooding was an ongoing problem for the low-lying lands around the mouth of the Arkansas—if not from the river itself, then from its tributary, the White River, which joined the Arkansas near its mouth, or from the Mississippi. Erosion and channel movement constantly reshaped the landscape and threatened riverbank settlements.

During the eighteenth century, this small settlement of traders and the neighboring Quapaws moved at least three times to escape overflows and respond to external threats from Chickasaw raiders and other political forces. The post was even temporarily abandoned between 1702, when Tonti's economic fortunes collapsed, and 1721, when the French government resettled a small garrison to assist John Law to establish a new colony of German immigrants nearby.

The first post was evidently situated on Little Prairie, a small detached remnant of the Grand Prairie and the first relatively high ground upstream from the mouth of the Arkansas. This location had been used for at least a thousand years by Native people. Subsequent post sites were primarily on low ground, where floods threatened dwellings and made attempts at farming difficult. In 1779 post Commandant Captain Balthazar de Villiers moved the post, both the garrison and the civilian settlement, to high ground on the edge of Grand Prairie, a location called Ecores Rouges briefly used previously by the Quapaws and the French.

Today's Arkansas Post National Memorial includes surviving portions of the post's colonial, territorial and state period communities. Villiers's plan created an orderly community for civilian residents with a lot and street arrangement, and designated neighboring locations for an Indian settlement and the fort. Unfortunately, even though the post was on high ground, it wasn't invulnerable to the Arkansas River, which began to eat away at the community almost immediately, forming an ever-narrowing peninsula on which the community plan was forced to undergo dramatic changes.

When Americans took control of the post in 1804, the community consisted of about 400 people, including about 60 black slaves, a few Spanish soldiers, and a multi-ethnic population that resided in the town and in small plantations in the neighborhood. Arkansas Post's population swelled briefly with new arrivals and economic opportunities in the new territory. When Arkansas was made a territory separate from Missouri in 1819, Arkansas Post was named the territorial capital, but entrepreneurs in 1821 succeeded in moving the capital upstream to Little Rock, which was centrally located and accessible by both dry land and river transportation. The territory's first newspaper, the Arkansas Gazette, followed the politicians, and Arkansas Post began a slow decline.

During the Civil War, the still-inhabited community gained strategic importance in Confederate efforts to defend the

Arkansas River from Union advances. Confederate Fort Hindman and nearby entrenched forces were shelled from bankside and river positions, the latter by Union ironclads. The Confederates surrendered on January 11, 1863. In the postwar period, the community continued to dwindle, and it finally lost its post office designation in 1941.

The Arkansas Post National Memorial has no standing structures. Historical and archaeological research have located parts the historic town site, including the Montgomery's Tavern and Arkansas State Bank sites, and the approximate positions of some other commercial and domestic sites. A walking trail and signage allow visitors to learn about the historic town and access the riverbank. The memorial also preserves elements of the wetland forest and swamp ecosystem, which had such an important effect on European and American efforts to settle this landscape. Signs also indicate the approximate locations of some lost town features, such as Fort Hindman, which was taken by the river not long after its surrender. A visitors' center contains exhibits and other information about the role that Arkansas Post played in

lower Mississippi valley and Arkansas history. A noncontiguous tract designated as the Osotouy Unit of the national memorial contains archaeological sites from the prehistoric and colonial eras, and will eventually be developed to interpret more completely the history of Quapaw relations with colonial residents.

Arkansas Post National Memorial can be reached from Arkansas Highway 165. Stuttgart is the nearest large town to the north, and Dumas is the closest town to the south.

Further Reading: Arnold, Morris S., *Colonial Arkansas, 1686–1804* (Fayetteville: University of Arkansas Press, 1991); Arnold, Morris S., *The Rumble of a Distant Drum: The Quapaws and Old World Newcomers, 1673–1804* (Fayetteville: University of Arkansas Press, 2000); Martin, Patrick E., *An Inquiry into the Locations and Characteristics of Jacob Bright's Trading House and William Montgomery's Tavern*, Archeological Research Series No. 11 (Fayetteville: Archeological Survey, 1977); Whayne, Jeannie M., et al., *Arkansas: A Narrative History* (Fayetteville, University of Arkansas Press, 2002).

Ann M. Early

THE HISTORIC PERIOD TUNICA INDIANS

Northwestern Mississippi and Eastern Arkansas
Adapting to and Surviving European Colonization

The Tunica were a powerful native presence in the lower Mississippi River valley during the early historic period. They were one of the most influential and organized tribes in an area that had suffered a catastrophic decline in population from prehistoric levels. The Tunica probably entered the valley from the west during the end of the prehistoric period and may have been heirs, at least in part, of the great Spiro phase in the Arkansas River valley.

Tunica ancestors were first encountered in 1541 in northwestern Mississippi and eastern Arkansas by the de Soto *entrada*. These people, identified as the Quizquiz and perhaps also the evocative-sounding Tanico, lived in large villages near the confluence of the Arkansas and Mississippi rivers. They participated in the Mississippian cultural tradition, which was characterized by dependence on intensive corn agriculture. Other characteristics of this culture include construction of earthen architecture in the form of mound building, complex sociopolitical development, and such specific artifact types, such as shell-tempered pottery. The corn subsistence base was supplemented by the rich riverine and terrestrial resources of the Mississippi River valley and its tributaries.

The Tunica were distinguished from their neighbors, however, by their distinctive language (Tunican), one that is not known to have been related to any other language group. This unique linguistic heritage is further evidence that the Tunica were recent immigrants to the lower Mississippi valley during the late prehistoric period.

Disease and population decline apparently led to a breakdown of social and political structures during the seventeenth century. Refugees from Quizquiz-Tanico migrated to the lower Yazoo River near its junction with the Mississippi River, where they were found living with other remnant groups in 1699 by the French, who first identified them as the Tunica (*Tonicas*). They resided at the Haynes Bluff mound site near Vicksburg, Mississippi, and perhaps even added to the mounds as late as the eighteenth century. The Tunica, then, like the neighboring Natchez, may have been among the last of the Native American peoples who built, as well as used, mounds.

The Tunica and the French established friendly relations, and during the next several decades the Tunica became important trading partners of the French and reliable allies in the latter's conflicts with the Natchez. In 1706 the Tunica

Bride-les-Boeufs, a chief of the Tunica during their occupation of Trudeau, and the wife and son of the great chief Cahura-Joligo, killed by the Natchez in 1731. Sketched from life by Alexandre De Batz in June 1732. [Peabody Museum, Harvard University, Cambridge, Massachusetts]

moved yet again to a point on the east bank of the Mississippi River opposite the mouth of the Red River in Louisiana. They lived at several locations near this important riverine junction for the remainder of the eighteenth century. Their most important settlement was the Trudeau site, which was occupied between 1731 and 1764. Trudeau was the provenience of the "Tunica Treasure," an extraordinarily rich collection of grave goods that were found with burials at the site. The wealth and diversity of European artifacts demonstrate the success of the Tunica in dealing with the French.

It is apparent that during this period the Tunica had a highly developed entrepreneurial system that was perhaps derived from their Spiroan heritage. They procured and controlled the distribution of resources, such as salt and horses, that were vital to their neighbors, Indian and European alike. The Tunica also continued to provide important services to the French as guides and military allies.

The Tunica were so closely associated with the French that when the English gained control of the Mississippi valley after the French and Indian War, they resorted to an uncharacteristic confrontation and attacked the first English convoy that attempted to ascend the river in 1764. The tribe briefly fled the Mississippi in fear of retribution but then returned and made peace with the English. They chose to establish themselves, however, as close as possible to the friendly French settlements. This was a time of diminishing economic and political influence for the tribe, and of increasing acculturation to European ways of life.

By 1800 the Tunica had moved west of the Mississippi River to Marksville, Louisiana, where a core group are still to be found today. They intermarried with peoples of other tribes, such as the Biloxi, Ofo, Avoyel, and Choctaw. They suffered a period of economic depression and social repression during the later nineteenth and early twentieth centuries, but have since undergone a renaissance after their federal recognition as the Tunica-Biloxi tribe in 1981.

This odyssey of the Tunica is documented in historical records and is supported by archaeological evidence. The salient feature reflected in these movements is the preference, at least during the early-middle historic period, for settlement at major junctions in the riverine system of communication. The selection of such control points enabled the Tunica to continue their entrepreneurial activities along established trade networks. When confronted with an adversarial situation, whether the antagonist was Native American or European, the typical Tunica response was to move to a new location that minimized the problem but still allowed them to succeed in

their adopted role as middlemen between the natives and Europeans in both economic and military ventures.

The Tunica are one of the few lower Mississippi valley tribes to survive from prehistory to the present. Their ethnic continuity has been due primarily to their adaptability to the new world of European influence, an entrepreneurial proclivity that enabled them to play an important role in that new world order, and their ability to make the right choices at times of stress.

Further Reading: Brain, Jeffrey P., *On the Tunica Trail*, Anthropological Study No. 1 (Baton Rouge: Louisiana Archaeological Survey and Antiquities Commission, 1977); Brain, Jeffrey P., *Tunica Treasure*, Peabody Museum of Archaeology and Ethnology Papers, vol. 71 (Cambridge, MA: Harvard University, 1979: Brain, Jeffrey P., *Tunica Archaeology*, Peabody Museum of Archaeology and Ethnology Papers, vol. 78 (Cambridge, MA: Harvard University, 1988); Brain, Jeffrey P., *The Tunica-Biloxi* (New York: Chelsea House, 1990); Day, Bill, *Tunica-Biloxi Today*, 3rd ed., Anthropological Study No. 1 (Baton Rouge: Louisiana Archaeological Survey and Antiquities Commission, 1994); Schambach, Frank F., "Some New Interpretations of Spiroan Culture History," in *Archaeology of Eastern North America: Papers in Honor of Stephen Williams*, edited by J. B. Stoltman, Archaeological Report No. 25 (Jackson: Mississippi Department of Archives and History, 1993); Truex, Faye, and Patricia Q. Foster, *The Tunica-Biloxi Tribe: Its Culture and People* (Marksville: Tunica-Biloxi Indians of Louisiana, 1987).

Jeffrey P. Brain

THE CHOTA AND TANASEE SITES

Eastern Tennessee

Cherokee Villages of the Eighteenth Century

In the eighteenth century, the Cherokee, often referred to as the Overhill Cherokee, occupied about sixty villages constituting four areas in western North Carolina, eastern Tennessee, and adjacent regions. Chota and Tanasee were two of ten villages along the lower Little Tennessee River that constituted the heart of the Overhill settlements. These were the most socially influential, economically significant, militarily important, and politically powerful Cherokee towns for much of the eighteenth century. Many prominent Cherokee leaders resided at Chota, and the town was regarded as the capital of the Overhill Cherokees for much of this period. In the mid-eighteenth century, the village was probably inhabited by 300 to 500 people.

The University of Tennessee conducted extensive archaeological excavations at the site from 1969 through 1974 in conjunction with Tellico Reservoir Archeological

Project. Excavations exposed approximately 2 hectares (roughly 4.9 acres) of the site, recording 37 structures, 736 refuse filled pits, and 117 burials belonging to the Cherokee occupation. Interpretation of the site is greatly enhanced by contemporary British records, especially the diary of Lieutenant Henry Timberlake, who lived among the Overhill Cherokee for four months in the early 1760s.

Historic records indicate that a small creek separated Chota from Tanasee and that Chota probably developed from, and then eclipsed in size and influence, its neighbor around 1720 to 1740. Archaeological materials from the two villages, however, are indistinguishable and indicate occupation from the late seventeenth through the early nineteenth centuries. Archaeological studies at the site identified two superimposed octagonal townhouses or council houses, a rectangular summer townhouse, and a village plaza. The earlier council

Artist's reconstruction of Chota about 1760.   [Drawing by Tom Whyte, courtesy of the Frank H. McClung Museum, University of Tennessee]

house was 15.5 meters in diameter, with four central roof supports, and a large central hearth. When the second townhouse was erected, the building was shifted approximately 2 meters from the footprint of the earlier structure. The second townhouse was 18.3 meters in diameter with eight major roof supports, a large central hearth and floor area, and postholes from interior bench supports. These provided seating within the building on seven sides, one for each of the seven Cherokee clans. The building was covered with bark and soil, and it probably stood more than 5 meters high at the center. A group of large pits, from which soil was recovered to maintain and repair the walls and roof, forms an arc on the structure's east side. The narrow corridor entrance, on the south side of the structure, projects about 2 meters beyond the outside wall before making a sharp right angle and extending another 1.5 meters. Immediately in front of the townhouse entrance are postholes representing a rectangular summer townhouse or pavilion. This structure measures 7 by 14.6 meters. Three adult burials—one unquestionably the remains of the great Cherokee war chief Oconastota, who was buried in 1783—are associated with this building. The village plaza occupies

approximately 0.25 hectares (about 0.6 acres), but few associated archaeological features are attributed to the ceremonial activities that the Cherokee conducted here.

By the mid-eighteenth century approximately sixty domestic structures and their associated activity areas surrounded the plaza and public buildings, and they stretched along the river for nearly 2 kilometers. Domestic structures were spaced 50 to 100 meters apart and consisted of paired winter and summer houses. At Chota and Tanasee ten pairs of winter and summer dwellings were mapped during the excavations. Winter houses, or hot houses, were circular or octagonal, measuring about 7 to 9 meters in diameter with four major roof support posts and a clay hearth. Except for internal bench support posts, few additional features occur within winter houses. These buildings were wattle-and-daub construction with a bark roof and stood about 3 meters high. Only a few meters away were summer houses, each consisting of a rectangular posthole pattern measuring about 8.8 meters long by 4.9 meters wide. They had bark-covered gable roofs and stood about 3 meters high. Most summer houses contained two to seven human burials. Exterior hearths, burned surfaces, smudge pits, refuse-filled pits, and additional burials occur near these structures. The shape and size of refuse-filled pits indicate their use for food storage as well as a source of soil for house construction, building repair, and pottery manufacture. Found at Chota, and virtually unique to the Overhill Cherokee, are large rectangular or oval pits with single or paired postholes at either end that supported a low roof. Often a small fired area is found at the center of the pit floor. Not described in historical sources, these facilities may have been used to store root crops introduced by European settlers, such as Irish potatoes. Each household also likely had a corn crib elevated above the ground by four posts, although it is impossible to isolate these among the hundreds of individual postholes. Additional clusters of refuse-filled pits, surface-fired areas, smudge pits, and additional human burials represent more widely placed activity areas likely shared among several households.

Also found at Chota and Tanasee are two other distinctive structure types. The first, only one of which was recorded, is a large rectangular house measuring 9.1 meters long by 3.5 meters wide and divided into three equal-size rooms with the entrance through the central segment. One end was probably used for storage, while the other end, containing interior storage pits and sometimes burials, was used for habitation. Comparative data shows that these buildings were more frequently used at several contemporary Cherokee villages, and they generally became more common after the mid-eighteenth century, as did the second kind of structure, a small cabin. Four such cabins, measuring about 5.6 by 4.4 meters, were recorded at Chota. They had vertical post walls woven with small saplings or rails and a gable roof. At one end was the entrance and at the other a hearth with an external wood and clay chimney. A rectangular cellar pit occurs inside one of these cabins.

Pottery shards (137,075 shards were recovered during the archaeological investigations) at Chota and Tanasee are predominantly Overhill Plain style (96.6 percent). Decorated Overhill types and Qualla ceramics characteristic of the Cherokee settlements in western North Carolina are each less than 1 to 2 percent of the assemblage. Studies of the stone artifacts (18,266 of these were recovered during the archaeological studies), corroborated by data from other Cherokee sites, show that although stone tool manufacture and use greatly diminished once European metal implements became available, the Cherokee never completely abandoned their stone tool technology. European artifacts (7,018 of these were recovered archaeologically) include a wide range of primarily British knives, axes, hoes, guns, and kettles obtained through the deerskin trade, which thrived for most of the eighteenth century. Also found at the site are decorative items such as silver earrings, broaches, and arm bands, as well as many different glass beads (72,772 were recovered). Parts of British military swords, fragments of cannons and cannonballs, and pieces of British ceramic tea sets surely found their way to Chota and Tanasee in 1760, when the Cherokee attacked and looted Fort Loudoun just a few kilometers downstream.

Faunal remains (65,299 pieces were recovered) from Chota and Tanasee indicate sustained use of native species such as deer, bear, raccoon, wild turkey, and other animals, and they reveal that the Cherokee incorporated European domestic animals, particularly pigs and chickens, into their diet. Cattle, sheep, and horses do not occur in great numbers before the 1780s. Native corn, squash, and beans were the prevailing agricultural crops, but archaeological data also documents the introduction of peaches and cow peas, for example, and historical sources record the use of Irish potatoes, sweet potatoes, cabbage, and other European plants.

The Cherokee suffered as allies of the defeated British in the American Revolutionary War. For this reason and because of continuing hostilities with the United States, Chota and Tanasee declined greatly in size, population, and regional influence. The town was burned in 1780. In 1784 the town had thirty houses, but only thirty-four people lived there in 1807. In 1819, when the town site was ceded by treaty to the United States, only a single Cherokee dwelling still stood there.

Tellico Reservoir flooded most Overhill Cherokee villages in the lower Little Tennessee River valley in 1979. Because Chota and Tanasee were subject to severe erosion by annual fluctuation of reservoir's level, the Tennessee Valley Authority covered the central part of the site with approximately 2 meters of fill. A memorial to the Cherokee people was erected nearby, concrete pillars were installed corresponding to the locations of the eight townhouse roof support posts, and a marker was the placed at Oconastota's burial site. Cherokee skeletal remains excavated at Chota and other Cherokee sites in the reservoir were re-interred near the Sequoyah Birthplace Museum a few miles away. At the museum are interpretative exhibits relating to Cherokee archaeology, and there are others at the Frank H. McClung Museum at the University of Tennessee, Knoxville, where the Chota and Tanasee materials are stored for further study.

Further Reading: Frank H. McClung Museum Web site, http://mcclungmuseum.utk.edu/; Schroedl, Gerald F., ed., *Overhill Cherokee Archaeology at Chota-Tanasee*, Department of Anthropology Report of Investigations No. 38 (Knoxville: University of Tennessee, 1986); Schroedl, Gerald F., "Cherokee Ethnohistory and Archaeology from 1540 to 1838," in *Indians of the Greater Southeast during the Historic Period*, edited by Bonnie McEwan (Gainesville: University Press of Florida, 2000), 204–241; Schroedl, Gerald F., "Cherokee Archaeology Since the 1970s," in *Integrating Appalachian Archaeology*, edited by Lynne Sullivan and Susan Prezzano (Knoxville: University of Tennessee Press, 2001), 278–297; Sequoyah Birthplace Museum Web site, http://www.sequoyahmuseum.org/.

Gerald F. Schroedl

THE CHALMETTE BATTLEFIELD SITE

Near New Orleans, Louisiana
The Last Battle of the War of 1812

On the Mississippi River some 4 miles below downtown New Orleans lies one of the most important historic battlefields in the United States. It was here on a muddy riverbank in 1815, at the end of the War of 1812, that the United States won the Battle of New Orleans. Historians often call this war the "Second War of Independence" because the overwhelming victory at New Orleans put an end to serious British ambitions to destroy the young republic. In spite of the recent encroachment of industrial development and associated residential sprawl, significant parts of the Chalmette Battlefield retain both geographical and archeological integrity. The best-preserved sections of the battlefield landscape are located in the Chalmette Unit of Jean Lafitte National Historical Park and Preserve, where the National Park Service protects the battlefield for the public.

The battle was fought in a rural setting of elegant sugar plantations and country homes. In the early nineteenth century, the better homes and mansions in this area were usually built in the local French-Spanish or Creole style. The lands of these country estates typically extended back from the relatively high ground beside the Mississippi riverbank, the natural levee, to low-lying cypress swamps located within a mile of the river's edge. Among the most dominant features of this near-level landscape were the numerous canals and drainage ditches that cut watery paths between the Mississippi and the swamplands.

An American gunboat attack on December 14, 1814, at the mouth of Lake Borgne northwest of New Orleans, began the battle. Here the United States Navy was soundly defeated while trying to stop an amphibious landing of British troops. By December 23, the British had made their way down the back waterways through the cypress swamps and had begun landing thousands of soldiers within 8 miles of New Orleans. General Andrew Jackson, in overall command of the American forces, went immediately to the attack with 2,300 men. In this ferocious fight and in two additional major fierce engagements, on December 28 and again on January 1, the Americans and British fought to a stalemate. The tide of battle finally turned on January 8, 1815. That was when some 5,000 Americans, ensconced behind a defensive earthwork, crushed a frontal attack by 10,000 British soldiers. After less than two hours of fighting, close to 3,500 British troops together with most of their senior officers lay dead or wounded. In contrast, the Americans had only 19 casualties. With little hope for success in future engagements, the sole uninjured British general called for an orderly and gradual retreat. By January 27, the British

had completed the grueling journey back through the swamps to their waiting ships and departed.

How did the Americans, who had up to this point fared poorly in the war with England, suddenly gain such an overwhelming victory? General Andrew Jackson deserves much of the credit for his expert and charismatic generalship. He managed to forge a disparate group of men—from New Orleans merchants to Choctaw Indians—into a truly formidable fighting force complete with effective artillery. Furthermore, top-of-the-line military engineers had constructed powerful defenses for the Americans. Superb leadership and fortifications won the day.

Beyond two small-scale investigations of the American defensive line in 1957 and in 1963, the Chalmette Battlefield received no serious archeological attention before the early 1980s. Between 1983 and 1985 the National Park Service conducted limited archaeological inventory and testing designed to find and protect any battle-related features and artifacts in the path of proposed construction. These studies, funded by both the National Park Service and the Corps of Engineers, discovered that only 180 feet of the American battle line had been lost to the Mississippi River, instead of the 800-foot loss estimated by earlier historians. It turned out that the entire 1964 National Park Service interpretive reconstruction of the battlefield was wrong. While a number of battlefield features were located, there were few artifacts, as is typical of eighteenth- and early-nineteenth-century battlefields. At that time the Industrial Revolution had barely started, so military equipment and supplies were limited and carefully husbanded by soldiers. In 2000 the National Park Service followed up on the first round of investigations with a systematic study that targeted the north central part of the American battle line, which received the main punch of the British attack. The exact location of this attack on today's battlefield was verified, and its pattern and outcome was graphically revealed in the mapped distribution of numerous buried musket balls and artillery rounds.

Today, approaching the Chalmette Unit from the east one can see the eroded brick ruins of De La Ronde House; the only visible remnant of the many plantation houses that played a major role in the battle. It sits in a small city park, isolated on a traffic island in the middle of the St. Bernard Highway, just over 2 miles east of the National Park Service entrance. This large mansion served both as a British headquarters and as a hospital for wounded troops.

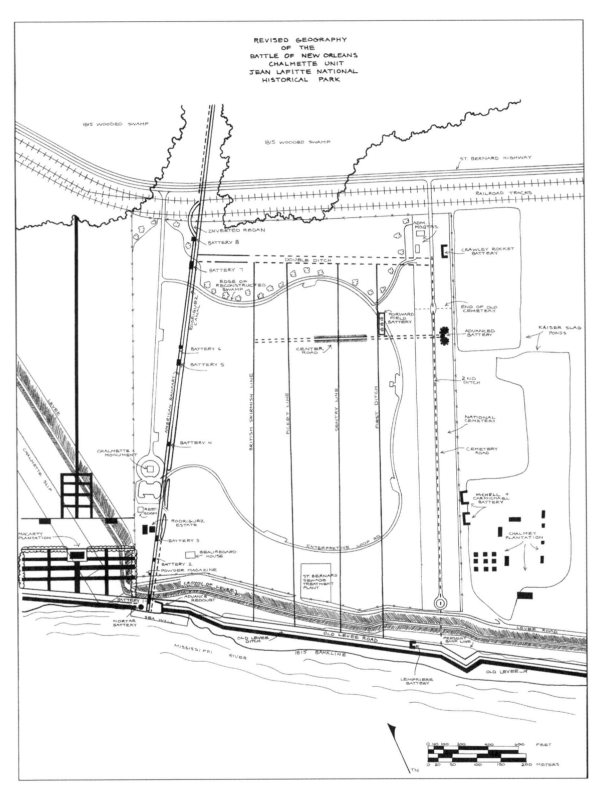

Revised geography of the Battle of New Orleans, Chalmette Unit, Jean Lafitte National Park and Preserve. [Drawn by Lyndi Hubbell for the National Park Service]

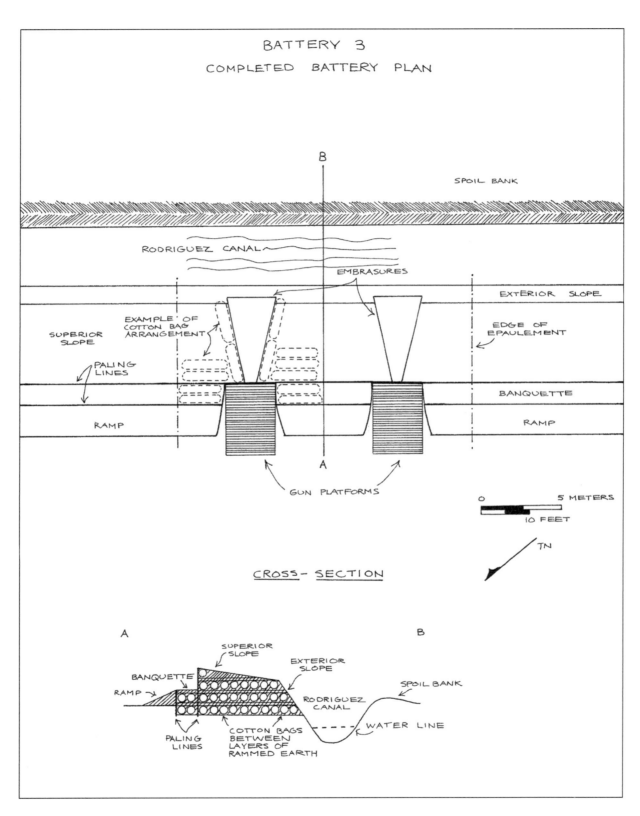

Battery 3 reconstruction: plan and profile of the completed battery emplacement. [Drawn by Lyndi Hubbell for the National Park Service]

5 CM

...l was found south of Battery 2, where the 7th Infantry Regiment held the line. A soldier probably lost his car-
...onal Park Service]

...ves the central and most signifi-
...ttlefield. The dominant battle-
...landscape is the Rodriguez
...hwesterly direction through
...former size, it is still the
...ark on the battlefield.
...ighting after December

23 to fortify this former logging canal that separated the
Rodriquez Estate from the adjacent Chalmette Plantation. A
close reader of terrain, General Jackson chose to fortify the
Rodriguez Canal because here the distance between the
swamp and the riverbank quickly narrowed from over a mile
to roughly a half mile, thus leaving little room for the British
to maneuver. Immediately behind the canal Jackson and his

men raised an imposing earthwork, 8 feet in height and 18 to 20 feet wide at its base. Today only a thin, buried soil layer of silty clay loam indicates the presence of the former great rampart. Much of its soil was removed for road building since the battle, and erosion took care of the rest.

Many of the American artillery batteries set in the defensive line held powerful naval guns. Two twenty-four pounders (cannons that shot 24-pound projectiles) were placed in Battery 3, which was discovered along the Rodriguez Canal in the southwest corner of the park. This is the battery that was commanded by Jean Lafitte, the feared Caribbean pirate. It was reinforced with alternating layers of cotton-filled bags and soil, an arrangement designed to absorb the shock of heavy British shot. As with the rest of the American line, its rear was strengthened with solid vertical cypress palings set deep into the earth. The lower ends of these palings were found in recent excavations, along with the faint impressions of smaller cypress staves that once supported the rear of the step-up that enabled troops to shoot over the high rampart. Fifty feet northwest of Battery 3 is the footprint of the Rodriguez House, its location still framed by four large oak trees. This house, commandeered by the Americans, took devastating fire from the British batteries.

In the National Cemetery at the northeastern edge of the Chalmette Unit is the remnant of the largest British battery. Built of rammed earth, it once held ten powerful cannons. Today it survives as little more than a low, broad mound. On January 8 it became the rallying point for the main British attack. A plantation road, called Center Road, passed through the battery, and it was along that road that 2,400 British troops marched in column to their deaths. When the moisture and vegetation are just right, the road is still visible

as it makes a straight approach toward the American line. Archaeologists have found one of the highest concentrations of lost and expended ammunition just to the north of this road. Here, in front of American batteries 7 and 8, is where the British attack stalled only 50 to 200 yards from the Rodriguez Canal.

Among the other battle-related features that have been identified are a series of north-south agricultural ditches that played a major role in the battle. The First Ditch and the Second Ditch, as the Americans called them, were used by the British as geographical landmarks for deploying troops and affording them protection from cannon fire. Two other ditches in the center of the Chalmette Unit provided sentry and picket lines for the Americans. Another, within just 100 yards of the Rodriguez Canal, concealed British skirmishers of the 95th Rifles.

Archival and archeological research at the Chalmette Battlefield has revealed the broad patterns of the battle landscape and the story it tells. However, much more needs to be done to fix the exact locations of many battle features and fill in important details about how the battle was fought and the men who both lived and died on the Chalmette Battlefield.

Further Reading: "At New Orleans" Web site, www.atneworleans. com/body/battlefield.htm; Cornelison, John E., Jr., and Tammy D. Cooper, *An Archeological Survey of the Chalmette Battlefield at J* *Lafitte Historical Park and Preserve* (Tallahassee: National Pa' vice, Southeast Archeological Center, 2002); Pickles. *Orleans 1815: Andrew Jackson Crushes the British, e* G. Chandler, Osprey Military Campaign Series Osprey, 1993); Remini, Robert V., *The Battle* York: Viking, 1999).

SHILOH NATIONAL MILITA

Northeast Mississippi and So

The Archaeology of a

Shiloh National Military Park comprises two units— southwest Tennessee and the other in northeast M; and preserves provocative cultural resources asso momentous military events during the American C and the prehistory of aboriginal Southeastern Indians. ney to Shiloh permits visitors to examine the intense hu drama on two of the more horrendous killing fields of the pi otal national American conflict; explore the complex issues, causes, and consequences of the Civil War as the defining crossroads in American history; understand what motivated Civil War veterans to preserve and commemorate the

This set of buck and tridge in the mud. [N

The Chalmette Unit pres cant part of the Chalmette B related feature in the park uni Canal, which runs in a south-sou the park. Though but a shadow of i most visible archaeological landr Jackson took advantage of lulls in the

This set of buck and ball was found south of Battery 2, where the 7th Infantry Regiment held the line. A soldier probably lost his cartridge in the mud.   [National Park Service]

The Chalmette Unit preserves the central and most significant part of the Chalmette Battlefield. The dominant battle-related feature in the park unit's landscape is the Rodriguez Canal, which runs in a south-southwesterly direction through the park. Though but a shadow of its former size, it is still the most visible archaeological landmark on the battlefield. Jackson took advantage of lulls in the fighting after December 23 to fortify this former logging canal that separated the Rodriquez Estate from the adjacent Chalmette Plantation. A close reader of terrain, General Jackson chose to fortify the Rodriguez Canal because here the distance between the swamp and the riverbank quickly narrowed from over a mile to roughly a half mile, thus leaving little room for the British to maneuver. Immediately behind the canal Jackson and his men raised an imposing earthwork, 8 feet in height and 18 to 20 feet wide at its base. Today only a thin, buried soil layer of silty clay loam indicates the presence of the former great rampart. Much of its soil was removed for road building since the battle, and erosion took care of the rest.

Many of the American artillery batteries set in the defensive line held powerful naval guns. Two twenty-four pounders (cannons that shot 24-pound projectiles) were placed in Battery 3, which was discovered along the Rodriguez Canal in the southwest corner of the park. This is the battery that was commanded by Jean Lafitte, the feared Caribbean pirate. It was reinforced with alternating layers of cotton-filled bags and soil, an arrangement designed to absorb the shock of heavy British shot. As with the rest of the American line, its rear was strengthened with solid vertical cypress palings set deep into the earth. The lower ends of these palings were found in recent excavations, along with the faint impressions of smaller cypress staves that once supported the rear of the step-up that enabled troops to shoot over the high rampart. Fifty feet northwest of Battery 3 is the footprint of the Rodriguez House, its location still framed by four large oak trees. This house, commandeered by the Americans, took devastating fire from the British batteries.

In the National Cemetery at the northeastern edge of the Chalmette Unit is the remnant of the largest British battery. Built of rammed earth, it once held ten powerful cannons. Today it survives as little more than a low, broad mound. On January 8 it became the rallying point for the main British attack. A plantation road, called Center Road, passed through the battery, and it was along that road that 2,400 British troops marched in column to their deaths. When the moisture and vegetation are just right, the road is still visible as it makes a straight approach toward the American line. Archaeologists have found one of the highest concentrations of lost and expended ammunition just to the north of this road. Here, in front of American batteries 7 and 8, is where the British attack stalled only 50 to 200 yards from the Rodriguez Canal.

Among the other battle-related features that have been identified are a series of north-south agricultural ditches that played a major role in the battle. The First Ditch and the Second Ditch, as the Americans called them, were used by the British as geographical landmarks for deploying troops and affording them protection from cannon fire. Two other ditches in the center of the Chalmette Unit provided sentry and picket lines for the Americans. Another, within just 100 yards of the Rodriguez Canal, concealed British skirmishers of the 95th Rifles.

Archival and archeological research at the Chalmette Battlefield has revealed the broad patterns of the battle landscape and the story it tells. However, much more needs to be done to fix the exact locations of many battle features and fill in important details about how the battle was fought and the men who both lived and died on the Chalmette Battlefield.

Further Reading: "At New Orleans" Web site, www.atneworleans. com/body/battlefield.htm; Cornelison, John E., Jr., and Tammy D. Cooper, *An Archeological Survey of the Chalmette Battlefield at Jean Lafitte Historical Park and Preserve* (Tallahassee: National Park Service, Southeast Archeological Center, 2002); Pickles, Tim, *New Orleans 1815: Andrew Jackson Crushes the British*, edited by David G. Chandler, Osprey Military Campaign Series, No. 28 (Oxford: Osprey, 1993); Remini, Robert V., *The Battle of New Orleans* (New York: Viking, 1999).

Ted Birkedal

SHILOH NATIONAL MILITARY PARK

Northeast Mississippi and Southwest Tennessee
The Archaeology of a Civil War Battlefield

Shiloh National Military Park comprises two units—one in southwest Tennessee and the other in northeast Mississippi—and preserves provocative cultural resources associated with momentous military events during the American Civil War and the prehistory of aboriginal Southeastern Indians. A journey to Shiloh permits visitors to examine the intense human drama on two of the more horrendous killing fields of the pivotal national American conflict; explore the complex issues, causes, and consequences of the Civil War as the defining crossroads in American history; understand what motivated Civil War veterans to preserve and commemorate the battlefield; and investigate one of the more pristine prehistoric Late Mississippian mound and village sites in the Southeast.

In the decade preceding 1900, America experienced a rebirth of patriotism and nationalism as citizens reflected on the honor and courage of previous American generations. The period witnessed the establishment of new museums and the creation and dedication of numerous commemorative monuments, memorials, and statues. With its social impact still immediate in the national conscience, the Civil War, fought only three decades earlier, became a primary focus of attention. Throughout the country, hundreds of stone and bronze statues commemorating Union and Confederate soldiers were erected on city courthouse squares and at county seats. In Washington, D.C., and Richmond, Virginia, massive bronze figures of the prominent military commanders who led the opposing armies were erected. More significant to the long-term preservation of the places where battles took place (Sellars 2005), Civil War veterans organized and championed a movement to establish a number of national parks, one of which was Shiloh, located in a rural setting on the west bank of the Tennessee River in Hardin County, Tennessee.

Union veterans, survivors of the bitter two-day carnage at Shiloh, argued that their comrades who served in other armies already had national parks commemorating their war service. In 1890 Chickamauga battlefield in Georgia and Antietam in Maryland were set aside by Congress as national parks, and legislative steps were being taken to establish another such park at Gettysburg, Pennsylvania. Why, asked the veterans of the West, was the same recognition not given to the contesting forces engaged at Shiloh? Furthermore, they argued that a park was necessary to protect the graves of soldiers buried on the battlefield in 1862. Although most of the Union soldiers who died at Shiloh had been exhumed and reburied in the National Cemetery created in 1866 at Pittsburg Landing, the remains of many Union troops were never recovered. Moreover, nearly all of the 1,728 Confederate soldiers killed during the battle still lay in graves scattered across the battlefield. Local farmers reported plowing up bones across the battlefield. So concerned veterans created the Shiloh Battlefield Association in 1893, which, in turn, moved to acquire options on land and lobbied for the establishment of a national park. The next year Congress passed legislation establishing Shiloh National Military Park, signed into law by President Grover Cleveland on December 27, 1894. Development of the new park was delegated to the secretary of war, who initially administered the park by means of a War Department commission composed of Shiloh veterans representing the one Confederate and two Union armies engaged at the battle. Roughly four decades later, on June 10, 1933, administrative responsibility for the park was transferred by executive order to the National Park Service.

Shiloh commemorates the scene of one of the major killing fields of the American Civil War, and the largest battle of the 1862–63 campaign for possession of the railroads of the western Confederacy and military control of the lower Mississippi River. In the early spring of 1862, Union forces under Major General Ulysses S. Grant pressed the campaign for control of the Mississippi River following quick victories at forts Henry and Donelson in northern Tennessee. In March Grant's army ascended the Tennessee River, establishing camp on the west side of the river at Pittsburg Landing, Tennessee. The Union camp extended 2 miles inland, encompassing a wilderness log church named Shiloh Meeting House. Grant awaited the arrival of the Union Army of the Ohio under Major General

Don Carlos Buell and made preparations to attack the strategic railroad junction at Corinth, Mississippi, 22 miles to the southwest. However, a Confederate army under General Albert Sidney Johnston, marching north from Corinth (April 3–5), surprised and engaged Grant's force at Camp Shiloh on April 6. In two days of bitter fighting, the contesting forces suffered heavy casualties—sustaining a combined total of 23,746 soldiers listed as killed, wounded, or missing out of the 109,784 men engaged. Among the dead was the Confederate commander, Albert Sidney Johnston, who bled to death from a bullet wound on the first day of battle. Reinforced by the arrival of a sizable portion of Buell's army, Grant launched a massive morning counterattack on April 7. Although the outnumbered Confederates, led by their new commander, General P.G.T. Beauregard, made a determined stand, the Southern forces were compelled to retire from the field and withdraw to their important base at Corinth. The awful carnage experienced by the Shiloh combatants shocked the American people, bringing the horrors of war home to citizens North and South. The ferocity of the fighting experienced at Shiloh forecast an increasingly bloody and protracted war.

To record the history of the battle and suitably mark the field with markers and monuments, the War Department commissioners used the surface remains of the Union camps, soldier burials, and the surviving evidence of conflict to locate the original battle lines and mark defining historical features. Recent archaeological investigations conducted by the National Park Service confirm the accuracy of the early commission's investigative efforts to locate troop positions and the lines of combat, and also identified a relative lack of disturbance of the Civil War archaeological resources preserved within the battlefield landscape.

Today, however, Shiloh is a "place of peace," as its biblical Hebrew name implies. The battlefield terrain consists of small to medium-size agricultural fields, rugged ravines, marshy creeks, and natural springs. Much of the site is covered by open forest, mostly made up of oaks and hickories. This pastoral character of the landscape provides a tranquil and strikingly beautiful memorial setting, permitting visitors with an opportunity to slip easily back into the past. One important development arising from the long-term preservation and stewardship of this nationally significant Civil War site has been the preservation of an oasis of biological diversity (a variety of terrestrial and aquatic animal and plant species) within the park boundaries. It is an outstanding example of the crucial role the National Park System plays in preserving the vanishing rural American landscape and its associated native wildlife.

With legislation passed in 1996 and 2000, Congress expanded the purpose of Shiloh National Military Park, creating a new unit in Corinth, Mississippi, and mandating development of a Corinth Civil War Interpretive Center. This state-of-the-art interpretive facility, which opened in 2004, focuses on events and conditions in northern Mississippi and southwest Tennessee, covering topics such as slavery, emancipation, and the privation experienced in this area during the war. It explains the key role of Corinth in the western theater, when for more than six months in 1862 this vital railroad junction ranked second only to the Confederate capital at Richmond in terms of strategic importance. The land surrounding the community was heavily fortified by Confederate and Union forces during the conflict, and both a siege (May 1862) and a fierce battle (October 3–4, 1862) were waged for possession of the crossroads. The remains of these earthworks are among the best preserved in the nation.

Long before the Civil War, prehistoric Native peoples left their imprint on Shiloh in the form of numerous mounds and house sites on the steep bluffs overlooking the Tennessee River. They occupy equal status in national significance alongside the more famous Civil War resources preserved within the park, and are protected by the Shiloh Indian Mounds National Historic Landmark, established in 1989. This extensive prehistoric village and mound complex, inhabited by American Indians from AD 900 to 1300, is the best-preserved Mississippian town site in the Tennessee River valley. This 45-acre prehistoric village was once surrounded by a defensive wooden palisade. The principal remains so far identified include seven large mounds, six residential or ceremonial and one burial, in addition to many low hillocks that are the remains of small dwellings. An embankment to the west of the mound area indicates the former existence of a defensive palisade, and further excavation revealed the remains of several dozen houses and other subsurface features.

There are also a number of important ancient sites near the Shiloh and Corinth parks. One such place is Savannah, Tennessee, now destroyed by the present-day town; nevertheless, Shiloh artifacts are displayed there at the Tennessee River Museum. Other mound sites in the vicinity include Pinson, Chucalissa, Bear Creek, Tishomingo, and Pharr, which can be visited by the public. For many years the Shiloh mounds have been a source of great interest to archaeologists and antiquarians, professional and amateur alike. One authority has called them "the principal, and really only notable group of mounds on the (Lower) Tennessee River." Yet despite the interest the mounds have aroused, and the exploration that has been made of them, very little is known about the ancient people and culture that produced them.

Students of prehistoric American cultures have identified the mound builders as possible ancestors of the Chatt-Muskogee tribes—embracing the Choctaws, Chickasaws, Natchez, and other tribes indigenous to the Southern or Southeast region of this country. Archaeologists cite the indigenous peoples of this region as possessing one of the richest cultures found north of Mexico. At the time Europeans first came to the New World, many Indian groups in the interior Southeast had economies that combined farming with hunting and gathering, organizing themselves into relatively complex political units, to build large towns and monumental ceremonial centers (such as the Shiloh mounds), and developing a rich symbolism and an expressive art style.

In the years immediately following the establishment of the park at Shiloh, some exploration was made of the mounds under the direction of the National Military Park Battlefield Commission. While this work was conducted with more zeal than skill, one interesting find made by the commission was an effigy pipe found in the large burial mound by Commission Chairman Cornelius Cadle in 1899.

The most extensive, although not the most rigorous, archaeological exploration occurred in 1933–34 as a federal Civil Works Administration project under the direction of Dr. Frank H. H. Roberts, an archaeologist of the Smithsonian Institution. Over the last decade, National Park Service archaeologists from the Southeast Archaeological Center in Tallahassee, Florida, have conducted a number of investigations to learn more about the ancient mounds and the society that built them. This work was made necessary because of riverbank erosion on the eastern boundary of the mound and village complex. That erosion threatened the largest mound, which is known as Mound A. The information from this investigation produced substantial data on how individual architectural stages were constructed and when that construction took place. Radiocarbon 14 and archaeomagnetic dating established that the most intensive prehistoric activity at Shiloh took place from AD 1050 to 1300.

Currently, the National Park Service holds more than 4,133 of the roughly 6,000 acres authorized by legislation for inclusion in the park. Managers administer a progressive land protection plan to coordinate further acquisition of the remaining historic properties located outside national park boundaries held under private ownership. The park is open daily (closed only on Christmas Day) to the public (a small entrance fee is required) and park rangers are on duty to aid visitors in understanding the significance of Shiloh battlefield, the Indian mounds, and the Corinth Interpretive Center. Shiloh remains a uniquely special place where many who tramp across the now peaceful landscape often exclaim they "can still hear the guns roar."

Further Reading: Allen, Stacy D., *Shiloh! A Visitor's Guide* (Columbus, OH: Blue & Gray Enterprises, 2001); Cunningham, O. Edward, *Shiloh and the Western Campaign of 1862*, edited by Gary D. Joiner and Timothy B. Smith (New York: Savas Beattie, 2007); Sellars, Richard West, "Pilgrim Places: Civil War Battlefields, Historic Preservation, and America's First National Military Parks, 1863–1900," *CRM: The Journal of Heritage Stewardship* 2(1) (2005); Shiloh National Military Park Web site, National Park Service, www.nps.gov/shil (online 2007); Smith, Timothy D., *This Great Battlefield of Shiloh: History, Memory, and the Establishment of a Civil War National Military Park* (Knoxville: University of Tennessee Press, 2004); Sword, Wiley, *Shiloh: Bloody April* (New York: William Morrow, 1977), rev. ed. (Dayton, OH: Morningside Press, 2001); Welch, Paul D., *Archaeology at Shiloh Indian Mounds, 1899–1999* (Tuscaloosa: University of Alabama, 2006).

Stacy D. Allen

THE CSS *HUNLEY* SHIPWRECK

Charleston Harbor, South Carolina
The Recovery and Investigation of a Civil War Submarine

On February 17, 1864, at 8:45 pm, the Confederate submarine *H.L. Hunley* maneuvered 4 miles offshore to destroy the USS *Houstonic*, a 207-foot Union steam screw sloop-of-war guarding an approach to the harbor of Charleston, South Carolina. *Housatonic* sank in a matter of minutes, and *Hunley* became the first submarine to successfully sink an enemy warship. Unfortunately for its crew, the *Hunley* also was sunk in this operation, at an unknown location. In 1995 a dive team funded by best-selling author Clive Cussler discovered the lost sub after a search that lasted 15 years. Dr. Robert S. Neyland, U.S. Navy Underwater Archaeologist, directed archaeologists from the Naval Historical Center, National Park Service, and South Carolina Institute of Archaeology as part of a diverse group that included engineers and commercial divers who planned for and successfully raised *Hunley* on August 8, 2000.

The American Civil War stimulated many technological innovations, including experimentation with submarines by both Union and Confederate engineers. *Hunley* was constructed in 1863 in Mobile, Alabama—the third in a line of submarines built by Southern engineers and investors led by Horace Lawson Hunley, a New Orleans lawyer and Southern patriot. The first was aptly named *Pioneer*, and was scuttled in New Orleans. The second, sometimes referred to as *Pioneer II* but more likely called *American Diver*, was lost while under tow in Mobile Bay. Neither *Hunley* precursor saw battle. *Pioneer* was given a letter of marque signifying it was a private vessel; however, Hunley and his men transferred to Mobile, Alabama, where they are identified as members of the Confederate Secret Service.

The submarine arrived in Charleston, South Carolina, later in 1863 and began its sea trials. The danger of operating this submarine was tragically clear, for it sank on two separate occasions, claiming the lives of thirteen men. The second sinking claimed the life of Hunley himself and the Mobile engineering team. The submarine would bear his name thereafter. *Hunley* was raised and put under the command of Lt. George E. Dixon, a Confederate Army engineer from Mobile who was convinced that the submarine could be successful. Dixon obtained a volunteer crew that he put through rigorous training. Lt. Dixon's plan succeeded: *Hunley* planted a barbed torpedo in the starboard stern quarter of the USS *Housatonic* and detonated a 95-pound explosive charge. *Housatonic* sank quickly, but *Hunley*, despite signaling with a blue light to Confederate sentries ashore, was also lost.

ARCHAEOLOGY OF *H.L. HUNLEY*

Hunley was one of the Confederacy's secret weapons; therefore, none of its original drawings or plans survived the Civil War. The vessel recovered in 2000 differs significantly from the sketches and replicas made after the war. Once thought to be merely a converted steam boiler, it was found to have a far more sophisticated sleek, hydrodynamic shape, possessing a hand-crank–powered propeller, hand pumps that could shift water between the sub's forward and aft ballast tanks, a joystick for steering the rudder, diving planes on either side of the hull, and iron frames for stiffening the riveted hull to prevent buckling from water pressure during dives. The propeller shaft was counterweighted to prevent uncontrolled spinning, and a hand brake would bring its motion to a halt. A wooden force bellows was used to pump fresh air into the crew compartment from the surface through two 5-foot snorkels. Perhaps the most innovative invention was the spar-mounted torpedo used to destroy *Housatonic*.

Prior to the recent work, little was known about the crew except for an incomplete list of names put together after its loss. Historical accounts reported a nine-man crew, but there were in fact only eight. The skeletal remains and personal effects of the men discovered within *Hunley* tell the unwritten story of these men. Studies of the bones by forensic anthropologists reveal a crew who varied in origin, age, and stature. Only four of the crew were United States born; the other half were of European origin. Carbon isotopes 12 and 13 were used to distinguish a European, wheat-based diet from an American one of corn.

The four Europeans were identified as Miller, a sailor between 40 and 45 years of age who had only been in the country a short time; Arnold Becker, in his early 20s and the youngest crew member, also a recent immigrant; Cpl. J. F. Carlsen, a 20- to 23-year-old who was also a recent immigrant; and Lumpkin, a seasoned sailor 37 to 44 years old with a carbon isotope signature indicating he had been in America for some time. American-born crew members included Lt. George E. Dixon, who was in his mid-20s. Dixon was not Southern and perhaps hailed from the Midwest. Joseph Ridgeway was a 31-year-old Maryland-born seafarer. Frank Collins was 24 years old and was born in Virginia. James A Wicks, like Lumpkin, was a seasoned sailor, 45 years old, and was born in North Carolina. Wicks was a Union sailor who "went South." Many of the men were taller than expected, with three crewmen 5 feet 10 inches and one over 6 feet tall—not the heights of

Rear view of Lt. Dixon's gold coin.   [Friends of the *Hunley*]

Underwater view of the *Hunley* in the conservation tank.   [Friends of the *Hunley*]

men one would expect to have wrapped themselves around a hand crank in a sub less than 4 feet high and 3½ feet wide.

The men's bones exhibit evidence of working-class lives. *Hunley* sailors Lumpkin and Miller both had healed injuries indicative of a hard seafaring life. Arnold Becker, although young and physically strong, had damaged his vertebrae, revealing he had overtaxed his considerable strength. Lumpkin's teeth were heavily stained from tobacco and were worn where he clenched his tobacco pipe. A previous foot injury had left him with a permanent limp. Frank Collins had "tailor notches" in his front teeth, not surprising since both his grandfather and uncle were cobblers.

Personal possessions carried by each crew member answered questions about social status, habits, and health. The most valuable items were associated with the remains of Lt. George Dixon. A mangled twenty-dollar gold coin confirmed historical accounts of Dixon being wounded at the Battle of Shiloh and the coin taking the impact of the bullet and saving his life. Sixteen-year-old Queen Bennett of Mobile, Alabama, reportedly gave the coin to Dixon when he left Mobile to fight in the Civil War. Dixon considered the gold coin to be his good luck piece. Following his recovery from the wound, Dixon had the reverse side of the coin engraved with the following words:

SHILOH
April 6, 1862
My Life Preserver
G.E.D.

However, a diamond broach and ring were unexpected discoveries, as was a gold watch with chain and Masonic fob. Dixon also carried a pair of leather-covered brass binoculars, a folding rule, and a penknife.

Lt. Dixon's crew carried possessions indicating the common lives of sailors and soldiers. The few objects that they had were of little monetary value. Personal items included four tobacco pipes, one complete and one damaged folding knife, a leather wallet that might or might not have contained money, and canteens. Joseph Ridgeway from Maryland had tied around his neck the dog tag of Connecticut-born Union soldier Ezra Chamberlin, presumably a battle souvenir.

The work of operating the submarine was better understood with the discovery of a compass in a wooden box, iron wrenches and hammer, a mercury depth gauge, a wax candle still in its wooden holder, and a signal lantern. The latter probably generated the blue light reported by eyewitnesses shortly before *Hunley* disappeared.

Many questions about *Hunley* remain to be answered. The life of Lt. Dixon is largely unknown prior to his arrival in Mobile, Alabama, in 1860. How well *Hunley* operated as a seagoing vessel has yet to be determined, although this will be done by a thorough analysis of the hull's hydrodynamic abilities and its equipment. Of course, the greatest mystery surrounding *Hunley* is why it and its crew never returned to shore.

The *Hunley* and select artifacts can be viewed by the public at the Warren Lasch Conservation Center located in north Charleston, South Carolina. Although principally a research and conservation laboratory, it is open to the public for tours every Saturday and Sunday. More information on the

Lowering *Hunley* submarine onto recovery barge.   [Friends of the *Hunley*]

submarine, its recovery, and ongoing research can be found at Friends of the *Hunley* Web site, www.hunley.org.

Further Reading: Conlin, David L., ed., *USS Housatonic Site Assessment* (Santa Fe, NM: National Park Service, 2005); Hicks, Brian, and Schuyler Kroft, *Raising the Hunley: The Remarkable History and Recovery of the Lost Confederate Submarine* (New York: Ballantine Books, 2002); Murphy, L. E., ed., *H.L. Hunley Site*

Assessment (Santa Fe, NM: National Park Service, 1998); Oeland, Glenn, "Secret Weapon of the Confederacy," *National Geographic* (July 2002): 82–101; Ragan, Mark K., *Union and Confederate Submarine Warfare in the Civil War* (Mason City, IA: Savas, 1999); Ragan, Mark K., *The Hunley* (Orangeburg, SC: Sandlapper, 2006); Walker, Sally M., *Secrets of a Civil War Submarine: Solving the Mysteries of the H.L. Hunley* (Minneapolis: Carolrhoda Books, 2005).

Robert S. Neyland

ANDERSONVILLE NATIONAL HISTORIC SITE

Andersonville, Georgia

The Archaeology of a Civil War Prisoner-of-War Camp

Between 1864 and 1865, the Confederate States of America transported over 40,000 Union prisoners to a newly built prisoner-of-war compound at Andersonville, Georgia. A little over one-third of these prisoners never left. During its years of operation, it constituted the largest concentration of people

in all of south Georgia. Not allowed by Confederate commanders to build adequate shelters, captured Union prisoners dug shallow holes and caves into the landscape's red clay soil. At the height of Andersonville's operation, over 100 Union soldiers died each day. In the years following the close of the war, Union soldiers recounted the horrific conditions of the prison camp through diaries and photographs taken after their liberation by Northern forces. In the early 1970s, Andersonville was brought into the National Park Service as a National Historic Site by an act of Congress. In 1998 the site also became the location of the National Prisoner of War Museum. The historic site and museum are located on approximately 500 acres of land.

BACKGROUND AND HISTORY

Andersonville is located on a predominantly marshy area of land where a small tributary flows westward into Sweet Water Creek. Natural springs also occur there, opening and closing at periodic intervals. The land sloping toward the tributary has a steep grade of 12 percent until it levels off approximately 50 feet above the marshy plain. The open area of the site includes the former stockade, prison fortifications, and the footprints of Civil War–era structures, including the commandant's house and a hospital.

During the Civil War, Andersonville was both a community and prison. The community, which numbered approximately twenty-five persons by 1863, was situated along the Southwestern Railroad, a line that connected southwest Georgia to the city of Macon in central Georgia. In November 1863, W. Sidney Winder was dispatched by Confederate authorities to assess the possible location of a new prisoner-of-war camp in Sumter County. The Confederacy desperately needed a new prison camp because it was overwhelmed with Union prisoners after having backed out of an exchange program that would have traded African American soldiers for white soldiers. With freshwater from the stream, the accessibility of rail transport, and a location deep in the South, Andersonville was chosen by Winder as the best site for the new compound. By December 1863, Confederate engineers using slave labor began constructing a prison camp designed for 10,000 persons.

The camp was originally rectangular, measuring 1,010 feet by 780 feet, and had hewn-pine walls 17 to 18 feet high. Along the western wall two gates were positioned with a rail line leading directly to the doors. With the gates closed, the tightly constructed hewn-pine walls completely shut out the outside world. Within the compound, a deadline fence was placed approximately 15 feet from the pine wall. It discouraged potential escapees from approaching the main wall by delineating an area where prisoners could be shot on sight. The rectangular compound was cut in half by what was little more than a ditch. The steep slopes rose out to the east and west walls. On high elevations outside the compound's walls, four cannon placements and numerous earthworks surrounded the camp. These cannons were all the prisoners could see of life outside the compound.

Although designed for 10,000 prisoners, Andersonville's population swelled to overflowing almost immediately after the camp's opening. By June 1864 the prison population

numbered 23,000. To accommodate the burgeoning population, Union prisoners and slaves were ordered to extend the camp's main walls, adding approximately 10 acres to the compound. Less than three months after compound's walls were extended, the camp held a population of over 30,000 in an area of less than 30 acres.

When Andersonville was liberated by Union forces under William Sherman in 1865, approximately 100 prisoners were dying daily from the effects of inadequate shelter, malnutrition, and disease. In the months and years immediately following the end of the war, photographs of emaciated prisoners horrified civilians throughout the Northern states. Even in the South, some diarists who happened to travel through Andersonville would write of disturbing conditions in the camp. Following the surrender of all Confederate armies, Andersonville prison's commandant, Captain Henry A. Wirz, an immigrant from Switzerland, was executed. Wirz was the only person to receive the death penalty for crimes related to the Civil War. By the end of the nineteenth century, no structural remains were left of Andersonville prison, as rot and reuse had claimed most of the building materials.

After the end of hostilities, Clara Barton, the founder of the American Red Cross, entered Andersonville with plans to rebury and name those who had died. Aided by approximately three dozen men, Barton was able to use numbered burial rolls to identify the prisoners. From the late nineteenth century into the twentieth, the Andersonville site was owned by various people and organizations, and eventually became marked by monuments. Two freed African Americans purchased much of the site in the 1870s and planted cotton there. In the early 1890s, the African American farmers sold the land to the Grand Army of the Republic of Georgia, a local chapter of the national fraternal veterans' association composed of former Union soldiers. A few years later, the land passed to the National Women's Relief Corps, which took up the responsibility for the grounds and adjoining cemetery. During the 1910s former prisoners and soldiers would travel to Andersonville to pay respects to fallen comrades at the cemetery and grounds. In 1910 a large granite monument was constructed over the site of a natural spring that was said to have burst from the ground in late 1864. Known as Providence Spring, the clean water of the spring was believed to have saved hundreds of prisoners. Also during this time Northern state governments and private fraternal societies began commissioning monuments for the Andersonville site, large Victorian-influenced obelisks inscribed with a state's name. In the 1930s the Civilian Conservation Corps, a New Deal–era youth work program, began erecting drain culverts in order to retard soil erosion. In 1971 the site was brought into the National Park Service as Andersonville National Historic Site. Twenty-seven years later, the site name was expanded to include the National Prisoner of War Museum, dedicated to the memory of American soldiers incarcerated in all of America's wars.

CONTESTED LANDSCAPE

In the years that followed the Civil War, as Northern commemorative groups were constructing monuments at the prison, the United Daughters of the Confederacy (UDC) and, later, the Sons of Confederate Veterans (SCV) were erecting monuments to a different version of history. Within the community of Andersonville, the UDC erected in 1909 a monument to Henry A. Wirz dedicated to his service to the Confederacy. Believing that the numbers of dead prisoners had been inflated, or that the North was itself responsible for the deaths of its soldiers due to the blockade of Southern ports, these groups contended that Wirz did his best under impossible circumstances.

Into the early 2000s Andersonville the National Historic Site and Andersonville the community continue to tell much different stories of this area's role in the Civil War. At the National Park Service site, the historical narrative focuses on loss and remembrance as monuments and museum pieces weave a story of both human suffering and perseverance. In the community, however, Confederate flags abound as storefronts in the historic area sell rebel memorabilia under the shadow of the UDC's Wirz memorial.

ARCHAEOLOGY

Since becoming a part of the National Park Service, numerous archaeological excavations have been undertaken at Andersonville. Some of the earliest excavation work was conducted by Lewis Larson and Morgan R. Crook, who worked to outline the perimeter of the former prison site. Since the late 1980s, however, the National Park Service's Southeast Archaeological Center (SEAC) has performed the archaeological investigations at the Andersonville site. The excavations are unearthing valuable information concerning the historical events that took place at the site. The original dimensions of the prison walls and the extent of the compound's expansion, for example, are largely known due to the work of field archaeologists and historical researchers.

One of the intriguing components of SEAC's archaeological work has been the investigation of the prison's wall and gate. The trenches dug to hold the pine walls contained an unusual stratification of soil compared with that found at the expansion wall. The original trenches were tri-colored, with light and darker varieties of soil bounding the decaying material of the wooden post. It seems that the slaves, working under a gang system, were uniformly digging the holes, and as one slave dug from one side and another across from him, the trench was refilled accordingly. This left the tri-colored fill seen upon excavation.

According to various accounts, as many as 10,000 slaves were forced to work on military installations during the Civil War. Since the actual community of Andersonville had only twenty or so known inhabitants, the slaves were most likely brought in to do the construction work. One account of slave resistance can be found in the diary of John McElroy, one of the first Union prisoners, who witnessed the construction of the original walls. McElroy noticed that the slaves usually seemed unable to comprehend what they were told by Southern officers. Once the Southern officers left, however, the slaves would talk and joke freely with the Northern prisoners.

The expansion of the prison was undertaken by Northern prisoners, as documented in the official logs of the camp. The new wall was dug more haphazardly than the earlier stockade, as indicated by the multi-layered stratigraphy of the trench that held the wooden wall. Additionally, the trenches were not as deep as those originally dug by the slaves. On the surface, it might appear that Union prisoners were too overcome by heat, hunger, and disease to build a substantial wall. However, the archaeological excavations uncovered something interesting: an escape tunnel that the prisoners had dug at about the same time. The largest part of the tunnel was approximately 3 feet wide and less than 2 feet high. Following the tunnel to the stockade wall, archaeologists discovered that it had collapsed, frustrating the escape attempt less than yard from the other side of the wall.

The artifacts recovered at Andersonville include pig, cow, and rabbit bones, various pieces of military buckles and insignias, as well as buttons and glass. Included in the artifacts of the 1990 excavation was a silver filigreed band with an attached eraser. Given the abundance of letters and diaries written either from or about Andersonville, the eraser is a poignant reminder of men who faced unspeakable hardship and were able to leave us an account of their suffering.

Further Reading: *Archaeology at Andersonville*, National Park Service, Southeast Archeological Center Web site, www.nps.gov/seac/andearch.htm (accessed April 16, 2008); Blair, William A., *Cities of the Dead: Contesting the Memory of the Civil War in the South, 1865–1914* (Chapel Hill: University of North Carolina Press, 2004); Marvel, William, *Andersonville: The Last Depot* (Chapel Hill: University of North Carolina Press, 1992); Prentice, Guy, and Marie C. Prentice, "Far from the Battlefield: Archaeology at Andersonville Prison," in *Archaeological Perspectives on the American Civil War*, edited by Clarence R. Grier and Stephen R. Potter (Gainesville: University of Florida Press, 2000).

Mark Barron

GLOSSARY

Accelerator Mass Spectrometric (AMS) Dating. A method of radiocarbon dating precise enough to count the proportion of carbon isotope (carbon 14) atoms directly and reducing the size of the sample of material required for accurate dating dramatically.

Anasazi (Ancestral Puebloan) Cultural Tradition. A well-known ancient cultural tradition that existed in the "Four Corners" area of the Colorado Plateau, around the common corners of Colorado, Utah, Arizona, and New Mexico, beginning about AD 900 and lasting until about AD 1300. Anasazi is the older and more traditional term used by archaeologists to refer to Ancestral Puebloan people. Many well-known sites are associated with this tradition, for example, the ancient architectural sites of Mesa Verde, Chaco Canyon, and Canyons of the Ancients National Monument (see the essays by Steve Lekson, Wirt Wills [on Shabik'eschee Village site], Paul Reed [Overview of Chaco Canyon], Jill Neitzel, Tom Windes, LouAnn Jacobson, John Kantner, Cathy Cameron, and Mark Varien in the Southwest section).

Archaic. A general term used to refer to a time period that encompasses the early Holocene from about 10,000 to 3,000 years ago, but varying in different regions. Developments during the Archaic included the manufacture of ground stone tools, the beginnings of food cultivation, and initial settled life. In some parts of North America this time period is divided into three sub-periods: the Early, Middle, and Late portions.

Assemblage. A group of artifacts recurring together at different places or times. Assemblages may be associated with particular activities or with a cultural tradition.

Atl atl. A spear-, arrow-, or dart-throwing tool. These are composite tools usually with several parts, including an antler or wood handle, a weight, and a hooked end. The atl atl works as a lever to propel the projectile for greater distance and with greater force.

Avocational archaeologist. Individuals with a serious interest in archaeology, but who do not engage in the discipline as their profession. Many avocational archaeologists have made important archaeological discoveries and contributions to our understanding of the ancient or historic pasts.

Basketmaker. A term used to refer to the early portion of the Ancestral Puebloan cultural tradition. Early Basketmaker people relied on hunting and gathering for much of their food, but during this period, domesticated plants, such as corn, beans, and squash, were added to the diet. During this period, ways of life became more settled and more permanent houses, called "pithouses" because they were dug partly below ground became common. Coiled and twined basketry also is common, and people began to make plain pottery for the first time.

Biface. A stone tool that has been chipped on both sides to shape and thin it.

Blade tool manufacture and technology. Blade manufacture is a quite different method of making flaked stone cutting and piercing tools than that employed in making chipped stone tools, such as a bifacial point or knife. The latter involves shaping, thinning, and sharpening a single piece of stone. In blade manufacture, a nodule of stone is carefully prepared to form a core so that multiple, long, narrow, parallel-sided flakes with very sharp edges can be struck. These "blades" then are used as knives for cutting, or snapped into segments that can be inserted into slots on the sides of antler or wooden points to form the cutting edges. Knives can also be made this way. One advantage of this technique over biface manufacture is that large cutting and piercing tools can be made using small pieces of stone when large pieces are not available.

Cation ratio dating. Cation ratio dating is used to date rocks that have a modified surface such as prehistoric rock carvings (petroglyphs). This is a relative dating technique that is not considered an accurate method of dating by some professional archaeologists.

Rocks are covered by a kind of varnish, a chemically-changed layer caused by weathering that builds up over time. The change in the rock varnish is due to calcium and potassium seeping out of the rock. The cation ratio is determined by scraping the varnish from the carved or petroglyph surface back to the original rock surface and making a comparison of the two. The technique relies on change due to weathering of the stone over long periods of time, so geographically distinctive patterns are needed to compare the original surfaces with the modern suface that show the results of weathering.

Chert. A type of very fine-grained stone rich in silica. It is often found in or weathered from limestone deposits. It was shaped into chipped stone tools, and sometimes for blade tools, using stone and bone or antler hammers.

Chipped Stone tools. Tools shaped and thinned by systematically flaking exterior portions off. Typically this manufacturing technique is used with very fine-grained stone (e.g., obsidian, chert, or flint) that can be flaked relatively easily because it fractures smoothly in a way that can be controlled manufacturing techniques skillfully applied.

Clovis. Clovis is a term used to name an archaeological culture, a time period, and a particular variety of fluted stone spear points or knives. The name derives from Clovis, New Mexico, near which is located the type site, Blackwater Draw. Clovis spear points have been found in direct association with extinct megafauna in ice age gravel deposits The Clovis culture is known to have occupied many parts of North America during the Paleoindian period. The distinctive Clovis spear point has a vertical flake scar or flute on both faces of the point that extends about 1/3 its length. Sites containing Clovis points have been dated across North America to between 13,500 and 10,800 years ago. In western North America Clovis points have been found with the killed and butchered remains of large animals like mammoth or mastodon. As a result, Clovis peoples are assumed to have targeted large game animals, although how much of their diet actually came from hunting, much less from large game, is unknown (see the essays by David Anderson in the Southeast section and Bonnie Pitblado and Dennis Stanford in the Great Plains and Rocky Mountain section).

Component. A culturally homogenous stratigraphic unit within an archaeological site.

Core. A lithic artifact used as the source from which other tools, flakes, or blades are struck.

CRM (Cultural Resource Management). This activity includes archaeological investigations done as part of public project planning required by federal or state laws to ensure that important archaeological sites are not wantonly destroyed by public undertakings. CRM also includes the long term management of archaeological resources that are on public lands and for which legal protections and preservation is required of the public agencies that administer these lands (see the general introduction for more details abut contemporary CRM in North America).

Dalton. Term used to refer to an archaeological culture dating to the end of the Paleoindian period and the beginning of the Archaic time period. Dalton artifacts and sites are recognized in the Midwest, Southeast, and Northeast of North America. The point distribution shows that there was a widespread Dalton lifeway oriented toward streams and deciduous forests. Dalton culture people were hunters and gatherers using a variety of wild animal and plant foods over the course of each year. Timber and nuts were important as raw materials and food. Like Paleoindians, Dalton groups probably consisted of families related by kinship and mutual dependence (see the essay by Dan Morse in the Southeast section).

Debitage. Stone debris from chipped-stone tool manufacturing or maintenance activities.

Desert Culture. Ancient cultural groups that occupied the present-day Great Basin and Plateau regions. They created a distinctive cultural adaptation to the dry, relatively impoverished environments of these regions. The Cochise or Desert Archaic culture began by about 7000 BC and persisted until about AD 500.

Earthfast foundation. Earthfast (also known as "post-in-the-ground") architecture was the most prevalent building tradition of 17th-century Virginia and Maryland. At its core, the typical "Virginia House" (as dwellings of this type were sometimes called) consisted of pairs of hewn wooden posts set into deep, regularly-spaced holes dug into the ground. Once set in the ground and backfilled, these posts were either pegged on nailed together with cross beams to form the sides and gables of a rectangular, A-framed structure. The exterior "skins" of such earthfast structures varied. Some were both roofed and sided with riven wooden clapboards. Others were sided in wattle-and-daub and roofed with thatch. Irrespective of their construction, earthfast structures tended to be rather impermanent, lasting no more than perhaps a decade or two at most in the hot, humid Chesapeake region.

Effigy pipes. A variation on the plain stone tube pipe carved in the likeness of an animal. A wide variety of animal images—birds, mammals, and reptiles—are used for these pipes which are frequently associated with the Adena and Hopewell cultures in the Midwest region.

Feature. Usually refers to types of archaeological deposits related to a particular focused activity or event. For example, hearths, garbage or trash pits, storage pits, and foundations or other architectural remnants are referred to generally as features.

Flotation. A technique for recovering very small organic remains, such as tiny pieces of charcoal, seeds, bone, wood, and other items. A soil sample is placed in a drum of water, sometimes mixed with other liquids. The liquid is agitated to loosen any soil from the organic material. This material, being lighter than water, floats to the surface and can be skimmed off using a fine mesh screen. The organic materials can be used in a variety of analyses, for example, to interpret diet, subsistence activities, for dating, and to determine use of wood for tools or structures.

Gorgets. Made of copper, shell or polished or smoothed stone these thin, often oval artifacts were often perforated by two or more holes and worn around the neck.

Hohokam Cultural Tradition. Hohokam refers to the Sonoran Desert region of Phoenix and Tucson in southern Arizona and further south. The Hohokam region witnessed remarkable cultural developments beginning about AD 900. In this general area, about 200 sites with large oval, earthen features (interpreted as local expressions of Mesoamerican ball courts) have been found. A distinctive cluster of large sites in the area of modern Phoenix clearly represent the Hohokam center. Hohokam had red-on-buff pottery, large towns composed of scores of courtyard groups (three to five single-room thatch houses facing inward into a small courtyard or patio), and ball courts. There were regular markets for the exchange of goods supported by canal-irrigated farming (see Steve Lekson's essay on the classic period ancient Southwest).

Holocene. The most recent geological epoch, which began about 10,000 years ago. The period after the last glaciation in North America.

Hopewell Cultural Traditon. An archaeological tradition of the Midwest dated to the Middle Woodland period (about 50 BC to AD 400). The Hopewell tradition is known for a distinctive burial patterns and a wide-ranging exchange among communities. Communities hundreds, even thousands, of miles from one another participated in this exchange system and raw materials, as well as finished products were exported and imported. The Hopewell tradition also is known for the mounds that they built for ceremonial and burial purposes. It is known to be one of the most considerable achievements of Native Americans throughout the ancient past. These mounds, especially in the Ohio River valley are large complexes incorporating a variety of geometric shapes and rise to impressive heights (see essays in the Midwest section by George Milner, Douglas Charles, N'omi Greber, William Dancey, and Bradley Lepper).

Horizon. A set of cultural characteristics or traits that has a brief time depth but is found across multiple areas or regions.

Kiva. Among modern Pueblo Indian communities in the Southwest, a kiva is a nonresidential structure or room that is owned and used by specific social groups, such as clans or religious societies. The activities that take place in kivas are different than the daily, domestic activities—such as food preparation and pottery manufacture—that occur in dwellings. Because of this historic affiliation of sociopolitical functions with kivas, archaeologists use this term to refer to large pit structures lacking evidence for domestic functions that may have been used as public buildings, rather than household dwellings.

Lithic. Stone.

Loess. Fine-grained windblown sediment deposited as soil layers on areas not ice-covered during the last glaciation.

Megafauna. Large mammal species, such as mammoth, mastodon, bison, giant beaver, giant ground sloth, and stag elk that lived in North America during the late glacial and early post-glacial time periods. Many megafauna species have become extinct.

Midden. The archaeological remains of a human settlement's garbage and trash deposits. Middens typically are an accumulation of decomposed organic refuse usually very dark colored that frequently also contains thousands of discarded pieces of stone artifacts and ceramics, animal bones, nutshells, and other remains.

Mimbres Cultural Tradition. The Mimbres cultural development occurred in the Mogollon region of western New Mexico between about AD 900 and 1150. It is most famous for its remarkable black-on-white pottery. While the majority of Mimbres bowls are painted with striking geometric designs, images include depictions of people and events using an artistic style that merits inclusion in the world's major art museums. Images also show Mimbres' wide interests: Pacific Ocean fish, tropical birds from western Mexico (and, perhaps, monkeys from the same area), and armadillos (see essays by Steve Lekson [Classic Period Cultural and Social Interaction], Karen Schollmeyer, Steve Swanson, and Margaret Nelson, and J. J. Brody in the Southwest section).

Mississippian Cultural Tradition. A widespread tradition centered on Midwestern and Southeastern North America beginning about AD 1000 and lasting in some places until AD 1600. Typically societies that were part of this cultural tradition had chiefdom level political organizations, had subsistence systems based on intensive agricultural production of corn, beans, squash, and other domesticated plants, and built settlements that incorporated earthen architecture, typically various kinds and sizes of mound architecture. Mississippian chiefdoms flourished across much of the Eastern Woodlands: as far north as Illinois and southern Wisconsin; as far west as eastern Oklahoma; as far east as the Carolinas and Georgia; and south to Florida and the Gulf Coast (see essays by Robin Beck in the Southeast section and Mary Beth Turbot in the Midwest section).

Mogollon Cultural Tradition. An ancient Southwestern cultural tradition dating between about A.D. 200 and 1450. The tradition is found in a vast, ecologically diverse geographic area in southwestern New Mexico, southeastern Arizona and northwestern Mexico. Mogollon takes its name from the mountain range and highlands that separate the Anasazi and Hohokam regions. The Mogollon area witnessed remarkable cultural development referred to as the Mimbres after the river in southwest New Mexico where this development was centered (see essays by Steve Lekson [Classic Period Cultural and Social Interaction] and Wirt Wills [the SU site] in the Southwest section).

Paleoindian (Paleoamerican) Cultural Tradition. The Paleoindian time frame extends from approximately 13,500 to 9,000 BC and is found in almost all parts of North America. It is the earliest widely recognized archaeological cultural tradition in North America. The Clovis culture is the earliest Paleoindian culture, but there are increasing numbers of investigations of sites that are purported to be older than the Clovis or Paleoindian tradition.

Pit. A hole in the earth constructed and used for cooking, storage, or garbage or trash disposal. Pits are a common kind of archaeological feature.

Pithouse. Pithouses typically are single room dwellings, although some have antechambers. Pithouses are semi-subterranean dwellings in which some portions of the walls consist of the sides of an excavated pit. They are constructed by excavating a large hole or pit, building a timber framework inside the pit, then covering the framework with the excavated dirt, resulting in a house that is very thermally efficient, but prone to rapid deterioration, depending on the climate, from the effects of moisture, as well as vermin infestation.

Pleistocene. The geological epoch dating from 1.8 million to 10,000 years ago. During the last part of the Pleistocene human populations began to migrate into North America. The end of this epoch is a period of repeated glaciations in North America. It is succeeded by the Holocene era.

Postmolds. The archaeological remains of timbers, posts, saplings, or other wood structural elements of former buildings or dwellings. Depending on the age and soil conditions, posts placed in the ground ultimately will decay into fragments or mere stains indicating where these portions of buildings once existed.

Prehistory, prehistoric. Regarded by some as a demeaning term indicating primitive, but, most often used simply to refer to the general period of time prior to written records. As such, the length of the prehistoric period for different parts of North America varies according to when written records are available, generally associated with the beginning of European contact with aboriginal cultures.

Radiocarbon Dating (also known as Carbon-14 [^{14}C] Dating). An absolute dating method that measures the decay of the radioactive isotope of carbon (^{14}C) in organic material.

Steatite (Soapstone). A metamorphic rock, composed largely of the mineral talc and relatively soft. Steatite has been used as a medium for carving for thousands of years. Steatite also was carved out in ancient times to create bowls, in particular in places and at times before pottery had begun to be produced.

Taphonomy. The study of the process of fossilization. Used in archaeology to examine the human and natural changes that produce the archaeological record. For example, changes to organic materials after the death of the organism, such as how bone is changed by chemical, mechanical or animal processes after burial.

Tradition. An archaeological concept indicating a consistent set of cultural characteristics and traits that has great time depth and covers a recognized area.

Wattle-and-daub construction. A building technique using poles placed vertically in the ground and then plastered over with mud to construct the walls. Usually structures of wattle and daub were topped with thatched roofs.

Woodland Time Period. A time period term used mainly in the eastern North America south of Canada between roughly 1000 BC and AD 1000. In the Midwest region the Woodland period is regarded as the centuries between Archaic times and the Mississippian period. During this long period, the technology of pottery developed and spread, social and political complexity increased, cultivated plants changed from a supplemental part of diet to dietary staples, and settlements grew from small groups of residences to some of the largest cities in the world at that time.

Younger Dryas. A cold climatic event that took place from 12,900–11,600 years ago. It was a rapid return to glacial conditions during the longer term transition from the last glacial maximum to modern climatic conditions.

Sources used for definitions: The definitions in this glossary are derived from a number of sources, including essays in this encyclopedia, and the following texts:

Renfrew, Colin and Paul Bahn (2000). *Archaeology: Theories, Methods, and Practice*, third edition. Thames and Hudson, London and New York.

Thomas, David Hurst (1991). *Archaeology: Down to Earth*. Harcourt Brace Jovanovich College Publishers, Fort Worth and New York.

INDEX

A page number followed by *i* indicates an illustration; *m* indicates a map.